A WORLD HISTORY OF WAR CRIMES

A WORLD HISTORY OF WAR CRIMES

FROM ANTIQUITY TO THE PRESENT

SECOND EDITION

Michael Bryant

BLOOMSBURY ACADEMIC
LONDON • NEW YORK • OXFORD • NEW DELHI • SYDNEY

BLOOMSBURY ACADEMIC
Bloomsbury Publishing Plc
50 Bedford Square, London, WC1B 3DP, UK
1385 Broadway, New York, NY 10018, USA
29 Earlsfort Terrace, Dublin 2, Ireland

BLOOMSBURY, BLOOMSBURY ACADEMIC and the Diana logo are trademarks
of Bloomsbury Publishing Plc

First published in Great Britain 2021

Cover image: The Narmer Palette
(© World History Archive / Alamy Stock Photo)

A catalogue record for this book is available from the British Library.

Library of Congress Cataloging-in-Publication Data
Names: Bryant, Michael., 1962– author.
Title: A world history of war crimes : from antiquity to the present / Michael Bryant.
Description: 2nd edition. | London, UK ; New York, NY : Bloomsbury Academic, Bloomsbury
Publishing Plc, 2021. | Includes bibliographical references and index.
Identifiers: LCCN 2020036909 (print) | LCCN 2020036910 (ebook) |
ISBN 9781350106604 (hardback) | ISBN 9781350106598 (paperback) |
ISBN 9781350106611 (ebook) | ISBN 9781350106628 (epub)
Subjects: LCSH: War crimes–History. | Crimes against humanity–History. | War (International law)
Classification: LCC KZ7145 .B79 2021 (print) | LCC KZ7145 (ebook) | DDC 341.6/909—dc23
LC record available at https://lccn.loc.gov/2020036909
LC ebook record available at https://lccn.loc.gov/2020036910

ISBN: PB: 978-1-3501-0659-8
       HB: 978-1-3501-0660-4
       ePDF: 978-1-3501-0661-1
       eBook: 978-1-3501-0662-8

Typeset by RefineCatch Limited, Bungay, Suffolk
Printed and bound in Great Britain

To find out more about our authors and books visit www.bloomsbury.com
and sign up for our newsletters.

For Shirley Crowe and Brenda Sparks,
The best of all aunts

CONTENTS

Contents

Contents

ILLUSTRATIONS

Illustrations

PREFACE TO THE SECOND EDITION

When Bloomsbury approached me a couple years ago about doing a second edition of this book, my reaction was excitement mixed with trepidation. On the one hand, I was thrilled by the prospect of adding new materials to a book that had done little more than scratch the surface of an enormously complex subject. On the other, I blanched when confronted by the challenges of such an undertaking. The very topic of the book—the human species' efforts over millennia to normalize warfare, to bring the business of fighting and killing into alignment with cultural conceptions of how the world works or should work—seemed to me to require a writer far more talented than myself. The subject demanded a Homer, Tolstoy or Melville to tell humankind's story of organized violence in its infinite richness. It should be painted, as Booth Tarkington said of a book by Charles Fort, with a "brush dipped in earthquake and eclipse." Shaking off my reservations, I reasoned that, having already written a first edition, I could only improve my history with publication of a second.

If there is an analytical perspective holding this book together, it is the view that rule-based limitations on warfare become explicitly humanitarian only in the nineeenth century, and that before this time the limitations imposed on war—on both its declaration and the conduct of its participants—were largely determined by cosmo-religious belief systems. I had arrived at the realization that contemporary scholarship underrated the degree to which religion had affected the Law of War. Skewed, perhaps, by the sensible Enlightenment position that we are essentially rational rather than religious, and convinced that religion would eventually dissipate like morning mist in the scorching rays of reason's sun, modern intellectuals had discounted the power of religious belief in human psychology. When the repressed returned it exacted a heavy price for this miscalculation. In our own time, the butcher's bill would include the global spread of ethno-nationalism, militant Islamic fundamentalism (the Taliban, Al Qaeda, and the Islamic State), 9/11, the Iraq War, and a right-wing evangelical movement that has provided the vital jet fuel to extremist politics in the USA. Even in a "secular age," religion and quasi-religious manias persist as a driver of human behavior.

My reading of the Law of War confirmed not only the centrality of religious belief to warfare in ancient societies but its decisive impact on the thinking of perpetrator groups today like ISIS. I sought to capture this truth in the first edition of the book and to reaffirm it in the second. The reader will find new sections of Chapter 1 devoted to warfare in prehistory, ancient Egypt and Mesopotamia, China, and Israel. New chapters have been added: the new Chapter 2 tackles the Law of War and war crimes in Pre-Columbian America; the new Chapter 5 describes war crimes in the context of European relations with indigenous peoples; the new Chapter 10 explores the causes of war crimes in light of world historical methodologies. The illustrations accompanying the text have been substantially increased.

After reading this new edition, it is hoped that students of the Law of War will appreciate its many facets in world history. From imitating the gods' creation of the world to ensuring the victory of order over chaos, from punishing sin, enforcing feudal obligations, and preserving good order and discipline to resolving legal questions through violence, the Law of War has evolved toward humanitarianism as its crowning purpose. The Law of War, much like every artifact of human fabrication, will continue to change and evolve based on human perceptions of the goods in urgent need of defense. The direction of such changes is unknown, but given our current predicament it is not hard to imagine the Law of War someday criminalizing the heedless destruction of non-human species or the environment. Might the military forces of nation-states defend the planet's ecology from the predations of industrial capitalism? The prospect seems utopian but so, too, at one time did the idea of protecting minorities from attack by their own governments. Everywhere in world history, cultures have invested warfare with their deepest existential concerns. Might we not have space for hope that soldiers in the not too distant future may fight for nature's preservation, inspired not by bloodlust but love of the physical world that has mothered all of us, as expressed by Chief Seattle in 1854?

> We are part of the earth and it is part of us. The perfumed flowers are our sisters; the deer, the horse, the great eagle, these are our brothers. The rocky crests, the juices in the meadows, the body heat of the pony, and man—all belong to the same family.

Michael Bryant
Harrisville, Rhode Island
January 29, 2020

INTRODUCTION

At some point in distant time, the human mind discovered that the crude weapons it had fashioned to hunt and fell animals could be turned against human beings with the same deadly effect. From that point forward, the business of war has been about killing.[1] However, so far as we can tell based on anthropological study of premodern societies, the violence of warfare was rarely boundless. To be sure antiquity witnessed martial bloodbaths, yet war, even at its most extreme, was typically regulated by a strict code of behavior, a web of injunctions and prohibitions that varied from one era to another and from one culture to the next. While the cultural logic informing these codes of action and the worldviews expressed in them often differed, few were the world's civilizations that did not recognize a limit to what could be done to the enemy.

Certainly this does not mean that premodern peoples entertained the concept of "war crimes" or endeavored to suppress them through criminal punishment. Indeed, both the idea of "crime" and its derivative "war crimes" are much later inventions of the human imagination in its efforts to construe the social world. In no civilization of antiquity was a distinction ever drawn between civil and criminal law. The tendency of premodern civilizations to overlook something basic to our modern understanding of law—namely, the difference between civil wrongs and crimes warranting punishment—is due in significant degree to the non-emergence in these cultures of a critical dichotomy in the modern mind, that between public and private law. Public law, understood as rules applying to the individual's relationships with the State and other persons that directly concern society, makes possible the classification of certain kinds of behavior as "criminal" when in violation of written laws. Private law, by contrast, almost wholly concerns relationships between individuals—torts (violations of due care causing harm) and contracts (legally enforceable agreements between two or more parties). When a criminal law is violated, the State responds by imposing a sanction on the offender in the name of society. When a private law is violated, the State responds by requiring offenders to pay restitution to injured parties for the purpose of "making them whole." A legal action for a civil wrong is conducted not in the name of society as a criminal trial is but on behalf of the plaintiff.

Clearly, societies that conflate private and public law, and therefore tend to treat what we today call "torts" and "contracts" interchangeably with intentional acts harmful to society as a whole, cannot be said to subscribe to a notion of the "criminal act" as the term is understood today. At least in the cultures of Western Europe, the very idea of crime as a subset of socially injurious actions warranting special consideration did not truly arise until the revival and elaboration of the Roman canon law in the eleventh and twelfth centuries CE. The Church's lawyers were among the first to regard actions meriting stern ecclesiastical censure as a substantive and separate body of Church law. In ensuing centuries, this theological distinction between grave sins and other actions subject to canon legal jurisdiction seeped into secular law at a time when the monarchs of Europe were building their kingdoms. Particularly in Germanic societies, the theological concern with the "intent" of the wrongdoer was translated into the secular doctrine of *mens rea* ("guilty mind"), which graded as criminal a deleterious act committed with the full intention of the wrongdoer. To be punishable and not merely correctable through the payment of damages, the criminal act had to be not only a violation of a social norm defined either by the Church or the State; it also had to be the product of the violator's will. By the sixteenth century, the punishability of the criminal act was narrowed even further through stipulations that wrongdoers could not be sanctioned if they acted from self-defense or a physical/psychological disability.[2]

The origin of the phrase "war crimes" occurred still later in world history. Some scholars of the Law of War hold that war crimes as a legal term only dates back to 1906, when jurist Lassa Oppenheim coined it in his influential treatise *International Law*.[3] This may be true as it pertains to English language publications, but the first use of the term appears to have been in Johann Caspar Bluntschli's 1872 work *Das moderne Völkerrecht der civilisierten Staaten als Rechtsbruch dargestellt*. (American jurist Francis Lieber, author of the Lieber Code, used the phrase still earlier but never in print.[4]) Bluntschli's treatise, written in German, refers to violations of the Law of War as *Kriegsverbrechen* (translated as war crimes). His understanding of war crimes, however, is not the same as later definitions of the term. By *Kriegsverbrechen* Bluntschli meant actions by civilians in occupied territory who illegally armed themselves to fight against the occupier. Such persons, Bluntschli asserted, could be prosecuted in courts-martial as unlawful combatants; if found guilty, they could be executed. In short, the first mention of war crimes as a category of crime did not refer to illegal acts by combatants during war. It referred instead to illegal acts in occupied territory by civilians.[5]

Similarly, Oppenheim's conception of war crimes set forth in 1906 differed from later views. He considered four acts to be war crimes:

1. Violations of the law by military forces acting without orders.

2. Hostilities carried out by non-military persons.

3. Espionage and treason committed during war.

4. Marauding acts (typically committed by soldiers who have left their duty assignment).[6]

Remarkably, instance (1) above only recognized the criminal liability of persons violating the accepted Law of War when they acted without orders. If orders were involved, on the other hand, the only remedy available to a state was reprisals against the offending state. The individual perpetrator, in other words, could not be punished for war crimes. As the authors of a recent article defining war crimes have commented, these earliest written statements on the subject by Bluntschli and Oppenheim were conceptually discontinuous with the meanings attached to it in subsequent decades.[7]

Thus, while the term "war crimes" was available in the scholarship of prominent international jurists before 1914, no consensus existed, either among scholars or nation-states, about what precisely war crimes were or how they should be treated. Despite the outrage surrounding German military practices during the First World War, the Treaty of Versailles (1919) never charged the Kaiser with war crimes but with a "supreme offence against international morality and the sanctity of treaties." Elsewhere in the treaty, Article 228 did provide for the trial of German soldiers "accused of having committed acts in violation of the laws and customs of war," who were subject to being punished if convicted. None of these provisions was ever realized, however, and a robust legal confrontation with war crimes would have to wait until 1945.

Even during the Second World War, in the very midst of Japanese and German acts of official brutality, Allied policymakers acknowledged that, in the words of a 1944 memorandum for the US Judge Advocate General, the term "war crimes" had "no well-established meaning in military or international jurisprudence." Groping for a definition, the memo's author wrote that war crimes were "violations of the laws and customs of war which constitute offenses against person or property, . . . *which outrage common justice or involve moral turpitude*" (emphasis added). He attached an "Illustrative List of 'War Crimes'" that is worth reproducing here.

Disguised poisoning of wells or streams.
Refusal of quarter, or directions to give no quarter.
Treacherous request for quarter resulting in illegal wounding or killings. Deliberate
    killing of bearers of flag of truce.
Killing or cruel treatment of wounded or prisoners of war.
. . .
Murder and rape arising in connection with military operations or occupation.
Wanton devastation or destruction of property.
Deliberate destruction of hospitals and religious, charitable, education, or historic
    buildings and monuments when not required by legitimate military necessity.
Pillage and plunder.
Attack on or destruction of hospital ships.
. . .
Torture in any form of troops or civilians.
Causing death by willful starvation of populations, by excessive removal of
    foodstuffs.
. . .
Abduction of girls and women with the object of prostitution. Wholesale uprooting
    of peoples in occupied territory.
Omission of a superior officer to prevent war crimes when he is aware of their
    commission and is in a position to prevent them.[8]

Nearly every act on this list was charged as a war crime against Japanese and German defendants after the Second World War.

The author of the memo quoted above correctly notes that in 1944 there was no coherent, consensus-based definition of war crimes in military or international law.

When war crimes were addressed at all, the wrongdoers were punished by national states or their armed forces under their own national law, and not under international law.[9] This state of affairs would change dramatically in 1945 when for the first time war crimes were defined legally as violations of international law for which offenders, whether acting on orders or not, were criminally liable as individuals.

Given the relative recency of "war crimes" as a legal concept, the reader may ask why so much of this book is devoted to war crimes predating the Second World War. The answer is that a broad and allusive approach to war crimes guides the coverage of this study. Too often, discussion of the subject takes place in a truncated context divorced from its deep historical roots. Just as conceptions of crime in world history are profoundly joined to religious ideas about sin, intent, and the purity of the will, so is the concept of the "violation of the laws and customs of war," as the 1944 memo for the Judge Advocate pointed out: war crimes, whatever else they are, "outrage common justice or involve moral turpitude." Japanese and German war criminals were not punished merely because they violated international law; they were punished because their crimes were considered appalling and reprehensible at a visceral level.[10] This "shocking to the conscience" criterion holds as true today as it did after the Second World War, as recent prosecutions by the International Tribunal for Yugoslavia confirm. Without the element of moral turpitude, war crimes would likely be dealt with through ordinary administrative and legal processes (such as courts-martial), if they would be addressed at all. This is not to say that offenses against a society's normative construction of warfare are invariably treated as shocking acts of moral depravity. Quite to the contrary: for many societies from antiquity until the nineteenth century, violations of the rules governing warfare were treated in different ways based upon that culture's self-understanding—the manner in which a given society constructed its knowledge of how the world works.[11] As a general rule, the more ancient the society, the more stylized and ritualistic will be its view of the proper way to conduct war. As the peoples of China, India, and Greece grew into populous urban-based societies, they developed codes of war designed to maintain a religiously-conceived cosmic order. Rules prescribing who a soldier could attack or what property he could plunder were not in origin humanitarian; from the beginning they were deeply interlinked with religious ceremonialism. The cosmic order observable in the heavens and in nature—the procession of heavenly bodies along regular tracks in the night sky, the rising and setting of the sun, the growth and death of vegetation, the unvarying recurrence of the seasons, the annual migration of animals—had to be reproduced in the social world in a bid to uphold the cosmic harmony. Rules determining behavior in all kinds of human intercourse, including war, sought to capture this regularity of the cosmos and integrate society with it. In no sense were such restrictions on warfare driven by an ethical or humanitarian concern.

The actual practice of war was largely divorced from humane concerns until the latter part of the nineteenth century, when the Swiss humanitarian Henri Dunant, shaken by the suffering of wounded and dying soldiers at the Battle of Solferino, helped establish the Red Cross as an international relief organization. The first of a series of Geneva Conventions followed one year later. Until that time, myriad cultural logics underlay the constraints on warfare in world civilization; few of them were ethical/humanitarian. Religious ceremonialism and the enforcement of boundaries between social groups were the usual source of restrictions on warfare. This was the reality at the level of day-to-day *practice*. However, in the *theory* of permissible warfare, matters were quite different. It is suggested in this textbook that an alternative source of the Law of War gradually arose during the first millennium BCE in several world civilizations, among them China, India, the Middle East, and Mediterranean Europe. This alternative source was not cosmo-ritualistic nor socially particularist but humanitarian and universal, and while it rarely manifested itself as a restraint on the battlefield, it did sometimes have practical, real-world effects. Wherever it appeared, this new, universal, and ethical view discounted the absolute authority of the monarch, demanding that royal power be subordinated to a higher principle of right. According to its teachings, the supreme good in the world was action in accordance with justice and truth, and these conceptions of justice and truth were in turn conceived as universal in scope.

From the earliest hunting and gathering social units, human beings had always observed a degree of restraint in their interactions within their kin group. Antisocial behavior was dealt with informally through counseling or, for the repeat offender, ostracism. During the first millenium BCE, the human mind began to think of these duties of restraint as extending beyond the kin group and running to persons outside it. In China this notion reached the level of a universalist ethic in the thought of Mozi, whose doctrine of universal love redefined the Chinese cult of filial piety by emphasizing the importance of concern for persons outside the family, thereby creating the basis for a pacifistic theory of just war. In other ancient cultures, too, we encounter similar notions: in the *Manusmriti* (India), the prophetic books of Hebrew Scripture (Israel), and the writings of the Stoics (Greco-Roman culture). The period between 800 BCE and 200 BCE witnessed a profound reorientation in the thinking of cultures that had little or no contact: China, India, Israel, and Greece. The focus of this shift entailed a re-examination of social life in light of normative insights; the givenness of the world (the "is") was increasingly challenged on behalf of higher truths (the "ought"). The association between kingship and divinity atrophied to the point where kings became accountable to principles of right and justice transcendent to their governance. In this process, an essential foundation of the Law of War was laid—the idea that the ruler and military commanders had to respect limitations in their waging of war. Although humanitarian considerations rarely limited the battlefield in antiquity, they sometimes mitigated the ferocity of warfare. More importantly, the concern with minimizing the unnecessary suffering of war achieved a foundational status in world civilization, one that would eventually bear fruit in the legal revolutions of the nineteenth and twentieth centuries.

For much of its existence, however, approaches to warfare were as mercurial and diverse as the many societies that manufactured them. In fact, it might be more accurate to refer to the "Law of War" in the plural—as the "laws" of war, inasmuch as every culture has imposed limitations on when and how it may be conducted. This book will not contend that a single Law of War has endured in world history over the span of several thousand years. Rather, it will introduce the reader to the broad spectrum of world societies that have produced their own unique Law of War. These pages will propose a conception of the Law of War as a cultural hoodoo, planed by the forces unique to specific cultures in the world, sheared by their religious beliefs, economic lives, social conflicts, and general worldviews into sometimes fantastic, sometimes incommensurable, and sometimes comparable forms. On the other hand, even as we acknowledge the irreducibility of world cultures, we should be aware of a universal reality human beings have always faced: we are mortal beings who suffer and die in war. This means that the variable laws of war, while evolving unique features determined by their cultural belief systems, also share important similarities of form and function grounded in the desire to impose restraint on an activity destructive of human well-being.

What exactly is a "world history of war crimes"? What are the methodologies of such a study? One method for studying world history posits that the human mind during the first millennium BCE came to believe that the received world of human action, particularly in the political and ethical realms, had to be reassessed vis-à-vis a transcendental vision of the right, good, and just. This supernova of the ethical into human life burst forth in one civilization after another at roughly the same time, in a mysterious process of alignment without visible contact that the Swiss psychologist Carl Gustav Jung once termed "synchronicity."[12] In this textbook we are unconcerned with synchronicity as an explanatory tool. Instead, we will pinpoint decisive outbreaks of the ethical in world history that were relevant to the conduct of war then and retain their relevance for warfare today. Underpinning the approach of this textbook is William McNeill's conception of "the main drive wheel of social change" in world history—that is, "encounters with strangers" and the clash of cultures such encounters engendered. No theories of synchronicity are needed to explain remarkable convergences in human thinking about the Law of War; we need only recall that, in McNeill's memorable phrase, "human beings were rovers from the start." Had they not been, humans would never have left Africa to people almost every corner of the earth. Swidden agriculturalists brought wheat from the Near East to China prior to 2000 BCE. From southeast Asia rice moved into India and China by the first millennium BCE. Precious metals flowed between the ancient city-states of Sumer and traders in Romania's Carpathian Mountains, carried overland in caravans drawn by pack animals. Mesopotamian charioteers conquered the riparian civilizations of the Near East and India around 1500 BCE, making inroads as far as Europe and China. A vital artery of trade linking the east and west, the "Silk Road," was opened in 114 BCE by Han traders, and for centuries it served as a conduit between Rome and China not only for goods but also technologies, disease, and religious and philosophical ideas. By 300 CE a caravan-based trading network embracing Eurasia and Africa was firmly established, abetted in no small degree by the introduction of camels, and by 1000 CE an "ecumenical world system" had arisen.[13]

The point is that, despite the absence of demonstrable intersecting paths of influence between ancient civilizations in their approach to warfare, such exchanges were not only possible but even probable. Indeed, some of these cultural encounters are backed by solid evidence. Near Eastern ideas concerning covenants and the depiction of the ruler as a servant of God directly influenced the ethical monotheism of ancient Israel. The immunity of heralds and ambassadors was an international norm recognized in both Greece and Persia during the first millennium BCE. At trial in peregrine praetorian courts the folk law of non-Roman litigants was absorbed into the "law of nations," which then crept into the Roman civil law as a gap-filler called "equity." Greek Stoicism underlay the Roman theory of natural law, and the religious thought of an obscure Middle Eastern sect became the cradle of Roman just war theory—an analysis of the circumstances justifying the legal resort to war (*jus ad bellum*) that continues to the present day.

In short, a world history of war crimes is to a significant degree the story of encounters between disparate cultures exerting reciprocal influence over long spans of time, particularly in their conceptions of where the boundaries between the permissible and the forbidden in warfare should be drawn. In other cases we will examine, more geographically isolated civilizations evolved unique forms of the Law of War. Chapter 1 explores the roots of the Law of War in world history with reference to some of the major civilizations of the ancient world: Mesopotamia, Egypt, China, India, Israel, and Greece. In their earliest stages, these cultures of the ancient world were identified with the gods and the cosmic order, lending an absolute authority to the pronouncements of sovereign authority. Archaic peoples sought to emulate the gods by defending their notions of order against the forces of disorder, often identified with enemy armies. The primal violence retold in the creation myths of world cultures had to be reproduced in actual social practice, leading to acts of bloodshed that modern standards would brand as war crimes. These included the sacrifice of war captives and, in some instances, ritual cannibalism. Such acts, so repellent to us today, were believed to sustain the world and ensure victory over chaos and darkness. Ancient civilizations throughout the world subscribed to these views of the importance of killing the enemy. The foreign soldier's death was a direct imitation of divine models and can thus be accurately characterized as an act of sacred violence.

As inheritors of sacred authority charged with defending the cosmic order against chaos, kings broadcast their power through feats of violent machismo—lion hunting, the slaughter of war captives, and retainer sacrifices. When their authority came under challenge during the first millennium BCE, a space was created in the human mind for subordinating the earthly ruler to higher principles of justice. However, humanitarian considerations in wartime behavior would have to await a later age for their historical moment. In antiquity limitations on warfare tended to be ceremonial and religious rather than ethical; their purpose was to reaffirm the divinely given social order as exemplified in structures like the caste system of India. Although limits existed as customary (oral) rather than positive (written) norms, these injunctions and prohibitions in the conduct of war qualify as law, insofar as they entailed disagreeable consequences for violators—that is, they were coercive—and elicited broad obedience in the ancient world.

Chapter 2 explores the Law of War in ancient civilizations untouched until the late fifteenth century CE by Europe: the cultures of the Maya, Aztecs, and North American Indian tribes (the Five Nations, the Plains Indians, and the Pueblo). In Mesoamerica the religious drive to secure sacrificial victims was fundamental to Mayan and Aztec warfare, resulting in the stylized execution of war captives. The Maya sacrificed their prisoners to open the portal to the Otherworld, the Aztecs as a propitiatory rite for their sungod, Huitzilopochtli. In North America the logic underlying warfare and the treatment of war captives is murkier, yet the cosmo-religious motives behind tribal warmaking are undeniable, appearing in the Iroquois "mourning-wars" and Pueblo "scalp societies." A linkage of warmaking with cosmic processes, such as the "Tlaloc-Venus warfare" introduced by the Mayan king Great-Jaguar-Paw, is evident in the archaeology and ethnography of the Americas—proof that, contrary to later colonial European assumptions, Indian peoples *did* possess a sophisticated Law of War, no matter how much it differed from European practice.

Chapter 3 charts the continued unfolding of the Law of War in the civilizations of ancient Rome, Islamic society, and medieval Europe. The principal legal constraint on the resort to war during the Roman Republic was the "fetial" system, a formal procedure officiated by designated priests that appears to have originated from Roman interactions with the peoples of central Italy. Aside from the fetial system, the Romans acknowledged few restraints in their conduct of war. As all of the Italian peninsula fell under Roman control, the fetial system began to fall into desuetude. As it did, however, a new concept of universal law, the *jus gentium* (law of the peoples), gradually took shape. It seems to have consisted of heterogeneous elements, among them a customary commercial law regulating trade between Rome and other Italian peoples, Roman religious ideas, and Greek Stoic philosophy. Under the impact of the peregrine praetor, a legal official who heard cases involving Roman and non-Roman parties, the *jus gentium* became a catchment for the diverse beliefs and folkways of the far-flung Roman Empire. Built on the customary law common to the peoples of the Roman world, the *jus gentium* demonstrates the importance of cultural encounters to the history of the Law of War. Nonetheless, the "law of the peoples" had no impact on the Roman way of war, which remained brutal and implacable well into the twilight of the empire.

Chapter 3 also examines the Muslim Law of War, focusing on Islamic legal doctrines of war captive treatment and just war. The early Islamic policy of sparing war captives and enemy civilians as Muslim armies united Arabia prompted seventh- and eighth-century Islamic jurists to uphold the inviolability of prisoners' lives. As Islam spread in later centuries through the Middle East, Asia, Africa, and Europe, this tolerant policy of sparing prisoners was abandoned, but even then Islamic jurists insisted that captives could not be executed when guarantees of safety had been made or the interests of Muslim society opposed execution. Similarly, *jihad* (holy war) was to be waged against non-Muslim pagans, who were confronted with the choice of either converting or being put to the sword. Like prisoner execution, *jihad* was subject to limitation: in their dealings with Jews and Christians, Muslim conquerors demanded either conversion or payment of a community tax. If the tax was paid regularly, Jews and Christians could live peacefully as religious minorities within the Islamic state, free to practice their religion as they chose.

The topic of Islamic *jihad* furnishes the bridge in Chapter 3 to discussing its rough medieval European counterpart, just war theory. In the hands of the Bishop of Hippo, St. Augustine, the just war theory of the Romans was reinterpreted; thereafter, it was approved not only as a means of securing damages from offender nations but of punishing sins against God. Augustine in effect Christianized just war theory, transforming it into a doctrine of holy war that by the High Middle Ages would support the Crusades and the Church's wars against heretics. Consistent with his Roman sources, Augustine showed concern only for the conditions justifying resort to war, not with how war should be waged once it began. By the thirteenth century CE, however, some Roman canon jurists were beginning to lay down principles of accountability for launching an illegal war, arguing that a ruler fighting without just cause was liable for the property damage he caused and, most strikingly, that soldiers who killed in support of an unjust war should be put on trial for committing homicide. None of these Roman canon scholars, as the chapter notes, produced an enforceable Law of War; this remained to the secular authorities in Europe who did the actual fighting. By the 1300s, a body of law had arisen to govern the conduct of hostilities between noblemen, the "law of the knights." While not applicable to combat between the nobility and commoners, the law of the knights captured basic principles of chivalry like the right to quarter and enforced them in formal court proceedings. The records of these trials, many of which have been preserved, reveal that most involved disputes that are obscure for the modern observer. The litigants were often soldiers bound by oaths of loyalty to different sovereigns, accused of treason by one of their lords. Occasionally, a matter arose in a court of chivalry that more closely resembled a trial for war crimes; such cases tended to be the exception. At no time, it is emphasized, did medieval chivalry or the law of the knights ever develop into an international body of law.

Chapter 4 makes clear that the first fruitful attempts to constrain the actions of belligerents were undertaken by national governments and were effected by means of domestic laws and military orders issued to soldiers in the field. Some of these provisions, which date back as early as the thirteenth century, prohibited robbery, plunder, and rape and even created categories of protected persons—unarmed women, children, clergymen, and the peasantry. None of these laws sought to enforce international norms; an ordinance promulgated by King Charles VII that forbade "pillage and abuses," for example, threatened to punish violators for high treason. The English Crown issued similar laws in the seventeenth century prohibiting rape, robbery, and desecration of churches while enjoining English soldiers to pay fair value for any food they seized. Further, the laws imposed on the English army the duty to give quarter;[14] failure to comply with this obligation was punishable by death. Comparable ordinances issued by the Scots in the 1640s not only recited the prohibitions of rape, murder, and plunder, but stated that matters not squarely addressed by the ordinances should be interpreted "by the light and law of nature." Despite these and other progressive installments in the Law of War, macabre battlefield excesses characterized early modernity, driven by a higher incidence of siege warfare, rebellion, and religious conflict. By the mid-seventeenth century, however, the extreme violence of the previous era had spent itself, its vigor sapped by deconfessionalization, war-weariness, and a growing appreciation for the benefits of reciprocity. It was in this tumultuous era that the great Spanish Law of War theoreticians composed the most thoughtful treatises on the subject up to that time: Vitoria, Ayala, Suárez, Gentili, and Grotius.

Chapter 5 charts the catastrophic encounter of New World peoples with European colonists in the early modern period. To the deadly admixture of racism, cultural chauvinism, technological advantages, rapacity, and epidemic disease, Europeans added the notion characteristic of their wars against heretics, Muslims, and the Irish that New World peoples were pagan barbarians ineligible for the protections of chivalry. Assimilating them to subhuman animals, devils, and predators, Spanish and English armies waged indiscriminate war against Indian men, women, and children with the aim of either enslaving or exterminating them. The deeply entrenched idea of Indian inferiority became a fixture of European and American thought about Native Americans well into the nineteenth and early twentieth centuries, conditioning and coarsening the attitudes of politicians, government officials, and legal scholars toward them.

Chapter 6 chronicles the emergence of sovereign nation-states in world history and their impact on the Law of War. The Peace of Westphalia ending the Thirty Years War produced the European system of sovereign countries presided over by powerful kings like Louis XIV—kings who transformed the desultory warfare of past ages into a focus of royal action, waged by national armies recentered on a strict chain of command and instilled with military discipline. For much of the eighteenth century, these European armies fought dynastic wars on behalf of their kings with little effect on the common people. This priority would change with the rise of "citizen" armies in the late eighteenth century. Particularly in France after 1789, armies reorganized to accentuate talent rather than family connections were imbued with a new national consciousness. By the nineteenth century, these developments began to yield increasingly destructive wars, especially when combined with improvements in the technology of warfare. The enhanced lethality of warfare made possible by these changes led to the first international efforts to restrain the unnecessary suffering of war through treaties, among them the Geneva and Hague Conventions.

Although this new humanitarian concern with taming the worst excesses of war was genuine, it stood in counterpoint to the doctrine of military necessity espoused by the Great Powers. The failure—or refusal—of powerful nation-states to accept the tenets of international humanitarian law[15] would lead to ghastly atrocities during the First World War, including the first European genocide of the twentieth century: the extermination of Turkey's Armenian population. Chapter 6 emphasizes that, while we tend to think of the Law of War as a body of international legal principles, in fact it has historically been enforced at the level of national governments and their armies. A leading proof of this assertion is the codification of the Law of War undertaken by Columbia law professor Francis Lieber under the orders of President Abraham Lincoln. Lieber's Code, which for influence on subsequent approaches to the Law of War may be unrivaled, underscores the falsity of the view that the "customs and usages" of war have historically lacked any criminal enforcement. For centuries the Law of War was codified and enforced as military law governing armies in the field. What the Law of War lacked was not criminal enforcement, but *international* criminal enforcement.

Concerted efforts to cure this defect were first made only in the twentieth century. The mixed results of these endeavors are the subject of Chapters 7 and 8. The spectacular failure of the Allies after the First World War to achieve any of their plans to punish war crimes committed by the Central Powers—plans that included trial of the Kaiser and his top officials by an international tribunal—became an object lesson for their descendants during the Second World War. With the negative touchstone of the First World War before them, Allied officials formulated a uniform war crimes policy envisioning the prosecution of lower-ranking Axis offenders in national courts and by 1945 the trial of "major war criminals" in an international military tribunal. The jurisprudence created by Allied tribunals would become the essential foundation of modern international criminal law. Their foundational concepts would be applied after 1945 to war crimes committed across the world, from Cambodia and Iraq to the former Yugoslavia and Rwanda.

Chapter 9 surveys developments in the Law of War since the immediate postwar era. It briefly touches on some of the knottiest problems addressed in the leading international conventions after 1945, such as the status of guerrillas and the treatment prescribed under modern treaties for fighters associated with independence movements. The chapter then shifts its attention to the formation of ad hoc United Nations (UN) tribunals and a permanent international criminal court at the end of the twentieth century. The chapter concludes with a series of reflections on terrorism and the resort to torture in the US "global war on terror."

The final chapter of the book, Chapter 10, tries to understand war crimes as a world historical phenomenon, using the methodologies of world history to probe the cross-cultural, trans-regional, and trans-temporal forces that have molded culture and human psychology, enhancing their susceptibility to extreme wartime violence. Avoiding mainstream criminological analysis as inappropriate to world historical study, we will focus on deep structures underlying the commission of atrocities in warfare. Our foray into the long-term causes of war crimes will expose us to David Livingstone Smith's dehumanization theory, Jan Assmann's theory of total religion, the dispositional and characterological theories of Theodor Adorno and John Steiner, theories that attribute war crimes to structures of modernity (such as those of Hannah Arendt and Zygmunt Bauman), and social-psychological approaches pioneered by Stanley Milgram and Philip Zimbardo, whose researches have affected later theories advanced by Christopher Browning, James Waller, and Dave Grossman.

This book does not regard every advancement toward constraint as a simultaneous victory for a more humane warfare. The fact that modern nations like France and the USA would revive the medieval practice of torture as official policy debunks this cheerful thought as an illusion. Rather, it is hoped our global journey through several thousand years of the Law of War will enable the student to understand that human civilizations have always imbedded warfare in a larger interpretive framework. When we use the word "constraint" in this book, we do not mean by it a blanket prohibition of violence during war. We mean what the Franco-Latin roots of the word signified in the fourteenth century: a "binding together" or "drawing tight." The forces that "bound together" or "drew tight" the violence of war have varied depending on the variables of time and place. In one it was religious ritual, in another it was the recouping of damages for injury done; in still another, it was reaffirmation of social class, military discipline, or a sense of fair play. Occasionally but infrequently, it was humanitarianism. Because the dominant constraint on war today is humanitarian, we may be tempted to believe that all limitations on battle in world history were antique forerunners of our own. Such an assumption is erroneous. Nonetheless, the persistence of constraints on warfare gives us reasonable cause for hope. Standing in the shadow of weapons that could destroy all human life on this planet, the inborn tendency of our species toward moderating the worst effects of its own violent behavior is no trivial matter.

CHAPTER 1
THE ROOTS OF THE LAW OF WAR
IN WORLD HISTORY

Stone Age warfare

On August 11, 1880, William Tecumseh Sherman, the commanding general of the United States Army and former Civil War general, stood before a cheering crowd of five thousand veterans in Columbus, Ohio. The gales of applause that greeted Sherman were ill-matched to the somber message he would offer his listeners—particularly the youths among them—in his impromptu speech. "There is many a boy here today," Sherman cautioned, "who looks on war as all glory, but, boys, it is all hell. I look upon war with horror, but if it has to come I am here."[1] Sherman, who had spent the last two years of the war burning much of Georgia between Atlanta and Savannah to the ground, had not converted to pacifism. Yet, the old general expressed a view of war echoed in the assessments of countless other military men through the ages—a view that takes the full measure of war as a cruel, dehumanizing, and murderous affair coldly indifferent to human values, an activity inimical to all touched by it and ready at any moment to debase everyone and destroy everything connected with it.

Well before history's first world empire arose in Mesopotamia, the soldiers of hostile armies were butchering each other with frightful effectiveness. Although we tend to associate war with states, Stone Age societies were by no means strangers to indiscriminate violence, as the archaeological record convincingly shows. Stone Age massacre victims, however, rarely numbered above several dozen. Excavation of graves at Djebel Sahaba in Sudan dating to the Upper Paleolithic (12,000–10,000 BCE) have yielded the remains of fifty-nine men, women, and children bearing the marks of traumatic injury from blunt objects and projectiles—victims who appear to have perished in a Stone Age massacre.[2] A later killing site was excavated in the 1980s in Talheim (Baden-Württemberg, Germany). It consists of a mass grave of thirty-four victims—eighteen adults and sixteen children—dispatched from behind with both thin- and thick-bladed stone axes.[3] As David L. Smith has observed about such Stone Age atrocities, the lack of concentrated population centers tended to check the scale of the carnage. However, with the onset of the agricultural revolution some 12,000 years ago, which gradually transformed hunter-gatherers into farmers and pastoralists and thereby laid the foundation for sedentary and growing populations, the lethality of military conflict swelled.[4] This development was the essential precondition to the martial holocausts of late antiquity. John Keegan describes the role of the agricultural revolution in the history of warfare:

Hunters and gatherers may have "territory"; pastoralists have grazing and watering-places; agriculturalists have land. Once man invests expectations of a regular return on his seasonal efforts in a particular place . . . he rapidly develops the sense of rights and ownership. Toward those who trespass on the places where he invests his time and effort he must equally rapidly develop the hostility of the user and occupier for the usurper and interloper Pastoralism, and agriculture even more so, make for war.[5]

As Neolithic populations increased, they converted the weapons used by their Paleolithic forbears to hunt game into deadly military arms. By 8000 BCE, a revolution in military technology had emerged alongside the revolution in agriculture. At this time, Neolithic peoples invented the sling, dagger, mace, and—most importantly—the bow, a weapon unknown to Old Stone Age hunters. Converting human muscle into mechanical power, the bow enabled its Neolithic users to fell speedy animals as they roamed over regions opened by the retreating glaciers. It also became a formidable weapon for use in Neolithic battles between the new agriculturalists and hunter-gatherers covetous of their land. Keegan, in fact, interprets Site 117 at Djebel Sahaba as the outcome of a clash between farmer-pastoralists and nomadic hunters. Archaeological excavations at Jericho (Jordan) have revealed the existence of an agricultural community of 2,000 to 3,000 residents as long ago as 9000 BCE. Encircled by a ten-foot-thick, thirteen-foot-high wall crenelated with towers and girdled with a moat, Jericho was clearly built to withstand military assault, proving that warfare did not originate during the creation and expansion of Near Eastern empires but already conditioned settlement patterns at the dawn of agriculture 11,000 years ago.[6]

While wholesale changes wrought by farming, animal domestication, and technological innovation significantly enhanced the destructiveness of warfare, the rise of strong kings able to organize large armies and mobilize them against their enemies brought the science of mass killing to unprecedented levels. The success of these kings in seizing, consolidating, and expanding their vast power was itself made possible by the agricultural revolution and the surplus produced by farming populations, especially in Mesopotamia and Egypt.

The human imagination and the quest for cosmic order

One of the main obstacles facing us as we try to understand constraints on warfare is our remoteness from the psychology and worldview of premodern peoples. The modern mind is an analyzer and fragmenter; it "disenchants"[7] the world, stripping it of unity, cohesion, and purpose. In short, as the scholar of religion Mircea Eliade has written, modernity "desacralizes" nature. Negation of the sacred relegates everything to the realm of "profane existence," in which "man feels no responsibility except to himself and to society." Eliade continues:

For [modern man], the universe does not constitute a cosmos—that is, a living and articulated unity; it is simply the sum of the material reserves and physical energies of the planet … By contrast, the premodern person "always puts himself in a cosmic context." His personal experience lacks neither genuineness nor depth; but the fact that it is expressed in a language unfamiliar to us makes it appear spurious or infantile to modern eyes.[8]

Unique in the animal kingdom, humans from the start possessed a fertile imagination, one that conjured meanings and invested the material world with them. Insofar as imagination and meaning-production are prelinguistic, it would seem that both are more basic to the human mind than language. To comprehend them, therefore, we cannot always rely on written texts for evidence, particularly in hunting/gathering cultures and early agrarian societies devoid of a written language. Hence we are thrown back onto the archaeological and anthropological record for traces of a given culture's worldview.

Paleolithic material culture attests to a soaring human imagination expressive of a symbolic consciousness. Cave paintings at Lascaux, Trois Frères, Chauvet (France), and Alta Mira (Spain) reveal Old Stone Age artists affirming through their portrayals of wild animals a connection with these creatures and the higher, transhuman forces imbuing them. The near inaccessibility of the cave interiors chosen to display these paintings suggests that they were intended to serve a spiritual function.[9] According to one view, parietal art was the work of shamans pursuing "vision quests" by torchlight in European caves.[10] Stone Age cave art betokens, in the words of Dutch archaeologist Henri Frankfort, "man's intimate and reciprocal relationship with the animals, and beyond these, with the divine."[11] Prior to language, prior to writing, prior to the rise of agriculture, cities, and centralized rule, humans were religious beings who translated their spiritual yearnings into images daubed with ochre and charcoal onto the walls of rock shelters. Appearing in the fossil record before nearly every other form of culture (with the possible exception of tool-making), these impulses are fundamental to human beings at the earliest stages of their development.

The modern mind grapples to understand such religiosity. Eliade writes: "The man of the archaic societies tends to live as much as possible *in* the sacred or in close proximity to consecrated objects."[12] The world of ancient peoples was suffused with spiritual meaning. The closer their proximity to the sacred, the greater their experience of the real. In sharp contrast with later interpretations of the divine, archaic peoples did not wall off the sacred from everyday existence; rather, they lived the totality of their lives in its midst. By means of ritual the mundane world could be brought into contact with the divine. Long before Christian theologians preached the imitation of Christ (*Imitatio Christi*), archaic peoples sought to imitate their own gods through ceremonial acts operating as conduits of absolute reality. In their cultures the *axis mundi*—the "axis of the world" believed to support the earth, heaven, and the underworld—was reproduced by a sacred pole or pillar at the center of a building. The sacred pole was also likened to the "cosmic mountain" located at the world's midpoint, linking the earth with heaven. In Harappa and Mohenjo Daro as well as ancient Mesopotamia, the ziggurat[13] was a homology of the cosmic mountain.[14]

Figure 1 Charcoal images of four horses drawn on the wall of the Chauvet Cave in southern France, circa 30,500–35,500 years ago. © Wikimedia Commons (public domain).

Because the gods were creators of the cosmos, archaic peoples could participate in the sacred by imitating their creative act. According to Eliade, "every construction or fabrication has the cosmogony [i.e., creation of the cosmos] as paradigmatic model. The creation of the world becomes the archetype of every creative human gesture, whatever its plane of reference may be."[15] Thus the Algonquin and Lakota Indians constructed their sacred lodge in imitation of the cosmos: the roof was the sky, the floor the earth, the four walls the points of the compass. Eliade observes that in building the sacred lodge to correspond with the spatial dimensions of the cosmos, native peoples were reenacting its creation. This "founding of a world" denoted the reclamation of order from disorder, of meaning and life from chaos and death. For this reason, armed defense of sacred space became an effort to prevent chaos from engulfing cosmic order.[16]

In view of such a way of seeing reality, transcultural myths of the gods' victory over dragons and monsters take on a different hue. The ancient Egyptians, Persians, Mesopotamians, and Hebrews all retailed these stories. As an agent of darkness, water, night, and death, the dragon must be conquered and dismembered to allow the birth of the cosmos. The gods' victory was reproduced each time an invading army was repelled: the victory over the hostile power not only beat back chaos and death but reenacted the gods' creation of the cosmos. Eliade speculates that fortifications like trenches and ramparts surrounding human settlements began as "magical defenses" against attack by demons and ghosts (symbols of agents of disorder). He sees residues of this archaic idea in the North Indian practice of keeping the evil spirits of disease out of a town by drawing a circle around it. Similarly, medieval Europeans understood their city walls as barring the entry of Satan, disease, and death.[17] In these and other examples, the parallelism between military invasion and the divine cosmogony is striking: in triumphing over an armed foe, ancient peoples participated with the gods in world-creation and preservation.

Archaic mythologies demanded a blood sacrifice in order to both create and sustain the cosmos. The elements of the world were harvested from the body of the slain Norse giant Aurgelmir—his flesh became the earth, his teeth stones, his bones mountains, his blood the seas, his skull the sky, his brain the clouds. In India the primal man Purusha was sacrificed, and from his body grew the four *varnas* (classes) of Hindu society. Similarly, the Daoist Chinese cosmogony focused on the primal man Pan Gu, a monstrous horned and tusked figure covered with hair, from whose vast corpse the universe was created. Following the examples of their gods, archaic peoples offered human and animal sacrifices to consecrate their homes and temples. These *Bauopfer* (building sacrifices) typically involved the burial of a sacrificial victim under the floor of a newly constructed domicile. Because the house was supposed to represent the cosmos, its creation had to reenact these spectacular, world-generative killings; without them, the building would just be an ordinary structure, not an "image of the world" (*imago mundi*). Such a structure, one patterned after the gods' own sanguinary creative act, is truly at the Center of the World, and "to live near to a Center of the World is … equivalent to living as close as possible to the gods."[18]

Murder, killing, immolation, sacrifice, and dismemberment, while incised in the creation myths of archaic cultures, are also staple themes in the soldier's breviary. These are deeds that later times will consider to be war crimes. For archaic peoples, however, they were the means by which the gods created the cosmos from chaos. In order to align oneself with the gods and share in their spiritual power, primordial violence had to be recalled and emulated. An example is ritual cannibalism, a behavior abhorrent to the modern sensibility. As with other acts of premodern humans, cannibalism served a ritualistic function. The gods, whose killing and consumption of a victim's body created and maintained the world, set the example. Particularly after the agricultural revolution and the rise of sedentary farming, archaic peoples imitated their gods by spilling blood and eating the decedent with the aim of guaranteeing the growth of plants. The killer/cannibal is not a deviant in such societies; he is shouldering a weighty social responsibility based on "divine, transhuman models." Eliade exhorts us to remember the religious character of acts we find morally obnoxious; archaic peoples carried them out in the belief they were following the gods and defending their world from dissolution.[19] This insight will be critical as we later delve into the practices of premodern armies involving mass execution, decapitation, ritual cannibalism, and blood-letting. Removed from the grammar of religion, such practices appear irredeemably cruel. When seen in light of the actors' quest for cosmic order, they become, if not more sympathetic, then at least more understandable.

The rise of kingship and the excesses of warfare

It is hard to envision that human societies before the rise of states were ever perfectly equal. If anthropological studies of more recent higher hunting and gathering cultures accurately capture the social makeup of their prehistoric ancestors, then the evolution of kinship-based "bands" into "tribal states" creates a group of authoritative political leaders, the "chieftains." These figures enjoy a status exalted above the tribes over which they preside. As anthropologist E. Adamson Hoebel once noted, a marked tendency toward hereditary succession begins to emerge at this point in social development. With the rise of the chieftain, human society began to advance steadily toward kingship. The transition from tribal states ruled by chieftains to territorial states ruled by kings likely occurred when the agricultural revolution produced a surplus that could be expropriated by these powerful elites.[20]

What might enable a single individual to justify his claim to supremacy over a large, increasingly differentiated society? With this question, we enter to a certain degree into the realm of speculation. According to Lewis Mumford, we can piece together the origins of kingship by looking at two world civilizations in which kings first appear on the stage of history: Mesopotamia[21] and Egypt. When we do, we find recurrent portrayals of the king as a prolific hunter of lions and other dangerous animals. With the advent of the first kings, the hunter's weapons previously described—the mace, sling, dagger, and bow—are turned against people to compel their obedience to the king's commands. Mumford observes that Assyrian kings equated hunting with warfare and identified both of these activities with themselves.[22] The supreme hunter is also the supreme ruler, and

Figure 2 Ashurnasirpal II hunting lions. © Wikimedia Commons (public domain).

those who defied his authority would suffer the fate of the big game depicted on Egyptian and Mesopotamian stelae—carcasses skewered with the king's arrows.

The king's status as preeminent hunter was insufficient by itself to secure the obedience he demanded. In order to justify expropriating the taxes and tribute needed to maintain an army and a bureaucracy, another element had to be introduced: the fusion of the king's person with the sacred. The institution of divine kingship is found everywhere in the ancient world, in civilizations as geographically disparate as Old Kingdom Egypt, Mesoamerican Indian cultures, and Shang China.[23] Wherever it existed, the identification of the king with the gods bolstered his claim to superior authority. In ancient Egypt, the Pharaoh was not only a fearsome warrior par excellence but was himself a god whose very person integrated society and the cosmos. The outward manifestation of this integrative function of the Pharaoh was his responsibility to ensure performance of religious ritual and to preserve the temples where ritual was enacted. By means of ritual, the Pharaoh maintained the cosmic order of Egyptian life, from the movement of the sun through the heavens to the annual flooding of the Nile River.[24] This melding of secular and religious powers conferred on the Pharaoh an awesome majesty: the living embodiment of his community, his life and prosperity were synonymous with those of his subjects. When he thrived, so did society. Clearly, the commands of such a figure must in all circumstances be obeyed.

One sign of the Pharaoh's deification and the immense power flowing from it was human sacrifice, a practice found throughout world civilizations in antiquity. Human sacrifice assumed different forms in the ancient world; the most common were "retainer" sacrifices, in which the wives and attendants of the deceased king were interred with him. Retainer sacrifices typify royal burials in the First and Second Egyptian Dynasties but, as in Mesopotamia, the practice vanished thereafter from the historical record. In Egypt these sacrifices of the Pharaoh's *ménage*—his wives, officials, and servants—are charnel house reminders of his power: only the king as a divinity could take his own household with him into the next world.[25]

A similar conjunction of royal divinization and retainer sacrifice characterized early states in Mesopotamia and China. In Sumer, where kingship arose more or less contemporaneously with Egypt, the institution of the king was held at least as early as the Middle Bronze Age (ca. 2100–1550 BCE) to have been "lowered down from heaven," a phrase used in the Sumerian King List. Unlike Egypt, however, the Mesopotamian king was not typically deified; instead, he was considered a "great man" (*lugal*).[26] This restriction notwithstanding, Mesopotamian kings were closely associated with the gods and, much like the Egyptian Pharaohs, were expected to maintain the harmony of material society and the cosmos. In the preamble to the Code of Hammurabi, the king states that the chief deity of the Babylonians, Marduk, "had given me the mission to keep my people in order and to make my country take the right road." In the epilogue, Hammurabi returns to his self-portrayal as an agent of the gods: "The great gods have called me, and I am indeed the good shepherd who brings peace, with the just scepter." Hammurabi is a man, not a god—but he is an intermediary of the chief god, communicating Marduk's commandments to his people. Babylonian iconography represents Hammurabi conversing with the gods on terms of relative equality. Such evidence suggests that the importance of Mesopotamian monarchs, while a step down from that of the divine Pharaoh, is nonetheless considerable, and we should therefore not be surprised when we find retainer sacrifices in the Early Dynastic royal tombs of Mesopotamia. The most notable was the Great Death-pit of Ur excavated by Sir Leonard Woolley, in which members of the royal household—six guards and sixty-eight women— were dispatched with blows to the head and placed in the tomb to accompany Queen Pu-abi into the afterlife.[27]

Human sacrifice was also practiced in Shang China (ca. 1766–1122 BCE), but there the sacrificial victims were more diverse. The royal tombs at Anyang, the last and most powerful capital of the Shang Dynasty, contain the decapitated skeletons of both servants and prisoners of war. As in Egypt and Mesopotamia, these unfortunates were expected to serve the Shang king in the afterlife. The inclusion of prisoners of war as sacrificial victims highlights a prominent theme in ancient religion: the interplay between sovereignty, religion, and the ceremonial killing of war captives. In Shang China, the king was not a god; however, he would become an exceedingly powerful ancestor after his death, and for this reason he was a seminal force in Shang ritual. Although priests typically carried out human sacrifice, they did so on behalf of the king as the intercessor

Figure 3 Basalt stele of Hammurabi talking with Marduk. © Wikimedia Commons (public domain).

between the community and the gods. Ritual was of paramount significance to ancient peoples like the Shang. In fact, according to geographer Paul Wheatley, Chinese cities first came into being as ritual centers, or "cosmo-magical cities," in which religious ritual was offered to the gods as a means of integrating society and the cosmos. For the Shang rulers, the sacrificial victims required by these rituals could be obtained only through warfare. The oracle bones—our primary source on the history of Shang China—report that the Shang mounted military expeditions of as many as 13,000 troops, seizing after one battle 30,000 prisoners of war. Three hundred of the captives were sacrificed. If our interpretations of the archaeological evidence are correct, then religious ritual to ensure the harmony of heaven and earth was the driving force behind urbanization and armed conflict in ancient China.[28]

This nexus between the slaughter of war captives and regal power is explicit in Egyptian antiquity. Retainer sacrifices of the Pharaoh's household are evident in the First and Second Dynasties, but disappear thereafter.[29] Nonetheless, evidence spanning thousands of years of Egyptian history suggests that prisoners of war may have been sacrificed ritualistically at the end of battle. John Keegan juxtaposes two representations of the Pharaoh separated by nearly two millennia: that of Menes, the legendary unifier of Upper and Lower Egypt, and Ramses II. The figuration of Menes is found on the Narmer palette (ca. 3000 BCE) (Figure 4). On one side, Menes towers above his defeated enemy, holding

Figure 4 Relief from the Narmer palette, *c.*3100 BCE. On the one side, the Pharaoh strikes the classic "smiting of the enemies" pose; on the obverse side, the decapitated bodies of the Pharaoh's enemies lie sprawled before him. Some commentators believe that both images portray the victory of the Pharaoh over chaos and evil.

aloft a mace[30] that will deal the coup-de-grace. On the reverse side, Menes has assumed truly superhuman stature: a Goliath-sized figure twice as large as his dwarfish attendants, he hulks in regal profile, reviewing a field of decapitated enemy soldiers. Seventeen hundred years later, a Nineteenth Dynasty fresco portrayed Ramses II in a similar posture, looming over a Nubian captive whom he is in the process of killing. For Keegan, the remarkable persistence of this image is not purely conventional; rather, it hints at a practice of ritualistic human sacrifice of captives on the battlefield when retainer sacrifice had been either discontinued or was being phased out. The heroic proportions of both Pharaohs likewise convey a message to those who behold these images even today. For scholars Jean Guilaine and Jean Zammit, the Narmer palette (and, by implication, the death-dealing image of Ramses) "symbolizes the omnipotent sovereign overpowering all who challenge him. Massacre is shown to be a symbol of authority."[31]

The massacre of enemy soldiers at the hands of a ruler conceived as the preserver of cosmic order is the all-too-frequent marker of kingship in the ancient world. The"cylinder seals" of Uruk, the leading city-state of Sumer (ca. 4000–3100 BCE), portray early kings beating kneeling war captives with sticks in preparation for their execution.[32] The Assyrian king Sennacherib (705–681 BCE) exulted in the slaughter of Elamite soldiers, vaunting that he "cut their throats like sheep" and "filled the plain with corpses of their warriors."[33] More than a millennium before their defeat at Sennacherib's hands, the Elamites had sacked the ancient city of Ur (ca. 1950 BCE), stacking the bodies of the slain on the city gates and strewing Ur's boulevards with their heads. According to a Mesopotamian poet, the Elamites "made the blood of the Land flow down the wadis like copper or tin. Its corpses, like fat left in the sun, melted away of themselves."[34] These atrocities may or may not have been done for ritualistic purposes, but they unquestionably projected the immense authority of the ruler, a person seemingly unbound from ethical constraint.

The softening of royal power

No exertion of the imagination is needed to grasp that the commands of monarchs in the ancient world were absolute. In the Babylonian cosmogony told in the Enûma Eliš, Marduk demands that all of the other gods obey his orders unconditionally. We may presume that the absoluteness of Marduk's commands extended to those of his representative, the Babylonian king.

The functional need for such obedience may be debated. Without doubt, kings furnished vital services to their communities, such as rationing and allocating scarce resources, as well as coordinating the manpower of separate communities to perform essential tasks that would have been impossible had they acted alone. On the other hand, the very absoluteness of the king's will foreclosed any critical evaluation of the actions carried out on his authority. The royal and religious imperatives of the ancient world prior to the first millennium BCE were ceremonial, but not ethical.

This being said, there are occasional glimpses of an alternative view of royal authority even before the extraordinary challenges to absolutism that will erupt between 800 and 200 BCE. It is visible at points in the epilogue to the Code of Hammurabi, which presents a nuanced portrait of regal power. Hammurabi is a confidant and ambassador of Marduk, and thus must be obeyed unconditionally; at the same time, the king refers to himself as a "good shepherd who brings peace." In language that presages the Hebrew Book of Isaiah, Hammurabi proclaims he has "harbored" his people "to prevent the powerful from oppressing the weak, in order to give justice to the orphans and the widows."[35] Similarly, as Jan Assmann has argued, the emphasis in the Egyptian conception of the Pharaoh as a god metamorphosed over time into the son of god and later into the servant of god.[36] While the Pharaoh retained his divine status, this emphasis on his role as a servant of god already involves—at least implicitly—a subordination of the king to a higher power. In Robert Bellah's words, "it was the god who was the real ruler."[37]

Something new was gradually emerging in world history, a sprig of green thrusting forth from the seemingly impenetrable crust of absolute kingship: the notion that worldly power and the divine will were not identical. The rest of this chapter will focus on six world civilizations of the ancient world: Egypt, Mesopotamia, China, India, Israel, and Greece. We will see that in these cultures the idea of constraining the conduct of warfare had its roots in religious ceremonialism. At the same time, we will also come to appreciate that monumental changes in the sovereign's ability to wage war were afoot during the first millennium before the Common Era.

Ancient Egypt and the Law of War: the centrality of ma'at

With an eye fixed firmly on twentieth-century autocracies, modern people today might think that a society governed by an absolute ruler like the Pharaoh must have been totalitarian. The Pharaoh's divinity—he was associated with Amun-re, and unlike Mesopotamian kings was not merely a vicar of the gods but was himself divine—invested the Egyptian state with supreme authority, an authority that, as Frankfort notes, "subjects the people unreservedly to the ruler's command."[38] In the Egyptian cosmogony the Creator God was also the first king. After bringing the cosmos[39] into being, God transferred his role as Creator and Preserver of the cosmic order to the first Pharaoh as his son. The clear implication is that kingship in Egypt was not historical but existed from the beginning of time.[40]

In fact, our commonsense assumption of Egyptian totalitarianism would be a misjudgment of Egypt's social and political order. Writing in 1956, Frankfort cautioned that "nothing would be more misleading than to picture the Egyptians in abject submission to their absolute ruler."[41] In sharp contrast with other civilizations we will consider, the Egyptians accepted and supported their system of governance for three thousand years. We have no evidence that their theocratic polity was imposed on them; rather, it seems to have developed incrementally over vast spans of nearly unimaginable time, affording them a sense of quiet stability accompanied by the reassurance that their God-King would sustain the cosmos. Not until the Greeks did ancient civilizations distinguish between a higher or sacred order of being and their own social world. For the Egyptians, society and the cosmic order were fused. There was no separation of religion and statecraft, of God and society. As German Egyptologist Jan Assmann describes it, "the Egyptian gods are not only *in* the world, they *are* the world."[42] Hence the Egyptian political system with the divine Pharaoh at its head was not only political but religious as well; it was a "theopolitical order"[43] reflected in the Pharaoh's status as both god and king.

The Pharaoh was associated with fearsome creatures that conveyed his majesty: the lion, bull, and falcon. From at least the time of Amenophis II (reigned ca. 1426–1400 BCE) he was identified with the sungod Amun-Re. Amenophis III (reigned 1390–1353 BCE) built a temple in Nubia, the land closest to the sun from the vantage point of Egypt, in which he could be worshipped as a sun king. (Tutankhamen and Ramesses II both emulated his example and constructed temples for their own worship as solar monarchs.) The depiction of Amenophis in cultic images with a falcon head and a solar disk asserted his identity with Re.[44] In this role as sungod, the Pharaoh restrained the chaos and disorder that threatened to engulf Egypt. It is noteworthy that the sungod Re had always been worshipped as a bulwark against chaos. The Egyptians extolled his creation of the world as a victory over disorder, as expressed in the formula, "He [Re] put order [ma'at] in the place of chaos." Similarly, Tutankhamen's restoration of traditional Egyptian religion after his father's heresy was celebrated with nearly identical language: "He put ma'at in the place of falsehood."[45]

In our efforts to grasp the Egyptian Law of War, we must reckon with this term "ma'at" and its close affiliations with the Pharaoh. The defense of ma'at was the purpose of Egyptian warfare, and whatever rules governed Egyptian military practice were derived from ma'at. Jan Assmann asserts that ma'at can only be approximately translated into other languages as "truth, justice, right, order, wisdom, authenticity, honesty." He continues:

> [Ma'at] relates to morality and manners in human communal life, to the divine justice of the final judgment, to the daily victory over chaos by the cosmos-creating sun god and the cosmos-creating laws of his earthly likeness, the king.[46]

According to Assmann, ma'at is not only the "social justice" that should prevail within Egyptian society but "justice as world order."[47] Ma'at had to be continually sustained in order to bind the world together and keep chaos at bay. As the sun king the Pharaoh was the defender and upholder of ma'at on earth, and he discharged this inestimably vital function through hunting dangerous animals and waging war on foreigners.

Dangerous animals and foreigners are on their face radically dissimilar, yet for the Egyptians they were functionally the same. Both represented the forces of chaos and evil that the sun king had to subdue in his bid to preserve the cosmic order. Like other ancient peoples following their "divine, transhuman models," the Pharaoh reenacted Re's defeat of the serpent Apophis (symbolic of chaos) by defeating foreign armies. His victory over Egypt's enemies both replicated the sun's victory over the serpent and guaranteed the world's survival.[48] The expectation that the Pharaoh would put chaos to rout was tangible enough that every Egyptian king—including more dovish Pharaohs like Hatshepsut and Akhenaton—demonstrated his (or, in Hatshepsut's case, her) military prowess soon after ascending the throne. The ritual "smiting of the enemies" motif likely arose from this cultural norm of the Pharaoh as an antagonist of world-destroying disorder rather than from military or geopolitical factors.[49]

Figure 5 Panel from funerary chest, tomb of King Tutankhamen, *c.*1323 BC, representing the youthful Pharaoh slaying the enemies of Egypt. © DEA / W. BUSS / Getty Images.

Figure 6 Panel from the same funerary chest, depicting King Tutankhamen hunting gazelles from his chariot with a bow and arrow. Note the topos of the Pharaoh as both hunter and warrior conveyed in these conjoined images. The Pharaoh's victory over big game and enemy armies reenacted Re's victory over chaos. © Werner Forman / Getty Images.

Along with foreign enemies, game animals represented the forces of chaos that had to be contained. The nexus in ancient societies between warfare and hunting reappears in ancient Egypt, where the Pharaoh is both a master hunter and superior warlord. In fact, together with his role as supreme builder, the attributes of hunter and warrior are the Pharaoh's defining qualities. These characteristics are closely intertwined in Egyptian iconography. On King Tutankhamen's funerary chest, for example, the youthful Pharaoh is portrayed in one panel standing in his chariot, killing his enemies with a bow and arrow (Figure 5). In a separate panel of the chest, Tut appears in the same chariot and pose, slaying animals with the same weapon (Figure 6). Obverse depictions of war and hunting are commonplace in ancient Egypt. Erik Hornung tells us that one side of a ring belonging to Amenophis II contains a scene of the king doing battle against Egypt's enemies while the other side depicts him killing a lion.[50] Juxtaposition of such imagery conveys the message that the Pharaoh is the salvific figure who defeats the chaos represented by foreigners and wild animals. His importance to success in battle or in the hunt dwarfs the contributions of any other person or group, as Egyptian texts readily attest. Only the Pharaoh's exploits are significant (they are described as "more efficient than millions of soldiers"). They alone are recounted and celebrated while the achievements of his underlings are unmentioned.[51] As defender of ma'at, the sun king shares credit with no one.

I [Amun-Re] came to let you tread on those of Asia . . .
I came to let you tread on eastern lands . . .
I came to let you tread on western lands . . .
I came to let you tread on lowlanders . . .
I came to let you tread on islanders . . .
I let them see your majesty as the avenger . . .
I came to let you tread on earth's limits . . .

Poetical Stela of Thutmose III, quoted in Cox, Just War, 374

Fending off chaos and establishing ma'at were the purpose of Egyptian warfare. Before military campaigns Pharaohs visited cult centers like the Temple at Karnak, where they received grants of authority from the gods to wage war. Acting on behalf of Amun-Re, the Pharaoh regarded the armed resistance of his enemies—whether internal or external—as rebellion so heinous that it justified any measure taken to suppress it. Punishing rebels, so far as it restored ma'at to the realm, was a "just cause" for going to war. The belief that enemy armies would destroy the cosmic order of ma'at in turn licensed horrific violence against them. Egypt's armies slaughtered the "rebels" against Amun-Re, their wives, and their children by burning them alive or sawing their bodies into pieces. As Egypt became an imperial power during the Middle Kingdom, the Pharaohs increasingly framed their conflicts with foreigners as campaigns to suppress insurgency. Thutmose I (1504–1492 BCE) declared his intention to invade Nubia in order to crush rebellion; Thutmose III similarly vowed to "kill the treacherous ones" in Megiddo. The Egyptians referred to the Hittites at the Battle of Kadesh (1274 BCE) as rebels, a characterization lacking any factual basis yet serving to justify their harsh treatment at the hands of Ramses II.[52]

Much as in ancient Rome, in Egypt there were few constraints on a war backed by "just cause" once it started. At the commencement of battle deceit, ambush, and the use of all manner of weapons were fair game. Because the Egyptians viewed foreigners with contempt, they treated enemy captives with a casual brutality, butchering the men and enslaving the women and children. Genocide forks across Egyptian annals like bursts of heat lightning, as when Thutmose III gloats over his conquest of the Naharin, "I desolated his towns and his tribes and set fire to them. I captured all their people, carried off as living prisoners . . . and their goods as well. I took away the very sources of life." Egyptian malice toward enemy combatants extended even to their corpses. Return of the bodies of fallen soldiers was commonly practiced in late archaic and Classical Greece, yet it never became normative in Egyptian warfare. Instead, Egyptian armies mutilated the corpses of enemy soldiers for hands, ears, and sex organs. These body parts were used both as means to count the enemy dead and as trophies presented by soldiers to their commanders. Rory Cox comments on the deliberately transgressive nature of mutilating the dead: "Given the importance that Egyptians attached to the preservation of the flesh for burial, the mutilation of enemy corpses . . . must have been understood by Egyptians as a deliberate act of violation . . . [that] conveyed a message of humiliation, retribution, and warning."[53] Braced by such an attitude, the Egyptians considered all war captives to be the property of the Pharaoh. For enemy leaders they reserved a special fate, one described by Amenophis II on his stelae in the Temples of Amada and Elephantine:

> His majesty returned in joy of heart to this father Amon, when he had slain with his own mace the seven princes . . . who had been put upside-down at the prow of his majesty's falcon-boat . . . Then six men of these enemies were hanged on the face of the wall of Thebes, and the hands as well. Then the other foe was taken upstream to the land of Nubia and hanged to the wall of Napata, to show his majesty's victories forever and ever in all lands and all countries.[54]

The rank-and-file soldiery fared little better. Under the Pharaoh Merneptah (19th Dynasty, 1213–1203 BCE) Libyan war captives were impaled and burned alive while others had their hands cut off, their eyes gouged out, and their ears removed. Analogous treatment of Nubian prisoners during the reign of Akhenaton (d. 1335 BCE) may indicate that such atrocities were customarily imposed on Egypt's adversaries. The venue for their performance was likewise significant: brutalization of enemy soldiers was a public spectacle performed in Egypt for the edification of the Egyptian people. The message conveyed was that the Pharaoh had through his conquest and destruction of foreign enemies restored ma'at to the world. The extreme violence inflicted on captives communicated this point to the intended audience of the public spectacle, the people of Egypt. Visual erasure of the enemy as a threat to ma'at was the essential condition of world-maintenance; without a clear and dramatic enactment of the enemy's destruction, the cosmos might lapse into chaos. Accordingly, captives possessed no legal status at all (the Egyptian word for "captive" translates as "like one who had never existed"). They could be enslaved, bound, branded, and used as forced laborers. They were also liable to being tortured and ritually executed. Enslavement and branding followed for the wife and children of the war captive.[55]

What was true for the Pharaoh's power over enemy war captives applied to enemy property as well. The Egyptian army looted or consumed moveable property; agricultural resources were destroyed in order to deny sustenance to enemy troops. The modern emphasis on discrimination and proportionality had no purchase in the battlefield conduct of the Egyptians. Likening Egypt's practices to the vandalism of the Hundred Years War and Sherman's March to the Sea, Rory Cox writes that the "purpose [of these ravaging operations] was to terrorize foes into submission, to destabilize the political authority of the opponent, to cripple an enemy's economy in order to reduce military capability, and to acquire booty for the army."[56]

In the end, and despite the harshness of their wartime conduct, the Egyptians did observe a Law of War founded upon their conception of justice. That their conception is radically different from our own understanding of the word should not obscure this fact. The Pharaoh's subjugation of chaos as represented by foreign enemy soldiers was the just cause that legitimated Egypt's permissive approach to warmaking. As with other civilizations we will encounter, the justice underlying the resort to war, or *jus ad bellum*, tended to sanctify all measures used to wage war, or *jus in bello*. Surpassingly important ends justified all means to achieve them. The tendency of an existential just cause to devour *jus in bello* will emerge subsequently in ancient Israel, Rome, and medieval Europe. In the modern era, we will glimpse it in European imperial relations with non-Western peoples, the law of "double effect" in Catholic ethics, and the Salafi jihadism that inspired the attacks of 9/11. The persistence and diachronicity of "just cause" thinking is telling. Its appearance at the very origin of human civilization, more or less contemporary with the rearing of the pyramids and at a time when the Sphinx first gazed with unblinking eyes upon a desert world, portends that the legitimizing force of a just cause is unlikely to fade away anytime soon.

Ancient Mesopotamia and the Law of War

Just cause reasoning to legitimize warfare is also apparent in Mesopotamia, a roughly contemporary civilization of Egypt. Evidence of a Mesopotamian *jus ad bellum* reaches back into the Early Dynastic Period IIIb (2500–2335 BCE). The Babylonians demanded that before war could be waged it had to be both declared and supported by just cause. An example of a declaration coupled with a justification is found in a letter of the king of Yamhad, Yarim-Lim (reigned ca. 1780 BC – ca. 1764 BC), to the king of Dēr, Yašub-

Yahab, in which Yarim-Lim backs his forthcoming war against Dēr with accusations of treachery against Yašub-Yahab. "You are continually responding to me with lies and provocation," Yarim-Lim wrote. He continued:

> I swear to you by Addu, my city's god, and by Sin, my own god: [may I be punished] should I ever go away before annihilating your land and you! Now therefore, I shall come at springtime and shall pitch camp at your city's gate. I shall have you witness the galling weapons of Addu and Yarim-Lim.[57]

Historian Amnon Altman comments on this letter that "the accusation of ungrateful behavior seems to provide a justified casus belli [reason for war]."[58]

As in ancient Egypt, so in Mesopotamia kings sought the approval of the gods for their military campaigns. When Rim-Sin, the king of Larsa, raided Babylonian territory, the king of Babylon, Hammurabi, turned to the gods for authorization of his counterattack. Hammurabi's complaint about Rim-Sin's offense was directed to "divine judges," who would investigate the charge and render a verdict in the form of a prophetic oracle. This practice was from all appearances de riguer among Mesopotamian city-states. An oracle given to king Zimri-Lim of Mari bespeaks the necessity of securing divine sanction for warmaking: "If you go [off] to war, never do so [wi]thout consulting an oracle. [W]hen I become manifest in [my] oracle, go to the war. If it does [not] happen, do [not] go out of the city gate."[59] Whatever formidable powers the king enjoyed, he was still limited in his freedom to wage war by the will of the gods. Once divine favor was enlisted, Mesopotamian armies dealt as severely with conquered enemies as other peoples in the ancient world did. This was particularly the case in the earlier periods of Mesopotamian history—that is, at a time when the city-states of the region had rudimentary economies with little surplus or division of labor. The Mesopotamian example furnishes an analytical foil to the Egyptian Law of War: in Egypt, the ideology of ma'at underlay the resort to warfare and the treatment of foreign war captives. In Mesopotamia, by contrast, a more socio-economically focused approach to why war captives were treated as they were may have more explanatory heft. This is so because we can observe marked differences in the treatment of captives between periods of Mesopotamian history based on their respective levels of economic and social advancement.

[The] king of Larsa harried my land with repeated pillage attacks. . . . I have granted the man of Larsa many favors but he did not reward me (even) for one favor. Now, I complained to the gods Šamaš and Marduk, and they answered me with 'Yes!'. I would not have launched this attack without the (consent of the) god!

Report of an anonymous official to Zimri-Lin, the king of Mari,
quoting Hammurabi's declaration; cited in Altman, Tracing, *9*

Our earliest sources on a Mesopotamian *jus in bello* date back to the reign of the second king of Akkad, Rîmuš (reigned 2284–2275 BCE). Rîmuš boasts in writing of killing thousands of men in his wars against the cities of Babylonia, as well as capturing thousands of prisoners from each of the defeated cities. According to Assyriologist I. J. Gelb, the Sumerian terms for "captive" (LÚ + KÁR) were associated with "rope" and "binding." Sumerian reliefs portray male captives being led away in neckstocks. Their destination was unclear but potentially ominous. Rîmuš's own description of his actions records that he "caused x men to go out (from the cities) and placed (them) in the camp." Gelb points out that the Sumerian word for "camp," *karāšum*, carries a secondary meaning, "destruction." Thus, in the sentence above, "camp" may also be translated as "the place where men are killed." The term is layered with additional meanings of "catastrophe" and "slaughter." The latter interpretations gain credence from Rîmuš's other boasts of his treatment of enemy soldiers in his wars against Parahšum and Zahara. In these campaigns, he roisters, he killed some of the enemy, captured others, and "heaped up a (burial) mound over them." Gelb draws the somber conclusion "that in addition to killing enemy warriors in battle, the Mesopotamian rulers may have been in the habit of gathering enemy males and probably others and putting them to the sword at some place within the territory of the conquered cities."[60] In other words, we may be witness here to the use of a death camp to dispose of unwanted enemy combatants.

In the early phases of Mesopotamian history, the women and children of the conquered enemy were taken prisoner as a form of war booty belonging to the state. Sometimes they were given as offerings to the temples of the conqueror. Administrative texts from Ur III (ca. 2200–2100 BCE) suggest that hundreds of women and children captives may have been used as forced labor in the construction of the palace of Bur-Sin.[61] Enemy soldiers spared death either during or after battle were roped or confined in neck stocks. The existence of warrior prisoners in their midst posed challenges of control to Mesopotamian conquerors: women and children could be managed with few problems beyond the immediate need to feed them, but captured soldiers were constant security threats. The use of ropes and neck stocks were one solution; another, well attested during the Early Dynastic Period (ca. 2900–2350 BCE) and continuing into the New Assyrian Period (911–609 BCE), was to blind male captives in order to make them more docile. Archaeologist J. N. Postgate writes that "[blinded war captives] could serve perfectly adequately, like Samson on the grindstone, to move water from a well or canal to the fields or gardens, with just a bucket and rope."[62]

As the city-states of the fertile crescent became more economically differentiated, war captives became more serviceable to and controllable by an increasingly complex and far-reaching state authority. Male captives were set free to work as farmers, guards of the king, mercenaries, and laborers. A royal inscription from the reign of Samsu-iluna (ca. 1750–1712 BCE) describes the sparing and freeing of war captives. The changing policy toward captives is furthermore reflected in linguistic usage. The terms for war captives immediately after capture, *sag* and *arád* (both translated as "slave"), gave way to the new words *erín* (worker) and *guruš* (man), which denoted captives after their disposition had been decided. For Gelb the improvement in treatment was due to the new opportunities to integrate war captives into the emerging surplus state with its court retinue, expanding bureaucracy, and resource-intensive army.

The example of Mesopotamia indicates that more advanced stages of socio-economic development can moderate *jus in bello* because foreign captives are more readily assimilated into the economy. This tendency is not, however, invariable; sophisticated ancient cultures like Greece and Rome continued to kill, enslave, and oppress enemy war captives despite their limited surplus economy, as did higher Mesoamerican civilizations.

Ancient China and the Law of War

The rulers of ancient China under the Zhou Dynasty (ca. 1046–256 BCE) adhered to a highly ritualized conception of military campaigns that imposed in-built constraints on their conduct. These constraints were both ceremonial and non-ethical. Mark Lewis has described the ritualized nature of warfare under the Zhou: "Every stage of the campaign was marked by special rituals that linked actions in the field to the state cults and guaranteed the sacred character of the battle." Such rituals included instruction of the warriors before battle about why fighting was required by Heaven, duty, the state, and their ancestral spirits. Following this instruction, oracles were consulted, a war prayer intoned, and a ceremonial command (*ming*) issued.[63] Other rules stipulated that gifts should be given to invaders and, in the event a river crossing threw an army into turmoil, the opposing army had to refrain from attacking until order was restored. An invader was obliged to retreat if the ruler of the state being invaded died; the rationale for such a rule was to avoid deepening the mourning process.[64]

As we will see throughout our study of the Law of War, principles often do not coincide with practice. Yet, it would seem that the constraints the Zhou imposed on warfare *were* observed on the battlefield. Keegan recounts an illustrative episode from the war between the rival states of Ch'u and Sung sometime in 638 BCE. Outnumbered by the Ch'u army, the Sung noticed that their adversaries were in disarray, prompting a Sung commander to request permission to attack while the Ch'u were vulnerable. This request was denied. Predictably, the Sung suffered military defeat. The duke who had rejected the order to attack subsequently defended his decision on the grounds that "the gentleman does not inflict a second wound, or take the grey-haired prisoner . . . I would not sound my drums to attack an enemy who had not completed the formation of his ranks."[65] Devotees of expedience may boggle at this story; they will be no less incredulous to learn that Chinese aristocrats (who dominated warmaking in the Zhou Dynasty) complied with self-imposed prohibitions on attacking an enemy in retreat struggling with his chariot. The hapless adversary could even be given assistance.[66]

Despite these limitations, it would be inaccurate to describe Zhou principles of chivalry as grounded in either law or ethics. Instead, they were part of a larger ritual system that included religion, sacrifice, and hunting—activities reserved along with warfare for the exclusive administration of the Zhou aristocracy.[67] As elsewhere in the ancient world, hunting and warfare for the Zhou were often synonymous. They regarded the hunt as a form of military training, and so closely identified were the two that a military campaign could mutate into a hunt or a hunt into a military campaign. Hunting and warfare moreover shared a common vocabulary—the term for the hunt (*lie*) also applied to armed attack. Prior to the hunt or battle, participants took collective oaths that were legally enforcible against the oathtaker. Hunting was so intimately linked with warfare that violation of an oath taken before the hunt was enforcible through military law. The law was employed, however, to uphold a ritualized politics based on sacrifice.[68] Warfare and hunting supplied the sacrificial victims that enabled the maintenance of this ritual complex.

Whether in the form of animals obtained through hunting or war captives seized in battle, the sacrifice was an important expression of ancestor worship for the Zhou. As religious rituals, Zhou military campaigns were launched at ancestral temples amid sacrifices conducted by the rulers at the *she* altar. At this altar the general of the army was given both his command and a meat offering, as well as a bow or an ax by the ruler. Zhou soldiers likewise met at the *she* altar; after the performance of the necessary rituals, they decamped for the campaign. As they marched toward battle, the army continued to observe religious rituals, including a "travel sacrifice" to appease the gods of the territories through which they passed, a pre-combat meal, and ceremonies to conjure the ancestors and tutelary deities of their state. On the cusp of battle, the soldiers completely leveled their camp as a sign of their resolve to die in combat.[69]

Historian Mark Lewis identifies the "solemn declaration" or "oath" as the most important of the pre-battle religious ceremonies of Zhou armies. The declaration was formulaic: it consisted of a summary of the enemy's crimes along with the assertion that the declarant was carrying out the will of Heaven. It instructed the soldiers on the rules for proper behavior and threatened retribution for violators. Sometimes, the declaration dangled promises of reward for success in battle or the punishment that awaited a defeated commander. In one head-turning example, the commander of an army supporting the lord of Jin, Zhao Yang, declared that "should I be guilty [of defeat], then may I be punished by strangulation, may I have only a thin coffin with no outside layers, may it be drawn by an unornamented horse and wagon, and may I not be buried in the graveyard of my lineage."[70] Warfare has always been a serious matter in the cultures that wage it, but the commander's acceptance of a catastrophic personal fate in the event of his defeat is unintelligible outside a religious framework. This rich ceremonial texture of Zhou warfare represents an ancient Law of War—here, a *jus ad bellum*—woven from the strands of Chinese religion, especially ancestor worship. Warfare was not simply killing; it was an activity buoyed by the will of Heaven, the honor of the state, and the duty of each soldier to fulfill the demands of the ancestors.

Devotees of pragmatism, then and now, can only react with baffled disbelief to such a stylized and wildly impractical attitude toward warfare. As in ancient India (see below), so in Zhou China the constraints imposed on warmaking by ceremonial religion invited trenchant criticism. In the twilight of the Spring and Autumn period (770–476 BCE), a military theorist and general for the state of Wu, Sunzi (Romanized as Sun Tzu), authored *The Art of War*, the first study of military science in world history. Sun Tzu, like his Zhou predecessors, insisted that constraints be respected in battle, particularly the humane treatment of war captives. In contrast with earlier thinking, however, Sun Tzu did not defend the need for constraints with reference to their place in an all-embracing ritual system. Rather, he justified them as the most efficient means to prevail in war.[71]

The realism of Sun Tzu was a counterpoint to the ritual system of Zhou China. He rejected the subordination of the commander to the ruler on the view that it would detract from success in battle. For the same reason, Sun Tzu approved of deceit in warfare, a teaching at odds with conventional morality.[72] Realists in other cultures like India's Kautilya and Renaissance Italy's Niccolo Machiavelli agreed with Sun Tzu's concept of amorality in support of military victory.

If there is a linchpin around which the culture of ancient China revolved, it was ritual (*li*). Our oldest sources of information about China all underscore the centrality of ritual to the worldview of the ancient Chinese going back at least to the Shang Dynasty. By the spring and autumn period, however, the proliferation of small territorial states had fostered rampant military conflict. The stylized character of warmaking described above gave way to a sharper, more pragmatic approach as larger states conquered and assimilated smaller ones. Inter- and intra-state wars exceeded the ability of Zhou rulers to contain them. Warfare under the Zhou had been dominated for centuries by noble lineages that owned the land, government offices, a segment of the enserfed population, military leadership positions, and ancestral temples. The internecine conflicts between these lineages had wiped many of them out by the end of the fourth century BCE. With the waning of these noble lineages the long-standing ritual system began to unravel: in place of Heaven or the will of one's ancestors, wars were increasingly fought for territorial control.[73] The crisis of the Chinese ritual system in the face of social chaos became the occasion for the greatest of all Chinese thinkers, Confucius, to reformulate a primary foundation of Chinese civilization, one that has endured in China until the present day.

Like many of the world's great moral reformers and spiritual leaders, Confucius (a Romanization of Konfuzi, 551–479 BCE) committed nothing to writing. What we know of his teachings was reduced to writing by his students as a series of aphorisms entitled the *Analects*, in which Confucius set forth the main categories of his religio-ethical thought: *ren* ("goodness") and *li* ("ritual").[74] These are complementary terms in Confucian thinking; they are not synonymous. Heiner Roetz interprets *li* as conventional morality and *ren* as universal ethical principles.[75] Although *ren* is the decisive standard for assessing the moral quality of an action, the substantive part of Confucius's thought was *li*, understood as a proper appreciation of each person's rightful place in society. Such an understanding could be obtained only by studying "The Way" (*Dao*, not to be confused with the use of the same word by Daoists) of the ancients, as preserved in their classic texts. Earnest study of classic Chinese literature would enable comprehension of *li*, and with this comprehension students would develop the knowledge of how to act virtuously no matter the situation confronting them. For Confucius, the ideal society would remain under the control of the king but he would not use force to compel the obedience of his subjects; rather, a citizenry properly educated to virtue would internalize its responsibilities and spontaneously obey them, thereby dispensing with the need for coercion.[76]

We ought not be misled into thinking that Confucius was espousing an anti-monarchical viewpoint, for this was assuredly not the case. The high value he attached to deference to authority emerges clearly in his just war theory. According to Confucius, the virtue of the ruler united the virtue of a people involved in military conflict. All preparations for battle, including the rituals (*li*) surrounding it, had to originate from the ruler as the Son of Heaven. The centrality of the ruler to legitimate warfare was fully consistent with his supremacy in preserving social order, which he accomplished through ritual performance. For this reason, Confucius rejected the position of Sun Tzu and the military realists who demanded the scission of the military commander from the ruler. For the realists, command authority was vested entirely in the masterful commander, a figure trained in the intricacies of strategy and possessing an almost uncanny capacity to deploy his troops to the maximum advantage. All matters touching on military affairs were left to him and him alone, and even the ruler was forbidden to intervene. Such a doctrine was anathema to Confucius. To sever the link between the ruler and warfare would deprive the army of its ability to satisfy the preconditions for a just war—namely, proper ritual observance—and ultimately lead to an unsuccessful outcome. The realist argument that warfare and civil society were radically discontinuous found no home in the thought of the Confucian school.[77]

Robert Bellah, following Roetz, argues persuasively that Confucius's thinking aspired to universalism. The virtue of the "gentleman" (*junzi*) acting in harmony with ritual would become transformative of the world around him—even in his interactions with non-Chinese people. In the *Analects* we read: "The Master wished to live among the barbarian Nine Tribes. Someone said, 'They're uncouth. What about that?' He said, 'If a gentleman lived among them, what uncouthness would there be?'"[78] Echoes of this universalism can be heard in Confucius's repeated invocations of an ethics of empathy that anticipates the Christian Golden Rule by nearly five centuries:

> Zhonggong inquired about *ren*. The Master replied, "In your public life, behave as though you are receiving important visitors; employ the common people as though you are overseeing a great sacrifice. Do not impose on others what you yourself do not want, and you will not incur personal or political ill will.[79]

Bellah's summation of Confucian ethics would appear to be well-founded: it is "intended to be human ethics, not Chinese ethics."[80]

Confucius died two years after the outbreak of the "Warring States period" in Chinese history, a 260-year epoch of civil war and dynastic struggle that would ultimately lead to the collapse of the Zhou Dynasty in 256 BCE. The upheavals of a society *in extremis* are registered not only in Confucius's appeal to restore an imperiled tradition, but also in the ethical thought of Mozi. Beginning as a Confucian, Mozi (470–391 BCE) later established his own philosophical/religious movement, Mohism. Mozi's thought, like that of Confucius, was a response to the disintegration of traditional Chinese mores, particularly the deeply engrained convention that violence was a means to preserve honor or satisfy the will of Heaven. As large territorial states crystallized at the expense of smaller political units and the countryside increasingly fell under the sway of centralized authority, violence became a tool for enforcing obedience to new authoritarian hierarchies. Indeed, the philosophical school of Legalism arose during the Warring States period as an ideological justification of ruthless centralized power—a theory perfectly adapted to the totalistic imperial rule of China's first emperor, Qin Shi Huangdi, who established the Chinese Empire in 221 BCE. Mozi was long dead by the time Huangdi inaugurated the Chinese Empire, but the spirit of his thought was a rejection of everything Huangdi would later stand for. For Mozi, society could only flourish under rulers educated in the "right" views instilled in them by the will of Heaven. When rulers embodied such views, they had to be obeyed. However, according to Mozi, the source of obedience was "Heaven," not the "Son of Heaven" (i.e., the king). In other words, a standard for right conduct existed beyond the will of the ruler.[81]

Distinctive of Mozi's thought is the doctrine of universal love (*jian ai*), a concept that nudged the Chinese cult of filial piety toward a greater concern for others outside the family. Mozi articulates this doctrine in a reflection on the ethics of warfare:

> how can partiality be replaced by universality? If men were to regard the states of others as they regard their own, then who would raise up his state to attack the state of another? It would be like attacking his own. If men were to regard the cities of others as they regard their own, then who would raise up his city to attack the city of another? It would be like attacking his own ... Now when states and cities do not attack and make war on each other ... is this a harm or a benefit to the world? Surely it is a benefit.[82]

The overt meaning of this passage is to condemn unjust war, which Mozi might define as waging war without sufficient regard for *jian ai*. Never content with armchair theorizing, Mozi and his disciples traveled among the patchwork of kingdoms during the Warring States period, aiding states who were defending themselves against aggressors.[83]

Remarkably, Mozi expressed a humane view of just and unjust warfare nearly a millennium before the just war theories of medieval Christian theologians. His dichotomy preceded by some 2,500 years the first international efforts to abolish the resort to war (the Kellogg-Briand Pact, 1926) and to criminalize aggressive warfare (the judgment of the International Military Tribunal at Nuremberg, 1946). The extraordinary novelty of his thought—its insistence that universal love trumped the particularist love of one's family— seems jarringly dissonant with not only Confucianism but the entire tradition of Chinese history. This incongruity notwithstanding, Chinese scholars until the second century BCE referred to Confucianism and Mohism as the two most significant schools of thought.[84] Together with Confucius, Mozi represents a moment in Chinese history when the givenness of social, religious, and political life was called into question.

The third of the Chinese thinkers to subordinate the king's will to a higher principle of right and to insist on the universality of ethical concern was Mencius (371–289 BCE). Mencius shares with Confucius and Mozi a concern with the moral legitimacy of political power, an issue that bulked ever larger as the Warring States period telescoped into the totalitarian emperorship of Huangdi in 221 BCE. The seemingly perpetual warfare of Mencius's era grated on him, provoking comments that have lost none of their shock value over the millennia since their utterance. About the conflict raging during the Warring States period Mencius remarked:

> In wars to gain land, the dead fill the plains; in wars to gain cities, the dead fill the cities. This is known as showing the land the way to devour human flesh. Death is too light a punishment for such men.[85]

When King Xuan asked Mencius about the permissibility of killing Zhou, a brutal Shang Dynasty ruler, he responded:

> A man who mutilates benevolence [ren] is a mutilator, while one who cripples rightness is an "outcast." I have indeed heard of the punishment of the "outcast Zhou," but I have not heard of any regicide.[86]

Mencius's words here, denying legal legitimacy to an immoral ruler, resonate with the statement of the Roman statesman Cicero that an immoral law lacks legal validity.[87] For both Mencius and Cicero, the laws of kings were measured by their conformity to eternal laws of justice. Mencius, however, went a step beyond Cicero in elevating not only the will of Heaven above the king but recognizing the "gentleman" (junzi), the person who practices benevolence (ren), as superior to the immoral king as well.

By the third century BCE, the Chinese had arrived at the belief that the ruler's actions on earth had to conform with processes in the heavens and in nature overall. Because the natural world "died" during the autumn and winter months, this period was set aside as the "killing time" of the year. Rulers accordingly launched their military campaigns in the fall and winter; to depart from this custom and wage war during the spring and summer was an egregious breach of the ruler's duties to imitate nature. The calendrical system dictated what the ruler could and could not do during a given month, and he was expected to comply with this system. Contemporary commentators like Sima Qian describe as "evil" those kings who had violated the calendrical system and thereby set themselves at odds with the patterns of nature. These "evil monarchs," for example, fought both in the seasons reserved for death and punishment and those dedicated to growth and the harvest. To be just, warfare had to harmonize with the annual cycles and rhythms of nature. To act otherwise was to break with the cosmic Way prescribed by Heaven.[88]

The Chinese Law of War involved the adjustment of military practices on earth to cosmic and astral models. The proper subordination of individual caprice to these models created civilization and full human beings. We see this idea of civilization- and humanity-building through right action in the Chinese concept of qi. Appearing for the first time during the Han dynasty (206 BCE – 220 CE), qi is an elusive term to define. Anthropologist Bruce Trigger defines it as "the formless but configuring primal energy present in everything that existed."[89] As applied to people qi was associated with passion, anger, and belligerence. These are not commendable properties but actual vices exposed as such in the figure of the warrior. The "man of combat" is driven by *qi* into rash and unnatural acts that reduce him to the level of a beast, cutting him off from human society. It falls therefore to the sage commander—that is, the general—to restrain, discipline, and redirect the *qi* of his soldiers by bringing it into alignment with the cosmic qi. The commander achieved such mastery through the sheer force of his intellect (*shen*), a force that reproduced the creative powers of the cosmos that had brought the physical world into being. The military commander, then, followed the model of Heaven and Earth, and in so doing reconciled his army's behavior with the cosmic will.[90]

How did the sage commander align military action with the will of Heaven? The Huang Lao manuscript (early second century BCE) relates that wars could only be fought during the killing season (fall/winter). Furthermore, only certain targets could be attacked: the obstinate who refused to yield and those persons who had committed crimes. In addition, and more abstractly for modern readers, harmonizing an army's *qi* with the cosmic *qi* could be accomplished by means of music and so-called "pitchpipes." Each of these contributions disciplined the *qi* of every soldier in the royal army, drawing it into consilience with the *qi* of Heaven and Earth. In the Han theory and practice of *qi* as it relates to warfare, we are confronted with an exotic yet unmistakable Law of War that tempered royal prerogative and erected limits to when, against whom, and under what conditions war might legitimately be fought.

Ancient India and the Law of War

In contrast with ancient China, in ancient India[91] no imperial power ever held unified control over the diverse kingdoms and republics of the subcontinent until the time of the British Raj. (The Mauryan Empire established in 321 BCE for a time ruled over much of the subcontinent but never extended its control into southern India.) Consequently, the numerous political units formed by Indo-European immigrants between 1000 and 600 BCE retained their autonomy. These territorial chiefdoms, called *janapadas*, began as kinship-based groups that ripened into states with political bureaucracies and urban capitals. Sixteen *janapadas* had developed by 500 BCE; when Alexander the Great made his incursions into India (327 BCE), four of the largest groups had grown to dominate the smaller ones.[92] The multiplication of these city-states virtually guaranteed military conflict.

Although the *Dharma-shastras* and the *Artha-shastras* of Kautilya are our main sources for the Law of War in India, the earliest Indian texts, the Vedas, established the ideological framework in terms of which Indian constraints on warfare developed. In order to explore how ancient Indians may have conceived of these limitations, we need to appreciate the enormous impact on Indian thinking about war of two interrelated doctrines—caste and *dharma*.

The mythic origin of the Hindu caste system is portrayed in the *Rigveda*, the oldest and most sacred of the four Vedas. Composed by Brahman priests between 1500 and 1200 BCE, the *Rigveda* is the product of an Aryan tribal society that had not yet organized itself into political units. This notwithstanding, the *Rigveda* clearly affirms the existence of a rigidly stratified society dominated by the king and the Brahman priesthood.

In addition to discussing animal sacrifice on sacred altars, the *Rigveda* traces the caste system to the sacrifice of Purusa, the primal man whose body, carved into four sections in a primordial sacrifice, produced the four divisions of the Hindu caste system (*varnas*): the military or ruling class (the *Kshatriya*), the priests and teachers of law (the Brahmans), the merchant-farmers (the Vaisha), and the servants (the Sudra).[93] In this fashion, the *Rigveda* anchors the Indian social hierarchy firmly in the cosmological hierarchy. The rites of worship and sacrifice expounded in other portions of the text were designed to uphold the harmony of society and cosmos. A crucial aspect of this balance was the set of role responsibilities assigned to each caste. The *Kshatriya* as a distinct class bore the obligation of defending the community against armed aggression. As one commentator on Vedic India notes, there is little evidence at this time of a code of rules governing the conduct of warfare. At some point, however—probably in the interval between the Vedic era and composition of the great epics—customs originated that imposed restrictions on warmaking.[94] Growing out of the notion of caste set forth in the *Rigveda*, these conventions prescribing the king's duties and the obligations of the *Kshatriya* would be reduced to writing in the *Dharma-shastras*.

Of equal importance for understanding the Indian approach to the Law of War is the doctrine of *dharma*. Many scholars have commented on the difficulties of translating *dharma* into English;[95] it is a non-Western concept resistant to the binaries characteristic of Western thinking. Adding to the complexity is the kaleidoscopic plasticity of *dharma*'s meaning as it has been appropriated and redefined by successive Indian cultures in time and space: Vedic India, Indian Buddhism, and Jainism. *Dharma* is the central tenet of the *Rigveda*, the conceptual glue that holds together the early Hindu understanding of reality; yet even here, the construction of *dharma* in the Vedic tradition reflects the perceptions and interests of a single group, the Brahman caste.[96] The Sanskrit root of *dharma* is *dhṛ*, meaning "to support, uphold, maintain." As its etymology suggests, in its Vedic usage *dharma* referred chiefly to the performance of religious rituals believed to "uphold"the cosmic order; *dharmas* (in the plural) were the rituals of cosmic maintenance. The linkage of *dharma* with rites of cosmic importance indicates its prescriptive character. Indeed, the *Rigveda* itself expands the term with additional meanings, to include broader social norms and even statutory law.[97]

Subsequent elaboration of Vedic Hinduism sharpened the focus of *dharma*, equating it with the doctrine of caste. Henceforth in traditional Hinduism, *dharma* was inextricably bound up with *varṇāśramadharma*, the network of specific rules and duties assigned to both one's caste and to the stages of a person's life. Wilhelm Halbfass stresses that the rules and duties prescribed by *dharma* were not reducible to "a general principle of behavior." Rather, they were exquisitely particular, and applicable solely to Hindu society.[98] Despite the restrictive scope of *varn. āśramadharma*, it eventually became an all-embracing principle with cosmic reach, "in which," according to anthropologist Clifford Geertz, "each sort of being in the universe, human, transhuman, infrahuman alike, has, by virtue of its sort, an ethic to fulfill and a nature to express—the two being the same thing."[99] For Geertz,[100] this emphasis on status—on one's position within a social order that itself "is transcendentally defined"—is the unique quality distinguishing

Indian legal thought from that of other cultures. "It is the *dharma* idea ... that sets the Indic case apart."

As one of the original *varṇas* in classical Hinduism, the *Kshatriyas* were subject to an elaborate array of duties that conditioned every aspect of their lives—from their education as children and proper execution of sacrifice to their style of dress and conjugal practices.[101] Among these rules of conduct were principles of just and unjust warfare. The distinction between them first appears in the Indian epics, which distinguish between the *dharmayuddha*, or war fought in accordance with the principles of *dharma*, and the *kutayuddha*, or war waged at variance with *dharma*. Remarkably, our sources indicate that Indian warriors were trained in both kinds of fighting. (Commentators disagree on the permissibility of *kutayuddha* in the epics.[102]) *Dharmayuddha* prescribed chivalric principles binding on all members of the military caste, from the king to all of his military subordinates, and governing both the circumstances in which war could be declared as well as caste-acceptable behavior for fighting (particularly the treatment of prisoners of war and civilians). *Dharmayuddha* permitted resort to war only when (1) there was no other alternative; (2) the aim of fighting was just; and (3) the appropriate rules for waging war were observed and no forbidden weapons or tactics were used by either side.[103] Many of the Indian sources—the *Mahābhārata*, the *Dharma-shastra*, and (at times) Kautilya's *Artha-shastra*—permit warfare, but only if it is waged in accordance with *dharma*. Even the Buddha, who taught an ethic of nonviolence, allowed participation in warfare so long as the cause was "righteous" and only "after having exhausted all means of preserving peace."[104]

As we consider the extraordinarily detailed rules of warfare in ancient India, it is essential to recall that *dharmayuddha* was a code specific to the warrior caste, not a set of norms held to be universally binding on all people. We should not overlook that the *dharmic* principles of action were rituals designed to "uphold" or "maintain" the cosmos; hence, warmaking was yet another stage on which the balance between society and cosmos was carefully enacted by means of ritual performance. The markedly ceremonial character of the Indian Law of War sets it apart from the natural law theories of Greco-Roman Stoicism and medieval Thomism. As we have seen, the bedrock of the Vedic concept of *dharma* was caste, a construct that permeated every feature of the Indian thought-world. Unsurprisingly, caste figures quite prominently in battlefield practices based on *dharmayuddha*. For one commentator,[105] the "cardinal canon" of Indian warfare was its insistence that like could only do battle against like—that a king could only fight against another king (and never against "warriors of inferior status"),[106] an officer was forbidden to fight against a foot soldier, mounted cavalry could only engage other mounted warriors, elephant riders were allowed to fight only against other elephant riders.[107] These rules applied, however, only to the *Kshatriya*; they were not believed to be universally obligatory.

Although such principles were imbedded in a context of religious ritual, other rules of warfare appear to have been motivated by more humanitarian concerns. Both the *Ramayana* and *Mahābhārata* prohibit the use of hyperdestructive weapons by their heroes. In the *Ramayana*, Rama's younger brother, Lakshmana, had at his disposal a super-weapon that would have devastated the enemy, both the warriors and noncombatants. Rama counseled his brother that the Indian Laws of War forbade the use of such a weapon against an enemy—even when the enemy was fighting an *adharmic* style of warfare. Similarly, in the *Mahābhārata*, the Indian Law of War prohibited the hero Arjuna from using a hyperdestructive weapon, Pasupathastra, because the conflict had been limited to conventional weapons and Arjuna's opponents had not violated this restriction. Were he to unleash Pasupathastra, it would cause indiscriminate carnage.[108] Centuries later, Manu would extend the prohibition of unconventional weaponry found in the epics to poisoned arrows.

Analogous concerns surface repeatedly in the *Mahābhārata*. The principle of avoiding indiscriminate violence as exemplified in the story of Arjuna and Pasupathastra applied more generally to all relations on the battlefield. Enfeebled or injured warriors were to be spared, as were warriors who did not have a son or those whose weapons had been rendered useless. Immunity from attack also covered enemy forces in retreat, as well as warriors already engaged in battle with another warrior. The text explicitly requires that quarter be given, a rule that had to be followed even if the vanquished was "a wicked enemy." According to the prescribed custom, the surrendering warrior was entitled to quarter when he announced "I am yours" to his opponent, brought his hands together in supplication, or discarded his weapon. At this point, the surrendering warrior could be taken prisoner.[109] Wounded enemy warriors were to be given medical attention and released upon recovery.[110] The *Brāhmanas*, Brahmanic commentaries on the Vedas dating from 900 to 700 BCE, relate that prisoners of war were chained and sent to the outskirts of the kingdom. Sometimes the prisoner of war consented to become a slave of his captor, in which case he was enslaved for one year; at the end of this time, the captive's freedom was restored to him.[111] Composed at a much later date, the *Mahābhārata* includes reference to the treatment prescribed for young women taken as prisoners of war: they were to be dealt with courteously and persuaded to marry men of their captor's choice. If, however, the offer was rejected, they were returned safely to their homes.[112]

The epics and *Dharma-shastras* articulate other high-minded protections that drew a clear line between combatants and noncombatants. The *Mahābhārata* prohibited killing women, children, or the elderly, declaring that any Aryan warrior who did so was "no son of the Vrishni race."[113] Other protected persons included envoys, Brahmans, arms-bearers, car-drivers, spectators, farmers, and the menial laborers of the enemy army. Likewise, the Indian Law of War forbade military attacks on the enemy's cemeteries, temples, civilian houses, gardens, and farmland. Writing in the late fourth century BCE, the Ionian historian and diplomat Megasthenes marveled at the Indians' refusal to despoil enemy lands during war.[114]

What are we to make of these and other constraints on warfare in ancient India? First, it is noteworthy that a certain tension between mercy and lethal violence exists in uneasy counterpoint in the epics. On the one hand, the *Mahābhārata* at times equates *dharma* with *ahiṃsā*, meaning "non-injury" or "the sparing" of others. Some of the restrictions on warmaking listed above may have been based on *ahiṃsā*; if this is indeed the case, then a universalist ethic of compassion in warfare may have emerged in India well before the Buddhist emperor Ashoka. Bellah rightly points out, however, that "these tendencies never until modern times gained ascendency." He reminds us that the holiest part of the *Mahābhārata*, the *Bhagavad Gītā*, embraced quite a different rule of behavior, *svadharma*—that is, the role responsibilities imposed by one's caste.[115] In the *Gītā*, Arjuna hesitates to kill his relatives in battle. Arjuna's charioteer, the god Krishna, instructs him that he should act according to the duties of his warrior caste, but should detach himself from the outcome of his actions (thereby avoiding their injurious karma). In short, the ancient Indian Law of War seems to be driven less by a universalistic ethic of compassion than by the role responsibilities appropriate to one's place in the Indian social order.

This interpretation gains strength when we consider the high importance attached in ancient India to martial valor and success in battle. At the dawn of Indian history, concern with military success was already uppermost in the minds of Indian military commanders. W. S. Armour points out that "from the earliest times there was another school of thought [other than chivalry] which argued that the enemy has to be killed in war, whether this is conducted according to the rules of morality or otherwise. By these every argument for fair play was frankly ridiculed." In Armour's view, the various rules regulating battle were "quite impracticable, and suggest ... the tournament rather than the battlefield"; the record of military conflict in India suggests that the principles of restraint and actual practice frequently diverged.[116]

Much later, this strain of Indian realism filtered into the thought of Kautilya (ca. 300 BCE), whose *Artha-shastra* (the "Science of Material Gain," composed between 321 and 300 BCE) set forth a Machiavellian account of inter-state relations based not on *dharma* or *ahiṃsā*, but solely on considerations of power. Similar to Machiavelli, too, was his active participation in the politics of his time, in which he served as a counselor to Chandragupta, the founder of the Mauryan Empire in northern India. Kautilya's real-world, first-hand involvement in power politics and imperial state-building may have led him to become, in H. S. Bhatia's words, "a ruthless exponent of the principle of expediency" and a premier advocate of utilitarianism in ancient India.[117] For Kautilya, the king's overriding duty was preservation of the state and his own power, and to this supreme value all else was subordinated. Thus, Kautilya encouraged the king to resort to *kutayuddha* (unjust, or *adharmic*, war) if necessary to preserve his kingdom, particularly where his smaller state was threatened by a larger and no alliances with a protector state were possible.[118] The lengths to which Kautilya would go in defending the state are breathtaking, as evidenced by his recommendation that spies be used for various nefarious ends, including assassination of enemy kings, commanders, and other officials. Spies were urged to wreak havoc on enemy forces by adopting false identities: masquerading as merchants, they were encouraged to sell toxic liquor to enemy troops; impersonating servants, they could peddle contaminated grass and water to poison enemy cattle, horses, and elephants; posing as prostitutes, they might seduce high- ranking political and military leaders, who would then be ambushed and murdered.[119] Where the *Mahābhārata* unconditionally forbade poisoning wells, Kautilya justified it on grounds of state necessity. His *Artha-shastra*, however, was not a counsel to commit evil for evil's sake; rather, much like his Italian counterpart Niccolò Machiavelli, Kautilya approved amoral methods when necessary to secure the well-being of the state.[120]

A very different paradigm of statecraft and warmaking is offered by the Mauryan Emperor Ashoka (reigned ca. 265–238 BCE; an alternative date is 273–232 BCE), the grandson of Chandragupta. Early in life, Ashoka displayed a viciousness reminiscent of Kautilya, who might have continued as an advisor to Ashoka's father, Bindusara. If Ashoka's intrigues to claim his father's throne are any indication, he was an apt pupil of Kautilya's jugular style of politics: he is suspected of murdering one or more of his brothers in order to succeed Bindusara.[121] As king of Magadha, Ashoka for a time governed with a hard hand, torturing prisoners in Magadha's main prison, a dungeon called "Ashoka's Hell" because the jailer was told no one should ever emerge from it alive, and extending the conquests of his father and grandfather. He waged a pitiless *adharmic* war against Kalinga, a region south of Magadha in east-central India. This military conflict became the occasion of one of the most remarkable conversions in world history. Much of our knowledge of Ashoka's reign is inscribed on so-called "rock edicts"— petroglyphs etched on stone columns strewn throughout Mauryan territory, narrating episodes from Ashoka's life. On the famous 13th Rock Edict, we read that 100,000 Kalingas perished during the war and 150,000 more were deported. The immense suffering of the war against Kalinga moved Ashoka to regret the invasion and to embrace Buddhist principles of nonviolence (*ahiṃsā*) henceforth as the official policy of Magadha. Incredible for our jaded sensibilities today, Ashoka ordered that all the war captives be set free, the Kalingas' lands restored to them, and an official apology conveyed to them. According to the rock edicts, he thereafter wore the clothing of a Buddhist monk, renounced hunting, and became a vegetarian and an active Buddhist. He also ordered that "Ashoka's Hell" be destroyed and the criminal law made more humane.[122]

Ashoka's renunciation of war is a working out of the axial turn in India in the realm of statecraft and armed conflict. Bellah holds that the first "axial breakthrough" in ancient India occurred with the *Upanishads* (ca. 500 BCE), a movement further developed by the teachings of the Buddha (ca. sixth to fourth centuries BCE) and later incorporated into state policy by Ashoka. In Richard Gombrich's assessment, the Buddha appropriated the particularist Brahmanic tradition he inherited but "turned the Brahmin ideology upside down and ethicized the universe." For Gombrich, this "ethicization of the world" was a "turning point in the history of civilization."[123] Ashoka's achievement was to apply the universalist ethics of Buddhism to his own actions as emperor. Weighed in the Buddhist scales and found wanting, Ashoka, overcome with remorse, abolished war and reconstructed his state on the principle of nonviolence. The question remains, however, whether Ashoka's policies amounted to a body of law we can identify with the Indian Law of War. This is far from certain, inasmuch as Ashoka's ethical commitment to Buddhist ideas never hardened into a durable core of legal principles. Indeed, with the evanescence of Buddhism from India (third to thirteenth centuries CE), the political teachings of Kautilya's *Artha-shastra* and the *Dharma-shastras* became the ideological cornerstones of Hindu kingship.[124] Realism, state necessity, and self-preservation ultimately carried the day. It should be borne in mind, however, that the legacy of Ashoka in India may exist less in actual laws than in a continuing and powerful morality of peaceful coexistence. Such was his influence that India's first prime minister, Jawaharlal Nehru, compared modern India's policies of foreign relations in the mid-twentieth century to those of Ashoka.[125]

The final source we will consider for the ancient Indian Law of War is the *Dharmashastra* of Manu (ca. 200 BCE – 100 CE), also called the "Code of Manu" or "Laws of Manu" (*Manusmriti*). Among their diverse purposes, the Laws of Manu sought to mitigate the harshness of war by regulating its conduct. They instructed the king to shun the use of poisoned or flaming weapons, to spare the lives of war captives, disarmed warriors, and spectators, and to refrain from attacking noncombatants. The Laws also reiterated the older principles of equality in fighting (officers could only fight other officers, mounted warriors were forbidden to engage unmounted warriors). These archaic rules were, as we have seen, originally based on caste distinctions. In the *Manusmriti*, however, a heightened concern for fairness as well as caste seems to underlie the prohibitions. The Laws proscribed forms of military attack that have little to do with caste, such as collective assaults on single warriors or killing a warrior suffering from a disadvantage (e.g., being unarmed or lacking armor). They permitted the taking of spoils by both the warriors and the king, but advised them to refrain from looting the conquered area. Manu forbade vengeful reprisal against the defeated enemy, insisting that the victorious king should grant amnesty to anyone who surrendered.[126]

In sum, the ancient Indian Law of War existed in delicate equipoise, balanced between clashing traditions of realism and humanitarianism, caste responsibilities and universalist ethics, Brahmanic ritual and personal salvation. This curious stovepiping of archaic particularism and humane transcendentalism has characterized Indian approaches to limiting warfare until the present day.

Ancient Israel and the Law of War

In contrast with China and India, little is known about the ancient Hebrew Law of War, insofar as our earliest sources discussing warfare in Israel, i.e., Deuteronomy, Chronicles, and Kings, are all post-monarchical (ca. seventh to sixth centuries BCE). These sources purport to describe the military practices of the ancient Hebrews as, moving into the land of Canaan in the late second millennium BCE, they clashed with the aboriginal people living there. Prior to this time, the Hebrews were nomads caught between the giant millstones of two great empires, the Egyptian and Hittite. The decline of these imperial powers under the impact of foreign invasion enabled the rise of numerous smaller states like Israel. Before the monarchy was established under Saul, Israel was an acephalous collection of kinship-based groups loosely joined in common defense against attacks by their neighbors, among them the Ammonites and Philistines. The Books of Chronicles and Judges state that from early in Israel's history in Canaan, Hebrew law recognized differences in the legal status of Israelites and non-Israelites. The ancient Hebrew approach to war drew even finer distinctions between the "Seven Nations"—the indigenous inhabitants of Canaan[127] expelled or exterminated by the Hebrews under Moses and Joshua—and other non-Hebrew peoples. According to Deuteronomy, no quarter would be given to the peoples of the Seven Nations. Moses communicated to the Israelites Yahweh's instructions for dealing with them:

> When the LORD your God brings you into the land which you are entering to occupy and drives out many nations before you—Hittites, Girgashites, Amorites, Canaanites, Perizzites, Hivites, and Jebusites, seven nations more numerous and powerful than you—when the LORD your God delivers them into your power and you defeat them, you must put them to death. You must not make a treaty with them or spare them . . . But this is what you must do to them: pull down their altars, break their sacred pillars, hack down their sacred poles and destroy their idols by fire.[128]

The wars of annihilation against the Seven Nations stood in stark contrast with the treatment Yahweh demanded of other foreign peoples:

> When you advance on a city to attack it, make an offer of peace. If the city accepts the offer and opens its gates to you, then all the people in it shall be put to forced labour and shall serve you. If it does not make peace with you but offers battle, you shall besiege it, and the LORD your God will deliver it into your hands. You shall put all its males to the sword, but you may take the women, the dependents, and the cattle for yourselves, and plunder everything else in the city. You may enjoy the use of the spoil of your enemies which the LORD your God gives you.[129]

As he imparted these orders to the Israelites, Moses again emphasized that the people of the Seven Nations were to be treated far more harshly:

> That is what you shall do to the cities at a great distance, as opposed to those which belong to nations near at hand. In the cities of these nations whose land the LORD your God is giving you as a patrimony, you shall not leave any creature alive. You shall annihilate them—Hittites, Amorites Canaanites, Perizzites, Hivites, Jebusites—as the LORD your God commanded you.[130]

Hebrew military practice was equal to the severity of Yahweh's commands. In their war against Midian, the Israelites slaughtered all the Midianite men, captured the women and children, seized all the cattle as booty, and reduced the cities of Midian to ashes.[131] Time and again in their conquest of Canaan, the Hebrews denied quarter to the peoples of the Seven Nations. The refusal to spare the soldiers of the enemy also extended to their kings, the royal family, and all enemy civilians.[132] According to the Book of Samuel, this practice continued even after the Israelites had settled in the land of Canaan. The prophet Samuel, the anointer of Saul as the first king of Israel, ordered Saul to "go now and fall upon the Amalekites and destroy them, and put their property under ban. Spare no one; put them all to death, men and women, children and babes in arms, herds and flocks, camels and asses." Saul flouted Samuel's command by sparing King Agag and plundering the livestock. Samuel reproved Saul for his violation, ordered that the Amalekite king be brought to him, and "hewed Agag in pieces before the Lord at Gilgal."[133] Sometimes, the Israelites dismembered their war captives, as they did the Canaanite king, Adoni-bezek, whose thumbs and big toes were cut off after his capture.[134] David removed the foreskins of 200 Philistines killed in battle and gave them to Saul as the price demanded for his daughter Michal's hand in marriage.[135]

Even for many believers, the extreme violence of the Old Testament is troubling. Some scholars hold that the mayhem recounted in the Scriptures—particularly Joshua and Deuteronomy—does not describe real historical events in the Hebrew settlement of Palestine but circumstances of the authors' own time and place.[136] Whatever the historicity of these books, the "solemn ban" (*herem*, found for example in Numbers 21:1), whereby everything in the conquered city—men, women, children, livestock, real and personal property—is destroyed, appears to be a genuine phenomenon.[137] Trying to understand its cause and function within ancient Hebrew society is a tricky matter. The practice may have begun as a sacrifice to Yahweh that was later transferred to relations with defeated peoples. On this view, captured in the Biblical story of Jephtha's vow, the Israelites contract with Yahweh to give him all the spoils if he would grant them victory over their enemies. By the time of the Deuteronomic historians (seventh to early fifth centuries BCE) the idea of *herem* had become identified with Yahweh's justice, which demanded the extermination of Israel's enemies because of their idolatry and uncleanliness.[138] According to Jan Assmann, the Deuteronomists were the key figures demanding "total religion"—a subjection of politics, the religious cult, and all of society to an intolerant, all-consuming monotheism. For Assmann monotheism from ancient Israel to modern-day Salafism has been one of the historical engines driving barbarism in warfare.[139] We will explore this theme in greater depth in Chapter 10.

Other Biblical scholars interpret *herem* as the war of Yahweh against chaos. The ancient Hebrews may have been influenced by the ideology of Assyrian warfare as set forth in the *Enuma Elish*, in which the god Marduk became king by defeating chaos. The Assyrian king imitated Marduk by waging war against the representatives of chaos, enemy foreigners; in defeating them, the king restored order to the world. If this interpretation is correct, then for at least some period of Israel's history, i.e., the late monarchy, the sacred ban was a means of fighting against chaos (*Chaoskampf*) and saving the world from disaster.[140] In its own ideology of just war, the Hebrews were in continuity with the battles against chaos fought by the Egyptian Pharaoh and Assyrian kings.

As Thomas Alfred Walker noted in his 1899 study of the Law of Nations,[141] ancient Israel was no more violent in its conduct of war than the civilizations surrounding them in the Near East. In fact, Israel likely absorbed the concept of *herem* from other Near Eastern Peoples. The Philistines' treatment of Saul's corpse was hardly a model of decency and restraint: he was decapitated and his headless body nailed to the wall of Bethshan.[142] The prophet Elisha summarized the all-too-common practice of ravaging civilians and their cities in his tearful prophecy to the king of Damascus, Hazael, of how the Syrians would deal with the Israelites: "I know the harm you will do the Israelites: you will set their fortresses on fire and put their young men to the sword; you will dash their children to the ground and you will rip open their pregnant women."[143] And yet, despite the parade of horrors characteristic of warfare in the ancient Near East, we occasionally see glimmers of an alternative vision—an approach that imposes some constraints on waging war. When the king of Israel asks Elisha whether he should kill the Syrians at Samaria, the prophet replied: "No, you must not do that . . . You may destroy those whom you have taken prisoner with your own sword and bow, but as for these men, give them food and water, and let them eat and drink, and then go back to their master." The king followed Elisha's counsel and released the Syrians after feeding them.[144] The source of this episode is the Second Book of Kings, which, together with the Books of First Kings, Joshua, Judges, Deuteronomy, and 1 and 2 Samuel, are the core of the Deuteronomic history written during the Babylonian exile (ca. 550 BCE). The Deuteronomic historians are important because they center Judaism on the covenant between Yahweh and the Jewish people.

Prior to this time, the idea of a covenant was by no means unknown in Judaism; in fact, it was a commonplace notion in many Near Eastern cultures.[145] However, the covenant in Israel was originally between Yahweh and the house of David. With the Deuteronomic historians, the contracting parties were recast as Yahweh and the Jews rather than the divinely appointed king. In other words, limits on warfare are implied in texts that reinscribed the essence of the Jewish faith in a relationship between God and the Israelite nation. The covenantal relationship—specifically, the adherence of the Jewish people to the Torah (the Jewish Law) and the cultic practice in Jerusalem—was the key, not the role of the king as a mediator of God.

As in many of the world civilizations considered in this chapter, so in ancient Israel the idea of taming the unbridled fury of warfare arose from challenges to the king as a god or representative of the divine. The centering of Judaism on the covenant between Yahweh and the nation of Israel necessarily eroded the authority of the king. The Deuteronomic historians were explicit about the king's subjection to the Law. They attributed to Moses a set of instructions he issued to the Israelites before their settlement in Canaan, in which Moses tells them that, while they have the freedom to appoint a king, he must punctiliously follow Yahweh's Law, "neither exalting himself above other members of the community nor turning aside from the commandment."[146] Bellah describes the conception of kingship set forth in Deuteronomy as resembling a "constitutional monarchy . . . hardly recognizable in Near Eastern terms."[147] For Bellah, the Deuteronomic historians' revision of the covenantal relationship to embrace Yahweh and the Israelite people, rather than Yahweh and the Israelite people *through the person of the king*, marks an epoch-making "breakthrough in Israel."[148]

Why did this happen? In an article published in 1975 in *Daedalus*, Eric Weil speculated that great breakthroughs were enabled by great "breakdowns." According to Weil, the collapse of once solid cultural structures discredits the status quo, the inadequacy of which is made self-evident.[149] A gap opens between the givenness of the social world and the people who inhabit it, a seam that invites critical reflection and ultimately change. Weil's theory may have relevance to the situation in Israel when the Deuteronomic history was taking shape: a period when the northern kingdom had fallen to the Assyrians and the southern was being swept away by the Babylonians. The convulsions wracking Israel during this time, as Israel faced immediate threats to its very existence, may have opened the door to a fundamental rethinking of Judaic religion and culture.

The era of the great Israelite prophets was a direct outgrowth of these tumults. We have already seen how the prophet Elisha referenced a principle of right above the will of the king. Other Hebrew prophets would follow suit: Amos, Hosea, Isaiah, Jeremiah, and Ezekiel all embrace understandings of the covenant that, either explicitly or implicitly, demoted the role of the king as moral preceptor and intermediary of God. The Jews became a people ruled not by a traditional king but by divine law. Not coincidentally, we can discern in the midst of this extraordinary sea change the stirrings of something resembling—if not a fully formed Law of War— then at least the embryo of it. In the same passage in Deuteronomy in which Moses instructs the Israelites on the solemn ban, we are told that he cautioned them to spare the trees as they laid siege to enemy cities, "for they provide you with food; you shall not cut them down."[150] A modest prohibition, to be sure, but one reminiscent of the ban on destroying agriculture we previously encountered in ancient India.

The Law of War in Archaic and Classical Greece

Our modern prejudices about the nature of law may blind us to the existence of law in cultures remote in time and space from our own. The absence of treaties, statutes, or formal enforcement mechanisms can mislead us into assuming that these ancient civilizations lacked a Law of War. While premodern cultures may not have had positive (i.e., written) laws or a criminal justice system to enforce conformity to them, it would be an error to assume that a Law of War did not exist, or that it was unable to elicit obedience from combatants in the field. In ancient Egypt, Mesopotamia, China, India, and Israel, there were generally observed restraints on warfare despite the absence of formal codification. These restraints were based primarily on religion and ritual practice. A similar Law of War regulated the battlefield in Archaic and Classical Greece.

The crucial point here is that customary law in Greece, as elsewhere in the ancient world, was not considered inferior to statutory law and treaties. Indeed, the capacious Greek term *nomos*, meaning "law," applied to both customary and written law. The Greeks did not equate law with written (positive) law; rather, they considered written law as supplementing customary law.[151] Rosalind Thomas has suggested that reducing law to writing may have been a Greek strategy for solemnizing rules that had not yet attained the level of respect accorded to customary law.[152] For Adriaan Lanni, "if anything, customary law may have enjoyed *more* respect than positive law in ancient Greece."[153] The norms underlying the customary Greek Law of War were derived from religion, a force that permeated Greek society from the Archaic period to the Classical Age. Once again, our modern legal consciousness, particularly in the United States where the First Amendment to the US Constitution strictly separates the political order from religion, is ill-equipped fully to grasp the inextricability of law and religion in Greek (and, indeed,

"Law and religion are twins that, everywhere we look in history, spend their childhood years in the most intimate companionship, reciprocally aiding and complementing each other."

Rudolf von Jhering, Geist des römischen Rechts, Vol. I, 256

world) history. Arguably the greatest Greek thinker of them all, Plato, asserted that to serve the laws is to serve the gods.[154] The divine authority attached to law in civilizations as diverse as China, India, Israel, and Greece likely accounts for its peremptory character, even when no formal sanction was meted out to the violator.

What were these informal religious rules that governed combat in ancient Greece? Already in Archaic Greece (800–480 BCE), customs had arisen that protected religious objects and guaranteed uninterrupted performance of religious rituals and ceremonial events. These included immunity from attack during wartime of religious structures and anything belonging to the gods, such as altars, sanctuaries, valuables, livestock, and land. Sanctuaries were especially tempting targets during wartime because they were repositories of treasure offered to the gods. The immunity afforded religious objects extended to religious officials such as priests, soothsayers traveling with Greek armies as they campaigned, religious ambassadors, participants in the panhellenic festivals like the Olympics, and even the Spartan kings, who had a triple function as monarchs, military commanders, and religious officials. This immunity, a particularly durable restraint on warfare from Homeric Greece until the Hellenistic era, was so authoritative that an army that enslaved or killed the people of a conquered city was obliged under the customary Law of War to exempt the city's religious functionaries.[155] Both panhellenic and local religious festivals were off-limits to marauding armies, which Greek custom forbade from either attacking a city celebrating a local festival or deploying their soldiers while their own city celebrated its local festival.[156]

The evidence from antiquity indicates that the customary Laws of War regarding the inviolability of religious objects, persons, and events were often followed. Plutarch reports that the Spartans' Greek opponents refrained from harming Spartan commanders because of their status as religious officials.[157] Thucydides relates that the Syracusans declined to pursue the fleeing Athenians until after their festival had concluded.[158] Herodotus recounts the best known example of this customary rule: the refusal of the Spartans to reinforce the Athenians against the Persians at Marathon because Sparta was celebrating a festival at the time.[159] Adriaan Lanni observes that Greeks complied with the custom even when compliance was detrimental to achieving military success: "It seems safe to say that when Greek states complied with the norm, even when doing so would place the physical security of the state or its allies at risk, their decision was not made for instrumental reasons, but because it was prohibited by the laws of war."[160]

Other immunities appear also to have been religiously inspired. An international norm upholding the immunity of heralds and ambassadors[161] existed in the ancient world, accepted by both the Greeks and the Persians. The benefits of protecting these officials from harm may have had a secular aim: the mutual observance of their immunity enabled communication and negotiation between different city-states. However, our primary sources tell us that heralds were deemed "messengers of the gods and of men" falling under the aegis of Zeus. To do harm to a herald invited punishment from the gods and from men.[162] Similarly, treatment of the bodies of fallen soldiers was governed by norms that had religious roots and secular benefits. Although dead soldiers were routinely plundered for their armor, Classical Age Greeks regarded desecrating the corpse of the fallen as a violation of their Law of War. This norm appears to have originated in the Classical Age; it was alien to Homeric Greece, where indignities to the enemy dead were not uncommon.[163] The custom acquired such an urgency in Classical Greece, however, that it even applied to wars with barbarians (non-Greeks) who were otherwise removed from coverage under the Greek Law of War. Conquerors were expected to surrender the bodies of dead enemy soldiers upon request of the vanquished army. In this way, the appropriate funerary rites could be held and the dead interred as demanded by the gods. The sources emphasize that this norm was both a divine and a Greek law that was seldom violated.[164]

As in the other archaic societies discussed in this chapter, so among the archaic Greeks these religiously-based norms were not motivated by a humanitarian concern to avoid unnecessary suffering during war. Instead, they were rules imbedded in a ritual practice intended to fulfill divine commands. Religion, however, was not the only concern guiding behavior during battle; the honor attained through military victory was a major spur to behavior in combat. The dictum of "helping one's friends and hurting one's enemies"[165] summed up the goal of Greek warfare, a code of conduct elastic enough to permit almost any means conducive to success. Treachery, brutality, enslavement, and ransom were all fair game under the Greek Law of War. The view that the victors could do with the troops and civilians of the losers whatsoever they wanted was predominant, a "winner take all" principle of warfare that is well-attested in our sources. The fifth-century Greek historian Xenophon averred "that whenever a city is taken in warfare, both the people and their possessions belong to those who captured the city," an assertion corroborated by Aristotle's recognition that "the things conquered in war are the property of the conquerors."[166] Enemy soldiers could be put to the sword even when they tried to surrender; the conqueror had the choice of killing, enslaving, or ransoming them, and each of these options was elected at different times, according to our sources.[167] The manner of killing could take barbarous forms: the Spartans and Athenians respectively burned alive and stoned to death surviving enemy soldiers.[168] At least one source, Euripides, suggests that it was forbidden to put surrendered soldiers to death once they were removed alive from the battlefield. Lanni cautions that this prohibition is not found elsewhere, and that the absence of corroboration may indicate that the mention of it was "propaganda" to deflect criticism of Athenian imperialism.[169]

No prisoner of war status as defined by the Geneva Conventions existed in ancient Greece. The term for a war captive was at best hazy; both Greek and Latin refer to men and property in the hands of the triumphant army with the same word. The winner had three options: to execute war captives, to enslave them, or to liberate them after first detaining them. If the decision was execution, the killing could be done when the city was sacked or later on after the conflict had subsided. If the captive was put to death later, the motives for execution were various. A war captive might be executed in reprisal, out of the victor's anger, or as a human sacrifice (particularly in Archaic Greece). In 25 percent of the cases documented in our sources from Homeric times, war captives were simply executed; the rest were enslaved. The practice of enslaving war captives continued into the Classical Age, but it was usually restricted to conflicts between Greeks and barbarians (non-Greeks).[170]

The most fundamental immunity under modern international humanitarian law—the prohibition on targeting noncombatants—was absent from the Greek city-states. A civilian's best chance of avoiding harm during battle was to withdraw behind the walls of a fortified city and leave the fighting to the armies outside. If, however, the city fell to invaders, the well-established custom was to grant *carte blanche* to the victors, who were free to kill all the men and enslave the women and children. If they chose, conquerors might also enslave the entire population. In effect, a victorious army had an absolute right of property to everything and everyone in the defeated city—so long as the victor had not agreed to a negotiated surrender with the city's inhabitants beforehand. In the latter case, the population could be spared the worst of military subjugation. This notwithstanding, all of the citizens under the agreement were obliged to vacate the city, leaving behind their possessions as booty for the victors.[171]

As we have seen, the rules governing the conduct of warfare in Archaic Greece were largely based on religion. However, other features of the Greek Law of War are likely attributable to more secular purposes. Some of these may have arisen in connection with the hoplite phalanx, a transformative military formation consisting of heavily armed warriors fighting in a compacted mass. The hoplite soldier wore a helmet, a breastplate, and greaves to protect his shins, and carried both a sword and a six-foot-long thrusting spear. Informal rules emerged to govern the deployment and actions of these hoplite soldiers. Some of these rules crept into the Greek Law of War between 700 and 450 BCE, earning recognition with other battlefield constraints as the "common customs of the Hellenes" (*koina nomina*). Historian Josiah Ober argues that these principles were specifically connected to the unique interests and requirements of the hoplites, such as the injunction that non-hoplite arms be limited or that pursuit of retreating opponents be discontinued after a short time.[172] Ober subscribes to the traditional account of the Greek Law of War associated with Victor Hanson,[173] holding that the "common customs of the Hellenes" served the interests of the men who filled the hoplite ranks, mostly farmers with enough wealth to purchase expensive armor and to ensure their prominent status in the polis. On this social historical interpretation, the "common customs" were forged between 700 and 450 BCE by the social elites within the hoplite armies. As Greece spiraled into civil war during the fifth-century clash between Sparta and Athens, these rules tended to break down, chiefly because fewer of the traditional elites served as hoplite soldiers and the style of warfare characteristic of hoplite battle was drastically changing.[174] In short, for adherents of the traditional view, the Greek Law of War did not express a humanitarian concern with alleviating unnecessary suffering; rather, it encoded the privileges of a socially powerful group, and when that group's interests changed, so did observance of the Law. By the time of the Peloponnesian War, the role of these historical elites in warfare had receded to the point where the common customs of the Greeks were no longer followed. The atrocities of the panhellenic civil war of the fifth century, such as the destruction and enslavement of the people of Melos by the Athenians and the execution of Plataean war captives by the Spartans, were proof positive that the Law of War had been discarded.

Other scholars have challenged the traditional account. For Adriaan Lanni, the abandonment of constraints on warfare during the Peloponnesian War was due to changes in military tactics—specifically, the increased use of siege methods throughout the year (and not just during the summer season) as a means of breaching fortified cities.

In view of the reduced protections accorded to civilians under the long-standing Greek Law of War, the enhanced incidence of successful siege warfare necessarily entailed the exposure of vulnerable noncombatants to the whims of their conquerors. Quoting Aristotle, Lanni affirms that "such harsh treatment of civilians did not violate international law, which provided that 'that which is conquered in war is the property of the conquerors.'"[175] Because civilians had precious few immunities under the Greek Law of War prior to the Peloponnesian conflict, documented instances of massacres, enslavement, and the complete destruction of enemy cities did not violate Greek international law. She does, however, agree with the traditional account that the exceptional bitterness of the war, inflamed by the belief of the participants that they were fighting for their very existence, contributed to the war's many excesses.[176]

One of the main objections to recognizing international law as law in the accepted sense of the word is the absence of a mechanism to enforce compliance with it. This objection has dogged international humanitarian law well into the twentieth century. However, as it pertains to ancient Greece, the criticism falls wide of the mark because plenty of evidence from antiquity exists for the binding quality of Greek constraints on war. Three of the primary mechanisms of enforcement were reprisals, reputational damage, and divine punishment suffered by violators.

Greek views on the treatment of civilians during wartime

Xenophon: ". . . it is a law established for all time among all men that when a city is taken in war, the persons and the property of the inhabitants belong to the captors."

Plato: ". . . If any fall alive into the enemies' hands we shall make them a present of him, and they may do what they like with their prey . . . all the goods of the vanquished fall into the hands of the victors."

Aristotle: ". . . those vanquished in war are held to belong to the victor . . ."

Garlan, War in the Ancient World, 69

It was commonly accepted among the Greeks that a city-state could retaliate against an adversary if it violated the Law of War. When the Athenians desecrated the Boeotians' temple at Delium, the Boeotians retaliated by refusing to hand over the Athenian dead as required under Greek customary law.[177] Thucydides relates a similar account in the Theban attack on the Plataeans in 431 BCE. At the time of the military assault, the Plataeans were celebrating a religious festival—meaning that the Thebans had violated a norm of the Greek Law of War. When the Plataeans eventually prevailed, they captured and later executed more than a hundred Theban soldiers. After the Plataeans surrendered to the Thebans and Spartans years later, they raised the defense at trial that their execution of the prisoners had been legitimate under the Law of War: the Thebans had not only attacked them during a time of peace established by treaty, "but it was in the period of a religious festival that they seized our city, and in making them suffer for it we acted rightly and in accordance with the general law that one is always justified in resisting an aggressor."[178] The Greek historian and statesman Polybius (200–118 BCE), however, writes that the Greeks imposed limitations on the right of reprisal. These chiefly concerned a ban on retaliation against religious buildings or objects.[179]

One form reprisal sometimes took was hostage-taking. This practice likely has archaic roots that long antedate the Classical era of Greek history. It is imbedded in a worldview of collective solidarity and responsibility, in which the victim had a right to demand reparation from the entire community for the harm done by a single member of that community. After indemnifying the victim, the community was expected to seek compensation from the wrongdoer. Both the Greeks and the Romans recognized the need to defuse potential conflict by permitting an aggrieved party to take hostages. The law code of the Athenian legislator Draco (ca. 621 BCE) explicitly provided that the family of a homicide victim could "take and hold hostages [from the perpetrator's kin group] until they either submit to trial for blood guiltiness or surrender the actual manslayers." Draco limited the hostages to no more than three.[180] What was good for kin groups in their interactions was also good for city-states in their mutual dealings. The principle justifying hostage-taking applied not only to instances of violent death, but to other legal matters as well. A fourth-century BCE inscription from Cyrene, a Greek colony in Libya, related that the colony dispatched agents to Peloponnesian city-states to pay off the debts owed by Cyrenean debtors, an act designed to avert reprisals that might be taken against the entire community.[181]

In addition to reprisal, violators of the Law of War could suffer damage to their reputation, a severe penalty in a culture that placed a high value on honor and status. Lanni points out that reputational damage was not just an intrinsic evil to be avoided; because the reputation of a city-state affected all of its dealings with other city-states, the loss of honor triggered by the commission of war crimes could impair the offender's ability to negotiate treaties, conduct trade, and form alliances. In other words, there was genuine pressure to conform to the common customs of the Hellenes, a pressure exerted at the summit of the city-state government and radiating downward through the ranks.[182] Finally, the threat of divine sanction may have sometimes deterred armies from flouting the norms of the Law of War. As we have seen, many of these norms were religiously-based; hence, the Greeks regarded their violation as *hybris*—a prideful defiance of the will of the gods. Herodotus tells us that the gods punished the Athenians and Spartans for transgressing one of the most important and widespread international rules in the ancient world: they killed the Persian envoys at the onset of the first Persian War.[183] Pausanias reports that the Megarians murdered an Athenian herald, a brazen contravention of the Law of War, for which the gods consigned them to eternal poverty.[184] Although Greek history abounds with stories of hereditary curses engendered by violations of religion-based customs and transmitted in perpetuity through the generations,[185] our sources suggest a weakening of this belief as skepticism about traditional religion mounted in the fifth century BCE. Nonetheless, the persistence of traditional religious beliefs well into and beyond the Classical Age suggests that the threat of divine sanction very likely deterred some potential wrongdoers from violating the Law of War.

Herodotus's account of the Greek killing of the Persian envoys highlights a central feature of the Greek Law of War: it was usually deemed inapplicable to wars between Greeks and non-Greeks (barbarians). The Greeks' repudiation of the Law of War as it pertained to non-Greeks may have reflected their xenophobia, an attitude well-documented in the literature. According to Coleman Phillipson, non-Greeks "were considered barbarians,—aliens not only in the political sense, but also in the intellectual and moral, and what is still more important, in the ethnic and religious sense."[186] Aristotle believed that barbarians were by their nature suited to be enslaved by the Greeks.[187] His view was not exotic. Non-Greek war captives had been enslaved at least since Homeric times, and even when the reduction of prisoners to slavery began to abate amidst criticism of its harshness in the late Classical Age, the practice and policy of enslaving barbarians continued in force.[188] The upshot of such thinking was to withhold the Greek Law of War from conflicts between Greeks and non-Greeks.[189] The Persian Wars are illustrative on this point: the Greeks deviated time and again from the Law of War, executing the Persian envoys and undertaking neither a formal declaration of war nor the customary exchange of war dead. Contrary to earlier custom, the Greeks pursued fleeing Persian soldiers doggedly at Marathon and put them to the sword. The Persian survivors of the Battle of Plataea were all executed.[190]

To sum up, as in ancient China, India, and Israel, the Greek Law of War consisted of rules derived from religion interfused with other principles that may have served secular purposes (such as the interests of powerful social classes within the hoplite armies). The consensus of scholars is that the common customs of the Hellenes did not express a humanitarian concern for reducing the dreadful suffering of war. These are modern concerns, and it is anachronistic to read such concerns back into an age and a people who did not share them. Nonetheless, it is also notable that the ancient Greeks insisted military conflict *was* subject to constraint. And while the Law of War in Greece was harsh as measured by contemporary standards, we see flashes in the Classical Age of an attitude of mercy that may foreshadow future developments in the history of law and war. Thucydides recounts the gripping story of the efforts by the city of Mytilene to break away from the Athenian empire during the Peloponnesian War. When the revolt was crushed, the Athenians dispatched a ship with the message that all Mytilenean men were to be executed and the women and children slaved. Reconsidering its decision a day later, the Athenian assembly sent a second ship on a frantic errand to overtake the first one and countermand its order of mass executions.[191] As Adriaan Lanni observes, a sense of compassion seems to have impelled the Athenians' change of heart.[192] At least on this one occasion, public opinion was able to temper the harsh Law of War in Greece.

Conclusion

In *The Province of Jurisprudence Determined* (1832), the English jurist John Austin argued that "customary law" should not be considered law until a state authority either codified it statutorily or established it judicially. Until that time, custom rated as no more than "positive morality." Austin's position was that, in the absence of formal promulgation by the sovereign, custom lacked the "imperative" quality distinguishing positive law from other general rules of conduct like etiquette or international law.[193] As this chapter has demonstrated, however, conceptions of law like Austin's do not adequately explain the Law of War in world history. In each of the cultures we have discussed, constraints on warfare emerged from religion and ritual rather than from a sovereign authority's decrees, and they were performed as a means of placating the gods or of preserving cosmic order. Although rarely written down, these constraints were yet able to elicit obedience, however imperfectly, and did so without a formal criminal justice system to punish acts of non-compliance.

In his 1899 study of the law of nations, T. A. Walker conceded that international law in the ancient world "was rude and primitive enough." This aside, it was "an improving law" that, for all its shortcomings, upheld the belief that "the intercourse of men, members of diverse communities, was not absolutely lawless."[194] Limits had always been set to the ferocity of armed conflict based on cosmological belief systems and the rituals they inevitably produced. Additional limitations arose when kings were no longer identified with the gods, a realization that dawned on ancient peoples in the course of the first millennium BCE. Once the person of the king was separated from the will of Heaven, the potential for principles of right, justice, and truth separate from the edicts of a ruler became available, against which the actions and commands of worldly rulers and military leaders could be measured. As a result, during the first millennium BCE societies in China, India, Israel, and Greece began to display an interest in curbing the unnecessary violence and destruction of warfare. Constraints on war were sometimes construed as being universal in scope—as applying not only to one's own society or culture but to outsiders as well. A new tradition of the Law of War, one based less on religious ritual than on compassion for the casualties of battle on all sides, was slowly coming into being.

CHAPTER 2
THE LAW OF WAR IN PRE-COLUMBIAN AMERICA

With respect to the civilizations covered in Chapter 1, none was hermetically sealed off from influence by others. At some point in their histories they were all brought into conjunction with one another, whether by means of trade routes linking eastern and western entrepots or the military conquests of the Assyrians and Babylonians, the Persians, Alexander the Great, Greek colonists, and the Roman legions. Such was not the case with the civilizations that are the topic of this chapter. Not until the voyages of Christopher Columbus and their ruinous aftermath were any of them—so far as evidence tells us—exposed to the cultures of Europe, the Near East, or Asia. They thus present an intriguing and revealing glimpse of sophisticated peoples who, because of their geographical position, were able to develop apart from the civilizations of Eurasia. Although no transformative watershed occurred during the first millennium BCE in the ancient Americas as it did in Eurasia to mark a cognitive boundary between the socio-political worlds and the gods, pre-Columbian civilizations adhered to a Law of War entirely of their own stamp, one that bears astonishing similarities with but also impressive differences from their Eurasian counterparts.

Mesoamerica

The Maya

Kings as Shamans   To get at Mayan understandings of conflict, we must first familiarize ourselves with their cosmology, for warfare and the laws underlying it are the tendrils of Mayan religion. As Mesoamerican scholars Linda Schele and David Freidel have argued,[1] an understanding of the Maya can be acquired only with the knowledge that "the Maya codified their shared model of reality through religion and ritual rather than economics." For modern Westerners whose frame of reality is materialist and economic, a culture that primarily construes the world in non-material spiritual categories is so exotic as to be nearly incomprehensible. Our task in this chapter, as throughout the chapters on premodern peoples, is to render the forbidding and enigmatical more accessible to the modern mind with its own biases of place, time, and circumstance.

In addition to economistic materialism, the Judaeo-Christian theological tradition poses a further obstacle to understanding Mayan conceptions of war. The dominant Western model of God's nature emphasizes God's *aseity*, or independence and self-subsistence. God does not rely on anyone or anything for God's being: God has existed from all eternity and will continue to exist without the need of refreshment from earthly sources. This is a dualist conception of God's relationship to the world and humankind.[2] The Mayan cosmology, by contrast, was strongly anti-dualist. It emphasized that the physical world was a "material manifestation of the spiritual and the spiritual … the essence of the material." Thus the spiritual realm caused health or disease, success or failure, victory or defeat on the earthly plane, and the actions of living people reciprocally affected the flourishing of beings in the other world. People on earth alone could nourish the gods and spirits of dead ancestors resident in the afterlife. There was no First Amendment in Mayan culture to divorce religion from the state; instead, Mayan kings functioned as shamans arbitrating between the two worlds, seeking to balance through their performance of ritual the needs of the here and now and the afterlife.[3]

The Mayan cosmology consisted of three dimensions of existence—heaven (the "Otherworld"), the earth (Middleworld), and the Underworld (Xibalba). At night Xibalba swung into the heavens and became the starry night sky. An axis (*Wacah Chan*, "six sky" or "raised sky") ran through these vertical levels, symbolized by a tree with roots thrusting into the watery Underworld and branches reaching upward into heaven. This axis, in the figuration of which we may discern Eliade's axis of the world, provides the vital link joining the human realm with the Otherworld. As with other cultures we have considered, for the Maya the axis does not have a fixed geographical placement; rather, it could be evoked anywhere in the Middleworld through ritual. Standing on the summit of a pyramid-temple (a homology of the cosmic mountain joining heaven and earth), Mayan kings practiced blood-letting ceremonies that conjured *Wacah Chan* in the form of a "World Tree" growing through the center of the temple. The World Tree opened the portal into the Otherworld. Through this portal departed ancestors and Mayan gods entered the human realm to commune with the king. In contrast with some ancient cultures we have already studied, the Mayan king was not divine; he was instead a shaman, the link between this world and the next.[4]

Although Mayan kings were not divine, they did manifest the earthly forms of gods from the Otherworld like the Twins, the main heroes of Mayan mythology. Their story is a complicated one; what follows is a simplification of a much more intricate tale. In brief, the twins were called to account in Xibalba because of their excellent yet rambunctious style of playing the Mayan ball game. Through their ingenuity they escaped a series of traps laid for them by the Lords of Death; these traps involved decapitations and dismemberments of the Twins as well as their immolation in a fiery pit. In the end, however, the Twins were always resurrected, a feat that duly impressed the Lords of Death. They asked the Twins to be killed and resurrected just as they had been. The Twins obliged, killing the Lords but abstaining from resurrecting them. In this way the Twins outwitted Death, affording human beings a glimmer of hope for their own immortality. Mayan kings would reenact the Twins' victory over Death by means of ritual performed through blood-letting, dismemberment, and decapitation.[5] By the Classic period (begins ca. 120 CE), this ritual was the cornerstone of Mayan life, pervading everything the Mayans did—including their style of war.

Sometimes, Mayan kings drew blood from their own bodies through cuts made with a keenly sharp obsidian blade. However, the most satisfying boon to the gods and ancestors of the Otherworld was the blood of high-born victims. Images carved on stelae and painted on temple frescoes portray captured enemy soldiers of noble background being sacrificed through decapitation. Waged under the sign of the jaguar adorned with waterlily scrolls, this kind of Mayan warfare was conceived as a royal hunt ending in the capture of aristocratic enemies and their blood sacrifice, used to open the portal to the Otherworld. In the Classical Age it had become so regular a feature of Mayan warfare that we can speak of a "war-sacrifice complex," one that dominates the imagery of the Temple of the Sun at Palenque (a major Mayan city-state). Deeply intertwined with it was the Mayan ballgame and its playing field, the ballcourt. Highborn captives were often compelled to play this game in front of a crowd of spectators; the losers were beheaded, their bodies trussed into a ball and thrown down the temple steps. In the symbolic world of the Maya, the game was likened to the Twins' victory over the Lords of Death.[6]

The Tlaloc-Venus Complex The Maya were not a unified territorial empire like Akkad, Assyria, Persia, or Rome. Rather, they were a patchwork of city-states divided by language barriers yet sharing significant cultural affinities. No one city-state could unify the Maya under its own imperial rule. Hence, Mayan history from 200 CE to the arrival of the Spanish was the story of city-states locked in mutual struggles for regional hegemony.[7] One such rivalry between the city-states of Tikal and Uaxactún came to a fateful head in January 378 CE.

The military clash between the two city-states inaugurated a revolution in warfare among the Maya. Long before the final conflict between them, the Maya had offered sacrifices of noble war captives to their gods and ancestors. These prisoners had been captured after the traditional mode of Mayan fighting—namely, hand-to-hand combat of highborn warriors seeking both the prestige of conquest and sacrificial victims for their gods. Great-Jaguar-Paw, the ruler of Tikal, decisively upset this tradition of battle in his war with Uaxactún. The modest goals of winning prestige and securing prisoners as sacrifice were eclipsed by an overriding new priority: the destruction of the enemy kingdom and its annexation by the winner. Great-Jaguar-Paw modeled the new approach in his ceremonial garb, the elements of which were borrowed from the central Mexican cultural center of Teotihuacán. The regalia became an emblem henceforth for the king's role as conqueror/warrior and the new paradigm of total war that Great-Jaguar-Paw had introduced. The costume consisted of a balloon-shaped headdress, spearthrowers, a flexible shield, owls, a jaguar mosaic, and a jaguar bodysuit. Wherever seen in Mayan iconography, these elements of the king's regalia signified the new style of total war as it emerged in Tikal's conquest of Uaxactún.[8]

Schele and Freidel call this new kind of total war the "Tlaloc-Venus complex." It was associated with Tlaloc, the rain god venerated at Teotihuacán and (much later) Tenochtitlan. His image appears in representations of the regalia worn by Mayan kings adhering to the new style of warfare. "Venus" in the compound noun "Tlaloc-Venus" refers to the Mayan concern to synchronize their new, ruthless warfare with the Eveningstar's cycle (the first appearance of Venus in the west). Warfare was also

Figure 7 Five figures of Tlaloc appearing in the Codex Borgia. © Wikimedia Commons (public domain).

coordinated with the fixed positions of Jupiter and Saturn in the night sky. While Tikal's conquest of Uaxactún on January 16, 378 does not seem to have been aligned with the cycle, within forty years of Tikal's victory the association of the new warfare with Venus is certain. The pattern established by Great-Jaguar-Paw and his war chief Smoking Frog would be widely imitated by other Mayan kings as well as subsequent Mesoamerican tribes like the Mixtec and Aztec.[9]

For the royal clans subjected to Tlaloc-Venus warfare, the outcome was often extirpation. Uaxactún's royal officers not killed in combat were taken prisoner; none would be ransomed. Instead, all of them would be tortured and killed. Their biological deaths were obviously a catastrophe for the defeated army, yet an even graver loss than their lives faced the royal clans of Uaxactún: the irremediable loss of their portal to the Otherworld. Many cultures in world history have fought total war but none have waged it in the style of the Tlaloc-Venus complex. The complete subjugation of the enemy city-state and the destruction of its leadership also involved the capture of the loser's portal. Conquest was, in other words, not only of the royal clan and their city but also of their ancestors and gods.[10] Defeat was a disaster for a fallen Mayan city-state so awful in its galactic boundlessness as to be scarcely comprehensible for us today.

We know of the treatment of war captives from Mayan artwork—glyphs carved into stelae and lintels and images painted on temple frescoes. In these panels the degradation of war captives is prominently figured. Unlike Mesopotamian representations the Maya often portrayed their war captives as individuals lying supine under the feet of the conqueror, whose triumph earned him prestige pleasing to the gods and departed ancestors. Mayan kings (*ahauob*) had an incentive to identify the royal identities of their captives because it enhanced the glory of their victory. The Tlaloc-Venus complex would continue for several more centuries; archaeologists have uncovered its footprint in other Mayan military conflicts, including Caracol's conquest of Tikal (May 1, 562 CE) and Narranjo (December 27, 631 CE), Toniná's sack of Palenque (711 CE), Dos Pilas's defeat of Seibel (735 CE), and Piedras Negras's conquest of Pomona (793 CE). Particularly in Tlaloc-Venus wars fought in later centuries, war captives designated for sacrifice were dressed in a characteristic uniform. Stripped of their battledress, they were clothed with a kilt and paper or flowers as ear ornaments. They were then painted the color of sacrifice, blue.[11]

For more than half a millennium, the Maya fought each other over land, resources, and prestige. They also fought each other for spiritual reasons that seem unfathomable to us today. It may be a stretch to refer to a Mayan *jus ad bellum* and *jus in bello* in the accepted meaning of those terms. At least with the Egyptians and Mesopotamians, there were efforts to justify warfare with declarations of a just cause, an urge that the Maya did not share. Nonetheless, by the late fourth century CE the Maya had come to the idea that war should be aligned with the positions in the night sky of Venus, Jupiter, and Saturn and for the purpose of seizing war captives for sacrifice. Only in this way could the shaman-kings of the Maya pry open the portal to the Otherworld and sustain the life-giving contact with their gods and ancestors. Warfare for the Maya was not pure anarchic bloodsport anymore than it had been for the Egyptians, Hebrews, Mesopotamians, Chinese, Indians, or Greeks. It was an activity deeply conditioned by their religious conception of the cosmos and their belief in the interaction of the supernatural realm with the material world—an interaction lubricated by violence, blood-letting, and ritual.

The Aztecs

Human sacrifice and the cult of Huitzilopochtli Among the powerful heirs to the Mayan tradition of warfare and human sacrifice were the Aztecs, a people who had forged a sprawling, multi-ethnic territorial empire in Mesoamerica by the early sixteenth century CE. The Aztecs were at first a coalition of three city-states forming a triple

"[Moctezuma II] had over two hundred chieftains in his guard, in other rooms close to his own, not that all were meant to converse with him, ... and when they went to speak to him...they had to enter barefoot with their eyes lowered to the ground, and not to look up in his face.... [When they left him] they did not turn their backs, but kept their faces towards him with their eyes to the ground, and they did not turn their backs until they left the room."

Bernal Díaz del Castillo, The True History of the Conquest of New Spain, *vol. II, 60*

alliance: the Mexica (or "Chichimec" in Nahuatl, the language of the Aztecs), Texcoco, and Tlacopan. In 1428 this alliance attacked and conquered the dominant city in the Valley of Mexico, Atzcapotzalco, thereafter gaining control over most of the Valley. The Mexica eventually emerged from this triumvirate as the preeminent city-state from their perch on an island in Lake Texcoco called Tenochtitlan. With the reins of power firmly in hand, they burst out of the Valley and subdued nearly all of central Mexico. By the first decade of the sixteenth century, few were the Mesoamerican tribes that were not tributaries of the Aztec empire.[12]

As the Aztecs led by the Mexicas acquired dominance over central Mexico, so too did the Aztec ruler. A step in the direction of the ruler's increasing independence was taken by Itzcoatl, the king when the Aztecs launched their surprise attack on Atzcapotzalco. Itzcoatl stripped the *calpulli* and *altepetl* councils of their authority to choose future rulers, transferring it to a circle of his advisers called the "Council of Four." A further augmentation of the ruler's power occurred in the late fifteenth century when Moctezuma II combined in his person the offices of king and high priest, a heady blend that Latin American colonial scholar Benjamin Keen called "a mixture of theocracy and royal absolutism."[13] Moctezuma II became the first Aztec ruler to associate himself with their primary god, Huitzilopochtli, a deity of war and the sun. Huitzilopochtli recalls the salvational, chaos-battling warrior gods of other cultures we have discussed—the sun-king Pharaoh in his struggle against foreigners and wild animals, Marduk's victory over Tiamat, the monster of primordial chaos, and Yahweh's war against chaos as reflected in the sacred ban. A legend describes Huitzilopochtli's efforts to save the life of his mother, the earth-goddess Coatlícue, from a plot hatched by his sister, the moon-goddess Coyolxauhqui, and his brothers, the stars (Centzonhuitznahuac). He decapitated his moon-goddess sister and routed his star-brothers. Much like the Egyptian Re, Huitzilopochtli had to renew his battle against his siblings each morning as he rose as the sun in the east. His victory over the forces of night and chaos guaranteed life for human beings on earth. If the sun was one of his aspects, the other was war. It was this facet of Huitzilopochtli's divinity around which the Aztecs constructed their cult of human sacrifice.[14]

The cult of Huitzilopochtli and its relation with Aztec warfare presents challenges to the modern understanding of why human beings wage war against each other. Our common sense assumption that war is bound up with territorial aggrandizement and the

Figure 8 The Techcatl, or Aztec sacrifice altar. Mexica room of the National Museum of Anthropology (Mexico City). © Wikimedia Commons (public domain).

seizure of resources is largely inapplicable to the Aztecs. Their motive for attacking and conquering other peoples in central Mexico was, so far as we can tell, the acquisition of enemy soldiers as fodder for the mill of Huitzilopochtli's cult of sacrifice. Mesoamerican scholar and anthropologist Nigel Davies relates that Moctezuma I and Tlacaelel, the main architect of the triple alliance, decided they would wage constant warfare against the cities of the Valley of Puebla-Tlaxcala to guarantee an uninterrupted flow of sacrificial victims. According to Davies, the aim was not conquest; rather, the antagonists would agree to fight a battle at a pre-arranged time and place, in which prisoners would be taken on both sides and offered as sacrifices on the altars of each. These "Flower Wars," as they came to be known (because guests invited to attend the sacrifices would sit in spectators' boxes festooned with flowers), would provide a perpetual source of victims without the need to wage wars in distant locales. After Moctezuma and Tlacaelel had agreed to this policy, Moctezuma declared that war was from that moment forward the chief activity of the Mexica. The expansion of the Aztec Empire through force of arms was thus driven primarily by religious and cosmological motives: to appease the gods (especially Huitzilopochtli) and to reproduce ritualistically his victory over chaos and darkness.[15]

In addition to war captives, the sacrificial victims were criminals, slaves, and persons given by tributary cities to the Aztecs. They were slaughtered in elaborate ceremonies atop the Great Pyramid of Tenochtitlan (later destroyed by Hernando Cortes), their hearts ripped from their chests by priests wielding an obsidian blade. The conclusion of victory ceremonies sometimes involved eating the victims' flesh. The advent of the Flower Wars marked an important transition in the Huitzilopochtli cult: whereas prior to the Flower Wars sacrifice was individual, afterward it consisted of mass offerings, some on a scale rarely if ever seen in world history. At the dedication of the Great Temple in 1487, for example, sources tell us that 80,400 persons were sacrificed, a figure historians have called into question. Most of the secondary literature cites a figure of 20,000,[16] itself extraordinary and without precedent. Davies himself argues for a fraction of the legendary number; he suggests dropping a zero and accepting a ballpark figure of 8,400.[17]

The Feast of the Flayed God Captured prisoners were also sacrificed in connection with the Feast of the Flayed God, Xipe Totec, held during the second month of the Nahuatl year. On this sacred occasion, the staging of the sacrificial act differed from the norm. The prisoners were dressed as sacrificial victims; feathers were attached to their heads, their lips darkened with cosmetics and their faces covered with chalk. The priest in charge gave the prisoner a shield and a wooden club adorned with feathers as well as four wooden balls that could be used as weapons. In this attire he would now face four gladiators wearing the costumes of eagles and ocelots, who advanced on the prisoner one

Figure 9 Xipe Totec mask, the flayed god, created between 1325 and 1521. © Wikimedia Commons (public domain).

after the other. Each gladiator was armed with a wooden club spiked with an obsidian blade. (There would be no parity of arms in this ceremony.) Most of the time the victim was slain by the first gladiator and his heart torn from his chest as an offering to Huitzilopochtli. When the ritual was over the priests flayed the victims, donning their skins for twenty more days. The victim's captor made the rounds of the shrines on the island with the blood of the victim in a green bowl. He sprinkled blood on the lips of the gods' effigies in each shrine as if to nourish them. Remarkably, the rules of sacrifice were such that the captor was forbidden to partake of the victim's flesh, which he regarded as being his own flesh. At the time of capture he addressed his prisoner as his "beloved son"; the prisoner returned the sentiment by calling his captor "my beloved father."[18]

This outré element of Aztec sacrifice has few if any parallels in world history. At the same time, it draws our attention to the dense, counterintuitive symbolism that encrusts the phenomenon of Aztec human sacrifice. It is a commonplace in historical writing on the Aztecs to describe their victims as sacrificed *to* Huitzilopochtli; I have used such a locution in this chapter. In reality, however, the Aztecs and the victims themselves believed that the victim *became* the god to which he was sacrificed. As Davies notes, the identification of the victim with the god helps account for the lack of resistance in the chronicles of Aztec sacrifice. Incredible as it may sound to a modern observer, the captive regarded his capture as an election of himself by the god. The god had chosen him for sacrifice, and from all appearances the prisoner felt honored by the god's choice. That the prisoner voluntarily embraced his own killing flies in the face of the instinct for self-preservation yet there is abundant evidence for it, including the demands of two young Aztec men captured by Pedro Alvarado, Cortes's deputy who ordered the massacre of Aztec aristocrats and priests in Cortes's absence. When Alvarado offered to set them free, they insisted on being sacrificed.[19]

Although some experts have emphasized other factors in Aztec imperial expansion,[20] a consensus has gathered around the view that ritual sacrifice imbedded in a religious cosmology was the principal cause of Aztec warfare. Indeed, the two phenomena of war and sacrifice were interpenetrating, as American anthropologist George C. Vaillant observed years ago: "War led to sacrifice and sacrifice led back to war, in ever-widening circles."[21] The Aztecs were not innovators in human sacrifice; in Mesoamerica the practice antedated them by a good millennium, reaching back into what may have been the cradle of Mesoamerican human sacrifice—the cultural center of Teotihuacán.[22] Nor were the Aztecs unique in world civilization; many other cultures of the ancient world sacrificed human beings to ensure a good harvest or to propitiate their gods. As these cultures matured and complexified, however, they tended to discard human sacrifice. Not so the Aztecs, who, as their merchants created and then dominated a regional trading network in central Mexico, accelerated the volume and tempo of their sacrifices. In this regard most scholars agree that the Aztecs were singular. Yet we ought not judge them too harshly, for despite the grimness of human sacrifice the Aztecs were a people with sensitivities and moral standards. They were appalled that the Spanish would burn people alive for committing crimes or for heresy. They were offended at the Spanish custom of branding slaves and denying them rights as human beings. Davies points out that the very idea of torturing a ruler to extract information from him about the whereabouts of fabled gold would have been abhorrent to the Aztecs.[23]

The Aztec example discloses, I would suggest, the potential for extreme violence within human collectivities when two forces converge: the conviction that an inestimably important good hangs in the balance that can be achieved only through mass killing and a militaristic drive for territorial expansion. We will encounter this theme again in our study of war crimes in world history, especially as we turn our attention to Salafism and jihad in Chapter 10.

North America

Compared with the Maya and Aztecs, the cultural practices and belief systems of pre-Columbian North America pose significant obstacles to modern scholarship. Our sources on Mayan and Aztec cosmologies and how they affected warfare are well-attested in contemporaneous accounts as well as in the material culture of both civilizations—frescoes on temple walls, glyphs carved into stelae, iconography adorning pyramid sites, and even ancient written records like the Mayan Popol Vuh (in which the myth of the twins is recorded). The evidence of religious beliefs and martial customs among North American tribes before European contact is far more scant. We have some rock art, particularly among the ancestors of the Plains Indians. Osteological evidence—the condition of skeletons of pre-contact native Americans who perished in battle—affords what one scholar has called "a direct measure of brutality."[24] Fortifications in the communities of Amerindian farmers designed to repel attack likewise bear witness to armed struggle in pre-Columbian America, as do the accounts of native peoples and early European explorers and missionaries. Ultimately, however, our knowledge of the material and cosmo-religious reasons for waging war is fragmentary for prehistoric North America as compared with Mesoamerica.

Plains Indians

Traditional studies of pre-contact and early post-contact warfare among Plains Indians—tribes that include the Comanche, Kiowa, Apache, the Sarsi, the Blackfoot, Atsina, Arapaho, Cheyenne, Crow, Teton Dakota, and Assiniboin, among others—have stressed the view that war was above all a game in these societies. A leading anthropologist of native peoples in the first half of the twentieth century, Robert Lowie, denied that territorial expansion or securing access to resources motivated Crow Indian warfare. Such explanations could not address why a Crow warrior earned more prestige from lightly touching an adversary than killing him.[25] For Lowie "the motives of primitive warfare rather seldom coincided with those familiar to us." Instead, war was a game played according to "established rules," and only when one's kinfolk were killed did the conflict escalate through reprisals to homicidal levels.[26] Other twentieth-century anthropologists tended to agree, holding that "utilitarian" (i.e., economic) motives for

Figure 10 Three Sioux Indians on horseback with rock formation in background, *c.*1905. ©
Buyenlarge / Getty Images.

warfare were secondary to cultural ones. As the ethnographer of the Plains Indians Clark
Wissler wrote in 1941, "so far as we can see, the Assiniboin, the Ojibway and the Cree on
the one hand and the Dakota on the other thought of the feud in terms of horses, captives
and scalps, symbols of glory and social distinction."[27]

Meanwhile, dissenters from this view held that more familiar explanations of
territorial expansion better accounted for the growing incidence of warfare on the Plains.
One expert, Bernard Mishkin, argued that "cultural motives" for warfare might differ
from "individual motives" like the quest for personal glory.[28] University of Texas
anthropologist W. W. Newcomb endorsed Mishkin's position. For Newcomb, adherents
of the "game" theory of Plains warfare confused individual motives for fighting with the
actual *causes* of warfare, which for Newcomb were almost always economic. So long as
tribes lived as nomadic hunters within bounded territories, what little conflict existed
between them might remain low-level, game-like exercises. When, however, tribes
strayed over into each other's hunting grounds or horticultural centers, as occurred
when the Sioux and Ojibway clashed over land claims in 1800, conflict escalated to fully
violent levels that merited the descriptor of "serious warfare."[29]

As contemporary experts on the Plains Indians have noted, the incidence of true warfare
on the Plains grew appreciably between ca. 1100 and the time of European colonization.[30]
In Middle Missouri defensive fortifications appear in the eleventh and twelfth centuries. At

the Crenshaw site in Arkansas the jaws and skulls of native peoples were seized—apparently as trophies—by more distant tribes. European colonialism does appear to have sharpened conflict between Great Plains tribes by pitting them against each other in contests over land and resources, as well as injecting into their wars the deadly additive of firearms. Europeans also displaced native peoples, driving them out of ancestral lands and into territories occupied by other tribes and thus virtually assuring armed struggle between them. For some anthropologists, the kind of "genocidal warfare" associated with tribal conflicts chronicled by European observers—warfare with the aim of seizing land or annihilating an enemy people—did not begin until the era of European colonization.[31] Other scholars of the Great Plains Indians reject this view in part if not in whole, contending that ethnohistories of the region flatly contradict their thesis that only with European colonialism did Great Plains Indian warfare become truly destructive. An early study of Northwest Plains ethnography by Frank Secoy found that two forms of warfare characterized the Northwest Plains Indians: (1) massed shield lines combat, which yielded few casualties; and (2) the systematic destruction of small native communities. Both forms of warfare predated sustained contact with European settlers, proving that hyperviolent wars of destruction involving the mass murder of men, women, and children were sometimes waged on the Great Plains before colonialism.[32]

The thesis that pre-contact warfare on the Great Plains could be hyperlethal gains support from a comparison of two massacre sites in South Dakota separated by 400 years or more: the Arikara Larson site in Walworth County and the Crow Creek site near Chamberlain. Comparison of the two sites is instructive because Crow Creek is pre-contact and Larson post-contact.

Crow Creek Crow Creek was a horticultural (simple agricultural) village built ca. 1325 by Coalescent Indian tribes above the Missouri floodplain. In 1978, 486 skeletons of the Crow Creek population were discovered in a trench, exposed by erosion to the light of day after 700 years. Osteological evidence revealed that the entire village (likely aside from some young women) had been massacred: 23 percent of the skeletons had broken teeth; 50 percent of the skulls were fractured; and 90 percent had been scalped. Every one of the skeletons recovered from the bone bed bore signs of mutilation. The hands and feet of many of the skeletons had been removed, presumably as war trophies. Paleo-anthropologists believe the attack was launched by the ancestors of the Mandan and Hidatsa Indians. Extreme violence was not restricted to pre-mortem assaults on the villagers but extended to post-mortem mutilation of their bodies. It is theorized that the killers left the bodies where they fell and that another group, possibly one that had had cordial relations with the victims, interred them in the trench where they were discovered 700 years later.

Accounting for the high degree of superfluous violence at Crow Creek is no straightforward matter. Anthropologists have posited that cooler and drier conditions depressed food production in the region in the fourteenth century, fostering a competition between native tribes for resources, including arable land. Such a theory might explain inter-tribal conflict; it is less satisfactory in revealing why the Crow Creek attackers savaged their victims as they did. To shed light on the excess, other factors might have to

Figure 11 An Arikara village on the Missouri River, painted by George Catlin in 1841. © Wikimedia Commons (public domain).

be considered, among them the very real possibility that military conflict, as in analogous situations everywhere in history, led to a dehumanization of the enemy tribe that facilitated extreme brutality.[33]

The osteological evidence moreover indicates that women were singled out for especially harsh treatment. Paleo-anthropologists examining the remains in light of three independent variables of violence—the number of cut marks per skull, the incidence of gashes on the frontal bone, and the breadth of gashes on the frontal bone— have determined that the sexual identity of the victim correlated with more severe cranial blows. This fact, in the view of anthropologist and paleo-forensic expert Ashley Kendell, suggests that women "experienced higher levels of brutality during the Crow Creek massacre."[34] The reasons for disparate treatment of women at Crow Creek are lost in the mists of antiquity. Kendell alights on several theories, none of which is authoritative: trophy-taking synergizing with depreciatory attitudes toward Arikara women, the fact that scalping a female victim would have happened after the attackers had breached the village's defensive perimeter and penetrated into its center (allowing for more time to slaughter and scalp the victims), the special honor attached to killing an adversary's wife and children, concepts of "social substitution and collective liability" (women as bearers of a group's guilt for alleged offenses), the high value accorded to a female victim, and differences in hairstyle between Arikara men and women (the men's hair being easier to scalp than women's).[35] The ultimate reason for heightened brutality against women at Crow Creek, however, is unknown.

Larson Another massacre of Arikara Indians took place at the Larson site, located on the Missouri River in South Dakota, some 400 years after the Crow Creek slaughter. The Larson site massacre was imbedded in a tumultuous context of European settlement and mass displacement of native American tribes. One such tribe was the Lakota, a hunting people driven westward by the Europeans. As they trekked to the west the Lakota collided with farming tribes living along the Missouri River. Armed conflict broke out between them, often centered on efforts to secure access to European trade goods, especially weapons. This was the broader context when the Lakota attacked the Arikara earthlodge village at the Larson site around 1785.

Arikara oral traditions report that they customarily retreated into their homes when an enemy invader had penetrated their outer defenses. Barricaded inside their homes, stronger family members strove to defend their weaker relatives. This was likely what happened at the Larson site insofar as the victims' skeletons were located inside their homes, in which they were apparently struck down. All together the Larson site yielded up the bodies of seventy-one victims: of this number, sixty-one were found inside their houses while ten were killed outside. Ages ranged from four to fifty years old. Both men and women were represented among the victims (although the absence of young women between 20 and 29 suggests they may have been abducted as concubines). Cut marks on the remains reveal a fate not dissimilar from the carnage at Crow Creek. The attackers scalped, decapitated, and disemboweled the victims, pulverizing their faces and skulls and harvesting their hands and feet regardless of age or sex. After the slaughter the town was set on fire.[36]

It may be reckless to draw too many confident inferences from our comparison of the two massacre sites. We do not know, for example, how typical of pre-contact Plains Indian conflicts Crow Creek was; it may have been an outlier.[37] This possibility notwithstanding, the striking parallels between the two massacres imply a grisly continuity of extreme violence rising to the level of genocide *avant la lettre*, stretching from colonial North America to the time before European colonization. Post-mortem mutilation of the victims of all ages and genders is common to both periods, as are the peculiar forms such mutilation took—scalping, crushing the skull and face, removing hands and feet, decapitation. We can only speculate about the motives for such excess, but one fact does seem clear: genocidal warfare between Indian tribes was not the unique effect of European influence. Rather, it appears to have preexisted white settlement by several centuries.

The Iroquois Confederation

Discussion of battlefield constraint and excess among the tribes of the Iroquois Confederation—the Five Nations of the Seneca, Cayuga, Onondaga, Oneida, and Mohawk—must take some measure of the havoc wrought by epidemic diseases on their lives.

European diseases had wiped out 50 percent of the Five Nations peoples by the 1640s. The need to replenish their populations gave primacy to the "mourning-wars" of traditional

Figure 12 Map of the initial nations of the Iroquois Confederacy, from *History of the Five Indian Nations Depending on the Province of New-York* by Cadwallader Colden, 1755. © MPI / Getty Images.

Iroquois warfare. Disconsolate persons unable to come to terms with a relative's death might obtain relief by participating in raids and seizing war captives from enemy tribes. Typically incited by the grieving female kinfolk of the departed, the raids were specifically intended to seize war captives, whom the mourners could either select as a replacement for their deceased relative or for torture and execution as scapegoats for the decedent's death. Mourning-war produced an elaborate ritual that ended either with the POW's adoption or death. As the prisoners arrived at the entrance to the victors' village, they faced a double row of villagers armed with clubs, sticks, and weapons of various kinds, who beat the prisoners on arrival. They were then stripped of their clothing and led to a platform in an open area of the village. Here the village's older women presided over another round of torture, this one involving the removal of fingernails and poking the prisoners with sticks and firebrands. After their ordeal the prisoners were allowed to recover with food and drink as they awaited the verdict of the village leaders. Iroquois headmen assigned the captives to bereaved families; the leading women of these families made the final call about whether to adopt or execute them. In either case, the seizure of war captives was designed to allay the grief of families mourning their dead relatives.[38]

If the decision was to execute the prisoner, then he was nonetheless adopted and assigned a familial title ("uncle" or "nephew") and the death sentence raddled on his face in red and black paint. In the next several days the condemned gave his death feast, during which he was permitted to enumerate his military accomplishments. On the day designated for his execution the doomed man was tied to a stake with a short rope. The villagers burned him from the feet upwards with firebrands and other searing implements. Before death he was scalped and hot sand thrown on his skull before he received the coup-de-grace—a knife thrust into his chest or a hatchet buried in his neck. Stripped from its bones and cooked in kettles, the corpse's flesh became a repast for the entire village. Historian Daniel K. Richter believes that the feast "carried great religious significance for the Iroquois," but the precise nature of its meaning is lost to us today.[39]

Disease and the decimation occasioned by European arms had a catastrophic impact on the mourning-war custom of the Iroquois. By the mid-1600s warfare was impelled as much by the quest for captives to replenish sagging tribal populations as by conflict over the fur trade. A contemporaneous Catholic publication, *Jesuit Relations*, reported that by 1657 "more Foreigners than natives of the country" lived in Iroquois villages. For a time, then, it appears that mourning-war among Iroquois tribes had ended in the decision to preserve the lives of war captives through adoption. By the late 1670s, however, it was clear that the practice could not replace the enormous casualties of settler and inter-tribal violence and epidemic disease. The Mohawk alone witnessed a decline in their warrior population between the 1640s and the 1670s of some 40 percent or more. The stresses of mass death extending over several decades began to erode the orderly rituals of the mourning-war. One missionary related that Iroquois warriors killed and cannibalized 600 enemy warriors in the Illinois country. On another occasion, Onondaga headmen had to intervene to shield war captives from attack by drunken braves "who observe[d] no usages or customs." Onandaga leaders exhorted their people to follow normal procedures for disposition of captives because "it was contrary to custom to ill-treat prisoners on their arrival, when they had not yet been given in the place of any person . . . and when their fate had been left undecided by the victors."[40]

Pueblo Indians

Ethnographic data on the Pueblo Indians reveal a vivid religious dimension to scalping enemy peoples during an armed conflict. A Spanish missionary in New Mexico, Alonso de Benavides, reported about the Tewa Indians that "whenever they went to war they offered meal and other things to the scalps of the enemy nation which they had brought back as trophies . . . In this way they persuaded themselves that they would obtain great victories."[41] A religious cult, called a "scalp society," surrounded the taking and honoring of enemy scalps in wartime. According to American anthropologist and sociologist Elsie Clews Parsons, a scholar of the Taos Pueblo, the scalp society consisted of the scalp taker (the "first man") and various other participants, whose status in the society derived from the time at which they reached the corpse of the dead enemy warrior ("second man," "third man," etc.). Together they constituted a group called the *Talana* that organized a scalp dance.[42]

The significance the Pueblos attached to scalp-taking reaffirms the ubiquitous relevance of religion to warmaking in world cultures. Swiss-born American anthropologist

Figure 13 Puebloan Granaries at Nankoweap, Colorado River, Grand Canyon National Park, Arizona. © Thomas Gotchy / Getty Images.

Adolf Bandelier held that "religion . . . was essential to warfare" in Pueblo society, a truth demonstrated by the metaphysical properties the Pueblo assigned to enemy scalps. He continued:

> In securing the scalp of the dead, the captor secures the faculties, mental as well as physical, of him whom he has slain, and renders them so to say tributary to himself and to his tribe. The Pueblos scalped, they danced with the scalp, and honored it.[43]

The centrality of warfare—and by implication of its religious importance—to the cultures of the Pueblo Indians finds corroboration in Zuni mythology. These stories are replete with armed attacks of one pueblo on another and of supernatural beings on pueblos, with the effect in each case being the utter annihilation of the besieged community. The Zuni origins story of the war gods Matsai'lema and U'yuyewi describes a primal battle scene set in motion by what in later times might be described as a war crime:

> The A'shiwi had proceeded less than a day's journey from Ko'thluwala'wa, coming to the place that they afterward called Han'lipinkia, when smoke was discovered in the distance. "Ha!" exclaimed the Kia'kwemosi, "there is a village. I wonder who these people are?" "We will see" said the Divine Ones; and two members of the Ne'wekwe ti'kili (Galaxy fraternity) were told to go ahead and hunt a trail. They

refused, saying: "We are fighting men and we may meet some one and kill him, and thus get you into trouble." But the Divine Ones dispatched the two men, who had not gone far when they observed two women on the bank of a stream washing buckskin. They killed the women, who belonged to the village whence the smoke came; and as soon as the strange people learned of the murder they were enraged and as one attacked the A'shiwi, who fought two days, but without success. Then Kow'wituma and Wats'usis, having grown weary with fighting, for they had many conflicts during their journey from the far northwest, requested their Sun Father to send two others to take their place as warriors.

[The reinforcements were U'yuyewi and Matsai'lema. They fight to a stalemate against the village of the murdered women.][44]

The Zia Pueblo recount a similar myth of their war gods, Ma'asewe and U'yuuyewe, who explored the earth in the shape of two hungry boys. When only one

Figure 14 Painting of Pookongahoya, one of the twin war gods of Hopi myth, in the Desert View Watchtower, Grand Canyon National Park, Arizona, USA. © Lee Rentz / Alamy Stock Photo.

family in the village of Oraibi gave them food, the two gods wiped out the village by turning everyone save the family that fed them into stone. When their mother reproved them for destroying the village, the boys told her about the Oraibi villagers' refusal to feed them. The lack of hospitality of the Oraibians effected an about-face in their mother's attitude: "It is good!" [she exclaimed.] I am glad you destroyed the people, for they were mean and bad." The boys later repeated their genocidal gambol through the world, obliterating another village by turning nearly all its inhabitants into stone.[45]

The boys' rampage did not go unpunished. The Santa Ana Pueblo's origins myth relates how their killing spree gave rise to a Pueblo Law of War (as retold by American anthropologist Leslie White):

Masewi and Oyoyewi [twin war gods], full of zest, go about the country "killing people for nothing." This angers the gods and they decide to teach the twins a lesson. They cause a hideous corpsewoman (a ko'ok'o) to pursue them to the four corners of the earth. At last the boys are spared. The gods now lay down the rules for killing and scalping people. They instruct Masewi and Oyoyewi in all that pertains to war: how the scalping is to be done, how to fast and observe continence, how to dance for the scalps and how to take care of them. Chastened, the war gods organize the Opi (Warriors) society and teach the people how to take scalps, how to fast and observe continence, how to take care of the scalps and how to dance for them. In this way Keresan war customs were established.[46]

The oral traditions of the Hopi also describe the destruction of Pueblo villages by other Pueblo Indians. A dispute between witches and the Coyote Clan (represented by Coyote Boy) led to the witches practicing black magic to harm the Clan's village, Sikyatki. In a bizarre inversion, the Sikyatki headman plotted with another pueblo to destroy his own village. The plan was to lure Sikyatki's men away from their homes through a bogus "harvest party" and set fire to their houses during their absence. When they rushed back to put out the fire, the warriors of the enemy pueblo would strike them down. The scheme unfolded as planned, and only a remnant of the Coyote Clan survived to be absorbed into another community, Oraibi.[47]

As often with long-standing oral and written traditions (we need only bring to mind Heinrich Schliemann's excavation of Troy inspired by his reading of The Iliad), the tale of Sikyatki's destruction contained a nucleus of historical fact. The actual village of Awatovi was annihilated by Hopi attackers in the late eighteenth century, likely because of conflicts between converted Christian Hopis living in the village and their traditionalist neighbors. (Hopi versions of the attack attribute it to the morally licentious lifestyle of the Awatovi villagers.) In the Hopi version of Awatovi's destruction, the chief of the village invites other communities to attack Awatovi, dangling the reward of women, girls, and land as inducements. The village was indeed attacked, the men all killed, and the women dispersed across other Hopi communities. The site of Awatovi was never reoccupied; it remains an abandoned ruin on the Hopi reservation until today.

Conclusion

The Maya, Aztecs, and North American Indian tribes demonstrate the radical incommensurability of their military cultures with our own moral and legal norms. Although some specialists have stressed more common rationales for intertribal violence (e.g., territorial expansion, struggles over resources), the force of religious beliefs in indigenous warfare is simply too well-supported in the archaeological and ethnographic evidence to be denied. For the Maya shamanism, and in particular prying open the sacred portal between this world and the next by means of human sacrifice, was the chief determinant of when and how war should be conducted. For the Aztecs war was chiefly waged to procure high-born victims for sacrifice to appease the gods and to reenact the victory of their sungod, Huitzilopochtli, over the powers of darkness. For North American tribal peoples, war was sometimes a game and sometimes a genuinely deadly and internecine affair; the form it assumed could depend on ecological factors like access to buffalo herds or arable land. While the quest for individual honor and prestige in battle motivated many of the participants, the actual causes of warfare may have been more materialistic. This notwithstanding, it is impossible to subtract religious motives from native American warfare, as the case studies of the Plains Indians, Iroquois Confederation, and Pueblo Indians prove. Particularly among the Pueblo, ethnography confirms the central role of warfare and scalp societies to Pueblo Indian culture.

These civilizations did not lack a kind of Law of War so far as we construe the term "law" broadly to mean a constraint eliciting wide-spread obedience. In the face of contrary evidence, European observers who encountered New World peoples charged them with barbarism, thereby identifying them with lawless infidels to whom no duty of restraint or mercy was owed. Infidels they may have been, but the civilizations of North and Mesoamerica were far from lawless. Suspending the norms of humane treatment in their dealings with Nearctic populations, European colonizers laid the track on which the awful locomotive of disease, war crimes, and genocide would barrel into the Americas, crushing everyone in its path.

CHAPTER 3
THE LAW OF WAR IN ROME, THE ISLAMIC WORLD, AND THE EUROPEAN MIDDLE AGES

The Romans and the Law of War

The fetials

Considered from the vantage point of the Law of War, ancient Rome presents a remarkable contradiction in its approach to warfare, an approach compounded of restraint and decorum on the one hand and savage barbarism on the other. As in ancient Egypt, China, Mesopotamia, India, Israel, Greece, Mesoamerica, and North America, the earliest constraints on war in Rome were related to religious ceremonialism. During the Roman Republic (ca. 509–27 BCE), these limitations were vested in the hands of a group of priests called the "fetials." Dionysius of Halicarnassus tells us that the institution of the fetials was created by the pre-Republican King Numa (ruled 715–673 BCE) as a means of peaceful resolution to a brewing conflict with the Fidenaean people.[1] Members of the fetial college were selected from the leading families in Rome and appointed to their positions for life. Their rituals focused on ensuring that the Roman resort to war was just, particularly when the potential opponent was a city allied with Rome. Before the waging of war could be deemed just, the Roman fetials were sent to the offending nation to demand redress (*res repetendas*) for the alleged wrong. The demands were made every ten days for thirty days. If the offending nation failed to meet their demand, the fetials returned and declared war by throwing a blood- drenched spear into the offender's territory.

Similarly, if an ally demanded justice of Rome for an alleged wrong committed by a Roman citizen, the fetials would consider the claim; if they found it had merit, they ensured that the accused would be handed over to his accusers. In addition, the fetials solemnized treaties by killing a pig with a flintstone and entreating Jupiter, the king of the gods, to punish the Romans if they were the first party to violate the agreement. As elsewhere in the ancient world, so in Rome ambassadors were protected by the gods. Defending their divinely given immunity fell under the jurisdiction of the fetials, who investigated allegations of offenses against ambassadors. Once again, as with accusations against Roman citizens by allied nations, the fetials determined the merits of the claim and, if confirmed, ensured that the guilty person was delivered to the ambassador's home state. The extradition of offenders by the college of fetials had a twofold purpose: to fulfill the just demands of the outraged state and to placate the gods.[2]

The belief system underlying the ritual performances of the fetials is one of communal responsibility. The notion that an entire community was responsible for the harm done to a foreign victim by one of its own was a fundamental tenet of archaic justice, as we saw in

Chapter 1. It undergirded the Greek practice of reprisal and hostage-taking, and its influence is clearly visible in the ceremonial actions of the Roman fetials. Their solemnization of treaties bound all of the Roman people; their demands for reparation were made on all of the members of an outside community harboring an accused wrongdoer; and their extradition of Roman offenders had the effect of extinguishing any further responsibility of the Roman people for the offenders' wrongs.[3] As Alan Watson has observed, however, the fetial system "was geared to a very particular situation: related communities with a shared religion but no joint political structure, and who had differences of interest and neighboring enemies."[4] Watson points out that the system assumed the existence of fetial priests within all the states involved in the dispute. The problem, of course, was that the fetial system was unique to central Italy. When Rome, having conquered all of central Italy (ca. 509–290 BCE), set its sights on bigger game, the fetial system began to unravel. Between 290 and 262 BCE, the rest of Italy fell under Roman dominion, and by 133 BCE the Romans could call the Mediterranean "our ocean" (*Mare Nostrum*). The role of the fetials was to resolve conflict between the various Latin tribes in central Italy, not to enable Roman colonial expansion into and beyond the Mediterranean basin. Livy reports that the fetial system began to break down as early as 322 BCE in the war between the Romans and the Samnites. (The latter people had no fetials.[5]) Although we have evidence of their usage as late as 359 CE,[6] it is clear that resort to the fetials declined as Rome became an imperial power.

Roman warfare

As far as it pertained to armed conflict, the fetial system could only certify that the conditions for a just war existed. Determining what standards would regulate battlefield conduct lay outside its authority. (In other words, the fetials determined *jus ad bellum* but not *jus in bello*.) It is noteworthy that a people so concerned with the procedures surrounding the declaration of a just war could wage war as ferociously and remorselessly as the Romans did. What seems counterintuitive at first makes more sense on further inspection. From early on in their history, the Romans demanded that every war they fought be justified.[7] Once the formal imprimatur of a just war had been secured, however, the prosecution of that war was without restraint. In their campaigns of conquest against the peoples of Italy (particularly the Faliscians, Capenatians, and Volscians), the Roman historian Livy reports that the Romans adopted a scorched earth policy of war, "leaving not a fruit-tree nor a vegetable" in enemy territory. After their victory over the Auruncians they executed their war captives on the spot. Towns laid under siege faced a grim fate when eventually taken: all the combatants involved in resistance were executed, while the civilians were sold as slaves to the merchants who followed the Roman armies.[8] Historian John Keegan's verdict on the ruthlessness of Roman warfare likens it only to that of the Mongols: "Like the Mongols, [the Romans] took resistance, particularly that of besieged cities, as a pretext justifying wholesale slaughter of the defeated."[9] Livy reports that an especially gruesome treatment was reserved for the leaders of the resistance: prior to execution, they were whipped and their bodies mangled. Similar treatment would be dealt to hostages seized from the defeated city if resistance to the Romans by the conquered population continued.[10]

The extreme violence of the Romans in their conquest of other Italian tribes nonetheless paled beside their wars with non-Italians. Whatever meager limitations based on a common cultural heritage may have existed to temper Roman war in Italy were swept away when the Romans battled foes outside the Latin cultural sphere. Polybius describes the Roman conquest of New Carthage (Spanish Cartagena) in 209 BCE:

> [The Roman general Scipio Africanus] directed [his soldiers], according to the Roman custom, against the people in the city, telling them to kill everyone they met and to spare no one, and not to start looting until they received their order. The purpose of this custom is to strike terror. Accordingly one can see in cities captured by the Romans not only human beings who have been slaughtered, but even dogs sliced in two and the limbs of other animals cut off. On this occasion the amount of such slaughter was very great.[11]

Such extremity was not an outlier but a regular occurrence as the Romans expanded throughout the Mediterranean. Enemy soldiers were not only denied quarter; after summary execution on the battlefield their corpses were dismembered, a fate that befell Macedonian soldiers fighting against the Romans in 199 BCE. The killing and dismemberment of fallen soldiers horrified the Greeks, who regarded proper burial of the dead—including the enemy dead—as a sacred duty. Archaeological excavations at Maiden Castle in Dorset, England, show that the Romans carried this practice with them in their invasion of Britain during the first century CE.[12]

The absence in classical Latin of a word for "civilian" that might have fostered a distinction between combatants and noncombatants was tailor-made for wars of extermination. In his campaigns against the German tribes, the Roman general Germanicus put to the sword men, women, and children. Almost four centuries later, Roman legions followed Germanicus's example in their battles against the Germans, ravaging the countryside and killing soldiers and civilians alike. When Emperor Valentinian's legions invaded the territory of the Guadi, a Germanic people settled in modern-day Moravia, they slaughtered every person encountered on their march.[13]

Stoicism, natural law, and the jus gentium

One of the ironies in the Roman Law of War is that the process of territorial expansion which doomed the fetial system simultaneously engendered a universal conception of law. This conception became known as the *jus gentium*, or "law of the nations." However, the term *jus gentium* emerged early in Roman history and only through subsequent mutation did it slowly acquire the meaning of universal law.

In the first centuries of the Roman Republic, the concept of the *jus gentium* appears to have been linked with customs and cultural practices common to both the Romans and other Italian tribes. The perception of affinities among the diverse cultures of Italy was more anthropological than legal. At some point, according to nineteenth-century British legal historian Sir Henry Maine, the term *jus gentium* was also applied to a customary commercial law that, much like the "law merchant" of the Middle Ages, informally governed trade between the Romans and other Italian peoples.[14] The great German scholar of Roman law, Frederick Carl von Savigny, agreed with this view about the intimate connections between the *jus gentium* and customary commercial law, as did a leading nineteenth-century expert on Roman history, Theodor Mommsen.[15] More recent scholarship, on the other hand, has emphasized the origins of *jus gentium* in the religious ideologies of ancient Rome. The historical record reveals that ambassadors enjoyed immunities granted them under the *jus gentium*. Classicist Clifford Ando contends that these protections were grounded in "sacrality," a fact suggesting that the Romans during the Republic regarded the authority of the *jus gentium* as deriving from religion.[16] An offense against an ambassador invited intervention by the fetials and, if their demands for restitution went unheeded, a declaration of war.[17]

The great watershed in Roman interpretation of the *jus gentium* occurred during the middle and later years of the Republic, when the meaning of the term was revised in light of Greek philosophical thought. Aristotle's distinction between "universal" and "particular" law in the *Rhetoric* was of particular importance to the Roman understanding of the law of nations. According to Aristotle, particular law was the "written and unwritten law" developed "by a particular people for its own requirements." By the phrase "written and unwritten," Aristotle presumably meant statutory and customary law. He contrasted particular law with the "law of nature," which he considered to be "universal." Aristotle continued: "For there exists, as all men divine more or less, a natural and universal principle of right and wrong, independent of any mutual intercourse or compact."[18] To drive home the distinction between man-made and natural law, Aristotle quoted Sophocles's Antigone, who justified her defiance of King Creon's orders in terms of a higher principle of duty—a duty "not of today nor yesterday . . . but ever hath it life, and no man knoweth whence or how it came."[19] Aristotle pursued this topic further in *The Nicomachean Ethics*, where he demarcated "natural" from "conventional" justice. Natural justice was that part of the law found in all cultures, the validity of which did not hinge on its particular expression, while conventional justice was time-bound and local.[20]

Aristotle's important distinction between relative human law and universal natural law became a cornerstone of Stoicism, one of the two leading philosophical movements of the Hellenistic period (the other being Epicureanism). Founded in Athens by Zeno of Citium (ca. 335–263 BCE) and elaborated by Chrysippus (ca. 280–206 BCE), Stoicism had by the second century BCE made inroads into the Roman mind, gaining a sympathetic audience through the works of the Roman statesman, scholar, and lawyer Marcus Tullius Cicero. In its original form, Stoicism embraced the teachings of Socrates, particularly his belief in a world governed by a divinely-ordained reason. Aristotle's dichotomy between man-made and natural law also filtered into Stoicism, where it was encapsulated in the Stoic view that human beings shared with the divine a capacity for "right reason" (*recta ratio*), in the light of which we can conform our behavior to the God-given rational order of the natural world. We fulfill the natural law by using our right reason to live in accordance with our natures as rational beings—beings who understand the difference between particular law that varies according to time and place, and the eternal, unchanging law of nature which transcends man-made law.

Marcus Tullius Cicero (106–43 BCE) appropriated this Greek Stoic tradition and transformed it into an overtly legal and ethical system. His clearest and most systematic exposition of Stoicism as a kind of jurisprudence is found in *On the Laws* (*De Legibus*, 51 BCE), presented in the form of a dialogue between three characters: Marcus, Quintus, and Atticus. In this work, Cicero seeks to extrapolate his Stoic conception of law and ethics from the nature of the human being. Following the Greek Stoics, he states that the essence of the human being is reason, a faculty humans share with God. When humans apply their reason to "command and prohibition"—that is, to what we must do and what we must refrain from doing—it is "right reason" (*recta ratio*). God has "implanted" right reason in Nature as well as in the human heart; in conforming to it, we attune ourselves not only to the natural harmonies of the physical world, but also realize the most vital essence of our very being. So far, Cicero's ideas reprise the basic themes of Greek Stoicism. He steps decidedly beyond Greek Stoicism, however, when he defines the content of right reason in terms of a principle that strongly resembles a universalist conception of ethics. Discussing justice and friendship, Cicero's mouthpiece Marcus states:

> . . . when a wise man shows toward another endowed with equal virtue the kind of benevolence which is so widely diffused among men, that will then have come to pass which . . . is after all the inevitable result—namely, that he loves himself no whit more than he loves another.[21]

Responding to Marcus's dissertation on justice and friendship, Atticus says he is convinced "that all men are bound together by a certain natural feeling of kindliness and good-will."[22]

Universalism was always present in Greek Stoic thought, but in Cicero's revision of it—and, indeed, in the Roman reception of Stoicism beginning with Cicero and handed down to its other great proponents, Epictetus, Marcus Aurelius, and Seneca—we are exhorted to do more than to act in accordance with nature. Rather, Cicero teaches that we should break through to the realization that our nature is to be compassionate toward the human race as a whole and not just to our family members, friends, and neighbors. This point is made with still more clarity in *On Duties* (44 BCE), where he writes:

> There are others again who say that account should be taken of other citizens, but deny it in the case of foreigners; such men tear apart the common fellowship of the human race. When that is removed then kindness, generosity, goodness and justice are utterly destroyed. Those who destroy them must be judged irreverent . . . [,] for the fellowship among mankind that they overturn was established by the gods.[23]

Cicero's Stoic jurisprudence follows from his anthropology. Principles of justice do not depend on circumstance, on utility, on egoism, or on the whim of the legislator; they are, as principles of reason imbedded in nature and shared by God and human beings, eternal and unchanging. Cicero cites an infamous incident from ancient Roman history to convey this truth, the rape of Lucretia by Sextus Tarquinius. The issue was whether a crime had occurred because no written law prohibiting rape was in existence at the time. For Cicero, the non-existence of a written law was inconsequential because Tarquinius's rape violated the "eternal Law." "Reason," Marcus affirms, "did exist, derived from the Nature of the universe,urging men to right conduct and diverting them from wrongdoing, and this reason did not first become Law when it was written down, but when it . . . came into existence simultaneously with the divine mind."[24]

Eternal principles of justice existed whether or not there were laws prescribing certain acts and proscribing others. But what was the status of written laws that clashed with these eternal principles of right? Cicero does not mince his words in declaring that such laws are not law at all:

> [Unjust laws] no more deserve to be called laws than the rules a band of robbers might pass in their assembly. For if ignorant and unskillful men have prescribed deadly poisons instead of healing drugs, these cannot possibly be called physicians' prescriptions; neither in a nation can a statute of any sort be called a law, even though the nation, in spite of its being a ruinous regulation, has accepted it.[25]

This passage resonates with Aristotle's distinction between "particular law" and the "law of nature." Cicero has taken Aristotle's view of law, however, and joined it to Stoic naturalism to produce something new in Greco-Roman legal history: the doctrine that official but unjust laws are invalid because they are repugnant to our nature as rational beings, and hence lack obligatory power. His emphasis on universal compassion has parallels with the Confucian and Christian Golden Rule and Mozi's doctrine of universal love (*jian ai*). Moreover, Cicero's refusal to concede validity to unjust laws invites comparison with Mencius's insistence that the political conditions of the moment can be judged with reference to a higher ethical standard, as well as with the Hebrew prophets and their subordination of secular rulers to a higher law.

In summary, the concept of the *jus gentium* appears early in Roman history, but it is untethered to any single definition, assuming at least three distinct forms: (1) the common beliefs and practices of the various Italian tribes during Roman expansion throughout Italy; (2) commercial customs that regulated trade between these groups; and (3) a more philosophical theory of law influenced by the Stoic distinction between relative man-made laws and universal principles of justice based on reason. Each of these understandings of the law of nations was a byproduct of Roman territorial growth. As Rome passed from its Republican into its imperial stage, the *jus gentium* underwent a fourth shift of meaning, one associated with the enhanced stature of a Roman legal official called the "peregrine praetor." First created in 367 BCE, the office of the praetor was divided in two in 242 BCE. The "urban praetor" decided legal cases in which both parties were Roman citizens—that is, they presided over the so-called "quaestiones," or jury, courts of the late Republic and early Empire. The "peregrine praetor" heard cases in which the parties were of mixed citizenship: one Roman, the other non-Roman. Court cases involving foreigners and Roman citizens presented unique problems that were ultimately solved through the institution of the peregrine[26] praetor. As Rome conquered by the sword the tribal peoples of Italy and cemented them into its growing empire, it extended the rights of Roman citizenship to the nations living in territories close to Rome. These persons could sue or be sued in the urban prefect's jury courts under civil law (*jus civile*).[27] To more remote peoples, however, the Romans often did not grant full rights of citizenship under Roman law. Instead, these subjects of Rome retained local self-rule—meaning that they enjoyed few, if any, rights under the Roman civil law. The Romans established the office of the peregrine praetor in order to adjudicate cases to which the civil law was inapplicable by virtue of the litigants' diverse citizenship.[28]

The peregrine praetor toured cities in Italy much like circuit riders, hearing cases in far-flung territories involving Roman and non-Roman citizens (or sometimes cases in which both parties were non-Romans). Because he was not empowered to apply the civil law, the peregrine praetor had to decide cases based on legal principles outside the Roman civil law that would be accepted as fair by all of the litigants. Over time, this ad hoc quality of adjudication matured into a systematic body of law, the primary tenets of which were culled from the praetors' sense of equity and maxims of law common to the parties. In short, the work of the peregrine praetor was eminently practical: he studied the law governing disputes that each litigant brought with him into court based on his cultural background, selected those principles common to each, compared them with the praetor's own sense of justice, and decided the case accordingly. The peregrine praetor eventually acquired the authority not only to adjudge cases (*jus dicere*), but to issue edicts setting forth rules to decide cases involving foreigners (*jus edicere*). This is an important moment in the history of Roman law, for it marks the point at which the peregrine praetors as legislators were able to elaborate a system of law based not on the Roman *jus civile* but on the customary law common to the peoples of Italy.[29]

As a result, two legal systems were operative in late Republican and early imperial Rome: that of the Roman civil law and that of the law of the peoples. In the meantime, the urban praetor began to incorporate principles of the *jus gentium* into the civil law, particularly in cases where the latter was either deficient or produced an unjust outcome. Ironically, a jury-rigged body of law used to resolve disputes involving foreigners and non-citizens crept into the civil law's regulation of conflicts between Romans. The *jus gentium* became a supplement to the *jus civile*, a supplement which Roman citizens gradually recognized as a much-needed alternative to the limitations and injustices of their ancient law. A clear sign of the rising prestige of the law of the peoples among the Romans was the attribution of the term *jus aequum*, or *aequitas*—the law of equity—to principles of the *jus gentium* applied to decide cases unsuited to the civil law. Roman legal scholar William Morey has cautioned, however, that the *jus gentium* was not viewed as "a standard of abstract justice, but as being a branch of positive law more even and fair in its provisions than the *jus civile*, and better suited to protect the interests of all persons."[30] For the Romans, as practical a civilization as any the world has seen, the *jus gentium* was not primarily abstract and philosophical, but expedient and pragmatic.

Under the impact of Stoicism, however, this practical, administratively oriented view of the *jus gentium* acquired a metaphysical hue that it has retained till the present day. For Cicero and the leading jurists of imperial Rome, the *jus gentium* expressed natural law, and not merely the sum total of widely shared norms reflected in the edicts of the peregrine praetors. The general customs of the numerous peoples living within the Roman Empire, so far as they were studied and juridified by the praetors and later imported into the civil law, became synonymous in the Roman legal mind with the law of nature. The cogitations of natural reason affirmed the *jus gentium* as superior law. Actually existing law could be compared with it and, where it failed to measure up, reformed so as to align it with the law of the peoples. The great imperial jurists, such as Gaius, Ulpian, and Paulus, followed Cicero in declaring that the laws of the state were authoritative only when they were in harmony with the moral principles disclosed by natural reason—that is, with the *jus gentium*.[31]

What is the relevance of the *jus gentium* to the Roman Law of War? As it turns out, not much at all! There is scant evidence that natural law theory acted as an emollient on the Romans' remorseless conduct in battle. William Harris draws attention to the incongruous pairing of political sophistication and military barbarism that characterized ancient Rome: "In many respects, [the Romans'] behavior resembles that of many other non-primitive ancient peoples, yet few others are known to have displayed such an extreme degree of ferocity in war while reaching a high level of political culture."[32] Such truculence was not confined to the pre-Stoic years of the early Republic; it epitomized Roman warfare well into the imperial period, if the incursions into Germany by the legions of Emperors Julian and Valentinian are any indication. The account of Roman war crimes recorded by the historian Ammianus Marcellinus (330–395 CE), which describes Roman soldiers ambushing and killing the Saxons as they returned home under a truce, suggests that neither the *jus gentium* nor Christian ethics fundamentally altered the severity of Roman warmaking.[33]

The relevance of the *jus gentium* to the Law of War does not reside in its short-term effects on Roman military conduct, which were negligible. Rather, its lofty ideas would span centuries of historical change to influence the Roman Church's just war doctrine, the codes of chivalry of medieval Europe, and the jurisprudence of the early modern exponents of international law—Grotius, Gentili, de Vattel, Suárez, and Ayala. The notion that universal law existed beyond the treaties and statutes of sovereign powers, enjoying a validity independent of government fiat, traversed the millennia to affect the Preamble to the Hague Convention IV of 1907—perhaps the most important document in the history of humanitarian law. The effects of the *jus gentium* on the Law of War proved to be long term, and the impact would be profound.

Piracy and the jus gentium

Already in the ancient world of the Greeks and the Romans, the idea had taken root that certain actions could violate a higher principle of justice even when committed by sovereign rulers. An intriguing question, however, is thereby raised: did the Romans ever regard violators of universal norms as war criminals? An answer to this question is not readily apparent. On the one hand, we have no evidence that the Romans branded their adversaries as war criminals and punished them accordingly. On the other, we do see in Roman history the rise of a class of persons who were criminalized for their defiance of the customary practices and usages of the ancient world: pirates.

Before the rise of powerful states able to curb them, pirates roamed freely in the Aegean Sea and the Mediterranean basin. In fact, as Thucydides tells us, pirates during the Archaic period were not the criminal reprobates they would later become: "No disgrace was yet attached to such an achievement [of piracy], but even some glory."[34] Some Greek peoples became professional, full-time pirates, particularly if they lacked arable land. Rocky or marshy coastlines near commercial lanes invariably produced pirates, who could launch nimble raids in small boats and retreat safely into their well-concealed ports. Piracy flourished wherever the navies of powerful kingdoms were unavailable to suppress them. In the fifth century BCE, the Athenians, the naval superpower among the Greek *poleis*, took measures as the leader of the Delian League to combat piracy in the eastern Mediterranean. Others stepped forward over the next couple of centuries to suppress piracy, including Alexander the Great and the Ptolemies. By the mid-fourth century BCE, the Romans had begun counter-piracy campaigns in the western Mediterranean, which they would extend to the entire Mediterranean basin during the Empire.[35]

With the rise of strong imperial states like Athens and Rome, the status of pirates began to change. In a world of weaker states with underdeveloped customs of mutual interaction, piracy could burgeon, achieving a degree not only of acceptance but of romantic *panache*. However, as international norms arose like the "common customs of the Hellenes" and the fetial system of the Romans, tolerant acceptance of piracy, began to fade. Scholars have stressed the essential ambiguity of piracy in a world bound together by customary international practice. For the Romans, warfare was a just and religiously-based activity designed to secure restitution or the deliverance of an offender to the injured state. Failure to satisfy either of these demands became a cause of war, a prerequisite to declaring and waging a just war. Piracy could not be assimilated to the Roman framework of just war because it lacked any motive save the unjust enrichment of the plunderers. Cicero condemned piracy on these grounds, arguing that the anarchic quality of piratic violence removed it from legitimate warmaking.[36] In short, for the Romans pirates stood outside the *jus gentium* because they made resort to illicit violence.

The upshot is that pirates were akin in Roman history to war criminals—that is, persons who, in wielding illicit violence across territorial boundaries, had violated acceptable limits on armed conflict. Rather than being put on trial, however, pirates—particularly the piratic states of the Mediterranean—were attacked and suppressed by the Roman military. Without exaggeration, it can be said that pirates were the first war criminals in world history. Centuries later, their notorious status as international offenders would be revived in the early modern period.

The Islamic world and the Law of War

For many contemporary Americans and Europeans horrified by gruesome, Islamist-inspired atrocities, the impression has taken shape that Islam preaches a savage gospel of cruelty and murder. Such an impression is regrettable because it contradicts the actual theory and practice of constraining warfare in early Islamic history. Two themes in the Islamic Law of War illustrate this point: traditional Muslim attitudes toward captured prisoners and civilians, and the Muslim conception of *Jihad*.

According to our sources,[37] as Muhammad and his forces struggled to unite Arabia between 622 and 632 CE, they fought two battles in which the treatment of enemy war captives was at issue. The first, the Battle of Badr, was between the Muslims under Muhammad and the Quraysh people in 624 CE. In the years preceding the battle, the Quraysh (a pagan Arab people) had frequently harassed the Muslim community in Mecca. The outcome of the Battle of Badr was a resounding victory for the Muslims, who killed seventy of the enemy, captured an equal number, and dispersed the rest. Muhammad consulted two of his lieutenants about how the captives should be treated. The first advocated ransoming them; the second favored execution. Muhammad chose to ransom them. He "divided the prisoners amongst his companions and said, 'Treat them well.'"[38] When a destitute prisoner requested his liberty, Muhammad released him on the condition that he cease fighting against the Muslims. The other prisoners were given food and clothing, then set free with or without ransom.[39] The second battle fought by the Muslims under Muhammad, the Battle of Hunayn, was waged in 630 CE and resulted in the Muslims' defeat at the hands of a Byzantine army. The Muslims initiated the fighting after Northern Arab tribes under Byzantine tutelage had executed Muhammad's emissaries. The Muslim army reportedly captured both combatants and noncombatants (women and children), but released all of them without ransom.[40] Muhammad's refusal to execute war captives after the Battles of Badr and Hunayn suggests an early policy of sparing the lives of prisoners captured in combat. In their description of raids during Muhammad's life, the hadīths buttress this interpretation: one hadīth relates that Muhammad ordered the release of an enemy leader captured in a raid, while another characterizes the sparing of war captives' lives as a divinely imposed duty.[41]

Consistent with the practice delineated in the ancient sources, early Islamic jurists held that prisoners of war could only be set free or ransomed, but their lives had to be spared. Lena Salaymeh points out, however, that some Islamic jurists dissented from the majority view. An Umayyad caliph, 'Umar ibn 'Abd al-Azīz (680–720 CE), reportedly

---

"Therefore, when ye meet the Unbelievers (in fight), smite at their necks; at length, when ye have thoroughly subdued them, bind a bond firmly (on them): thereafter (is the time for) either generosity or ransom."

Qur'ān 47:4[41]

---

banned killing prisoners but ordered one captive to be executed. Legal scholars during and after Umar's era sometimes allowed prisoner execution; indeed, one of them, Mujāhid ibn Jabr (645–722 CE), argued that Qur'ān 47:4 (see text box), which apparently forbade executing prisoners, had been derogated by another verse, Qur'ān 9:5. The latter verse stated: "But when the forbidden months are past, then fight and slay the pagans wherever ye find them, and seize them, beleaguer them, and lie in wait for them in every stratagem (of war)."[42] According to Mujāhid, verse 9:5 enabled Muslim leaders to entertain several options for dealing with war captives—enslavement, ransoming, liberation, or execution. These permissive attitudes toward executing prisoners appear to have been minority views. In the main, seventh- and eighth-century Islamic legal commentators agreed that killing war captives was strictly prohibited.

In the ensuing centuries, as Islam embarked on its dizzying gallop through the Middle East, Asia, Africa, and Europe, Islamic scholars increasingly shifted to the view that prisoner execution was sometimes allowed. Among the earliest jurists to endorse prisoner execution was Muhammad ibn al-Ḥasan al-Shaybānī (750–805 CE), considered the founder of Islamic international law. In his treatises on the Islamic Law of Nations, Shaybānī reproduced the views of his teachers, Abu Hanīfa and Abū Yūsef, on the prisoner issue. According to Shaybānī, Hanīfa held that an imām (a Muslim religious leader) was free to decide whether to take war captives "to the territory of Islam to be divided and killing them ... [The Imām] should examine the situation and decide whatever he deems to be advantageous to the Muslims."[43] A tenth-century Islamic jurist, Al-Qayrawānī (922–966 CE), agreed that war captives could be put to death, but he insisted on limitations to this rule: "It is not wrong to kill a non-Arab unbelieving prisoner, but no one is to be killed after being given a guarantee of safety (amān), and treaties with the enemy are not to be violated."[44] Thirteenth-century commentators supported the execution of war prisoners subject to qualification, such as the interests of Muslim society. Shāfiī jurist Al-Nawawī and H. anbalī jurist Ibn Taymiyah both provided for it. Representatives of each of the four mainline Sunnī schools of jurisprudence regarded prisoner execution as axiomatic, despite clear prohibitions of the practice in the Qur'ān and Ḥadīth.[45]

How can we explain this shift from condemnation to endorsement (subject to limitations) of executing war captives? One theory is that the tumultuous era of Islamic expansion brought the Muslims into contact with adversaries like the Byzantine Christians who supported prisoner execution. In his tenth-century treatise on war, for example, the Byzantine Emperor Nikephoros II Phocas appears to support it.[46] In the course of the many wars fought between the Byzantines and the Arabs, did the more permissive attitudes of their foes toward killing war captives gradually influence Muslim jurists to approve the practice? We cannot know for certain, but the impact of the Byzantine military on Arab thinking about prisoner execution is a distinct possibility, suggesting that both adversaries in a protracted conflict will often abandon humanitarian restraint when one of them has taken a step toward barbarism.

As we have witnessed in our discussion of Greco-Roman wars against "barbarians," the branding of a group of outsiders as inimical to values considered ultimate by the branding culture frequently works as an accelerant to martial violence. Paradoxically, the concept of a "holy" or "just" war tends to produce extremism—a willingness to go *à l'outrance* so long as the war at its inception has been declared justified.[47] The Romans, as the prime example of this tendency, were at pains to secure the all-important title of "just war" for their armed conflicts, a designation mediated by the fetial system of the Roman Republic. Once the fetial priests had deemed the conditions ripe for a just war, the Romans waged pitiless, unsparing war against their foes—particularly against the non-Italian peoples encountered during their expansion into the Mediterranean. A similar concept arose among the Muslims in their conquests of Arabia, Persia, Syria, Egypt, and North Africa: the idea of *jihad*.

Few terms in Islamic theology have produced more misunderstandings in the contemporary Western world than the word *jihad*, loosely translated as "holy war." The term arose during a time when Muhammad and his followers were seeking to establish Islam in Mecca amidst a polytheistic society. *Jihad* originally meant the "struggle" or "exertion" of a devout Muslim to advance belief in the Islamic God, Allah. At the core of *jihad* is the notion of obligation: it was the solemn duty of all Muslims to exert themselves to propagate Islam. Such efforts, as clarified by later Muslim jurists, consisted of four types of struggle: (1) by the heart; (2) by the tongue; (3) by the mind; and (4) by the sword.[48] *Jihad* "by the sword" was holy war to compel non-believers to submit to the revealed truths of Islam. ("Islam" is an Arabic word meaning "submission" or "surrender.") War must not be waged, according to Muhammad, by Muslims against fellow Muslims. Rather, as the Prophet declared in his final visit to Mecca in 632 CE, war should be waged against non-Muslims until they accepted Allah as the one true God. The full fury of *jihad* would fall on idolaters, pagans, and polytheists, such as those, like the Quraysh, who opposed Muhammad and his followers. Against the so-called "Peoples of the Book of Scriptures" (*Ahl-al-Kitab*)—persons like Jews and Christians who believed in Allah, but in a distorted manner—a milder form of *jihad* would be pursued. As Islam expanded its territorial control, Muslim conquerors encountered both of these groups. To the pagans, the Muslims issued the demand to convert or face extermination. To "Peoples of the Book" who fell under Muslim hegemony, the offer was to either convert to orthodox Islam or pay a community tax (the *Jazia*). So long as they submitted to Muslim rule and paid their tax, Jews and Christians were protected by Islamic law, and even allowed to practice their own faiths.[49]

Medieval Europe and the Law of War

The just war in medieval theory and practice

In Western Europe, too, a doctrine of "just" or "holy" war had crystallized by the High Middle Ages (ca. 1000–1299) that would prove fateful to warfare and the extremity with which it was fought. Although the concept of "just war" in the West dated back to Aristotle,[50] the most important exegete of just war theory for medieval Europe was the fifth-century bishop of Hippo, Aurelius Augustinus, better known to history as St. Augustine. In forging a synthesis of Classical Greco-Roman thought with Judaeo-Christian theology, Augustine (354–430 CE) created a basic framework for analyzing Christian participation in organized killing, one that later became the dominant influence on the medieval theory of just war from the eleventh century onward.

The paradox of Christian piety, which became distressingly acute after the Emperor Constantine's conversion, was the clash between Christian pacifism and the inevitable violence required to administer an imperial state. The early Church condemned warfare as anathema to the ethical teachings of Jesus. Church fathers like Origen (ca. 185–254 CE) deflected the charges of critics who cited the Old Testament as evidence for divinely-ordained killing, replying that Old Testament wars should not be interpreted literally but as allegories of spiritual combat against Satan.[51] Historian Frederick Russell notes, however, that such revulsion against violence began to recede once the Roman state under Constantine recognized Christianity as a legitimate religion in 337 CE. Constantine's own bishop, Eusebius of Caesarea, divided Christian believers into two groups—those who abstained from entanglements in the secular affairs of the state, devoting themselves singlemindedly to God, and those who participated in the hurly-burly of Roman life, including its just wars. In similar terms, the Christian fathers, St. John Chrysostom and St. Jerome, granted license to Christians to serve in the Roman army, insisting that enforcement of the *Pax Romana*[52] by Roman arms was prefigured in the prophecies of the Book of Isaiah and the New Testament.[53] The receptivity of churchmen to participation by the faithful in Roman wars acquired a significant boost when Christianity became the official religion of the Roman Empire in 381 CE. At this time, the Roman state emerged as the defender of Christian orthodoxy against heretics.[54] Ensuing laws imposed civil disabilities on non-conforming Christians; in extreme cases, the death penalty could be inflicted. Heresy eventually became a public crime equated with treason. Unsurprisingly, the Christian Church swung its support behind the coercive policies of a Roman state that punished dissenters from orthodoxy. An important precedent had been set: the religion of the pacifist from Galilee endorsed the violence of an imperial state now identified with its interests.[55]

Augustine shared with many other Church officials of his era the belief that violence exercised in a just cause was not only permitted but morally obligatory. The context of his thinking is critical to understanding Augustine's theory of just war. He was writing at a time when the things he treasured most were under siege: the Roman polity was embroiled in a losing military struggle with pagan Germanic tribes (the Visigoth chief, Alaric, would sack Rome in 410 CE), while the Church's authority was being assailed by heretical groups like the Manicheans. Manichaeism was a threat to Christian orthodoxy on multiple fronts. One of its more potent challenges, based on the irreconcilability of the spiritual life with acts of violence, impugned the alliance between the Roman state and the Church. Augustine's theory of the just war was a response to Manichean pacifism, a doctrine that still appealed to many Christians uneasy with the violence of Roman wars. In his effort to refute the Manicheans and to legitimate military service, Augustine drew on two sources—the Bible and the Roman statesman Cicero. Augustine mined the

Old Testament for instances in which the Israelites waged holy war against their enemies with God's approval. For Augustine, Joshua's war with the people of Ai was just because it was commanded by Yahweh. Because Yahweh ordered the war and Joshua obediently carried out Yahweh's order, Joshua was merely the tool by means of which God destroyed the city of Ai. Joshua and the Israelites were fully justified in destroying Ai insofar as they acted in strict conformity to Yahweh's will; in killing the people of Ai, they were motivated by love for Yahweh, not by malice. With this and other examples from the Bible, Augustine harmonized Christian ethics with warfare. A Kantian 1,400 years before Kant, he held that the pivotal criterion was the intention with which the Christian soldier acted, not the external act itself. A pure intention absolved the soldier of any guilt for killing during wartime.[56]

In his appropriation of Cicero, Augustine incorporated the Roman conception of just war into his own doctrine but radically transformed it, thereby creating a novel justification of armed conflict based on its moral quality. Cicero had mainly recapitulated the Roman idea of "just causes" as an essential prerequisite to waging just war. At the root of this conception is the law of contract: just as breach of contract between private parties gave rise to an action for damages by the non-breachor, so in inter-state relations a failure of one state to fulfill its obligations toward another—or, for that matter, the infliction of unwarranted harm by one on the other—gave the non-offending party a claim to compensation. If the offending state refused to pay, the aggrieved state was justified in declaring war. Following the Roman understanding, Cicero asserted that all just wars were efforts to recover damages. "Consequently," Russell comments, "warfare was not a willful exercise of violence but a just and pious endeavor occasioned by a delict or injustice of the enemy." Augustine agreed with Cicero that the aim of a just war was to obtain damages for wrongs done, either in the form of lost property or harm caused by the subjects of a state. However, he went beyond Cicero in expanding the scope of just war to include not only securing damages but punishing sins against God. Augustine's innovation was to combine the Roman interpretation of law as "justice"—a secular term that involved giving to people their due—with "righteousness," a religious word describing divine principles of right conduct. In Augustine, the High Medieval identification of law and religious morality is fully adumbrated.[57]

Although Augustine's conception of just war went beyond the narrower Roman view, in his approval of unlimited violence to wage a just war he was true to Roman norms. All means, including treachery and aggressive war, were permissible to defend righteousness against its enemies. Furthermore, like the Greeks and the Romans, Augustine did not distinguish between combatants and noncombatants. If the enemy had truly sinned, it did not matter whether individual subjects were personally innocent; they could be struck down with impunity alongside the guilty. Frederick Russell observes that this aspect of Augustine's thought, combining Cicero's just war based on restitution with a theological concept of war as a tool for punishing collective sin, provided a ready-made justification for the holy wars and crusades of the High Middle Ages. The example of Joshua in his dealings with the Amorites was instructive for Augustine: the Amorites' refusal to grant the Israelites passage through their territory was a sin meriting divine punishment at the hands of the Israelites. Mere refusal to allow passage seems a flimsy pretext for levying war against a people; but in Augustine's view, justification of the war did not hinge on the distinction between offensive and defensive war. Rather, it was determined by the justice of the Israelites' cause. Since Yahweh wanted to punish the Amorites, the Israelite conquest and seizure of their lands were irreproachable, whether or not the war was aggressively initiated.[58] The justice of the cause sanctified all methods to achieve it.

An implicit corollary of Augustine's theological conception of just war was that the Christian warrior did not carry the stain of innocent blood on his hands, so long as his actions were harnessed to the cause of righteousness. What responsibility, however, did the soldier bear to ascertain whether the war he participated in was just? On this point, Augustine was ambivalent. On the one hand, he adhered to the general norm in the ancient world of the warrior's unconditional obedience to the ruler's orders. This duty of obedience extended to profane kings engaged in fighting unjust wars: even under these conditions, the Christian warrior had to carry out his monarch's commands. On the other hand, Augustine wavered on the categorical nature of the soldier's duty. If the ruler issued orders clearly at odds with divine law, then deviation from such orders was permitted. Overall, however, Augustine declined imputing to the soldier any guilt for homicide if he spilled blood during battle. Augustine was even more extreme on this issue, for he not only absolved the righteous warrior of blood guilt; he held further that any soldier who refused an order to kill committed treason. Augustine's position here seems to be grounded in his distrust of human passions. Were the warrior to follow his own impulses, the field would be cleared for rampaging individual emotions—the very thing Augustine feared, and condemned, as the highway to sin. Better that the soldier strictly follow orders and be acquitted of wrongdoing than that the passions be given free rein.[59]

Augustine's remarkable approval of military violence despite his sincere belief in the Christian religion strikes a less dissonant chord when we recall the times in which he lived. To his mind, attacks from without on the very structure of the Roman state by the Germanic tribes were braided with attacks from within on Church orthodoxy by heretics and schismatics. One of the latter groups, the Donatists, carried their religious zeal to the point of attacking orthodox African Christians and their churches. Augustine, as a devout Christian, confronted a dilemma: that which he cherished the most was under siege, yet the Church was forbidden to take up arms to defend itself by the sword. Augustine's solution was to enlist the Roman emperors to protect the Church against the existential threats it faced. With the eventual collapse of the western Roman Empire and its supercession by Germanic kingdoms in the fifth century CE, the Augustinian solution was to a large extent forgotten. Much like Augustine's turbulent era in North Africa, however, the chaos and insecurity of the ninth and tenth centuries, unleashed by the fragmentation of centralized authority under the strain of Magyar, Viking, and Arab invasions, revived interest in his rapprochement of Church and State. The reasons for the renewed engagement with Augustine's just war theory are multiple. Continued armed struggle against the Muslims on Europe's borders and the growing insistence by the papacy on its independence from secular rule contributed to the revival. As in Augustine's time, men of violence were needed to protect the Church against its enemies, as well as to establish it as a self-governing institution removed from lay interference. By the eleventh century, popes and bishops had taken to leading their own armies into battle. (Historian Christopher Tyerman notes that some bishops even donned armor and participated directly in combat.) Just war theory could be readily invoked to justify the Church's involvement in armed conflict. Pope Leo IX (1048–54) was at the head of a papal army that fought the Normans in southern Italy. When the Normans campaigned against the Muslims in Sicily (1060) and invaded Anglo-Saxon England (1066), the invaders were given papal banners.[60]

Some idea of the magnitude of changes in ecclesiastical attitudes toward Christian participation in war between the time of the pacifist Origen and the High Middle Ages may be gathered from Pope Gregory VII's favorite motto, "Cursed be he that keepeth back his sword from blood" (Jeremiah 48:10). Gregory VII (r. 1073–85), whose struggle with Emperor Henry IV over the right to invest clergy set the Church on the path toward "papal monarchy," was so adamant about the need to fight against the Church's adversaries that he tried to raise his own army, the *militia Sancti Petri*. Gregory compared his papal soldiers and their defense of Christianity with Christ's suffering on the cross, thereby equating the violence of holy war with the pacific self-sacrifice of Jesus.[61] Gregory's militancy, which was on the cusp of the Crusades and, indeed, foreshadowed them, represents a decisive repudiation of Christian qualms about participating in war-related killing. By the late twelfth century, the Church had created new "fighting" orders, the Templars and the Hospitallers, devoted among other duties to fighting the Muslims in the Holy Land. The Templars and Hospitallers inspired formation of similar orders in Spain to battle the Muslims and in Germany to fight the pagan Prussians and Lithuanians.[62] The guiding principle in these wars was explicitly Augustinian: violence deployed to defend righteousness was divinely approved, hence participation in such violence was a religious act. This rationale was to be routinely deployed by the Church in armed struggle against the Muslims and heretics like the Albigensians. By the late fourteenth century, one of the leading commentators on law and war, Honoré Bonet, invoked these arguments in his *Tree of Battles* (1387) to justify warfare against the Muslims. "By what law or on what ground can war be made against the Saracens?" he asked, and answered his own question with conventional just war theory.[63] In this fashion, the medieval Church and its apologists were able to escape the dilemma of shedding blood while remaining loyal to Jesus's ethical teachings. The key for the Church, as it was for Augustine, was to treat all wars to defend Christianity as sanctioned by God and therefore permissible.

One of the major conduits through which Augustine's just war theory was transmitted to the Roman canon lawyers of the High Middle Ages was the sixth-century Archbishop of Seville, St. Isidore (560–636 CE). As the medievalist Maurice Keen has indicated, Isidore essentially reproduced the basic points of Augustine's theory while relying on different authorities. Where Augustine's touchstones were the Church fathers and Greek philosophy, Isidore relied on Roman law and Cicero. He defined just war as being "waged on valid authority, either to regain things lost or to drive out invaders."[64] Isidore displays the influence of Cicero when he portrays an unjust war as "that which results from passion, not from lawful reason; as Cicero explains in his Republic, unjust wars are those on which men enter without good reason."[65] In the twelfth century, Augustine's and Isidore's definitions of just war were adopted by the Benedictine monk and leading systematizer of Roman canon law, Gratian (?–1159?), whose work conveyed their thinking about just war to the leading Roman canon lawyers, particularly Raymond of Pennaforte. Raymond's appropriation of Gratian (and through him, of Augustine and Isidore) influenced other Roman canonists—e.g., Henry of Segusio (also called Hostiensis), Monaldus, John of Legnano, and Baldus de Ubaldis, among others.[66]

Gratian's *chef d'oeuvre*, his twelfth-century compilation of Roman canon law, the *Decretum*, betrays the influence of Augustine's and Isidore's approaches to just war. Like his predecessors, Gratian adopted a moralistic solution to the problem of Christian involvement in martial violence. How should Christians deal with evil men? Gratian characterizes it as "terribly wrong" not "to deprive immoral persons of the opportunity to continue their conduct, or in order to preserve the peace of the church, so as to serve the well-being of many." For Gratian, Christians were positively obliged to wage war in defense of others. He writes: "It is sometimes right to take up arms to oppose the wicked and [to resist] injuries to our associates, so as to deprive evil people of the chance to do wrong, and to give the virtuous a free opportunity to seek the assistance of the Church. He who does not do this consents [to iniquity]."[67] As it was for Augustine, so for Gratian the Christian warrior is justified because his motives are pure: "One who corrects or chastises does so out of love, not hate." From this duty to combat the wicked Gratian arrived at the conclusion that the Church had authority to use force when needed to attain its spiritual purposes. When it did, the Church used "sacred violence"—a form of coercion that differed in kind from "carnal" wars. The chief distinction between the two kinds of warfare is that sacred violence is sanctioned by God, while carnal violence is driven by selfishness and cupidity.[68] In drawing this contrast, Gratian demonstrates the unmistakable influence of Augustine.

By the second half of the twelfth century, the Roman canonists had begun to absorb Gratian's writings on just war. One of them, Master Rolandus, not only agreed with his main tenets, but went beyond them to affirm the justice of taking up arms against the wicked as an act of ministry to God. The notion that slaying one's enemy can be an act of Christian love goes back to Augustine and his interpretation of Joshua's destruction of Ai. Because such violence was virtuous, the Christian warrior performed a religious service for God and the Church. In Gratian's view, Christians did not need to perform a rite of purification when they returned from battle, a ritual adopted by Christian soldiers in the late Roman Empire and still practiced during the Middle Ages. (The penitential articles prescribed for soldiers at the Battle of Hastings contained a provision on lustral purification.) With their endorsement of Augustine via Isadore and Gratian, the canonists framed a religious justification for the Crusades (which had been long under way at the time), the persecution of heretics, and the forthcoming wars of annihilation fought against native peoples in the New World.

Subsequent generations of canonists refined the concept of just war they received from Augustine and Gratian. According to the Roman canon lawyer and Italian jurist John of Legnano (1320–83), just war could assume one of four types. The first, the "Roman War" (*guerre mortelle*, or "mortal war"), was waged by the Church on non-believers. John and subsequent canonists believed the rules of this form of warfare held sway over Rome's wars in antiquity. It was a no holds barred kind of war, in which the privilege of ransom did not exist and no distinction was drawn between combatants and civilians; all prisoners were subject to being put to death. The primary examples of Roman War were the armed conflicts fought against the Muslims in Spain and in the Middle East. Rarely would Christian knights wage Roman War against each other.[69] John's second and third types of war were waged on the authority of a prince and a judge, respectively. The fourth category of just war, necessary war, was fought in self-defense. Other canonists rejected three of John's four types of just war, holding that the only just war was one fought on the king's authority (John's second category). As Keen notes, this is an Augustinian idea. In his *Epistolae* (*Letters*), Augustine had written that "the final object of war is peace."[70] Because the aim of the sovereign was to maintain the peace, only the king could declare war. Elsewhere, in *Contra Faustum* (*Against Faustus*), Augustine declared that "the natural condition of mankind, which is attuned to peace, demands that the decision and authority for making war should lie with the prince."[71] This notion appears to have influenced the writings of medieval canonists. Bartolus tells us, for example, that "only he who has no superior can declare a just war." Nicholas of Tudeschi follows this line of thought, asserting that "wars which are not declared by a prince are not properly wars."[72]

The viewpoints of the canonists, of course, represent attitudes about the Law of War among only one group of thinkers during the High Middle Ages. In fact, the actual customs and usages of war evolved gradually over time, and sometimes they diverged from John of Legnano's four types of just war. Medieval armies developed a semiotic system to communicate their right to wage war. Keen writes that four states of war could be signified:

1. **War to the death (*guerre mortelle*)** This form of warfare closely resembled John of Legnano's first category, Roman War—a virtually unrestricted, remorseless style of battle. Medieval armies announced they were fighting a war to the death by displaying a red flag or banner. The French at Crécy exhibited a red banner, the Oriflamme, announcing that no prisoners would be taken. According to Keen, the Oriflamme was unfurled in the 1300s and 1400s in times of emergency; at such junctures, no quarter would be given. The color red appears to have been deliberately chosen, insofar as in heraldry red symbolized ferocity and mercilessness in battle. When a *guerre mortelle* was fought between Christian armies, contemporary witnesses expressed surprise—such wars were typically reserved for "enemies of the faith." The Burgundian chronicler of the Hundred Years War, Lefèvre de St. Rémy, remarked testily that the Armagnacs carried with them the Oriflamme when they invaded Artois in 1414 "as if against the Saracens." (The banner, however, was not unfurled.)[73]

2. **Public (open) war (*bellum hostile*)** Public war involved war between two Christian princes. Spoils were allowed and captives taken for ransom. Captives enjoyed a right to ransom rather than being executed. Such a war was inaugurated by the display of a prince's banner. From this moment on, a legal state of war existed between the two antagonists.[74]

3. **Feudal or covered war (*guerre couverte*)** This category pertained to private wars fought not between two sovereigns but between two feudal lords holding lands from the same prince. The medieval Law of War permitted the combatants on each side to kill those on the other, but certain actions—burning, plunder, and ransom—were forbidden. Feudal war was declared by a battle cry rather than the display of banners. Further, the combatants could establish no legal rights in the property seized from their enemies. As Robert Stacey notes, the denial of property rights in private conflicts furnished an incentive to feudal lords to connect their "covert war" with a public one, thereby authorizing ransom, burning, and plunder. By the late Middle Ages, this trend had resulted in the phasing out of private wars altogether: a soldier wishing to share in plunder had to register his name in a prince's official muster lists.[75]

4. **Truce** Signified by display of a white flag in the hands of the king's heralds, a truce suspended the war either as a whole or in designated areas. In addition to the white flag, a herald carried a white wand indicating his immunity from attack. Other participants in the conflict ensured their exemption from hostilities by carrying a piece of white paper in their helmets, such as prisoners held as hostages. The most typical sign of a truce was a white baton, which guaranteed safe conduct in enemy territory. If a garrison surrendered a town, it was often given free passage through the surrendered region to an allied area. In this case, the garrison's soldiers carried a white baton to ensure their immunity from attack. Keen observes that soldiers afforded free passage under such circumstances were rarely if ever molested.[76]

The four forms outlined above, each denoted by a special insignia to justify its occurrence, were the kinds of warfare that armies in the field recognized as legitimate during the High Middle Ages. However, we should understand that the Law of War observed in the field was a separate body of rules from the just war theory of medieval churchmen. As we have seen, the medieval just war theory inherited from St. Augustine was primarily concerned with the circumstances that rendered armed conflict appropriate, and even obligatory, for Christian soldiers. It paid scant attention to the rules governing how war should be conducted. In other words, to phrase the issue in the parlance of modern international law, just war theory had to do with *jus ad bellum*, and rarely with *jus in bello*. This did not mean that Roman canonists did not periodically advocate limits on the extent of violence inflicted on the enemy. Gratian himself had denied the anything goes interpretation of just war. He held that some actions, although carried out in furtherance of a just war, were prohibited. These included arbitrary killing or killings motivated by revenge, merciless pursuit of a defeated opponent, and aggressive (i.e.

unprovoked) warfare. While Gratian did acknowledge some limits to how a just war was prosecuted, he followed Augustine in approving certain acts that, if committed outside a just war, would be considered morally abhorrent—e.g., the employment of ambush, treachery, and tactical surprise.[77]

The Truce of God and the Peace of God

The two canons on the Law of War proclaimed by the Third Lateran Council of 1179, the *Treugas autem* and the *Innovamus*, codified earlier proclamations that tried to introduce constraints into warfare. The predecessors of the *Treugas autem* were the various "Truces of God" of the eleventh and early twelfth centuries, which, like the *Treugas autem*, forbade armed conflict during specified time periods. These were set forth by a succession of Church synods, bishops, and even popes throughout continental Europe. The efficacy of the Truce in reducing warfare is questionable. By the thirteenth century, whatever influence the Truce possessed had cratered as strong monarchs exerted their control over the nobility, substituting the "King's Peace" for that of the Church.

Like the *Treugas autem*, the *Innovamus* expressed a much earlier principle of Church law, the "Peace of God," which actually predated the Truce of God (the latter evolved from it). Dating back to a tenth-century Church council, the Peace of God was reasserted by succeeding Church councils. Medieval soldiers in northern France and the Rhineland swore public oaths to defend churchmen and their property. Over time, additional groups were considered immune to attack: women, merchants, and noncombatants in general. Although neither the Truce of God nor the Peace of God delivered on its promise to shield civilians from harm, each publicized the important distinction between combatants and noncombatants, emphasizing the inviolability of civilians during times of war.

The Roman Church supplemented Gratian's limitations on just war with additional restrictions set forth at the Third Lateran Council (1179). There Pope Alexander III and his bishops promulgated two laws: the *Treugas autem* and the *Innovamus*. The first of these banned armed conflict during Lent and Advent, and required knights to abstain from fighting from Thursday through Sunday each week. The second of the laws, the *Innovamus*, identified categories of persons immune from military attack: Church members (e.g., priests and monks), merchants, and peasants involved in farming (along with their livestock, which was removed from depredation). The Council stipulated that violators of either law would face excommunication. According to historian James Brundage, the Pope and bishops who drafted the two laws were seeking to tease out the allusive yet sketchy statements about just war found in the *Decretum*. After their promulgation, both laws filtered into the reference works and textbooks assigned to students studying canon law in European universities. In addition, a third law originally announced at the Second Lateran Council in 1139 was revived, the *Artem illam*. Although Gratian had neglected to include it in the *Decretum*, the *Artem illam* began to appear in compilations of canon law beginning in the late 1170s. When Pope Gregory XI published the official digest of canon law after Gratian in 1234, the *Liber Extra*, the *Artem illam* was incorporated into its pages along with the *Treugas autem* and the *Innovamus*. Like its companion laws, the *Artem illam* aimed to impose limitations on combat; unlike them, however, its focus was not on restricting war to specified periods of time or designating classes of persons as off-limits. Rather, the law represented the first (and, according to Brundage, the only) effort by the Church to outlaw classes of weapons considered unduly violent even in this era of sanguinary warfare—the crossbow and the ballista. These weapons were essentially armor-piercing devices that could be deployed by ordinary infantrymen against armored cavalry. Brundage suggests that the crossbow and ballista were socially subversive: mere commoners could now butcher knights on horseback who typically hailed from the ranks of the nobility. On May 29, 1176, the crossbow-equipped soldiers of the Lombard League defeated Emperor Frederick Barbarossa's cavalry at the Battle of Legnano, a victory that sent shock waves rippling across aristocratic Europe. Shortly after the Battle of Legnano, the scarcely-remembered prohibition of the crossbow and ballista by the Second Lateran Council in 1139 was reinvigorated by canon lawyers. By 1215 the insurgent English barons at Runnymede had joined the canonists in condemning the use of the crossbow; among the demands they extracted from the beleaguered King John was a concession to expel his crossbowmen from England.[78]

The *Artem illam* anticipates this revulsion against the leveling social implications of the two weapons. Moreover, the ban applied only in wars between Christian combatants. In wars of Christian armies against heretics and Muslims, the *Artem illam* permitted their use. Subsequent canon lawyers took note of the exception, declaring, as did Bernard of Pavia in the late twelfth century, that Christians might use the crossbow in their struggles with "pagans and persecutors of the Christian faith." Who were these "pagans and persecutors?" Bernard left no doubt about their identities: not only Muslims (called "Saracens") but also pagan peoples at odds with the Germans—Livonians, Letts, and Estonians. Another canonist, Raymond of Pennafort, confirmed Bernard's interpretation but pushed it even further with a throwaway remark: "Some people say that this weapon [the crossbow] can be used in a just war against Christians."[79] Raymond did not ally himself with this position; he merely observed that "some people" advocated it. These advocates, who included both theologians and canon lawyers, detected the loophole to the general prohibition of the crossbow in the *Artem illem* and pursued it to a remorseless conclusion—namely, that the crossbow was permitted *if the war were a just one*. As James Brundage tells the story, the canon lawyers on the faculties of medieval universities adopted this view despite the clear intention of the law's framers at the Second Lateran Council.[80] Thus, a canon that forbade the use of the crossbow in warfare between Christian antagonists was stood on its head by the late thirteenth century to allow deployment of the crossbow by a righteous army. The justice of the war *ab initio* legitimated weapons that would otherwise be illegal. The canonists were perilously close here to declaring that just wars could be fought as Roman wars, that is, as wars fought without formal restraints. In other regards, however, the Roman canonists laid down principles of individual accountability remarkably advanced for their era. Although Cardinal Hostiensis (d. 1271) declared that a just war was in essence a Roman War, he insisted that a ruler fighting without just cause was liable for all harm caused by his troops. He argued that aggrieved parties should be able to sue the prince in a canon court to obtain compensation for property lost or destroyed during the war. Incredibly, Hostiensis and other canonists went a step farther and, in diametrical opposition to Augustine, asserted the right to prosecute soldiers who killed in connection with an unjust war. Augustine, we will recall, was so enamored with obedience to orders that he denied the accrual of fault to soldiers for their conduct in battle, even when they were acting on the orders of an unrighteous commander. Hostiensis and the canonists agreed with Augustine in acquitting combatants fighting a just war of blame for causing deaths, but they staked new territory with their claim that slaying others during an unjust war exposed the killers to charges of criminal homicide.[81]

Similarly, the approach of John of Legnano to the issue of liability during wartime turned on the critical distinction between just and unjust war. For John, neither princes nor soldiers needed to fear incurring liability for participation in a just war; authors of an unjust war, however, were liable for the damages they caused. It appears John thought that the risk they might have to pay damages would deter princes from launching unjust wars: the prospect of an interminable sequence of lawsuits stretching on forever, in Brundage's words, "might well strip victory of its savor and its profit."[82] Of course, such liability inured only to those who waged unjust war. For righteous warriors, the benefits of combat grew rosier with the waning of the Middle Ages. Where earlier canonists— including Gratian—had followed the Romans in prohibiting the taking of private spoils, subsequent interpreters revised this tenet, holding that the legality of plunder depended on whether the conflict was just or not. While victors of an unjust war had no legal title to enemy property, spoils acquired in the course of a just war were fair game. Pope Innocent IV did the canonists one better when he asserted that the victor received legal title to both property *and* persons on the losing side. Innocent softened his position, however, by recognizing the legal right to compensation of persons suffering deprivation of their property as a result of an unjust war.[83]

Chivalry and the law of arms: the military courts of medieval Europe

For all their earnest engagement with just war theory, Church officials, lawyers, and theologians never developed—save in condemning the use of the crossbow and ballista, and this only inconsistently—a systematic body of humanitarian law. As Robert Stacey has observed,[84] the Church in the Middle Ages was chiefly concerned with justifying the conditions under which Christians might participate in the deadly business of warfare; in other words, its focus was on *jus ad bellum* rather than *jus in bello*. The medieval authorities who did articulate a set of judicially enforceable principles of conduct in war were princes and their commanders in the field—that is, the secular authorities of medieval Europe.

By the late eleventh century CE, hard lines had been drawn within European armies between the heavily armed noblemen fighting on horseback and the "unarmed rabble" (*inerme vulgus*), or commoners relegated to the infantry. The gap between noble and "vulgar" soldiers gave rise to a new military social order with its own protocols of behavior—the knights. As knights rose to prominence as a distinct elite, long-established but informal principles governing the nobility's conduct during battle were extended to them. By 1100 social position and military profession had been effectively fused in this new class—a class acting in accordance with an ethical/legal code that prescribed its members' behavior in both peacetime and wartime. The code of conduct came to be known as "chivalry." When knights defeated during combat in later centuries surrendered and besought their conquerors, as did three French knights at Limoges in 1370,[85] to "act to the law of arms," they were appealing to this venerable body of chivalric rules.

Chivalry was decidedly *not* intended as a universal set of principles offering timeless instruction for the conduct of armies everywhere. In this regard, chivalry should not be confused with the Roman concept of the *jus gentium*. It is perhaps an index of the strangeness of the medieval world as compared with our own today that chivalry only applied to the nobility (i.e., knights) in their battles with one another. Equality before the Law of War was never a concern. The nobles reserved a certain hauteur for the common people; if commoners had the temerity to take up arms, they were, in a sense, trespassing the proper boundaries of their social station. The result was that knights suspended the chivalric Law of War when they fought against common soldiers, a law that would ordinarily oblige a knight to capture an opposing knight and—if the prisoner so requested—ransom him. When the antagonist was a commoner, on the other hand, he could be struck down as the knight saw fit.[86] (Stacey notes that the Church did not subscribe to this viewpoint.) The overriding point here is that the medieval Law of War was a secular, rather than religious, institution, the principles of which should be distinguished from theological notions of just war.[87]

By the 1300s, the customs and practices of chivalry had become encapsulated in a body of formal law called the *jus militare*, or "law of the *milites*" (Latin for knights). In our discussion of ancient civilizations and their approaches to the Law of War, we encountered similar principles of proper conduct during battle, such as the differences drawn in Vedic India between just and unjust methods of waging war (*dharmayuddha* and *kuttayuddah*). In both Vedic India and medieval Europe, rules of chivalry were context-specific and caste-based; injunctions and prohibitions were in each instance directed solely to the warrior class (in India, the *Kshatriyas*; in Europe, the knights). Yet, what sets medieval chivalry apart from previous efforts in world civilization to constrain warfare was the development of formal military courts, in which alleged violations of the Law of War might be adjudicated. The venues for enforcing the Law of War were not international; rather, they were courts administered by the sovereigns of European states. These were not, however, part of the ordinary court system. Because the parties to a case based on the Law of War typically hailed from different feudal allegiances, the conventional courts were unsuitable for their trial.[88] In England, from at least the reign of Edward III (1327–77) onwards, they were tried directly before the sovereign—be he king, duke, or prince—and his council, a group consisting of his military lieutenants: namely, the sovereign's constable and marshals. Keen suggests that over time the English king transferred authority to hear disputes arising from the Law of War to the members of his council. These men were not professionally trained judges but military officers well acquainted from personal experience with the uneven fortunes of war. What they lacked in judicial expertise they made up for with their knowledge of combat, and an aggrieved party could expect a sympathetic hearing from them. The sovereign's council gained permanent jurisdiction over disputes involving the law of arms; the court organized by the council stood open to hear complaints at all times, whether in peace or war. In England, it became known as the Court of Chivalry, a body that sat at Westminster Abbey; in France, it was called the Courts of the Constable and the Marshals of France, a body meeting at the Table de Marbre in Paris.[89]

Who were the complainants, and what kinds of cases might they pursue in the chivalric courts of England and France? By necessity, the parties to the suit were soldiers bound by oaths of fealty to different sovereigns. To complicate matters still further, the parties often owed duties of allegiance to multiple lords; a knight might for example owe such a duty to both his liege lord and the lord for whom he was temporarily fighting. Thus, a potential litigant might seek redress against an alleged breachor of the chivalric code by applying either to the breachor's liege lord or to his sovereign. Each of these lords could grant relief, but the complainant's best bet was to file suit with the breachor's sovereign. Before creation of the courts of chivalry, the complainant would personally mount his case in the presence of the accused's prince. After establishment of the prince's council, the case would lie with its courts and their personnel. Appeals could be lodged directly with the king.[90]

To appreciate the kinds of suits tried in these courts of chivalry, it is helpful to gain acquaintance with the nature of the substantive law applied in them, and the nature of the feudal ties that bound a soldier to fight on behalf of his liege lord.

1. The law applied in chivalric courts was an amalgam of military customs—many of them derived from local usage—and chivalric principles enforceable in warfare between Christian armies, as set forth in Honoré Bonet's *Tree of Battles*. A Roman canonist, Bonet's treatise on the Law of War borrowed liberally from John of Legnano. In effect, the substantive law applied in these courts consisted of local military custom, canon law principles, and civil law precepts (the latter two sources conveyed by Bonet's treatise). According to Maurice Keen, Bonet and his copier, Christine de Pisan, digested the esoteric legalese of professional lawyers and translated it into a comprehensible form for a lay audience. Knights accepted the scholars' interpretations as expressing a time- honored code of military behavior.[91] The result of this synthesis of military customs, canon law, and civil law was, as Keen writes, the emergence by the mid–1300s of "a set of rules . . . accepted as decisive in the trial of disputes arising out of war, no matter where they were tried or by whom."[92]

2. The feudal relation between the soldier and his lord is of equal importance to understanding the kinds of offenses triable in chivalric courts. Medieval knights, although self-consciously fighting as members of a Christian military profession, nonetheless waged war as individuals who both enjoyed certain rights against and owed certain duties to their adversaries. In general, knights furnished their own equipment and servants, and while they received meager wages from their

lord and his captains, they rarely received compensation adequate to their maintenance. Rather, knights expected to make up the shortfall through participation in the spoils of war, to which they were contractually entitled. Robert Stacey points out that medieval war bore comparison with a joint stock company, in which soldiers enjoyed a legal right to plunder seized during battle, as well as to a portion of ransoms received by the captain and his lord. Today, we tend to think of the Law of War as protecting the integrity of prisoners of war and civilians; in the Middle Ages, by contrast, the majority of cases based on the Law of War related to the proper division of spoils.[93]

Keen furnishes an instructive hypothetical to illustrate how such cases often unfolded. He bids us imagine a medieval soldier who has taken prisoner his adversary after a bitterly-contested struggle. The soldier now releases the captive after receiving his promise in writing to pay a prescribed amount of gold and other items of value as ransom. The former captive, however, defaults on paying the promised ransom, and the soldier presses his claim with the delinquent's prince. In this hypothetical case, which is based on numerous actual cases, the aggrieved party would seek an audience directly with the prince if possible; if not, then with the prince's council. Under the medieval Law of War, the erstwhile captive was a prisoner *en parole*—i.e., one who gave his word that he will pay ransom if his captor released him. (Our contemporary practice of "parole" is based on this prototype.) Until he fulfilled his promise, the parolee was obligated to return to his captor when summoned, and his duty to respond to such a summons trumped all others he owed to his own sovereign and captain.[94] Numerous claims against delinquent prisoners *en parole* were filed in chivalric courts during the Hundred Years War. In one case, an archer seized Berengar of Mont Blanc in France, releasing him only when he agreed to pay ransom. When Berengar reneged on his promise, the archer filed a claim with King Edward II's council. Similarly, King Henry VI's council presided over a case involving Louis de Berthalot and his French prisoner, Olivier de Coitevy, whom de Berthalot had taken prisoner in Bordeaux in 1452. The councils of the Duke of Burgundy, the Kings of France and Aragon, and the Black Prince all heard cases filed by knights alleging non-payment of ransom by their former prisoners.[95]

Claims based on the spoils of war resemble civil disputes rather than criminal acts, yet the annals of medieval chivalric courts abound with them. Other claims pursued in these courts, however, more closely resemble crimes, even when they were not described in such terms. As we have seen, the social world of the High Middle Ages was thickly woven with personal relationships. A knight did not fight as the representative of a nation-state but rather for his liege lord, to whom he owed an indefeasible duty of loyalty. Given the primacy of personal ties, we can readily comprehend why the Law of War regarded a breach of fealty as a peculiarly grave offense, one chargeable against the offender as treason. A prominent case involved Edward the Black Prince and the Marshal d'Audreham. At the Battle of Poitiers (1356), Edward took d'Audreham prisoner, eventually releasing him when the parolee made two promises: to pay his ransom and to abstain from fighting against either Edward or the King of England until his ransom was paid. Eleven years later, d'Audreham fell again into Edward's hands at Najera after taking up arms against the Black Prince. Edward verified that d'Audreham's ransom had not been fully paid and charged him with treason. Both parties agreed to submit their dispute to a court consisting of twelve knights chosen from Edward's troops.[96]

At trial, Edward charged d'Audreham with committing a serious offense against chivalric honor in taking up arms against him in violation of his word. The Marshal countered with a legalistic argument: he claimed he had not truly fought against Edward because the Black Prince was not the "head of the war," and thus did not participate in the battle of Najera as a public person. The chief of the war was Edward's lord, Pedro of Castile, for whom the Black Prince fought at Najera as a captain. Hence, d'Audreham concluded, he had fought not against Edward but against Pedro of Castille, and he therefore could not be convicted of violating his word as a knight. The panel of twelve knights agreed with the Marshal, and his acquittal followed—an outcome that even Edward celebrated, insofar as a conviction for treason would have entailed d'Audreham's execution.[97]

Breaking your word as a knight could invite a charge of treason in a court of chivalry, as could other kinds of actions. An example was the surrender of a town while it still retained the ability to resist a siege. As a general rule, siege was fraught with peril for combatants and noncombatants alike, regardless of how they acted. If they resisted an invader, they were virtually assured of harsh treatment when the city fell to the enemy. If they surrendered, they could expose themselves to a charge of treason for giving up without a fight. Keen affirms that the Law of War regarding towns laid under siege was singular in its "savage severity," possibly because of the enormous effort required to breach the formidable walls of medieval fortresses.[98] Custom dictated that the commander of a siege dispatch his herald to the enemy garrison, who, once admitted, communicated the demand that the garrison and town be surrendered to his army. Accompanying the demand of capitulation was an unvarnished threat of dire consequences should the townspeople refuse. On one occasion during the Hundred Years War, the commander's emissary was denied entry to the garrison, provoking a warning from him that "if [the townspeople] were taken, they would be dealt with so that others should learn by their example, for the Duke of Bourbon would hang every man of them by the neck."[99] The threat had its effect, for the garrison immediately agreed to surrender. Keen emphasizes that such threats were perfectly legitimate within the medieval law of armed conflict, which authorized a commander to deal harshly with the resisters once the siege had formally started. The customary practice in such situations was a Roman War without quarter, although the commander could decide to negotiate terms with the defeated enemy. Moreover, exceptions could be made at the commander's election, and ransom was frequently accepted from war captives. All of this, of course, resided within the discretion of the commanding officer; when the city fell to the invaders there were few practical legal limits to the harm that could be visited on the inhabitants. Keen writes:

> Only churches and churchmen were technically secure, but even they were not often spared. Women could be raped, and men killed out of hand. All the goods of

the inhabitants were regarded as forfeit. If lives were spared, it was only through the clemency of the victorious captain; and spoliation was systematic.[100]

A steel-eyed logic informed the medieval law of siege. Rejection of a prince's demand to surrender was deemed an insult to his authority, an act of defiance that merited draconian punishment. The conqueror sometimes allowed the compliant within the town to retain their possessions unmolested, while seizing the goods—and often the lives—of the obstreperous "at the King's pleasure," as Henry V did to the people of Falaise in 1418. In such situations, plunder was not a violation of the Law of War; rather, it was a fulfillment of the law, insofar as pillaging a resistant town was considered a legal sanction for contumacy. Keen comments: "The king could divide the spoil as he wished, or even promise it in advance, but it was all at his disposition, because it was forfeit for rejection of his authority."[101]

Unfortunately, in the skein of relationships characteristic of feudal society, a too hasty decision to surrender, while preserving the lives and belongings of the townspeople, could simultaneously invite retaliation by the surrendering party's own lords. In this regard, a condition of siege differed considerably from engagements on the battlefield: a knight was able to surrender without adverse effect to himself (his bodily safety was guaranteed by the Law of War), whereas the decision by the leader of a town under siege to surrender—particularly if taken before commencement of battle—exposed the captain and everyone in his garrison to the charge of treason. Because the sign that a siege had begun was the discharge of cannon or "siege engines," the absence of bombardment prior to surrender was evidence presumptive of treason in chivalric courts. Thus John Talbot, the Earl of Shrewsbury, indicted the Earl of Stafford in 1433 for surrendering La Ferté "without assault and without [siege] engines," as Talbot's indictment read. Stafford had violated his oath as a knight to protect the town and deliver it only to the king—a crime against the king's majesty as well as the code of knighthood.[102]

While death and confiscation levied on captains for abandoning—or failing to abandon—a city to the enemy may strike modern observers as extreme, such punishment is nonetheless comprehensible as a violation of the Law of War. Other offenses, on the other hand, are so exotic and time-bound as to resist our efforts to translate them into roughly analogous categories of law existing today. Such cases often arose from the intricate network of feudal loyalties binding vassals to their sovereigns and lords. Oaths of allegiance were consummated in two kinds of instruments: statutes of orders of chivalry and confraternities of knights, and contracts of service. Knights, no matter how hard-boiled, often refused to take up arms in the service of another if their liege lords' interests, which they had pledged to preserve, would be thereby compromised. On one occasion, an archpriest declined participating in battle at Cocherel; were he to fight, he would be waging war against the King of Navarre, one of whose commanders, the Captal de Buch, had assigned lands to the archpriest. In another case, a mercenary soldier from Auvergne refused to fight for the Count of Armagnac because he was the enemy of the mercenary's lord in Béarn. In each of these cases, fighting would have made the knight liable to a charge of violating the medieval Law of War—a war crime unimaginable for us today.[103]

At other times, however, violations of the medieval law of arms closely resemble a war crime of the twenty-first century. An example is the trial in 1420 of the Seigneur de Barbasan for the murder of John the Fearless. Unfolding before Henry V, the proceedings ended with Barbasan's conviction and sentence to death. He appealed his case to Henry's heralds, generally recognized in military circles as learned experts on the Law of War. Barbasan argued that before his capture he had fought Henry hand-to-hand in a mine beneath the city's walls. Adverting to the principle that no one could put "a brother-in-arms" to death, Barbasan was able to persuade the heralds his life should be spared. They agreed, and the king commuted his death sentence to a prison term for life. This case is remarkable on a couple of scores: not only because it concerned, in Keen's words, "a matter tantamount to a war-crime," but also because it reveals a Law of War binding on the king. Henry V did not balk at the verdict of his heralds. Instead, he accepted them as authoritative and superior to his own judgment.[104] Without stretching the comparison, we may reasonably see here the extension of a diachronic principle common to the great ethical traditions of China (Mozi, Mencius), ancient India (Ashoka and Manu), Israel (Moses), ancient Greece (Aeschylus and Aristotle), Rome (Stoicism and Cicero), and the High Middle Ages (Cardinal Hostiensis): the idea that the ruler, no matter how exalted, had to submit to a law higher than his own will. Keen phrases the issue crisply: "It was the law, and not any man or any court, which was truly sovereign."[105]

The limits of chivalry: the wars against the Muslims

Although the Law of War was sovereign in medieval Europe, its application was restricted to warfare between Christian knights who were social equals. Even between Christian armies, noblemen routinely disregarded the Law of War in their dealings with enemy foot soldiers. The nineteenth-century German historian Jakob Burckhardt recounts the story of a Renaissance nobleman, Paolo Vitelli, who gouged out the eyes and cut off the hands of the commoners responsible for firing the arquebus, the late medieval forerunner of the rifle. Vitelli's motive for this atrocity was to retaliate against plebeians for dispatching their social betters with so ignoble a weapon as the arquebus. Nor was his abhorrent act a violation of chivalry, a body of principles that only covered battlefield relations between noblemen.[106]

The social inegalitarianism of chivalry underscores the fundamental difference between the medieval Law of War and the Roman conception of the *jus gentium*. So far as we can tell, medieval chivalry never acquired the aura of universality that grew to envelop the "law of the peoples" during Roman times. Knights of the Middle Ages never regarded chivalric principles as an expression of natural law, binding on all people everywhere as revealed by the operations of natural reason; rather, it applied only among the social elites of medieval Christian armies in their conflicts with each other. Unlike the *jus gentium*, moreover, chivalry had a measurable effect on the conduct of Christian armies in the field. While it did not apply to warfare between the nobility and common soldiers or between Christians and non-Christian combatants, chivalry provided a normative framework for the proper conduct of hostilities, one that not only constrained how war was fought but envisioned punishment for violations of its injunctions. Herein resides the significance of the medieval law of arms: despite its limitations, it represents the first sustained efforts to impose judicial restraint on inter-tribal warfare.

The imperfections of medieval chivalry considered as an international body of law are poignantly demonstrated in the behavior of Christian armies during the Crusades. When the Crusaders conquered Jerusalem in 1099, they ran through the city's streets massacring every man, woman, and child they met. Some of Jerusalem's Muslims found refuge in the Mosque of al-Aqsa, but they ultimately surrendered to the Norman leader Tancred, promising to pay an exorbitant ransom if he spared their lives. Tancred accepted their offer and displayed his banner over the mosque. Tancred's banner, however, had no effect as a shield against attack, for the Crusaders later broke into the mosque and slaughtered all of its refugees. When Jerusalem's Jews took refuge in their main synagogue, the Crusaders set fire to the building, incinerating everyone within. This, in the thinking of the Crusaders, was just punishment for alleged Jewish support of the Muslims.[107]

Muslim refusal to emulate Christian excesses suggests that not all parties to the religious wars of the Crusades would resort to wholesale butchery of the enemy.[108] Before recapturing Jerusalem in 1187, the Muslim military leader Saladin entered into an agreement with the Christian commander of the Jerusalem garrison, Balian of Ibelin, promising to ransom each man in the city for ten dinars, each woman for five dinars, and every child for a single dinar. When it became clear that some 20,000 inhabitants would be unable to afford the ransom, Saladin agreed to a single payment of 100,000 dinars, a sum that was reduced still farther to 30,000 dinars to ransom 7,000 of Jerusalem's residents. A leading historian of the Crusades, Steven Runciman, describes the situation when Saladin entered Jerusalem:

> The victors were correct and humane. Where the Franks, eighty-eight years before, had waded through the blood of their victims, not a building now was looted, not a person injured. By Saladin's orders guards patrolled the streets and the gates, preventing any outrage on the Christians.[109]

Saladin's example of good faith and restraint made little impression on his adversary, King Richard I (the "Lion-Hearted"), when he conquered the city of Acre in 1191. After a bitter siege, the garrison leaders sued for peace; the Crusaders accepted the terms offered. These included the complete surrender of Acre and its contents, payment of 200,000 gold pieces to the Christians in three monthly installments, and the release of 1,500 Christian war captives. The war captives included a hundred "prisoners of rank" to be "specifically named." As surety, the Crusaders took hostage the Muslim garrison; they were to be released after payment of the first installment of gold. Thereafter Saladin, who had not personally negotiated the capitulation, confirmed its terms and organized the captives and gold for delivery to the enemy. The money was satisfactorily handed over, but Richard objected that the "prisoners of rank" designated by name had not been released; he therefore refused to liberate the Muslim hostages. When Saladin offered a modus vivendi pending final resolution of the issue, Richard's ambassadors rejected it, demanding full payment of the first installment—a demand Saladin refused to honor until his soldiers were set free. Nine days later, on August 20, 1191, Richard announced Saladin had reneged on his word and ordered that the 2,700 hostages be executed—a commandment which Richard's knights performed gleefully as an act of vengeance for their comrades who had fallen during the siege. Runciman describes the piteous end of the hostages and their families: "The prisoners' wives and children were killed by their side. Only a few notables and a few men strong enough to be of use for slave-labour were spared."[110]

The nadir of Crusader barbarism, however, may have been reached during the sack of Constantinople in 1204. As Theodore Draper has observed,[111] the savagery of Christian armies during the sack is indefensible in terms of medieval chivalry. Under the Church's teachings, previous crusades against the Muslims were by definition holy wars fought outside the customs and usages of the Law of War. The defenders of Constantinople, by contrast, were Christians, and defense of their city can only be characterized as an effort to repel a wanton war of aggression motivated by the desire for plunder. When the city fell on April 12, 1204, the Crusaders "rushed in a howling mob down the streets and through the houses, snatching up everything that glittered and destroying whatever they could not carry, pausing only to murder or to rape." Millennia-old Greco-Roman *objets d'art* were obliterated as the marauders vandalized both palaces and common homes in the city. Blood ran in rivers through the streets, purling around the mangled bodies of women and children. The sack and pillage of Constantinople lasted three interminable days, in the course of which this event took its place—when measured by both loss of life and the destruction of invaluable heirlooms—as one of the worst carnages in world history.[112]

Conclusion

Neither the Roman *jus gentium* nor the medieval code of chivalry softened the brutality of warfare, particularly when the cause was consecrated as "just" and the enemy was a true outsider. What, then, did they accomplish? The impacts of both the "law of nations" and chivalry were in the *longue durée* and coincided with two momentous historical events: the rise of European nation-states, for whom the observance of restraints in warfare paid reciprocal dividends, and the concomitant professionalization of national armies. Not only was a salaried military no longer thrown back on plunder for its compensation and survival; it also developed an ethos of mutual respect, honor, and fair play in its confrontations with opposing armies. To the rise of nation-states and professional armies we might also add the emergence of democratic politics in the seventeenth, eighteenth, and nineteenth centuries. One of the lamentable shortcomings of chivalry was the refusal of medieval knights to recognize its principles when the opponent was a non-noble. As the medieval model of knighthood gave way to a very different paradigm based on the unifying idea of a nation-at-arms, the ancient social distinctions that once justified Paolo Vitelli in severely maiming his commoner prisoners were no longer tenable.

Some scholars have found archetypal residues of chivalry in modern humanitarian law. Theodore Draper sees in the medieval tournament's condemnation of surprise attacks a forerunner of the Third Hague Convention's prohibition of initiating war without first declaring it or issuing an ultimatum.[113] Similarly, he traces the modern immunities enjoyed by diplomats to the protections afforded heralds and emissaries during the Middle Ages.[114] In fact, the notion that war could be started only after appropriate ritual observance was common to many of the civilizations of antiquity we have examined. Ancient Egypt, Mesopotamia, China, India, Greece, and Rome, as well as medieval Europe, all had some conception of procedures and ceremonies prescribed for the licit resort to war. Similarly, many of these cultures extended protections and immunities to foreign heralds and diplomats. Neither of these aspects of the Law of War was particularly novel, even during the era when chivalry was coalescing as a distinct code of military behavior. I would suggest that the chief contribution of chivalry to subsequent elaboration of the Law of War was the juridification of it—the idea that those who breached its precepts could be placed on trial as *war criminals*. Once the local and caste-based system of chivalry merged with the universalism of the *jus gentium* in later centuries, the result would be to confect an international concept of the Law of War. Rather than courts of chivalry, violations of international norms would be tried in national and military courts and (by the twentieth century) international tribunals.

The path toward this legal revolution, however, is a twisted one, snaking through eras of world history in which the special venom of religious hatred, racial and ethnic chauvinism, and imperialist rapacity poisoned the interactions of opposing armies. This notwithstanding, deep cultural channels were in place to guide warfare along a jagged trail toward legal restraint.

CHAPTER 4
MAKING LAW IN THE SLAUGHTERHOUSE OF THE WORLD: EARLY MODERNITY AND THE LAW OF WAR

The practice of the Law of War, 1300–1648

With the waning of feudalism and the rise of professional armies, the customs enforced in chivalric courts would require a new foundation. This new point of anchorage was found in the national ordinances of Europe's premier centralizing monarchies, England and France. Before the 1800s, the Law of War was codified in only two forms: bilateral treaties (i.e., treaties between two nation-states) and the national law of individual sovereign states. The codifications of the Law of War we are most familiar with today— that is, multilateral treaties (agreements between multiple countries)—are of far more recent origin. The first multilateral treaty designed to limit warfare was the Paris Declaration on Maritime War (1856), an agreement some 600 years later than the first national law imposing restrictions on warmaking—the English King John's "Constitutions to be Made in the Army of our Lord the King." As Theodor Meron has asserted, "national ordinances were the principal means for developing and codifying the Law of War" previous to the nineteenth century.[1]

King John's Constitutions of 1214 instructed the king's marshals to verify that the army respected supplies kept in churches and churchyards—locations in which the peasants sought refuge during times of war, both for themselves and their property (including cattle). The clear thrust of the Constitutions was to broaden the immunities of the Church in wartime so as to include the peasants and their possessions, thereby marking them as a class of protected persons.[2] According to Meron, more significant than John's Constitutions were the Ordinances of War promulgated by King Richard II at Durham in 1385, which banned robbery, plunder, and killing or capturing unarmed women and members of the clergy. Richard's Ordinances also forbade contact with the pyx (the container in which the Eucharist was kept), an offense which, along with rape, was punishable by hanging. When Henry V issued his Ordinances of War at Mantes in July 1419, they were modeled on Richard's Ordinances, particularly the prohibition of rape, killing/capturing unarmed women and clergymen, and pillaging churches.[3]

It is not the English, however, who are credited with the most systematic and far-reaching effort to regulate the conduct of war in the late Middle Ages. That honor goes to the French King Charles VII, whose Ordinance to Prevent Pillage and Abuses by Soldiers was decreed at Orléans on November 2, 1439. The twist in Charles's Ordinance was that the "pillage and abuses" it sought to prevent were those inflicted by French mercenaries on French civilians. The purpose of the decree was to abolish these mercenary forces, which for too long had remained outside the king's control, and to lay the foundation for a professional army in France. The Ordinance cited a raft of prohibitions, including the plunder, imprisonment, or ransoming of people either in their homes or on public roads, as well as taking the livestock, carts, and tools of merchants and peasants, or otherwise tampering with them. Furthermore, the Ordinance proscribed destroying food stuffs and their storage bins (wheat, cornfields, fruit-trees) and banned the common practice of soldiers extorting payments from the civilian population by ransoming their produce, either prior to or after harvest. Charles threatened to punish violations as a form of *lèse-majesté* (high treason against the king), a sanction involving "loss of all honours and public offices and of all rights … for the offender himself and his descendants, and confiscation of his property"[4]

The Ordinance of Charles VII went on to affirm a remarkably advanced principle of command responsibility, according to which a captain was accountable not only for the crimes of his subordinates but for his failure to punish their offenses. In addition, the Ordinance deemed as accomplices any soldiers or other persons who, observing commission of such crimes (e.g., robbery), failed to report them to the authorities. These persons would "be held responsible for the offence as accessories to it and shall be punished in the same manner as the offenders."[5]

Although unwilling to venture as far as the French did in imposing vicarious liability on their troops, the English well into the seventeenth century adopted law codes to govern the behavior of their soldiers in the field. Drawing on Henry V's Mantes Ordinances, King Henry VIII proclaimed the Statutes and Ordinances for the Warre in 1544, which forbade desecrating the pyx and depriving a person with proof of ownership of his possessions without first securing the approval of senior officers. Perhaps actuated by a desire to remove the most common motive for plunder, Henry VIII's Statutes required officers to pay their soldiers on a regular basis. Robbing merchants engaged in supplying English troops was banned, as was putting to the torch a city and its houses "except the king's enemies be within it, and cannot be otherwise taken." Peasants could not be expropriated of their livestock without authorization from senior officers; the Statutes reserved the death sentence for this offense. Territories that surrendered to the English king were under his authority, meaning that their mistreatment through robbery, plunder, or capture was forbidden "upon peyne of death." Women and children enjoyed explicit immunities: women and their property were not to be molested, while children under the age of fourteen—so long as they were not the children of lords, captains, and the wealthy—could not be taken prisoner.[6]

The English Crown preserved a remarkable degree of continuity over time in its rule-making for armies in the field. In 1639 it promulgated the "Lawes and Ordinances of Warre, for the Better Government of his Majesties Army Royall, under the Conduct of … Thomas Earle of Arundel and Surrey," which sustained the prohibitions of rape, burning houses, and plundering merchants found in previous English ordinances. The inhabitants of a territory that had surrendered to the king could not be harmed. Prefiguring the Martens Clause of the Fourth Hague Convention of 1907, the Lawes and Ordinances of Warre affirmed that, in cases of first impression, recourse should be made to the "ancient course of marshall discipline." Additional laws were issued that adopted many of these earlier rules but imported new ones as well. In 1640, the Earl of Northumberland decreed his "Lawes and Ordinances of Warre Established for the Better Conduct of the Service in the Northern Parts." Northumberland's laws reprised the themes we have heard in earlier ordinances—namely, the prohibition of rape, desecrating churches and religious objects, robbery, murder, and harming farmers or their possessions. Farms, barns, trees, ships, and carriages all enjoyed protection under the laws; none could be burned or destroyed without orders. Soldiers had to pay fair value for the food they seized. Northumberland's laws went on, however, to chart new territory in the English Law of War by ensuring the right to quarter. The penalty for failing to give quarter to a yielding adversary was death. As Meron notes, the right to quarter was acknowledged in the customary law of medieval warfare, yet it was absent from English martial decrees at the time of the Battle of Agincourt (1415). Northumberland's reassertion of quarter was the most innovative element of his decree. Less original, but of equal significance, was the insistence in Northumberland's laws—like that found in Charles I's Laws and Ordinances of War— that "[a]ll other faults, disorders and offences, not mentioned in these articles, shall be punished according to the general customes and laws of warre," a passage which also evokes the Martens Clause of the Fourth Hague Convention.[7]

From the standpoint of humanitarian concern for the well-being of war captives, Meron regards the subsequent proclamation by the Scots of their "Articles and Ordinances of War for the Present Expedition of the Army of the Kingdom of Scotland, by the Committee of Estates [and] the Lord General of the Army" (1643) as the equal of the Nuremberg jurisprudence. The Scottish Articles contain familiar prohibitions of rape, murder, plunder, and the affirmative duty to pay for food seized by the army. They also ordered soldiers to give quarter to any surrendering enemy. In matters not addressed by the explicit language of the Articles, the concluding provision looked not only to the customs of war as a gap-filler, but to the "law of nature":

Matters, that are clear by the light and law of nature, are presupposed; things unnecessary are passed over in silence; and other things may be judged by the common customs and constitutions of war; or may upon new emergents, be expressed afterward.[8]

Despite the humane provisions of the English and French ordinances of war, early modern Europe between 1550 and 1700 was a theater of cruelty during wartime. Historians pondering over why this was so have identified three primary causes for the increased savagery: the higher incidence of siege warfare and rebellion in this period, both of which had always been met with draconian repression; and religious conflict arising from the upheavals of the Protestant Reformation. We consider each of these accelerants to the violence of warfare below.

Siege warfare

Dating back at least to the time of the Greeks and the Romans, siege warfare had always been the occasion for inflicting wholesale violence on civilians. Acting on the widely-accepted principle that"that which is conquered in war is the property of the conquerors,"[9] Greek armies during the Peloponnesian War stormed fortified cities, massacring and enslaving their inhabitants. Similarly, a city that defied Roman arms in the midst of a just war faced virtual extermination—the razing of the city, the execution of resistance leaders, and the enslavement of everyone else. The harshness of siege warfare continued well into the Middle Ages, an era in which conquerors of resistant cities were fully justified under the Law of War in putting the vanquished to the sword. The fierceness of siege warfare persisted into the early modern period, demonstrating an impressive arc of continuity that reached from Classical Greece to the English civil wars of the seventeenth century.

Why was siege warfare so bitterly destructive? In the Middle Ages, as we have seen, the refusal of a town to capitulate was regarded as an insult to the prince's authority, an act of defiance meriting forfeiture of all possessions within the town—and sometimes of the townspeople's lives. Today, such a policy would be considered a war crime, but in the medieval era the total subjugation of a resistant city was deemed a fulfillment of the Law of War rather than a violation of it. Other explanations dwell less on the medieval Law of War than on basic human psychology in combat. Military historian Geoffrey Parker argues that "the catharsis of passing through the killing ground of the breach and emerging unscathed" may have driven conquering armies to "indiscriminate violence" against the besieged city's defenders. At the same time, as Parker notes, the history of sieges records many incidents in which a sense of stunned paralysis fell over the town's inhabitants once it fell to the invaders. In these cases human behavior may be imitating the animal kingdom, where the panic-stricken torpor of a cornered animal can incite its hunter to zestful violence. Parker retells the story from the English Civil War of Cirencester's conquest by the Royalists in 1643. When the King's soldiers stormed the town, the Parliamentary garrison "stood like men amazed, fear bereft them of understanding and memory" as they were slaughtered. A similar outcome occurred during the siege of Lincoln, which fell to Parliamentary troops a year later. At Lincoln, the royal soldiers tossed aside their weapons and, as one observer recorded,"cried out for quarter, saying they were poor Array Men [conscripts]." Their surrender and pleas for merciful treatment fell on deaf ears, as the witness tersely concludes his account of the battle: "We slew fifty of them."[10] The phenomenon of the frozen passivity of the defeated

---

"I believe that it has always been understood that the defenders of a fortress stormed have no claim to quarter."

The Duke of Wellington, letter to George Canning, February 3, 1820, quoted in Parker, Early Modern Europe, 48

---

and bloodthirsty avidity of the victor appears to be transcultural: comparable behavior on both sides is observable in the storming by the Qing armies of cities loyal to the Ming in the seventeenth century.[11]

The growing importance in the sixteenth and seventeenth centuries of siege to ultimate success in battle boosted the frequency of atrocity. Parker writes that throughout Europe "battles became relatively rare and sieges constituted the hinge of success and failure."[12] The heightened significance of siege warfare had already begun during the Hundred Years War, when it became clear that a territory could only be successfully occupied by controlling fortresses and fortified cities.[13] What followed was a military equivalent of the principle of coevolution in biology: as attackers massed larger numbers of soldiers and improved artillery against fortresses, the defenders pioneered new techniques of fortification,[14] which in turn spurred efforts to increase troop strength and wall-piercing siegeworks. The prodigious ingenuity, manpower, and time needed to take a heavily fortified city—as demonstrated forcefully in the Dutch siege of Breda in 1637, a fortified town conquered after six months of blockade and bombardment by 23,000 cannon balls, and only after 5,000 Dutch soldiers had erected double earth-walls as protection—guaranteed a hefty price would be paid by the defenders. If no surrender occurred before the battery was brought up, then the city's inhabitants could expect no quarter when the town fell to the attackers. Shakespeare's Henry V, in a passage that describes the writer's own era as much as early fifteenth-century Europe, warns the townspeople of Harfleur to surrender or face total destruction:

If I begin the batt'ry once again,
I will not leave the half-achieved Harfleur Till in her ashes she lie buried.
The gates of mercy shall be all shut up
And the flesh'd soldier, rough and hard of heart, In liberty of bloody hand shall range
With conscience wide as hell, mowing like grass Your fresh fair virgins and flow'ring infants.
What is't then to me if impious war,
Array'd in flames, like to the prince of fiends, Do, with his smirch'd complexion, all fell feats Enlink'd to waste and desolation?[15]

Such threats were far from idle in the early modern period. In 1572 the garrison town of Mechelen in the Netherlands refused the Duke of Alba's demand for surrender—an act of defiance for which it would pay dearly. Quickly taking the city, Alba watched as his soldiers sacked Mechelen for three days, acting, in the words of one eyewitness, "as if this religious capital of the country were a Muslim city and all the inhabitants barbarians. The desolation was so complete that not a nail was left in a wall."[16] In the lead-up to the May 1631 sacking of Magdeburg, one of the wealthiest cities in the Holy Roman Empire, Magdeburg's authorities had committed a threefold primal sin: they had rejected insertion of an imperial garrison, forged an alliance with Sweden's Gustavus Adolphus (an adversary of the Holy Roman Emperor), and refused the demands of Count Tilly, commander of the imperial siege army, for the town's surrender. When Tilly's army breached the innermost wall of the city on May 20, 1631, his soldiers poured into the interior, indiscriminately slaughtering thousands of Magdeburg's inhabitants. Although Parker views the carnage as driven by "strategic necessity" and conducted "according to the laws of war," the German historical writer Jörg Friedrich presents a far darker assessment:

> Not innocent childhood, nor helpless old age, nor youth, nor gender, nor class, nor beauty could appease the rage of the victor. Women were ravished in the arms of their husbands and daughters at the feet of their fathers, and the defenseless sex had only the prerogative of serving the two-fold fury [of the conquerors]. Fifty-three females were found in a church, beheaded. The Croatians enjoyed throwing children into the fire and Pappenheim's Walloons spearing infants at the breasts of their mothers.[17]

According to Friedrich, Tilly deflected pleas to stop the bloodbath with the reply, "Return in an hour, then I'll see what I'll do." Tilly was in no position to quell the violence because he had agreed beforehand with his men to grant them three days of uninterrupted plundering once Magdeburg fell.[18] Some 30,000 of Magdeburg's population met their end during the city's sack.[19]

Sieges of other European cities in the early modern period produced similarly woeful results. Friedrich recounts the civilian deaths: one-third of Maastricht's population killed by Spanish units in 1579; 7,000 mowed down in Antwerp in 1576. While Parker and

Figure 15 Tilly's siege of Magdeburg, line engraving (1637). © Wikimedia Commons (public domain).

Friedrich disagree about the motives for and scope of the butchery in Magdeburg, they agree about a major factor contributing to the extraordinary violence unleashed in all of these sieges: namely, the near-impossibility of readily distinguishing military from civilian targets inside the fallen cities. For Parker, "civilians who militarized their homes by accepting a garrison in effect presented an undifferentiated target to the besiegers," to the point where civilian belongings and military property became indistinguishable in the eyes of the invaders. Likewise, according to Friedrich, "in a condition of siege, in contrast with the battlefield, the military, the defenders, and civilians are inseparable." When we draw together the various factors conducing to violence—the bitterness and protracted length of siege warfare, the long-standing tradition of refusing quarter to refractory cities, the practice of compensating soldiers through plunder, and the difficulty of distinguishing military from civilian targets once a city has fallen—the brutality and devastation of this siege-prone era become more understandable.

Rebellion

We will postpone our discussion about the theory of the Law of War in early modernity until later in this chapter. As always in the history of legal norms, there was a significant gap between the teachings of legal scholars and the practice on the battlefield. However, it is worth mentioning here that, when it came to rebellion, there was a seamless coincidence of legal opinion and military practice. Reaching back centuries (at least) to the Church's war on the Albigensians in France, Christian Europe had fought "Roman" wars against heretics—literal wars of extermination waged without mercy and removed from the meliorative influence of the Law of War. The same rule applied to the treatment of rebels. For the sixteenth-century legal scholar Balthasar Ayala, rebellion was so monstrous that he equated it with heresy. Like heresy, rebels had no right to make war against their superiors, and when they did (again like heretics) they enjoyed no protections under the Law of War, such as *postliminium*[20] and the rights enjoyed by war captives. In short, rebels could be enslaved or even put to death summarily; all of their property was liable to seizure.[21]

As we have seen, sieges were on the rise in early modern European warfare. So, too, were rebellions, driven in part by religious dissension and the demand for political change that accompanied it. The growing incidence of sieges and rebellions during this time virtually guaranteed extreme brutality in clashes from which the restraints of law had been stripped. In Spain's expedition to annex the Azores in 1582, the Spanish commander subjected his prisoners of war to summary execution on the ground that his was a police rather than a military action, a designation that effectively denied Spain's opponents any protection under the Law of War. Seven years later, possibly with events like the annexation of the Azores in mind, Alberico Gentili, an Italian jurist widely recognized as the founder of international law, asserted that the "chief incentive to cruelty [in war] is rebellion." Once again, on this point the theory and practice of the Law of War were in harmony. Indeed, the tendency to treat rebellion as an event so heinous as to be disqualified from legal protection under the Law of War persisted well into the eighteenth, nineteenth and twentieth centuries. The suppression of the Jacobite revolt in 1745 is an illustrative case: after the Jacobite army was defeated at the Battle of Culloden, the English executed scores of war captives; others were hunted down and slaughtered. Thirty years later, there were calls from British officers to deal with the American rebels in 1774–45 as England had with the Jacobites—that is, with unvarnished ruthlessness. Parker discerns in subsequent government responses to other insurrections a recurrence of the pattern Gentili had long ago noticed: the suppression of the Paris Commune in 1871, the Nazis' destruction of Warsaw in 1944, the Soviet crushing of the Hungarian uprising in 1956, and the starvation and mass death associated with the Biafran war (Nigeria) of the late 1960s all ring the changes on an archaic military practice while preserving its essential core.[22]

Religious conflict

The military scholar François de La Noue wrote in 1587 that the frequency of rebellion was a leading cause of brutality in the wars of his era. To rebellion, however, La Noue added another force of social disruption that sharpened the claws of violence in early modern warfare: religious strife.[23] Centuries-old precedent for lashing out with unbridled ferocity against Muslims, Jews, and heretics already preexisted the sixteenth century's wars of religion, so that, when Europe split into two hostile Christian camps after the Protestant Reformation, the antagonists could readily slot their enemies into the category of "unbelievers," thereby justifying the suspension of law and the infliction of unlimited harm on them. As Theodor Meron has observed, the Reformation in effect "blurred" the distinction between a non-Christian and "Christians of another branch of Christianity,"[24] resulting in the treatment of both groups as infidels undeserving of chivalrous treatment. Religious wars raged throughout Western Europe in the late sixteenth and seventeenth centuries. In Catholic France a series of religiously inspired conflicts engulfed society, none more breathtakingly vicious than the St. Bartholomew Day's Massacre in August 1572. A plot hatched by members of the Catholic nobility and the French king's mother, Catherine de Médicis, to exterminate the Huguenot leadership came to fruition at the wedding of Marguerite de Valois and the future French king, the Huguenot Henry of Navarre. Many of France's Huguenot nobility were in attendance, presenting a rare opportunity to the cabal around Catherine to wipe out the Huguenot leaders at a stroke. When the bell of Saint-Germain-l'Auxerrois announced the dawn on August 24, 1572, the conspirators put the Huguenot guests to the sword, including Henry of Navarre's attendants (Navarre himself was spared). As it has in many other genocidal massacres in world history, this initial burst of localized killing quickly spread to other parts of the city, where Huguenot homes and shops were overrun and pillaged, their occupants brutally murdered and their bodies flung into the Seine river. The wave of bloodshed swelled outward into the provinces, inundating Huguenot populations in Rouen, Lyon, Bourges, Orléans, and Bordeaux. The violence did not end until early October 1572, by which time as many as 70,000 Huguenots may have been killed. (Some scholars have estimated a death toll of 3,000 in Paris alone.) Among Europe's Catholic monarchs there was little wringing of hands over the unchivalrous nature of the massacre nor fretting about violations of the Law of War. Rather, Philip II of Spain applauded the butchery, while the Pope struck a medal to commemorate it.[25]

Materialist explanations of human behavior often fail to appreciate the power of religious motives. This is especially true when we consider the motivation for Spain's attempted invasion of England by sea in 1588. Philip II's marshaling of the Spanish Armada was influenced by the Pope's suggestion that he destroy "the infidels and heretics" by either invading England or attacking Muslim Algiers. After conferring with his theologians, Philip opted to invade England—a decision that Geoffrey Parker calls an instance of "messianic imperialism."[26] The result was disastrous for Spain: dispersed by a storm, some of the Armada's ships ran aground on the coast of western Ireland. Sailors who survived the wrecking of their ships and made landfall were hanged by supporters of England. Gentili, ever an advocate of granting quarter to soldiers *hors de combat* (removed from combat), condemned the summary execution of the sailors "as if they were robbers and pirates," recommending that the self-appointed executioners be punished for violating the Law of War.[27]

Today, such atrocities would be considered illegal under international humanitarian law, but at the time they were deemed permissible. Even clergymen egged on soldiers to wipe out their religious antagonists, using race-baiting invective to dehumanize them. In a sermon delivered in 1645 to Parliamentary troops on the verge of attacking Basing House (the redoubt of a Catholic peer), a military chaplain exhorted his listeners to exterminate the Catholics as "open enemies of God," "bloody papists," and "vermin." Drawing upon the analogy of the Second World War, Parker likens such military chaplains to "political commissars" responsible for keeping the embers of religious hatred glowing among the soldiers, and thereby preventing any empathic feeling toward the Catholic Other. Nearly every one of those holed up in Basing House was put to the sword.[28]

The growing incidence of siege warfare, rebellion, and religious conflict interacted with permissive attitudes to foster a climate generative of extreme violence. Yet, if we conclude that early modern Europe was little more than a boundless slaughterhouse, fashioned after Joseph de Maistre's image of the world as "a vast altar, upon which all that is living must be sacrificed without end," we would be mistaken.[29] In fact, Geoffrey Parker regards the period between 1550 and 1700 as a historic watershed in the norms mitigating the dreadful brutality of warfare—a change expressed both in theory and practice.[30] Although public opinion throughout Europe condoned acts during the sacking of a city performed under the arousal of a sudden, breakthrough victory, matters were different once the battlefield frenzy had abated. When Protestant soldiers took Mechelen, Belgium, in 1580, they spared a convent full of nuns because, in the words of a contemporary chronicler, "the fury was over and they no longer had license [to kill]."[31] The distinction between "hot-blooded" and "cool-blooded" action arose in a sermon of 1644, delivered by a Royalist preacher during the English Civil War. Addressing Charles I's soldiers, he advised them that "you neither do, nor ... suffer to be done, in coole blood, to the most impious rebels, any thing that savours of immodesty, barbarousnesse, or inhumanity."[32]

These and other anecdotes suggest that, while the age was scarred by hair-raising atrocities committed in combat, in the minds of early modern Europeans *some* limitations were acknowledged, and even expected, in battle.

Popular attitudes toward warfare are critical to taming its orgiastic destructiveness, yet they are a far cry from prosecuting offenders in duly appointed courts. Interestingly, such trials did indeed occur in the late sixteenth century. In 1574 the Spanish king, Philip II, launched an investigation into charges that the Duke of Alba had employed unnecessary force to suppress the Dutch rebels. The result was the acquittal of Alba but the conviction and banishment from the royal court of his senior officials. Two years later, after the Spanish sack of Antwerp resulted in the deaths of 8,000 civilians and the destruction of a thousand of the city's houses, the Spanish crown ordered a judicial investigation to ascertain responsibility for the carnage. By the latter half of the seventeenth century, the English had installed a court of claims in Ireland with an explicit mandate to inquire into alleged war crimes by Oliver Cromwell's occupation troops.[33] Such examples indicate that early modern Europeans not only rejected the view of war as a licentious arena of never-ending barbarism, but insisted increasingly that such limits were enforceable through military tribunals within the army or judicial process outside it. Violations of such limiting norms were more and more regarded as war crimes meriting some form of punishment.

As always in historical study, we must grapple with the reasons why so momentous a change in European attitudes and practices developed in early modernity. One possible explanation is that, with the passage of time, the class of persons claiming protection under the Law of War was substantially enlarged. As we have seen, a regrettable feature of medieval chivalry was its exclusivity: it applied only to members of the nobility in their clashes with one another. In the eyes of the medieval Law of War, social status was everything. By the late sixteenth century, however, what had been the exclusive preserve of aristocrats in their private wars was opened to all combatants, no matter their social background. It is remarkable that the first stirrings of this egalitarian approach to the Law of War occurred in the midst of a rebellion—i.e., the revolt of the Dutch against Spain beginning in 1566.[34] Rebellion, that form of military conflict most conducive to brutal excess, paradoxically became the cradle of legal accountability for war crimes. By the end of the 1500s, Spain and the Dutch Republic had signed a treaty requiring each side to ransom all war captives within twenty-five days. The agreement envisioned a cost-free swap of prisoners of equal rank; for all others, ransom would be paid in the amount of the prisoner's monthly pay plus a per diem charge for maintenance during his detention. The convention was periodically reviewed and amended to account for inflation. When Spain and France later went to war, this protocol regulating prisoner ransom/exchange was introduced into the conflict, along with a proviso stipulating that ill or wounded war captives would be protected and sent back to their own countries. As Parker observes, what in the Age of Chivalry had been a purely private matter between contending sovereigns and liege lords now fell under regulation by the State.[35]

Another factor that may have contributed to efforts to prevent plunder was the creation of funds by local communities, which were used to pay protection money to

Figure 16 Engraving of the statue of Fernando Álvarez de Toledo in Antwerp by Jacques Jonghelinck. From Nederlantsche Oorloghen by Pieter Bor. © Wikimedia Commons (public domain).

uncompensated soldiers. Precedent for such payments stretched back into the Hundred Years War, with one crucial difference: during that conflict, payments made to an individual commander ensured the town's immunity from attack *by that commander*, but not by others. In the language of contract law, there was no privity of contract beyond the local community and the commander to whom the money was paid. Parker notes, however, that as State power grew through the sixteenth and seventeenth centuries, the system of prearranged protection money and the immunity it bought was imposed on *all* troops, and not just the army with which the town had struck the deal. The system was not a dead letter; in the Netherlands, for example, it was enforced by"protection troops." In the deprecatory words of a Spanish officer to his superiors in 1640, the protection troops thwarted Spanish attempts to gain intelligence on the enemy, thereby "giv[ing] rise to many inconveniences for His Majesty's service." One of these "inconveniences" was the protection troops' habit of arresting Spanish soldiers in the area "as spies." According to the Spanish officer, the protection troops also enabled the peasantry "to bring in their crops safely and provide full aid and assistance to the enemy."[36]

Behind both of these contributory factors to constraining warfare bulked the growing power of the State. The old feudal system of using unremunerated soldiers on the assumption they would seize plunder when victory was secured gradually gave way to armies mobilized and supplied by strong centralized governments. Although mercenaries were widely used during the early modern period, the trend was away from "military entrepreneurs"[37] who rented out troops to governments and toward financially well-heeled state authorities able to sustain their own army. Once soldiers could expect regular compensation, a primary goad to plunder and pillage was eliminated—that is, the penury of the unpaid soldier, which confronted him with the necessity to loot "as a survival strategy."[38]

To be sure, other factors likely affected this extraordinary change in the theory and practice of battlefield conduct. Parker discusses three of them: the"deconfessionalization" that gained ground in Western Europe after the Peace of Westphalia (1648) formally ending the Thirty Years War; the war-weariness of Europeans grown disenchanted with the ruinous consequences of the wars of religion; and the dawning realization that reciprocity in ensuring the welfare of enemy prisoners paid dividends when one's own troops were captured.

1. **Deconfessionalization** The end of the Thirty Years War in 1648 stabilized confessional boundaries between Protestants and Catholics. Thereafter, Europeans ceased to war against each other for religious motives. When war broke out between European states, it often led to inter-confessional coalitions that were quite literally unthinkable during the earlier wars of religion. Thus, in 1700 Louis XIV's efforts to dominate Europe were rebuffed by a coalition army backed by Catholic and Protestant leaders, including the Calvinist William of Orange and the Catholic Prince Eugene of Savoy. Parker points out that, while atrocities still took place, they were no longer impelled by religion, and everywhere they were condemned. This process of religious

"deconfessionalization," as Parker terms it, gathered even more momentum during the eighteenth-century Enlightenment.

2. **War-weariness and disenchantment** The Thirty Years War was an unmitigated disaster for Germany. As much as one-third of its population perished during the war. Most of the fatalities were not direct war casualties but victims of the plague and starvation, in comparison with which war-related deaths were relatively few.[39] A Swabian peasant family Bible records the doleful entry, "We live like animals, eating bark and grass. No one could imagine anything like this could happen to us. Many people say that there is no God." Although deaths caused by plague and starvation dwarfed those attributable to combat operations, Europeans at the time understood that the war itself was the ultimate reason for their suffering—and that it was not so much a sign of "God's wrath" as a product of human intention and will. Lurid but truthful accounts of extreme violence circulated throughout Europe. Civilian deaths in individual battles were not in the single digits but in the scores. Tilly's troops killed forty-six civilian inhabitants of the mining town of Zellerfeld in 1625. More than eighty noncombatants died when Calw was taken in 1634, and even more perished in the fire that swept through the town. Soldiers demanded money from civilians and when they refused they were liable to being killed, a fate that befell a woman, the widow of a man murdered by soldiers, who had failed to meet their demands.[40] Such incidents of killing directed against civilians reflected old-fashioned cupidity: if you met the soldiers' extortionate demands for money you effectively purchased the right to quarter; if not, homicidal violence was the not-infrequent sequel.[41]

Other killings, however, were clearly and notoriously fueled by religious hatred. For centuries, members of the clergy had enjoyed legal immunity to attack during wartime on the principle of *Nolite tangere unctos* ("For God wants to have his anointed ones untouched").[42] The Thirty Years War, however, represented a sharp break with this long-standing prohibition on violence against the clergy. In fact, according to historian Otto Ulbricht, Catholic soldiers specifically targeted Protestant ministers for persecution. "Whereas mayors in the cities and villages," Ulbricht writes, "were often taken hostage to enforce the payment of contributions . . . pastors were victims of violence since they personified the root of all trouble to the common soldier. To them, the war was a religious one." Thus, pastors caught fleeing Catholic troops were often beaten, tortured, and left for dead. The minister of Poppenhausen was struck on the head, forced to drink dung water, and lowered into a local river after first having his legs and left arm bound with a rope. He was then repeatedly hauled up to the bridge railing and dropped again into the river. When the pastor was drawn up to the bridge railing, his tormentors beat him.[43] Everywhere in Europe, the reaction to the Thirty Years War after 1650 was one of revulsion. Parker likens this reaction to the "no more war" mood of the international community after the First World War, which, of course, spawned unprecedented attempts in the interwar period to restraint the conduct of war.[44] This generally critical view was fertile soil for the growth of later constraints on warfare.

3. **Reciprocity** For notions of reciprocity to operate effectively as constraints on war, the antagonists in armed conflict must be capable of retaliation. Absent the ability of one side to inflict reprisals on the other, reciprocity would scarcely occur to the superior party as a reason to treat captured enemy soldiers with decency. A case in point is the revolt of the Dutch against Spain in 1566. In the early phases of the revolt, it was standing Spanish policy to hang all war captives. By the fall of 1573, however, the rebels captured one of Alba's most capable officers, the count of Bossu, and communicated to Alba that, unless he stopped the summary execution of Dutch prisoners, they would accord Bossu the same treatment. The two sides negotiated an exchange of prisoners (Bossu and other Spaniards for Dutch rebels in Spanish captivity). This negotiated prisoner exchange appears to have wrought a sea change in Spanish attitudes toward the rebels: thereafter, when they fell into Spanish hands they were treated not as rebels but as soldiers. A parallel sequence of events occurred during the English Civil War, in which the royal army abandoned its policy of hanging all Parliamentary prisoners as traitors when Parliament threatened to hang Royalist prisoners in reprisal.[45]

Restraint based on reciprocity moved forward in land warfare, but the process was soon under way in naval war as well, albeit at a slower pace. As late as the mid–1620s the Dutch sent to the gallows or threw overboard Flemish privateers.[46] They suddenly discontinued the practice, however, when some 1,500 Dutch sailors fell into the hands of the "Dunkirkers."[47]

In none of these developments can it be said that European behavior was guided by an international body of norms. Rather, moderation in how combatants and noncombatants were treated during wartime originated from the policies of governments and their militaries. A sense of decency (particularly regarding civilians), concerns for reciprocity, disenchantment with the pointless and ruinous fallout of religious war, and the compensation of soldiers either through prearranged protection money or through governmental paymasters were all important contributors to limiting warfare. The norms underlying these contributory factors, however, were internal to the societies that adopted them; they were assuredly *not* international principles of right conduct superior to the municipal laws of the day. When soldiers were put on trial for committing war crimes, their actions were considered violations of their army's rules of engagement or of their sovereign's own domestic law. In our own era, conditioned as we are by the Nuremberg war crimes trials, the various ad hoc UN tribunals, and the permanent International Criminal Court, we may tend to think of war crimes as violations of international law. In the history of war crimes, by contrast, the most common forum for enforcing the Law of War has been the courtroom of the nation-state and its battlefield avatar, the military court-martial, and the most common charge against the accused war criminal has been violation of the national or military law of the defendant's own country.

The charges against some of the best known accused war criminals—Sir William Wallace, Harry "Breaker" Morant, the My Lai massacre defendants Lieutenant William Calley and Ernest Medina, and the Andersonville commandant Henry Wirz, to mention only a few—were for murder, and they were based on national military law. (The murder charge against Wallace was for committing atrocities against civilians, but the gravamen of the charges he faced was treason—an offense against English royal law.) The idea that people could be prosecuted for violating international legal principles beyond the rules of their country's domestic or military law was alien to the statecraft of early modernity. Matters were different, however, in the realm of theory.

The theory of the Law of War in early modernity

Francisco de Vitoria

Every so often in world history, great theologians cross disciplinary boundaries and become highly influential political and legal theorists. Confucius, Mencius, Augustine, Thomas Aquinas, the great medieval canonists, Martin Luther, and, in the twentieth century, Reinhold Niebuhr were as widely read for their political and legal insights as for their theological thought. The same may be said of Francisco de Vitoria (1486–1546), a Spanish Dominican friar and professor of theology at Salamanca University. Perhaps due to his eclectic education, Vitoria ranged far beyond theological issues in his intellectual pursuits. He weighed in on the wars between Spain and France, warning that the conflict could be an internecine disaster, and censured the behavior of the political and religious luminaries of his day. In keeping with the legal and philosophical temper of his and earlier ages, Vitoria believed that war was permissible among Christian states so long as it was just. Thus a Christian prince could declare war without violating his legal or religious duty, but only if it was fought for the good of the country rather than the private benefit of the prince. Vitoria went on to draw the rarest of all boundaries in the premodern world: the point beyond which armies could not venture in their actual conduct in battle without violating the law. For Vitoria, it was expressly forbidden to kill women and children, a prohibition that extended not only to Christians but to Turkish civilians as well. Seizing the property of innocent civilians, on the other hand, was allowed, but only if military necessity required it. If an enemy population that has committed a wrong refuses to provide compensation, then the wronged party may obtain restitution by confiscating the possessions of enemy noncombatants, including the property of those who are in no way responsible for the victim's loss. Vitoria cautioned that such action was justified only when there was no other alternative available to secure redress.[48]

In battle, soldiers were allowed to kill all combatants who offered resistance, and were even justified in killing them after the battle was over in accordance with Deuteronomy 20. As with so many of his teachings on the Law of War, Vitoria makes such treatment contingent on proportionality: killing after the conclusion of battle was allowed only when the enemy soldier posed grave security risks. In such circumstances, execution was a form of punishment designed to maintain the peace and security of one's own troops. An army could resort to it only when no other alternative was available and only when death was a punishment commensurate with the offender's offense. On the same theory and with the same reservations, war captives could be put to death. Vitoria also held that armies might take hostage combatants and noncombatants alike as pledges for agreements with the enemy. In the event that the adversary behaved treacherously, however, Vitoria forbade the execution of hostages unless they had been combatants. Under no circumstances in a war between Christian armies could the vanquished be enslaved. This immunity, however, did not run to wars with the Muslims.[49]

So far as plunder was concerned, Vitoria reproduced the basic position of antiquity and medieval Europe—namely, everything could be seized as compensation for losses and expenses sustained by the victor, and all "movables" (personal property) were liable to confiscation even if their value exceeded the amount of the victor's damages.[50] On the issue of conduct during and after siege, Vitoria followed the prevailing views of his age but imposed limitations consistent with his general emphasis on military necessity. On initial examination, his attitude seems severe enough: citing Deuteronomy, he holds that when a defiant city has finally been captured, "all who have borne arms against us" could be slain.[51] Vitoria's view here likely reflects the hard line taken in the Middle Ages against rebels, recalcitrant cities, and oath-breakers. He went still further and affirmed that, even if a city surrendered unconditionally, the victor could execute "the more notorious offenders" if the conditions of capitulation did not mention anything about the population's safety.[52] He softened his position by adding that enemy troops "presumed" to have fought "in good faith," whether or not the conflict was just, should be spared.[53]

Vitoria's thinking on siege warfare was guided by the principle of military necessity. Thus he conceded the legality of plundering a city when it was "necessary for the conduct of the war or as a deterrent to the enemy or as a spur to the courage of the troops."[54] In his teachings on the Law of War, Vitoria approached very close to justifying virtually any action if it served the interests of military necessity. Thus, while he counseled commanders to forbid their soldiers from committing rape during a sack, Vitoria conceded that sacking an enemy town was legal if required by "the necessities of war," and even if rapes were inevitable.[55] In all matters military, necessity ruled with an iron hand.

Lest we dismiss Vitoria as an apologist of cruel necessity, it is important to recall how advanced his conception of the Law of War was for its time. Attacks on women and children were strictly off-limits, a prohibition that extended to Muslims; enslaving the vanquished—so long as they were Christians—was forbidden; enemy soldiers fighting "in good faith" should be given quarter; executing troublesome prisoners was justified, but only if no other means to secure the occupation was at hand; under no circumstances could civilian hostages be executed for breaches of faith. In the context of its era, Vitoria's Law of War was remarkably restrained and humane.

In taking Vitoria's measure as a forerunner of international humanitarian law, moreover, some degree of circumspection is in order. For over a century now, scholars have acclaimed Vitoria a founder of international law. According to James Brown Scott,

Vitoria's great achievement was to replace "Christendom" with a universal community of individual states bound together "regardless of geography, race, or religion."[56] In fact, as Wilhelm Grewe has forcefully argued, this view of Vitoria is mistaken. However much he may have anticipated certain principles of subsequent international humanitarian law, Vitoria remained faithful to the medieval vision of a world society governed by the Church; and while he may have used the language of natural law to describe it, his ideal remained a futuristic world order "embracing sky and world"—as Grewe terms it, "the Church in its totality."[57] The Church in its totality would come into being only after all the earth's peoples had converted to Christianity and their political leaders governed society as Christian rulers. Once this happened, the total Church encompassing all the world would arise. It is not the global community of individual nation-states bound together by the law of nations that imbued Vitoria's thinking; rather, it was the universal Church spread across the earth's continents and peoples which formed the axis of his thought. As Vitoria himself wrote, the final world community he envisioned was the *res publica Christiana* (Christian republic), midwifed by missionary conversion and the abolition of non-Christian cultural forms—the medieval Church grown to a planetary legal community.[58] Before such a universal Christian republic, the "law of the peoples" would have little if any significance.

Balthasar Ayala

One of the more divisive of the early modern experts on the Law of War, as measured by disagreements among later scholars about the originality of his thought, is Balthasar Ayala (1548–84), a Spanish military judge attached to forces under the command of the Prince of Parma in the Netherlands. The reason for the split in opinion concerning Ayala resides in the uneven quality of his views on the Law of War—views that are marked by bland conformity to the prevailing norms of his times and bold departures in the direction of more humane means to wage war.

On the more orthodox side, Ayala set forth a theory of just war that copied the mainstream views of his age. The most important criterion for a just war was the authority of the person or persons who fought it. Only a sovereign had the right to wage war, and when he did so he stood beyond judgment. For Ayala, the formal authority of the belligerent was the indispensable condition of legal legitimacy; if you were a sovereign, your resort to war was inherently and indisputably just. Ayala's refusal to consider the substantive nature of a decision to go to war may have been grounded in his inexorable condemnation of the Dutch revolt against Spain. Because the Dutch rebels were not a sovereign authority, they could not by definition instigate a just war. In Ayala's eyes, no consideration of the rebels' reasons for fighting against the Spanish crown was necessary; the formal criterion of sovereignty was the final determinant of legitimacy, and it was precisely this attribute that the rebels lacked.[59] Having expounded the bedrock foundation of just war, Ayala reverted to a conventional list of "just causes" to wage war: "for defense of ourselves or our allies," "to regain from the enemy something which he is forcibly and unjustly detaining," refusal to permit a neighboring country to cross one's territory in peace, and suppression of heresy or rebellion.[60] Ayala hastened to add, however, that these "just causes" had to do more with morality than with law.[61]

To meet the criteria of just war, then, it was only required that the war be initiated and conducted by a sovereign authority. The traditional catalogue of just causes Ayala cited merely defined the moral scope of warmaking but in fact had no bearing upon its legality. There flows from Ayala's principles here the thesis that a conflict fought between sovereign powers was a just war on both sides. Theodor Meron thoughtfully points out that, in Ayala's theory, "the whole moral foundation of the just war doctrine lost its credibility," insofar as "both belligerents could claim, as they usually did, that their war was just."[62] Much later Abraham Lincoln would disagree, holding that both sides "in great contests" *might be* wrong but one side *must be* wrong—a proposition that, Meron says, overlooks the Renaissance awareness that war could be just on both sides.[63]

Since neither belligerent could be charged with fighting an unjust war, a certain degree of restraint had to be used in dealing with the enemy, both during and after the conflict. In other words, each antagonist in the struggle had to treat the other as a legitimate enemy (*justus hostis*). This in turn meant that legal duties were imposed on such practices as reprisals, postliminium, and the obligatory power of agreements (fidelity to treaties). Regarding reprisals, Ayala held that the ancient Greek practice of androlepsy—detaining as many as three citizens of a city when one of its citizens has killed a Greek abroad, and holding them as hostages until the offender was delivered—had withered over time, eventually yielding to reprisals. Ayala forbade reprisals against innocent persons but conceded that seizing their property was allowable if done under the sovereign's authority and for a just cause. Christians were forbidden to enslave Christian prisoners of war, a rule that did not apply in wars against the Muslims. Promises exchanged between two Christian sovereigns had to be honored. Thus, both sides were obliged to honor treaties and truces, and promises of ransom had to be fulfilled by both the ransomer and the prisoner being ransomed.[64]

So far as noncombatants were concerned, Ayala's thinking displays the experience-hardened sobriety of his practical work as a military judge. He wrote that the Law of War prohibited attacks on "clergy, monks, converts, foreigners, merchants, and country folk" during wartime. In the same breath, he affirmed that these protections had in the actual conduct of war been frequently disregarded, a statement of empirical fact highlighting the chronic gap between law "in the books" and law "in practice."[65] Ayala's realism notwithstanding, he did appear to support the legal category of a protected person, in which he also classified ambassadors.[66]

Ayala regarded the immunity of ambassadors as existing independently of any agreements between the belligerents; rather, he appears to have believed it was rooted in customary law (i.e., the "Law of Nations"). He also seems to have viewed the immunity as non-derogable; it could not be set aside even if the enemy had harmed the prince's own envoys. Presumably, the same customary rule was applicable to the treatment of the clergy, farmers, tradesmen, and the like, whether or not their immunity was routinely violated in practice.[67]

Whatever restraint Ayala urged in dealing with noncombatants and envoys he abandoned in his counsels on suppressing heresy and rebellion. Wrapping his arguments in Yahweh's commands from Deuteronomy 20, Ayala argued that "wars of fire and blood" should be unleashed against heretics, in which quarter would be denied, the property of all heretics confiscated, and any survivors enslaved. For Ayala, rebellion was tantamount to heresy, and should be met with the same degree of ruthlessness.[68] In his discussion of rebellion, he fell back on the chief criterion distinguishing a just from an unjust war: the sovereign authority of the belligerent. Because rebels lacked such authority (and were in fact locked in a death struggle with it), they had no right whatsoever to wage war; by presuming to instigate hostilities, rebels forfeited the protections of a legitimate combatant under the Law of War. According to Ayala, rebels

ought not to be classed as enemies, the two being distinct, and so it is more correct to term the armed contention with rebel subjects execution of legal process, or prosecution, not war . . . For the same reason the laws of war, and of captivity, and of postliminy, which apply to enemies, do not apply to rebels.[69]

Given that Ayala served as a military judge in the service of the Spanish king during an armed insurgency by the Dutch, we can hardly boggle at his severity toward rebels. Moreover, there exists an uncanny affinity between his extreme prescription, on the one hand, and the responses of armies to revolts by subject peoples, ranging, as we have seen, from Spain's summary execution of prisoners captured in the Azores in 1582 to the savage repression of insurgency in our own time.

Ayala was unfazed by the possible justice of rebels' demands. So adamant and uncompromising was his position that he confronted rebels with a catch–22: he conceded that a tyrant might be legitimately resisted, but denied that a sovereign authority could ever be considered a tyrant. No amount of persecution, abuse, torture, or mistreatment— no matter how extreme—could ever justify rebellion against the sovereign. Instead, beleaguered subjects had to bear up under an oppressive ruler, hopeful, perhaps, that the Pope would intervene to depose him, but otherwise forbidden to resist his rule.[70]

Over the years, assessments of Ayala's contributions to the growth and maturation of the Law of War have been mixed. Some commentators have attributed Ayala's reputation as the founder of international law to his good fortune in being recognized by Hugo Grotius. In a 1921 essay W. S. M. Knight wrote that, but for Grotius's reference to him as a formative early thinker, Ayala and his work "would have been almost entirely unknown at the present day."[71] Along the same lines, the English scholar John Westlake, who translated Ayala's *De iure et Officiis Bellicis et Disciplina Militari* into English in 1912, discounted the originality of Ayala's thought, insofar as it "ran on the lines which had been handed down for many ages and demanded no rearrangement of the traditional signposts by which its course was marked out."[72] Ayala fares better in the appraisals of other scholars like Wilhelm Grewe. For Grewe, Ayala's claim to recognition as an innovator rather than an imitator rests on his groundbreaking effort to formulate a Law of War uncoupled from moral theology. The result was a novelty in scholarly reflection on the Law of War: Ayala based his just war theory not on sacred motives and divine purposes as previous thinkers had, but on one central criterion—the sovereign status of those who waged it. "Seen in this light," Grewe concludes, "Ayala appears as an author who, on the one hand, prepared the ground for a doctrine of the laws of war which attributed equal rights to both belligerents in the quality of *'justi hostes'* (just enemies)."

> He thus paved the way to a limitation, moderation and humanizing of war. On the other hand, in respect of the exceptional case of a war against rebels, Ayala delivered a justification for discrimination as was prevalent in medieval "holy wars" against heretics and infidels.[73]

Grewe's evaluation of Ayala's significance underscores its essential ambivalence in the history of humanitarian law. The limitations Ayala advises in wars between "just enemies" should be discarded when the enemy is a rebel or a heretic. In the duality of his thinking about the constraints on warfare, Ayala was very much a man of his age. The basic template underlying his views would be applied as guidelines to military conduct during the Thirty Years War, as well as serve as a touchstone for Europeans in the colonial wars of ensuing centuries. The removal of native peoples from the category of "just enemies" generated some of the worst atrocities to stain the blood-drenched annals of warfare in global history.

Francisco Suárez

The Spanish Jesuit Francisco Suárez (1548–1617) shared with Thomas Aquinas and Vitoria the rare achievement of contributing in equal measure to theological speculation and the theory of the Law of War, treating the latter subject in *De Triplici Virtute Theologica, Fide, Spe, et Charitate* (*The Three Theological Virtues, Faith, Hope, and Charity*), a treatise published posthumously in 1621.[74] In alignment with the leading theorists on the Law of War from Roman times until the modern age, Suárez was mainly concerned in his writings on war to delineate the preconditions for a just war. His perspective on just war carries with it a whiff of modernity lacking from Ayala's blunt, authority-based conception. For Suárez, a king could wage a just war only to right a wrong that has been done. Even in these circumstances, however, the king was justified only if no other alternative to war was available. Suárez imposed on the kings of his day the legal and moral duty to exhaust all non-violent remedies before turning to war as a last resort.[75] He went still further and demanded that wars could be initiated solely when the wrong to be addressed through war was sufficiently serious. "It would be contrary to reason," he wrote, "to inflict very grave harm because of a slight injustice."[76] The problem, of course, was that each of the belligerents in a war would naturally claim that theirs was a legitimate cause—a problem that Ayala waved aside with his affirmation that *all* wars waged by sovereign authority were just. With this proposition (shared also by Gentili), Suárez was in fundamental disagreement. In his view, the mere assertion of a just cause was not enough to justify recourse to war; to hold otherwise would be "entirely absurd," insofar as "two mutually conflicting rights cannot both be just." With this argument he rejected the proposition that wars were just if fought by sovereign authorities, countering that, at most, only one of the belligerents could be acting from a legitimate cause. Anticipating Abraham Lincoln's wry assertion that in every conflict one side must be, and both sides may be, in the wrong, Suárez affirmed the possibility that both belligerents were fighting an unjust war.[77]

Suárez's skepticism about the inherent rightness of sovereign authority was likely influenced by his deep affiliation with the Roman Catholic Church. The Pope himself asked Suárez to write defenses of Church doctrine, a request he fulfilled with the publication of *De Virtute et Statu Religionis* (1608–09) and *Defensio Fidei Catholicae* (1613). In these apologetic works, Suárez rejected the English theory of the divine right of kings, which held that the English king enjoyed absolute sovereignty as God's hand-chosen representative on earth. The Stuart king James I, a champion of the divine right theory, responded by burning Suárez's *Defensio* on the steps of St. Paul's Cathedral. Suárez may have had an ax to grind against the exorbitant claims of European monarchs, but his insistence on the limited authority of kings may be equally considered as part of an ancient chorus of voices at odds with royal absolutism in global history.

Our discussion thus far has dwelled on Suárez's account of the conditions making for a just war (*jus ad bellum*). What can we say about his approach to the rules governing the actual conduct of the war after it has started (*jus in bello*)? Like many scholars of his time, Suárez held that the "innocent" should be exempted from violent attack. By the "innocent" he meant one of three classes of persons protected under three sources of law: (1) women, children, and those unable to fight (such as the elderly or the disabled), protected under natural law; (2) ambassadors, who enjoyed immunity under the *jus gentium*; and (3) clergymen and members of religious orders, protected under Roman canon law. Everyone else in the adversary's state was viewed as an enemy subject to being killed.[78] Suárez agreed with Vitoria that after victory was secured the "guilty," whom Vitoria called "the more notorious offenders," could be executed as a means of deterrence to onlookers. Suárez wrote: "[T]he slaying of a great multitude would be thus permissible only when there was most urgent cause, nevertheless, even such slaughter may sometimes be allowed, in order to terrify the rest."[79] While the captured soldiers of a sovereign waging an unjust war could be put to death (because unprotected by the *jus gentium*), Suárez maintained that mercenaries should be spared, insofar as they were ignorant of the justice involved on either side. The key point here, as Theodor Meron aptly describes it, is that no one associated with fighting an unjust war "had standing in law."[80]

Throughout our study, we have often seen the snug interaction of just war theory with the norms considered binding on combatants during and after battle. The example of Suárez presents yet another example of this impressive *pas de deux*. He opined that if the war was unjust then all participation in killing by the unjust side was strictly forbidden. If, however, it was just, then killing did not offend the Law of War—a principle of action so elastic that it extended to clerics, who had traditionally been prohibited from fighting by the canon law. For Suárez, a clergyman might "kill" or "mutilate" an opponent while fighting on behalf of a just cause, but only "in absolutely necessary defence of his life."[81]

As it has throughout history and from one culture to another, a just cause tended to consecrate all means in support of it.

Suárez is best known for his vision of a vast world legal community comprising all the human race. Other scholars before Suárez (like Vitoria) had envisioned an international legal community, centered on the Christian nations of Europe. What set Suárez apart from these earlier conceptions was the breadth of his ideal, one that encompassed not only Christian Europe but all of the world, as well as his belief that all nations were bound together by natural law rather than the "law of nations" (*jus gentium*). In arguing for an international legal community that included but surpassed the European cultural sphere, Suárez looked not to the *jus gentium* but to natural law as the adhesive holding the nations together. He distinguished between two kinds of the law of nations: the *jus gentium inter se*, or international law, and the *jus gentium intra se*, or the domestic (municipal) laws that individual states incidentally shared.[82] We should remember that Suárez was writing in the heady years of the Age of Exploration, as Iberian Europe was colonizing central and South America. Neither of the two meanings of *jus gentium* was relevant to the numerous Amerindian peoples of this new continent, peoples entirely outside Christian Europe both geographically and culturally. Instead, Suárez invoked natural law as the tie that unified all peoples everywhere, expressed in "the natural command of mutual love," an idea that is traceable directly back to Cicero.[83] Where natural law and a cultural understanding based on common denominators like religion, language, and legal principles—that is, *jus gentium intra se*—bound Christian Europe together, only natural law in the form of mutual love could serve as a bonding agent beyond Europe's borders. This universal law of love, for Suárez, should govern the relations of Europeans with aboriginal peoples in Asia, Africa, and the New World.[84]

Wilhelm Grewe poses an important question regarding Suárez's ideal of a world legal community: does it "represent the origin of the modern conception of a universal international legal community of mankind?"[85] Grewe provides a cogent answer to his own question: the premises of Suárez and other Spanish scholars were firmly moored to medieval Christianity, the Church, and the Spanish monarchy as it expanded into the New World. None of the Spanish scholars, not even Suárez, could avoid treating Christian Europe and its colonies as two distinct legal realms.[86] While rejecting the forced conversion of native peoples advocated by Major and Sepulveda, Suárez nonetheless held that the Church had a "special right" to evangelize them. This right originated in Christ's absolute (because divinely given) right to preach the gospel to all human beings, a right that devolved from Christ at his death to his apostles and finally to the Church. In his treatise *De Fide* (*On Faith*), Suárez drew from the Church's right of evangelism the conclusion that it enjoyed the prerogative to defend its evangelists and to punish those who stymied their preaching through physical attack.[87] Ironically, he grounded his theory in the *jus gentium*, which recognized the right of a republic to defend the innocent from assault by the powerful. It goes without saying that Suárez would not have approved of non-Christians invading European territory to preach their religions to a Christian audience, nor countenanced the right of Aztec armies to punish any Europeans who offered violent resistance to heathen proselytizing. This lack of reciprocity in Suárez's thought, despite the extraordinary humanity and broadmindedness characteristic of so many of his ideals, illustrates the degree to which he moved in orbit around a traditional Christian worldview, able sometimes to strike out in bold new directions but ultimately, and fatefully, controlled by the gravitational field of late medieval Christianity.

Suárez's conception of a world legal community of nations unified by the *jus gentium* and natural law may not in the final analysis mark the emergence of a modern international legal community. This aside, the tensions within his ecclesiocentric ideals are object lessons on how *jus gentium* and natural law, when deployed as categories in the Law of War, may lead to both good and ill effects. Long before Suárez, the Stoics had championed the essential unity of human beings as a repudiation of the view that some men were slaves by their very nature (a position advocated by Aristotle). Following Thomas Aquinas, Paulus Vladimiri had defended the right of non-Christian Lithuanians to their own state against canonists like Hostiensis, who rejected the political autonomy of non-Christian peoples. During the Age of Exploration, natural law was advanced by scholars such as Suárez and Bartolomé de Las Casas in defense of native peoples against Spanish imperial domination. Similar criticisms based on natural law were voiced as the trans-Atlantic slave trade sprang into baleful life. Rarely, however, did the ideal of the universal brotherhood of the human race advance beyond the theorist's salon to influence policy in the conduct of war.[88]

Not only did natural law theory fail to reduce the violence of political and military practice in the epochs of world history mentioned above, but it achieved quite the opposite; natural law theories of commerce and property reinforced the casual brutality with which war was waged against non-European peoples. The tendency to identify natural law with commerce and property rights arose in the early modern period and continued well into the nineteenth century. Vitoria had invoked the "right to commerce" (*jus commercialis*) as a prime justification for Spanish subjugation of the West Indies. In the centuries after Vitoria, this ideology became a rationale for dispossessing native peoples of their land and, not infrequently, of their cultures and their lives. The patron saint of classical liberalism, John Locke, set forth in the *Second Treatise of Government* (1690) his cultivation theory of property, whereby people could acquire property rights, confirmed by natural law, by mingling their labor with objects in the world. Through farming and improvement of land, a farmer acquired property rights. The corollary of Locke's theory of ownership was that those who did not cultivate their land had no rights to possess it and could be driven off it. If they refused to leave, they could be forcibly ejected or killed. Locke explicitly applied his theory to native peoples in the Americas.[89] His ideas became a powerful ideological justification for westward expansion in North America during the eighteenth and nineteenth centuries, where they were cited as "Rules of natural Justice." When native Americans, unmoved by the logic of Locke's ideas, fought back against their own dispossession, the result was mutual atrocities and genocide committed on native peoples by settler militias.[90] (See Chapter 2 for an in-depth discussion of settler genocide of North American native peoples.) By the mid-nineteenth century, a similar ideology was adduced to legitimize Great Britain's military efforts to open China to trade. Not to be outdone by their ex-colonial masters, the United States sent its own expedition to force Japan to accept diplomatic and commercial relations with the West. The ideology of cultivation and commerce was merely one variation on an enduring theme of colonial domination.[91]

Whether it was conceived as the right to preach the Gospel, to convert the heathen, to cultivate land, or to engage in commerce, the alleged right was couched in the form of an unassailable, and irresistible, natural law. The aim of those citing it was to establish a universal community based on the dominion of the West over indigenous peoples. The role of natural law as an ideological prop to justify the expropriation, mistreatment, and genocide of non-Europeans reveals its essential ambiguity. It also shows how distant Suárez's ideal of a world community of nations is from the modern "family of nations" based on the consent and cooperation of each state.

Alberico Gentili

Outside of Hugo Grotius, who, as we will see, adopted many key tenets from him, none of the sixteenth-century thinkers covered in this chapter sound as contemporary to the modern ear as the Italian jurist Alberico Gentili (1552–1608). Born in San Ginesio and educated at the University of Perugia, Gentili was banished from Italy because of his Protestantism in 1579, landing on his feet two years later as a professor of law at Oxford University. In 1587 he was appointed to the Oxford chair of Regius Professor of Civil Law. From then until his death in 1608 in London, Gentili produced three volumes of his celebrated treatise, *De Jure Belli* (*The Law of War*). (Volume 1 was published in 1588, volumes 2 and 3 followed a year after.)[92] Although neither Hugo Grotius nor Gentili was Spanish, both men were deeply influenced by the Spanish Law of War scholars of the late sixteenth century.[93] Hence, it is unsurprising that many of the same themes arise in Grotius and Gentili that we have previously encountered in the work of Vitoria, Ayala, and Suárez. In Gentili appear the same age-old concerns with just war and its definitions, the permissibility of reprisals, ransom, and hostage-taking, proper conduct during and after a siege, the treatment of war captives and noncombatants, and the nature of war with non-believers. Gentili's originality was to follow these well-worn paths for a distance before bolting from them in search of new perspectives. He was like a skilled mariner wintering in safe and familiar harbors who suddenly hoists sail and scuds into the vast watery unknown. An example is his approach to the subject of the just war, a topic on which discourse about the limits of warfare had centered for at least two millennia. He begins by recognizing a conventional justification for waging war, i.e., to defend oneself or others. Gentili takes up Augustine's argument that your enemy's unjust cause transforms your conflict with him into a just war, thereby legitimating all means employed to secure the just cause. At first, Gentili seems to agree that only one side can have a just cause, insofar as only one of the parties to the conflict can truly be right. He then does a quick about-face and rejects Augustine's view, protesting against it with reference to a stunning, clear-eyed realism. He points out that no matter who is ultimately right or wrong, each of the parties will invariably claim justice for itself. Ayala had made a similar claim, but the two scholars' conceptions are quite different.

Ayala's assertion that both sovereigns involved in a war were just was based on his deference to sovereign authority, an authority which could not be questioned once the decision to go to war had been made. By contrast, Gentili's recognition that both sides will declare themselves virtuous and their enemy wicked was not driven by a statist bias. While a single justice might nestle somewhere within the intricate tangles of the conflict, it could rarely be discerned by self-interested human beings able to convince themselves of the overriding goodness of their own actions. Gentili is refreshingly forthright: because we can seldom know for sure who is right and who wrong, we should assume that both parties are fighting for a just cause. It follows that neither side can be accused of injustice.[94]

We ought not overlook the critical implications of Gentili's position. With his argument that the justice of a war was ultimately irresolvable, he decoupled just war theory from the rules governing conduct during and after combat. Because the antagonists would insist on their own rectitude, the restraints prescribed by the Law of War should be observed by each side on the assumption that the enemy *might* be fighting a just war. The coinherence of *jus in bello* and *jus ad bellum*, a relationship dating back at least to the fetial system of ancient Rome, was finally broken — if not in practice, then in the thinking of one of early modernity's most prescient commentators, whose views would shape the Law of War in the ensuing centuries. In divorcing the notion of military constraints from just war theory, Gentili did not rely on theology or metaphysics but on a refreshing pragmatism based on empirical observation of how the world of men actually operated. Men saw things from their own perspective, and none of us looking through the glass darkly could ever know for certain who was acting justly. Not only does our sinful humanity blur our ethical perceptions, but our experience in the world teaches us that the unjust cause frequently prevails. The observable triumph of evil, for Gentili, bolstered his contention that the conduct of war, both in the midst of battle and afterwards, should be regulated by humanitarian considerations.[95]

Although Gentili presumed that both armies were fighting for a just cause, he did insist that a sovereign had to declare war before initiating it. His principle here was based on fairness: the enemy had to be put on notice before armed conflict could begin. In defending this requirement, Gentili cited the customary practice of the Greeks, the Romans, and the Germans, as well as the maxims of Roman canon law. All of these sources attached great importance to the declaration as a *sine qua non* of just war. Even in his analysis of an archaic norm of battle, Gentili's purposes were qualitatively different from his sources. The declaration of war was not simply a ritual or formality for Gentili; rather, it served as a cooling-off period that afforded to the antagonists a window for peaceful settlement of their differences. He stipulated that after declaration an interval of thirty-three days had to elapse before commencement of war. Grewe regards Gentili's prescription as the first "war moratorium" in world history, a device intended to create one last chance to avert war.[96] According to Gentili, governments that neglected the compulsory declaration were per definition waging an immoral and unjust war. Their failure to make the necessary declaration moved them into the category of pirates and brigands—that is, persons removed from the protections of the Law of War.[97]

Gentili's discussion of *jus in bello* is impressive and capacious (Grewe describes it as "a comprehensive Law of War").[98] In general, he emphasized the sanctity of promises, whether in the form of treaties with the enemy, which had to be concluded in good faith, or a pledge by a prisoner of war released on the condition that he would not fight his captor again. In both instances, however, Gentili's treatment is subtle, and his general doctrine of promise-keeping subject to qualification. Treaties had to be concluded with an opponent in good faith but a government's representatives could lie during negotiations, much as a physician was allowed to deceive his patient. A prisoner released on the condition that he abstain from waging war on his former captor might avoid his promise if it violated the Law of War or his duties to his country. Gentili's discussion of *jus in bello* here and elsewhere is marked by continuity with—and innovative departure from—the received wisdom of medieval and early modern scholarship. Where the fourteenth-century Italian jurist Baldus de Ubaldis (1327–1400) had taught that poison could be deployed against the enemy, Gentili firmly rejected it as a criminal act, just as he did Baldus's assertion that the enemy could be murdered anywhere he was found. Gentili considered Judith's murder of the Assyrian general Holofernes as recounted in the Book of Judith a monstrous act of murder. Similarly, he defended the integrity of promises against other commentators like the Spanish bishop and jurist Diego de Corvarruvias, the French political philosopher Jean Bodin, and the French jurist François Hotman, all of who maintained that such promises were not obligatory.[99]

Gentili devotes a considerable portion of his treatise to the proper treatment of prisoners of war. He emphasized that, while they were prisoners, war captives were not convicts—meaning that their lives had to be preserved, whether or not they had fought tenaciously against their captors and regardless of the inconvenience involved in guarding them. He allowed some exceptions to this rule, as in cases of prisoners who had acted wrongfully. Examples were cruel or treacherous actions by prisoners or acts illegal under the Law of War, such as desertion or going over to the enemy.[100] Gentili further held that agreements to exchange prisoners be negotiated in good faith; any leader captured in battle should be treated with decency and his detention had to be temporary, even though his captor feared victory would be short-lived were he to be released. Gentili forbade enslavement of prisoners in wars between Christians but allowed it if the enemy was non-Christian. His view, which was consonant with many of the medieval and early modern commentators (including Thomas Aquinas), was based on Turkish practice: because the Turks enslaved their Christian prisoners, Christians were justified in returning the favor. Hostages could be taken to ensure that the enemy behaved in good faith; when he failed to do so, they could be executed. Gentili took the edge off this harsh tenet by adding that the wise commander would reject the execution of innocent hostages.[101]

Gentili was among the first modern scholars of the Law of War to regard the denial of quarter as a serious crime. It was a criminal act to execute soldiers "who surrendered themselves and threw down their arms on the ground . . ." He conceded that siege warfare might call for a different rule, but added that "if there is no such cause, it surely seems right to accept it; otherwise we have a war of extermination." In general, he held that "when victory was assured the slaying of the enemy should cease."[102] Gentili's conception of the relationship between captor and captive was strikingly legalistic: he wrote that an implied contract came into existence when a warrior surrendered to his enemy, which Gentili portrayed as "a bargain with the enemy for his life." When this occurred, the "rights of humanity and the laws of war ... order the sparing of those who surrender."[103] On this point, Gentili adopted the rationale from his position on the duty to preserve prisoners of war; the risk posed by surrendering warriors did not justify their killing. Gentili praised commanders who "did not slay their captives, no matter how great danger threatened them." He contrasted such enlightened belligerents with King Henry V's slaughter of French troops after his victory at Agincourt in 1415.[104]

Civilians enjoyed a special status of immunity in Gentili's thought. He referred to them not as "civilians" but as "innocents," a term also employed by other scholars in the Spanish tradition (such as Vitoria and Suárez). By "innocents" Gentili meant women, children, the elderly, clergymen, peasants, and merchants. For Gentili, a trio of authoritative laws shielded innocents from harm: divine law, natural law, and positive (man-made) law. As in so many of his meditations on the Law of War, Gentili acknowledged exceptions to this class of protected persons, such as instances in which women fought as combatants.[105] The same immunity applied to clergymen and monks: so long as they avoided fighting, they were off-limits to armed attack. Similarly, unarmed peasants, merchants, and travelers were protected persons. Reprisal could not be inflicted on travelers or resident aliens; property found in enemy territory that did not belong to the enemy was not subject to confiscation by the victor.[106]

We previously saw that Vitoria counseled commanders not only to prohibit rape while sacking a city, but to take steps to prevent its outbreak. However, Vitoria dithered on the permissibility of rape when the "necessities of war" rendered its occurrence inevitable.[107] Gentili, in stark contrast to Vitoria, espoused an absolute line on the issue of rape: it was forbidden under all circumstances.

> [T]o violate the honour of women will always be held to be unjust. For although it is not contrary to nature to despoil one whom it is honourable to kill, and although where the law of slavery obtains it is permitted according to the laws of war to sell the enemy together with his wives and children, yet it is not lawful for any captive to be visited with insult. ... I make no allowance for retaliation ...

Gentili continued:

> At some time the enemy [who allows raping women] ... will surely render an account to ... the rest of the world, if there is no magistrate here to check and punish the injustice of the victor. He will render an account to those sovereigns who wish to observe honourable causes for war and to maintain the common law of nations and of nature.[108]

In this extraordinary passage, Gentili suggests that commanders who condone rape should be prosecuted as war criminals for violating the Law of War.

In view of his concerns to protect noncombatants from attack, it may be surprising that Gentili was receptive to hostage-taking and the principle of collective responsibility. He addressed the two facets of collective responsibility in his treatises on the Law of War: the liability of a state for the wrongs of its citizens and of individual citizens for the wrongs committed by their state. Concerning the former, Gentili held that the wrongs of private citizens could not be imputed to their community when the wrongful acts did not result "by act of the state." However, he added that the community did incur responsibility if it neglected to punish or make amends for the wrongful act, a principle of blame based on the community's authority to "hold its citizens to their duty." If the state breached its duty to prevent wrongful acts by its own citizens, then"the state, which knows because it has been warned, and which ought to prevent the misdeeds of its citizens, and through its jurisdiction can prevent them, will be at fault and guilty of a crime if it does not do so." He laid down a rule of imputation that, as Theodor Meron notes, is a foreshadowing of modern international humanitarian law:"A state is liable for such offences of its citizens as are not for the moment but are successive and continuous; but even then, only if it knew of them and could have prevented them."[109]

The principle of collective responsibility continued in force after hostilities had ended. When treaties or other agreements between warring states were signed, hostages were sometimes exchanged as a guarantee of fidelity to the agreement. If one of the parties breached its word, the other was justified in killing the hostages in its custody. Under the medieval Law of War the execution of hostages in such circumstances was permitted, and Gentili upheld this customary practice as a method of inducing each side to abide by the agreement. His approach here, much like his conception of the relationship between a captor and the captive who has surrendered to him, was conceived as a legalism: the right to punish hostages was implied in the agreement between the two states. While acknowledging the existence of an individual's right to life, Gentili's cost-benefit analysis weighed it against the public good derived from promise-keeping: "Every great principle has some element of injustice, in which the loss of the individual is compensated by the public advantage."[110] At first blush, Gentili's acceptance of hostage execution strikes the modern sensibility as harsh. I would suggest, however, that his interpretation of this archaic practice (if not the result at which he arrives) is quite modern—particularly his acknowledgment of an individual right to life, as well as his prudential balancing of competing societal interests.

Executing hostages is a form of reprisal, a practice generally approved during the Middle Ages and early modern period.[111] Gentili's approach to reprisals was consistent with his attitude toward killing hostages: while counseling armies to exhibit mercy "towards those who really suffer [retaliation] for the faults of others," his overall acceptance of collective responsibility led him to endorse reprisals. For Gentili, the greater principle (collective responsibility) assuredly contained the lesser (reprisals). He wrote:

[I]t avails not in this case to say that those who were punished were not the ones who acted cruelly, and that hence they ought not to have been treated cruelly; for the enemy make up one body, just as an army is a single body [T]he individuals are responsible, even if a fault was committed by all in common.[112]

The Dutch jurist Hugo Grotius, who otherwise follows Gentili on many points, will later take issue with his predecessor's acceptance of retaliation against innocent prisoners, dismissing the idea of collective responsibility as "a sort of fiction."[113]

On the issue of piracy, moreover, the normally humane Gentili took a tough stance evocative of ancient Roman policy. Like the Romans, he regarded piracy as a form of unjust warfare, meaning that pirates stood outside the *jus gentium* and hence could not lay claim to its protections. "Piracy is a violation of the law of nations and is against the foundations of human society," he wrote. "Pirates therefore should be attacked by everybody, because violating that law is injuring everybody and therefore every individual can feel injured."[114] Gentili, like Grotius after him, was influenced by Cicero's well-known dictum that "pirates are the enemies of the human race."[115] Their noxious actions were so extreme that they fell not only outside the Law of War but beyond the pale of law itself, that is, they were "outlaws" (*hors-de-la-loi*) who could be attacked by anyone chancing to encounter them, and both their property and their lives could be violently taken from them. For so moderate a thinker, Gentili's approach to piracy was militant and unbending; all means for their repression, including treachery, were fair game. As he did on the question of reprisals, Grotius differs with Gentili on the treatment of pirates, contending that their possession of a common humanity required adherence to any treaties signed with them.[116]

Hugo Grotius

In his magnum opus *De jure Belli ac Pacis* (*The Rights of War and Peace*, 1625), the Dutch jurist Hugo Grotius set forth his main reason for undertaking so massive a treatise on the Law of War. His motives were neither academic nor philosophically ethereal; rather, they flowed out of the real-world conflicts of nations in collision, the fallout of which too often were desolated cities and shattered human lives. Grotius wished to refute the deeply entrenched belief that relations between countries were by necessity amoral and lawless. The most effective vehicle for his refutation would be a systematic exposition on the Law of War, showing once and for all that the affairs of human beings were governed not by brute force but by law. Grotius wrote:

Such a work [as this] is all the more necessary because in our own day, as in former times, there is no lack of men who view this branch of law with contempt as having no reality outside of an empty name. On the lips of men quite generally is the saying of Euphemus, which Thucydides quotes, that in the case of a king or imperial city nothing is unjust which is expedient. Of like implication is the statement that for those whom fortune favours might makes right, and that the administration of a state cannot be carried on without injustice.

Furthermore, the controversies which arise between peoples or kings generally have Mars as their arbiter. That war is irreconcilable with all law is a view held not alone by the ignorant populace; expressions are often let slip by well-informed and thoughtful men which lend countenance to such a view.[117]

Grotius was challenging a common attitude of amoral expediency in warfare, one with roots stretching back into the free-wheeling massacres of the Peloponnesian War as described by Thucydides, memorably expressed in Cicero's rueful aphorism, "In times of war, the law falls silent." An idealist as well as a world-class jurist, Grotius found the macabre excesses and cruelties of war disturbing, particularly when their apologists chalked them up to the natural order of human beings in conflict. For Grotius no degree of alleged necessity legitimated the killing of women, children, or war captives. His aim was to demonstrate the utter indefensibility of such crimes, once and for all, in the light of a systematic theory based on the law of nature.

An extraordinary project such as the one Grotius entertained required an equally extraordinary mind, and by dint of experience, education, and native intellect, Grotius was equal to the demand. He was born in 1583 in Delft, Holland, and grew into a child prodigy who took up his studies in law at the University of Leyden at the age of eleven. He finished his degree of Doctor of Laws at the University of Orleans, France, when he was fifteen. In The Hague he practiced law for a time but abandoned his legal practice for a political career. He became embroiled in the fierce political conflicts of his day, leading to his arrest and consignment to prison for life in 1618. Smuggled out of jail in a chest of books, he made his escape to Antwerp and then to Paris, where he found protection under King Louis XIII until 1631. It was during his decade in France that Grotius wrote perhaps the most important work in the history of scholarship on the Law of War, *De jure Belli ac Pacis* (*The Rights of War and Peace*).[118]

The cornerstone of his study was natural law, a concept that for Grotius was inseparable from human nature. Rational creatures like human beings were in their essence non-violent. When people behaved violently, they violated their true natures as rational beings, and thus acted unnaturally (as primitive and non-Christian peoples did). Violent acts, in other words, placed the actor at variance with "the natural social sense which exists among all men"[119]—a phrase virtually indistinguishable from Cicero's analysis of human nature in his classic dialogue *Laws*.[120] Further, again like Cicero, Grotius held that humans were endowed with "right reason," a faculty that enabled them to understand the occasions when they acted at cross-purposes with their pacific nature. Despite his insistence that human nature is peaceful, Grotius did not categorically forbid war; there were circumstances that justified resort to it. Application of our right reason to an individual instance of war would reveal whether it was just or unjust, and hence whether the war was consistent with the law of nature. Grotius believed that military force could be used to enforce a legitimate right or to impose judgment on offenders whose strength precluded a judicial proceeding, as he wrote in his Prolegomena.[121]

Following Cicero and Augustine, both of who approved of war to punish wrongs or in self-defense,[122] he identified the three causes of just war: self-defense, recovery of property, and punishment.[123] Once a just cause existed to wage war, only one of the two opponents could be justified.[124] In upholding this tenet, Grotius parted company with Ayala and Gentili and generally hewed to the traditional just war theory of the Middle Ages. This notwithstanding, he acknowledged the fallibility of human perception, particularly when obscured by the fog of war. Although the justice of a cause was clear in some cases, in others it was not readily apparent who possessed moral superiority. The flawed understanding of human beings meant that the actual participants in an armed conflict might not discern the injustice of their root cause. Thus, while he believed in right reason and natural law, Grotius grasped that the application of natural law to real-world conflicts was often a very tricky matter.[125] One conclusion he drew from the above premise was that the assignment of criminal responsibility for fighting an unjust war had to be done carefully. There was a difference, he wrote, between "those who were responsible for a war and those who followed the leadership of others [i.e., the 'innocent population']." The latter group could be absolved of wrongdoing. Even the instigators of unjust wars might be pardoned if such conflicts "may deceive persons who are by no means wicked."[126]

Twelve years before the publication of Grotius's treatise, Francisco Suárez had tried to distinguish the *jus gentium* (law of nations) from natural law. Natural law "prescribes the performance of good acts, but also prohibits all evil acts in such a way as to be tolerant of none; whereas the *jus gentium* may permit some evils ..." Much like the civil law of individual states, the *jus gentium* was a "human system of law" that sometimes "tolerated" forms of injurious action prohibited by natural law.[127] In Grotius's analogous distinction between the *jus gentium* and natural law, the influence of Suárez is unmistakable. However, there are important differences in the two scholars' interpretations of this contrast. For Grotius, the *jus gentium* was not strictly separate from the natural law; rather, its status was ambiguous. The *jus gentium*, while conceptually distinct from natural law, might coincide with it. On the other hand, the *jus gentium* might constitute nothing more than human positive law (which Grotius called "voluntary law").[128] During a war, for example, one or both sides might employ modes and degrees of force repugnant to natural law, as revealed by the deep moral reason of human beings. Nonetheless, Grotius held that such a manner of waging war might be permitted if the ancient customs of the law of nations did not forbid it. Scholars have taken Grotius to task for trying to have it both ways, i.e., asserting the existence of a transcendent principle of right while condoning violations of that right so long as they were customary and of long duration.[129] Although he may be vulnerable to the charge of floundering in the weeds of the elusive distinction between voluntary and natural law, Grotius clearly condemned actions revealed by right reason to be violations of the law of nature that did not command the consent and practice of nations.[130]

Despite the complications involved in disentangling natural law from the *jus gentium*, Grotius clung to natural law as the vital foundation of his jurisprudence. Without it, there could be no universal legal order in which specific norms of conduct could find anchorage. Curiously, warfare played an essential role in cementing legality into his international community of nations. Grotius thought of warmaking as governed by the same logic that controlled the use of police power within a state. Thus, both in warfare between states and within civil polities, armed force could be deployed to punish wrongdoing. We should "lean towards peace,"[131] because this is our nature as rational beings; but, when crimes have been committed by "armed criminals," the ruler is authorized to punish the wrongdoer, if need be by capital punishment. The right of sovereigns to punish criminals at home through law enforcement and abroad by means of war was based on the "right of Rhadamanthus"—a principle of proportionality under natural law, according to which people should suffer the same amount of pain as they have caused.[132]

The same question that we raised in connection with Suárez presents itself here: did Grotius advocate participation by sovereign states in international organizations to enforce the norms of natural law? Some portions of his work open themselves to this interpretation. He called, for example, on Christian princes to meet in conference for the purpose of averting the outbreak of war. The balance of opinion among scholars, however, inclines toward answering the question above in the negative. Edwards regards Grotius's proposal as arising from his belief in the natural law duty of Christian princes to preserve law and order. At no point did Grotius propose the creation of a formal international organization to resolve conflict or punish violations of natural law. Indeed, Grotius himself ruled out the idea of such world government on the grounds of administrative impossibility, writing: "For as a ship may attain such a size that it cannot be steered, so also the number of inhabitants and the distance between places may be so great as not to tolerate a single government."[133] Grotius's jurisprudence, as Edwards aptly describes it, unfolded "within the framework of a natural human order" divorced from considerations of "international organization."[134]

Whether the war was fought for self-defense, to recover property, or to punish wrongdoers, Grotius required that a public declaration be made setting forth the reasons for war, "in order that the whole human race as it were might judge of the justness of it." Grotius equivocated on the need for a declaration of war under the law of nature, but he averred that it was still "honourable and praiseworthy to make it" even if natural law did not require it. His reason was that a formal declaration might open the door to peaceful resolution of the underlying conflict, thus giving effect to his injunction that war be a last resort after all other means of reconciling the parties had been exhausted.[135] All of this notwithstanding, there is no trace in his work of a "crime against peace" chargeable against a country for waging illegal war such as we will later encounter at the Nuremberg trials.[136]

For a man acclaimed as the "father of international law," some of Grotius's tenets may make the contemporary student of international humanitarian law wince. In Book 3 of *The Rights of War and Peace*, he affirmed that history was a chronicle of "the destruction of whole cities, of the leveling of walls to the ground, the devastation of fields, and conflagrations. [They were] permissible also against those who have surrendered." Grotius did not approve of indiscriminate killing of enemy soldiers, either during combat or siege; he urged that "those [persons] who yield upon condition that their lives be spared" should not be slain.[137] However, he agreed with Gentili that the law of nations permitted the execution of hostages taken as a pledge of adherence to an agreement.[138]

While admitting that such killing contravened the natural law (unless the hostage deserved punishment), Grotius in effect legitimated hostage execution on the ground of the historical longevity of the practice as well as the consent of the nations to it.[139] Here we encounter the contradiction in Grotius's thought between the *jus gentium* and natural law: the former often allowed what the latter forbade. This antinomy surfaces again in Grotius's conception of the right of a belligerent to attack and kill enemy soldiers, subjects, and persons lingering within enemy territory after war has been declared. According to the law of nations, these three groups were all fair game. Where the law of nations prohibited harm to them on neutral soil, Grotius indicates that the prohibition had nothing to do with a protected status; rather, their immunity was based on the rights of non-interference enjoyed by a sovereign government on its own territory.[140]

Grotius's concessions to realism are of a different order than, say, those of Machiavelli, on whom normative constraints scarcely registered. By contrast, Grotius is deeply concerned about the gap between the law of nations and natural law—so concerned, in fact, that closing the fissure between customary practice and natural justice was the driving force behind his treatise. In the third book, Grotius urged respect for so-called *temperementa*, or rules of moderation, which natural law demanded in situations of military conflict sanctioned by the law of nations. These rules of moderation were not obligatory in such a war; instead, Grotius held them out as aspirational rules, in the light of which the "volitional" (positive) law could be reinterpreted and amended. For Grotius, man-made law (a term that included both domestic, or "municipal," law and the *jus gentium*) was an improving body of principles subject to refinement and growth over time. The *jus gentium* had come into existence by the mutual consent of the nations, and by the mutual consent of the nations it could be altered or even abolished. Grotius looked to the political elites of his day—to "those who hold sway over the Christian world"—to bring man-made law into alignment with his rules of moderation.[141]

What were these rules? They included the exemption of children and women from military attack, as well as other persons shielded under the law of nature, if not the law of nations: priests, scholars, farmers, merchants, hostages (if innocent of a crime), and prisoners who have surrendered without conditions. Natural law required further that quarter be given, both in battle and after siege.[142] The law of nations allowed each of these groups to be killed as part of the absolute dominion of the victor over the vanquished. Natural law, however, counseled that they be treated humanely. Grotius's rules of moderation also applied to enemy property, which could be destroyed so long as it induced the enemy to seek a peaceful end to the conflict. The victor could seize enemy property in payment of a debt owed or to defray the expenses of the war, but not as a form of punishment.[143]

In addition to his title as the founder of international law, Grotius has been hailed by at least one influential scholar as the first advocate of humanitarian intervention.[144] Grotius's statement in support of intervention appears in Chapter XV of Book II, where he considers whether war was justified against an abusive ruler in order to protect his subjects from gross mistreatment. On the one hand, Grotius denied to the subjects themselves any right of armed resistance against their sovereign, on the grounds that such resistance would endanger the social stability essential for civil society.[145] On the other hand, Grotius recognized as one of his first principles that violations of natural law and the law of nations, much like serious crimes within a society, had to be punished. Grotius located the right to punish serious crimes in both the natural law and the *jus gentium*. Because a ruler's subjects were generally precluded from violent resistance, the grave crimes he committed would go unpunished unless a third party outside the offending country could intervene. Grotius's thesis here suggests not only a right to intervene on behalf of sorely oppressed peoples, but something resembling an actual *duty* to intervene—an obligation demanded by natural law. In such circumstances, only other sovereigns—figures who "are themselves subject to no one"—were entitled to stop egregious wrongdoing by another ruler. Grotius wrote:

> The fact must also be recognized that kings, and those who possess rights equal to those of kings, have the right of demanding punishments not only on account of injuries committed against themselves or their subjects, but also on account of injuries which do not directly affect them but excessively violate the law of nature or of nations in regard to any persons whatsoever. For liberty to serve the interests of human society through punishments, which originally . . . rested with individuals, now after the organization of states and courts of law is in the hands of the highest authorities, not, properly speaking, in so far as they rule over others but in so far as they are themselves subject to no one. For subjection has taken their right away from others.[146]

We should not overlook the nature of Grotius's double meaning in the passage above: he advocates not only armed intervention to stop flagrant violations of law, but actual punishment of the ruler responsible for them. Legal scholar Theodor Meron discerns in Grotius's words "an important precursor to the recognition in modern international law of universal jurisdiction over . . . genocide, war crimes and crimes against humanity."[147] Grotius's statement may be interpreted, moreover, as an early modern version of a principle with a venerable pedigree in world civilization: the notion that the king and his law are subordinate to a higher principle of right.

Conclusion

The early modern period was rife with paradoxes at every level, as befits an era burdened with the mortgage of a ruthless Roman military practice and a Christian religious tradition anxious to reconcile that practice with its own ethics. The higher incidence of siege warfare, rebellion, and religious schism guaranteed that the dogs of war would run without a leash and that cruelty, death, and devastation would be plentiful. Yet, an age of such extremity was also a turning point in the history of the Law of War. The transition from mercenary and uncompensated armies to a professional military trained, maintained, and paid by strong centralized states removed much of the incentive to plunder cities when they fell after a siege. These same professional armies gradually developed codes of military justice that enforced discipline among their troops, holding accountable not only individual soldiers for their crimes but also commanders for failing to punish their subordinates' offenses. Prohibitions of rape, desecration of religious objects and churches, murder, harming farmers or their property, robbery, and plunder all filtered into these early military codes of conduct, as did the right of quarter. By the mid–1600s, other factors accelerated the process toward greater restraint, including deconfessionalization, widespread disenchantment with the ruinous effects of religious war, and a growing awareness of the benefits of reciprocity.

Early modernity was notable, too, for the exquisite quality of legal and philosophical reflection on the Law of War as typified by the writings of Vitoria, Ayala, Suárez, Gentili, and Grotius. However, the influence of their thought was negligible in tempering the fury of armed conflict. Rather, the major source of real-world restraint during and after battle was the national law of powerful governments, whether expressed in statutes, orders for armies in the field, or military penal codes. This would continue to be the case until the rise of international criminal jurisdiction in the aftermath of the Second World War, and even today international prosecution of war crimes functions chiefly as a backstop to national enforcement, serving as a gap-filler when the nation-state is either unable or unwilling to prosecute.[148]

The period from 1500 to 1700, notwithstanding the ferocity of warfare during this era, was a soil rich in the nutrients required for the modern Law of War to strike root. The constitutional revolutions of the seventeenth and eighteenth century in Great Britain, the USA, and France undoubtedly affected Western thinking about the possibility of bringing an activity often characterized by lawless, unbounded violence under formal legal constraint. At the same time, changes in society, politics, military organization, and technology would aggravate the destructiveness of warfare, boosting it to unprecedented heights. These factors, along with the immense suffering they will cause, would push modern people in the next two centuries to re-evaluate Cicero's weary maxim that "the laws fall silent during wartime."

CHAPTER 5
COLONIALISM AND THE LAW OF WAR:
IRELAND AND THE AMERICAS

In 1925 an alliance of the Druze and Syrian nationalists revolted against the French mandate installed in Syria with the backing of the League of Nations. Although the only military force defending Syria's capital of Damascus was French, France nonetheless retaliated with a bombing campaign in October 1925, leading to the deaths of several hundred civilians. In the pages of *The American Journal of International Law* two scholars addressed the legality of French actions: University of Chicago Professor Quincy Wright and Elbridge Colby, identified in his article only as "Captain, United States Army." The ultimate conclusion the two men reached was more or less the same: neither believed the French bombing violated international law. The reasoning through which they arrived at their conclusion, however, was significantly different. For Wright the question of legality was determined by the fact that Syria was not a state but a protectorate; hence, the conflict was not international and France was justified in suppressing an insurgency within its own territory. For Colby France's actions were unobjectionable because they targeted non-Europeans beyond the pale of international legal protection.

Colby's logic was straightforward if blunt. All "uncivilized peoples" were combatants because all of them fought in one degree or another in a military conflict. This rendered them subject to attack as soldiers. Because only "civilized nations" like the Europeans and their cognates distinguished between combatants and noncombatants, the immunities of civilians under the Law of War protected only their populations and did not extend to "savages." To add grace to his declaration of open season on non-Western peoples, Colby quoted Vitoria's approval of exterminating "all who can bear arms" among the heathen while cautioning that "in a war with Christians this would not be allowable."[1]

Colby's was not a deviationist position. Many of his contemporaries shared his thinking about the exceptional harshness with which wars against non-Western peoples should be fought. "In small wars against uncivilized nations," wrote Colonel J. F. C. Fuller in *The Reformation of War*, "the form of warfare to be adopted must tone with the shade of culture existing in the land, by which I mean that, against peoples possessing a low civilization, war must be more brutal in type."[2] American judges voiced similar views, denying the status of legal belligerence to Indian tribes like the Bannocks and holding they should be treated like "gangs of pirates, bandits and marauders," none of whom enjoyed protections under the Law of War.[3] Even the most authoritative source on international law in Britain at the time, the multi-volume *Law of Nations*, declared that international law applied only to conflicts "between civilized nations, where both parties understand them and are prepared to carry them out." In wars between Western powers and "uncivilized States and tribes" international law was inapplicable, and it was left wholly to the "discretion" of the commanding officer how to conduct operations.[4]

The thesis that non-Western peoples not only stood beyond the Law of War but were deserving of especially harsh treatment is deeply rooted in world history. In this chapter we review Western colonization of North and South America vis-à-vis the assumption that native peoples were pagan barbarians to whom few if any restraints were due under the traditional norms of warfare.

Central America

Hispaniola

Elbridge Colby's view that the Law of War did not extend to cultural and religious outsiders would have been warmly received by apologists of Spanish rule in the Americas. Juan Ginés de Sepúlveda, a rhetorician from Córdoba and staunch defender of Iberian colonialism, argued along Aristotelian lines that the Indians of the New World were

Figure 17 A 1598 portrayal of Ovando's massacre of Queen Anacaona and her people on Hispaniola. © Wikimedia Commons (public domain).

"natural slaves" inferior to the Spanish. His *Democrates segundo; o, de las justas causas de la guerra contra los indios* ("Concerning the Just Cause of the War Against the Indians", 1544) invoked biblical scripture and Greco-Roman history in support of waging just war against native peoples. Both the Romans and the Hebrews had fought just wars to exterminate their enemies; in fact, he affirmed, such wars against inferior peoples were demanded by the "law of nature." Furthermore, any effort by the Indians to resist Spanish domination should be met with a just war to compel their obedience.

From the onset of the Spanish Conquest such attitudes were pervasive in the thinking and practice of Spanish colonizers.[5] Genocide scholar Ben Kiernan argues that they and other Europeans considered New World peoples ripe for plunder, domination, and murder because they were believed incapable of cultivating the land.[6] This belief based on the Indians' supposed ignorance of farming would be echoed later on by the English philosopher John Locke, widely viewed as an intellectual patriarch of—perhaps paradoxically—revolution, liberal democracy, and colonialism. One must be cautious, however, in tracing vectors of causality between an idea and an alleged effect. The human mind is devious, fully capable of weaving bogus justifications for actions that were instead driven by other, less visible motives. While the ideological makeup of Spanish behavior in the Americas can be debated, the colonizers' real-world activities are clear enough. In Hispaniola the Spanish governor Nicolás de Ovando crushed a revolt of the Taino Indians, provoked to rebellion when the chief of the Taino's fourth kingdom, Higüey, was killed by a Spanish fighting dog set on him by the Spaniards. Bartolomé de Las Casas, a Dominican friar and later defender of the Indians who participated as a young man in Ovando's campaigns against Higüey, wrote that the governor confined several hundred Taino Indians in the chief's house, where he had them all knifed to death. Ovando then ordered the corpses be taken to a nearby public plaza for counting. He capped off this massacre by hanging the queen of Higüey. His bloodlust merely whetted by the carnage, Ovando attacked the fifth kingdom of Hispaniola, Xaraguá, hanging its queen, burning hundreds of nobles alive, and killing "a countless number of the common people." Survivors were sold into slavery.[7] (Las Casas himself was given a slave by Ovando.)

The worst of the violence on Hispaniola, however, erupted after Queen Isabella I's death in 1504. Las Casas, who lived on the island until 1506, was an eyewitness to the bloodbath. In his own words, "there were countless people that I saw burned alive or cut to pieces or tortured ... They also made slaves of many Indians." Las Casas said the Spanish "treat[ed the Indians] like some stupid animals. Natives perished, working in the gold mines as well as in agricultural work. The colonists exploited them without compassion or consideration, and the iron discipline, oppression and fatigue killed native workers."[8]

The Pre-Columbian population on Hispaniola has been estimated at 1 million people. Eighteen years after Columbus's arrival, that number had plummeted to 46,000. One tribe, the Arawaks, was completely exterminated from the island by the mid–1600s. Still more breathtaking declines occurred on the nearby islands of Jamaica, Cuba, and Puerto Rico, where the population between 1509 and 1552 was reduced from 600,000–1,000,000 to 200. These shocking decimations of native peoples can be documented everywhere the Spanish (and later the Portuguese) ventured: in Mexico, Venezuela, Brazil, Peru, Florida, and

"We shall take you and your wives and your children, and shall make slaves of them ... and shall do all the harm and damage that we can, as to cassals who not obey ... and we protest that the deaths and losses which shall accrue from this are your fault."

The Spanish Requierimiento

Panama. Witnesses in Panama accused the Spanish of dismembering Indians "like butchers cutting up beef and mutton for market" and of subjecting them to nearly unimaginable acts of cruelty: "Some Indians they burned alive; they cut off the hands, noses, tongues, and other members of some; they threw others to the dogs; they cut off the breasts of women." Dominican friars protested to Charles V that Indian children were torn to pieces by dogs before their mothers' eyes; others were grabbed by the legs "and hurled ... against the rocks, or flung ... into the jungle so that they would be certain to die there."[9]

As always when talking about human-caused mass death on this scale, issues of motive and intent cloud the discussion. Las Casas himself denied that the Spanish willed the destruction of Indian life; rather, "they kill them because they want to be rich and get a lot of gold, which is their sole aim, through the labor and the sweat of the tortured and the unfortunate."[10] Kiernan's analysis of the issue is spot-on. He rightly points out the legal distinction between motive and intent. Acquisition of wealth may have been the motive of the Spaniards' actions, yet their intent was quite clearly to destroy Indian life as a means to effect their purpose. In their profligate cruelty toward native peoples, Spanish perpetrators were as guilty of murder—or, in this case, genocide *avant la lettre*—as a poisoner who kills a rich uncle in order to accelerate the process of his own inheritance.[11]

Mexico

Christian apologists of empire had for centuries quoted the scriptures to justify military aggression. Augustine legitimated the violence of the Roman legions with reference to Joshua's war on the people of Ai. Within this just war tradition, the sanctity of a righteous cause opened wide the floodgates to all manner of doing harm to the enemy so long as God approved it. In 1513 the Spanish crown embraced the just war tradition as a vehicle for removing the native peoples of the New World from their ancestral lands. The device, called the *Requerimiento* (Requirement), was a proclamation inspired by Joshua's destruction of the inhabitants of Jericho for refusing to forfeit their land to the Israelites. Since the Pope had delivered the New World into the hands of the Spanish monarchy,[12] Christian rulers were justified in proselytizing the Indians and demanding their allegiance to the Spanish crown, if need be at the point of a sword. In 1512 the policy was reduced to writing and thereafter read aloud by the conquistadores to the New World's puzzled inhabitants. Often read in Spanish to non-Spanish speakers, the text threatened its listeners with armed attack for non-compliance, admonishing them that "the deaths and losses which shall accrue from this are your fault, and not that of their highnesses, or ours, or of these soldiers who came with us."[13] This, along with the enserfment of native peoples on their own lands that were divided among Spanish settlers (called *repartimiento*, introduced by Spain in 1514), led to a mass die-off of 90 percent of Hispaniola's Indian population over a span of twenty-two years. While many of the deaths may be attributed to epidemic disease caused by Old World microbes, a large and undetermined number were due to direct military assault and the atrocious conditions of slave labor.

In Mexico the Stygian ferryman of Mesoamerican peoples was Hernando Cortes, a notary and conquistador in Hispaniola who received assignments of gold mines on Cuba after its conquest in 1511. His appetite for gold unsated, Cortes arrived on the Mexican coast with a force of several hundred soldiers in April 1519. Arriving in the province of Tlaxcala, a tributary of the Aztec empire that had recently revolted against the Mexica, Cortes delivered the *requerimiento* through his interpreters. When the Tlacalans failed to accept his demands to surrender, conflict broke out between them and the conquistadors, in the course of which Cortes put more than ten villages to the torch. When women and children ran unarmed from their homes, the Spaniards attacked them. (Cortes later said that as they emerged naked running into the streets he "began to

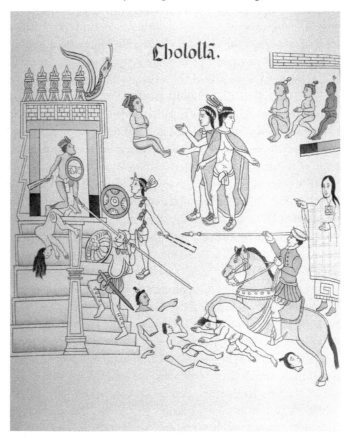

Figure 18 Attack of Cortes on the Quetzalcoatl temple in Cholula, October 1519. Painting by Diego Munoz Camargo, 1585. © Heritage Pics / Alamy Stock Photo.

do them some harm.")[14] Thereafter Cortes sent emissaries to the Tlacalan chiefs, threatening that if they did not agree to peace on Cortes's terms he and his men would kill all of them and destroy their country. The credible threat of genocide persuaded the Tlacalans to sue for peace. Five thousand of the Tlacalan warriors then joined the Spanish for their impending campaign against the Mexica in Tenochtitlan.

Were these acts war crimes? Not in the view of the Spanish. Operating within a just war tradition that legitimized every action so long as it served a righteous cause, most of the conquistadors believed their treatment of native peoples not only unobjectionable but normative. This was as true in conflicts with heretics, Muslims, Jews, and reprobate European armies as it was in wars against New World Indians. The seeming insouciance with which the Spaniards carried out shocking acts of depraved violence against native men, women, and children supports the view that they did not consider any act too wicked or extreme if perpetrated against an enemy fighting on the side of an unjust cause. Such was the case in Cortes's destruction of Cholula, an atrocity that, despite its abhorrent character, scarcely registered on the Christian consciences of the Spaniards. In a pattern that would repeat itself in other massacres of native peoples, the conquistadors summoned the leading citizens of Cholula, a rival city of Tlaxcala, to attend a supposedly peaceful meeting. Arriving unarmed, the Cholulans soon found themselves the prisoners of the Spaniards, who blocked the entrances of the building and adjoining courtyards where the meeting had convened. At a prearranged signal—the discharge of a musket— the Spaniards fell on their captives, killing three thousand of them within a couple hours. Reinforced by 5,000 Tlaxcalans, the conquistadors set to pillaging the city of Cholula. Cortes ordered that houses and towers allegedly used as launching pads for attacks on the Spaniards be set on fire. Priests holed up in one of these towers refused to surrender and were simply burned alive. Cortes and his men spent two days razing Cholula to the ground. Estimates of the death toll range between 6,000 and 20,000 Cholulans.[15]

The great prize still dangled before Cortes's eyes—the island capital of the Aztec empire, Tenochtitlan. His defeat of the Tlaxcalans and Cholulans had impressed the Aztec ruler, Moctezuma II, who welcomed Cortes and his men into the capital. Cortes repaid this hospitality by taking Moctezuma hostage on the assumption the Aztecs would refrain from attacking him if he held their king as surety. During Cortes's absence from Tenochtitlan, his deputy commander, Pedro de Alvarado, provoked a rebellion when he murdered numerous Mexica nobles during a ceremonial feast. Driven from Tenochtitlan, the Spaniards regrouped under Cortes and launched an all-out attack on the capital. The campaign began with the conquest of the lakeside outpost Ixtapalapa, a town of 10,000 Indians. According to Cortes's own account, more than 6,000 native men, women, and children were killed in the assault. The Spaniards moved on to the pièce de résistance, Tenochtitlan, which they took after a 93-day siege. Aztec warriors fought desperately against the invaders, yet the contest revealed the tragic mismatch between Indian and early modern European approaches to warfare. The natives, equipped with stone-age military technology, sought to capture the conquistadors alive for disposal as victims of ritual torture and sacrifice. The Europeans by contrast wielded iron-age swords and cannon, both on foot and on horseback, with the aim of killing as many Indians as

"The whole land is in turmoil and the Indians greatly aroused because of the cruelties and maltreatment of the Christians. . . . Their hands are bloody with slaying and cleaving asunder children, hanging Indians, cutting off hands, and roasting to death certain Indian men and women . . . all because they will not tell them where to find gold."

Fray Tomás de Toro, bishop of Cartagena, in a letter to
the Spanish king, dated May 31, 1535

they could. The Spaniards penetrated the city's final defenses on August 21, 1521, capturing the surviving warriors and forcing them to build a Spanish city on the ruins of Tenochtitlan. They also enslaved the younger and more attractive women and young boys, branding them on their cheek with an insignia of the conquerors. Cortes ordered Aztec priests be torn to pieces by dogs. Two years later he hanged Moctezuma's successor, Cuauhtemoc, together with his allies from neighboring cities.[16] With his death the line of Mexica rulers ended.

In 1523, the year the Spaniards executed Cuauhtemoc, Cortes sent his deputy Pedro de Alvarado with an army of 420 men southward on a voyage of conquest. Alvarado's bloody trek through Guatemala and Columbia proved both exterminatory and extortionate for the Indians he encountered. Despite his friendly reception by the king and a retinue of nobles, Alvarado demanded that the ruler of the Quiché Indians, a Mayan tribe inhabiting the midwestern highlands of Guatemala, give him a rumored supply of gold. The Quiché were a sophisticated people: they lived in large population centers reposing on a complex social system, speaking a language later written down in the Popol Vuh. None of this mattered to Alvarado. When Quiché leaders failed to satisfy his demand, he had them tortured and burned alive. (The Mayan chronicles making this accusation find corroboration in Alvarado's own report to Cortes about his expedition.) Alvarado then embarked on a killing spree through Guatemala, demanding gold and tribute from Mayan Indians and exterminating entire tribes when their rulers failed to deliver. The rapacity and violence of the Spanish provoked resistance from native peoples, which the conquistadors then adduced as a reason to wage further wars of annihilation on their populations. In spring 1524 Alvarado and his army nearly obliterated the Tz'utujil Maya and the Mayan denizens of Acat. After the Spanish had conquered Honduras, he arrived there to attack and exterminate the Maya of Choloma and Tzutzampan, among other cities.[17]

The Spanish harvest of death in central America beggars the imagination. In Guatemala, Las Casas affirmed that the conquistadors—particularly Alvarado and his men—had killed between 4 and 5 million Mayan Indians, a substantial percentage of the pre-contact population (the exact number of which is unknown). Kiernan observes that this figure, if true, "would almost constitute a holocaust in scale as well as in name."[18] In Mexico the term "holocaust" seems even more descriptively fitting insofar as the

Figure 19 Q'umarkaj, capital of the *Quiché* Mayan kingdom. Pedro de Alvarado (1485–1541), Spanish conquistador and governor of Guatemala, burnt Q'umarkaj to the ground and executed its rulers in 1524. © Wikimedia Commons (public domain).

estimated pre-contact population of 12 million was reduced by 85 percent *within three years* (1519–21). I emphasize the time span here because as measured by lethality it far surpasses the Nazi Holocaust, which in its genocidal phase ground on for four years and yielded fewer victims. Assuredly many of these deaths were due to military casualties and smallpox, yet the deliberate mass murder of Indian prisoners and civilians contributed substantially though to an undetermined extent to the reduction. Furthermore, the documented intentionality of mass death is beyond dispute (although its degree is still debated). The Spaniards did not just unwittingly infect Indians with deadly disease or kill them as enemy soldiers in battle; as in the case of the Nazi Holocaust and other genocides, cruelty and sadism were often on prominent display in European treatment of New World peoples. The conquistadors trained large, powerful dogs to attack and eviscerate the Indians; the dogs' reward was to devour the victim's corpse.[19] Las Casas describes the extreme, cavalierly inflicted violence of the Spaniards:

> It was a general rule among Spaniards to be cruel; not just cruel, but extraordinarily cruel so that harsh and bitter treatment would prevent Indians from daring to think of themselves as human beings ... So they would cut an Indian's hands and leave them dangling by a shred of skin and they would send them on saying "Go now, spread the news to your chiefs." They would test their swords and their manly strength on captured Indians and place bets on the slicing off of heads or the cutting of bodies in half with one blow.[20]

How can we account for such superfluous violence—violence far beyond the amount needed to secure any legitimate military objective, a violence unnecessary for biological survival and evincing an attitude of malicious contempt for Indian lives along with a zestful eagerness to cause them profound physical and emotional suffering? We will ponder this question in far greater depth in Chapter 10. Here we pause long enough to note the racist quality of the New World holocaust. Spanish racism was not the primary rationale behind these and other cruelties; the conquerors' motive appears to have been the acquisition of land, slaves, and gold. (Here the conquistadors decisively part company with Nazi genocidaires, who by the end of the Second World War desired the destruction of Jewish life for its own sake.) Rather, racism was a critical enabler of the entire process of dispossessing the Indians of their homes, their freedoms, and their lives.

Devaluing Native Americans as bearers of basic rights under the Law of War facilitated their destruction, much as it did the persecution of ethno-racial groups on the European continent itself. The Age of Discovery overlapped with a growing intolerance in Iberia of Muslims and Jews. Forced into conversion, the newly Christianized Jews and Muslims of Spain nonetheless became objects of mistrust. Converted Jews (called *conversos*) were suspected of practicing their forbidden Jewish religion in secret. Underlying these suspicions was a belief that Jewish ancestry rendered a person hostile toward decent, God-fearing Christians. By the 1500s a religio-political doctrine had emerged called the "purity of blood" (*limpieza de sangre*), inspiring in different parts of Spain the enactment of blood purity laws. These laws barred *conversos* from admission to religious orders and civil institutions. To obtain access, an applicant had to produce a certificate of pure blood vouching for his family history. Only full-blooded Christians—that is, individuals with proven Christian ancestry— were permitted to become conquistadors or missionaries in the New World. The late historian George Frederickson held that the Spanish purity of blood dogma was a milestone in Western attitudes about race, marking a fateful transition from religious to racial discrimination.[21] In the *limpieza de sangre* we can glimpse the larval impressions of modern Western racism.

Spanish colonization coincided with the rise of a racially defined animus toward religious outsiders. It was a logical and predictable extrapolation from such thinking to the conclusion that the Indians were inferior to the Spanish. As early as 1510 Scottish theologian John Mair, whose writings were widely circulated in Spain and adduced in debates to deny indigenous people's rights, invoked Aristotle's notion of "natural slavery" to insist the Indians of the Caribbean "live like beasts" and thus could be enslaved. Such ideas surfaced, as we have seen, in the thought of influential colonial figures like the arch defender of Indian enslavement, Juan Ginés de Sepúlveda. In 1550 he debated Las Casas at Valladolid on whether the Spanish were justified in enslaving the Indians and seizing their land. Against Las Casas's plea for humane treatment of native peoples, Sepúlveda countered that the difference between Indians and Spaniards was nearly commensurate with the difference between monkeys and men. He likened their intellectual capacity to "bees and spiders," a likely cross-reference to Aristotle's *Physics* (in which Aristotle distinguished between the behavior of the lower animals patterned by instinct and that of human beings governed by reason).[22] Indians were not fully human, although he conceded that over time "our laws and customs" might allow them to "become more human."[23]

Sepúlveda's racist bigotry permeated the thinking of the conquistadors. Bernardino de Minaya, a missionary and defender of native rights, wrote that they regarded the Indians as "not true men, but a third species of animal between man and monkey created by God for the better service of man." He noted that some Spaniards considered them "talking animals" and "beasts in human form."[24] In view of such attitudes, it is hardly surprising that the Spaniards would remove Native Americans from the immunities of their Law of War. The ferocity of the Spanish conquest of Mexico is borne out by the frightful statistics: by 1600 only one million Indians remained. Some 10 to 11 million indigenous people had perished in eighty years of Spanish rule.

North America

British colonization of Ireland as imperial prototype

Much as Spanish experience in the New World was shaped by events on Iberian soil (the persecution of Jews and Muslims), so, too, were English colonial ideas forged in smithies close to home. Over the last seventy odd years, historians have rightly insisted on the interconnections between English colonization of Ireland and English colonization of North America, two incursions that happened at roughly the same time.[25] In many ways, English experience in Ireland became a touchstone and archetype for their wars in the New World. Colonial settlers in New England would draw upon the campaigns to subjugate Ireland as precedents for dealing with native peoples.

Scholars differ over England's decision to reconquer Ireland in the sixteenth century. According to an older school of interpretation represented by Irish historian Nicholas Canny, the crown claimed title to Ireland's land by virtue of the right of conquest acquired by the Normans in the twelfth and thirteenth centuries. Thus Sir John Davies, the attorney-general of Ireland and a leading legal apologist of British imperial rule, could declare in 1612 that "our Kings of *England* haue borne the Title of *Soueraign Lords* [of Ireland] for the space of foure hundred and odde yeares."[26] For English officials, the success of the Irish in resuming occupation of the land in the ensuing centuries had no bearing on the primacy of English title because Irish occupancy never matured into legal title. Hence, in their eyes the Irish were trespassers on land that belonged by right to the descendants of the Normans—the English. In virtually every case save one,[27] English colonization of Ireland was predicated on this strained legalistic argument.

More recent scholars of early modern Ireland like David Edwards have stressed the Tudors' desire to extend their reformist ambitions into Ireland by resuming Norman claims to it. While high-minded reform may have fired the ideals of English officials in Dublin, the situation outside that city and in the provinces was considerably different. Benignly conceived programs of assimilation were enforced at this level with a Procrustean severity represented by the introduction of martial law in 1556. Growing resistance to English rule in the provinces elicited savage repression by English commissioners, men who interpreted any act of opposition as rebellion and thus liable to deadly countermeasures. For Edwards, martial law wielded by these commissioners became a warrant for despotic violence against the Irish population, hastening in the final years of Elizabeth's reign "the completion of the Tudor reconquest of Ireland."[28]

The colonizers were not professional soldiers but members of the English gentry and the second or third sons of English aristocrats excluded from inheritance by primogeniture. At first the English goal was to acquire control of Ireland while simultaneously Anglicizing the Irish. This could be accomplished by ousting the Gaelic (Scottish) chieftains, abolishing their law, and converting the native Irish into English subjects. Queen Elizabeth herself regarded the Scots in northeast Ulster as trespassers the English could eject without ceremony from their lands; the Irish, on the other hand, should in her words be "well used" as subjects of the crown.[29] As we will see, this patronizing yet non-genocidal attitude toward the Irish would shift dramatically by the mid–1570s.

The governor of Ulster, Walter Devereux, the first Earl of Essex, mounted an ambitious expedition to control and colonize parts of northeast Ulster. Acting under Elizabeth's

Figure 20 Walter Devereux (1539–1576), first Earl of Essex, dated 1572. © Wikimedia Commons (public domain).

orders to crush the Gaelic chieftains, Essex sought to "extirpate" the "Rebell" Scots "within two years" by garrisoning 1,300 English soldiers in Ulster towns. (There were only 2,000 English soldiers in Ireland at this time, a number that underscores the extraordinary commitment of the English to suppressing the Ulster Scots.) Sensing opposition from the head of the most powerful Gaelic family in Ulster, Turlough Luineach O'Neill, Essex resolved "to expulse him, and utterlie to roote him out, or else so to weaken him by taking awaie his dependanntes (for which the warre muste be the instrument)."[30] Essex made good his threat when his soldiers butchered 200 hundred Clandeboye[31] O'Neills in Belfast at a Christmas celebration in 1574. Essex's soldiers did not discriminate between men, women, and children but put all of them to the sword. Essex sent the sept (family) leader Brian MacPhelim O'Neill, his wife, and his brother to Dublin, where they were executed. Queen Elizabeth approved Essex's action, lauding him as a man who would "oppose yourself and your forces to them whom reason and duty cannot bridle." The murders of the O'Neill clan were the prelude to his troops' extermination in July 1575 of the 600 Scots inhabiting Rathlin Island off the coast of County Antrim in northern Ireland.[32]

Nicholas Canny believes that the Essex expedition was a turning point in the crown's attitude toward the Irish. He discerns in Elizabeth's commendation to Essex a proof of this change. In it she referred to the native peoples of Ireland as a "rude and barbarous nation" that Essex knew how to "allure and bring ... to civility," whether by peaceful measures or extreme violence. In Canny's view the Queen's choice of words reflects the new position of the English government that the Irish along with the Scots were now subject to mass killing without trial.[33] Both the acts of the killers and the language they used afterwards to describe them tend to support Canny's thesis. By the late 1570s English proprietors in the midlands talked explicitly of "the utter extirpation of all the landless septs in the plantation" who had rebelled against the English. Waves of mass killing surged across the midlands as some of the leading Irish families were mown down. In 1577 Sir Henry Sydney, the Lord Deputy of Ireland, could declare "the total extirpacion of" Rory Og O'More's wife, relatives, and followers. In 1578 Sydney boasted that "I waste hym and Kyll of his men daylie." The reaper's scythe fell heavily in March of that year when Francis Cosby, Sydney's lieutenant, invited the O'More clans to a peace parley at his castle on the hill of Mullaghmast. The supposed parley was a trap: as soon as the clans were assembled, Cosby's forces encircled them, killing every one of the clan members. Sydney's report to the Queen stated the massacre had reduced the O'More clans "from 500 to 50." The English killed Rory Og O'More himself in battle three months later.[34]

"Out of every corner of the woods and glynnes they came creeping forth upon their hands, for their legges could not bear them; they looked like anatomies of death, they spake like ghosts crying out of their graves; ... that in a short space there were none almost left, and a most populous and plentifull country suddainely left voyde of man and beast."

Edmund Spenser, English poet and eyewitness

We ought not overlook the fact that Cosby's slaughter of the O'More clans was not a deviant act committed in the frenzy of combat. It was backed by a commission of martial law dated March 18, 1577, and bearing the signature of Lord Deputy Sydney. No less than the mass murder of the O'Neill clan and the eradication of the Scots on Rathlin Island, the slaughter of the O'Mores was an atrocity by policy. It was, in David Edwards' terminology, an act "of mounting state terrorism" carried out with the Crown's approval. The perpetrators were rewarded for their efforts, Essex being considered for the lord deputyship after Clandeboye, Cosby being knighted after the killings at Mullaghmast.[35]

The 1580s witnessed a tripling of English military forces in Ireland to 8,000 soldiers. The increase was inversely proportional to the size of the native population, which fell by 30 percent during this time as the English army ravaged Irish towns and the countryside. Massacres of Irish septs like the Kavanaughs were commonplace. In Munster the Earl of Desmond (head of the Fitzgerald sept) led a rebellion that provoked swift and draconian reprisal from the English. "We consumed with fire all inhabitations and executed the people wherever we found them," a commanding officer of the English troops in Munster wrote of their expedition of March 1580. According to another commander, the Earl of Ormond, the English troops killed forty-six Irish leaders, 800 "traitors," and 4,000 "common people." The Irish perspective on the bloodshed was less elliptical. An Irish publication, *Annals of the Four Masters*, charged the soldiers with killing not only combatants but also "blind and feeble men, women, boys and girls, sick persons, idiots and old people."[36]

Outright premeditated killing was not the only method of wiping out the population of Munster, for the English complemented military assaults with policies to prevent the Irish from farming the land. In the city of Cork thousands of Irish natives died of starvation between January and March 1582. In other parts of Munster twenty to seventy people perished each day during this period. The effects of willful famine converged with unrelenting massacres to depopulate the province. An English investigation in 1584 determined that 97 percent of the previous inhabitants of the Desmond estates had died. English settlers arriving to colonize the area found it an unpeopled wasteland. The few native survivors were walking skeletons whose emaciation shocked the colonists. One of them described the survivors as "the poorest creatures ... so lean for want of food as wonderful."[37]

As the wretched denizens of Munster were starved and slaughtered, elsewhere the English waged a pitiless war against the Irish population. In 1586 the president of Connacht (a western province of Ireland), Richard Bingham, ambushed and killed more than a thousand Scottish supporters of an Irish chieftain in their encampment. The slaughter included unarmed noncombatant men, women, and children found in the camp. He later killed thirty alleged rebels after discovering their hideout. He decapitated the bodies and sent the heads as a gift to his brother. In other instances, Bingham's troops confiscated alleged rebels' livestock and hanged them without trial. Some English officials came to regard with consternation Bingham's depredations, such as William Fitzwilliam, his successor as president of Connacht, as well as the archbishop of Dublin, Adam Loftus.

Both men denounced Bingham for his excesses. Another official wrote in 1590 that Bingham's victims were "non but women, children and churls destroyed."[38]

The practice of head-taking was not original to Bingham. Among the Irish, references to it in the Irish Annals reach back into the Middle Ages. In the 1530s a chieftain of the Burkes in Connacht earned a fearsome nom de guerre, *Ulick-na-gceann*, or "Ulick of the heads." However, decapitation among the Irish, David Edwards cautions, was not routine and appears to have been restricted to a ruler's enemies—that is, to the upper classes engaged in warfare. Civilians were exempted from it. In light of this limitation, the charges of barbarism against the Irish based on allegations of head-taking made by Elizabethan and Jacobean playwrights like William Baldwin and John Webster seem to have been calumnies. So, too, were their claims that Irish warfare had no aim other than sadistic bloodlust, expressed in the desire for a "deadman's heade" as a trophy of battle (Baldwin) or for recreational use as a football (Webster).[39]

In fact, head-taking appears to have existed on both sides of the conflict. Among the English soldiers sent to Ireland as recruits in the 1540s, many had previously fought on the English-Scottish border, a frontier where decapitation of the enemy had been carried out for centuries. The customary practices of these army veterans may have been reinforced in Ireland by the Tudor law of treason, a crime punished by beheading. As the Tudors increasingly came to regard their efforts to control Ireland as counterinsurgency measures, decapitation may have been normalized as a way to deal with resisters. Regardless of the origins, prominent English commanders employed the practice to intimidate the Irish population. As colonel of Munster (1569–71), Sir Humphrey Gilbert beheaded entire Irish communities and planted their heads on the path to his tent as terrifying symbols of his awful power. Local chieftains approaching Gilbert's tent to negotiate their surrender to him had to traverse a "lane of heddes."[40] This is indeed a form of state terrorism, as Edwards correctly diagnoses it. Gilbert's atrocities were not renegade operations like Mr. Kurtz's in the jungles of the Congo. Rather, they reflected an official policy of draconian action to subdue an allegedly refractory land, and may for this reason be considered an aspect of England's civilizing mission in Ireland.

Unsurprisingly, such repression invited blowback. A new round of rebellions erupted in Ulster in 1591, giving rise by 1594 to the "9 Years War" (1594–1603). The conflict was internecine on both sides: 2,600 English soldiers were killed while 6,000 Irish rebels and noncombatants were either killed or wounded. Bingham's penchant for displaying the severed heads of accused rebels spread to other colonial officials. In 1597 the Lord Deputy of Dublin complained that Dublin's air was being polluted with the decomposing heads brought to the city for exhibition each day. After martial law was reintroduced in 1596, English commissioners decided to execute all prisoners jailed for alleged sedition no matter whether they had received a trial or not. When rebels succeeded in destroying the Munster plantation and driving English settlers out of the territory, colonial authorities stiffened their resolve to crush the rebellion. Extermination of the Irish through scorched earth tactics became official policy. Essex's successor in Ulster, Lord Mountjoy, dispatched his commander Chichester on a search-and-destroy mission in November 1601 that blazed a fiery and bloodstrewn path through the north. "We have burnt and destroyed along the Lough," he later said, "in which journeys we have killed above one hundred people of all sorts, besides such as were burnt, how many I know not. We spare none of what quality or sex soever, and it hath bred much terror in the people." Chichester's approach was one of spoliation and mass murder: foodstuffs were torched, houses destroyed, and peasants struck down by the hundreds. He subsequently reported that in the northern Irish county of Tyrone he and his troops "found every where men dead of famine, in so much that Ohagen protested unto us that between Tullogh Oge and Toome there lay unburied a thousand dead, and that since our first drawing this year to Blackwater, there were above three thousand starved in Tyrone."[41]

Even for twenty-first-century readers accustomed to gruesome atrocity stories, English warfare against the native population of Ireland remains bloodcurdling. It raises the question that Nicholas Canny seeks to address—namely, how could the English settlers conceive such a fiercely malevolent attitude toward the Irish? Canny cites several possible contributory factors before alighting on the one most pertinent to this chapter: the English view that the Irish were pagan barbarians removed from the protections of the Law of War. A royal official in Ireland, Edmund Tremayne, accused the Irish in Munster of irreligion: they were neither "Papists nor Protestants but rather such as have nether feare nor love of God in their harts that restreyneth them from ill. Thei regarde no othe, thei blaspheme, they murder, commit whoredome, hold no wedlock, ravish, steal and commit all abomination without scruple of conscience." The Lord Deputy of Ireland, Sir Henry Sidney, shared Tremayne's gloomy view of the Irish, likening them to "unreasonable beastes" for whom "perjurie, robberie and murder counted alloweable." Sidney doubted whether the Irish were truly Christian because he saw no evidence of either baptism or a belief in the afterlife among them. Spenser likewise held that the population, though nominally Catholic, were "so blindly and brutishly informed for the most part as that you would rather think them atheists or infidels." Canny presents these and other proofs to argue that English settlers, and indeed Englishmen as a whole, became convinced that the Gaelic Irish were pagans.[42]

Belief in Irish paganism was important to the English colonial project because it allowed the government to declare the Irish barbarians. They were compared with the great barbarian peoples of history—the Huns, Vandals, Goths, and Turks—and even accused from time to time of the ultimate symbol of barbarism in English eyes, cannibalism. (The charge of Irish cannibalism was a recurrent theme of early modern English discourse.) The initial plan of Anglicizing and "civilizing" the Irish—"to reduce that countrey to civilitie and the maners of England," as one colonial official expressed it—disappeared as English perceptions of the Irish darkened by the 1570s. There were no efforts to reform the Irish; instead, at the faintest hint of resistance, the colonizers destroyed Irish property, burned Irish farmland, and slew Irish men, women, and children by the thousands. In each case, bestializing and barbarizing the native population provided justification for extreme violence. To such a "wicked and faythles pepoll," as an official in Belfast, Edward Berkeley, derided the Irish,[43] the principles of chivalry did not apply. English colonists would carry these ideas about native inferiority with them to North America, where they would soon condition their attitudes toward Native

Americans and eventually lead both groups on a downward spiraling path toward wartime brutality.

The Pequot War

The pattern of "civilizing" the savage Other, then striving to exterminate the "barbarians" when they offered resistance, trailed after the English as they advanced into North America. It is notable that historian Frederick Jackson Turner's thesis[44] that the United States was formed culturally, intellectually, politically, and socio-economically in relation to a frontier really begins on foreign shores with England's conquest of Ireland. Much of US history—particularly as it relates to wars against cultural outsiders—can be interpreted as the effects of a frontier perpetually moving westward, from Ireland to the East coast of North America and beyond.[45] Whatever else the frontier signified to Euro-Americans, it certainly meant a liminal zone between civilization and barbarism, Christianity and paganism, higher culture and debased devil-worship. In short, it was an area where the Law of War had no place.

Although colonial Virginia is not our focus here, it is worth pointing out that the supervisory council of the Virginia colony at Jamestown consisted of veterans of the Irish campaigns. Among them were Sir Ferdinando Gorges, sergeant major of the English army in Ireland; the Earl of Southampton, an associate of Essex in Ireland; Lord De La Warr, a lieutenant of the second Earl of Essex; and the Lord President of Munster, Sir George Carew, the commander of English forces responsible in 1602 for massacring the defeated garrison at Dunboy Castle. Carew collaborated with Mountjoy's truculent commander in Ireland, Lord Chichester, in preparing Virginia's political system.[46] After an Indian uprising in 1622 in Virginia, the colonists retaliated by killing native men and women without discrimination. No limitation was recognized in suppressing the Indians, including the universally condemned resort to poison. The colonists murdered more than one hundred Indians invited to an alleged peace conference by serving them wine laced with poison. Such insidious dealings even appalled the London Company, whose counsels of moderation provoked the colonists' retort that against "barbarous and perfidious enemys" like the Indians, no means was "injuste, that may tend to their ruine ... with these [enemies] neither fayre Warr nor good quarter is ever to be held, nor is there any other hope of theire subversione."[47]

Events in Virginia were a meteor presaging similar exterminatory violence—and similar exterminatory mentalities—in Puritan New England. The similitude is not accidental; like the Virginians, the colonists in New England carried with them to New World shores the memories and methods of Ireland's conquest. Sir Humphrey Gilbert, the governor of Ulster and an English commander who denied quarter to Irish resisters (including women and children), advocated killing noncombatants on the theory their deaths would disrupt the supply line to the rebels. Both Gilbert and Sir Richard Grenville, a sailor and privateer involved in English colonization efforts in Ireland, participated in England's settlement projects on the northern east coast of North America.[48] Initial attitudes toward the Indians were not hostile—the Puritans viewed them, in the words of the founder of Massachusetts Bay Colony, John Winthrop, as "innately fair-skinned and wholly human." Their plan was not to harm the Indians but to convert them to Christianity. The Colony explicitly adjured colonists to avoid injuring "in the least kinde" the native people. In their conduct, according to the Charter issued by King Charles I, the colonists were to lead exemplary lives that would bring the Indians "to the knowledge and obedienc of the onlie true God and Savior of mankinde."[49] The mission to evangelize the Indians was a restraining force on the degree of violence to which the "heathens" could be subjected. This, together with the non-expansionist mindset of the Colony, tended to stabilize relations between the two groups (with some notable exceptions)[50] through the 1620s and early 1630s.

By the mid-1630s, however, the colonists' attitudes began to darken considerably. When war eventually came with the Indians it would center on the Pequots, an aggressive tribe that dominated the Connecticut country. The origins of deteriorating relations between the Bay Colony and the Pequots are murky but appear to lie in trade disputes between the Pequots and other native tribes. For a time the Pequots had enjoyed a monopoly on trade in the area until the Dutch and Plymouth colony established trading posts on the Connecticut River. When other tribes traded with the Dutch the Pequots retaliated against them, prompting the Dutch to abduct and later murder the Pequot grand sachem. The Pequots responded in 1634 by attacking a ship under the command of a dodgy merchant previously expelled from Massachusetts Bay Colony, John Stone, and killing everyone on board. This event did not at the time raise the ire of Bay Colony authorities because the massacre was not within their jurisdiction. This notwithstanding, as a condition of the "Connecticut Settlement" with the Pequots, the Puritans subsequently demanded the surrender of all the Pequot men involved in Stone's death. The Pequots' failure to meet this demand in 1636, bizarre as it may sound (insofar as Stone and his crew before their demise had been expelled from the Colony), would become the casus belli to the Pequot War.[51]

In July 1636 the Bay Colony ordered the Connecticut governor John Winthrop Jr. to publicly censure the Pequots for failing to turn Stone's killers over to them as "the very condition of the Peace betwixt us." Winthrop was told that, in the event the Pequots persisted in their refusal, he should inform them the peace treaty was nullified and the Puritans would "reuenge the blood of our Countrimen as occasion shall serue." When the Pequots did not produce Stone's killers, the English revoked the peace treaty and mustered a military force of ninety men under John Endecott, the commander, and his deputy commander John Underhill. This force was first dispatched to Block Island with the charge to kill all the Indian men and enslave the women and children. (They attacked Block Island first because the dismembered corpse of John Oldham, a well-respected trader from the Bay Colony, was found in his boat off Block Island's coast.) The peculiar order must have alerted Endecott and his men to the singular nature of the warfare they were soon to undertake. It would be an irregular style of fighting not against other soldiers in conventional battle but against rebels, who were to be cut down without trial on the assumption they were guilty of Oldham's murder. As Ronald Dale Karr concludes, "before the army took to the field, it had already been decided that the law of arms would not apply when fighting these Indians."[52]

Figure 21 Period engraving depicting the attack by Massachusetts Bay Colony and its Mohegan allies on the Pequot village on May 26, 1637. The inner ring consists of Colony musketeers, the outer ring of the Mohegans. The engraving clearly shows the intent on the part of the attackers to destroy the lives of noncombatant villagers. © Wikimedia Commons (public domain).

As it turned out, the Block Island Indians fled Endecott's army by retreating into the swamps, denying him the opportunity to kill all of their men and enslave the rest. Instead, the English burned down their houses and destroyed their corn. In a final indignity, the soldiers slaughtered the Indians' dogs that had been left behind. They then turned to deal with the Pequots. Their ships dropped anchor at the mouth of the Pequot River, and Endecott conveyed their demands to a Pequot envoy—the heads of the warriors who had killed Stone and his crew. The envoy explained that the killings had been retaliation for the Dutch murder of a Pequot sachem; the Pequots had simply made a mistake by confusing Stone and his crew with the Dutch. Unmoved by the envoy's words, the English came ashore and demanded to speak with their sachem. The Pequot envoy said the sachem was away, and then invited Endecott to a parley. Endecott's response was to set on fire the Pequots' cornfields. The Pequots interpreted this and ensuing English raids as a declaration of war.[53]

"[Indian] Warres are farre lesse bloudy, and devouring then the cruell Warres of Europe; and seldome twenty slain in a pitcht field: partly because when they fight in a wood every Tree is a Bucklar. When they fight in a plaine, they fight with leaping and dancing, that seldome an Arrow hits, and when a man is wounded, unlesse he that shot followes upon the wounded, they soone retire and save the wounded."

Roger Williams, Key into the Language of America *1643*

The Pequots, like North American Indians in general, did not wage war for the sake of imposing their dominion on a defeated foe. Roger Williams reported that the typical motives for Indian armed conflict were "pride" (honor offenses) and retaliation for a real or imagined offense. Of these two, according to Williams, retaliation was the most common motive for going to war. In such cases conflict between groups ended when satisfactory retribution was served on the offender. In other cases compensation would be paid to the winners, thus bringing the war to a close. Their form of warfare—again, according to Williams—was less destructive than the European way of war.[54] Rarely fighting pitched battles, North American Indians staged guerrilla raids and ambushes. They employed formal declarations of war as well as diplomacy in negotiations with enemy forces, and did not sexually assault women.[55] In contrast with evidence of pre-contact massacre sites like Crow Creek, the natives of the eastern seaboard typically spared the lives of women and children. Historian Francis Jennings asserts that the Pequots long adhered to this traditional practice of preserving the lives of non-combatants until the outbreak of their war with the Bay Colony. Once they learned that the English might attack their own women and children, the Pequots issued threats to return the favor by killing the colonists' noncombatants.[56] A clearer example of how the lawlessness of one party can spread to its enemy, leading each to escalating abandonment of all restraint, would be difficult to find.

After attacks on Fort Saybrook in the fall of 1636, the Pequots adopted a different strategy in the spring of 1637 that focused on raiding settler outposts, in the course of which thirty settlers were killed and two women abducted. On May 1 the Connecticut General Court followed the Bay Colony in declaring war on the Pequots and raised a militia of ninety men under the command of Captain John Mason. Joining forces with their Indian allies the Narragansetts, Mason and his men advanced to the outskirts of a Pequot village near the Mystic River. According to Ben Kiernan, Mason was made aware that the village contained women, the elderly, and children, the warriors being away at the Pequots' main fort. Mason's orders from the Connecticut General Court have not survived; however, as some historians have argued, the surrounding circumstances of the expedition suggest Mason and his men embarked with the clear idea of taking the war to the entire Pequot population and not just its warriors.[57] He arrayed his troops in concentric circles surrounding the village: his Narragansett allies formed the outer circle, the Connecticut militiamen the inner. The attack, when it came, was launched at nighttime as the Indians slept. Setting fire to the village, the militiamen waited as the flames spread and the Indians, awakening in the midst of their blazing homes, fled in terror from them. As they emerged from their wigwams they were mown down by English musketry and swords. Some of the inhabitants ran in panic from the soldiers back into the fire; their fate was to be burned alive. In total as many as 700 Indian noncombatants perished during the attack.[58]

In June 1637 the Bay Colony dispatched troops to the Connecticut country for the express purpose of exterminating the remaining Pequots. Two hundred surrendered to the Narragansetts, who handed the prisoners over to the colonists (after killing two of them). The men, separated from the women and children, were put on a ship and taken

Figure 22 Destruction of the Pequot Village by Connecticut Militiamen and their Indian allies, May 1637. A print from *Cassell's History of the United States* by Edmund Ollier, *c.*1880. © Print Collector / Getty Images.

just outside the harbor, where all of them were murdered. The women and children were sold into slavery. The extremity of this and other attacks drove the Pequots out of Connecticut. Roger Williams reported that "[n]ot a Pequt is to be found, it is said . . . they are gone farr and finally." As they fled their homeland in small groups, the Pequots were constantly harassed by colonial soldiers who killed or captured them. On one occasion the militiamen beheaded two Pequot sachems. On another, in a swamp near New Haven, colonial soldiers encircled 280 Pequots. They killed the men and enslaved the elderly, women, and children; some of the boys were sent to the West Indies to spend the rest of their days as slaves. By the end of the Pequot War one witness summed up the doleful situation: "The Pequetans now seem[ed] nothing but a name."[59] As it turns out, even the name "Pequot" was to be eradicated along with the people it designated. The Treaty of Hartford in 1638 formally ending the Pequot War mandated that the word "Pequot" be eliminated from the river bearing its name, which was changed to the Thames, and the site the Pequot occupied be renamed New London.[60] In this manner, the Puritans sought to void the Pequot people from history, and very nearly did so.

Statistics can sometimes be misleading, but in this case the numbers eloquently communicate the dreadful plight of the Pequot Indians. In 1637 the population numbered as many as 4,000. By 1638 at least 35 percent of that number had been killed (Kiernan thinks the figure is higher). As Kiernan tells the tale, by the 1800s only forty Pequots were alive.

The elegiac story of the Pequots was chosen for this chapter because it represents in miniature the catastrophic outcome of Indian and European military conflict. Many other tribes on the eastern seaboard met with similar, if not always fatal, treatment at colonial hands. How can we account for the ghastly violence of these encounters— violence so brutal and wanton that it appalled the Puritans' Indian allies, the Narragansetts, and even disturbed some of the Puritan soldiers who were party to it? Adam Hirsch tries to account for the brutality in terms of a clash of "military cultures," in which a European style of warfare based on pitched battles between uniformed armies encountered a markedly different Indian style consisting of guerrilla tactics, raids, and ambushes. On this theory, the refusal of the Indians to fight pitched battles enraged colonial forces, prodding them to suspend the ordinary constraints of chivalry.[61] The implication of Hirsch's argument is that European violence toward the Pequots was excessive and aberrational as measured by customary practice on the Continent. He writes:

> Certainly the most startling characteristic of colonial operations during the Pequot War was their sheer wantonness. The slaughter of noncombatants at Mystic village, the ruthless pursuit of the vanquished tribe, the enslavement or execution of prisoners, all represented an approach to warfare more suggestive of the twentieth century than the seventeenth.[62]

Against Hirsch's view Ronald Karr argues that the Europeans' behavior was hardly "unprecedented." Rather, the European military culture Hirsch references not only observed codes of restraint derived from medieval chivalry but also provided for departures from those codes when circumstances called for them. In wars with heretics, Muslims, rebels, the refractory inhabitants of besieged cities, and persons (like Mesoamerican Indians and the Irish) considered inhuman pagan barbarians, European military culture justified war without mercy. According to Karr, Hirsch's claim that European wars of the seventeenth century were limited affairs "fought between armies, not entire populations" is simply wrong on its face because European armies often attacked civilians and executed war captives during unconventional wars. "The primary difference between conventional and unconventional wars," Karr explains, "was political: the former . . . were extensions of diplomatic maneuvering to secure limited concessions from a rival power; the latter sought total victory over an illegitimate and immoral foe."[63]

In English eyes the Pequots were illegitimate and immoral for two reasons. First, they were rebels against the dominion of the English sovereign in the New World. Karr contends that the English expected the Pequots to submit to English rule. Thus, the killings of Stone and Oldham were not only acts of war but violations of English Common Law. The Pequots had become "lawless subjects" inviting whatever force was needed to achieve their subjugation—including, in Karr's words, their "utter destruction."[64] Second, the Pequots (and Indians generally) were considered godless pagans increasingly identified in the colonial imagination with the Devil. Underhill called them "wicked imps . . . Like the devil, their commander, they run up and down as roaring lions, compassing all corners of the country for their prey."[65] Puritan leaders celebrated the destruction of the Pequots as a divinely ordained victory over an evil enemy. Plymouth governor William Bradford rhapsodized about their annihilation as a "sweet sacrifice," praising the Puritans' god as acting "wonderfully for them, thus to enclose their enemies in their hands and give them so speedy a victory over so proud and insulting an enemy."[66]

As in Ireland so in New England a diabolical enemy was owed none of the protections afforded by the Law of War. Played out to ferocious effect in Ireland, this pattern would now influence colonial, and later US-American, attitudes toward native peoples for the next two centuries. In one interpretation advanced by Yale law professor John Fabian Whitt, Euro-Americans construed Indian "mourning wars"[67] as evidence of barbarism, drawing the fateful conclusion that native peoples stood beyond the compass of battlefield chivalry.[68] Such attitudes conditioned the hard-nosed European approach to warfare exemplified in the Pequot war. They surface in the colonial writings of prominent American religious leaders like the Reverend Solomon Stoddard, the minister of a

Figure 23 Cotton Mather, American Puritan minister (1663–1728). "So ... the infant colonies of New-England, finding themselves necessitated unto the crushing of serpents, while they were but yet in the cradle, unanimously resolved, that with the assistance of Heaven they would root this 'nest of serpents' out of the world." From *Magnalia Christi Americana* (1702), quoted in Brantlinger, *Dark Vanishings*, 49. © Wikimedia Commons (public domain).

Congregational church in Northampton and grandfather of Jonathan Edwards. In a 1701 letter Stoddard wrote, "If the Indians were as other people are, and did manage their war fairly after the manner of other nations, it might be looked upon as inhumane to persue them [in a manner contrary to] Christian practice. But they are to be looked upon as thieves and murderers, . . . they don't appeare openly in the field to bid us battle, they use those cruelly that fall into their hands." In the same letter Stoddard later compared native peoples to "wolves" who "are to be dealt withal as wolves." His clear implication was that the Indians should be exterminated.[69]

A similar language of dehumanization implying genocide appears in the writings of the age's best-known Congregational minister, theologian, and author, Cotton Mather. For Mather the Indians were "nations of wretches, whose whole religion [is] the most explicit sort of devil-worship." Mather conjured feverish visions of the Indians' demonic treachery; in his paranoid worldview the Indians wanted to carry out the Devil's plan to wipe out the Bay Colony and exterminate the Puritans. To counter the threat from Satan's hoardes, Mather urged the destruction of all native peoples.[70]

Adam Hirsch and John Whitt both argue that this perception of Indian barbarism radicalized Euro-American warfare with native peoples, a perception reflected in the "extinction discourse" used by Stoddard and Mather.[71] As we have seen, English colonizers routinely employed such language to describe the Irish, and with comparable effect— shockingly grisly massacres of native peoples. The use of bestial or diabolical imagery to devalue an opponent furnished ideological cover for war crimes in both Ireland and the New World. However, the more fundamental truth is that European warfare in other theaters could be just as violent when the enemy forfeited his status as a legitimate combatant, as rebels, heretics, heathens, and tenacious defenders of besieged cities did. When by the 1630s the Indians in New England presented themselves as demoniacs and rebels to the colonial imagination, English settlers applied well-worn categories from European military practice to remove them from the conventional Law of War.

Over time the doctrine that "savages" were not protected persons would congeal in the thinking of seventeenth-, eighteenth-, and early nineteenth-century Western legal experts. For both Hugo Grotius and the Swiss jurist Emer de Vattel, the Law of War did not apply in "unjust wars," rebellions, wars against enemies who disregarded the Law of War, and conflicts with "savages" or "heathens." In his influential 1758 treatise *The Law of Nations* Vattel declared that "all nations have a right to join in a confederacy for the purpose of punishing and even exterminating those savage nations."[72] American legal scholars hewed to a similar line. James Kent wrote in his *Commentaries on American Law* (1794/1826) that Indians' "savage state" rendered them unable to fulfill their duties under the Law of War, implying that they therefore stood beyond its protections. American jurist Henry Wheaton enunciated the same point in his *Elements of International Law* (1836), arguing that the Law of War applied only "among nations . . . united by ties of similar origin, manners, and religion." He expressly excluded the American Indian.[73] The wells from which later commentators like Elbridge Colby would draw their water were very deep, indeed.

In view of the vast cultural differences between the Europeans and the Indians, was such extreme violence inevitable? It may be that discrepancies in religion or worldview were not the decisive factor, nor was the Pequots' refusal to submit to the Puritans' demands. Ronald Karr's analysis of the question is highly suggestive. Karr argues that, in situations in which wars with heretics or rebels involved antagonists who were evenly matched, reciprocity (i.e. mutual self-limiting behavior) was a not infrequent result. He cites the example of the Dutch rebellion against the Spanish Habsburgs, an act that in most circumstances would have elicited a drastic and bloody crackdown. While the Duke of Alva initially waged a war of terror against the rebels in Rotterdam, Mons, Mechlin, and other Dutch cities, his approach moderated significantly in 1573 after one of his top lieutenants was captured. Karr writes, "Faced with the imminent execution of his colleague, Alva halted his practice of executing all captured rebels and opened negotiations with the Dutch nationalists."[74] Eventually the two sides arrived at formal agreements through a series of parlays that established basic ground rules for the conflict. These agreements came into being despite the refusal of each side to acknowledge the legitimacy of the other. Similarly, in the latter phases of the English Civil War, royalist and Parliamentary troops met in formal sessions and agreed to observe the Law of War. But for rough parity of arms between the belligerents, there would have been little incentive for the superior to restrain itself in crushing an inferior opponent.

Karr's thesis suggests that the lack of parity in arms between colonial forces and native groups like the Pequots strongly tilted their wars toward excess. Convinced of the barbarism, perfidy, and deviltry of the Indians, as well as accusations of Indian cannibalism,[75] the Puritans had scant reason to follow the Law of War, particularly when their weaponry and tactics gave them a nearly insuperable technological advantage. The long-standing practice of suspending restraints when dealing with barbarians or rebels could now flow without check. To be sure, the Puritans' use of extreme violence against the Pequots shook native peoples to their core. The understanding dawned on them that their conflict with European settlers was a literal fight for survival. Metacomet (King Philip) believed, and with good reason, that "he could expect no mercy" from the Puritans if he lost the war.[76] New England Indians learned this bitter lesson from the tragedy of the Pequots and applied it in one of the most destructive wars fought in North American history, the so-called "King Philip's War."

King Philip's War

Armed conflict again flared up between New England Indians and European settlers in the mid–1670s, sparked by acts of reciprocal violence. Massachusetts and Plymouth declared war on the Wampanoag sachem Metacomet, called "King Philip" by the English, and the Wampanoag people. Before long other Indian tribes were drawn into the war on both sides, among them the Mohegans, Nipmucs, and Narragansett warriors (the Narragansett tribal leadership tried to remain neutral in the conflict). In the final analysis, it mattered little whether an Indian tribe participated in the war or not because the colonists attacked native peoples indiscriminately. Despite their efforts to avoid entanglement the Narragansetts were targeted by the English, who attacked their main fort on an island in a frozen swamp near modern-day West Kingston, Rhode Island.

Overrunning the fort, the militiamen set fire to Narragansett homes and food supplies, in the process killing or burning to death 150 Indians, a large number of whom were women, children, and the aged.[77]

Colonial forces picked up where they had left off forty years before, savaging the Indians wherever they were found. One commander ordered that an Indian woman captured in Hatfield be torn to pieces by dogs. The English brazenly violated pledges made during negotiated surrenders, as they did with an Indian group promised exemption from enslavement if they gave themselves up. When the natives surrendered under these terms, their captors reneged on their agreement and sent the prisoners to Plymouth, where they were sold as slaves and transported out of North America. Meanwhile hundreds of Wampanoags were sold into slavery in Bermuda. After Metacomet's death in August 1676, some of his followers surrendered on the condition they would not be enslaved. The English, who apparently felt no need to fulfill explicit promises made to their Indian prisoners, sold the men, women, and their children into slavery.[78]

Figure 24 Colonial village of Brookfield, Massachusetts, burnt by Native Americans during King Philip's War, 1675. Engraving by Van Ingen Snyder, *c*.1860. © Universal History Archive / Getty Images.

As historians of King Philip's War have cogently argued,[79] the ruthlessness of colonial authorities during the Pequot War left a lasting impression on the minds of New England's Indian population. Confronted with an utter lack of restraint or mercy from the English, they discarded their own Law of War in 1675 and repaid the colonists in their own bloody coin. An Indian military force under the Narragansett sachem Canonchet launched a winter offensive in 1676 that pushed back the frontier and destroyed all white settlements in western Rhode Island. Providence, the capital of Rhode Island, was burned in March 1676. However, the Puritans' ability to recruit Native American allies to join their campaign against the Wampanoags, Narragansetts, and Nipmucs ultimately proved decisive. Death from military attack, disease, and starvation combined with enslavement and transportation to the Caribbean to devastate these native groups. By the time of their defeat in September 1676, 30 percent of the Indian population had perished while hundreds were enslaved and moved out of the country. On the English side, six hundred soldiers were killed during the war; seventeen settlements were razed and fifty more badly damaged.[80]

Conclusion

A common thread spans the history of wartime carnage recounted in this chapter: the idea prevalent among Europeans that certain groups were ineligible for the protections of the customs and usages of war as these had crystallized in medieval chivalry. In conflicts with heretics, Muslims, Jews, rebels, and pagan barbarians, the Law of War would be suspended. The clash of European armies with such groups unfolded in the shadow cast by the just war tradition that medieval Europe had inherited from Greco-Roman culture and St. Augustine. In their dealings with the Maya, the Aztecs, the Irish, and New England's indigenous populations, European colonists acted pursuant to the Greco-Roman conviction that all means to defeat an enemy in a just war were allowed. To this formula Augustine had added the fatal notion that extreme violence was acceptable if used to punish sin, a strand of the medieval Law of War that would eventually creep into Europe's colonial wars against native peoples. Even when territorial acquisition was the chief motive (as it was in the colonization of Ireland and Mesoamerica), the religious justification of extreme violence—including actions many observers would describe today as genocide—was a ubiquitous enabling condition of brutality.

The absence of a rough parity of arms between the two sides meant that reciprocity rarely braked the headlong velocity toward non-utilitarian violence. The triad of greed, cultural chauvinism, and religious fanaticism became an agent of mass murder cloaked in the guise of just war theory. When much later Elbridge Colby summed up four centuries of mainstream legal thought in denying the Law of War's protections to "uncivilized peoples," this just war tradition was the nervure around which his argument was molded.

CHAPTER 6
THE LAW OF WAR IN THE EIGHTEENTH AND NINETEENTH CENTURIES: EUROPE AND THE UNITED STATES OF AMERICA

The eighteenth century

Sovereignty and warfare heading into the eighteenth century

In Europe one of the important offshoots of the Peace of Westphalia formally ending the Thirty Years War was a continent-wide assertion of the principle of sovereignty. The idea of sovereignty harked back to the Roman jurists of the early imperial period, who had argued that law drew its obligatory force not from custom, usage, or precedent but from the recognized authority of the lawmaker. The Romans called this authority *majestas* (sovereign power), a legislative power that resided in the emperor. For the Romans, the binding force of law was *ex officio*; it inhered neither in caprice nor custom but in duly constituted imperial authority.[1]

In the decades ensuing after the Thirty Years War, sovereignty acquired many of the characteristics we associate with the word today. Among the first thinkers to develop a modern concept of sovereignty was Jean Bodin (1530–96), a French political philosopher who published his *Six Books on the Republic* (1576) during the upheavals of the wars of religion. The Middle Ages were characterized by a quilt-work of coexistent, overlapping, and sometimes competing aggregations of power: the Church, municipal authorities, the Holy Roman Emperor, secular princes, the guilds, and the legal system all enjoyed supremacy within their limited jurisdictions. For Bodin, however, sovereignty was far more than supreme authority over a small corner of society; it was absolute political power over society as a whole. Modifying the Roman *majestas*, Bodin shifted the focus of sovereignty from properly constituted authority to supreme political control of a state. The basis of his argument was the necessity for a pre-eminent lawgiver, one whose uncontested authority would promote the well-being of the state by binding together the diverse elements that it comprised. Although Bodin's theory of sovereignty would find a warm reception from the absolute monarchs of the seventeenth century, it was not restricted to autocratic governments (Bodin himself acknowledged the applicability of his theory to democracies).[2] In fact, his conception of sovereignty as supreme, exclusive authority within a state has persisted as the dominant view among governments, democratic and authoritarian, until today.

The peace settlement ending the Thirty Years War—signified by the treaties of Münster and Osnabrück—created the conditions in which the modern understanding of sovereignty could flourish and grow. In stemming the Counter-Reformation in the

German lands, the Peace of Westphalia scotched the threat of European domination by the Habsburgs. More than 300 German states now became sovereign powers with the right to conclude treaties and conduct foreign relations with other countries. The vital sinews of the Holy Roman Empire, namely, its ability to tax the estates, exploit them as a source for recruiting soldiers, and pass laws to constrain their actions, were irrevocably sapped. Contemporary Europeans spoke of "German liberties" after 1648, a phrase given substantial credence by the recognition of German states' rights in the public law of Europe. These newly independent states were incorporated into a European system of sovereign countries (*Staatensystem*), the members of which were fully independent of each other. None was beholden to a superior; none recognized a common tie with other states capable of hampering its own sovereign power. As R. R. Palmer and Joel Colton once wrote, "No one any longer pretended that Europe had any significant unity, religious, political or other." Rather, Europe now thought of itself as "a large number of unconnected sovereignties, free and detached atoms, or states, which moved about according to their own laws, following their own political interests, ... alternating between war and peace, shifting position with a shifting balance of power."[3]

One of these "unconnected sovereignties" whose hand the Peace of Westphalia immensely strengthened was France. Along with Sweden, the Peace of Westphalia had appointed France as a co-guarantor of the 1648 settlement. Although Sweden would be unequal to the demands and opportunities of its role, such was not the case for France; it enjoyed the legal right to intervene in Central Europe for the next 150 years.[4] Under its flamboyant king Louis XIV (r. 1643–1715), France became the archetype of the powerful, post-Westphalian European state. In his famous dictum "L'état, c'est moi" ("As for the state, it is myself") he summed up the view of early modern sovereignty in Europe. No matter how balkanized a society might be, no matter how fractured by class, region, or religion, a single powerful individual monopolized control over its legislative processes and armed forces. Such control led to stability and order at home. However, the situation was quite different in France's dealings with other sovereign states, insofar as the French monarch could not legitimately claim in foreign relations a transcendent right to law-making and military force. No theory of "divine right" as elaborated by apologists of royal power like Jacques-Bénigne Bossuet (1627–1704) could bolster the king's claim to supremacy beyond the borders of his kingdom. Louis XIV's response was to devote the resources of the state to perpetual warmaking and war preparation.[5]

By the mid-1600s, the arcane network of feudal allegiances was in free-fall. Throughout the medieval period, princes and kings shared military authority with noblemen. Feudal obligations to a liege lord could effectively veto a knight's participation in a battle on behalf of a king when their interests clashed. In France as well as central Europe, aristocrats had often commanded their own private armies; in other cases, the captains of an armed force were commissioned by a government, but the captains themselves recruited and outfitted their soldiers. As a result, these forces not seldom eluded the control of the governments for whom they were nominally fighting. This byzantine system disappeared in the face of strong kings like Louis XIV. Where war was "a kind of aimless and perpetual violence" during the Middle Ages, Louis transformed it into "an activity of the state."[6] The disjointed segments of the army were knitted together into a unified structure consisting of ranks and grades, all of them subordinated to a chain of command. At the apex of the chain was Louis; fanning out below him was an officer corps devoted to the king's service. Louis brought to heel a class of officers accustomed to freelancing independence (many had spent their time not in military drills but loitering at court), requiring that they supervise their troops and minimize financial irregularities. In 1675 he established the *ordre de tableau* (Table of Ranks), thereby ensuring that his officers would earn their rank based on seniority rather than their family origins. Further down the chain of command stood the mass of soldiers, a group now clothed in uniforms, drilled to march in unison, and quartered in barracks. Louis not only instilled his army with military discipline, but significantly expanded its size from around 125,000 men in 1659 to 400,000 by the 1690s.[7]

From dynastic to national wars: the Law of War in the age of nationalism

A recurrent thesis in the literature reaching back into the 1700s is that warfare in pre-revolutionary Europe was limited and relatively tame, chiefly because it lacked the passion of armed conflict inflamed by nationalist rancor. On this theory, the transition from dynastic to national wars between 1792 and 1815 marked a descent into barbarism, as the fervor of a dawning national consciousness swept away the decency and restraint of the pre-revolutionary period. In its place nationalist warfare substituted a military style based on ideological fervor. Where pre-revolutionary wars in Europe were fought over territory, the wars waged by the "nations in arms" were impelled by abstract ideals like freedom, liberty, and the brotherhood of humankind. Enemies were no longer to be treated with consideration after the cessation of war, but as existential threats to ultimate values that had to be eradicated. The reputation of the pre-revolutionary period for milder, more civilized conflicts could inspire nostalgia in historians writing after the cataclysm of the First World War—historians who pined for a golden age of limited warfare, made possible by "an aristocratic and qualitative society" thrown into the dustbin of history by the French Revolution.[8]

Among the earliest proponents of this view was the Prussian general and military theorist, Carl von Clausewitz (1780–1831). Writing in the shadow of the Napoleonic wars, Clausewitz affirmed a causal relationship between the nature of a society and the style of war it was prone to wage. The older aristocratic society produced limited wars tempered by long-standing norms of military behavior. With the democratization of

---

"At the present war is conducted by regular armies. The ordinary people take no part and as a rule have nothing to fear from the enemy."

Emmerich de Vattel (1714–67), on the nature of warfare during the ancien régime

---

society during the Napoleonic era, however, the common people "became a participant in war"; as a result, "the whole weight of the nation was thrown into balance," leading to an abolition of constraints and an explosion of violence. The Law of War became purely discretionary, and more often than not it was honored in the breach.[9] Clausewitz's view has contributed to what military historian Roger Chickering calls a "master narrative" governing modern military history—i.e., the notion that the French Revolution and Napoleonic era were the cradle of "total war."[10] On this interpretation, total war— which taps all of a population, mobilizing it through ideologies that dehumanize the enemy and seek not just victory but the total collapse or destruction of the enemy's army—began in 1792 during the French Republic's wars against the Austrians and Prussians. In the years immediately preceding the outbreak of war, the king's army dwindled away through mutinies and widespread resignation of the officer corps, particularly after Louis XVI's abortive attempt to flee the country in June 1791. The Republic rebuilt the military through voluntary enlistment, including the famous *levée en masse* in 1793. The *levée* was more than just general conscription; it envisioned harnessing the entire population of the country in support of the war, whether through fighting, production of munitions and supplies, service in hospitals, or inciting hatred of the opponent. These initiatives paid substantial dividends, for by mid-1794 the army had grown to a force of one million men, the socio-economic and geographical composition of which mirrored French society at the time. The French had realized Europe's first "nation in arms"—an ideal that would be widely imitated by other European countries in their struggles against Napoleon.[11]

According to the master narrative as Chickering describes it, the nineteenth-century Industrial Revolution added formidable material production to the ideal of the nation in arms, placing increasingly destructive weaponry in the hands of ever larger forces. At the same time, advances in rail travel and telegraphy enabled the coordination and transportation of enormous armies across vast territories. War was becoming all-encompassing: the French Revolution erased the boundaries between soldiers and civilians, while the Industrial Revolution would later erase many of the constraints on the size of the theater of operations and speed of troop movements, as well as on command and control. The omega point in this escalating process was the "Century of Total War" (First and Second World Wars), which achieved a territorial, demographic, and economic amplitude never before seen, a vastness of scale that "featured the calculated and systematic annihilation of civilians, both from the air and in the death camps."[12]

Clearly, the "total war" thesis portrays military developments from 1792 onward as marking a break with an earlier, more restrictive form of warfare. Chickering and other scholars have challenged this theory on the grounds that the *ancien régimes* of Europe were not as mild as the total war advocates claim. Louis XIV's war aims were no more modest than those of Napoleon, while the countries arrayed against Prussia in the Seven Years War intended to destroy it.[13] Chickering notes that a telltale sign of total war, i.e., general conscription, was already practiced in mid-eighteenth-century Prussia, Sweden, Russia, Spain, and portions of the Habsburg Empire. Furthermore, the master narrative cannot account for the ideologically-charged, sanguinary events of the Thirty Years War, which wrought enormous devastation, both incidental and deliberate, on combatant and noncombatant alike 150 years or more before the *levée en masse*.[14] Military historian Gunther Rothenberg makes a similar argument, contending that the image of a pre-revolutionary Europe bound by politesse and modest geopolitical aims, counterposed with an unruly nation-at-arms heedless of the Law of War and vowing extermination of the enemy at all costs, is a distortion. Rothenberg concedes that, in the absence of international treaties imposing limitations on the conduct of war, all Western European armies before 1792 had adopted rules prohibiting plunder and looting. These restrictions were driven less by humanitarian concerns than the urge to preserve discipline among the troops. Moreover, antagonists in battle generally agreed to treat prisoners of war and the wounded decently and to arrange for their exchange, and for the most part they suited their action to their word. However, Rothenberg asserts that this account should be balanced against those aspects of early modern warfare that are irreconcilable with the master narrative—specifically, the readiness of commanders to disregard the customs and usages of the Law of War when military necessity demanded it. He cites as examples the denial of quarter, destruction of civilian life, and laying to waste of enemy territory in the Rhineland-Palatinate (1675 and 1689) and Bavaria (1704). Whatever constraints come to light when we compare the pre- and post-revolutionary eras are due to "objective factors, limited manpower, economic, and agricultural resources" of the earlier period. Once these "objective factors" faded away by the late 1700s, "more intense and prolonged wars became possible."[15]

In fact, evidence can be adduced on both sides of this debate. An international and customary Law of War elicited widespread conformity before and after 1792. Despite the *levée en masse*, the French army in 1792–93 was replete with regular army units under seasoned commanders who adhered to the Law of War. With some exceptions, the Prussians and Austrians did the same.[16] Not until the summer of 1793, when Maximilian Robespierre and the Jacobins (who controlled the National Convention) announced the creation of an army that would replace "military honor" with "the honor of the revolutionary,"[17] do we see a significant abandonment of the Law of War. Lazare Carnot, a Jacobin leader and military commander, expressed the National Convention's new policy: "One should wage war *à l'outrance* or go home." In an address to his commanding officers, he exhorted his listeners to "exterminate [the enemy] to the bitter end." Thereafter, the National Convention issued proclamations denying ransom and ordering the execution of prisoners of war in order to convey "the vengeance of an outraged nation." Although few commanders or their troops obeyed the order, as many as 11,000 people may have been killed under its auspices until the order was repealed in 1794.[18]

One of the most shocking episodes of this troubled phase of French history was the civil war known as the "Vendée uprising" of 1793. The Vendée is an area located south of Brittany between the Loire valley and Sèvres, the population of which was disproportionately royalist and religious. Implementation of the conscription acts in February 1793 ignited rebellion among a people who had never fully accepted the Revolution. A joint peasant-royalist army of 30,000 men formed and captured several cities in the spring of 1793. In the fall, however, the insurgents were sent reeling by defeats at Cholet (October 17, 1793) and Le Mans (December 12, 1793). During and after the battle of Le Mans, some 15,000 rebels were killed and prisoners slaughtered by Republican forces under the command of General François-Joseph Westermann, prompting this report from Westermann to Paris notable for its calloused brutality:

> There is no more Vendée, citizens, it has perished under our free sword along with its women and children. I have just buried it in the marches and mud of Savenay. Following the orders that you gave me I have crushed children under the feet of horses, massacred women who at least ... will engender no more brigands. I have no prisoners with which to reproach myself. I have exterminated everything, and the streets of the countryside are strewn with corpses. In some places they form pyramids.[19]

Suppression of the Vendée uprising was purchased at the cost of 250,000 lives—roughly one-third of the region's population—which included combatants and defenseless civilians.[20]

The appalling bloodshed in the Vendée, while undeniably grim, should nonetheless be placed in its proper historical context. The insurrection occurred during a time when the National Convention perceived itself, with good reason, to be under attack from without and within. Involved in a struggle for its very existence, the Republic's armies responded to the rebellion in a manner not dissimilar from other eras in world history. In order to gauge the singularity of the Vendée massacres, we need only recall the Athenians' fearsome reaction when the island of Melos refused to join the Delian League, the Roman practice of taking and executing hostages at the first sign of resistance by subjugated peoples, or the exemption of rebellion from the Law of War in sixteenth-century Iberia, an exemption approved by Ayala, and one productive of such violence that Gentili would call rebellion the "chief incentive to cruelty."

The macabre bloodshed of the Church-sponsored war against the Albigensians (1209–29) may also be seen as the outgrowth of efforts to suppress a rebellion—in this case, the rebellion of a heretical Christian sect that rejected the Church's sacraments. In the words of historian Malcolm Barber, "this heresy was therefore much more than an argument over an intellectual conceit or even a fringe reforming movement which had overstepped the mark; to the papacy [Albigensianism] was an attack upon the very fabric of Christian society."[21] When the Albigensian town of Béziers fell to the Crusaders in July 1209, some of the townspeople sought refuge in a local church. The invaders beat to death every man, woman, and child found inside, then set the city on fire. In the conflagration, the rest of Béziers's population was burned alive. By the end of the sack, the deadly harvest amounted to 15,000 or more residents of the town. Nor was the fate of the denizens of Béziers unique: at Bram the Crusaders gouged out the eyes and sliced off the noses of the city's defenders, while after the castle of Montségur was taken, the victors forced 200 men and women into a wooden shed and burnt them alive.[22] These medieval atrocities are still able to curdle the blood, although they preceded the French Revolution and the onset of modern warfare by nearly 600 years.

The medieval destruction of the Albigensians replicates a pattern that has surfaced in all urban cultures *in extremis*: the tendency, as Carnot crisply phrased it, to "wage war *à l'outrance*" against rebels. The Crusaders did not regard their Albigensian opponents as men, women, and children, but as imminent threats to Christendom.[23] Similarly, Republican soldiers in the Vendée perceived the insurgents as a menace to the Revolution and the transcendent ideals of liberty, fraternity, and equality it symbolized. Roger Chickering points out that the worst fighting of the American Civil War took place in Missouri, a border state in which guerrilla and partisan warfare provoked stern repression by Union forces. Much of the violence, however, was irregular, and the targets were often individual families attacked by ambush or raiding parties. Chickering does not see the spoor of modernity in this piecemeal carnage; instead, he views it as a cascade of violent episodes dissociated from modern warfare, occurring outside the formal chain of command.[24]

In sum, the alleged line of demarcation between a milder premodern style of waging war and a harsher modern method ushered in by the French Revolution is, at best, a hazy one. Calling the separation even further into question is Napoleon's recognition of the Law of War in France's armed struggle against Austria. Napoleon, his generals, and their officers engaged in reciprocal gestures of respect toward their British and Austrian opponents, arranging for mutual assistance in the event they were captured as prisoners. Evidence exists that scouts on both sides of the conflict apprised each other of pending attacks and spared small parties of enemy soldiers. The French generally treated prisoners of war well, often repatriating them, sometimes in full uniform and armed, as was done after the battles of Jena (1806) and Tilsit (1807). Austrian and Prussian officers captured in battle were typically paroled; other soldiers were employed in agricultural or labor battalions, for which they were paid.[25] However, as it does in every armed conflict, bitter fighting often led to the deterioration of these standards, and military necessity sometimes eclipsed the Law of War. At the battle of Austerlitz (1805), perhaps the most important battle of the Napoleonic Wars before 1813, French forces denied quarter to Austrian and Russian troops. By 1813 the Prussians were able to repay Napoleon in his own coin at Katzbach (1813) and Waterloo (1815), beating to death and bayoneting wounded French soldiers on the battlefield. This curious duality in the Law of War—its mercurial character, which can change with whiplash abruptness—was dependent on the vagaries and shifting circumstances of combat. Emerich de Vattel, the eighteenth-century Swiss jurist and natural law theorist, recognized that military necessity could override the restraints typically observed in battle. What, however, constituted military necessity? Rothenberg briskly outlines the occasions when it arose: "Military necessity was invoked when supplies were low, when prisoners became a burden, or when commanders considered them a threat to their own troops."[26] Napoleon himself adopted different policies concerning prisoner treatment depending on the exigencies of the moment: in 1796 he responded to a food shortage by paroling 2,000 Austrian prisoners of war in French custody, yet three years later at Jaffa he ordered that thousands of Turkish prisoners of war be shot, claiming military necessity as justification.[27]

The unbridled savagery of the Peninsular War (1808–13) is sometimes advanced as proof of the new era of devastating warfare unleashed by the French Revolution and

Napoleon.[28] To enforce his "Continental System" designed to exclude British trade from Europe, Napoleon invaded Portugal (1807), then turned his attention to Spain, where he forced the abdication of the Spanish king and appointed his own brother Joseph Bonaparte as ruler (1808). What ensued was a fierce guerrilla war between French occupation troops and the Spanish population. The guerrillas staged attacks on French soldiers with the purpose of both terrorizing them and hampering their ability to live off the surrounding countryside. According to a contemporary report from a French staff officer, the guerrillas "attempted to destroy us in detail, falling upon small detachments, massacring sick and isolated men, destroying convoys, and kidnapping messengers."[29] The Spanish *Guerra de la Independencia* (War of Independence) spiraled rapidly into a pitiless fight to the death, in which guerrillas denied quarter to French soldiers they encountered, provoking vicious reprisals from the French. The "Spanish ulcer," as Napoleon bitterly termed it, inspired some of the most graphic and disturbing images of warfare ever portrayed in art—the "Disasters of War" (*Desastres de la Guerra*) of the Spanish painter Francisco de Goya (1746–1828). Goya's etchings not only capture the horror, devastation, and suffering of the Peninsular War, but eerily prefigure the excesses of the "people's wars" of subsequent times. The battle of Zaragoza was one of the many episodes of this conflict that powered the dreadful intensity of Goya's art noire. When the city fell in February 1809 after twenty-three days of house-to-house fighting, French soldiers vented their anger and frustration on Zaragoza's civilian population. By the conflict's end, some two-thirds of Zaragoza's population (34,000 people) lay dead.[30]

As we assess the validity of the "total war" theory, we should bear in mind that strands of the Napoleonic wars like the Spanish Peninsular War qualify as rebellions, a category of military conflict that has always elicited severe repression. When violations of the Law of War are weighed against evidence of conformity to it, it is by no means clear that combatants during the Napoleonic period were peculiarly inclined to abandon well-established customs and restraints. Rather, Gunther Rothenberg's conclusion that the Age of Revolution in France (1790–1815) exhibited "substantial continuities with the traditional patterns restraining war" seems to have the better of the argument.[31] And yet, the Age of Revolution does appear in retrospect to mark an important change in the history of warfare, a change which in subsequent periods will sharply increase the occurrence of war crimes. Roger Chickering, like Rothenberg, is skeptical of the total war thesis but acknowledges that the mobilization of the population in support of war as it developed in the late eighteenth century contributed to a long-term, deadly trend in warfare: the "calculated erasure of the bounds between combatant and noncombatant."[32] Twentieth-century "morale bombing"[33] is historically inconceivable without the previous transformation of the civilian population into a critical source of war production. If the idea of waging war directly on civilians did not occur to premodern generations, it was primarily due to the limitations of their technology. War has always been "a bad taste business," as the British journalist Martin Bell memorably describes it. Clausewitz understood that, in its pure essence, war was "primordial violence, hatred, and enmity."[34] From the Upper Paleolithic killing sites at Djebel Sahaba to the execution trenches of My Lai, the aim of war has always been the destruction of the enemy. Throughout the history of warfare, the enemy has at times been defined as every man, woman, and child belonging to the other side, particularly when the other side resists siege or revolts against established authority. Had Roman legionnaires or medieval knights possessed machine guns, high ballistic cannon, or atomic bombs, it is likely these weapons would have been deployed against civilian targets. It is the fateful confluence of hyperdestructive technology with the galloping increase in the size of armies, the latter process made possible by nationalizing military forces and incorporating the population into war production, which accounts for the horrific loss of human life in modern wars.

That this historical trend largely begins with the era of Napoleon is scarcely in doubt. The French Revolution's ideal of the "citizen soldier" bound to his nation's cause by personal conviction is a marker of the onset of nationalism. The French ideal spread throughout Europe as the countries invaded and occupied by Napoleon's armies imitated the new paradigm of warfare. To the Napoleonic wars can be attributed the reforms of the Prussian army undertaken between 1805 and 1809, set in motion by Prussia's defeat at Jena-Auerstadt in 1806. The major thrust of the reforms, in Prussia as in other states (such as the Austrian Empire), was to build a people's army in accordance with the French example. From 1808 forward, for example, Prussia restructured membership in the officer corps to emphasize talent rather than birthright. Napoleon's invasions, moreover, enkindled a new sense of national consciousness in the European countries he invaded. From the Iberian peninsula to Russia and radiating outward to Spain's colonies in the New World, nationalism emerged as one of the most potent psychological forces in modern world history. Under its influence wars would cease to be dynastic struggles between kings; rather, they became struggles between nations covering ever larger swaths of the earth's surface, in which much of the adult population participated and with which nearly all emotionally identified.[35]

Henceforth, wars would become more destructive. Where pre-revolutionary battles could produce casualties of nearly 20 percent,[36] the Napoleonic Wars resulted in the deaths of 20 percent *of all Frenchmen born between 1790 and 1795*—a mortality rate, John Lynn points out, slightly lower than that produced by the First World War, which wiped out one-quarter of Frenchmen born between 1891 and 1895. Of course, Napoleon and his adversaries lacked Big Bertha, machine guns, poison gas, and submarines. It is to these refinements in men's ability to kill each other rather than a disregard for the Law of War that we may ascribe the growing lethality of combat in the modern age, applied with a creeping inflationary tendency to civilian populations.

The nineteenth century

Technology

In *Moral Man and Immoral Society*, the American theologian Reinhold Niebuhr wrote:

> The very forces which lift man above nature give natural impulses a new and a more awful potency in the human world. Man fights his battles with instruments

in which mind has sharpened nature's claws; and his ferocities are more sustained than those of the natural world, where they are prompted only by the moods and the necessities of the moment.[37]

The "forces which lift man above nature" were of course human cognitive skills, lending an "awful potency" to "natural impulses" such as the struggle for survival. Nineteenth-century achievements of technical reason, ranging from breakthroughs in health care, dynamic sources of energy, and military science, were truly epochal. When technical reason heightened military destructiveness, it became a prime stimulus in efforts to restrain its most pernicious works. In the next section we will explore laws and treaties designed to curb the most baneful tendencies of modern warfare; here, we briefly consider the claws honed to razor sharpness by human ingenuity—the weaponry of the mid- to late nineteenth century.

Military historians have characterized the Crimean War (1853–56) as the first to showcase scientific advances in ballistic technology. Bullets hollowed at their base and grooved with helical cuts to accelerate their velocity,[38] called "minié" balls, tripled the effective range of rifled muskets from 100 to 300 yards.[39] Impressed by these refinements in artillery during the Crimean War, British industrialist William Armstrong extended the technology of rifling from bullets to cannon shells, enabling the manufacture of rifled cannon for the army and heavier guns for the navy. Further, Armstrong's rifled cannon were breechloaders, meaning that instead of being loaded from the muzzle the shells were inserted at the breech, thereby reducing the time needed for reloading. In Germany, the steelmaker Alfred Krupp engineered the development of steel guns, which by 1900 spanned calibers between 77 mm and 155 mm, reaching 420 mm by 1914.[40]

Few inventions in military technology before the First World War, however, could rival in sheer destructive impact the machine-gun. Although the French had devised a crude semi-automatic gun by 1870, the creation of a fully automatic weapon did not occur until 1884, when the American inventor and engineer Hiram Maxim produced the first true machine-gun, one that ejected 600 bullets per minute. The frightful destructiveness of Maxim's invention was not completely revealed until the First World War, a conflict in which every combatant nation deployed the machine-gun against its adversaries, and with appalling effect: able to cover a distance of 1,000 yards and 500 yards with accuracy, machine guns turned massed infantry assaults into suicide missions.[41]

The First World War also became the staging ground for the first widespread use of both lethal and non-lethal poison gas in wartime. Although explicitly prohibited by Hague Convention II of 1899, belligerents on both sides employed poison gas during the war. The first (non-lethal) gas attack was undertaken by the French in August 1914, when they deployed tear gas against the Germans. Two months later, the Germans attacked the British at Neuve Chapelle with a chemical irritant.[42] Neither the French nor the German attacks had a discernible impact on their intended targets. The first major poison gas attacks did not occur until 1915. In April the Germans lobbed 4,000 cylinders of chlorine at enemy lines in the Ypres Salient near Langemarck, with appalling effect: hundreds of Allied soldiers were mortally affected or rendered unconscious. The German army deployed poison gas again in May 1915, this time in Poland. In September of that year, the British for the first time used poison gas, firing 5,245 cylinders of chlorine during the Battle of Loos (France) that killed 600 German soldiers. In October the Germans strafed the French with shells containing chlorine and phosgene, killing 815 French soldiers and gravely sickening 4,000 more. While the use of poison gas would continue throughout the war, its effectiveness was limited, in part because of battlefield adaptations to gas attacks like the gas mask. Poison gas never played a decisive role in the outcome of the war.[43]

Treaties/conventions

The convergence of national armies supplied by industrial economies with the advent of ever deadlier weaponry helps account for the first multilateral treaties in the mid- to late nineteenth century. These treaties were efforts to codify the Law of War, which until that time had existed in diverse scattered sources—chiefly, the writings of legal scholars, the self-limiting practice of states, and (rudimentarily) the criminal codes of national armies. The drive to limit certain forms of warmaking by means of written instruments was undoubtedly affected by the rich, dynamic legal environment of the Age of Enlightenment and its aftermath. The late eighteenth and early nineteenth centuries witnessed an extraordinary flowering in the Western world of endeavors to codify law, endeavors that included William Blackstone's *Commentaries on the Laws of England* (1765) and the promulgation of criminal (1791, 1810) and civil law codes (1804) in France. In Germany, political fragmentation for a time impeded national codification, but scholars like Anton Friedrich Justus Thibaut (1722–1840) nonetheless pressed for a modernized, trans-German codification of civil law for all of the German lands. Coincident with this burst of interest in codification was a wave of written constitutions, first in Sweden (1772), then in the USA (1789) and France (1791). As historian James Sheehan has argued, during the nineteenth century "a constitution came to be regarded as the prerequisite for an orderly public life virtually everywhere."[44] In the view of Sheehan (as well as Max Weber, whom Sheehan follows), legality in the form of law codes, constitutions, court verdicts, and administrative decrees largely replaced royal and religious authority "as the most important source of political legitimacy."[45] Such legitimacy, however, was strictly enforceable only within the boundaries of a sovereign state. When considering the Law of War, the problems of legitimacy and enforcement are immediately evident: in wars, no written body of law decreed by a recognized authority and binding on all the belligerents set norms for conduct on the battlefield. Western governments would try to repair this deficiency through two sources: (1) codifying the Law of War in treaties and conventions, and (2) codifying the Law of War more robustly in national military law codes.

The first multilateral treaty related to constraining warfare was the 1856 Paris Declaration Respecting Maritime Law, which abolished privateering[46] and generally protected the integrity of neutral property. While few countries signed the Declaration, many non-signatories in ensuing decades complied with its rules, and it gradually acquired the status of customary international law.[47] (The USA, although a non-party to the treaty, nonetheless respected its terms, insisting in 1913 that as customary international law the Declaration bound all the belligerents in the First World War.)[48] The 1856 Declaration did not, however, prescribe humane treatment of prisoners of war or the wounded. Such regulation would not appear in a multilateral treaty until the Geneva Convention for the Amelioration of the Wounded in Time of War (1864). In the two centuries preceding the first Geneva Convention, hundreds of bilateral treaties had been signed by nation-states, providing for care to the wounded and immunity to capture of each side's army surgeons. These treaties, while important in maintaining respect for the Law of War, were valid only in conflicts between the parties to them, and their provisions lapsed once the particular treaty expired. Motivated by an eyewitness account of the immense and pointless suffering of the wounded and dying after the Battle of Solferino in 1859,[49] the president of the Geneva Society of Public Utility, Gustave Moynier, convened an international meeting in Geneva in 1863, attended by delegates of fourteen countries and four philanthropic organizations. The express purpose was to discuss how wounded soldiers could be better cared for on the battlefield. The upshot of the conference was the founding of a society, the International Committee for the Relief of the Wounded, committed to providing medical care to the wounded on all sides during wartime. (The Committee was renamed the "International Committee of the Red Cross," or ICRC, in 1875.) The ICRC's work would, of course, be stymied without the agreement of national governments that had always been jealously protective of their sovereignty. The translation of humanitarian ideas into humanitarian acts required the consent of these nation-states.[50]

The first step toward securing international support for the humanitarian ideals of the ICRC was taken one year after its creation. Prodded by the Committee's members, in 1864 the Swiss government held a congress of representatives from Europe and the Americas in order to convert the ICRC's concerns for the wounded into a binding treaty. The result was the first Geneva Convention, which the representatives of twelve countries attending the congress signed on August 22, 1864. The Convention obligated its signatories to spare field hospitals from military attack, to treat the soldiers of all the belligerents impartially, to protect civilians aiding the wounded, and to respect the Red Cross symbol as a protective insignia when attached to certain persons and equipment.[51] Over time other countries joined the Convention, so that it gradually met with almost universal acceptance.[52]

On the heels of the Geneva Convention followed other international treaties that sought to restrict warfare. All of them were infused with the deep humanitarian concerns informing the Convention. In 1863 the Imperial Russian Army employed a bullet to detonate ammunition wagons that exploded on collision with a hard surface. Four years later, the bullet was reengineered to explode on contact with soft surfaces. After the Imperial War Minister approached Czar Alexander II about banning this bullet from military usage, Alexander announced he would convene an International Military Commission in St. Petersburg to discuss the issue. Representatives from sixteen states met on three days in November 1868, producing the first international treaty to ban deployment of a weapon during wartime. Specifically, the "St. Petersburg Declaration" prohibited the use of projectiles less than 400 grams in weight that were either "explosive" or "inflammable," on the grounds that such weapons would "uselessly aggravate the sufferings of disabled men, or render their death inevitable." Clearly actuated by an overriding humanitarian concern, the language of the Declaration insisted that "the necessities of war ought to yield to the requirements of humanity," and implied that the utter destruction of the enemy's forces was not a "legitimate object" of warfare—rather, the only legitimate aim was "to weaken the military forces of the enemy."[53]

Tsar Alexander was not finished with his efforts to tame the rampant lion of war. In 1874 he and William I of Prussia sponsored an international conference in Brussels, Belgium, with the goal of adopting as a binding convention a Russian draft codifying the Law of War. Shadowed by controversy, the conference was unsuccessful in securing ratification of the draft as a treaty; however, the delegates' acceptance of a final declaration embodying nearly all of the Russian draft was a watershed in the history of the Law of War. It was the first time that European states agreed about the basic principles that should inform a codification of the Law of War.[54] These principles included several key themes that would subsequently influence *The Oxford Manual* (1880) and the two Hague Conventions (1899 and 1907), among them the insistence that the Law of War extended to civilians and militias (Arts. 9–11), a rejection of the view that belligerents could employ all means within their power to harm their opponents (Article 12), prohibiting the denial of quarter and weapons "calculated to cause unnecessary suffering" (Article 13), and forbidding military attack on undefended cities and villages (Article 15). Articles 23–34 dealt mainly with the duty to treat prisoners of war humanely.[55]

The significance of the Brussels Declaration should not be gauged by its direct impact on the Law of War (as noted, it was never ratified as a binding treaty). Rather, it resides in the Declaration's indirect influence on the Hague Conventions by way of *The Oxford Manual*. The Manual was the handiwork of the *Institut de droit international* (Institute of International Law), an organization co-founded in 1873 by the Red Cross president Gustave Moynier with the goal "to promote the development of international law" and "to become the organ of the civilized world's legal conscience."[56] Moynier and his colleagues sought to repair the deficiencies of the Declaration by establishing a commission to examine them. The commission ultimately recommended preparation of a code of war acceptable enough to secure international approval. Thereafter, the Institute formed in 1879 a second commission to work on the recommended codification. The result was *The Laws of War on Land*, or *The Oxford Manual*, which was published in 1880. The author of the Manual was the indefatigable Moynier. Less than a decade before he wrote the Manual, Moynier had campaigned for the creation of an international court to prosecute violations of the Geneva Convention of 1864, thereby gaining the distinction of being the first proponent of an international jurisdiction over war crimes. By 1873 he had modified his position, replacing his demand for an international court with a call on states to pass legislation criminalizing violations of the Convention.[57] This perspective deferential to the will of national governments pervaded the Manual when it was written in 1880. The Preface acknowledged that adherence to the Law of War as defined by the Manual could best be fostered through adoption of its tenets by national governments, rather than the unlikely ratification of an international treaty.[58]

The Manual was made up of eighty-six articles arranged in three sections. Two of the sections related to general rules governing hostilities, including conduct of troops in occupied territories, the treatment of prisoners of war, and the issue of prisoners in neutral countries. The third section, which Moynier convinced the Institute to retain in the final draft, would provoke a vehement, and revealing, backlash. According to Section III, Article 84 of the Manual, "If any of the foregoing rules be violated, the offending parties should be punished, after a judicial hearing, by the belligerent in whose hands they are. Therefore ... Offenders against the laws of war are liable to the punishments specified in the penal law."[59] Reinforcing this call for criminal punishment, Moynier lobbied for an international convention that would oblige states to align their criminal law with the Geneva Convention, and pressed for an international commission to investigate alleged violations of it. Opposition swiftly arose against Moynier's proposals. Few countries embraced the Manual; as David Crowe remarks, Argentina alone adopted it, and only for a short time.[60] Interestingly, in view of developments some thirty-four years later, the Germans were among the most vocal critics of Moynier's ideas. German rejection of his main tenets had surfaced already during the Brussels Conference in 1874, where German representatives clashed with other delegates over the degree to which military necessity allowed reprisals.[61]

To understand Germany's position on the Law of War—an attitude that framed not only its progressively lawless conception of war in the late nineteenth century, but also its dominant paradigm on the eve of the First World War—we should recall that the Brussels Conference took place scarcely three years after the Franco-Prussian War. Historians have traced the seeds of Germany's devaluation of international law to the impact on German thinking of Prussia's sensational, meteoric victories over a succession of enemies between 1864 and 1871. Within the space of seven years, Prussia defeated Denmark, Austria, and France, thereby enabling unification of Germany in 1871. For historian Isabel Hull, these impressive victories, which were secured by the chief of the Prussian general staff Helmuth von Moltke's strategy of concentrating maximum force on the enemy's army for the purpose of utterly destroying it, effected a critical change in the German interpretation of military necessity. At the heart of Moltke's scintillating triumphs was the goal of a "victory of annihilation" (*Vernichtungskrieg*), in which an offensive blow, massive and overwhelming, quickly vanquished enemy troops, resulting in a swift end to the conflict. Embedded in this "victory of annihilation" construct was the "idea of destruction"(*Vernichtungsgedanke*)—the notion that the goal of warfare was not just the political submission of the enemy (as Clausewitz had suggested), nor the weakening of the enemy's military strength (as the Brussels Declaration had asserted), but his physical obliteration.[62]

By the time of the Brussels Conference, the "idea of destruction" had decisively reshaped the German army's conception of the Law of War. The focus of this reformulation was the doctrine of military necessity. According to the modern view (as discussed by McCoubrey), "military necessity is a doctrine within the laws of armed conflict which recognizes the potential impracticality of full compliance with legal norms in certain circumstances, and, accordingly, may mitigate or expunge culpability for prima facie

COUNT VON MOLTKE.

Figure 25 Helmuth von Moltke, chief of the Prussian General Staff during the Franco-Prussian War. © Wikimedia Commons (public domain).

unlawful action in appropriate cases of armed conflict."[63] Typically, the "appropriate cases" that might legitimate otherwise illegal conduct were instances of self-preservation. Hull contends that the idea of destruction born during Germany's wars of unification led German policymakers to substitute success in battle for the criterion of self-preservation—thereby expanding the range of situations in which the Law of War might be ignored altogether. This was the view that Prussian Cavalry General Julius von Hartmann expounded in an 1876 article on "military necessity and humanity."[64] Because many jurists at the time regarded Hartmann as expressing the essential German view on the matter, we will delve into his perspective in greater depth.

According to Hartmann, war was "abnormal," an "exceptional state" (*Ausnahmezustand*), which negated "the bases on which civilization and culture rest." It "returns to conditions which grant to individual energy and power unlimited justification"—meaning that, "once war has started, then only the requirements of military necessity are operative."[65] The only persons who could limit military necessity were the commander and the troops under his command. While he supported the Geneva Convention of 1864, Hartmann firmly demurred to any other efforts to restrain military necessity through law, such as those contemplated by the Brussels Declaration. Hartmann did not construe military necessity narrowly as most non-German legal scholars of his era were inclined to do, who identified it with self-preservation as a rare exception to the general duty of compliance with the Law of War. Hartmann, by contrast, affirmed that whatever enabled an army to prevail qualified as an exception to the Law of War, a contention that commentators at the time assailed for removing any limitations on military necessity. By the late nineteenth and early twentieth centuries, leading German jurists had adopted Hartmann's desiccated understanding of the Law of War, prompting one of them, Johann Friedrich Ludwig Lueder, to proclaim the nihilist conviction that "when the exception [i.e., war] occurs, following its nature it cancels law, and *Kriegsraison* [military necessity] has precedence over *Kriegsmanier* [the Law of War]."[66]

Some of these jurists (including Lueder) cautioned that a situation of genuine military necessity was rare. This and similar caveats suggest that their endorsement of Hartmann's negationist view was driven by a desire to make international legal constraints on war acceptable to German military circles, insofar as the military perspective, to a greater degree than in other Western countries, shaped German perceptions of international law.[67] Spokesmen of the German position, after all, had nearly scuttled the Brussels conference by insisting that military necessity legitimated reprisals against civilians. German delegates to the conference likely affected the decision to strike provisions of the Russian draft that had imposed stringent restrictions on the right of reprisal.[68] Between the Brussels conference and the First World War, a uniquely German conception of the Law of War that conditioned its observance on military success became pervasive first in German military institutions and practice, then in Wilhelmine politics and society as well. Hull stresses that this conception is not primarily visible in military law treatises of the era. To find it, she advises, you must peer into the cultural practices of the German army.

Indifference toward the Law of War was already instilled in cadets during their training; the War Academy from 1907 to 1911 ignored it as a subject of instruction. A Reichstag survey conducted in the 1920s of prewar military instruction manuals found that only one of them contained a chapter on international law. Moreover, the sole official military handbook prior to the war was written by Major Rudolf von Friederich, who often disregarded the rules set forth in the Hague Conventions because his sources, which consisted of "the current general opinion" within German military circles, ignored them. Instead, von Friederich reproduced Hartmann's position and went on to conclude that military necessity abrogated not only the customs of war, but written law as a whole. Hull writes that other Wilhelmine manuals exhibited a similar hostility toward positive law as a constraint on war. She asserts—and this is a point crucial not only in our understanding of the Law of War at the turn of the century, but throughout world history—that "in the end it is less important what German representatives wrote or said than what German officers (and soldiers) did."[69] In Imperial Germany, the scholarship fell readily into alignment with a military practice profoundly agnostic, if not outspokenly hostile, toward the Law of War.[70] During the period stretching from the unification of Germany to the outbreak of the First World War, the army's novel equation of military necessity with success on the battlefield infiltrated other corners of German society, breeding a militarist ethos within a German middle class that had come to expect the kind of rapid, sensational victories the army had racked up against the Danes, Austrians, and French. As the notion of a fatal encirclement hardened in German thinking, out of which Germany could break only through a prodigious master-stroke to knock its enemies once and for all out of the war, law receded as a restraining force. As Hull grimly notes, the stage was being set for Imperial Germany's plunge into criminality and self-destruction during the First World War.[71]

While Imperial Germany drifted away from international law in the late 1800s, other countries were paddling steadily toward it. As he did at St. Petersburg and Brussels, the Russian Tsar led the way to the first multilateral codification of the laws of land warfare in world history, the Hague Conventions of 1899 and 1907. Paradoxically, Tsar Nicholas II's original aim had nothing to do with the Law of War; rather, he sought to reduce the stockpile of armaments throughout the world and thereby avoid a catastrophic war. Toward this end, in August 1898 the Tsar proposed an international conference to negotiate a treaty on general retrenchment of arms. In response to requests for more information on the agenda for the conference, the Russians presented an eight-point list of objectives, which included freezing military budgets, prohibiting development of powerful new weaponry and bombardment from balloons, and banning submarine torpedo-boats, among several other items.[72] The Dutch queen Wilhelmina offered to hold the conference at her summer residence in The Hague. Here 100 delegates from twenty-six countries convened the First Hague Conference from May 18 to July 29, 1899. In fact, the conference comprised three commissions devoted to different purposes. One commission worked on disarmament, another on affirming or amending the Geneva Convention and Brussels Declaration, and the third on resolving international conflict through arbitration.[73] The work of the first commission foundered on the opposition of the leading nations, particularly Germany. To the Tsar's overture that military budgets be frozen for five years (and navies' budgets for three), the German delegates rejoined that their country's military budget did not pose an undue strain on their economy, and that any adjustments disturbing the balance of armaments might lead to war. The British proved equally intransigent: their remit given before the conference began was to foil any initiatives that might weaken British naval superiority. As David Crowe notes, the first commission—whose task represented the Tsar's original purpose for the entire conference—produced little more than an effete declaration that reduction of "military charges" would be "extremely desirable."[74]

The second commission under the chairmanship of Fyodor Martens, a Russian jurist and diplomat, ultimately sent sixty-six articles to the conference for consideration, many of them based on the terms of the Brussels Declaration. The subcommittee agonized, however, over a contentious issue: the treatment under the Law of War of resistance within occupied territory. On the one side, proponents like the Belgian representative argued that resistance was a human right vested in the citizens of small countries invaded by larger ones. On the other side, critics like the German military delegate, Colonel Groß von Schwarzenberg, opposed legitimizing resistance fighters, demanding that every article of what would become the Hague Convention contain an exception based on military necessity. Martens finally resolved the stalemate by means of a clause inserted into the commission's draft, which would be subsequently incorporated into the Preamble to Hague Convention II of 1899. This passage, now known as the "Martens Clause," announced the delegates' intention to mitigate the "evils of war," yet conceded the impossibility of building consensus on "provisions embracing all the cases which occur in practice." The remainder of the clause struck a blow for the critics of military necessity and untrammeled command authority. We read:

> On the other hand, it could not be intended by the Conference that the cases not provided for should, for want of a written provision, be left to the arbitrary judgement of the military commanders.
>
> Until a perfectly complete code of the laws of war is issued, the High Contracting Parties think it right to declare that in cases not included in the Regulations adopted by them, populations and belligerents remain under the protection ... of international law, as they result from the usages established between civilized nations, from the laws of humanity, and the requirements of the public conscience.[75]

As both David Crowe and Adam Roberts point out, the Martens Clause did not solve the problem of whether resistance fighters qualified for protection under the Law of War.[76] From its inception until today, the Clause has been the object of varied interpretation by international jurists. In Chapter 8 we will see how it became a precarious ledge on which the novel charge of crimes against humanity was able to find a toehold at the Nuremberg war crimes trials.

The third commission, which focused on arbitration, produced a fifty-seven-article draft calling for, *inter alia*, mediation, international arbitration, and the creation of international commissions of inquiry. Its most visible achievement was laying the basis for subsequent creation of an International Commission of Inquiry, as well as a Permanent Court of Arbitration.[77]

Although public perception regarded the First Hague Conference as a failure given its inability to achieve meaningful disarmament,[78] the Conference in fact produced not only the historically consequential Martens Clause, but three conventions and three declarations. The participating nations had until December 31, 1899, to sign each of these documents, which would then become valid on September 4, 1900. Some of the participating countries signed the Final Act but declined signing the conventions and declarations. Others, like the USA, signed the Final Act but only some of the conventions and declarations. In sum, only France and Russia approved the Final Act and all the conventions and declarations. These results, on their face, may seem meager, but we should recall that Hague Convention II on the Law and Customs of War on Land was the first multilateral treaty to codify the Law of War in world history. (The Lieber Code, which is discussed below, was a national military code rather than a treaty.) Further, the arbitration provisions of Hague Convention I were invoked in the years after the Conference to end the Russo-Japanese War, in which US President Theodore Roosevelt served as the arbitrator, and for which he received the Nobel Peace Prize in 1906. Finally, the First Hague Conference was the indispensable prelude to a milestone in the history of the Law of War—the Second Hague Conference of 1907.[79]

Before the First Hague Conference dispersed, the delegates agreed to meet at a later date in order to revisit issues that had failed to gain acceptance. In 1904 Theodore Roosevelt proposed convening the sequel meeting to the 1899 conference. Absorbed with the Russo-Japanese War, the Tsar was in no position to pursue Roosevelt's suggestion until the summer of 1905. With US concurrence, the Russians circulated a proposed agenda in April 1906 for the second conference, listing as top priorities arbitration of international conflicts and further elaboration of the Law of War (especially in the area of how war was initiated, neutral rights, and maritime hostilities). The Second Hague Conference, when it met from June 15 to October 18, 1907, comprised 256 delegates from forty-four countries organized into four commissions. As with the First Hague Conference, the second did not succeed in limiting armaments—the putative reason for its existence—nor did it secure agreement to binding arbitration (German opposition here proved decisive). Nonetheless, by mid-October the Second Conference had adopted thirteen conventions and one declaration. Ten of the conventions concerned the Law of War; eight of them dealt with naval warfare.[80]

From the vantage point of the Law of War, the most important of the Second Conference's achievements was the Fourth Hague Convention of 1907. Although Hague IV was planned to supersede Hague Convention II of 1899 for States Parties to both conventions, eighteen states that had approved Hague II were not parties to Hague IV, and thus remained bound by the 1899 convention. As Adam Roberts observes, Hague IV largely copied the articles of its predecessor, adding only a small handful of meaningful changes.[81] Hague IV contained provisions relating to the definition of belligerents, the treatment of prisoners of war (strikingly, the prohibition of denying quarter), rules governing sieges, bombardments, flags of truce, capitulations, and armistices, and the authority of military government occupying enemy territory. Among the Convention's many articles, several stand out from the crowd with a prominence due to their long- term importance. First, the Preamble to Hague IV reprises the 1899 Martens Clause, asserting that soldiers and civilians remained under the protection of the "law of nations" even in situations not specifically addressed in the text of the Convention. Second, in line with its 1899 forerunner, Hague IV set forth a "general participation" (*si omnes*) clause in Article 2, rendering the Convention applicable only to conflicts in which all of the belligerents were States Parties to it. Nazi war criminals would later invoke Article 2 to nullify Hague IV as applied to the Second World War, insofar as Bulgaria was not a state-party to the Convention. Third, Article 22 of the Convention reaffirmed a principle of humanity found in the St. Petersburg Declaration, the Brussels Declaration, and *The Oxford Manual*—the principle that the right of an army to harm its enemy was "not unlimited." Fourth, while the Preamble to the Convention recognized "military requirements" (read: military necessity) as a potential check on efforts "to diminish the evils of war," military necessity could never, under any circumstances, justify such evils. These included the use of poison weapons, treacherously killing or wounding the enemy, denying quarter, or using weaponry designed "to cause unnecessary suffering" (all found in Article 23). However, seizure or destruction of enemy property was permitted if "demanded by military necessity," as were "ruses of war" needed to obtain information about the enemy (Article 24).[82]

The US delegation to the Second Hague Conference anticipated convocation of a third Hague conference in June 1914 that would further clarify and expand on the accomplishments of the first two. Their hopes died aborning as Europe descended into world war in August 1914. In the face of military necessity, the Hague principles entered into a period of eclipse that would pass away only when the war ended five years later.

Public perception of the Second Hague Conference at the time was far from uniformly positive. The main goals of both Hague Conferences, i.e., disarmament and averting an arms race, had not been reached. The government of the man who had been the driving force behind the Hague peace conferences, Tsar Nicholas II, refused to support disarmament in the fear it might prevent Russia from reconstructing its army after the Russo-Japanese War.[83] These failures notwithstanding, the Hague Conventions would take their place among the most important documents in the history of the Law of War. They would influence the 1949 Geneva Conventions (particularly Article 135, Convention III and Article 154, Convention IV), the 1977 Geneva Protocol I, and the 1980 Convention on certain conventional weapons.[84] Just as significant, military law codes would incorporate elements of the Hague Conventions, providing a vital conduit through which the Hague rules could shape the education, training, and discipline of army members throughout the world. National military codes and war manuals had been the primary repositories of the Law of War for centuries. Historically, the most notable of these codes, General Orders, No. 100 of the Union Army of 1863, better known as the "Lieber Code," decisively influenced the Brussels Declaration, *Oxford Manual*, and Hague Conventions, and now enjoys a reputation among scholars as the modern genesis of these humanitarian documents.

Military law codes: General Orders, No. 100

When considering the Lieber Code as a leading source of the Law of War, we must bear in mind that the code was not an aspirational set of lofty principles that the author wished the US Army to follow. Rather, as the statesman and lawyer Elihu Root recognized in 1916, the Lieber Code sought to describe "what the laws and usages of war were," not "what the writer thought they ought to be."[85] Its author, Francis Lieber (1798–1872), was a German-born professor of law at Columbia College in New York City. On August 6, 1862, he received a letter from Henry Wager Halleck, General-in-Chief of the Union Armies, requesting a public statement by Lieber on the law governing guerrilla warfare. The question of whether guerrillas were protected by the Law of War had become poignant because, as Halleck explained, "the Rebel authorities claim the right to send men in the garb of peaceful citizens to waylay and attack our troops, to burn bridges and houses, and to destroy property and persons within our lines." The Confederate government threatened that, if such persons were not accorded prisoner of war status by Union troops, the South would retaliate "by executing our prisoners of war in their

Figure 26 Bushwhacker attack on Lawrence, Kansas. *Harper's Weekly*, September 5, 1863. © Library of Congress (public domain).

possession."[86] Halleck was referring chiefly to guerrilla warfare in the border state of Missouri, where irregular guerrilla fighters called "bushwhackers" waged a savage war against Union sympathizers and their families, chiefly in the rural hinterlands of the state. Northern commanders were unsure whether such attacks were military operations covered by the Law of War or criminal actions removed from it. If the former, then bushwhackers like "Bloody" Bill Anderson and William Quantrill, if captured, would be entitled to treatment as prisoners of war; if the latter, they could be executed as murderers.

Responding to Halleck's request, Lieber penned his thoughts about guerrilla warfare in an essay, "Guerrilla Parties Considered with Reference to the Laws and Usages of War" (1862). Lieber contended that in the United States a "guerrilla party" was considered "an irregular band of armed men, carrying on an irregular war, not being able ... to carry on what the law terms a regular war."[87] What, however, constituted "an irregular band of armed men?" Lieber described the types of persons composing such a group:

> The freebooter, the marauder, the brigand, the partisan, the free corps, the spy, the rebel, the conspirator, the robber, and especially the highway robber, the rising en masse, or the "arming of the peasants."[88]

Elsewhere in his essay, Lieber adds to this list of guerrillas two other categories of irregulars: the rebel and the "bushwhacker." In the very word "rebel" is the etymological clue to why throughout history insurgents have been treated with draconian harshness. "Rebel" is derived from the Latin word *rebellis*, meaning "to renew a war." Lieber expanded this ancient definition with two additional elements: namely, that the rebel renewed war "after having been conquered," and did so "within an occupied territory." Harking back to the Augustinian tradition that interpreted the object of war as the restoration of peace, Lieber affirmed that rebels were everywhere dealt with harshly because they "essentially interfere[d] with the mitigation of the severity of war, which it is one of the noblest objects of the modern Law of War to obtain."[89] In other words, the rebel was particularly nefarious because he frustrated the very purpose of armed conflict: the restoration of peace as soon as possible. The second category of irregular fighter Lieber mentioned in his essay, the bushwhacker, was "a simple assassin, and will thus always be considered by soldier and citizen. ." Like all guerrillas, rebels and bushwhackers did not qualify for the protections afforded combatants under the Law of War.[90]

Lieber's denial of prisoner of war status to guerrillas no doubt found favor with Halleck and other Union commanders, for whom guerrilla attacks in Missouri and Kansas were a source of constant harassment. Another assertion in his essay, however, was likely less gratifying to them. This pertained to the definition of "partisans" and their treatment under the Law of War. Lieber observed in his essay that the term "partisan" was "vaguely used," insofar as it was sometimes considered synonymous with the "self-constituted guerrillero." More often, scholars tended to view the "partisan" as "detached from the main army." The weight of scholarly opinion ascribed to the partisan the aim of attacking the enemy in actions separate from the parent army.[91] Although working "outside of or beyond the lines of operation of his own army, in the rear and on the flanks of the enemy," the partisan was nonetheless "part and parcel of the army, and, as such, considered entitled to the privileges of the Law of War, so long as he does not transgress it."[92] The Union Army—including Halleck—inclined to regard partisans as little more than guerrillas. Their position, as Lieber himself realized,[93] turned on the notion of "self-constitution," that is, the organization and activities of a paramilitary force outside the main command structure. This view would justify treating captured partisans not as prisoners of war but as irregulars subject to being executed on the spot. Lieber challenged the Union position, countering that, while partisans performed a unique function within an army, they were not "self-constituted" in the way that guerrilla fighters were. Hence, partisans were entitled to treatment as prisoners of war under the Law of War. Historian Richard Hartigan points out that so-called "guerrillas" like Col. John Mosby, whose ranger band conducted assaults on Union supply and communication lines in northern Virginia and Maryland, would qualify as partisans under Lieber's criteria, although the Northern leadership regarded Mosby and his men as criminals rather than combatants.[94]

It was not, however, Lieber's essay on partisans and guerrillas that would become a cornerstone of the modern Law of War. That honor was reserved for his most celebrated statement on the topic, the eponymous Lieber Code. Even before writing his essay on guerrilla warfare, Lieber had contemplated preparing "a little book on the Law and Usages of War."[95] He returned to this ambition in a letter to Halleck in November 1863, writing that President Lincoln "ought to issue a set of rules and definitions providing for the most urgent cases, occurring under the Laws and Usages of War, and on which our Articles of War are silent." These "urgent cases" were offenses routinely punished by the world's criminal codes: homicide, maiming, assault, and arson. Lieber envisioned a military penal code that would criminalize such acts if committed by American soldiers on the civilian population of an enemy country. He suggested that a committee of three experts (with Halleck serving as chairman) be organized to prepare the code, a document that would set forth offenses under the Law of War as well as their punishment.[96] Halleck eventually agreed to Lieber's request, forming a committee along the lines Lieber had proposed,[97] with the twofold mandate of updating US military law (called the "Articles of War") and composing a code of rules based on "the laws and usages of War." As discussions among the committee members moved forward, they elected not only to revise the Articles of War but to systematize the sprawling body of rules pertaining to land warfare. The board appointed Lieber to work on a draft. Abraham Lincoln approved the final product—a document comprising 157 articles, entitled "General Orders, No. 100: Instructions for the Government of the Armies of the United States in the Field"— on April 24, 1863.[98]

One of the primary themes of the entire code, telegraphed in its earliest articles, was military necessity. It is important to remember that Lieber wrote his famous code in the shadow of a civil war that had torn the country asunder in 1861. Already in the 5th article of the Lieber Code, he indicated that "paramount to all other considerations" was the priority of "sav[ing] the country."[99] Lieber's discussion of military necessity should be considered in light of the overriding value he attached to the country's survival, to which every provision in his code was subordinate. He professed to define the doctrine of necessity as it was "understood by modern civilized nations"— namely, "measures which are indispensable for securing the ends of the war, and which are lawful according to the modern law and usages of war."[100] The latitude he recognized for military operations to "secure the ends of war" may make the modern reader squirm, but they were consistent with Lieber's emphasis on the centrality of national self-preservation. Thus, it was permitted under the Law of War to starve both the enemy's military forces and its civilian population in order to effect "the speedier subjection of the enemy."[101] While he conceded that the progress of civilization had engendered a distinction between combatants and noncombatants and the doctrine that unarmed civilians were to be spared, civilian immunity from military attack was far from absolute; the limits were determined by "the exigencies of war."[102] Similarly, he insisted that the modern practice was to uphold the right to quarter, yet qualified the prohibition by supporting the commander's authority to deny quarter "in great straits, when his own salvation makes it impossible to cumber himself with prisoners."[103] Retaliation against a conquered population was also permissible so long as it was carried out "as a means of protective retribution," "cautiously and unavoidably," and not "as a measure of mere revenge."[104] It is clear from these examples that Lieber, although carving out a space for humanitarian restraint in warfare, consistently balanced such restraint against the demands of military necessity. As dominant a role as military necessity played in the

Lieber Code, it, too, had limitations beyond which it could no longer justify certain forms of behavior. Lieber was especially emphatic on this point in condemning the use of poison "in any manner, be it to poison wells, or food, or arms." For Lieber, poison "is wholly excluded from modern warfare," and military forces that resorted to it placed themselves "out of the pale of the law and usages of war."[105] Like poison, torture was alien to the law of modern warfare, whether employed to extract information from captured enemy soldiers or to punish them.[106] Lieber's categorical prohibition of poison and torture appears to be grounded in his general rule that "military necessity does not admit of cruelty," the latter understood as "the infliction of suffering for the sake of suffering or for revenge, . . . of maiming or wounding except in fight." While deception of the enemy was allowed, "acts of perfidy" were forbidden. In a sentence redolent of St. Augustine, Lieber stated that military necessity cannot legitimate anything "which makes the return to peace unnecessarily difficult," inasmuch as the "ultimate object of all modern war" was the restoration of peace.[107]

As far as enemy possessions were concerned, Lieber held that all public property—money, "movable property," and rents accruing to real estate—could be seized by the

Figure 27 Francis Lieber. © Wikimedia Commons (public domain).

victorious army "for its own benefit or of that of its government." Title to enemy real estate would be suspended until after the war.[108] Lieber explicitly exempted from the meaning of "public property" the holdings of charitable institutions like churches, hospitals, schools, universities, etc., although they were all subject to taxation.[109] Private property was generally immune to confiscation unless required by military necessity, and even then, Lieber stipulated that the private owner must be compensated for the loss.[110] It was a violation of the modern Law of War to coerce the civilian population into forced labor unless the occupied territory was annexed to the victor's own country.[111]

Another salient theme of Lieber's code was the distinction drawn between lawful combatants entitled to prisoner of war status and unlawful combatants who were not. If an enemy population was mobilized in a *levée en masse*, they were protected by the Law of War—but only if the invaded territory had not yet been occupied. Once a victorious army occupied the area, however, civilians participating in a *levée* "are violators of the Laws of War and are not entitled to their protection."[112] An "act of perfidy," such as the deceptive use of a national flag or standard, stripped the offender of all protections under the Law of War.[113] Reiterating his argument from the essay on guerrillas, Lieber held that partisans were to be treated as prisoners of war when captured; guerrilla fighters, on the other hand, who stage attacks on enemy positions "without being part and portion of the organized hostile army," were to be dealt with "summarily as highway robbers or pirates." In the same manner, rebels "who rise in arms against the occupying or conquering army," if captured, fell outside the aegis of the Law of War.[114] In brief, so-called "war-rebels," guerrillas, civilians participating in a *levée en masse* in occupied territory, and "perfidious" actors were classified in the same category with "robbers" and "brigands": they were destitute of any legal protections whatsoever.[115]

After the Code was officially promulgated, Lieber had high hopes for it. In a letter to Halleck less than a month after its adoption, he took the measure of his brainchild as not merely an achievement of military law but "a contribution by the U.S. to the stock of common civilization," predicting that it would invite imitation by the English, French, and Germans.[116] Lieber's forecast proved to be accurate. The Prussian military embraced the Code as the basis for its field regulations during the Franco-Prussian War (1870). Through Lieber's long-time correspondent Johann Bluntschli, who sewed its articles' whole cloth into his own treatise on international law, the Code went on to influence the Brussels Declaration of 1874, prompting Fyodr Martens, the Russian delegate, to assert that the Declaration had its source in General Orders, No. 100.[117] Several years later, the Institute of International Law based its *Oxford Manual* on the Code and the Brussels Declaration. At the *fin de siècle*, the tide of its influence reached into the Hague Conventions (1899 and 1907), particularly Hague Convention IV on the Laws and Customs of War on Land. At Nuremberg in 1946, the International Military Tribunal stated that the Hague rules, and by implication those parts of the Lieber Code absorbed into the Hague Convention, were "declaratory of the laws and customs of war"—meaning that they had acquired the status of international customary law.[118] Following in the footsteps of the Nuremberg tribunal, a report of the UN Secretary-General to the Security Council in May 1993 declared that Hague IV of 1907 had risen to the level of customary law.[119]

Of course, not all of Lieber's Code rates as international customary law. As monumental an achievement as the Code was in its day, many of its articles are now superannuated. His recognition that an enemy may be starved into submission is a good example; today, deliberate starvation is forbidden under Article 54(1) of Additional Protocol I to the Geneva Conventions. While he insisted that cultural objects like artwork, libraries, telescopes, and hospitals should be preserved, he allowed the conqueror to confiscate them for his own "benefit." Article 56 of the Hague Convention interdicts this practice, requiring that such public property be treated as private (and hence protected against seizure under Articles 46 and 50). Furthermore, Lieber's willingness to suspend the right to quarter when military necessity demands it is repugnant to contemporary humanitarian law—specifically, Article 23(d) of the Hague Convention (characterizing it as "especially forbidden . . . to declare that no quarter will be given").[120]

The articles of the Code that grate on the ethical sensibility today ought not diminish the magnitude of Lieber's achievement. He was not engaged in the enterprise of stating the law *as he wished it to be*; he was setting forth his understanding of what the law *actually was*. Pushing against the harsher provisions of his Code was a vigorous cross-current of humanitarianism, expressed in his categorical repudiation of cruelty, torture, and poison. Lieber declared that, even in the midst of a struggle for existence, soldiers "do not cease on this account to be moral beings, responsible to one another and to God"—a principle of humanity that imbues the leading conventions of the nineteenth and early twentieth centuries. Lieber's humanitarian concern was transmitted from his Code to the Hague Conventions in a chain consisting of three intermediate links: Bluntschli, the Brussels Declaration, and *The Oxford Manual*. These vehicles of transmission prove that the affinity between Lieber and Hague IV was born of mediated influence. The Lieber Code, the Geneva Conventions, the Hague Conventions, and, indeed, modern international humanitarian law since 1907, all share a common ideological commitment: the belief that the right of belligerents to choose the means and methods of warfare is subject to constraint.[121]

Nonetheless, we will search in vain in the international humanitarian law of this era for an indication of the punishment awaiting offenders. Of course, Lieber's Code was a different matter; it was a national body of military law intended solely for application to the Union Army in the field. General Orders, No. 30, which was based on Lieber's essay on guerrillas, urged commanders and military judges in Missouri to try "brigands" by military commission and, if convicted, put them to death. In light of the fact that national military law codes incorporated the Law of War, enforcing its terms against their own troops and enemy soldiers,[122] it is misleading to affirm that no criminal jurisdiction for offenses against the law of nations existed prior to the twentieth century. On the contrary, as we have seen, prosecutions of war crimes in military courts stretch back into the Middle Ages. In the early modern period we even find a set of army instructions recommending the "ancient course of marshall discipline" as a gap-filler to decide unique cases. Comparable statements of punishment, however, are missing from the 1864 and 1906 Geneva Conventions and the 1899 and 1907 Hague Conventions. Article 3 of Hague IV did state that violators of the Convention must pay compensation, but only "if the case demands."[123] Other than punishment for disciplinary infractions by prisoners of war, the 1929 Geneva Prisoner of War Convention was barren of any penal provision, while the 1929 Geneva Convention for the Amelioration of the Condition of the Wounded and Sick in the Field contained only a tepid requirement that signatories persuade their legislatures to "repress" violations of the Convention.[124] In short, not until the Charter of the International Military Tribunal at Nuremberg was criminal punishment prescribed in an international document for offenses against the Law of War. Still less was support rallied for prosecuting violations in an international tribunal. Gustav Moynier initially backed such an idea, but later abandoned it in favor of national adoption and enforcement of international norms. Lieber himself favored domestic laws embodying the Law of War, contending that an international court would be inefficient.[125] The lack of precedent for punishing violations of international norms would bedevil efforts to prosecute war crimes for decades, inviting charges of retroactivity and *ex post facto* from their many critics—both after the First and Second World Wars.

The Lieber Code figured prominently in the prosecution of US commanders charged with war crimes during the Philippine-American War (1899–1902). After the USA's victory over Spain in 1898, the Treaty of Paris transferred sovereign control over the Philippines to the USA, an investiture of authority which Filipino revolutionaries rejected. Military conflict between US troops and Filipino regulars ensued. The aftermath found the Filipinos vanquished and in retreat under the president of their short-lived republic, Emilio Aguinaldo. From their sanctuaries in the northern mountains, the Filipinos staged guerrilla attacks on US forces throughout the provinces, provoking gruesome American counter-insurgency measures to crush the rebellion. During the war, mortality rates among Philippine combatants soared to levels unheard of in conventional combat. The most violent battles of the US Civil War never produced a ratio of dead to wounded soldiers higher than 1:5 (i.e., five wounded for every soldier killed). Even irregular conflicts like the Boer War leveled out at a dead-to-wounded ratio of 1:4. The ratio of dead to wounded Filipino guerrillas was 5:1, or five killed for every wounded guerrilla—a figure suggesting that US troops were refusing quarter to Filipino prisoners of war.[126]

A guerrilla surprise attack on an American garrison at Balangiga (island of Samar) took the lives of fifty-nine US soldiers in late September 1901. General Jacob Smith, a former Indian fighter and participant in the Wounded Knee Massacre of 1890, was dispatched to Samar to crush the uprising. At Balangiga Smith instructed his subordinate, Major Littleton Waller, that he "want[ed] no prisoners. I wish you to kill and burn. The more you kill and burn, the better you will please me. The interior of Samar must be a howling wilderness." Foreshadowing future US military policies in Southeast Asia, Smith demanded that all Filipinos on the island report to designated coastal towns. Anyone discovered outside these concentration points would be shot on sight. After the deadline had lapsed, the Americans destroyed 165 villages on Samar. News of Smith's draconian orders and the atrocities flowing from them eventually reached the USA, prompting a Senate committee investigation of the alleged war crimes.[127]

In the meantime, Major Waller had eleven of his Philippine porters shot for "treachery," an act for which he was court-martialed in Manila in March 1902. Charged with murder,

Waller intended to raise the defense that the killings were reprisals sanctioned by the Lieber Code. When, however, General Smith appeared as a witness for the prosecution, alleging Waller had executed the porters on his own initiative, Waller changed his strategy and rebutted Smith with a copy of his own written orders. The military court subsequently acquitted him of murder. Waller's successful effort to shift responsibility for the executions to Smith led to the latter's court-martial on April 2, 1902. The general, however, was not charged with either murder or war crimes; rather, the gossamer charge against him was "conduct to the prejudice of good order and military discipline." Much of his defense focused on racist portrayals of the Filipinos as "savages" undeserving of military courtesies. Major Waller, appearing as a witness at Smith's trial, voiced the argument he had rehearsed at his own court-martial: namely, that the Lieber Code allowed the Americans to repay Filipino "treachery" by shooting anyone "belonging to the band." Smith was convicted of "prejudicing officers" but escaped without punishment. He returned to the USA in August 1902 a free man.[128]

By the end of the Philippine-American War, more than 200,000 Filipino civilians, 20,000 Filipino troops, and 4,300 US soldiers were dead. (More than half of the American war dead perished from disease.) Despite outrage over the atrocities in US anti-imperialist circles, American military and political leaders repeatedly insisted the Law of War did not extend to "uncivilized races" like the Filipinos[129]—a suspension of legal restraint not dissimilar from other instances in world history we have previously considered.

Conclusion

The British scholar of Tudor history, G. R. Elton, once criticized the idea that legal rights grew out of human rights, such as those posited in the Declaration of Independence, the French Declaration of the Rights of Man and Citizen, and the UN Declaration of Human Rights. For Elton, gauzy philosophical avowals of human rights were sterile because they lacked "any demonstrably established or hereditary entitlement." On the contrary, history had taught human beings an important lesson about rights—namely, that they "grow out of law, not out of philosophical abstractions."[130]

Elton was not quite right about the historical provenance of law or rights. Rights do not grow out of law, as Elton maintained. Rather, both rights and law trace their origins to customary usage. Long before law was reduced to writing and sanctions meted out for criminal acts, human societies employed informal techniques of self-government, resident first in the clan structure of hunting and gathering groups, then in tribal leaders and councils of chieftains. As societies became more populous, economically differentiated, and politically centralized, social norm-setting migrated from the family to the office of the king. The "king's law" increasingly replaced the order of custom with a single law administered by the sovereign. When royalist societies came into conflict with each other, their violent clashes produced self-limiting norms that were over time recognized, if not always followed, by belligerent armies. Whether it was the *dharmayuddha* of Vedic India, the *koina nomina* of ancient Greece, the *jus fetiale* of the Roman Republic, the *Ahl-al-*

Kitab of ninth-century Muslims, the Peace of God of the High Middle Ages in Europe, the chivalry of Chinese warriors, Indian *Kshatriyas*, and medieval knights, or the reciprocity of early modern armies, civilizations evolved informal customs to mitigate the ferocity of battle. Some of these norms found their way into "ordinances of war" and military codes, which in turn transmitted them to the leading conventions of the nineteenth century. In each case, however, it was not the existence of law that gave rise to the restraint, but the restraint, as it developed in the cultural practice and self-limiting usage of world civilizations, that ultimately produced the law.

Despite impressive progress in the Law of War, it was unenforceable as an international criminal code when the world's nations blundered into the cyclone of the First World War. The Great War would reveal the tragic shortcomings of legal restraints on warfare. At the same time, from its tornadic winds would emerge, when the storm had finally broken, the beginnings of an international effort to prosecute violators of the law of nations—violators understood, for the first time, as *war criminals*.

CHAPTER 7
THE FIRST WORLD WAR AND THE FAILURE
OF THE LAW OF WAR

German crimes in the First World War

On the eve of the First World War, before a single German soldier had set foot on Belgian soil, the countries of the West already regarded Germany as the scofflaw of Europe. The scholarship on Wilhelmine Germany has typically focused on its churlish and provocative actions in the two decades prior to 1914. The scandal surrounding Kaiser Wilhelm's Kruger telegram,[1] the rampant naval race with Great Britain, German endeavors to subvert the *Entente Cordiale* between France and Great Britain (the "first" Moroccan crisis of 1905), the Bosnian crisis of 1908, and the dispatch of a German gunboat to Agadir to "protect German interests" (the "second" Moroccan crisis of 1911), all led to that country's political isolation in Europe, validating the belief in the minds of German leaders that they were encircled by their enemies—a "devil's circle of armaments and counter-armaments," as Bismarck's successor, Georg Graf von Caprivi, had characterized it, from which Germany could only break free through war.[2] What has often been missed in the conventional narrative of arrant German misjudgment in the lead-up to war is Germany's disruptive actions at the Second Hague Conference of 1907, which, as at the earlier Brussels Conference, advertised the German government's relegation of the Law of War to secondary status.

In an essay on Germany's responsibility for the First World War published in 1963, German historian Fritz Dickmann asserted that nowhere was Germany's "moral isolation most drastically demonstrated" than at the Second Hague Conference.[3] When the US delegate, Joseph Hodges Choate, pleaded for insertion of a mandatory dispute settlement clause into the Convention, the German delegates retorted that such a clause was incompatible with the sovereignty and autonomy of nation-states. Any restriction of military discretion by means of compulsory arbitration would eliminate Germany's primary tactical advantage: namely, its superior capacity for rapid mobilization, which would enable the Germans to escape encirclement by its enemies. The German delegation was amenable to binding arbitration with distant countries but rejected its application to Germany's relations with bordering states. For Dickmann, German obstructionism at the Hague Conference was particularly inexplicable because peaceful coexistence through binding arbitration actually favored a country like Germany that was surrounded by potentially hostile powers. In Dickmann's estimate, the German ear was tone-deaf toward the new harmonies arising in international affairs at the *fin de siècle*—the notes of international conciliation based on shared interests and a growing concern to restrain warfare. Dickmann wrote: "[Wilhelmine Germany] was lacking in any instinctive understanding that the world had changed, that the relations of the world's people's had grown closer, and consequently that their solidarity of interests had expanded as they developed a common interest in peace." Dickmann accused the Germans of clinging to an anachronistic "power politics" in an era of commercial and political integration—an "almost inexcusable and disastrous mistake."[4] The root cause was a "blindness toward the decisive tendencies of the time and the effects of [the Germans'] own behavior," expressed not only at the Hague Conference but in Germany's political actions between 1900 and 1914.[5] Dickmann's point is that even before the outbreak of the war, Germany's European rivals viewed it as an erratic and bumptious renegade nation.

The German contribution to the outbreak of the war in August 1914, in tandem with the subsequent conduct of German troops in the field, served to reinforce these negative perceptions. The immediate causes of the First World War have been often told, generating conflicting assessments of Germany's role as an instigator seeking to achieve its goals of world power under the cover of war.[6] Despite sharp differences of opinion on this issue, most of the antagonists would agree that Germany gave the Austrians full support in their impending war with Serbia, and that it declared war on both Russia and France when these countries ignored German warnings to desist from general mobilization. Disagreement may persist on the aims that impelled Germany's declaration, but its essential role in the outbreak of the war is beyond dispute. More importantly for our purposes, Germany's enemies regarded it as provoking the conflict—in their eyes, an act of brazen hubris only compounded when the German army, hard on the heels of its declaration of war on France and Russia, invaded neutral Belgium, thereby triggering Great Britain's entry into the war on August 4 (the British had guaranteed Belgium's neutrality). In the grip of their conviction that the vise of encirclement could only be broken by a lightning strike against France, the Germans dutifully followed the 1905 script written by the chief of the General Staff, Alfred Graf von Schlieffen (1833–1913), which envisioned a rapid advance of German troops through southern Belgium and into northern France. Once Paris was taken, France would be knocked out of the war, freeing Germany's hand to launch an offensive in the east against pre-industrial Russia, a country which, due to the slow pace of its mobilization, was ripe for conquest.

The Schlieffen Plan may have sparkled with the gloss of potential victory on paper. Nonetheless, the promise of success demanded perfect execution. Schlieffen had assumed that German progress through southern Belgium would be unhampered by Belgian resistance, an assumption that proved fatally wrong. Bitter fighting led to stern measures, particularly against Belgian civilians. By August 12, 1914, as many as 640 noncombatants had been killed around Liège near the Dutch and German borders. One week later, the civilian death toll in Aarschot, located ten miles northeast of Louvain, rose to 156, and in Andenne the following day 262 civilians were killed. However, the most notorious act of German violence toward civilians during the invasion was the burning of Louvain, an affluent university town sixteen miles east of Brussels. Aware of the frightful price noncombatants were paying for resistance, Louvain's authorities seized all weapons in the possession of town residents to remove any cause that might provoke German retaliation. Once Belgian troops had withdrawn from Louvain, the Germans occupied the city on August 19. Among other security measures, the Germans took hostages from among the city's government and university officials, persons who would guarantee with their lives peaceful obedience to the occupation. On the evening of August 25, a wild-fire panic swept over the occupation troops, fed in part by the counterattack of the Belgian army that forced German retreat into Louvain. Sporadic shooting erupted throughout the city. Alarms of *"die Engländer sind da!"* ("the English are there!") were raised in response to the arrival of a German troop train, misidentified by the occupation troops as British. German officers struggled to prevent their troops from panicked shooting into civilian homes and down into the streets from rooftops. The firing barrage likely planted in the soldiers' minds that Belgian civilians were attacking them, a misconception that led to a house-to-house search for so-called "franc-tireurs," a word the Germans had used during the Franco-Prussian War for French civilian guerrillas. Louvain residents expelled from their houses watched in horror as they were put to the torch.[7] Some of the ousted homeowners were beaten and killed. German soldiers herded others to an assembly point at the train station and city hall. Without orders, the soldiers shot some of the prisoners along the way, tossing their corpses into open-air trenches by the roadside. Historian Alan Kramer notes that the bodies of the victims, which the Germans later exhumed in January 1915, exhibited signs not only of gunshots but of bayonet thrusts—wounds suggesting they had been tortured before execution.[8]

Claiming that attacks on German troops were being coordinated from the university library, soldiers set the building on fire, reducing it to charred rubble in a blaze that lasted for days. After the library was gutted, German troops resumed their assault on Louvain's civilian population on August 26. By this time, human corpses and animal carcasses littered the streets of the city. In sum, the Germans killed 248 civilians during the tumultuous occupation of Louvain. A further 1,500 were packed into rail cars and deported to a German detention camp in Münster (this number included 100 women and children).[9] Destruction of property was immense: of the 8,928 houses in prewar Louvain, 1,120 were obliterated, a figure that included many of the city's most prominent private homes, public buildings, and businesses. A subsequent inquiry by the Prussian war ministry documented eyewitness accounts of widespread pillage by German soldiers.[10]

The blood-spattered pattern of German occupation policy set at Louvain recurred in the hamlet of Dinant, 90 kilometers southeast of Brussels. Dinant's civilian population did not participate in attacks on the Germans any more than Louvain's had, but German troops nonetheless believed they were involved. Alan Kramer notes that mass executions of civilians in and around Dinant appear to have been motivated by battlefield rage; German witnesses reported that, after someone fired on his troops, the officer who ordered one execution displayed a face "contorted with rage." Seventy-seven civilians were shot, although they were unarmed and in German custody at the time the soldiers came under fire. Many of them were women and children, including thirty-eight women and girls. Fifteen children were under the age of fourteen (seven were infants), and seven were men over seventy years of age.[11] In other mass executions at Dinant, the Germans were aware that the victims had not raised arms against their troops. Rather, the executions were apparently carried out in reprisal for alleged attacks by franc-tireurs on the principle of collective responsibility. In sum, the German army shot 674 civilians at Dinant—mass executions carried out against the backdrop of the looting and destruction of Dinant's oldest and most stately buildings.[12]

In England the press denounced the burning of Louvain as a "Holocaust" of the "Oxford of Belgium." Prime Minister Herbert Henry Asquith likened Louvain's incineration to the enormities produced by the Thirty Years War, while the Italians condemned the "cultural atrocities" committed by the Germans, which Italian journalists described as a "barbarity." The conduct of the German army in Belgium prefigured other notorious acts of senseless and counterproductive violence, further inflaming world opinion against Germany. In October 1915, the Germans executed by firing squad the British nurse Edith Cavell, a self-confessed spy, despite the efforts of US and Spanish envoys to persuade the German army to grant her clemency. As historian James Willis points out, the Cavell execution was symptomatic of the egregious misjudgment the Germans displayed time and again during the war. It poured kerosene on the fire of Allied propaganda and enraged the British public, which clamored for postwar justice against Cavell's executioners.[13] The German government followed up this blunder with another bewildering misstep—the execution of Charles Fryatt, the captain of a channel steamer captured by the Germans in June 1915. When they learned he had once tried to ram a German U-boat, the Germans court-martialed Fryatt and convicted him as a maritime franc-tireur. His execution on July 27 provoked howls of outrage in England, demanding that British officials vow to put the Kaiser and the court-martial members before a firing squad. In an address to the House of Commons on July 31, Asquith threatened the German High Command that "such crimes [as Fryatt's execution] shall not . . . go unpunished." He asserted Downing Street's intention after the war to prosecute those responsible, "whoever they may be and whatever their station," strongly hinting that top German leaders would be singled out as the leading defendants.[14]

In the wake of Fryatt's execution, British leaders began to sound out the other Allies about jointly placing the punishment of German war crimes at the center of their war aims.[15] During the war, Great Britain's partners were far from receptive to the British proposal. When the British Foreign Secretary Lord Edward Grey approached the French about a joint statement on war crimes, the French were noncommittal. Their main aim was to receive reparations from the Germans after the war, rather than seek punishment of individual perpetrators. The Russians evinced even less support for trials than the French; one Russian journalist charged the British with trying to recreate a kangaroo court along the lines of those they had used to try Mary Queen of Scots and Joan of Arc.[16] The British themselves retreated from their insistence on punishing German war crimes, particularly after the First Battle of the Somme (July 1 to November 13, 1916), in which the British army suffered 60,000 casualties, prompting David Lloyd George, at the time the minister of munitions, to confide in a colleague his belief that Britain would lose the war. Lloyd George rallied from his brown study when he replaced Asquith as prime minister, refusing any suggestions of a negotiated peace; however, there was at this time no further talk about prosecuting German war crimes. From then until the end of the war the Allies were mute on the subject, and not even reports in late October 1916 that the Germans were deporting Belgian citizens to Germany as forced laborers could nudge the British into renewing their call for trials. By 1917 the war crimes question had become a dead letter. When the Germans announced unrestricted submarine warfare on February 1, 1917, British officials declined issuing threats of future trials with the argument that previous warnings had been ineffective, and that in any case Great Britain was not in a position to carry them out.[17]

By the fall of 1918, as Germany staggered toward military defeat, the Allies had begun to rethink their views on war crimes trials. British parliamentarians agitated for insertion into the upcoming armistice, "as a condition of peace," a proviso requiring the surrender and punishment of Germans suspected of committing crimes on British prisoners of war. There was widespread support for this resolution within Parliament as well as from the British press. In late October the War Cabinet pressed Lloyd George, who was then in Paris discussing the terms of the armistice with Woodrow Wilson's main negotiator, Col. Edward House, and the French prime minister Georges Clemenceau, to include a war crimes clause in the document. Around the same time, the British government formed a Committee of Enquiry into Breaches of the Laws of War, which met for the first time on November 6. The Committee's task was to investigate violations of international law by German combatants and to determine responsibility for them. Moreover, the Committee was charged with preparing a charter for the tribunal that would preside over German war crimes. After the German surrender on November 11, the Committee's jurisdiction was enlarged to consider how Kaiser Wilhelm might be prosecuted for instigating the war.[18] On November 28, 1918, the Committee submitted its report to the War Cabinet. In their report, the authors acknowledged that no precedent existed in international law for extraditing and prosecuting a head of state. This notwithstanding, the Committee members—particularly the jurists among them, including Sir Frederick Pollock—asserted that "vindication of the principles of International Law" would be "incomplete" unless legal action were taken against the Kaiser. Failure to prosecute Wilhelm II might enable his subordinates to raise the defense of superior orders given by a commander unavailable for trial. For the Committee, it was a principle of basic fairness deducible from the common law tradition, and readily clear to "ordinary people all over the world," that the highest-ranking offenders be prosecuted and not merely their troops farther down the chain of command. As the chief of the German military, the Kaiser could and should be placed on trial for ordering violations of the provisions of the 1899 Hague Conventions. The report listed fifteen categories of illegal acts, among them unrestricted submarine warfare, executing hostages, and mistreating war captives. The report went on to recommend prosecuting Wilhelm for "having provoked . . . an aggressive and unjust war." All of these offenses, the Committee recommended, should be tried before an international tribunal consisting only of Allied judges, on the assumption that neutral judges would find both sides had committed war crimes.[19]

The collapse of the plan to try the Kaiser

On November 28, 1918, the Imperial War Cabinet unanimously approved Lloyd George's request for a trial of Wilhelm II. In early December the prime minister then tried to rally support for the plan from the Allies at an Inter-Allied Conference in London. Within a short time, Lloyd George, Clemenceau, and the Italian premier Vittorio Orlando had agreed to the Kaiser's prosecution. At the meeting the Allied leaders also discussed putting other accused war criminals on trial, including the crown prince Friedrich Wilhelm, the ex-chief of the German general staff, General Erich von Falkenhayn, and Talat Paşa, the leader of the Young Turks, who as minister of the interior was implicated in the mass murder of the Armenians during their deportation from the Ottoman Empire's eastern territories. The Allied leaders were unable to reach agreement on trials ancillary to the Kaiser's, but the decision to prosecute Wilhelm fulfilled Lloyd George's main objective for the meeting. The next step was to broach the plan with US President Woodrow Wilson and elicit his consent to it. Participants in the Inter-Allied Conference learned, however, that Wilson was still considering how best to deal with the Kaiser.[20]

In early 1919 the Allies met in Paris to create an agenda for the peace conference. At this time, Wilson was still dithering on the issue of trying Kaiser Wilhelm. Lloyd George suggested that a panel be convened to investigate the Germans' responsibility for starting the war. Wilson demurred on the ground that the Allied leaders, he believed, could resolve the issue on their own. In his history of Allied war crimes policy at the Paris Peace Conference, James Willis assumes that Wilson at this time would have agreed to a policy of outlawing and exiling the Kaiser, much as the European powers had dealt with Napoleon.[21] On the opening day of the conference, January 18, 1919, Lloyd George and Clemenceau arranged for German war crimes to occupy a position at the top of the agenda. Wilson's view that the Allies could themselves settle the issue was brushed aside, and a "Commission on the Responsibility of the Authors of the War and the Enforcement of Penalties" was formed to investigate the cause of the war, violations of the Law of War during the fighting, and the prospect of trying accused war criminals. In the ensuing months, the Commission would pursue its inquiry outside of the public eye.[22]

At roughly the same time as the opening of the conference and the origination of the Commission, Wilson received a memorandum from his legal advisor David H. Miller. Miller sharply differed with the pro-trial perspective of the British and the French on the Kaiser's criminal liability. Bracketing moral from legal considerations, the memo constructed its analysis on a bedrock question: at the time of the alleged crime, was it prohibited by a criminal law, i.e., a law that threatened punishment for violation? Miller answered this question in the negative, stating that in August 1914 international law did not criminalize aggressive warfare. In contrast with the other Allies, Miller held that general legal beliefs were irrelevant to the issue. The sole relevant factor was whether two sources of law were in existence at the start of the war: (1) codifications of international law, including treaties, which branded such acts as criminal, and (2) general international legal customs and practices indicating widespread consensus on the criminality of aggressive war. Like his American countrymen, Miller applied a strict legal positivism to negate the Kaiser's juridical responsibility for the outbreak of the war. In the absence of either codifications or general customary law and practice, no legal basis existed for trying Wilhelm II.[23] The memo then turned to the issue of other alleged breaches of the Law of War by the Germans. Miller affirmed that the violation of Belgian neutrality and the program of unrestricted submarine warfare were breaches of international treaties; however, they merely established the liability of the German state—not the individual criminal liability of German leaders. Miller based his statement on the fact that international law in 1914 did not recognize individual criminal responsibility for political acts carried out on behalf of the state.[24]

The position articulated in the memo could not have been more antithetical to the French analysis of the Kaiser's criminal liability. Like the British and the Americans, the French had sought the advice of legal advisors on the war guilt question. Immediately after the armistice, the government had recruited two French lawyers, Fernand Larnaude and Albert de Lapradelle, to assess the prospects of putting Wilhelm on trial for starting the war. The two jurists concluded, much as Miller had, that no precedents supported his indictment. Nowhere were acts like violating the neutrality of another country defined as a punishable crime. Furthermore, under international law the Kaiser as a head of state was immune from prosecution. From similar premises Miller had inferred that no legal basis existed for putting Wilhelm on trial. The French jurists, by contrast, recommended that he be tried in an inter-Allied court on the charge of violating not past law, but future law. According to Larnaude and Lapradelle, a new world legal order was emerging in the wake of the First World War, one characterized by Wilsonian principles of the self-determination of peoples, political and legal responsibility of state leaders for waging wars of aggression, and respect for the rule of law. Given the long-standing French insistence on non-retroactive legislation, an emphasis used in the eighteenth century to challenge the arbitrary laws of the *ancien regime*, the two jurists' conclusion that Wilhelm could be prosecuted under future rather than past law may be puzzling; however, they held that the norms underlying the Kaiser's criminal liability were not "new" in the sense of being "novel." Rather, these norms had existed for some time in the form of international custom, and all that was needed to give them legal effect was for the Allies to declare them officially. Larnaude and Lapradelle's views deeply affected French thinking about how German war crimes should be handled. In the eyes of some commentators, the French were the main advocates of putting the Kaiser on trial for aggressive war. It is little wonder, then, that on the first official day of the Paris Peace Conference, French President Raymond Poincaré's opening speech focused on Wilhelm II's war guilt.[25]

David Miller's report to Woodrow Wilson repudiated the French claim that the Allies could simply create new international law through fiat. Miller cited a US Supreme Court verdict from 1825 authored by Chief Justice John Marshall, holding that no state or group of states had authority to pronounce a generally accepted practice (in this case, slavery) a violation of international law. New international customary law could arise only through the unanimous consent of all states. As seen from this angle, the French contention that a general legal belief, coupled with a simple declaration of it by the victor-states, could establish international customary law was patently false. While ruling out a prosecution of the Kaiser on legal grounds, Miller's memo did leave open the possibility of dealing with Wilhelm II politically. A political solution, at least, could rely on precedent—specifically, the exile of Napoleon to St. Helena after the Hundred Days. This was the legal memorandum in President Wilson's possession when the Peace Conference opened on January 18, 1919. Miller's premises would ultimately shape the views of the Americans in Paris, contributing to the final collapse of the plan to put the Kaiser on trial.[26]

In fact, American opposition to trying Wilhelm II quickly emerged as the Commission on Responsibility began its deliberations. Its chair, the US Secretary of State Robert Lansing, entered upon his work with a deep-seated aversion to the very idea of international criminal law. Shortly after the Germans sank the British ocean liner *Lusitania* in May 1915, Lansing wrote in a privately circulated memo that the real standard of international conduct was not morality "but the necessity of the act in protecting national existence or in bringing the war to a successful conclusion." For Lansing, it fell to the armed forces alleged to have committed the war crime to determine whether the action was justified by military necessity. Lansing's main concern was that international prosecution of war crimes would engender precedents that could later be used against the USA, particularly in its future struggle against communism. Additionally, he argued that trying the Kaiser might weaken the German state, opening it to infiltration by the Bolsheviks.[27]

Lansing carried these preconceptions with him into his work with the Commission. In effect, even before that body began its inquiry, he was unshakably opposed to international jurisdiction over war crimes—a bias he concealed from other Commission members. Instead, he rebuffed the pro-trial arguments of the French and British representatives with an *ex post facto* argument: no precedent existed in international law for prosecuting a head of state on a charge of aggressive war, hence it was impermissible to try the Kaiser for starting the First World War. Three subcommittees were formed to investigate different aspects of the war crimes question. Lansing joined the third subcommittee, which was assigned the task of determining responsibility for offenses under the Law of War. The third subcommittee bogged down as Lansing and Sir Ernest Pollock clashed bitterly over the creation of an international tribunal. The American pursued a strategy of deliberate temporization that nearly paralyzed the subcommittee. When Pollock and the French delegate Larnaude began to discuss the prospect of trying German crimes in an international court, Lansing stymied the discussion with objections based on jurisdictional competence. Only when the exasperated Pollock demanded an immediate vote on the issue of the tribunal did Lansing momentarily concede defeat. The third subcommittee's report when it was finally drafted endorsed the trial of German offenses in an international tribunal.[28]

At this point, Lansing came clean with the other members of the Commission. He confessed his opposition to prosecuting Wilhelm II for any offense under the Law of War, drawing a sharp rebuke from Larnaude. Lansing's position was that no legal authority existed above the sovereign; for this reason, there could be no accountability of heads of state for violating international law. In mid-March 1919, Wilson instructed

Lansing that he should not merely dissent from the Commission's majority report, but compose a minority report that would reject both the formation of an international tribunal and placing the Kaiser on trial. Thereafter, the European delegates prepared their majority report while the Americans worked on their minority report. Fearing the potential consequences for monarchies of prosecuting the Kaiser, the imperial Japanese government ordered its delegates to join with the Americans. The Commission submitted its report to the Peace Conference on March 29; the American/Japanese report followed on April 4. The majority report recommended that: (1) actions that caused the outbreak of the war should not be punished, either legally or otherwise; (2) the Peace Conference should condemn by means of a public declaration the Germans' violation of Belgium and Luxembourg's neutrality; (3) actions that caused the war or violated the neutrality of other countries should be dealt with through "special measures" to include a "special organ"; and (4) punishment for future violations of international law should be promulgated. Although the Americans and Japanese dissented from much of the majority report (especially point 3), there were some areas of agreement. The minority report accepted that Germany had caused the war and willfully violated Belgian neutrality. Further, it concurred that a statement of penal liability for future violations of international law was desirable. The Americans also agreed to the principle of criminal responsibility of individuals who violated the Law of War (other than heads of state). The peace treaty could provide for their prosecution in Allied national military tribunals or, in cases in which the defendant committed crimes on multi-national victims, in mixed courts.[29]

What the Americans could not stomach was the creation of an international court, the prosecution of a head of state, or the principle of the "laws of humanity." The European delegates had appealed to the phrase "laws of humanity"—lifted from the gap-filling "Martens Clause" of the Preamble to the 1907 Hague Convention—to justify prosecuting violent acts that were not specifically prohibited by the Law of War. Uppermost in the Europeans' minds was the Turkish massacre of its Armenian population early in the war. For the Americans, however, the "laws of humanity" standard was arbitrary, and hence unenforceable. Against US objections to trying the Kaiser in an international court, the Europeans countered that such a trial would put future political leaders on notice that they would be held accountable for violating the international Law of War. The Americans would not budge. Instead, they cited Chief Justice John Marshall's opinion in *Schooner Exchange v. McFaddon and Others* (1812) for the proposition that all sovereigns were immune from the jurisdiction of other sovereigns. The US position was not that the Allied countries were unable to punish the Kaiser; on the contrary, the Americans granted them the right to impose whatever political penalties they considered appropriate. Legal punishment, on the other hand, was strictly out-of-bounds. As far as other German war criminals were concerned, the US delegates supported their prosecution in national military tribunals on the grounds that such trials were backed by precedent—e.g., the trial of Henry Wirz, commandant of the Andersonville concentration camp, who was prosecuted, convicted, and executed after the Civil War by a military tribunal.[30]

US resistance met with vigorous pushback from the Allies. Lloyd George told Wilson point blank on April 8 that Great Britain would not sign a peace treaty without a provision stipulating trial of the Kaiser. The prime minister was under growing public pressure in Great Britain to punish Wilhelm for starting the war, as well as for his methods of fighting it. In the House of Commons, Lloyd George was becoming a whipping post for his alleged "softness" toward the Germans. In the House of Commons 233 MPs dashed off a telegram to him, demanding that he compel Germany to acknowledge the harm it had caused. Agreeing with the prime minister, Clemenceau echoed Lloyd George's concern with raw public opinion, remarking that sparing Wilhelm from punishment was "something our peoples would never understand." Wilson responded that prosecuting the Kaiser would elevate him to the status of a national martyr, thereby keeping the door ajar for the revival of absolutism in Germany. In addition, Wilson declared that only a German court could try high-ranking members of the German government. He was not, however, able to shake Lloyd George from his insistence that Wilhelm be brought to trial, if not for starting the war, then for violating Belgian neutrality.[31]

Wilson asked for time to reflect on the Allies' demands. After conferring with Lansing that evening, he returned the following day with a draft of criminal articles proposed for inclusion in the peace treaty with Germany. According to the draft, military courts consisting of members from the Allied countries would prosecute German violations of the law of armed conflict. As for the Kaiser, his extradition would be sought from the Netherlands; once in Allied hands, he would be tried in a "special tribunal" made up of five Allied judges. However, Wilhelm would not be charged with a crime, but with "a supreme offence against international morality and the sanctity of treaties." Wilson's draft provisions on the punishment of German war crimes, with some changes, were adopted as Articles 227–230 of the Versailles Treaty. The "Council of Four"—the USA, Great Britain, France, and Italy—determined that analogous terms would be included in their treaties with the remaining defeated countries (Austria, Hungary, Bulgaria, and Turkey).[32]

On May 7, 1919, the treaty was presented to the German delegation in Versailles. Predictably, they were horrified by the "penal provisions" of the treaty, i.e., Articles 227–231. The focus of their dismay, however, was on Article 231, the "war guilt" clause, which obliged Germany to accept full responsibility"for causing all the loss and damage" arising from German aggression. The other provisions (Articles 227–230) closely tracked Wilson's draft. Germany would have to accept the following terms:

- Trial of the Kaiser for "a supreme offence against international morality and the sanctity of treaties" by a special tribunal composed of five judges from the USA, Great Britain, France, Italy, and Japan. A request for Wilhelm's extradition would be addressed to the government of the Netherlands. (Article 227)

- Trial by military tribunals of other Germans accused of violating the Law of War. This provision would apply regardless of the outcomes of any German proceedings against their own defendants. The Germans had to agree to deliver accused war criminals to the victors upon request. (Article 228)

- Crimes of German war criminals committed on the citizens of a nation would be tried by a military tribunal consisting of members from that nation. Where the victims were from different countries, the tribunal would consist of members from the affected countries. (Article 229)

- Germany would supply all evidence of crimes to the victors or the whereabouts of accused war criminals. (Article 230)

Widespread demonstrations rippled over Germany in protest against these clauses. Denunciation of the terms was not restricted to any one group; all parties across the political spectrum, except the Independent Socialists, opposed them. Even the German Chancellor, Philipp Scheidemann, struck a defiant note, proclaiming that Germany would never accept the treaty's conditions. On May 29 the German delegation in Paris rejected Articles 227–231 on the ground that they were an intolerable stain on Germany's honor. Instead, the delegates made a counterproposal: they would agree to the findings on accused German war criminals made by an international tribunal comprising members from neutral countries. The Germans reserved the right, however, to administer punishment themselves, and only if the Allies agreed to accept the tribunal's findings with regard to war crimes committed by their own soldiers.[33]

The Allies were not inclined to haggle with the Germans over the treaty's penal clauses. They gave Germany one week to sign the treaty or face renewal of the war and invasion of their country. Still, the German government wanted to reject the treaty. On June 18, Chancellor Scheidemann told members of his cabinet that they should retort to the Allied demand, "Do not think we can be your bum-bailiffs and hangmen among our own people." After formation of a new cabinet, the government conveyed to the Allies its willingness to sign the treaty, so long as Articles 227–231 were expunged from it. This was not unwarranted temerity on the Germans' part; they had reason to think, based on information provided them by French agents, that the Allies would relent on the notorious articles. However, the Allies did not act in accordance with expectation. The German counteroffer was rejected and a new ultimatum laid down: if the treaty were not signed within 24 hours, Allied forces would invade Germany. On the eve of the deadline, the new cabinet agonized over Germany's quandary in an all-night session. President Friedrich Ebert asked Field Marshal Paul Hindenburg and General Wilhelm Groener whether the Germany Army was capable of repelling the threatened invasion. Groener answered in the negative. Only minutes away from the deadline, the German government agreed to sign the treaty on June 23, 1919, thereby surrendering unconditionally.[34]

"The conclusion of peace and amnesty are so tightly bound one to the other that they are conceptually the same thing."

Immanuel Kant, Die Metaphysik der Sitten, *quoted in*
Hankel, Die Leipziger Prozesse, *32*

We may more fully grasp the magnitude of the Germans' shock when presented with the Allies' demands if we recall that, in previous centuries, the conclusion of peace generally excluded any criminal liability of the belligerents. From the seventeenth through the nineteenth centuries, the customary practice was to insert "oblivion clauses" into all peace treaties. These clauses in effect immunized all participants in the conflict from criminal trial by the enemy, on the principle that "in forgetting consists substantive peace." The first modern treaties to employ such language were the two treaties of the Peace of Westphalia ending the Thirty Years War, which relegated all occurrences of the war to a "perpetual oblivion and forgetting." According to German historian and linguist Gerd Hankel, the word "oblivion" signified that the events of the war would be forgotten; out of this act of forgetting flowed the "amnesty," meaning there would be no criminal accusations against the belligerents—although restitution for damages might still be sought. This principle was more or less tacitly assumed in European peace treaties until the First World War.[35] The progression of warfare as it scudded along its historical arc, from the "cabinet wars" of the eighteenth century to the "people's wars" of the nineteenth to the "total wars" of the twentieth, radically reoriented popular opinion in the nations directly affected by the Great War. Just as seventeenth-century Europeans had broken with classical and medieval just war theory, holding instead that wars of conquest were legitimate instruments of policy conducted by sovereign states, their modern descendants now rejected the *raison d'état* of early modernity.[36] As armies modernized and technology boosted the lethality of warfare, a version of just war theory crept back into European international relations. After a 262-year eclipse, just war doctrine re-emerged in the Versailles peace treaty—to the profound satisfaction of the French and the British, and to the deep chagrin of the Germans.

Nevertheless, external forces played havoc with enforcement of Article 227 of the Treaty of Versailles (providing for the Kaiser's prosecution). The Kaiser had sought refuge in the Netherlands, which now refused the Allies' request for his extradition. As the Dutch government persisted in its refusal, British interest in trying Wilhelm began to wane. Lord Curzon, the British Foreign Secretary, proposed an alteration to the request: The Netherlands might be asked to banish the Kaiser to Java rather than extradite him for trial. This suggestion likewise failed to bear fruit, as the Dutch made clear their opposition to Wilhelm's internment in an overseas colony. The Allies had little recourse beyond sending a démarche to Dutch officials, protesting their refusal.[37] On this anti-climactic note, the plan set forth in Article 227 to put Wilhelm II on trial collapsed.

The failure of the Allies to prosecute the Kaiser ought not discredit the genuine accomplishments of the penal clauses of the Treaty of Versailles. These provisions moved the community of nations closer toward the view that a sovereign and his agents could not simply wrap themselves in the time-honored robes of immunity and amnesty once a war was over; rather, punishment for war crimes became a proper epilogue to military conflict. Had the Dutch extradited Wilhelm to the countries of the Entente, history could have been different: the first head of state might have been hauled before an international tribunal for acts committed during the war. As James Willis notes, Dutch compliance with the extradition request might have been achieved had the Allies agreed to investigate war crimes committed *on all sides*, as Count Ulrich von Brockdorff-Rantzau, who led the German delegation at Versailles, had proposed.[38] The Allies, however, dismissed the Count's request, Germany signed the Treaty anyways, the Dutch refused extradition, and the plan to try the Kaiser went to ground.

The debacle of efforts to prosecute other German war criminals

Like the plan to try the Kaiser in an international court, the Allies' intention to prosecute other German war criminals in an international forum (Article 228 of the Versailles Treaty) failed to materialize. The reason was another perfect storm of converging forces and events. At first, the victors of the First World War were bent on seeing Article 228 enforced. On February 3, 1920, a list of 896 accused German war criminals—including the names of Generals Hindenburg and Ludendorff, Admiral Alfred von Tirpitz, and former Chancellor Bethmann-Hollweg—was served on the German ambassador in Paris, Baron von Lersner. The German government was expected to arrest these persons and ensure their delivery to the Allies to stand trial in an international tribunal for violations of the Law of War. As with the demand for the Kaiser's prosecution, the Allied list provoked a stormy response in Germany. Just over a month later, reactionary elements in Germany staged the Kapp Putsch, a coup designed to overthrow the Weimar government and install in its place an authoritarian regime. Although the immediate trigger to the Putsch was the decision of the German defense minister Gustav Noske to dissolve two powerful right-wing paramilitary groups (the so-called *Freikorps*), anxiety caused by the prospect of extradition contributed to its occurrence.[39] From the outset, the German government opposed the Allied demands, threatening to undermine them through passive resistance. Influenced by events at home, Baron von Lersner announced his resignation. The government in the meantime made a counterproposal: in lieu of extradition and prosecution in an international court, the accused war criminals should be prosecuted in the Reich Supreme Court in Leipzig.[40]

The German counterproposal met with a receptive audience, for the Allies were growing wary of the unwanted complications that might result from too strenuous an insistence on prosecuting German war criminals in an international court. The Kapp Putsch had highlighted the fragility of the Weimar government. The Allies feared that extradition would further weaken it, opening the Weimar system to violent attack from the right and from the left. (The recent Bolshevik Revolution in Russia weighed heavily in Allied leaders' minds.) They accepted the Germans' counterproposal, subject to the condition that the German trials could be nullified if they dealt too leniently with the accused. In such an eventuality, the Allies would bring German war crimes suspects to trial in an international tribunal, much as Article 228 had intended. Thereafter, the list of the accused was whittled down from 896 to forty-five names; the abridged list was then sent to the German government on May 7, 1920. The list included names of accused war criminals nominated by each of the Allied nations. The German war crimes trial program at Leipzig comprised two categories of cases. The first targeted defendants on the Allied list; the second implemented an earlier law passed by the National Assembly on December 18, 1919, the "Law for the Prosecution of War Crimes and War Derelictions" (*Gesetz zur Verfolgung von Kriegsverbrechen und Kriegsvergehen*, or KVVG).[41]

German trials based on the KVVG

The trials of alleged German war criminals before the Imperial Court in Leipzig began in January 1921. Curiously, the first trial did not involve defendants appearing on the Allies' list; rather, it was based on German domestic law (the KVVG). The defendants were three German soldiers accused of committing armed robbery on a Belgian innkeeper. All three were convicted and sentenced to varying prison terms. A similar case involving another German soldier followed, with comparable results. The pace of the German program was too slow for the Allies, however, who were already dissatisfied with German resistance to the disarmament and reparations provisions of the treaty. Reproached for obstructionism, the Germans were ordered to fulfill their responsibilities under the treaty on pain of being sanctioned. Continued German temporizing led to the Allied occupation of the Ruhr Valley in May 1921, over which the Fehrenbach Cabinet resigned. A new cabinet emerged, one now committed to meeting Germany's treaty obligations. A sign of the new policy of compliance was the resumption of war crimes trials three weeks after the Wirth Cabinet had formed.[42]

German prosecution of war criminals on the British list

The abridged Allied list included only seven names requested by the British for trial in Leipzig. Four of them were naval commanders charged with violations of the laws of maritime warfare, while the remaining three were members of the German army charged with mistreating Allied prisoners of war. Of the seven men appearing on the British list, only four would be prosecuted in Leipzig; the rest were either dead or otherwise unavailable for trial. The three German soldiers were accused of bludgeoning prisoners with their rifle butts and pummeling them with their fists. Although convicted, they received light sentences from the Leipzig judges (from six to ten month prison terms)— even though evidence was presented at their trial that some of the prisoners had died in their custody.[43]

The final trial of a British list defendant took place in June 1921. The accused was one of the naval officers identified on the list, Lieutenant Commander Karl Neumann, a former U-boat commander accused of torpedoing a British hospital ship called the *Dover Castle* on May 26, 1917. Neumann raised the defense of superior orders, arguing that the policy of the German Admiralty was to attack hospital ships in designated areas in retaliation for the Allies' practice of shipping soldiers and equipment on them. The Court accepted Neumann's defense, persuaded that, regardless of the objective illegality of Neumann's actions, he honestly believed his orders were binding. Sensing that the outcome of the case would be offensive to British trial observers, the

Germans promised a different result in another (non-British list) case scheduled for July 1921, in which a German U-boat commander clearly knew his egregious assault on another hospital ship was a criminal act. That case, the *Llandovery Castle* trial, got under way on July 9.[44]

The main culprit, who appeared as the number one war criminal on the Allies' first list, was the commander of U-86, Helmut Patzig, accused by the British of torpedoing the *Llandovery Castle*. After he had sunk the hospital ship, Patzig then fired on the lifeboats carrying the survivors in an apparent attempt to eliminate witnesses to the crime. Patzig, however, was unavailable for trial (he lived in Danzig, which was no longer part of German territory). Instead, the Germans invoked the KVVG to indict his lieutenants, Ludwig Dithmar and John Boldt. At trial it was found that U-86 attacked the *Llandovery Castle* on June 27, 1918 outside the free-fire zone established by the German Admiralty. The Leipzig Court was satisfied that Patzig knew the vessel was a hospital ship before he gave the order to torpedo it—a significant finding of fact proving he had exceeded his orders. Testimony at trial indicated Patzig believed American airmen were aboard the ship, which, if true, was a violation of international law. Although many of the *Llandovery Castle's* crew of medical staff went down with it, some crew members had found refuge in three lifeboats. Learning that US airmen had not been aboard the ship and fearing punishment for his crime, Patzig ordered the boats be shelled. Two of them were destroyed, while a third escaped under cover of night. In total Patzig's actions led to the destruction of 234 lives. The commander further sought to conceal his misdeeds by altering the logbook and extracting from his crew an oath of secrecy. At trial, Patzig's former lieutenants Dithmar and Boldt remained loyal to this pact and refused to testify. Boldt did break his silence to harangue the Court about their ex-commander's greatness, proclaiming that Germany would have won the war with more men like him.[45]

The atmosphere in which the trial unfolded was extraordinarily conducive to the men's defense. In the buildup to the trial, military veterans excoriated Dithmar and Boldt's prosecution. The former chief of staff of the German Navy, Admiral Adolf von Trotha, appeared as a witness for the defense. Chief Prosecutor Ebermayer struck a tristful note when he informed the court how difficult a challenge he faced having to "proceed against two German officers, who fought bravely and faithfully for their Fatherland."[46] In this hothouse of injured national pride, the Imperial Court issued its verdict on July 16, 1921. The Court acquitted the men for assisting in the attack on the *Llandovery Castle* because they merely followed the orders of their superior—orders which on their face appeared legitimate. Dithmar and Boldt were convicted, however, of participating in shelling the lifeboats, an act the men must have understood was illegal. The Court held that the two lieutenants might have deterred Patzig from launching the attack by threatening to expose his misdeed to the Admiralty. In view of these findings, an observer might have expected the Court to convict the defendants of murder, either as perpetrators or accomplices. Instead, holding that they had not premeditated the killings, the Court convicted them of manslaughter and sentenced each to a four-year prison term. Neither Boldt nor Dithmar served his full sentence: with the connivance of former *Freikorps* members, and possibly German officials, both men escaped their jail cells and were eventually pardoned (Boldt escaped in November 1921, Dithmar in January 1922). In response to Allied inquiries, the German government reported the fugitives had fled to Sweden.[47]

German prosecution of war criminals on the Belgian and French lists

In the select list of accused German war criminals sent to Berlin in early May 1920, the Belgians had identified fifteen names, the French eleven. The Imperial Court at Leipzig tried the first Belgian case shortly after the *Dover Castle* proceedings had ended. Like the *Llandovery Castle* trial soon to follow, the Belgian case occurred in an environment charged with rancorous emotion. One contemporary observer wrote that the witnesses for the prosecution "breathed hatred" toward the Germans, while the Belgian trial mission eschewed any courteous exchanges with their hosts. When defense counsel lambasted Belgium and France in their arguments, the German spectators erupted into applause. The omnipresent crowd outside the courtroom cheered the defendants and taunted the Belgians and French as they entered and departed the building. The trial involved a non-commissioned German officer named Max Ramdohr, the chief of secret military police in Grammont, Belgium, accused of falsely imprisoning and torturing several children aged nine to twelve in 1917. Believing the children had sabotaged railway lines, Ramdohr beat them and thrust their heads into pails of water. The Imperial Court, however, acquitted Ramdohr, holding that the children's accounts—the only evidence presented against the defendant—were grossly embellished and thus lacking in credibility. His acquittal on June 11 met with boisterous acclaim from courtroom spectators. The Belgians, on the other hand, received Ramdohr's acquittal with outrage. The Belgian contingent abruptly left Leipzig and informed their government that the trial was a farce. Withdrawing the evidence they had previously furnished the Imperial Court, the Belgians declared their support for reinstating the penal provisions of the Versailles Treaty.[48]

On June 29, the Imperial Court shifted its attention to the cases on the French list. The French were clamoring for the trial and conviction of General Karl Stenger, alleged to have issued an order to his soldiers to withhold quarter from French troops in August 1914. Standing alongside Stenger in the Leipzig dock was Major Benno Crusius, a subordinate of Stenger's, who had confessed to murdering French prisoners of war, some with his own revolver. Like other trials we have discussed, the prosecution of Stenger and Crusius took place in a courtroom thick with palpable emotion. Alsatian witnesses testifying for the prosecution were interrupted by the general's outbursts: "It is all a swindle! The witness is a lying Alsatian!" When US photographers attempted to shoot Stenger's picture outside the courtroom, pro-Stenger supporters attacked them. The proceedings were further envenomed by Major Crusius's decision to incriminate his former commander, a rare event in the Leipzig trials inasmuch as military members were expected to preserve a code of silence about each other's misdeeds. Instead, Crusius raised a superior orders defense, accusing Stenger of giving him the order to shoot

French prisoners of war—an allegation that Stenger emphatically rejected. Stenger did admit, however, to ordering that French soldiers using treacherous means to attack the Germans, such as firing on them while pretending to be dead or wounded, should be executed. Some of the other men in the unit vouched for Stenger's claim. After the general delivered an impassioned speech to the Court, the chamber burst into applause and calls of "bravo!"[49]

From judges working in a milieu of unbridled emotion and sparking malice it may be unrealistic to expect a judgment based on careful assessment of the facts. Unsurprisingly, the Court acquitted Stenger outright on the ground that Crusius had misunderstood the general's order. Crusius himself was acquitted of all the murder charges but convicted of manslaughter and given a two-year prison sentence. Exuberant crowds cheered Stenger as he left the Imperial Court building, showering flowers on him. The treatment accorded the French trial observers and witnesses was less welcoming: they were cat-called and spat on. The French government registered its protest by vetoing further participation in the Leipzig trials, an action that only backfired on the French because it deprived the Court of witnesses essential to prosecuting other German war criminals. Two German defendants charged with failing to check a typhus epidemic as it swept through their prisoner of war camp in 1915, Hans von Schack and Benno Kruska, were the immediate beneficiaries of the French decision— they were acquitted one day after the French withdrawal. In its verdict, the Court implicitly rebuked the French government: rather than war criminals as the French had alleged, the judges had found the two defendants to be brave and loyal soldiers who had done nothing wrong.[50]

Parallel with the trials held at Leipzig, the French and Belgians conducted courts-martial of accused German war criminals *in absentia*. The French trials were set in motion by an order of the French president, Raymond Poincaré, to prosecute 2,000 Germans appearing on the unabridged list. A "council of war" was stitched together to hear the cases at Lille, Nancy, and Chalons sur Marne. The proceedings yielded 1,200 convictions. Belgium, by contrast, only tried eighty such cases. For both the French and the Belgians, these trials were intended to mollify angry populations within the two countries. With Poincaré's departure from office in June 1924, however, the French ardor for war crimes trials began to cool. The new government pursued a more conciliatory policy with the goal of normalizing Franco-German relations. The courts-martial meantime slowed from a torrent to a trickle; by early 1926 the French government discontinued them altogether. Already in October 1925, the Belgians had apprised the Germans they would abandon their prosecution *in absentia* of accused German war criminals. The abatement of interest in further trials extended to the British, who years before had indicated their commitment to them was waning. Given the fierceness of British public opinion on the war crimes issue in 1919, it may seem odd that white-hot British resentment could chill so rapidly. By late 1921, the war crimes issue was displaced by the concern to repair relations with Germany and maintain them with France. A hard line on war crimes trials only detracted from both, at least in the thinking of Downing Street.[51]

The final results of the Leipzig trials were disappointingly meager. Of the 896 war crimes suspects on the original list, only twelve were placed on trial, and of this number only six were convicted. (A small handful of additional defendants were convicted based on the Germans' own law, the KVVG.) The sentences meted out were grossly disproportionate to the offense, and even these lenient punishments were never fully carried out.[52] Some seven years after their trial, the Imperial Court revisited the convictions of Dithmar and Boldt and, based on new evidence, determined they were not guilty, a verdict that was never disclosed to the public. Whatever remained of the Leipzig trials was then finally hollowed out by the Nazi government, which quashed all the war crimes trials on June 7, 1933.[53]

Turkish crimes against Armenians

Although this book focuses primarily on war crimes rather than crimes against humanity and genocide, we would be remiss if we neglected to mention the failure to prosecute Turkish perpetrators of the Armenian massacres committed during the First World War. The Allies had accused the Ottoman Empire of crimes against humanity as early as 1915 (the term, which would appear for the first time in an international legal instrument thirty years later, was coined by the Russian minister of foreign affairs, Sergey Sazonov).[54] With the signing of the armistice of Mudros (October 1918), the Sultan promised that the murderers of the Armenians, as well as other accused war criminals, would be court-martialed. Pressed chiefly by the British, whose main focus was on ensuring punishment of Turks for mistreating British prisoners of war, the new grand vizier, Damad Ferid, ordered that war crime trials be conducted by a special military tribunal. In April 1919 the tribunal convicted Kemal Bey and Major Tevfik Bey, two high-ranking officials of the former Turkish government accused of deporting, robbing, and killing Armenian civilians in the Yozgat district. Tevfik received a fifteen-year sentence at hard labor, Kemal a death sentence executed four days after the verdict was announced.[55] On the heels of its incendiary verdict against Tevfik and Kemal, the tribunal tried twenty former Young Turk leaders in Constantinople. Several of these ex-officials had sought refuge in Germany, and were therefore prosecuted *in absentia*. All were accused of participating in the deliberate plan to deport and murder the Armenians. By July 5 the court had produced an uneven verdict: only one of the defendants was physically present in the courtroom to hear his conviction to fifteen years at hard labor. Death sentences were meted out *in absentia* to the others. Several of the defendants were acquitted, while the court returned no verdicts on some of the accused (the British had taken them as prisoners to Malta).[56]

While the Treaty of Sèvres (August 10, 1920) contained provisions requiring the Turks to deliver accused war criminals for trial by Allied national or mixed military courts, the new Turkish government under Kemal Atatürk rejected it. In 1923 the Treaty of Lausanne replaced the Treaty of Sèvres. The successor treaty had no clauses pertaining to the trials of Turks suspected of crimes against the Armenians. During the interval between the two treaties, the will to punish Turkish perpetrators had ebbed. Turkish suspects were able to escape from British custody due to lax supervision of their detention centers. The remaining prisoners were subsequently exchanged for British prisoners of war held by Turkish nationalists, a prisoner swap that effectively signaled the end of Great Britain's interest in prosecuting those responsible for the destruction of the Armenians. British legal advisors insisted that no trials related to the Armenian massacre could be held until the Treaty of Sèvres had come into effect. The Treaty, of course, never became operative, and its successor dropped any reference to war crimes trials. The upshot was to guarantee that no further trials of Turkish perpetrators would take place.[57] The failure of law to achieve justice for monstrous crimes inevitably opens the door to vigilante justice. Thus a string of ex-officials involved in crimes against the Armenians was murdered by Armenian assassins in the early 1920s.[58] In quiet places far from any courtroom, the blood feud—a practice older than human civilization itself—wreaked its terrible vengeance, reminding perceptive onlookers that the refusal or inability of formal legal process to punish mass murderers often invites private redress.

Conclusion: the First World War and the quest for justice

The conventional view of efforts after the First World War to prosecute violations of the Law of War tends to be negative. The failure of justice enacted on so many levels has bolstered the argument that the postwar settlement, as seen from the vantage point of the Law of War, was a disaster. Yet the bitter experience of the war crimes debacle would leave an enduring mark on the minds of the planners who devised the trials of Nazi and Japanese war criminals twenty-five years later. They would learn from the Allies' mistakes after the Great War, and in the process forge a new paradigm of war crimes prosecution that would revolutionize international law.

The post-First World War settlement may have achieved its most important legacy as a case study in judicial futility. There are other legacies, however, that are far more positive. One of these was the long-term influence of the Imperial Court's verdict in the *Llandovery Castle* case. Although the Court applied only German domestic and military law in the trial, tribunals after the Second World War would cite its verdict in support of the proposition that the norms of international law should prevail over national law and military orders. The Imperial Court had rejected Dithmar and Boldt's superior orders defense on the ground that such an order was invalid under international law. It held that "the order [to shell the lifeboats] does not free the accused from guilt . . . if such an order is universally known to be against the Law."[59] The refusal of Allied tribunals after the Second World War to accept the superior orders defense harks back to the Imperial Court's position on subaltern criminal liability. In support of their judgments, these postwar courts sometimes referenced the *Llandovery Castle* verdict, such as the British Military Court that prosecuted Heinz Eck and four other U-boat crewmen in October 1945 (the *Peleus* trial).[60] To the Second World War and its lasting impact on the Law of War we turn in the next chapter.

CHAPTER 8
THE SECOND WORLD WAR AND
THE TRIUMPH OF THE LAW OF WAR

A reasonably comprehensive chronicle of German and Japanese war crimes committed during the Second World War would fill several library shelves. The transcripts of the International Military Tribunal (IMT) at Nuremberg (the "blue series") alone run to forty-two thick volumes, and this trial dealt only with a limited spectrum of Nazi wrongdoing. Similarly, the crimes of the Japanese, while commanding less public attention than their German counterparts, are neither less appalling nor less voluminous and extend over a longer time period, stretching from the 1931 invasion of Manchuria to the final desperate months of the Japanese occupation in the spring and summer of 1945. The summary of German and Japanese violations of the Law of War below focuses primarily on misdeeds that became the objects of Allied prosecution after the war.

German crimes in the Second World War

As historian Gerhard Weinberg has written, "war had been an intended and even a preferred part of National Socialist policy from the beginning."[1] Weinberg points out that, given Adolf Hitler's plans to roll back German territorial losses under the Treaty of Versailles and to expand Germany's borders, war was unavoidable. In both *Mein Kampf* (1925, 1927) and his so-called "second book" (1928), Hitler had declared that Germany had to fulfill its historical destiny through eastward expansion, which he called *Lebensraum* ("living space"). For Hitler, Germany's very survival depended on acquiring new land to feed and resettle its growing population. Germany's swelling population demanded additional agricultural land, which could only be seized in Eastern Europe. As it acquired this new land, the German people would flourish and continue to grow, requiring the annexation of still more territory needed to feed and accommodate them. Weinberg sees in Hitler's ideology of *Lebensraum* a "crude Social Darwinism" in which racial groups clashed over land considered necessary for national survival. Their struggle would also be a zero sum game: the Germans' failure to secure vital living space would only empower the Slavic "subhumans" (*Untermenschen*) in the USSR, who would someday attain the superior technology and colossal manpower required to destroy a Germany hobbled by its restricted territory and population size.[2]

Hitler's racialized portrayal of Slavic "subhumanity" was a persistent element of his foreign policy. Of at least co-equal rank in his thinking was anti-Semitism, a preoccupation that drove both his domestic and foreign policies. On the home front until 1941, anti-Jewish legislation aimed at removing the Jews from so-called "Aryan" society, whether through emigration or segregation. In foreign policy, Hitler regarded Marxism as a Jewish doctrine seeking global domination and the destruction of all higher culture. Along with securing *Lebensraum* in the east, then, Germany had to destroy "Jewish Bolshevism" in the Soviet Union. Hence, the three goals of acquiring *Lebensraum*, defeating the USSR, and combating the Jews were closely intertwined and to a large degree inseparable in Nazi ideology. They could only be achieved by waging war not only to recover territory lost after the First World War but to achieve far greater territorial accessions as well. In this respect, National Socialism was not simply bent on restoring Germany's prewar borders; its goal was to regain these areas *and to expand into new lands through military conquest*, enslaving or expelling indigenous populations in order to "Germanize" the newly acquired territory.[3]

In the Nazi worldview, the success of Germany's eastward expansion would hinge on the racial purity of the German people. The self-imposed problem for the Nazis was that the German people were stricken with racial interbreeding and physical degeneration. Purification of the Germans' racial stock would be undertaken through two methods— positive and negative eugenics. Positive eugenics involved boosting the birthrate and health of racially valuable Germans; negative eugenics involved sterilizing the hereditarily unfit and by the late 1930s removing them from society through mass killing (so-called "euthanasia"). It is no exaggeration to assert the intimate linkage of eugenics with the Nazis' plans for territorial expansion: the conquest of other countries and the subjugation of their peoples assumed a hale and virile "Aryan" Germany from which all racial contaminants had been purged.[4]

Obviously, Germany's geographical position in central Europe precluded an immediate invasion of the USSR. Instead, intermediate steps would have to be taken preparatory to the attack. The first was the conquest or absorption of nearby territories containing ethnic Germans—Austria and the Sudetenland of Czechoslovakia (both annexed in 1938), as well as Memelland in Lithuania (ceded to Germany in 1939). In 1938 Poland had rejected Hitler's demand for the cession of Danzig to Germany. The Germans would later cite the Poles' refusal to justify their invasion of Poland on September 1, 1939, thereby triggering the onset of the Second World War in Europe. From the start of the conquest of Poland, German brutality offered a harrowing glimpse of future policies in their occupation of Europe. Hitler's plan after Poland's defeat was to liquidate its ruling class, on the supposition that decapitating Polish society would scotch resistance and enable the Germans to tap the Polish peasantry as forced labor for the German economy. To implement this plan, "special action squads" (*Einsatzgruppen*) were formed, comprising members of the Nazi state security organizations—the Security Service (*Sicherheitsdienst*, or SD), the Security Police (*Sicherheitspolizei*, or Sipo), and the Protective Staff (*Schutzstaffel*, or SS). The SD and SS would later be declared "criminal organizations" at the Nuremberg International Tribunal, and for good reason: the *Einsatzgruppen* would be used in Poland, the Czech lands, and the USSR to eliminate "hostile elements," a term describing persons deemed to pose a physical or racial threat to the new German order. In Poland, by the end of 1939 the German army and the *Einsatzgruppen* had shot 50,000 Polish nationals, including 7,000 Polish Jews. In the spring of 1940, the Germans pursued their "general pacification" plan to exterminate the Polish intelligentsia by executing thousands of Polish political, religious, and cultural leaders, among them Roman Catholic priests targeted as symbols of Polish cultural identity. Numerous Polish priests and nuns were arrested and deported to concentration camps within the German Reich. As many as 2,600 priests and 263 nuns would perish in these SS-run pestholes.[5]

Of the many inhuman institutions conceived by the Nazi imagination, few surpass in cruelty or oppression the concentration camps. The first camp was erected in March 1933 at Dachau by Heinrich Himmler, the Munich police president and later head of the SS, as a detention center for Communists and Socialists. Transferred in April from the Bavarianstate police to the SS,control of the camp would remain under SS administration until the end of the war. In 1934 Dachau's commandant, SS *Obergruppenführer* Theodor Eicke, became the Inspector of Concentration Camps and Leader of the SS guard units (subsequently called "death's head units"). Under Eicke's leadership, Dachau would become the model for all other concentration camps in Germany: Sachsenhausen (1936), Buchenwald (1937), and Flossenbürg and Mauthausen (both in 1938), to mention only some of the more prominent ones. In July 1933 the Dachau camp held 27,000 prisoners, a number that dipped significantly by the early summer of 1935, when the total number of prisoners was 3,500. The prisoner population would spike, however, after other groups were incarcerated: homosexuals, "career criminals," Jehovah's Witnesses, Gypsies, abortionists, churchmen, and critics of the government. By December 1938 the concentration camp population had soared to 12,921 persons under "police preventive detention." In November 1938, in the wake of the *Kristallnacht* pogrom, some 10,000 German Jews were sent to Dachau, most of whom were released months later.[6]

With the start of the war and German subjugation of continental Europe, tens of thousands of prisoners from the countries Germany invaded were deported to German concentration camps. These included partisans, Jews, and persons unwilling to collaborate with the Nazis. Between 1939 and 1945, prisoners from more than thirty countries poured into Dachau. The camp commandant quickly tapped these prisoners as a source of forced labor. As the war ground on and war production became increasingly urgent, control over camp labor was vested in the SS Economic-Administrative Main Office (WVHA). As the chief of the WVHA, Oswald Pohl would later be convicted at the American National Military Tribunal in Nuremberg and executed in 1951. Over time, concentration camps became essential productive centers for the German war economy, a fact that encouraged the formation of additional camps throughout the Reich. Many of these were subsidiaries of larger concentration camps. Dachau, for example, grew into a concentrationary Jupiter around which eighty-five satellite camps revolved, all devoted to munitions production through slave labor. By the end of the Second World War, the Germans had constructed some 980 concentration camps and a stunning 30,000 slave labor camps throughout occupied Europe.[7] Although only a small handful of these were true death camps, camp conditions in all of them were intended to harass, dehumanize, and brutalize the prisoners, who had to dodge a fanged gauntlet of deadly threats from the casual violence of the guards to starvation and epidemic disease.

One hazard confronting hundreds of prisoners was the medical experiments performed by camp physicians like Dr. Claus Schilling, an expert in tropical diseases commissioned in 1942 to establish a malaria research center at the Dachau camp. While Schilling was at Dachau, an endless stream of prisoners was placed at his disposal as experimental subjects. Schilling deliberately infected the prisoners with malaria pathogens, and when they exhibited signs of the disease he treated them with a cocktail of medications. At first Schilling used "habitual criminals" as his guinea pigs; later his preference shifted to Polish priests and toward the end of his experiments to prisoners with heart defects, most of who were Polish and Russian nationals. Between 300 and 400 of them died either from the initial infection with malaria or from complications arising from the "treatment." Over and above Schilling's malaria experiments, a raft of SS medical programs was carried out at Dachau and Auschwitz-Birkenau in Silesia (formerly Poland). The Battle of Britain (1940) and the impending invasion of the Soviet Union (June 1941) had sparked Himmler's interest in aviation medicine, particularly the capacity of German pilots to endure high altitudes and hypothermia when shot down over the ocean. In 1941 Himmler authorized an SS medical officer in the Luftwaffe, Sigmund Rascher, to conduct high-altitude and hypothermia experiments at Dachau. In May 1942 the general inspector of the Luftwaffe, Erhard Milch, later to become the lead defendant in one of the Nuremberg successor trials,[8] authorized the use of Dachau prisoners for the hypothermia experiments. Rascher's program, which ran from March 1942 until August 1942, used 400 to 500 prisoners for the high-altitude experiments and 300 for the hypothermia experiments. Franz Blaha, a prisoner-doctor, testified at the 1945 Dachau trial that many of the high-altitude victims perished during the experiments, while the survivors were transferred to the invalid ward and subsequently killed there.[9]

In their conduct of the war, German forces demonstrated a degree of brutality unrivaled in modern warfare. Fearful that Italian misadventures in Greece would enable a British toehold in the Balkans, and furious that a military coup had overthrown the pro-German government in Yugoslavia, Hitler attacked the two countries on April 6, 1941, conquering both in short order. The Germans annexed swaths of territory in northern Yugoslavia, which they sought to purify by "re-Germanizing" the ethnic Germans living there while expelling everyone else. Shootings of innocent civilians soon galvanized two resistance movements: the "Cetniks," who staged limited sabotage actions against the occupation; and a partisan group under Josip Broz ("Tito"), which, particularly after the German invasion of the USSR, attacked the occupiers regardless of the ferocity of German retaliation against civilians. When they came, German reprisals for partisan attacks were swift and severe. On the orders of Field Marshall Maximilian Freiherr von Weichs, Supreme Commander of German forces in the occupation of Greece and Yugoslavia, 100 civilians were to be taken hostage and shot for every German soldier killed by partisans. Several thousand civilians were executed in connection with Weichs's orders. In Crete during the spring of 1941, the Germans razed entire towns and shot scores of civilians in reprisal for attacks on German troops.[10] War crimes against the civilian populations of Greece, Yugoslavia, and Crete would later be tried by the

Americans at Nuremberg (*U.S. v. List et al.*); the verdict would prove to be the most controversial of all the trials the USA conducted in that city.

As a springboard to the variegated forms of Nazi criminality, nothing can compare to the German invasion of the Soviet Union on June 22, 1941. Atrocities by policy on Soviet prisoners of war, the liquidation of Baltic and Soviet Jews in mass shooting operations, and the most notorious of the Nazis' crimes, the Final Solution, were the byproducts of Hitler's invasion and are inconceivable without it. Military preparations for "Operation Barbarossa," as the invasion was code-named, began in the summer of 1940. By December 1940 a concrete plan of attack had taken shape involving a three-pronged invasion led by Army Group Center, which would drive toward Moscow after taking Minsk and Smolensk. Army Group South would advance toward Kiev while Army Group North conquered Leningrad. Hitler's intention was to annihilate the Red Army in a massive, overwhelming stroke of concentrated military power, then turn to capture the Soviet Union's agricultural and industrial bases. The entire campaign, he believed, would be over by the summer or early fall of 1941. With the operational plan in place, the Germans spent the ensuing months fine-tuning the details of the invasion. On March 30, 1941, in a meeting with his top military commanders, Hitler described the upcoming invasion of the Soviet Union as a "war of extermination" requiring that all members of the German armed forces be ready to "make the sacrifice of overcoming their scruples."[11] He stressed that the special character of the impending conflict meant that the Law of War would be suspended for its duration. The chief of the Army General Staff, Franz Halder, recorded the *Führer's* words at this conference: "We must dissociate ourselves from the standpoint of soldierly comradeship. The communist is no comrade either beforehand or afterward."[12]

The High Command of the Armed Forces (OKH) issued a directive on May 13 consistent with Hitler's menacing words from his March 30 meeting. Under the signature of OKH's Chief of Staff, General Field Marshall Wilhelm Keitel, later to be prosecuted for crimes against humanity and war crimes at Nuremberg, the directive is so uncannily predictive of the German army's lawless conduct during Barbarossa that it warrants closer examination. It consisted of three sections. In section (1), the decree removed the jurisdiction of military courts over criminal acts committed by enemy civilians. "Irregular troops" were to be "ruthlessly" disposed of by the troops, whether in battle or in flight. Every other hostile civilian act against the German army should be met by the troops at the scene of the act "with the most extreme measures, including the destruction of the attacker." In situations in which this did not occur, the suspects were to be sent to an officer to determine whether they should be shot. The decree envisioned reprisals against towns from which "deceitful" or "treacherous" attacks on the German army were launched, particularly where the identity of the perpetrators could not be established. Where a region had been pacified, the supreme commanders of the army groups could coordinate trial of civilians by military courts. Section (2) of the decree allowed army commanders to suspend military law in cases involving German soldiers' attacks on enemy civilians. In the event that a soldier was court-martialed for such acts, the decree urged commanders to take into account certain mitigating circumstances—namely, that

Germany's miseries since 1918 were directly attributable to "Bolshevik influence," a fact that "no German had forgotten." In any event, the military judge should only order a trial of offenses involving "the preservation of discipline or the security of the troops." Examples of the latter included acts "indicative of a lack of sexual restraint" or a "criminal predisposition" that might "brutalize the troops." Finally, section (3) instructed troop commanders of their "personal" responsibility to ensure that all of the officers and legal advisors in their units be informed of the rules set forth in the decree.[13]

Keitel's decree was further amplified by top-secret guidelines issued by the Supreme Command of the German Armed Forces to its commanders on June 6, 1941. This document acquired a notorious name after the war: the "commissar order." In its preamble, the order recited language that in its dualistic tone might have been plucked from the pages of *Mein Kampf*:

In the struggle against Bolshevism we *cannot* expect the enemy will follow the rules of humanity or of international law. We may anticipate in particular a hateful, cruel and inhumane treatment of our prisoners of war by the *political commissars of all kinds* as the actual pillars of resistance. [Emphasis in the original.]

The order continued:

The troops must be aware that: (1) In this struggle quarter and respect for international law toward these elements are wrong. They are a danger for the security of our own troops and the speedy pacification of the conquered territories.

(2) The initiators of barbarous Asiatic combat methods are the political commissars.

These [persons] must therefore be dealt with in all severity and without the slightest hesitation.

They are therefore, when captured in battle or resistance, to be immediately shot.

After its issuance, the commissar order would circulate for two weeks among the top commanders of the German Army in the East without drawing a single objection. Despite the clear illegality of the order, German commanders relayed it to their troops in the days preceding the invasion. At Nuremberg after the war, German military officers would claim they had rejected the commissar order or sought to sabotage it, a claim partially validated by the US Chief of Counsel of War Crimes, Telford Taylor, who conceded that some of the commanders may have refused to pass the order on to their troops. In no small measure, as historian Felix Römer has argued, the Nuremberg trials contributed to the postwar myth of the "clean Wehrmacht," which portrayed the German army as innocent of involvement in Nazi crimes.[14] German historians of the 1960s largely endorsed the myth, assigning responsibility for the Third Reich's crimes to Hitler and the coterie surrounding him. By the 1970s, however, new scholarship challenged the myth of the German army's innocence, beginning with historian Christian Streit's conclusion "that the [commissar] order was implemented in most of the divisions of the [German Army in the East]."[15] While admitting that evidence of implementation at the divisional level did not prove each company consistently followed it, Streit found that Army and Tank Group reports listed 800 executions conducted under its terms.[16] In an unpublished manuscript widely cited in the literature, historian Detlef Siebert found 80 percent of the Army Corps (Army and Tank Groups) and one-half of all divisions had carried out the commissar order.[17] During the time the order was in force, i.e., from June 1941 to May 1942, Römer estimates that at least 3,430 commissars were executed under it.[18]

The decrees of May 13 and June 6 were catalysts to war crimes when the Germans invaded the Soviet Union. A third directive issued by Army Commander-in-Chief Walther von Brauchitsch on April 28, 1941 laid the foundation for mass shooting operations targeting civilians (especially Eastern European Jews) in the summer and fall of 1941. It set forth the details of an agreement between Reinhard Heydrich, the chief of the Reich Security Main Office, and Quartermaster of the Army Eduard Wagner regarding the interaction of the security police and security service with German army units in the forthcoming invasion. The Sipo/SD commandos were in fact the *Einsatzgruppen* used to terrorize civilian populations in Poland, the Czech lands, and Yugoslavia. They would be injected into army rear areas after the initial invasion, which they would comb for alleged security threats. Once found, these threats would be liquidated. The directive did not identify who precisely would be considered a threat meriting liquidation; it merely indicated that the *Einsatzgruppen* were authorized to take "executive measures against the civilian population."[19] However, when the directive is read in light of contemporaneous military orders, the identities of the targeted groups can be pieced together. An April 2, 1941 directive to the *Einsatzgruppen* being deployed to Yugoslavia instructed them to arrest "Jews and Communists" as potential threats. Moreover, a set of guidelines for the conduct of German troops in Russia issued on May 19, 1941 demanded "ruthless and energetic repression of Bolshevik instigators, franc-tireurs, saboteurs, Jews, and the complete removal of any active or passive resistance."[20] These groups would be the targets of the *Einsatzgruppen* during the invasion of the Soviet Union.

The Heydrich-Wagner agreement was the cornerstone of mass murder as a German military force consisting of 166 divisions and 4,306,800 soldiers plunged across the German-Soviet border on June 22, 1941. In the first six weeks of fighting the Germans captured hundreds of thousands of Soviet prisoners of war. By the end of the war, some 5,700,000 Soviet soldiers had fallen into German hands. Of this number, 3,300,000 perished in captivity—a mortality rate of nearly 58 percent.[21] Shortly before the invasion, German commanders ordered their troops to separate the commissars from other Soviet prisoners of war and send them to the rear for "treatment" by the SD. In all German army units, these orders appear to have been followed, and in some cases even exceeded: surrendering Red Army soldiers were often gunned down, and at the end of June a regiment of the 299th Infantry Division reported that, due to the "enemy's treacherous manner of fighting," quarter would no longer be given.[22]

Not all Red Army fatalities, nor even most of them, were inflicted by the *Einsatzgruppen*; rather, as the example of the 299th Infantry Division illustrates, Soviet prisoner of war executions were often carried out by the German army. During the opening months of the invasion, the Germans repeatedly encircled Red Army soldiers, cutting them off from the main body of the Soviet army. This meant that with the Germans' swift advance ever larger numbers of Soviet troops were behind the eastern front. Responding to this situation, OKH ordered on September 13 that Red Army soldiers found behind the front who had sought to re-group as a combat force would be treated as partisans and shot. The new policy was interpreted as applying to all Soviet soldiers encountered behind the front, whether or not they had tried to reorganize.[23] The high mortality rate among Soviet prisoners of war in German captivity was partially due to inadequate provision for their feeding, transportation, and maintenance. Thousands perished in forced marches spanning hundreds of miles; others died in open freight railroad cars fully exposed to the frigid winter. The deaths were not an oversight; German army commanders ordered the marches on foot and journeys in open freight cars with knowledge of the vast distances that would have to be traversed.[24] Similarly, inadequate or nonexistent food for Soviet prisoners appears to have been deliberate, leading to the mass die-off of Soviet prisoners from starvation during the harsh winter of 1941/42.[25]

As it did throughout occupied Europe, the German army carried out draconian reprisal shootings in the USSR. The practice was on display already in the opening month of the war, when the 110th Infantry Division shot sixty Russian soldiers and one commissar in retaliation for the mutilation of the corpses of German soldiers. In early October 1941, when the 61st Infantry Division exhumed the hastily buried bodies of three German soldiers bearing the signs of being murdered, the division headquarters ordered reprisal shootings of all prisoners in the regiment's custody—some ninety-three Red Army soldiers. A similar pattern was replayed at the end of October after the bodies of fifteen German soldiers were discovered. Analysis indicated that the men had initially been wounded, then subsequently killed with gunshots to the head. Reprisal for these murders was ordered by the division headquarters: all Soviet prisoners of war affiliated with the 1st Guards Division or the 100th Protective Division (both implicated in the killings) were to be shot—up to 230 men. Over the next several days, 160 Soviet prisoners of war were executed. Reprisals were not always initiated by division headquarters, but were often set in motion by the combat units, regiments, and battalions themselves. Moreover, execution of Soviet prisoners was widely dispersed across German army units; they were not confined to a handful of outliers. Mass shootings of prisoners of war continued with some ebbs and flows until the spring of 1942, when orders to treat them decently altered German policy. The new orders were motivated not by humanitarian but by pragmatic concerns: execution of Soviet prisoners of war was stiffening the resistance of Red Army troops.[26]

In most people's minds today, the tower of criminality the Nazis reared in Eastern Europe was less the execution of Soviet commissars or reprisals against Red Army prisoners; rather, it was the "Final Solution to the Jewish Question." The Final Solution—

the Nazis' program to murder every last Jewish man, woman, and child within their grasp by means of firing squads and poison gas—was an excrescence of German shooting operations against Jews in the USSR. As we have seen, the Heydrich-Wagner agreement tasked the *Einsatzgruppen* with liquidating alleged security threats like saboteurs, Jews, and communists. In the first, most critical phase of the *Einsatzgruppen's* activities (June to December 1941), Heydrich's four units conducted shooting operations against each of these groups as they scrambled to keep pace with the German army. The worst of these targeted Jews. In Lithuania, the first massacre of Jews was conducted by the *Einsatzkommando* Tilsit along the German-Lithuanian border, where 201 victims were shot. Waves of killings followed wherever the army set its bootprint: in Bialystok, Poland (2,000 Jews shot, June 27, 1941, and another 1,000 between July 8 and 11), Brest, Belorussia (4,000 to 6,000 Jews shot, mid-July 1941), and Kaunas, Lithuania (7,800 Jews killed by a combination of firing squads and pogroms carried out by local auxiliaries, early July 1941). By the end of July, the *Einsatzgruppen* had tallied 63,000 victims, 90 percent of who were Jewish. In their operational reports, the unit commanders adduced flimsy reasons for shooting Jews, depicting them as guerrillas and saboteurs—an identification that brought the victims within the scope of the men's orders.[27]

The first five weeks of Barbarossa were of critical importance to the unfolding of the Holocaust because they created, in the words of historian Christopher Browning, "a new point of reference for German occupation policy"—namely, the idea that the regime's goals of pacification and resettlement could be achieved through mass murder.[28] One sign of this new policy was the gradual erasure of the line between military-aged Jewish men and Jewish women and children. In the opening weeks of the invasion, German forces focused their shooting operations on Jewish men. By early July, however, German intelligence was reporting to headquarters that Ukrainian natives were killing "Jews and Russians including women and children" in pogrom-style attacks.[29] In Romania, the murder of Jewish women, the elderly, and children occurred even earlier: in late June, the Romanian 6th Mountain Regiment executed as many as 311 Jews in a pit the victims were forced to shovel out beforehand. The victims included women and children. By late July, the *Einsatzgruppen* followed suit and began to include many Jewish women and children in their shooting operations.[30]

Until this time, the escalation in the range and identity of victims appears to have been driven by local initiative. In late July, it was given official endorsement when Heinrich Himmler ordered his SS mounted battalions on the verge of sweeping the Pripet Marshes to shoot all Jewish men and "drive the female Jews into the swamps." A critical threshold had been crossed. By mid-August the *Einsatzgruppen's* shootings in the Baltic countries swelled, and thereafter included numerous Jewish women and children. At the Ukrainian city of Kamenets Podolsky they shot 23,600 Jews between August 26 and August 29. The frequency, intensity, and amplitude of Jewish massacres by mid- to late August 1941 are convincing proof that the German killers now understood that no Jewish man, woman, or child in the USSR was to be left alive.[31] By the fall, that policy would be revised to ensure the destruction of all European Jews within reach of the Germans.

Due to the psychologically taxing effects of mass shootings on the *Einsatzgruppen*, it was decided to relocate the killing process behind the barbed wire of camps in Eastern Europe. The new killing sites were inspired by two other repressive institutions in Nazi Germany: the concentration camp, where the regime's enemies were imprisoned, brutalized, and exploited as slave laborers, and the "euthanasia" centers, in which disabled patients bussed from mental hospitals throughout the Reich were murdered in gas chambers disguised as shower rooms. The "death camps" would be an amalgam of these forerunners. Like the Nazi state's political enemies, Jews would be confined in camps administered by SS guards. Like the mentally disabled, they would be transported to the camps (usually on trains, rather than busses) and killed with poison gas. What has since become known as the "Final Solution"—itself a distinctive phase of the larger Jewish Holocaust—in fact consisted of several programs targeting different groups of Jews. The Chelmno camp in the portion of Poland annexed to the Reich was the first of the operational death camps. Intended to murder the Jews in the Lodz ghetto and other parts of western Poland, Chelmno began gassing operations on December 8, 1941, and over the next four years 147,000 Jews and 5,000 Roma would die in "gas vans" originally designed to murder the disabled. A separate program, "Operation Reinhard," was devised in the fall of 1941 and placed under the direction of the SS Police Leader of the Lublin district of occupied Poland, Odilo Globocnik. Its goal was to kill the 2,284,000 Jews living in the five districts of occupied Poland (an area called "the General Government"). The program consisted of three death camps, all erected on the soil of the General Government and all located near rail lines and concentrated populations of Polish Jews. The three camps, Belzec, Sobibor, and Treblinka, would use carbon monoxide produced by gas or diesel engines to asphyxiate the victims in air-tight chambers deceivingly presented as shower rooms. The death toll of Operation Reinhard reached nearly 1.8 million Jews.[32]

The most infamous Nazi camp, however, was Auschwitz-Birkenau. Located in Upper Silesia, Poland, near the town of Oświęcim, Auschwitz did not begin its existence as a death camp, as had the Operation Reinhard camps. Rather, it had started as a Polish army base during the First World War named Zasole, which remained in Polish hands until the fourth partition of Poland in late September 1939. In the "secret protocol" signed by the Nazis and Soviets before the German invasion of Poland, the USSR had agreed to the resettlement of ethnic Germans in western Poland. Heinrich Himmler became the chief of the resettlement program on September 28, receiving the title of "Reich Commissioner for the Consolidation of the German Nation". His plan was to resettle 20 million German settlers in the German east over the next fifty to eighty years. As the settlers moved into annexed Poland, the original Polish inhabitants, including Jews, would be expelled farther east and their vacated homes given to the arriving settlers. In February 1940 the Germans ordered the creation of a concentration camp for Poles resistant to Germany's New Order. It was recommended that the old Polish army camp of Zasole be converted into a concentration camp. Himmler eventually approved their proposal, and in late April he appointed Rudolf Höß as its inaugural commandant. The first Polish prisoners arrived in the camp in June.[33]

Like its model, the original concentration camps in Germany, Auschwitz had the initial purpose of detaining and "reeducating" the prisoners, as well as terrorizing the local population. By September 1940, a new plan had formed: from this point forward, Auschwitz would be transformed into a production site for the German war economy. Toward this end, Höß was ordered to expand substantially the size of the prisoner compound to accommodate a permanent population of slave laborers. One of the buildings was converted into a prison called "Block 11." Prisoners designated for execution were taken naked into a courtyard to a black wall and shot in the back of the neck. The corpses were then incinerated in the camp crematorium. In Block 11, moreover, the Gestapo Summary Court held "trials" of Polish men and women labeled as resisters, who were interrogated, convicted, and executed at the Black Wall. These persons were never registered as camp prisoners; they were outsiders brought to the camp for the express purpose of execution. With time, camp personnel found it easier to perform killings in the camp mortuary and afterward dispose of the bodies in the crematorium next door. As 1941 passed into 1942, the categories of outsiders brought to the camp for killing spiraled outward to engulf Polish partisans and Russian prisoners of war. On February 15, 1942, the first transports of Jews arrived for liquidation.[34]

We can see, then, that early in its existence under the Nazis Auschwitz was a detention center that gradually acquired two distinct functions: to supply slave laborers for war production and to kill enemies of the Reich. In March 1941 the gigantic chemical conglomerate IG Farben, at the time the fourth largest company in the world, contracted with the SS to install a synthetic rubber and gasoline plant at Auschwitz, a site chosen because of its proximity to large coalfields. Himmler was captivated by the idea because it would promote his plan of German settlement in the east. According to the agreement, Farben would procure building materials for construction of the factory in exchange for slave labor—1,000 prisoners up front and 3,000 in 1942. The prisoners, who worked in a section of the camp named "Monowitz" (Auschwitz III), were driven by SS and Farben overseers to construct Farben's plant at a hectic pace, and at a considerable price. A judge in the US trial of IG Farben executives at Nuremberg, Paul M. Hebert, wrote in his concurring opinion, "It was Farben's drive for speed in the construction of Auschwitz which resulted in thousands of inmates being selected for extermination by the SS when they were rendered unfit for work." A German Jewish witness testified after the war that "the German IG foremen tried to surpass the SS in brutalities."[35]

In fulfillment of the agreement with Farben, the SS planned to increase the camp population to 30,000 prisoners. This slave labor force would be furnished by an anticipated influx of Soviet prisoners of war after the looming invasion of the USSR. By the end of 1941, however, it was apparent that the German army could not supply the 90,000 Soviet prisoners of war the SS was expecting. To fill the void, the SS—riven with the contradictory needs of ridding the Reich of its Jews and tapping them as a source of labor—decided to replace the missing Soviet prisoners of war with Jewish workers. This became the policy enunciated at the Wannsee Conference held near Berlin in January 1942, in which Heydrich acquainted the government's leading representatives with the fate reserved for European Jewry: the 11 million Jews of German-occupied Europe would be sent eastward, where they would be separated by gender and consigned to hard labor building roads. The harsh conditions would kill off "a large portion" of them, while the survivors would be liquidated. Throughout this process, Himmler would enjoy "primary responsibility for the handling of the final solution."[36] Shortly after the Wannsee Conference, in February 1942, an SS officer and bureaucrat in the provincial government, Albrecht Schmelt, sent 400 elderly Jews from Beuthen to Auschwitz. Schmelt was the organizer of a program bearing his name that mobilized Jewish forced labor in Upper Silesia. The "Schmelt Program" coordinated the labor of as many as 50,000 Jews. To rid himself of unproductive workers, and learning that the Gestapo Summary Court carried out executions in Auschwitz, Schmelt sent the elderly Jews to the camp. Several months earlier the SS had converted the crematorium morgue in Auschwitz 1 into a gas chamber with a capacity of 900 persons. The 400 elder Schmelt Jews were murdered in this gas chamber shortly after their arrival. The February gassing of the Schmelt Jews proved disruptive of the routine in the main camp. Executing prisoners convicted by the Gestapo Summary Court was one thing, but gassing hundreds of elderly people was intensely problematic for the SS. A different, more private site had to be found. The eyes of the SS fell on the satellite camp of Auschwitz-Birkenau.[37]

Birkenau's origins go back to Himmler's attempt in March 1941 to woo IG Farben into choosing Auschwitz for the site of its synthetic rubber/gasoline plant. At that time, Himmler made two promises to the Farben executives: he would enlarge the prisoner population in the main camp (Auschwitz I) to 30,000 and build a sprawling auxiliary camp of 100,000 inmates.[38] The auxiliary camp was Birkenau. Nearly a year later, faced with the (self-imposed) necessity of dealing with nonproductive workers, the SS decided to transform Birkenau into a camp not dissimilar from Chelmno—a center devoted to the destruction of nonworking Jews. Chief of SS construction Hans Kammler arrived in Auschwitz on February 27, 1942, and countermanded plans drafted back in January to install an expanded crematorium in the main camp. Instead, Kammler ordered that it be installed in the northwest corner of Birkenau. It would adjoin a vacant peasant cottage called "the little red house," a building reconstructed into two gas chambers later known as "Bunker 1." Bunker 1 would not employ carbon monoxide gas as a killing agent, as Chelmno did and as the Operation Reinhard camps were shortly to do. Rather, it used a highly toxic fumigant, Zyklon B. On March 20, 1942, another transport of nonworking Schmelt Jews became the first victims gassed there.[39]

By June 1942 Bunker 1 had proven to be unequal to the gassing demanded of it. Höß ordered that another cottage (the "little white house") be converted into a four-chambered gassing facility. Bunker 2, as it was called, began its deadly work on July 4. The victims were Slovakian Jews culled from a transport based on their unfitness for labor. Jews had been sent to Auschwitz from Germany's client state of Slovakia since February 1942. The early transports contained young, healthy male Jews tapped by the SS as forced laborers. Not until the opening of Bunker 2 were the Slovakian transports subjected to a "selection" and 638 Slovak Jews sent to the new gas chamber, carrying towels and soap in the misapprehension they were taking a shower.[40] In the ensuing months, the SS installed Crematoria II and III in Birkenau, then added two more (IV and V). (Crematorium I was in the main camp.) The first three crematoria were not originally intended as extermination centers; IV and V, on the other hand, were designed from the beginning as fully integrated killing sites, equipped with gas chambers, a morgue, and a furnace for incinerating the corpses. Over time, Crematoria I, II, and III were rebuilt as extermination centers.[41]

By January 1943, at a time when the war had turned against the Germans and Himmler's dreams of Germanizing the east were crumbling into dust, Auschwitz began to lose its function as a beachhead of industrial production and ethnic resettlement. A new focus now emerged: the destruction of the Jews for its own sake. Between March 1942 and November 1944, over one million Jews were murdered at Auschwitz, on average 32,000 to 34,000 per month. In 1944, as the German army was retreating on all fronts, the SS killed one-third of all the people murdered at Auschwitz. The victims were predominately Jews from all over Europe, including the Cracow ghetto, Salonika, and Hungary.[42]

The International Military Tribunal (IMT) at Nuremberg, 1945–46

Planning the Tribunal

A steady stream of reports about German atrocities flowed into Allied hands from the early years of the war. They drew public condemnations of German war crimes that hinted at future judicial punishment but never clearly warned of trials. Nonetheless, the Allies were determined to avoid the fiasco of miscarried justice that had occurred after the First World War, when little was done to hold German and Turkish perpetrators legally accountable. As the US and British governments diagnosed the problem of the postwar settlement, it resided in a trio of blunders: US and British policymakers vowed these failures would not happen again.

The lack of a concerted plan to address the war crimes question during the war The Allies during the First World War lacked a common policy on German war crimes. In fact, they made only one joint threat against a country for harming civilians—a 1915 declaration on the Armenian massacre. Never during the war was an international agency created to document German crimes and offer recommendations for future action by Allied policymakers. It was widely believed after the war that Allied disunity on the war crimes question gravely weakened the resolve to prosecute German war criminals. During the Second World War, by contrast, the British and Americans sought to coordinate their statements on German war crimes. Churchill and Roosevelt issued separate but complementary warnings about punishing German reprisal shootings in the fall of 1941. These statements energized the Allied exile governments in London, who issued their own joint declaration on January 13, 1942, at St. James's Palace, London. Their statement announced that a "principal" aim of the war was the prosecution of German war criminals for attacks on civilians.[43] The "St. James Declaration," as it was called, reflected a concern of the exile governments with British and American commitment to prosecute Nazi war criminals. While both countries had threatened "punishment," neither had defined with any detail what the word punishment meant. The USA and Great Britain were reluctant to make public announcements of future trials for fear they could lead to retaliation against their prisoners of war in German custody. Eventually, they changed their minds: in late 1942, the Anglo-Americans began for the first time to threaten the Germans with judicial punishment. The pressures brought to bear on them by the exile governments in London were decisive for this change in the Allies' tone.[44]

In October 1942, the USSR issued its own threat. The Soviets insisted that: (a) an international court should subject the Nazi leadership to criminal prosecution; (b) lower-ranking German war criminals should be tried in national criminal courts; and (c) the USSR was willing to cooperate in surrendering and extraditing war crimes suspects. One year later, the USA, Great Britain, and the USSR issued the Moscow Declaration, which, *inter alia*, provided that German war crimes suspects would be returned to the scenes of their alleged crimes after the war for trial by the newly restored governments. Further, it stated that major war criminals whose crimes "had no geographical location" would be punished by a joint decision of the Allies. At this time, what form the "joint decision" would take remained unspoken.[45] The Allies would later decide to try the major war criminals in an international tribunal, but in October 1943 that decision had not yet been made.

The absence of a fact-gathering agency to document war crimes during the war In August 1942, the British proposed to Roosevelt that a United Nations commission might be established to document Nazi atrocities against United Nations nationals. The proposed commission would forward the results of its investigations to the governments on whose citizens war crimes were committed. The report would include the names of suspected perpetrators, and only "organized atrocities," that is, crimes arising from official policy, would be considered. The affected governments would then decide whether to prosecute the accused. By early October 1942, the Americans had agreed with the proposal to establish this war crimes commission, which came into being in the fall of 1943.In its original form,the UN War Crimes Commission (UNWCC) was restricted to investigating war crimes committed by enemy nationals on citizens of the UN. By early 1944, the Commission members were urging the British Foreign Office and US State Department to expand its jurisdiction to investigate crimes committed by Axis nations on their own citizens.Both the Americans and the British opposed such an alteration in the Commission's authority.[46] As we will see, the Allies would ultimately finesse this issue by tracing the genocide of Jews—including the Jews of Germany and its allies—to German military aggression. This concession notwithstanding, the Holocaust would play a relatively minor role at the Nuremberg War Crimes Trial when it convened in the fall of 1945.[47]

Neglecting to create a mechanism to assure delivery of war crimes suspects to the Allies for punishment Proponents of prosecuting German war crimes remembered the fiasco of the post-First World War settlement. They blamed this failure in part on the absence of a war crimes provision in the armistice signed with Germany, as well as on the Kaiser's ability to find sanctuary in the Netherlands, thereby shielding him from extradition. As early as September 1942, the British were calling for insertion of a war crimes provision in any future armistice with Germany, which "should not be left over until after the conclusion of a peace treaty." For the British, failure to include such a proviso might make it "impossible, as after the last war, to obtain custody of the persons required." The provision would require "immediate capture or surrender of wanted criminals." All subsequent treaties with Axis nations would reproduce this provision.[48]

On October 7, 1942, Great Britain and the USA announced that terms for the surrender of accused German war criminals would be included in the armistice. In an address defining the authority of the UNWCC, Lord High Chancellor John Simon reaffirmed the British position, cautioning that the Allies' refusal to include a provision on war crimes in the 1918 armistice impaired enforcement of Articles 227–231 of the Versailles Treaty. Lord Simon vowed that "we do not intend to make the same mistake as was made by postponing this demand until the final treaty of peace has been signed."[49] Concern with the armistice issue led the UNWCC in June 1944 to insist that any peace treaty reached with Germany must demand surrender to the UN of all accused war criminals.

In addition to the armistice issue, the Allies strove to prevent a situation that would enable Nazi war criminals to find sanctuary from prosecution in other countries, as the Kaiser had in the Netherlands. Great Britain asserted in September 1942 that war criminals must be prevented from finding refuge in "neutral countries," thereby eluding the reach of Allied justice.[50] To avoid this possibility, the Allies warned neutral countries to refuse sanctuary to Nazi war criminals as the war drew down.[51]

In 1942 and 1943, the USA, Great Britain, and the USSR were all warning of future judicial punishment for Nazi war criminals. As far as the top Nazi leaders were concerned, however, the British and Soviets favored summary execution. From the summer of 1942 Foreign Office legal advisors had urged Prime Minister Winston Churchill to avoid trials of the leading Nazis due to the difficulties involved in creating an international court and the inevitable charge of "victor's justice" such a court would invite. Lord Simon stated his view to the War Cabinet in September 1944 that judicial proceedings of top Nazis were "quite inappropriate."[52] Already in late November 1943, at a meeting of Stalin, Churchill, and Roosevelt in Teheran, Stalin had suggested that 50,000 German officers and technicians, as well as the whole General Staff, be liquidated after the war. While in his memoirs Churchill would later claim Stalin's suggestion had offended him,[53] his conversation with Stalin at the Yalta Summit (April 1945) indicates a receptivity to the idea of summary executions. At Yalta Churchill raised the possibility of compiling a list of war criminals, arresting those on the list and after ascertaining their identity shooting them without trial.[54]

Although US officials would ultimately thwart this proposal, there was at least one high- ranking figure within the government who favored it—Secretary of the Treasury Henry Morgenthau Jr. In September 1944 Morgenthau urged that the UN draft a list of the German "arch-criminals," which would be given to the military with instructions to arrest them, verify their identity, and turn them over to a UN firing squad for execution. Morgenthau reserved trials by Allied military commissions only for lower-ranking war crimes suspects charged with offenses"against civilization." If found guilty by the commission, the convicted would be executed absent extenuating circumstances. No appeal from a guilty verdict would be permitted.[55] A doughty opponent of Morgenthau's proposal was the Secretary of War Henry Stimson, who only days after the Morgenthau memorandum authored a categorical rejection of summary execution. Stimson argued that the "arch-criminals" should be afforded a trial in an international court, in which they would enjoy US-style legal rights—notification of the charge, the right to defend themselves, and the right to call witnesses. The accused would be charged with "offences against the laws of the Rules of War." Lower-ranking suspects would be sent back to the scenes of their crimes for trial by national military commissions as stipulated by the Moscow Declaration. The memorandum made clear that no crimes unrelated to the conduct of the war, such as crimes committed by Germans on German victims, would be prosecuted. Military tribunals"would be without jurisdiction in precisely the same way that any foreign court would be without jurisdiction to try those who were guilty of ... lynching in our own country."[56] Hence, from early on, the Americans opposed prosecuting any atrocities unrelated to the conduct of the war. Such atrocities were off-limits to international jurisdiction.

By the early fall of 1944, Stimson's plan was supplemented with an approach to the war crimes issue advocated by Lieutenant Colonel Murray Bernays, the head of the War Department's Special Projects Office and (as a civilian) a lawyer for the Securities and Exchange Commission. Bernays tackled the question of how the Allies would deal with the administrative challenges of prosecuting thousands of German war crimes suspects individually. His solution—a novelty in European as well as international law, but one routinely used in the USA to prosecute SEC and Smith Act violations—was to identify as"criminal organizations" the leading Nazi agencies implicated in war crimes. Thereafter, anyone belonging to these organizations could be charged with conspiracy to commit the crimes perpetrated by their various members.[57] By January 1945 US officials had devised a war crimes program based on Stimson's and Bernays's ideas. It contemplated charging both Nazi leaders and Nazi organizations with war crimes and conspiracy to commit them. After the leaders and their organizations were convicted before an international court, lower echelon suspects would be prosecuted in what US officials called "subsequent trials," in which membership in a criminal organization was presumptive evidence of guilt.[58] After Roosevelt's death on April 12, 1945, his successor, Harry Truman, endorsed this plan. At the UN's founding conference in San Francisco, US representatives shared with their British and Soviet counterparts the details of their war crimes plan. The international tribunal would consist of a judge from each of the four victorious powers—Great Britain, the USA, France, and the USSR. Each country would designate a representative to serve on a committee to gather evidence for trial. In addition to trying individual defendants, the Americans proposed labeling Nazi agencies as criminal organizations, the members of which would be accused of conspiring "to control the world, to persecute minorities, to break treaties, to invade other nations and to commit crimes." Once an organization was convicted, everyone who had joined it voluntarily "would ipso facto be guilty of a war crime."[59] The British and Soviets agreed to the American proposal, as did the French shortly thereafter.

Alongside Stimson's and Bernays's proposals, 1944 produced a third seminal contribution to the Allied war crimes program: the notion of "aggressive war." On November 28, 1944, Colonel William Chanler, a close friend and legal associate of Stimson and the deputy chief of the War Department's Civil Affairs Division, sent Stimson a memorandum outlining the case for putting the Nazi leadership on trial for violating the Kellogg-Briand Pact of 1928. Starting as a bilateral treaty between the USA and France, the Kellogg-Briand Pact was eventually opened to signature by other countries; nearly every nation on earth subscribed to it. Signatories to the Pact agreed to renounce war as an instrument of national policy, as well as to settle disputes through peaceful mediation. Clearly influenced by the traumas of the First World War, the Pact is sometimes portrayed as "outlawing" war. This was not the case, insofar as the Pact acknowledged qualifications to its general prohibition, such as self-defense, military duties imposed by the Covenant of the League of Nations, the Monroe Doctrine, or treaties of alliance. Moreover, the Pact omitted any mention of sanctions for violations of its terms.[60] In his memo to Stimson, Chanler was not troubled by the absence of a penal provision in the treaty. For Chanler, Kellogg-Briand was binding international law for all countries, like Germany, that had signed it. For this reason, Germany's invasions of other countries were war crimes punishable "by any Allied military tribunal." He recommended that the Allies add the charge of aggressive war to any future indictment of Nazi leaders.[61]

By the summer of 1945, all of the legal elements for incorporation into an indictment of the Nazi leadership were ready to hand. On June 26, 1945, US representative Robert Jackson met with his British, French, and Soviet counterparts in London to make preparations for trial. Jackson presented the American plan to charge the major war criminals with war crimes, crimes of aggression, crimes against humanity, and conspiracy. On August 8, they produced a charter setting forth the charges against the major war criminals. The "London Charter," as it is called, would become not only the legal basis of the IMT at Nuremberg but the cornerstone of the indictment against the major war criminals. The most important section of the Charter was Article 6, which contained the substantive charges against the accused. Article 6 (a), "Crimes against Peace," involved "planning, preparation, initiation or waging of a war of aggression" or "in violation of international treaties," as well as participating "in a Common Plan or Conspiracy" to commit such crimes. Article 6 (b), "War Crimes," included "murder, ill-treatment or deportation to slave labor . . . of civilian population of or in occupied territory, murder or ill-treatment of prisoners of war . . ., killing of hostages, plunder of public or private property, wanton destruction of cities, . . . or devastation not justified by military necessity." Article 6 (c), "Crimes against Humanity," was among the most innovative of the substantive charges. In its original form, the Article condemned inhumane acts—"murder, extermination, enslavement, deportation"—inflicted on civilians, whether committed prior to or during the war. On October 6, 1945, however, the Berlin protocol substituted a comma for the semi-colon after the first clause of the Article. With a semi-colon, the four signatory nations of the London Charter appeared to be creating an international court with jurisdiction over humanitarian offenses, including those unrelated to waging war. With a comma, on the other hand, the authors made crimes against humanity dependent on the subsequent prepositional phrase "in execution of or in connection with any crime within the jurisdiction of the Tribunal." The only other crimes "within the jurisdiction of the Tribunal" were crimes against peace and war crimes, both of which were integrally connected to war. Thus, in binding the adjudication of crimes against humanity to war crimes and crimes against peace, the Charter's authors trimmed the scope of the offense. To meet the jurisdictional requirements, a prosecutor would have to show that an atrocity was somehow related to either the initiation of war or its conduct.[62]

Article 6 embodied Murray Bernays's conspiracy approach to Nazi crimes, insofar as it charged the Nazi leaders with participating in a "Common Plan or Conspiracy" to commit each of the crimes previously listed. Because the defendants were members of a conspiracy, each was "responsible for all acts performed by any persons in execution of such plan." Other articles of the Charter exhibited the influence of Bernays's theory of corporate liability. Article 9 empowered the court to declare that the government office to which a given defendant belonged was a criminal organization. If the court made such a determination, then according to Article 10 any of the Charter's signatories could subsequently prosecute other members of that organization solely on the grounds of their membership. These trials could take place in national, military, or occupation courts, in which the criminality of the affected organization would be assumed.[63]

With the statement of the charges, the Allies had notched their arrow on the bowstring, and all that remained was to determine a target. Who would be charged? In a report to President Truman on June 6, 1945, the head of the US prosecution team, Robert Jackson, set forth a rule of thumb that would guide the selection of defendants. The IMT would try the highest-ranking Nazis available, who would be charged with acting under a "master plan" to "incite and commit the aggressions and barbarities." Jackson explicitly ruled out trying crimes, no matter how "perverted," if they were disconnected from the Nazi master plan. Such crimes fell under the extradition provisions of the Moscow Declaration; upon application by the affected country, the Allies would send the suspects back for trial by its national court system.[64]

The indictment of the major Nazi war criminals was signed on October 6, 1945. The final list of defendants was the outcome of Allied negotiations in London during the previous summer. It included:

- **Prominent members of the Nazi Party/government:** Hermann Göring, Rudolf Hess, Joachim von Ribbentrop, Robert Ley, Wilhelm Frick, Baldur von Schirach, Fritz Sauckel, Martin Bormann, Franz von Papen, Albert Speer, Constantin von Neurath, Baldur von Schirach, Artur Seyss-Inquart, Fritz Sauckel, Ernst Kaltenbrunner, Walter Funk.

- **Leading military commanders:** Wilhelm Keitel, Karl Dönitz, Erich Raeder, Alfred Jodl.

- **Leaders in the civilian administration of Eastern Europe:** Alfred Rosenberg, Hans Frank.

- **Leaders of the German economy/industry:** Hjalmar Schacht, Gustav Krupp von Bohlen und Halbach.

- **Prominent propagandists:** Julius Streicher, Hans Fritzsche.

Three of the defendants listed in the indictment were ultimately unavailable for trial: Robert Ley, Gustav Krupp von Bohlen und Halbach, and Martin Bormann. Ley committed suicide in his jail cell on October 24, 1945; Gustav Krupp was examined by a US medical team and considered mentally incompetent to stand trial on account of a disabling stroke; and Bormann, although tried *in absentia* and sentenced to death, likely perished after leaving Hitler's bunker in the closing days of the war. Thus, when the IMT began its formal sessions on November 20, 1945, only twenty-one of the twenty-four defendants were present in the courtroom. In addition to the twenty-four named defendants, the indictment asked the tribunal to criminalize a handful of Nazi and German governmental organizations:

- The Reich Cabinet
- The Leadership Corps of the Nazi Party
- The SS
- The SD
- The Gestapo
- The SA (Sturmabteilung or "Storm Division"), i.e. the Brownshirts
- The General Staff and High Command of the German Armed Forces (OKH).

Eight judges would preside at the tribunal: one judge from the USA, Great Britain, the USSR, and France, plus one alternate for each of the principals. The president of the tribunal was the British justice Sir Geoffrey Lawrence.

The procedural law applied at the trial was a mixture of Anglo-American and Continental European law. Defendants were allowed to testify in court, but only subject to cross-examination—a practice familiar in US and British law yet absent from continental jurisprudence.[65] On the other hand, the defendants could make unsworn statements to the court and so avoid cross-examination, a feature of continental law unknown in Anglo-American criminal procedure.[66] Superior orders was denied as a defense against criminal liability but could be used in mitigation of guilt. Similarly, the defense of *tu quo que* ("you too"), while never directly ruled out by the tribunal, was deemed inconsistent with Article 18 of the Charter, and prosecutors like Jackson and his Soviet counterpart Roman Rudenko strove to exclude its invocation during the trial. The defense can be exceedingly powerful, as it argues that the defendant's accusers engaged in the same conduct for which he is being tried. Some of the defense counsel at trial successfully entered evidence into the record suggestive of *tu quo que*. The most striking may have been the success of Admiral Karl Dönitz's defense counsel, Otto von Kranzbühler, in securing admission into evidence of an interrogatory served on US

Figure 28 Nazi defendants sitting in the dock at the International Military Tribunal at Nuremberg. NARA 239, NT 620. © The Nuremberg Memorium, Nuremberg, Germany.

Admiral Chester Nimitz, Commander-in-Chief of the US Pacific Fleet during the war. Dönitz was charged with war crimes in connection with the German U-boat practice of unrestricted submarine warfare and failing to rescue the crews of torpedoed vessels. In his interrogatory, Nimitz answered that the US Navy pursued a similar policy against the Japanese. Nimitz's statement carried significant weight for the American judge Francis Biddle, who expressed reservations about convicting Dönitz for doing what the Americans had done in the Pacific. Although Dönitz was convicted on other counts and sentenced to a ten-year prison term, the tribunal absolved him of responsibility for breaches of the law of submarine warfare largely on the strength of the Nimitz interrogatory.[67]

A blow by blow description of the nine-month-long trial would explode the limits of this basic overview, and in any event such a summary would scarcely improve on the numerous studies of the day-to-day progress of the trial, to which the reader is referred.[68] Rather, what follows is a brief overview of some of the issues addressed in the trial that would have long-term resonance in the Law of War after 1945.

Significant features of the trial

German objections to the IMT's jurisdiction The putative legal bases of all the Nuremberg trials were the Geneva and Hague Conventions (especially Hague Convention

Images from Nuremberg

Figure 29 Alfred Jodl on the witness stand. NARA 238, NT 761. © The Nuremberg Memorium, Nuremberg, Germany.

Figure 30 Judges presiding over the International military tribunal at Nuremberg. NARA 238, NT 311. © The Nuremberg Memorium, Nuremberg, Germany.

Figure 31 Defendants in the dock at the American Einsatzgruppen trial in Nuremberg, Germany. The figure with the faint smile on his face turned toward the camera is Otto Ohlendorf. NARA 238, OMT. © The Nuremberg Memorium, Nuremberg, Germany.

IV). Early on, the defense made a "*si omnes*" ("if everyone") objection to the tribunal's jurisdiction. While obsolete today, *si omnes* clauses, also called "general participation" clauses, often appeared in Law of War treaties prior to 1945. According to the clause, a treaty applied to a military conflict only if all the belligerents were parties to it. Hague IV contained a *si omnes* clause in Article 2. The defense counsel at Nuremberg cited Article 2 in arguing that Hague IV was inapplicable to the Second World War because Bulgaria had not subscribed to it. The IMT judges rejected this argument, holding that in the decades since its passage Hague IV had acquired the status of international customary law, and hence was binding on all participants in the conflict. As Theodor Meron notes, the judges' ruling here was the only means of salvaging the trials from the "general participation" objection.[69] Previous versions of the Geneva Conventions likewise contained *si omnes* clauses, but Article 82 of the 1929 Geneva Convention had expunged the general participation requirement, asserting that the Convention was binding on parties to it even when other belligerents in the conflict had not subscribed to it. Accordingly, the IMT dismissed the defendants' argument that the Geneva Conventions were inapplicable to the war in the east because the USSR was not a party to the Geneva Prisoner of War Convention. This convention, signed by forty-seven States in July 1929, had effectively replaced its predecessors (i.e., the 1864 and 1906 Conventions). It required that sick or wounded persons officially attached to an enemy army be given adequate medical care regardless of their nationality. This principle of international law, along with the humanitarian provisions of Hague IV, were held by the IMT to be declaratory of international customary law and thus binding on the Nazi government despite the *si omnes* clauses found in earlier conventions.[70]

Treatment of the conspiracy charge The IMT judges agreed with the Prosecution that a conspiracy to wage aggressive war did indeed exist as early as November 1937. They chose this date because of the "Hossbach Memorandum," a document the Americans had found in the summer of 1945. It consisted of notes taken by a Hitler adjutant, Colonel Friedrich Hossbach, at a meeting in the Reich Chancellery on November 5, 1937. At the meeting Hitler unveiled his "last will and testament" to an audience of his followers: he would seek *Lebensraum* for the German people and "overthrow" Austria and Czechoslovakia "in order to remove the threat to our flank in any possible operation against the West."[71] The Prosecution argued that the Hossbach memo decisively proved the existence of a conspiracy to commit crimes against peace. The IMT agreed not only with the Prosecution's interpretation of the memo but with its argument that Germany's *Anschluss* (union) with Austria and annexation of Czechoslovakia were the gambits in a plan to wage aggressive war.[72] The IMT did not follow the Prosecution's contention that a single, all-encompassing conspiracy drove its plans to wage aggressive war. Rather, the judges found "with certainty the existence of many separate plans rather than a single conspiracy embracing them all." For the judges, it was "immaterial" whether a unified conspiracy had been proven because "continued planning, with aggressive war as the objective, has been established beyond doubt." Their affirmation of a series of ad hoc conspiracies, attuned to exploit the variable opportunities of the moment yet geared toward accomplishing Hitler's plans for continental domination, was critical because the defendants had argued no such planning was possible in a totalitarian dictatorship like the Third Reich. "When [the defendants], with knowledge of [Hitler's] aims, gave him their co-operation," the tribunal held, "they made themselves parties to the plan he had initiated." The judges continued:

> They are not to be deemed innocent because Hitler made use of them, if they knew what they were doing. That they were assigned to their tasks by a dictator does not absolve them from responsibility for their acts. The relation of leader and follower does not preclude responsibility here any more than it does in the comparable tyranny of organized domestic crime.[73]

The judges refused, however, to recognize a conspiracy to commit war crimes and crimes against humanity as alleged in Count 1 of the indictment—not because the Prosecution had failed to prove it, but because Article 6 of the IMT Charter had only alleged a conspiracy with respect to aggressive war. The implication was that, lacking a statutory anchorage in its governing instrument, an alleged conspiracy to commit war crimes or crimes against humanity was beyond the jurisdiction of the tribunal.[74] Further, the IMT declined to exercise jurisdiction over any crimes against humanity before the outbreak of the war, on the view that Nazi persecution of Jews and other groups prior to September 1, 1939 was not sufficiently related to crimes against peace or war crimes.[75]

Treatment of the criminal organizations charge The indictment had requested that the tribunal declare certain agencies of the Nazi state to be criminal organizations: the leadership corps of the Nazi Party, the Gestapo, the SD, the SS, the SA, the Reich Cabinet, and the General Staff. According to the judges, a "criminal organization" was a group "formed or used in connection with the commission of crimes denounced by the Charter." Mere membership alone was not sufficient to convict a defendant for belonging to a criminal organization. To convict, it had to be shown the defendant either knew of the "criminal purposes or acts of the organization" or personally contributed to them. The judges then declared the Nazi leadership corps, SS, SD, and Gestapo to be "criminal organizations." They declined to grant the Prosecution's request regarding the SA, Reich Cabinet, and General Staff, chiefly because they were not persuaded these groups were formed for the purpose of committing crimes against peace, war crimes, or crimes against humanity.[76]

The verdict of the IMT

On October 1, 1946, the tribunal announced its verdict. It found all the defendants save Schacht, von Papen, and Fritsche guilty of one or more of the four counts. Twelve of them were sentenced to death by hanging (Göring, Ribbentrop, Keitel, Kaltenbrunner, Rosenberg, Frank, Frick, Streicher, Sauckel, Jodl, Seyss-Inquart, and Bormann), three to a life term in prison (Hess, Funk, and Raeder), and four to prison terms ranging from ten to twenty years (Doenitz, Schirach, Speer, and von Neurath). After confirmation by the Allied Control Council for Germany, the sentences were executed: those condemned to death were hanged,[77] those sentenced to prison terms were interned in Berlin's Spandau prison.[78]

The American National Military Tribunal (NMT) at Nuremberg

Article 22 of the IMT Charter provided for a series of Nazi war crimes trials to be prosecuted by the tribunal—the first at Nuremberg and subsequent trials at locations to be determined later. Due to the logistical difficulties of international trials, the decision was made to entrust responsibility to each zone of occupation to prosecute Nazi offenders. The legal basis of these "subsequent" trials was a law passed on December 20, 1945 by the Allied Control Council. Called "Control Council Law No. 10," the decree authorized each of the four zonal commanders to arrest war crimes suspects and try them in "appropriate tribunals." While the Soviets, who conducted a wholesale purge of ex-Nazis from the professions and bureaucracies of their occupation zone, did little to implement Law No. 10, policies were different in the western zones. The French conducted a high-profile trial under Law No. 10 in their military tribunal established at Rastatt, targeting the German industrialist Hermann Röchling. French authorities also conducted lesser known proceedings against other Nazi defendants. The British meanwhile were holding their own trials under the Royal Warrant of June 14, 1945, which charged the accused with violations of the laws and usages of war. The cases involved a diverse congeries of defendants, ranging from Wehrmacht General Nikolaus von Falkenhorst (who had planned and commanded the invasion of Denmark and Norway), Luftwaffe Field Marshall Albert Kesselring (charged with ordering the execution of 335 civilians and inciting the killing of others in Italy), and Luftwaffe General Kurt Student (charged with mistreating and in some cases murdering prisoners of war in Crete) to concentration camp guards from Bergen-Belsen. Elsewhere in liberated Europe, a broad spectrum of accused German war criminals was hauled into court. These defendants were tried in Belgium, Denmark, Greece, the Netherlands, Norway, Poland, Russia, and Yugoslavia. The tribunals in which they were prosecuted, moreover, presided over the trials of persons accused of collaborating with the Nazis.[79]

Most of the national trials mentioned above were not conducted under Control Council Law No. 10 but on the basis of the country's own military decrees or domestic law (such as murder or treason). The most ambitious of the trial programs explicitly based on Law No. 10 was the American National Military Tribunal (NMT) at Nuremberg. At the IMT, the chief of the US prosecution team had been Supreme Court Justice Robert H. Jackson. Once Jackson resigned as the head of the US trial program at Nuremberg in 1946, he was succeeded by his deputy, Brigadier General Telford Taylor.[80] Where the London Agreement and IMT Charter had furnished the authority and charges for the IMT proceeding, Control Council Law No. 10 supplied both the legal authority and charges for the American NMT.[81]

In fact, there was considerable overlap in the language and definitions of the IMT Charter and Law No. 10. This was far from surprising because the latter document was largely based on the former. Law No. 10 reproduced most of the Charter's definition of "crimes against peace," but expanded it to cover both "wars" and "invasions"—a change that, according to Taylor, afforded a basis for charging the *Anschluss* and the annexation of Czechoslovakia as crimes against peace.[82] Law No. 10 introduced a second revision that proved far more consequential. It is found in Law No. 10's definition of crimes against humanity. We will recall the "war nexus" in the IMT Charter's definition, which stipulated that acts of "murder, extermination, enslavement, deportation, and other inhumane acts," or "persecutions on political, racial, or religious grounds" could be prosecuted as crimes against humanity only if they were "in execution of or in connection with any crimes within the jurisdiction of the Tribunal." The other crimes within the IMT's jurisdiction were war crimes and crimes against peace, meaning that crimes against humanity could not be prosecuted without a provable relationship to aggressive warfare—the very essence of Nazi criminality, according to the authors of the Charter. The definition of crimes against humanity under the Charter, by contrast, deleted this prepositional phrase, effectively cutting them loose from their dependence on warfare and establishing them as a self-contained charge.[83] For the first time, the domestic policies of the nation-state as they bore on the treatment of its civilian population were

Figure 32 Defendants' gallery in the Doctors' Trial (U.S. v. Karl Brandt et al.), held in front of an American military tribunal at Nuremberg. NARA 238, OMT-1-D-58. © The Nuremberg Memorium, Nuremberg, Germany.

subjected to international criminal jurisdiction. The debacle of efforts to prosecute war criminals after the First World War would not be repeated.

According to Taylor, all persons to be indicted and tried by the NMT were chosen based on "substantial evidence of criminal conduct under accepted principles of international penal law."[84] Most of the accused war criminals were already in US custody; others were delivered to the Americans by the British, French, and Poles for prosecution. This was especially true for the first of the US successor proceedings, the "Doctors Trial" (*U.S. v. Karl Brandt et al.*),[85] in which the Americans' decision to devote an entire trial to medical atrocities prompted the British to send them SS and military doctors and other health care personnel in their custody.[86] The US medical case was illustrative of its approach to trying Nazi war criminals at Nuremberg—that is, to center prosecution on a specific occupational group complicit in Nazi crimes. The American NMT consisted of five occupational categories:

1. German professionals: doctors and lawyers (Cases 1 and 3: thirty-nine defendants)

2. SS and Police (Cases 4, 8, and 9: fifty-six defendants)

3. Industrialists and financiers (Cases 5, 6, and 10: forty-two defendants)

4. Military leaders (Cases 7 and 12: twenty-six defendants)

5. Government Ministers (Cases 2 and 11: twenty-two defendants).[87]

Unlike the IMT, which was a single integrated trial, the NMT comprised several trials running concurrently and involving different court members (judges, prosecutors, and defense counsel). At the onset of the trials in December 1946, only one trial of twenty-five defendants was held; over the next twelve months, as many as six proceedings against more than 100 accused occurred simultaneously. These courts were staffed with three or more American lawyers appointed by the US Military Governor. Most of the persons assigned as judges were either current or former state court judges; the remainder were well-known lawyers and a law school dean. In sum, there were thirty-two judges or alternates.[88] The diversity of the judicial personnel serving in the NMT trials helps account for the uneven outcomes in some of the judgments. This notwithstanding, the principles common to many of the trials have gone on to shape the development of the modern Law of War. We discuss some of the salient continuities and discontinuities among these cases below.

Notable features of the NMT trials

Rejection of the *ex post facto* challenge Early on in the NMT trials, defense counsel raised an *ex post facto* challenge to Control Council Law No. 10, arguing that the novelty of the charges was such that knowledge of wrongdoing could not be imputed to the defendants at the time they committed the crimes alleged against them. In the trial of Nazi jurists (*US v. Altstoetter*—Case No. 3), Military Tribunal III dismissed this contention on the ground that, in view of their participation in a "system of injustice … shocking to the moral sense of mankind," the defendants either knew or should have known that they would face punishment if they lost the war.[89] This constructive (rather than actual) standard of knowledge was consistently applied in the other NMT trials.[90]

Rejection of the superior orders and sabotage defenses Also at the jurists' trial, the defendants raised a superior orders defense that they had little choice but to comply with Hitler's orders whether or not they were compatible with international law. The NMT deflected the defense with the point of law already set forth in Article 8 of the London Charter.[91] A more strenuous defense was mounted by Franz Schlegelberger, the acting minister of justice under the Nazis charged with complicity in exterminating Polish Jews and non-Jews and terrorizing the civilian population of the eastern occupied territories. Schlegelberger claimed he had decided to remain at his post rather than submit his resignation in order to prevent a hardcore Nazi from succeeding him. The tribunal found this defense unpersuasive, countering that all evidence pointed toward Schlegelberger's zealous prostitution of the Ministry of Justice to Hitler's purposes of "exterminating the Jewish and Polish populations, terrorizing the inhabitants of occupied countries, and wiping out political opposition at home."[92]

Equivocations on slave labor and aggressive war Three of the NMT trials were devoted to the role of German businesses in facilitating the crimes of the Third Reich. The trials targeted forty-two defendants, nearly half of who were high-ranking corporate officers of the IG Farben chemical cartel. The remaining defendants were officers of the Krupp and Flick coal and steel concerns. In *U.S. v. Flick* (Case No. 5), Counts 1 and 2 of the indictment were based on the Law of War: Count 1 charged the six defendants with participating in the Nazis' slave labor program by using forced workers in their mines and factories, while Count 2 accused them of spoliation in confiscating property in France and the USSR. Friedrich Flick and his co-defendants argued that they were ensnared in a situation of duress, wherein they faced grave retaliation from the Nazis for refusal to use slave labor in furtherance of the war effort. In their closing arguments, the defendants also raised a *tu quo que* defense, insisting their actions were no more reprehensible than the Allied bombing of Hamburg and Dresden. Remarkably, Military Tribunal IV agreed with some of the defendants on most of the slave labor charges. In the Tribunal's view, a genuine situation of necessity existed to exonerate them from the charge. Flick and another co-defendant, however, were ineligible for the defense because of their "active steps" in procuring forced laborers for their plant, motivated not by fear of SS punishment but the desire to boost full capacity. Both were convicted on the first count.[93]

Another business-focused case, *U.S. v. Alfried Krupp von Bohlen und Halbach et al.* (Case No. 10), followed the Flick trial in yielding uneven results. From 1943 until the war's end, Alfried Krupp was the owner of Krupp Enterprises, a major supplier of armaments to the German military. Krupp and eleven of his underlings were charged with crimes against peace for their role in planning and waging aggressive war (Count One) and conspiracy to wage aggressive war (Count Four). The indictment further charged the men with a mélange of offenses: spearheading illegal rearmament during the Weimar Republic, helping Hitler become *Reichskanzler*, rearming Germany to enable it to launch wars of conquest, plundering the countries invaded by Germany, and enslaving the citizens of these countries. After the prosecution had rested, the defense moved for an acquittal on the first and fourth counts (pertaining to aggressive war), which the Military Tribunal granted on the rationale that the evidence failed to prove the defendants were fully aware of Hitler's aggressive plans. On Counts Two (spoliation) and Three (forced labor), six of the accused—including Krupp—were convicted, while the other four were acquitted. A significant element of its verdict was the Tribunal's rejection of the military necessity defense. According to the tribunal, whatever harm the men had caused through their actions far outweighed the potential evil they faced for disobedience.[94]

The principle expressed in the Tribunal's verdict that arms manufacturers could not be found guilty of aggressive war as a matter of law reappeared in the trial of IG Farben's corporate officers (*U.S. v. Carl Krauch et al.*, Case No. 6). Military Tribunal IV acquitted all of the defendants of the charge of planning and waging aggressive war (Count One) and conspiracy to plan and wage aggressive war (Count Five). Only five of the twenty-four defendants were convicted under Count Three (enslavement and mistreatment of prisoners of war, deportees, and concentration camp prisoners).[95]

Can you shoot hostages? The NMT's most controversial case In addition to professional men and industrialists/financiers/businessmen, the NMT prosecuted twenty-five German military leaders. One of these trials embraced twelve army commanders charged with war crimes during the German occupation of Yugoslavia, Albania, and Greece (*U.S. v. List et al.*, Case No. 7). All were accused of killing thousands of Yugoslav and Greek civilians under an order issued by General Field Marshal Maximilian Freiherr von Weichs, the supreme commander in the central sector of the Balkan campaign. Circulated at a time of growing partisan attacks on German forces in the region, his order provided for the execution of 100 civilian hostages for every German soldier killed by guerrillas. The primary issue was the permissibility of reprisals against civilian hostages under the Law of War.[96]

In his opening statement at the IMT, the French Prosecutor François de Menthon had condemned the execution of hostages as "the first act of terrorism on the part of German occupation troops."[97] He invoked Article 50 of the Hague Convention of 1907, which barred punishing civilians in an occupied territory for actions "for which they can not be regarded as jointly and severally responsible."[98] In fact, Article 50 prohibited only general reprisals against a civilian population and not the practice of taking hostages, as the IMT judges recognized.[99] Ironically, none of the Nuremberg tribunals accepted de Menthon's argument because reprisals against hostages were allowed under the Law of War prior to 1945. The Lieber Code had acknowledged the legality of retaliation under international law because "a reckless enemy often leaves to his opponent no other means of securing himself against the repetition of barbarous outrage." Lieber did impose restrictions on retaliation, however: he expressly ruled out any resort to it for purposes of "mere revenge," but only after a "careful inquiry" to verify the need for "protective retribution."[100] In the eyes of Telford Taylor, the Law of War prior to the Second World War was unsettled on the issue—a fact suggesting that no clear consensus had gathered around it. The US Army field manuals of 1914 and 1940 both endorsed taking hostages from among the civilian population of a conquered territory, who were subject to execution if "unlawful" attacks were staged on the occupying army. Both versions recognized the right of military commanders to order the destruction of villages and houses on the principle of "collective punishment" when the assailants could not be identified.[101] Writing on the eve of the First World War, Oppenheim took a harder view on the hostage rule than Taylor. Oppenheim agreed that hostages were often exchanged in premodern times to ensure mutual compliance with treaties, surrenders, and armistices, but he asserted that "the practice has totally disappeared" in modern times.[102]

The Military Tribunal presiding over the *List* trial endorsed the view that hostage-taking was allowed prior to 1945. The Tribunal made clear its lack of sympathy with the rule, yet added that "it is not our province to write international law as we would have it,—we must apply it as we find it." The judges believed an occupying army under the Law of War could take hostages to ensure the peace, and even shoot them "on a theory of collective responsibility" if occupation troops were attacked. However, they went on to impose qualifications on the hostage rule, insisting that hostages could only be taken if there was a connection between the assailants and the population from whom the hostages were drawn. If no such connection could be proven—if, for example, attacks were carried out "by isolated persons or bands from distant localities without the knowledge or approval of the population or public authorities"—then the Law of War forbade hostage-taking. Furthermore, the occupation authorities were obliged to announce publically the names and addresses of the persons seized as hostages and to declare that any further attacks on the occupation would result in their execution.[103]

The court went on to find that the Germans failed to satisfy the preconditions under customary law that legitimized hostage-taking. For the judges, most of the defendants had exploded all reasonable limitations of the hostage rule. The practice of shooting 100 hostages in retaliation for the killing of a single German soldier was grotesquely excessive; to be acceptable under the Law of War, the number of hostages shot could not surpass the severity of the attacks which the reprisal sought to deter. On the contrary, List and his co-accused routinely disregarded this restriction, amassing "a record of killing and destruction seldom exceeded in modern history." Mass executions, civilian enslavement, and indiscriminate destruction of property were all designed to terrorize the population. Accordingly, the Tribunal convicted List and seven others of war crimes and crimes against humanity, handing out prison terms from life to as few as seven years. Two of the defendants were acquitted, while two others were unavailable for prosecution.[104]

The *List* verdict provoked bitter criticism throughout Europe, but nowhere more than in the Soviet zone press, which assailed the punishment of the defendants as overly lenient. The focus of the criticism was on the Tribunal's admission that hostages could be taken and, under the right circumstances, executed, as well as its ruling that partisan fighters could be denied combatant status under the Law of War (on the theory that they were illegal combatants). Ex-members of anti-German resistance movements throughout Europe deplored the verdict for agreeing with the defendants that irregular fighters were not entitled to legal protection. The Norwegians were meanwhile incensed by the partial acquittal of General Lothar Rendulic, the commander of German troops in Norway, Finland, and Yugoslavia. Counterintuitively, Telford Taylor found no fault with the Tribunal's findings and judgment; instead he lauded the "admirable workmanship" of the verdict and defended the court for merely applying the Law of War as it existed prior to 1945.[105] In any event, it is notable that the controversial holding of the Military Tribunal, no matter how admirably crafted or historically accurate, did not long survive its statement: Article 3 of Geneva Convention I of 1949 explicitly prohibits hostage-taking.

How far up the chain of command does responsibility go? The high command case The second of the military cases tried at the NMT, *U.S. v. Wilhelm von Leeb et al.* (Case No. 12), produced a verdict that is hard to reconcile with the rulings in an earlier trial by military commission in the Far East, *U.S. v. Yamashita* (discussed below), or for that matter the analysis of its sister tribunal in *U.S. v. List*. In terms of the subsequent development of commanders' responsibility for the actions of their subalterns, *Leeb* may be an aberration. Given its prominence in the NMT jurisprudence, we briefly discuss it here.

Field Marshal Wilhelm Ritter von Leeb and his twelve co-defendants were all high-ranking German military leaders charged with participating in Hitler's plans to wage wars of aggression, as well as with war crimes and crimes against humanity. Like Jodl and Keitel, many of the defendants in the *Leeb* case were present at conferences in which Hitler had communicated his intention to attack other European countries. Jodl and Keitel's attendance at these meetings had led to their conviction at the IMT; US prosecutors at the *Leeb* trial must have thought that proving the generals' presence at the same meetings would produce comparable results. While not all of them had attended the conferences, they had all either known about or actively contributed to preparing for the invasions. These facts notwithstanding, Military Tribunal V acquitted the defendants of the aggressive war charge, holding that mere knowledge of the *Führer's* plans to wage aggressive war was not enough to convict. According to the tribunal, to sustain the charge the prosecutors would have to show not only that the accused knew of Hitler's intentions, but were "in a position to shape or influence the policy" of waging aggressive war. Because no such proof had been offered, Leeb and his co-defendants could not be found guilty of the charge.[106]

While all the accused were acquitted of crimes against peace, eleven of them were convicted of war crimes and crimes against humanity for their involvement in either drafting or implementing the commissar and "commando" orders. The former we have already described *in extenso*; the latter was a Hitler decree issued in October 1942 to German forces in Europe and Africa, ordering that all captured Allied commandos be executed without trial. The issue facing the tribunal was whether the accused were criminally liable for transmitting the commissar and commando orders to their subordinates for implementation. The court held that to incur criminal liability a commander "must have passed the order to the chain of command and the order must be one that is criminal upon its face, or one which he is shown to have known was criminal." The tribunal's position was that a commander was not responsible for the war crimes of his troops without his own "personal dereliction," an act or omission to act equivalent to an endorsement of their offenses. The judges reasoned:

> Criminal responsibility is personal. The act or neglect to act must be voluntary and criminal. The occupying commander must have knowledge of these offenses and acquiesce or participate or criminally neglect to interfere in their commission, and [the] offenses committed must be patently criminal.

In other words, the judges refused to apply a constructive standard of knowledge ("knew or should have known") to the assessment of command responsibility.[107]

Even under this rigorous standard of proof, only two of the accused—Field Marshal Sperrle and Admiral Schniewind—were acquitted of all charges. The *Leeb* case has been broadly criticized in the secondary literature for its incompatibility with the *Hostage* and *Yamashita* cases—both of which imputed constructive knowledge to commanders in the field.[108] Moreover, the *Leeb* verdict bucks the trend in international law since 1945 toward affirming criminal responsibility of superiors for the crimes of their subordinates. The late Italian jurist Antonio Cassese notes that the principle of accountability, which after the Second World War spread from military commanders to civilian and political authorities, has risen to the level of a customary rule in international law. According to the rule, superiors are criminally liable "for failure to perform an act required by international law," that is, of violating their internationally imposed duty "to prevent or suppress crimes by subordinates." The standard applied is constructive knowledge: commanders are liable if they knew or should have known of their subordinates' crimes.[109] The customary rule today comprises three parts. A superior is criminally liable for the wrongdoing if:

1. The superior "exercise[s] effective command, control, or authority over the perpetrators;" or—

2. The superior knew or should have known his subordinates would commit international crimes; or—

3. The superior "failed to take action necessary to prevent or repress the crimes," as he must according to international law.[110]

As measured by modern international customary law, the *Leeb* verdict would appear to be an anomaly.

Inconsistency on the war nexus question: comparing cases We will recall that the IMT Charter had insisted on a causal link between illegal warfare and the various charges lodged against the major war criminals. Control Council Law No. 10, a decree that furnished the basis for the NMT at Nuremberg, deleted this requirement and established crimes against humanity as an offense independent of crimes against peace and war crimes. Despite the uncoupling of crimes against humanity from illegal warfare, the various tribunals at the NMT were inconsistent on the issue. In the *Flick* and *Ministries* cases, Military Tribunal IV refused to exercise jurisdiction over prewar atrocities committed against Jews, holding that such acts were insufficiently connected to waging or planning aggressive war. By contrast, Military Tribunal II in the *Einsatzgruppen* trial (*U.S. v. Ohlendorff*, Case No. 9) explicitly affirmed that crimes against humanity were "not limited to offenses committed during the war."[111] Similarly, Military Tribunal III in the Justice case (*U.S. v. Josef Altstoetter*, Case No. 3) upheld the legal independence of crimes against humanity, stating "it can no longer be said that violations of the laws and customs of war are the only offenses recognized by common international law."[112]

The US Army military trials in Europe

Coincident with the IMT and NMT trials in Nuremberg, the US Army was conducting its own trials of Nazi war criminals before military commissions and military government courts. These trials, because most were held at the site of the former concentration camp at Dachau, Germany, are collectively called the "Dachau trials" and form the third major

Military commissions: a brief history

The US Army did not invent the military commission in 1945. Rather, the institution has roots reaching deep into the nineteenth century. The first documented instance of military commissions dates to February 1847, when General Winfield Scott appointed "councils of war" to try violations during the Mexican-American War. Scott's councils of war were resurrected as "military commissions" during the Civil War and tasked with prosecuting the Confederates and their supporters. According to the US Supreme Court in an 1866 judgment, *Ex parte Milligan*, the commissions were proper only in a state that had been a theater of war and only when the civilian courts there were not yet functioning. Commissions were used to try Captain Henry Wirz, the commandant of the Andersonville prisoner of war camp, and President Lincoln's assassins. As many as 200 trials of civilians were held in the occupied South during Reconstruction. The US Army convened military commissions to try rebellious Dakota and Modoc Indians as well as Philippine insurgents many decades before they were employed to prosecute accused German and Japanese war criminals after the Second World War.[114]

---

war crimes program of the USA in Europe. Particularly after D-Day (June 6, 1944), Supreme Headquarters–Allied Expeditionary Forces handled all reports of war crimes committed against Allied nationals. Until the spring of 1945 the US Army did not plan on significant investigations of war crimes unless the victims were American soldiers. This changed after liberation of the concentration camps by the US Army. Pressure then mounted to investigate and try these cases. Thus, while the focus initially was on prosecuting crimes of Germans against US servicemen, American investigation gradually shifted to other kinds of Nazi atrocities.[113]

On July 8, 1945, the US Joint Chiefs of Staff issued Directive 1023/10 to the Commander of US Forces/European Theater. The directive instructed the Theater Commander to take steps to investigate and arrest all persons suspected of involvement in the following crimes:

1. Atrocities and offenses against persons or property constituting violation of international law, including the laws, rules, and customs of land and naval warfare.

2. Initiation of invasions of other countries and of wars of aggression in violation of international laws and treaties.

3. Other atrocities and offenses, including atrocities and persecutions on racial, religious or political grounds, committed since January 30, 1933.

The directive authorized the Theater Judge Advocate to try these war crimes suspects for violations of the Law of War in "specially appointed military government courts." This decree was followed by an order of July 16, 1945 issued by Dwight Eisenhower, the Commander of US Forces–European Theater after Germany's surrender, instructing commanders of the 3rd and 7th Armies to establish special military government courts in their respective districts to prosecute war crimes committed before May 9, 1945. Although most of these trials would be held at Dachau (some 489 proceedings), a handful convened elsewhere, including Augsburg, Darmstadt, and in Austria. The Dachau trial program focused on four categories of war crimes, described as violations of the Hague and Geneva Conventions:

- attacks on US airmen and soldiers;
- killing of US soldiers by the 1st SS Panzer Division during the Ardennes offensive;
- murder of ill Eastern European workers at the Hadamar mental hospital
- atrocities committed in Nazi concentration camps in Germany.

Several military commission trials of German civilians involved in murderous attacks on US airmen occurred as early as the summer of 1945.[115] The first major Army trial of concentration camp war criminals, however, was held from November 15 to December 13, 1945 at the site of the Dachau camp. In *U.S. v. Martin Gottfried Weiss et al.*, US Army prosecutors charged forty former camp personnel with two counts of acting "in pursuance of a common design" to commit violations of the Law of War against Allied civilians and prisoners of war, in the form of "killings, beatings, and tortures, starvation, abuses and indignities." The accused were a motley assortment of camp staff, from commandant and deputy commandant to medical officers, orderlies, guards, and prisoner functionaries. The "common plan or design" charge was a version of the conspiracy allegation leveled at accused Nazi war criminals at Nuremberg. Common plan was easier to prove than conspiracy: the prosecution did not have to show an actual meeting or agreement between the conspirators to commit criminal acts but the existence of a "community of intention," which required only that participants in the common plan knew of the illegal acts committed in the camp *and* actively encouraged them through their own behavior.[116]

Different conceptions of the ideological motivation for concentration camp crimes underpinned each of these theories of corporate liability. At Nuremberg, the Americans portrayed the Nazis as conspiring to commit aggressive war; war crimes and crimes against humanity were perpetrated in order to enable them to invade and subjugate other countries. At Dachau, the Americans interpreted the common plan as a program to inflict war crimes for their own sake on the camp prisoners. In other words, they viewed Nazi crimes in the concentration camps as motivated by sadism, with the ultimate goal of exterminating entire groups of people. In this fashion, the American prosecutors misidentified camps like Dachau and Buchenwald as death camps. The UNWCC summarized the American view of the purpose of the Dachau camp: "The case for the prosecution was that all the accused had participated in a common plan to run these camps[117] in a manner so that the greatest numbers of prisoners would die or suffer severe injury."[118] This portrayal of concentration camps on German soil was distorted: although murders, gratuitous deaths, beatings, and mayhem occurred at all of them, the camps within the Reich were not intended as extermination centers like the death camps of

Poland. Nonetheless, conditions in the camps were appalling enough to ensure conviction of all forty of the defendants at the *Weiss* trial. Thirty-six received death sentences (a handful were commuted on review to hard labor for life), while the others received prison terms from life to hard labor for ten years.[119]

U.S. v. Martin Weiss, as the first of the American concentration camp trials, received the title of the "parent case." There followed a succession of trials at Dachau of other crimes committed in the camp during the war, as well as in the sister camps of Buchenwald, Flossenbürg, Mühldorf, and Mauthausen. As the "parent case," the *Weiss* trial established important precedents for these subsequent prosecutions. In addition to "common plan/design" to commit war crimes, the first of the concentration camp cases implied that mere presence as a staff member raised a presumption of complicity in war crimes. In the Mauthausen "parent" case,[120] a US military government court made explicit the suggestion of presumed complicity by issuing "special findings" to accompany its conviction of all sixty-one of the Mauthausen defendants. According to the special findings, it was impossible for an employee of the Mauthausen camp to have spent time in the camp without acquiring "knowledge of the criminal practices and activities therein existing." The court concluded that, as members of the Mauthausen staff, all the defendants either knew or were presumed to have known of the atrocities committed within the camp, and were therefore guilty of war crimes. In effect, the court found that the Nazi concentration camp was a criminal organization, the members of which must have been aware of its "criminal purposes."[121]

The special findings in the Mauthausen case may have influenced a directive on war crimes trials issued by the US Headquarters/US Forces-Europe on June 26, 1946. According to the directive, additional perpetrators were to be tried after the principals were convicted in a given parent case. In these later trials, the findings of the parent case "that the mass atrocity operation was criminal in nature" and that the defendants participated in a "common design" to commit war crimes would be assumed. Further, subsequent courts would presume that accused members of the camp staff were aware of the "criminal nature" of the camp. In its gloss of the directive, the UNWCC noted its similarity to the IMT Charter, Article 10, which affirmed the right of national, military, or occupation courts in their trials of accused war criminals to assume the "criminal nature" of groups declared by the IMT to be "criminal organizations." In these subsequent trials, the defendants would not be able to challenge the IMT's earlier findings. The UNWCC observed, however, that the evidentiary standard set forth by the IMT was more exacting than that of the military directive: where the IMT's verdict required that "knowledge of the criminal purposes or acts of the organization" be proven in later trials, such knowledge was presumed against former concentration camp staff.[122]

When the Dachau trials concluded in December 1947, they had prosecuted some 489 cases comprising 1,200 defendants. Of the 489 trials, 225 related to crimes committed in German concentration camps.[123] Although the Nuremberg war crimes trials command far more familiarity both among scholars and the general public, as measured by the volume of prosecutions and number of defendants the Dachau trials far surpass them. They are easily the largest trial program the USA has ever conducted on foreign soil.

Japanese crimes in the Second World War

While not seared into public awareness (particularly in the West) with the grotesque clarity of Nazi atrocities, Japanese war crimes are no less shocking than their German counterparts. Like German crimes, moreover, Japanese atrocities became the object of Allied trials after the war. Scholars have identified the Allied war crimes trials in Asia as a reaction to Japan's military expansionism in both the nineteenth and twentieth centuries.[124] In the late 1800s until the eve of the First World War, Japan seized control of the Kuril Islands, Karafuto (Sakhalin island), and the Liáodōng Peninsula (northeastern China).[125] After 1914, it acquired German colonies in the Pacific. The expansionism that ultimately sparked the Second World War in the Pacific began in 1931, when Japanese officers detonated the southern Manchurian railroad, an event subsequently called the "Mukden Incident." In its aftermath, the Japanese wielded control over Manchuria, installing a puppet government, Manchukuo, in the spring of 1932. Already in the early part of that year, the Japanese military had launched an air raid and naval bombardment of Shanghai, an act regarded by one historian as the first air raid of a large civilian target, "setting the precedent for Guernica and the Second World War."[126] The ensuing years saw Japanese penetration into northern China and Mongolia. By 1937 a clash between Japanese and Chinese soldiers near Beijing emboldened Chiang Kai-shek to seek to drive Japanese forces out of China. The Chinese failure to oust the Japanese from Shanghai after a three-month battle was the prelude to the Japanese "Rape of Nanking," an orgy of mass killing, plunder, rape, torture, and destruction rarely equaled in the annals of military conflict.

As the Nationalist (Kuomintang, or KMT) Chinese capital from 1928 to 37, Nanking quickly became a target of the Japanese army's wrath after the city's capitulation on December 13, 1937. Estimates of the number of civilians murdered by the Japanese in Nanking between that date and early 1939 range from 100,000 to 350,000.[127] As many as 20,000 Chinese women were raped during this period, according to the postwar Tokyo International Military Tribunal for the Far East (IMTFE); scholars of the occupation, by contrast, argue for a much higher figure approaching 80,000. Chinese nationalist soldiers captured as they fled Nanking were shot in machine-gun executions—a manner of dealing with Chinese prisoners of war that became a trademark of the Japanese army's conduct throughout the war.[128] Japan's plan was to create a "Greater East-Asia Co-prosperity Sphere," a Japanese-dominated empire stretching from Manchuria to the Dutch East Indies, a vast swath of territory covering China, Indochina, Thailand, and Malaya, all of which would be reduced to satellites of Japan. Every trace of Western imperial and communist influence would be banished; the Sphere was to be Japan's private fiefdom. After securing their foothold in China, the Japanese invaded Indochina in 1940–41. In the meantime, efforts to resolve the US embargo on Japanese access to critical raw materials were scuttled, a diplomatic failure that bolstered Tokyo's decision to attack the US Pacific fleet at Pearl Harbor on December 7, 1941. Hard on the heels of Pearl Harbor, Japan mounted invasions of the Dutch East Indies and the Philippines.[129] Twenty-seven percent of the Allied soldiers unfortunate enough to fall into Japanese hands perished in captivity (as compared with 4 percent in German/Italian custody). As the Tokyo IMT found, prisoners were killed through shooting, decapitation, drowning, forced marches of ill or debilitated prisoners, slave labor, exposure to the elements due to inadequate housing, denial of medical care, torture, and beatings. The most infamous of the forced marches was the Bataan Death March in the spring of 1942, in which 76,000 Filipino and US prisoners of war were driven on foot to a Japanese prison at Camp O'Donnell. More than one-third of the prisoners died during the forced march.[130]

Most Japanese atrocities were fueled by a racial ideology that regarded Japan's enemies as inferior and contemptible. According to scholars David Crowe and John Dower, Japanese soldiers employed torture to demonstrate their dominance over their victims.[131] The IMTFE judges found that torture was neither exceptional nor maverick among Japanese soldiers but a common practice wherever the boot of Japanese occupation was felt. The profound contempt with which the Japanese regarded foreigners may help explain their willingness to deploy chemical and bacteriological weapons against military and civilian targets. In the summer of 1939 Japanese soldiers lobbed hundreds of bacteria-laden shells at Soviet soldiers. In addition to using infected ordnance, they contaminated waterways with intestinal typhoid bacteria with the aim of poisoning the Soviets. Crowe notes that the Chinese were the principal targets of most of these attacks, which in the fall of 1940 included airdrops of wheat onto Chinese territory impregnated with the plague bacillus—the first of several Japanese sorties pelting the Chinese with plague-infected wheat, rice, paper, and other objects. In the last stages of the war, the Japanese caused as many as 20,000 Chinese deaths by releasing pestiferous rats into Heilungschiang and Kirin provinces.[132]

Like the Nazis, the Japanese military conducted grievous medical experiments on human subjects at twelve biological warfare sites scattered across Asia. Unit 731, an organization created by a Japanese army doctor that provided the military with bacteriological weapons (such as the plague bombs dropped on Chinese territory), carried out the experiments on prisoners of war. At a 1949 Soviet trial of Japanese medical crimes, Lt. Col. Nishi Toshihide testified that the experiments included "replacing blood with sea water; excising [vital bodily organs]; interrupting blood flow from arteries to the heart ... and drilling holes in craniums, then inserting scalpels into the brain." Surgical techniques were sometimes carried out on conscious patients, a type of vivisection using "comfort women" (local women forced into prostitution) as the test subjects. Remarkably, the horrendous crimes of Unit 731 were never subjected to criminal prosecution because the US State Department found that the national security interest in the Unit's experiments outweighed the need for a war crimes trial. (The concern was that a trial would necessarily publicize details of the Unit's biological weapons program, which US officials desired to keep secret.)[133]

After the Japanese surrender on September 2, 1945, hundreds of trials of accused Japanese war criminals unfolded in Allied courts throughout Asia. In addition to proceedings conducted by the Americans, British, and Australians, lesser known Chinese trials were convened in China by the KMT and the Chinese Communist Party.[134] Allied military tribunals would eventually execute 920 Japanese war criminals and sentence

3,000 to lengthy prison terms; the British alone tried 304 cases.[135] The limited compass of this book does not permit a thorough overview of these proceedings. What follows is a summary of two key issues in the postwar Japanese war crimes trials, especially as they impinge on the Law of War after 1945: command responsibility in the *Yamashita* trial and the charge of conspiracy in the Tokyo IMTFE.

The trial of General Tomoyuki Yamashita, October 29 to December 7, 1945

After the fall of Prime Minister Hideki Tōjō and his cabinet in July 1944, in the fall of 1944 Tomoyuki Yamashita was given command of the 14th Area Army in its defense of the Philippines. The 14th Area Army consisted of 262,000 troops divided into three groups, each of which was assigned a section of the Philippines to defend. Although Yamashita ordered all his troops to vacate Manila and retreat into the Sierra Madre mountains in northern Luzon save for a token force of 3,750 men tasked with maintaining security, 16,000 Japanese sailors under the command of Navy Rear Admiral Sanji Iwabuchi moved into the city for the purpose of razing the ports and supply depots. Iwabuchi also assumed command of the security troops Yamashita had left behind. It was this combined force of Iwabuchi's sailors and Yamashita's security troops that waged a reign of terror in the capital city targeting Filipino civilians and American prisoners of

Figure 33 General Tomoyuki Yamashita and staff surrendering to the Americans in northern Luzon, Philippines, September 2, 1945. NARA, College Park, MD. © Wikimedia Commons (public domain).

war, in which 100,000 civilians and 1,010 American soldiers were killed in vicious street fighting that narrowed centripetally into building-to-building and then room-to-room combat. (All of Iwabuchi's 16,000 sailors perished.)[136] A Pacific theater veteran and biographer of Douglas MacArthur, William Manchester, somberly wrote that "of Allied cities in those war years, only Warsaw suffered more" than Manila. "Seventy percent of the utilities, 75 percent of the factories, 80 percent of the southern residential district and 100 percent of the business district were razed."[137]

By the time Yamashita surrendered to the Americans in early September 1945, more than 10,000 US soldiers had been killed and 36,000 wounded in the Philippine campaign. These figures, while striking, pale beside Japanese losses: 256,000 killed or dead from disease or starvation (two-thirds of Japanese forces in the Philippines), nearly 80 percent of them on the island of Luzon. General Douglas MacArthur, the Allied commander of the Japanese occupation (1945–51), proposed to President Harry Truman that Yamashita be tried for war crimes by a military commission. MacArthur was outraged by the senseless violence of the Philippine conflict in 1944 and 1945—the raping of hundreds of women, the pointless destruction of Manila (including MacArthur's former residence, which he watched with horror), and the unnecessary deaths and wounding of his own troops. MacArthur blamed Yamashita for failing to prevent his troops from committing such atrocities.[138] The White House agreed to MacArthur's proposal, and a military commission of five generals was convened to hear the case against Yamashita. He faced only a single charge: unlawfully disregarding and failing as a commander to control the men under his command, "permitting them to commit brutal atrocities and other high crimes against people of the US and of its allics and dependents."[139] Yamashita's prosecution at the time was without parallel: he was not charged with ordering war crimes nor even with knowledge of their commission. Rather, the indictment asserted his criminal accountability for being in charge of troops who committed war crimes. Before his trial, there had never been a case alleging the criminal responsibility of military commanders in the absence of a criminal act or omission to act by the defendant.[140]

From the beginning, the outcome of the trial was predictable. Reporters covering it had the impression that Yamashita's conviction was "in [the commission's] collective pocket" on the first day of the trial.[141] MacArthur exerted pressure on the commission members to move the proceedings along quickly, leading to dubious rulings that unfairly disadvantaged Yamashita.[142] Furthermore, the commission ignored substantial evidence of Yamashita's lack of control over his troops, particularly as their situation grew increasingly desperate and combat descended into furious, localized house-to-house fighting—fighting in which Yamashita and other Japanese commanders had little or no communication with their men. According to Richard Yael, the commission "failed to realize that such isolation, combined with intense combat and the fear that upon capture they might be enslaved, starved, or physically mutilated, might just create circumstances leading individual soldiers and squads to commit atrocities regardless of orders from higher authority."[143] Such facts, however, were immaterial to a tribunal that had already made up its mind to convict even before the trial had begun. On the fourth anniversary of Pearl Harbor, December 7, 1945, Yamashita was convicted and sentenced to death, a punishment upheld by the reviewing and confirming authorities. His attorneys, who had come to admire their client's quiet dignity and magnanimity, filed an appeal with the US Supreme Court. In an opinion that did not consider the military commission's shambolic fact-finding, the justices upheld the verdict and its punishment, holding that the Geneva and Hague Conventions imposed a duty of controlling their troops on military officers. Only six justices voted in favor of Yamashita's conviction; two others, Wiley Rutledge and Frank Murphy,[144] dissented from the majority view on several grounds, including the haste with which the trial was conducted and the simple fact that nowhere in world history had a commander been criminally charged under the Law of War for inadequately controlling his troops during combat.[145] His appeals exhausted, Yamashita was executed on February 23, 1946.

The legal analysis of *Yamashita* contradicts the subsequent verdict in the *Leeb* case. The principle underlying the military commission's verdict—namely, command responsibility for subordinates' war crimes based on an alleged failure to control them— was unsupported by the factual record of the case. Nonetheless, the principle survived the trial, appeal, and execution of the unfortunate Yamashita. Shortly after the verdict, a similar duty of supervision was imposed on Dr. Karl Brandt, Hitler's personal physician and Reich Commissioner of Sanitation and Health, for failing to prevent lethal medical experiments performed on concentration camp prisoners. (Brandt was convicted of war crimes and crimes against humanity and executed on June 2, 1948.) Other trials in the Far East reflected the fundamental reasoning, if not the egregious fact-finding, of the *Yamashita* military commission.[146] Modern international humanitarian law as a whole has moved in concert with the affirmation of command responsibility articulated in *Yamashita*. This trend appears in Additional Protocol I (1977) of the Geneva Conventions of 1949, Articles 86 (on failure to act) and 87 (on the duty of commanders). Paragraph (2) of Article 86 holds that commanders incur criminal responsibility for their subordinate's violations of the Convention "if they knew, or had information which should have enabled them to conclude in the circumstances at the time, that [the subordinate] was committing or was going to commit such a breach and if they did not take all feasible measures within their power to prevent or repress the breach." Article 87 imposes the duty on military commanders "to suppress and to report to competent authorities breaches" of the Convention or the Protocol.[147] This failure to act is responsibility by omission: the commander is criminally liable for failure to perform an action required by international law. In Cassese's view, responsibility by omission has risen to the level of a customary rule in international law.[148]

US military law later codified the *mens rea* ("guilty mind") element of international criminal law in the Army Field Manual (*The Law of Land Warfare*, FM 27-10, 1956 edition). The new standard of superior responsibility for war crimes committed by subordinates emphasized that commanders might incur liability if they either knew or should have known"through reports received" by them that their troops had committed or would commit a war crime, and they did not"take the necessary and reasonable steps to insure compliance with the Law of War or to punish violators thereof."[149] Remarkably, this standard of command responsibility was abandoned in the court-martial of Captain Ernest Medina, leader of the American infantry unit responsible for the My Lai Massacre in March 1968, in which US soldiers shot as many as 504 Vietnamese civilians. The killers belonged to Company C under Medina's immediate command. At his court-martial in 1971 Medina was charged with willfully allowing his troops to murder the villagers. In defense he claimed that he had neither ordered nor known of the atrocities committed by his men until the slaughter was well under way, at which point he was unable to halt their progress. The military judge presiding over Medina's trial, Colonel Kenneth Howard, instructed the jury members they could convict Medina only if they found "he [had] actual knowledge that troops ... subject to his control [were] in the process of committing or [were] about to commit a war crime and he wrongfully fail[ed] to take the necessary and reasonable steps to insure compliance with the Law of War." Howard continued with a gloss on the *mens rea* needed to convict: "You will observe that these legal requirements placed upon a commander require actual knowledge plus a wrongful failure to act ... While it is not necessary that a commander actually see an atrocity being committed, it is essential that he know that his subordinates are in the process of committing atrocities or about to commit atrocities."[150]

Despite the *Medina* court's rejection of the constructive knowledge criterion[151]—a court-martial, we should bear in mind, held in the maelstrom of the Vietnam War and with limited precedential value in international trials—the Law of War from the immediate postwar era until today has steadily moved toward imposing liability on superiors who either knew or (based on information available to them) should have known their subordinates have committed or would soon commit violations. A case illustrative of the modern trend is the 2001 trial of *Mucić et al.* before the International Criminal Tribunal for the Former Yugoslavia, in which the tribunal found the de facto commander, deputy commander, and a guard at the Čelebići prison camp in central Bosnia and Herzegovina guilty of murder, torture, and other violations of the Geneva Conventions. In convicting the de facto commander, Zdravko Mucić, for crimes committed by his subordinates, the tribunal found that he had information from which he could have concluded his men were committing war crimes or would shortly commit them, yet failed to act to prevent them. The information in Mucić's possession should have at the least "put him on notice of the risk of such offences by indicating the need for additional investigation in order to ascertain whether such crimes were committed or were about to be committed by his subordinates." Mucić was sentenced to a seven-year prison term.[152]

The Tokyo war crimes trials, 1946–48

The trials by military commission of Yamashita and several other high-ranking Japanese commanders[153] should be distinguished from proceedings held by the IMTFE, which began on April 29, 1946 in the Japanese War Ministry office in Tokyo. At the Potsdam Conference in late July 1945, the Allies had announced they would prosecute Japanese leaders for offenses against the Law of War. Not until January 19, 1946 did the IMTFE come into being, the product of a MacArthur executive order. In February he appointed nine judges to staff the tribunal, all of who were nominees of the Allied governments, then later added Filipino and Indian judges to the court. In addition, MacArthur approved a charter to serve as the tribunal's governing instrument. Modeled closely on the Nuremberg IMT Charter, it set forth procedural rules and the substantive charges against the accused, including crimes against peace, "conventional war crimes," and crimes against humanity, as well as conspiracy to commit each of these offenses.[154] The prosecutors chose to prosecute Japan's "principal leaders" primarily implicated in this array of crimes. They developed three categories of defendants: "Class A" war criminals, or the top leaders responsible for planning and committing crimes against peace; and "Class B" and "Class C" criminals occupying lower positions in the chain of command, in which they participated in war crimes and crimes against humanity. Much like their counterparts in Nuremberg, the Japanese defendants at the IMTFE were accused of formulating a "general policy" (in the words of Australia's associate prosecutor, Alan Mansfield) to wage aggressive war by means of war crimes and crimes against humanity. As the head of the US prosecution team at Tokyo, Joseph Keenan, averred in his opening statement, the atrocities committed by Japanese forces were all part of "one grand pattern" of imperial invasion and mass murder unleashed against "blameless and helpless individuals all over the world"—a plan of subjugation concocted by Japanese leaders and implemented by Japan's military forces.[155] In other words, each defendant participated in the conspiracy to commit crimes against peace by means of war crimes and crimes against humanity, and each was responsible for the crimes arising from the illicit agreement.

The trial lasted from May 3, 1946 to November 4, 1948—a period more than two and a half times longer than the Nuremberg IMT. All of the twenty-eight defendants, consisting of former government and military officials—among them Hideki Tōjō, the Japanese prime minister during most of the war (implicated in the decision to bomb Pearl Harbor)—were convicted in a mammoth 1,183-page verdict announced by the President of the court, Australian justice Sir William Webb. It sentenced Tōjō and six others to death; sixteen received life terms in prison (two others died during the trial, and a third was found mentally incompetent to stand trial). The condemned men were hanged on December 23, 1948 in Tokyo's Sugamo Prison. Although MacArthur defended the proceedings as a monumental step toward justice, other commentators on the trial have been far more critical.[156] The critics were by no means restricted to armchair scholars; even judges participating in the Tokyo IMTFE found fault with it. Justice Henri Bernard of France expressed doubt about the IMTFE's central finding of a conspiracy to wage wars of aggression; at the most, the evidence showed only a "desire" among Japanese elites to dominate other countries in East Asia. The most trenchant criticism of the tribunal's judgment was the 1,235-page dissenting opinion of India's Radhabinod Pal, which assailed the IMTFE's verdict from nearly every angle. Pal rejected the legal basis of the trial, dismissed the charges as a tissue-thin skein of *ex post facto* law barely concealing "a thirst for revenge," denounced Allied hypocrisy for leveling charges against their defeated foes that could just as easily have been hurled at the Allies themselves, and joined Bernard in casting doubt on the existence of a conspiracy to wage aggressive war.[157]

Conclusion: assessing the two World Wars as sources for the modern Law of War

While efforts to prosecute war crimes suspects after the First World War largely ran afoul of politics, they were not an unmitigated failure. For a time, there was both a desire and a plan to try war crimes in an international tribunal as codified in the treaties of Versailles and Sèvres. US, German, and Turkish resistance would ultimately thwart the fulfillment of this plan, but the intention to hold such trials was real. Moreover, the Leipzig trials, while often portrayed as a risible parody of justice, did produce a lasting impact on international law, chiefly in the *Reichsgericht's* rejection of the superior orders defense in the *Llandovery Castle* case.

The most important legacy of the First World War, however, may have been the degree to which its perceived failures stiffened the resolve of Allied officials during and after the Second World War to avoid a similar outcome. By preparing during the war to handle war crimes once it was over, forming an agency to document Nazi crimes during the war, and ensuring that suspects were delivered for punishment, the Allies obviated repetition of the failures that plagued the post-First World War settlement. The trials held in Europe and Japan undoubtedly invited charges of "victors' justice": the judges and prosecutors were appointed by the victors, the defendants were all nationals of the defeated countries. The tribunals themselves were not independent bodies but creations of the victorious nations. In particular, the IMTFE and the military commissions presiding over the trials of Yamashita and Homma approached the level of kangaroo courts in which the conviction and punishment of the defendants were foregone conclusions. These grave shortcomings aside, the trial programs in Europe and Japan were momentous developments. For the first time, international rather than national courts applied international law to the war crimes of political and military leaders. They valorized new international offenses—crimes against peace and crimes against humanity—never previously accepted under international law, and if the Allies made themselves vulnerable to the *ex post facto* criticism, their willingness to charge these crimes meant that their condemnation would gain increasing acceptance as international customary law after 1945. The jurisprudence of the Allied courts set forth legal doctrines that persist till the present day, such as the liability of heads of state, command responsibility, and the rejection of the superior orders defense. Finally, both the crimes committed during the war and their judgment afterward fostered a moral revulsion against extreme forms of state criminality in the postwar era, leading by the 1990s to the creation of ad hoc tribunals and, in an effort to establish a fair, permanent, and independent judicial body, an international criminal court. We will discuss these and other postwar developments in the next chapter.

CHAPTER 9
INTO THE TWENTY-FIRST CENTURY: WAR CRIMES AND THEIR TREATMENT SINCE THE SECOND WORLD WAR

The Geneva Conventions and the problem of irregular warfare

On the cusp of the Second World War, the Law of War as embodied in international treaties contained few explicit protections for civilians. The first of the Geneva Conventions (1864) rarely mentioned them; the Regulations annexed to Hague II (1899) and IV (1907) devoted little attention to them. The focus of these treaties was on protecting combatants rather than noncombatants. Devastating attacks on civilian populations during the First World War threw the deficiencies of the conventions into bas-relief. In the 1920s, the leaders of the ICRC urged the international community to rectify the matter. In 1929 the ICRC submitted a draft convention on civilian protection to an international conference of diplomats meeting in Geneva. The conference's purpose was to amend the 1906 Geneva Convention on wounded and sick armed forces in land warfare. The diplomats rejected the draft convention with a recommendation that it be considered later on after further study. They succeeded, however, in adopting the Geneva Convention Relative to the Treatment of Prisoners of War, an instrument supplementing the parts of the Hague Conventions touching on prisoners of war. Further efforts by the ICRC in the late 1930s in support of a Draft Convention for the Protection of Civilian Populations against New Engines of War—a document that envisioned creating safety zones for civilians in war-torn areas—were abandoned when Hitler invaded Poland in September 1939. Hence, the handful of protections afforded civilians in the Hague Convention of 1907 was the main treaty-based bulwark against attacks on civilians during the Second World War. These protections, as documented in the previous chapter, quickly proved their inadequacy.[1]

The Geneva Conventions of 1949 are best seen in light of the international community's renewed interest in expanding the scope of humanitarian law. The plight of civilians in war-stricken regions was a dominant concern. In 1948 the General Assembly of the UN approved the Convention on the Prevention and Punishment of the Crime of Genocide, a treaty that sought to criminalize genocidal attacks on civilian populations whether carried out in times of peace or war. One year later, an international diplomatic conference in Geneva representing sixty-four states approved four Geneva Conventions. The texts of the conventions were the handiwork of international legal scholars who had met at the seventeenth International Conference of the Red Cross in Stockholm in 1948. The experts had developed and refined their drafts for submission to the diplomatic conference planned for 1949. The Geneva conference had four primary goals:

- to revise the 1929 Geneva Convention for the Relief of Wounded and Sick in Armies in the Field;

- to revise certain parts of the 1907 Hague Conventions (especially as they pertained to marine warfare);

- to revise the 1929 Geneva Convention Relative to the Treatment of Prisoners of War; and

- to approve a convention to protect civilians during wartime.

Convening between April and August 1949, the diplomatic conference approved the ICRC drafts as four Geneva Conventions, as well as adopted a Final Act and eleven Resolutions on August 12, 1949. The 1949 Geneva Conventions comprised the following instruments:

1. Geneva Convention I for the Amelioration of the Condition of the Wounded and Sick in Armed Forces in the Field.

2. Geneva Convention II for the Amelioration of the Condition of the Wounded, Sick and Shipwrecked Members of Armed Forces at Sea.

3. Geneva Convention III Relative to the Treatment of Prisoners of War.

4. Geneva Convention IV Relative to the Protection of Civilian Persons in Time of War.

Of the four conventions, Convention IV may have been the most innovative; it was the first treaty in world history to focus exclusively on protecting civilians during wartime. In its approach to the plight of civilians, however, Convention IV was far from novel: it shared the concerns expressed in the earlier Nuremberg and Tokyo Charters with the mistreatment of noncombatants, an emphasis that would resurface a half-century later in the Statutes of the International Criminal Tribunal for the Former Yugoslavia (ICTY), International Criminal Tribunal for Rwanda (ICTR), and the International Criminal Court (ICC).

General features of the four Geneva Conventions of 1949

As their titles indicate, the four conventions extended protections to sick and wounded soldiers, prisoners of war, and civilians. Over all of them fell the shadow of atrocities committed during the Second World War. Convention III stipulated that prisoners of war had to be "humanely treated" and held free from "medical or scientific experiments . . . not justified by the medical, dental or hospital treatment of the prisoner concerned and carried out in his interest"[2]—a provision, we can reasonably assume, influenced by Nazi and Japanese medical experimentation on prisoners. Prisoners of war were to be spared "physical or mental torture," or indeed any "form of coercion" designed to extract intelligence from them. If prisoners of war refused to answer a question, they could not be "threatened, insulted, or exposed to unpleasant or disadvantageous treatment of any kind."[3] The language in Article 13 of Convention III, which strictly prohibits "reprisal against prisoners of war," betokens the framers' repudiation of the judgment in the *Leeb* case, which had allowed for measured reprisals against prisoners of war. The traumas of the recent war were also registered in Geneva Convention IV. Article 32 prohibited attempts during wartime to cause the "physical suffering or extermination" of civilians, and forbade murdering, torturing, mutilating, or physically punishing them. The framers trained their sights once again on the *Leeb* verdict in Articles 33 and 34, where "collective penalties" and "reprisals" against civilians or their property were outlawed. A trace of the German policy during the war of deporting forced laborers from their homes in the east to the Reich, where they were used primarily in agriculture, may have lingered in Article 49, which barred deportations "from occupied territory to the territory of the Occupying Power."

A long-standing obstacle to the enforcement of international humanitarian norms has been the difficulty of monitoring compliance with them. The authors of the Geneva Conventions sought a solution to this problem through creation of a monitoring system administered by "Protecting Powers." Each party to the Geneva Conventions was entitled to elect a neutral country to act as its own Protecting Power. The monitoring system was set forth in articles[4] common to each of the four conventions, meaning that it underpinned all of the Geneva Conventions of 1949. In some cases, a "humanitarian organization" like the ICRC was eligible to serve as a Protecting Power, particularly where the request of a party to the Convention for a Protecting Power "cannot be arranged."[5] Under each of the four Conventions, the Protecting Power was authorized to inspect prisoner of war camps, interview prisoners, and generally "to go to all places where protected persons are, particularly to places of internment, detention and work."[6] The Protecting Power system has not been free of roadblocks to its proper functioning. In the postwar era, the former Soviet Union dismissed the system as hindering its sovereignty. North Korea, North Vietnam, and China at different times refused to allow the ICRC to monitor their compliance with the Conventions. Today, if a State Party has recourse to the monitoring system, it will usually appoint the ICRC as its Protecting Power.[7]

The refusal of States Parties since 1949 to acknowledge the legitimacy of the Protecting Party system has been only one impediment to enforcing the Conventions. Another major barrier is the oft-repeated claim by States Parties that the conflicts in which they are embroiled are not of an "international character," and hence fall outside the scope of Convention protections. Denying the internationality of a conflict is attractive to nation-states because the Geneva protections largely apply to international hostilities alone. The framers of the Conventions were conscious, however, that many of the worst excesses of warfare occur when insurgent movements stage attacks on an occupying army, provoking severe repression by the occupier. Suppression of the Vendée uprising, the escalating violence of the Spanish Peninsular War, the butcheries of guerrilla warfare in Missouri during the US Civil War, and German retaliation for partisan resistance during the Franco-Prussian War and both world wars, exemplify the inhumane lengths of irregular warfare when it rages unchecked. Mindful of its destructive potency, the Conventions' authors inserted an article into each of the four conventions to cover irregular conflict. Because it is found in Article 3 of the four Geneva Conventions, in the years since 1949 the provision has become known as "Common Article 3." The Article seeks to shelter persons otherwise exposed to the anarchic vulnerability of lawless war—that is, those caught up in an "armed conflict not of an international character occurring in the territory of one of the High Contracting Parties." Common Article 3 protects "persons taking no active part in the hostilities, including members of armed forces who have laid down their arms and those placed hors de combat by sickness, wounds, detention, or any other cause." It demanded that such persons "be treated humanely" regardless of their "race, colour, religion or faith, sex, birth or wealth." Prohibited conduct included the following:

- violence to life and person, in particular murder of all kinds, mutilation, cruel treatment and torture;
- taking of hostages;
- outrages upon personal dignity, in particular humiliating and degrading treatment;
- the passing of sentences and the carrying out of executions without previous judgment pronounced by a regularly constituted court, affording all the judicial guarantees which are recognized as indispensable by civilized peoples.[8]

What exactly was an "armed conflict not of an international character" under Common Article 3? Since promulgation of the conventions, a consensus has developed that mere riots or violent internal disturbances do not qualify as an "armed conflict" under the Article. While civil wars clearly satisfy the test, the point at which other kinds of civil strife can ripen into an armed conflict covered by the Article is unclear. Governments confronting a violent domestic insurgency have resisted labeling it as an "armed conflict not of an international character," fearful that such recognition will confer political or legal legitimacy on the insurgents.[9] The issue gained special prominence as colonial peoples sought liberation from Western imperial powers after the Second World War. In the French colony of Algeria, the National Liberation Front (FLN, formed in 1954) and its armed wing, the National Liberation Army, launched an armed revolt against French colonial authorities, justifying their insurgency as self-defense—a ground recognized under the UN Charter of 1945 as a legitimate response to aggression. When this argument failed to convince, the FLN shifted to another rhetorical strategy, citing the right to self-determination as the justification for its rebellion.[10] In the view of the FLN, the insurgency was legal under international law; therefore, the rebels were protected persons under the 1949 Geneva Conventions.[11]

The French government held a starkly different view of the insurgency. It believed that Algeria was a part of France and the conflict akin to a civil disturbance, one requiring suppression through the normal channels of domestic law enforcement. Thus, the French refused to apply either the Hague or the Geneva Conventions to the Algerian war. This determination was controversial at the time; among others, the legal scholar G. I. A. D. Draper ascribed the French position to "political consideration" rather than an "objective assessment of the facts."[12] The ICRC itself held that Common Article 3 applied to the conflict. The French government eventually conceded that Geneva did apply—a concession that nonetheless failed to prevent egregious violations of the Convention by the French military. It can be legitimately asked whether the initial refusal of the French government to accept the Algerian war as an Article 3 armed conflict fostered the impression in the minds of French military officers that they were fighting a no holds barred type of war. George Andreopoulos writes that the most flagrant offense against international law committed by the French army, namely, the torture program installed by General Jacques Massu, commander of the 10th Paratrooper Division in Algeria, violated not only Article 3 of the 1949 Geneva Conventions, but also Article 5 of the Universal Declaration of Human Rights and paragraph 186 of the French Penal Code.[13] France was not an aberration in the postwar era. Many other countries have followed its example in insisting that their actions to suppress internal rebellions are domestic police actions beyond the pale of international law. A case bearing some comparison to the French in Algeria *mutatis mutandis* is the American experience in Vietnam. Unlike the French, the USA recognized the application of the Geneva Conventions to its conflict in Indochina. However, such recognition by no means ensured compliance with Geneva's terms.

The origins of the Vietnam War lay in the immediate postwar period, when the communist-inspired Viet Minh under their nationalist leader, Ho Chi Minh, fought to oust the French from Indochina. The armed struggle between the Viet Minh and the French military erupted in 1946 and continued until the French surrender at Dien Bien Phu in 1954. The Geneva Accords in 1954 divided Vietnam at the seventeenth parallel, the demarcation line between the French army in the South and the Viet Minh in the North. The French subsequently transferred sovereign authority to South Vietnam and withdrew. At this point, the USA stepped into the breach left by the French. Aiming to staunch the spread of communism in Asia, the Americans provided military assistance and economic aid to the South Vietnamese in a bid to stabilize their government, headed by the corrupt and ineffectual Ngo Dinh Diem. By the late 1950s, the Vietnamese communists in the South, called the Vietcong, were launching terroristic attacks on South Vietnamese officials. After the Vietnamese Communist Party adopted a resolution for the violent overthrow of Diem's government, South Vietnamese communists were brought to the North for special training in guerrilla warfare. The insurgents then infiltrated the South, injecting equipment and ordnance into their struggle against the Diem regime. Vietcong success in penetrating the rural communities of South Vietnam became one of the central preoccupations of the South Vietnamese government—and for the Americans after escalation of their involvement in the conflict, beginning in 1965.[14]

In fact, the presence of Vietcong guerrillas in southern villages was the sickness for which the American "Phoenix" program was the proffered antidote. A counter-insurgency initiative originally conceived by the CIA, Phoenix was designed to glean information by infiltrating the South Vietnamese peasantry and either arresting or killing Vietcong agents. In fact, the architect of the program's interrogation centers, the Saigon CIA chief Peter DeSilva, advocated terrorism in an irregular war as a way to dampen civilian support for the insurgents.[15] Members of the South Vietnamese army under the direction of the CIA and US Special Forces brought suspected Vietcong to the interrogation centers. Once there, detainees were often subjected to polymorphic torture, including rape, electric shock, suspending the detainees by their arms from a rope attached to the ceiling, beatings with rubber hoses and whips, and mauling prisoners with police dogs.[16] A former Seton Hall divinity student, Francis Reitemeyer, was assigned to Phoenix before filing an application for conscientious objector status. In his petition Reitemeyer recounted that he was told he would supervise eighteen mercenary soldiers in finding or killing all the Vietcong discovered in an area, whose whereabouts could be ascertained, if necessary, through "the most extreme forms of torture." His superiors defined the Vietcong as "any male or female of any age in a position of authority or influence in the village who were politically loyal or simply in agreement with the VC [Vietcong] or their objectives." Reitemeyer would be responsible for meeting a "kill quota" of fifty bodies per month. To illustrate how he should conduct his future assignment, he was told of a Vietcong suspect killed and dismembered, the body parts posed on his front lawn to terrorize other Vietcong sympathizers.[17]

The Phoenix program, which would ultimately neuter some 81,740 suspected Vietcong and their supporters, among whom between 26,000 and 41,000 were murdered, was a blatant violation of the Law of War. Reitemeyer's superiors understood as much: according to his petition, he was informed before assignment that in the event of his capture he could be prosecuted for war crimes based on the principles of Nuremberg and the Geneva Conventions. Phoenix was so freighted with Law of War violations that it could be an issue-spotting question for a law school exam. For starters, it breached Article 6 (b) (War Crimes) and (c) (Crimes against Humanity) of the IMT Charter and the parallel provisions in Article II of Control Council Law No. 10, all of which were considered international customary law by the 1960s. Further, Phoenix violated the Regulations to Hague Convention IV of 1907, Articles 4, 23, and 50, and Common Article 3 of the 1949 Geneva Conventions. We will recall that Common Article 3 *inter alia* forbade prosecution and punishment by extraordinary courts; to pass muster under the Convention, only a "regularly constituted court" was permitted to try the cases of captured prisoners, and only if it guaranteed the due process rights "recognized as indispensable by civilized peoples." A 1971 congressional investigation found that this lapse was a violation of the Geneva Convention. After visiting Vietnam, the conveners of the hearings expressed their concern that "the Phoenix program is an instrument of terror; that torture is a regularly accepted part of interrogation . . . and that the top US officials responsible for the program at best have a lack of understanding of its abuses."[18] In October 1971 *The New York Times* published the stunning statistic that in excess of 20,000 innocent civilians had been murdered in connection with the Phoenix program. In the same article, *The Times* reported that the congressional subcommittee had faulted the Pentagon for its failure to investigate allegations of war crimes.[19] For the anti-war movement, these disclosures transformed Phoenix into a malign symbol of American overreach in Vietnam. Some US military personnel involved in Phoenix disparaged the program less for its brutality than its corruption and epic profligacy. Unsurprisingly, much of the US aid appropriated for Phoenix was embezzled by South Vietnamese officials, who also accepted bribes from accused Vietcong suspects. The upshot was that 70 percent of suspects arrested as Vietcong or Vietcong sympathizers were released. The quotas had nonetheless to be filled. Innocent civilians were rounded up on the baseless accusations of interested neighbors, and when they failed to pay a bribe, they were liable to torture in one of the CIA interrogation centers.[20]

Given these dismal circumstances, why would US officials persevere in supporting Phoenix for eight years (1965–72)? The answer highlights a vexatious and recurrent problem facing the Law of War: the Phoenix program, in spite of its manifold inefficiencies, was remarkably successful in degrading the Vietcong's ability to fight. CIA director William Colby testified at the congressional hearings that Phoenix had scotched 60,000 proven Vietcong agents. A leading historian of the Vietnam War, Stanley Karnow, confessed that his initial skepticism about Colby's assertion yielded to acceptance when Madame Nguyen Thi Dinh, a Vietcong leader, confirmed after the war the deadly effectiveness of Phoenix, an assessment corroborated by other Vietcong and North Vietnamese military chiefs.[21] So long as the belligerents in a conflict believe that all-important values are at stake, as both France in Algeria and the USA in Vietnam did, the temptation will be to pursue militarily effective methods even when they contradict the Law of War.

"Grave breaches" under the Conventions

Military necessity notwithstanding, French and US counter-insurgency *could* have been prosecuted as "grave breaches" of the 1949 Conventions. Although neither the Hague nor Geneva Conventions prior to 1949 contained a penal provision, war crimes trials after the Second World War conclusively proved that violators of humanitarian law incurred international criminal liability.[22] Curiously, Geneva's drafters in 1949 opted to avoid explicit criminalization of the Conventions' provisions (the term "war crimes" does not appear in any of them), choosing instead to interlard them with reference to "grave breaches." These included:

- Willful killing (Conventions I, II, III, IV)
- Torture or inhuman treatment (Conventions I, II, III, IV)
- Willfully causing great suffering or serious injury to body or health (Conventions I, II, III, IV)
- Extensive destruction and appropriation of property, not justified by military necessity and carried out unlawfully and wantonly (Conventions I, II, IV)
- Compelling a prisoner of war or civilian to serve in the forces of the hostile power (Conventions III, IV)
- Willfully depriving a prisoner of war or protected person of the rights of a fair and regular trial (Conventions III, IV)
- Unlawful deportation or transfer of a protected person (Convention IV)
- Unlawful confinement of a protected person (Convention IV)
- Taking of hostages (Convention IV).[23]

While the Conventions themselves did not identify the foregoing acts as war crimes, they did create a penal system through which grave breaches could be prosecuted. States Parties were obliged to adopt domestic laws criminalizing the ordering or perpetration of such acts. If suspected war criminals were within its jurisdiction, a State-Party had to undertake a search for them; when found, they were to be placed on trial in a regular court or extradited to another State-Party to the Conventions.[24] In light of this language, the intention of the Conventions' drafters to criminalize the acts listed as grave breaches is irrefutable. Furthermore, while the Conventions did not flesh out their list of grave breaches, subsequent ad hoc tribunals interpreting the Law of War have done so, such as the ICTY.[25]

The prosecution of grave breaches in the national courts of States Parties raises the issue whether other breaches of the Conventions were also criminal. On this point Geneva was silent. According to the ICRC's commentary on the Conventions, criminal liability may still attach to violations beyond those identified as grave breaches; the criminalization of the latter, in other words, does not exclude the criminality of the former.[26] Additionally, both treaty interpretations and the holdings of authoritative bodies like the ICTY have enlarged the category of grave breaches to reach actions not originally on the list. In the early 1990s, for example, both of these mechanisms began to define rape as a grave breach. In a 1993 Aide-Mémoire, the ICRC declared that rape was a grave breach falling within the ambit of Article 147 of Geneva Convention IV ("willfully causing great suffering or serious injury to body or health"). That same year, the US State Department identified rape as a war crime or grave breach under international customary law warranting criminal prosecution. Yet another artifact from 1993, the Statute of the ICTY, branded rape as a "crime against humanity" (Article 5(g)); in their indictments before this ad hoc court, prosecutors have charged rape as, *inter alia*, a grave breach under the Geneva Conventions because it inflicted "great suffering" on the victims (a criminal offense under Article 2(c) of the Statute).[27]

Additional Protocols I and II: history and overview

At the diplomatic conference that adopted the Geneva Conventions in 1949, the delegates clashed over whether they applied to internal conflicts. This is far from surprising; as G. I. A. D. Draper notes, the Conventions were "backwards-looking to the experiences of World War II,"[28] in which prisoners of war and civilians in Europe and Asia were treated inhumanely in otherwise conventional, international wars. Although the diplomats would finally reject applying the Conventions to internal conflicts, their agreement was possible only through compromise—namely, the insertion into each of the four Conventions of Common Article 3, binding signatories to uphold certain restraints in an "armed conflict not of an international character." The frequency of low-intensity guerrilla conflicts and proxy wars in the postwar era, many of them construed by Western states as communist-inspired, quickly revealed the shortcomings of the Common Article 3 protections. Aware of these defects, the twenty-first International Conference of the Red Cross in 1969 adopted a resolution requesting, first, that the

ICRC formulate rules to supplement the Hague and Geneva principles and, second, that a panel of experts be assembled to consider them. The ICRC prepared two draft protocols, which were taken up for consideration by a conference of government experts meeting in Geneva in 1971–72. Their aim was to reassert and deepen humanitarian law, not to overhaul the 1949 Conventions. At its root, the ICRC's intention was to create a basis in international law for extending to internal conflicts the same protections afforded to international conflicts. A diplomatic conference followed the meeting of the government experts in 1974. Sponsored by the Swiss government and entitled the "Diplomatic Conference on the Reaffirmation and Development of International Humanitarian Law Applicable in Armed Conflict," it met in four sessions between February 1974 and June 1977. In addition to diplomats from across the world, the Swiss invited the representatives of national liberation movements to participate (only states, however, were allowed to vote).[29]

On June 8, 1977, the Diplomatic Conference adopted the ICRC drafts as the Two Protocols Additional to the Geneva Conventions of August 12, 1949.[30] Protocol I dealt with international conflicts as well as "armed conflicts in which peoples are fighting against colonial domination and alien occupation and against racist regimes in the exercise of their right of self-determination."[31] In both of these types of armed conflict, as Article 3 made clear,[32] the full coverage of the four Geneva Conventions applied. For signatory states that have also ratified the Protocol, this meant that the legal definition of "armed conflicts" binding on them during wartime was expanded to include not just international hostilities but wars of national liberation as well. This aspect of the Protocols has proven to be among its most controversial features, prompting powerful countries like the USA to decline ratifying them (although, paradoxically, the US government endorses many of their provisions as international customary law). No treaty in the history of the Law of War has produced more reservations by States Parties than Protocol I.[33]

The main purpose of Protocol I was to minimize the excessive and militarily pointless suffering of armed conflict, an aim to be consummated, in the words of Article 35, by prohibiting "weapons, projectiles and material and methods of warfare of a nature to cause superfluous injury or unnecessary suffering." Methods of warfare directed at civilians were forbidden under Protocol I. Article 54 outlawed the starvation of civilians through such measures as the destruction of food stores, crops, livestock, or drinking water, no matter the perpetrator's motives. This ban did not extend to sources of sustenance devoted exclusively to the maintenance or support of armed forces. Similarly, Protocol I forbade "widespread, long-term and severe damage" to the "natural environment" that may be reasonably expected "to prejudice the health or survival of the population." Part IV, Section III of Protocol I set forth the most concentrated articles on civilians, seeking to enhance their protection in an internal armed conflict. Article 69 enjoined humane treatment for such persons, "without any adverse distinction based upon race, colour, sex, language, religion or belief, political or other opinion, national or social origin, wealth, birth or other status." The Article further enumerated prohibited actions against civilians:

(a) violence to the life/health, or physical or mental well-being of persons, in particular:

(i) murder

(ii) torture of all kinds, whether physical or mental

(iii) corporal punishment

(iv) mutilation;

(b) outrages upon personal dignity, in particular humiliating and degrading treatment, enforced prostitution and any form of indecent assault;

(c) the taking of hostages;

(d) collective punishments; and

(e) threats to commit any of the foregoing acts.

Section III further demanded that a minimum level of judicial due process be afforded any protected person tried for an alleged crime related to war: the accused could only be punished "by an impartial and regularly constituted court respecting the generally recognized principles of regular judicial procedure." These "generally recognized principles" included informing defendants of the charges against them, enabling them to assemble a defense, prohibiting *ex post facto* prosecution, presumption of innocence, the privilege against self-incrimination, and other safeguards commonly observed in modern legal systems (Article 75 (3)(a)–(j)). The same section required that "special respect" be given to women and children (Articles 76 and 77, respectively) and amplified the definition of "civilians" under the Protocol to include journalists (Article 79).

We will recall that the 1949 Geneva Conventions, while avoiding the characterization of grave breaches as war crimes, nonetheless envisioned that States Parties would incorporate Geneva's provisions into their own legal systems and prosecute offenders domestically. Protocol I of 1977 not only expanded Geneva's list of grave breaches but advanced one step farther, designating them as war crimes. According to Article 85, an act could be graded as a "grave breach" (hence as a war crime) under Geneva only when committed on protected persons, identified in the Article as prisoners of war, refugees, stateless persons, the wounded, sick and shipwrecked, and medical or religious personnel. Article 85 went on to augment the category of protected persons to include the civilian population or civilian objects, which were to be immune to attack.[34] The Protocol's authors were not done, because in sub-paragraph 4, Article 85, they expanded the list of grave breaches still further, prohibiting the "willful" deportation or transfer of civilians within or outside of occupied territory, outrages on personal dignity arising from racial

---

"Without prejudice to the application of the Conventions and of this Protocol, grave breaches of these instruments shall be regarded as war crimes."

Article 85(4)(e), 1977 Geneva Protocol 1

---

discrimination (such as apartheid), or making centers or objects of a people's cultural identity objects of attack, among others. As with the Geneva Conventions, Protocol I imposed an affirmative duty on its States Parties to repress these breaches—presumably by enacting laws and prosecuting offenders in the criminal or military courts of the State Party (Article 8). States Parties, moreover, were obligated to instruct their military commanders to prevent or, if necessary, suppress grave breaches committed by their troops, as well as to report to "competent authorities" any violations known to them. As part of this obligation, military commanders had to provide training for their subordinates on the prohibitions of the Conventions and Protocol I (Article 87).

The companion to Protocol I was Protocol II, a treaty with a different emphasis from its cognate. Where Protocol I sought to protect the victims of international armed conflicts, Protocol II applied to non-international ones. In this regard, at least on its face, the rationale behind Protocol II would seem to resemble Common Article 3 of Geneva. Indeed, Article 1 declared that Protocol II "develops and supplements" Common Article 3; however, its definition of "armed conflicts" was narrower than that found in Common Article 3. The Protocol would apply only to conflicts between the armed forces of a state-party and "dissident armed forces or other organized groups." To qualify for protection, the "dissident" group had to be led by "responsible command" able to control a part of its territory to the degree required to support "concerted military operations and to implement this Protocol" (Article 1(1)). Application of the Protocol was explicitly withheld from civil upheavals like riots or isolated outbreaks of violence, which did not meet the definition of "armed conflict" under Protocol II. This did not mean Common Article 3 could not apply in such situations, insofar as the definition of an "internal armed conflict" under Article 3 was broader than that set forth in Protocol II; but Article 3 afforded fewer protections than Protocol II, and therefore protected persons, when suitably qualified, enjoyed more rights under its provisions.[35] The language of Protocol II restated many of the protections enumerated in the 1949 Conventions and Protocol I. They included "fundamental guarantees" of combatants and those rendered *hors de combat* (i.e., soldiers rendered unable to fight), children, and the wounded and sick (Articles 4 and 5). Attacks on civilian populations were categorically prohibited (Article 13(2)), as were attempts to harm the population through the impounding or annihilation of food supplies or devastation of agricultural areas (Article 14). In addition, civilians could not be displaced except to ensure their safety; in such circumstances, they had to be adequately quartered, fed, and protected (Article 17).

Neither Protocol II nor the part of Geneva it is intended to supplement, Common Article 3, delineated grave breaches for which offenders would be criminally responsible. Clearly, the Geneva drafters were unwilling to assert the criminal liability of violators in internal conflicts, nor did Protocol II address grave breaches or seek to criminalize offenses against its provisions.[36] We have seen the reluctance of powerful states to accept the principle of international criminal liability for atrocities committed during a domestic conflict. Such opposition may underlie the refusal of the US Congress to ratify either of the 1977 Protocols. As Steven Ratner and Jason Abrams remind us, the criminality of Common Article 3 and Protocol II violations will not be found in the treaty law, but in the customary law that has coalesced around these instruments since they were written. Until the 1990s national governments rejected the idea that internal atrocities were criminal offenses under international law. The USA was not singular in rejecting the 1977 Protocols; so, too, did the governments of lesser developed countries, who often looked askance on the Protocols as infringing their own sovereignty, particularly Protocol II.[37] Beginning in the mid-1990s, the governing instruments of two ad hoc UN courts, the International Criminal Tribunals for the Former Yugoslavia and Rwanda, adopted a different position. Article 3 of the ICTY Statute raised the possibility of charging persons suspected of war crimes with breaches of Common Article 3 and Protocol II perpetrated in the course of internal conflicts. This possibility became an actuality when the ICTY Appeals Chamber issued its well-known 1995 verdict in the interlocutory appeal filed by Duško Tadić, a Bosnian Serb leader ultimately convicted of crimes against humanity and war crimes in 1997. The appeal was based on his three-pronged argument that the Tribunal had no legal foundation, claimed wrongful primacy over national courts, and lacked jurisdiction *ratione materiae* (subject matter jurisdiction). At its core, Tadić's contention was that violation of international legal standards during an internal conflict did not support prosecution for war crimes. The Appeals Chamber rejected Tadić's appeal, holding that Security Council debates over Article 3 of the ICTY Statute, a provision asserting the authority of the Tribunal to prosecute violations of the Law of War, demonstrated Security Council members' intent to criminalize such violations. Hence, these offenses generally recognized as giving rise to criminal responsibility in international conflicts were also war crimes when perpetrated during internal conflicts. The implication was that such offenses were violations of international customary law.[38]

The ICTR reached the same result in the seminal case of Jean-Paul Akayesu, the former mayor of the Taba commune during the 1994 Rwandan genocide. Far more explicitly than its predecessor, Article 3 of the ICTY Statute, Article 4 of the ICTR Statute affirmed the authority of the Rwandan Tribunal to prosecute "serious violations" of Common Article 3 and Additional Protocol II of 1977. Akayesu, who stood accused of genocide, crimes against humanity, and violations of Common Article 3, was the ICTR's first case. In its verdict the Tribunal held that, based on its interpretation of the Tadić interlocutory appeal, serious violations of Common Article 3 and Protocol II were breaches of customary law. "The authors of such egregious violations," the Tribunal stated, "must incur individual criminal responsibility for their deeds." In regard to Protocol II, the Tribunal found that the list of prohibited acts under Article 4(2)— including collective punishment, hostage-taking, terrorism, slavery, pillage, etc.— expressed serious violations giving rise to criminal liability.[39]

Whether in international or internal conflicts, to be justiciable as a war crime an action must be, in the words of the ICTY, "closely related to the hostilities."[40] There must exist, in other words, a sufficient nexus between warfare and the alleged violation of humanitarian law. Thus, while Akayesu was charged *inter alia* with grave breaches of the Geneva Conventions of 1949, the ICTR acquitted him of the charge because his actions were not sufficiently linked to the civil war raging between the Hutu government and the Rwandan Patriotic Front (the rebel Tutsi army). (He was convicted of genocide and crimes against humanity.) As of April 2014, the ICTR had not yet produced a conviction for war crimes of any of the ninety-two people it has indicted. Beyond the war nexus, there are no further "contextual requirements" that must be proven in order to convict a perpetrator of war crimes; in contrast with crimes against humanity, neither Geneva nor Protocol I demands systematic government policy or mass action, and every violation of the treaties is chargeable against the perpetrator as a separate crime.[41]

Where do war crimes stand today relative to Geneva and the Protocols? A consensus has emerged that grave breaches of Geneva are indeed war crimes prosecutable under international law. Thus, for the citizens of States Parties to the treaties, their grave breaches give rise to criminal responsibility. Commentators have not yet reached agreement on precisely what actions committed during wartime are criminal; most concede that not every violation of the Law of War is a war crime. Instead, they hold that certain universally condemned practices of warmaking, such as those proscribed in the Hague Conventions as well as the use of biological weapons or poison, constitute war crimes under international law. Furthermore, for all people, whether or not their government has subscribed to the treaties, grave breaches furnish the legal basis to prosecute offenders for war crimes. Criminal responsibility will also exist for (1) Law of War violations identified as such by the IMT at Nuremberg or other authoritative postwar courts, and/or (2) acts universally recognized as crimes today. Examples of the second category appear in Article 3 of the ICTY Statute, itself based on the Hague Conventions. These include the use of poisonous weapons, "wanton destruction of cities," attacking undefended towns, villages, or dwellings, willfully seizing or damaging cultural facilities or historic landmarks, and plunder.[42] Presumably, other examples would be grave breaches of Protocol I that have been recognized throughout the world as war crimes (coercive medical experimentation, attacks on persons *hors de combat*). Finally, actions acknowledged as criminal by government officials during the drafting of the ICC Statute would arguably be justiciable as international war crimes (e.g., rape, the use of human shields, deliberate starvation of civilians).[43]

What is the current status under international law of atrocities committed during internal conflicts? While the norms imbedded in Protocol II have not risen to the level of customary law, the provisions of Common Article 3 have achieved this status. Despite the resistance of governments to admit its applicability to their internal affairs, Common Article 3 remains the most authoritative protection for soldiers and civilians enmeshed in intra-state conflict, so long as it meets the criteria of a "conflict not of an international character" set forth in the Article and the ICRC's official commentary on Geneva.[44]

Chemical weapons conventions: the legacy of the First World War in the postwar world

For millennia civilizations in world history have regarded the use of poison against an enemy as unconditionally forbidden. By the latter half of the nineteenth century, progress in ballistic technology had enabled armies to equip their shells not only with explosives but with poisonous gases like phosgene, chlorine, and cytotoxic agents (mustard gas). Refinements in this dismal technology of mass death galvanized efforts to ban poison gas by means of international treaties. Hague Declaration 2 of 1899 prohibited "the use of projectiles the sole object of which is the diffusion of asphyxiating or deleterious gases."[45] The ethico-legal principle here was the long-standing prohibition of weaponry that caused unnecessary suffering. This notwithstanding, and despite accession to or ratification of the treaty by France, Great Britain, Austria-Hungary, and Germany, poison gas was broadly deployed in the First World War. The pointless misery and torturous death unleashed by these weapons led to a flurry of legal instruments after the war seeking their complete interdiction. They included:

- Article 171, 1919 Treaty of Versailles (making illegal the use, manufacture, or importation into Germany of poison gas);
- The 1922 Washington Treaty Relating to the Use of Submarines and Noxious Gases in Warfare (prohibiting the use of poison gas; the treaty never became operative);
- The 1925 Geneva Protocol for the Prohibition of the Use in War of Asphyxiating, Poisonous, or Other Gases, and of Bacteriological Methods of Warfare (extending the prohibition to bacteriological weapons).

Among these treaties, the 1925 Geneva Protocol was by far the most significant and far-reaching. Numerous countries subscribed to it, but with the reservation they would comply with its terms so long as an enemy state did likewise—a proviso that in effect rejected an absolute ban, thereby leaving open the defensive resort to poison gas. In the decades following the Protocol, other chemical weapons conventions—the 1972 Convention on the Stockpiling of Bacteriological and Toxin Weapons and on Their Destruction, and the 1993 Chemical Weapons Convention—have further restricted not only their usage but their possession. These treaties have arraigned the thesis that poison or chemical weapons may be deployed in retaliation for a first-time use by an enemy army. Some states have accordingly withdrawn their reservations to the 1925 Protocol, affirming their avoidance of chemical and biological weapons under all circumstances.[46] The prohibition of hyperdestructive weaponry in world history retraces the path trodden by the Law of War since ancient times. Previous constraints grounded in religion (as in ancient India) or social hierarchy (as in medieval Europe) have given way to limitations based on humanitarian concerns. Today, the ban on chemical, biological, and bacteriological weapons stems from their patent violation of three cornerstone prohibitions under international law: the illegality of weapons that (1) cause unnecessary suffering or injury; (2) are indiscriminate, i.e., cannot be directed at a valid military target; and (3) are disproportionate to achieving a permissible military objective. By their very nature, poisonous weapons violate each of these criteria.[47] Their criminality, on the other hand, is more ambiguous. The Statute of the International Criminal Court, Article 8(2)(xviii), proscribes "asphyxiating, poisonous or other gases and all analogous liquids, materials or devices," but its language would appear to cover only chemical weapons. On this interpretation, the use of bacteriological weapons, otherwise forbidden under international law, would not be a crime within the jurisdiction of the ICC.[48]

International humanitarian courts: ad hoc and permanent

The insistence that violations of humanitarian law are war crimes that engender criminal liability would be of dubious value in the absence of a mechanism to punish the offenses. In world history, societies have punished violations of the Law of War through formal and informal means: reprisals (such as against hostages), reputational damage, the threat of divine retribution, and trial in courts of chivalry or national courts (including military commissions). Not until the twentieth century were international courts formed for the express purpose of punishing transgressions of humanitarian law. The first of these bodies, the IMT at Nuremberg, became the template and inspiration for both the ad hoc international tribunals established in the 1990s and the world's first permanent international tribunal—the International Criminal Court in The Hague.

Domestic courts continue to serve a crucial function in enforcing the Law of War, as they have for centuries. In the past two decades, for example, Canadian courts have successfully prosecuted accused war criminals. In *R. v. Finta*, [1994] 1 S.C.R. 701, the Supreme Court of Canada held that a 45-year delay in charging a defendant with crimes against humanity under the Canadian Penal Code was not "unreasonable" as defined by Canadian constitutional law.[49] More recently, in 2009 a Canadian Superior Court convicted a Rwandan national of genocide, crimes against humanity, and war crimes committed during the Rwandan genocide of 1994. The defendant had been charged under Canada's Crimes against Humanity and War Crimes Act (2000). Convicted and sentenced to life in prison in 2009, the defendant appealed his conviction, but in May 2014 a court of appeal in Quebec upheld the verdict.[50] In the USA, meanwhile, violations of the Geneva Conventions—among them, grave breaches of Common Article 3—are codified in federal law, 18 U.S.C. § 2441.[51] The federal statute, however, applies only to US military personnel and US citizens; in practice, it is rarely used.

Far more effective instruments for prosecuting Law of War violations in the modern era have been international tribunals. Spurred by the worst outbreak of war-related atrocities since the Second World War, the UN Security Council in 1993 created the first international court to prosecute humanitarian offenses since Nuremberg and Tokyo— the International Criminal Tribunal for Yugoslavia (ICTY). The ICTY originated during a time when the Bosnian conflict was in full swing. A former member of the Federal People's Republic of Yugoslavia, Bosnia and Herzegovina was a multi-ethnic society consisting of Muslims (called "Bosniaks," more than two-thirds of the population), Serbs (less than one-third), and Croats (one-sixth). As Yugoslavia disintegrated in 1991, the Bosnian government held a referendum to determine whether Bosnia would become an independent country. Nearly two-thirds of the electorate voted for independence in late February–early March 1992. Shortly thereafter, President Alija Izetbegović proclaimed Bosnia's independence, to the deep chagrin of Serbia and Bosnia's Serb population.

Bosnian Serb paramilitary forces, reinforced with elements from the Yugoslav army, responded by attacking Bosniak towns in the eastern part of the country. Their aim was to carve out separate Serb-controlled enclaves in Bosnia and Croatia. In a process later termed "ethnic cleansing," local Muslims were driven from their homes, leading to Serb control over two-thirds of Bosnia.

By 1994, 70 percent of Bosnia had fallen to the Serbs, who used their territorial dominance to thwart UN-brokered peace plans. Serb refusal to meet a UN ultimatum triggered NATO airstrikes, prompting the presidents of Bosnia, Croatia, and Serbia to agree to US-led peace talks held in Dayton, Ohio, in November 1995. The peace treaty formally ending the Bosnian civil war, the Dayton Accords, ended a conflict that had caused the deaths of 250,000 people and the displacement of 2 million more. The mass murder of civilians and systematic rape of Bosniak women in Serb concentration camps—crimes impelled by nationalist and ethnic motives—evoked sinister memories of Nazi genocide. These atrocities would be the focus of the ICTY.

Article 1 of the Statute governing the ICTY authorized the tribunal to prosecute "serious violations" of international humanitarian law committed in Yugoslavia since 1991. "Serious violations," in turn, were defined elsewhere in the Statute as: (1) grave breaches of the Geneva Conventions of 1949 (Article 2); (2) violations of the Law of War (Article 3); (3) genocide (Article 4); and (4) crimes against humanity (Article 5). Each of the foregoing articles specifies the elements constituting these four offenses. Although atrocities were committed by all sides during the Balkan conflict, Serb troops, in the view of a 1995 CIA analysis, "committed the worst and most numerous offenses." This same report suggested that the Serbian government may have contributed to "the purposeful destruction and dispersal of [the] non-Serb population [of Bosnia]."[52] Unsurprisingly, most of the ICTY's investigative and prosecutorial work has revolved around allegations of Serb atrocities.

The ICTY consists of three main offices: Chambers, the Office of the Prosecutor, and the Registry. Sixteen permanent judges elected by the UN Security Council to a term of four years make up the Chambers, as well as twelve *ad litem* judges. The judges are distributed among three Trial Chambers and one Appeals Chamber. Each Trial Chamber comprises three permanent and a maximum of six *ad litem* judges; the Appeals Chamber consists of five permanent judges (and two from the eleven permanent judges of the ICTR). The appellate judges from the ICTY and ICTR also make up the Appeals Chamber for the ICTR, but only five judges participate in a case under review. The judges, who are intended to represent the major legal systems of the world, consider documentary proof, testimony, and the arguments of counsel, formulate a verdict, and frame a sentence for the accused. They also draft the ICTY's internal legal regulations like its Rules of Evidence and Criminal Procedure. The Office of the Prosecutor (OTP), a body independent of any other UN, state, or international agency, comprises law enforcement officials, criminologists, forensic investigators, legal professionals, and trial lawyers. The OTP investigates allegations of breaches defined by the ICTY Statute, issues indictments, and prosecutes the accused. Finally, the Registry is a sub-office of the court that provides logistical and administrative support to the Tribunal (e.g., translating documents or interpreting the day-to-day proceedings of a trial). The Registry maintains the Tribunal's archives, administers a legal aid program for indigent accused, makes arrangements for protected witnesses, and oversees the Detention Unit. In sum, the ICTY and its subsidiary offices employ more than 1,100 persons. Its personal and subject matter jurisdiction, while shared with national courts, in fact has priority over national investigations and trials, which the ICTY may legally preempt.[53]

At the time of this writing, the ICTY is winding down its prosecutions in accordance with a "completion strategy" that emphasizes trying more senior officials accused of international crimes. The plan is to transfer lower-ranking suspects to the national judicial systems of states within the former Yugoslavia, who the ICTY would support in their efforts to conduct their own trials.[54] Now that the ICTY is preparing to disband, what are its achievements? Its jurisprudence since the mid-1990s has buttressed international humanitarian law and human rights law considerably. In addition to the Tadić interlocutory appeal (holding that international legal violations were criminal in internal conflicts), the ICTY has contributed to the development of international legal norms through its judgment in the Zejnil Delalić trial of November 1998. In its verdict, the ICTY issued two holdings important to the Law of War: (1) rape is a form of torture under international humanitarian law, and (2) command authority extends not only to military but to civilian commanders—that is, it imposes criminal liability on de facto as well as de jure exercises of authority.[55] More generally, in the capacious net the ICTY has used to seine top-ranking government officials accused of war crimes as well as common foot soldiers, the Tribunal has reaffirmed a chief tenet of the Nuremberg principles—the criminal liability under international law of heads of state and government officials.[56]

On November 8, 1994, the UN Security Council established another ad hoc international court, this one to prosecute allegations of genocide and "other serious violations of international humanitarian law" committed in Rwanda from January 1 to December 31, 1994.[57] The ICTR, which is sited in Arusha, Tanzania, closely resembles its twin in The Hague, consisting of sixteen judges and eighteen *ad litem* judges allocated among three Trial Chambers and an Appeals Chamber,[58] as well as an OTP and Registry. Similarly, the Statute of the ICTR invests the Tribunal with jurisdiction over genocide and crimes against humanity; however, because the Rwandan genocide occurred during a civil war (an internal conflict), the only war crimes over which the ICTR has jurisdiction are violations of Common Article 3 and Additional Protocol II— that is, the Tribunal cannot prosecute grave breaches under Geneva or offenses under the traditional Law of War.[59]

During its two-decade existence, the ICTR has achieved historic precedents. In 1998 the ex-Prime Minister of Rwanda during the Rwandan genocide, Jean Kambanda, became the first head of state to be convicted of that crime. Another 1998 case, the prosecution of former mayor Jean-Paul Akayesu, broke new ground in holding that sexual violence could be a crime against humanity or even genocide under international law.[60] Witnesses had accused Akayesu and other Hutu officials of being present when *interahamwe*[61] soldiers raped Tutsi women outside his offices in Taba; one witness reported hearing him order a militia member to rape a young female gymnast, another witness testified that he had orchestrated rape-murders of three Tutsi women.[62] On September 2, 1998, Akayesu paid for these and other crimes with a conviction and life sentence. He was the first person to be convicted and punished under the 1948 Genocide Convention, in part for his active role in the *interahamwe's* sexual assaults on Tutsi women.

The 1990s saw not only the creation of ad hoc international tribunals like the ICTY and ICTR but the world's first permanent international tribunal, the ICC headquartered in The Hague. The idea of a permanent court with jurisdiction over international crimes was not, however, a concept original to the decade of the 1990s. In 1870 the Red Cross president Gustave Moynier had campaigned unsuccessfully for the creation of such a court to prosecute violations of the 1864 Geneva Convention; however, an era of swelling nationalism and strong state authority was not a time propitious for erecting an international criminal court. A far more favorable moment arrived after the First World War. German violations of the Law of War opened many European statesmen to the idea of creating a permanent court with jurisdiction over international crimes. When a committee of jurists met in The Hague to write the Statute for the International Court of Justice, they also recommended creating a second court with jurisdiction "to try crimes constituting a breach of international public order or against the universal law of nations."[63] Nonetheless, support for the tribunal among the jurists appears to have been tepid, and their recommendation did not gain adherents at the first meeting of the Council of the League of Nations. In subsequent years, the idea was taken up by the International Law Association at a 1922 conference in Bueno Aires, where a draft statute creating an international criminal court was prepared and later adopted by the Association in 1926.[64] The notion of establishing an international criminal court was in the air throughout the 1920s. An international organization of parliaments, the Parliamentary Union, considered a proposal to establish a "Permanent Court of International Justice" in 1925, while at Brussels one year later the International Congress of Penal Law urged the creation of an international court with criminal jurisdiction. None of these organizations, however, represented governments, and not until the 1930s did some political leaders take up the idea.[65]

Shaken by assassinations of the Yugoslavian king Alexander I and the French foreign minister in 1934, the French government sought the passage of "international measures" to combat political crimes at a meeting of the Council of the League of Nations. A committee was formed to prepare a draft convention on "the repression of conspiracies or crimes committed with a political and terrorist purpose."[66] At Geneva in November 1937, the committee presented two conventions for signature: (1) the Convention for the Prevention and Punishment of Terrorism (signed by twenty states), and (2) the Convention for the Creation of an International Criminal Court (signed by ten European states). The second of these conventions envisioned a permanent court headquartered in The Hague, manned by five judges appointed by the Court of International Justice to terms of ten years. It would have jurisdiction over persons accused of committing violations under the proposed Terrorism Convention, including "willful acts causing death or grievous harm to heads of state or their spouses," "willful destruction" of public property, and manufacturing or supplying arms for the purpose of committing terrorist attacks, among other crimes. Prefiguring the IMT that would be formed in Nuremberg seven years later, the proposed convention also allowed a defendant to be charged with conspiracy. National courts could prosecute offenders, extradite them to other countries to stand trial, or send them to the ICC for prosecution.[67] The outbreak of the Second World War postponed any further discussion about a permanent international criminal court.

The issue was briefly revisited three years after the end of the Second World War. In its resolution adopting the Genocide Convention, the UN General Assembly appointed the International Law Commission (ILC) to investigate whether a permanent international court could be established to prosecute persons accused of genocide. Over the next fifty years, discussion within the UN about a permanent international humanitarian court was at best desultory. None of the intervening human disasters of the postwar era—Stalin's Gulag archipelago, Mao's Cultural Revolution, the mass slaughter unleashed by the Khmer Rouge in Cambodia, Pakistan's murder of hundreds of thousands in Bangladesh, General Suharto's annihilation of unarmed communists in Indonesia, the Guatemalan military's counter-insurgency targeting primarily Mayan Indians, and Saddam Hussein's gassing of Kurdish civilians[68]—eventuated in a permanent international criminal court. Given the frightful incidence of atrocity after 1945, it may be surprising that the immediate impetus for creating such a tribunal was a concern having little or nothing to do with these events. Rather, the occasion was a 1989 proposal by Trinidad and Tobago to establish an international criminal court to deal with the illicit drug trade and terrorism. A draft statute was forwarded to the ILC for its consideration. The ILC then sent an assessment of the draft statute to the UN General Assembly. The report went far beyond the modest parameters of drug trafficking and terrorism, envisioning a court with robust jurisdiction over a wide range of crimes under international law. Over the next several years, the General Assembly, non-governmental organizations, and other parties developed a blueprint on which the Rome Statute in 1998 was based. After a successful vote by the delegations to the Diplomatic Conference (120 in favor, 7 opposed, 21 in abstention), the Statute creating the world's first permanent international criminal court was opened for signature.[69]

Like the ICTY, the ICC is headquartered in The Hague. It consists of four sections: the Presidency, composed of three judges who oversee the administration of the Court; the Judicial Divisions, which comprise eighteen judges apportioned between the Pre-Trial Division, the Trial Division, and the Appeals Division; the OTP, authorized to receive referrals and evidence on crimes falling within the ICC's jurisdiction and to both investigate the charges and prosecute them before the Court; and the Registry, which, like its counterpart with the ICTY and ICTR, has responsibility for non-judicial aspects of the Court's administration. In addition to these four divisions, other semi-autonomous offices are affiliated with the ICC: the Office of Public Counsel for Victims and the Office of Public Counsel for Defense.[70]

The Preamble to the Rome Statute describes the ICC as a body authorized to punish "shocking" crimes that threaten global peace. According to Article 13(b), the

Court may begin an investigation when the UN Security Council refers an alleged violation to the ICC prosecutor. The substantive offenses over which the Court has jurisdiction are set forth in Articles 6, 7, and 8. Article 6 confers on the court jurisdiction over cases of genocide. The text of Article 6 reprises the elements of the offense in the UN Genocide Convention of 1948, i.e., acts committed with the "intent to destroy in whole or part a national, ethnical, racial, or religious group as such." Such actions include homicide, inflicting serious physical or mental harm, willfully imposing conditions of life designed to destroy the group, maiming, preventing births within the group, and "forcibly transferring children of the group to another group." Like the 1948 Convention, Article 6 excludes social or political units from its definition of "group."

In both form and substance, Articles 7 and 8 closely follow the charges against Nazi war criminals listed in the Charter to the IMT at Nuremberg. Article 7 invests the court with jurisdiction over crimes against humanity, including murder, torture, rape and other kinds of sexual violence, forced sterilization, enslavement, deportation, and similar acts causing severe and gratuitous suffering. To be justiciable, however, the prosecutor must show that such acts were both deliberate and "part of a widespread or systematic attack directed against any civilian population, with knowledge of the attack." Article 8 furnishes the ICC with jurisdiction over four categories of war crimes—i.e., "grave breaches of the Geneva Conventions," "serious violations of the laws and customs applicable in international armed conflict," grave offenses prohibited under Article 3 common to the four Geneva Conventions, and "other serious violations of the laws and customs" of war. In addition to these crimes, Article 5(1)(d) of the Statute asserts the court's jurisdiction over the "crime of aggression." Article 5, paragraph 2, however, recognizes that the court will not exercise jurisdiction over this offense until its elements are subsequently defined. At the Review Conference of the Rome Statute convened in Kampala, Uganda (May and June 2010), the Assembly of States Parties deferred final determination of the issue until after January 1, 2017, when the support of two-thirds of the States Parties and ratification by at least thirty of them will confer jurisdiction on the ICC to try crimes of aggression.[71] While the ICC's creation is an immensely important event in the history of international humanitarian law enforcement, superpower politics bedevil its operation. From the beginning, the USA has opposed robust operation of the Court, rejecting its model of universal jurisdiction in favor of one based on a state's voluntary acceptance. The US government also extracted a concession that the ICC could intervene only when the courts of the offender's host country refused to prosecute. Further, the ICC must abstain from prosecuting a case when it "is not of sufficient gravity to justify further action by the Court" (Article 17(1)(d)). Moreover, members of the Security Council can stymie the ICC by requesting a moratorium on investigations or prosecutions for one year (and renewable thereafter). These limitations notwithstanding, other features of the Court, particularly its permanence and rejection of immunity for heads of state (Article 27) and the defense of superior orders (Article 28), are cogent proof for the historic character of this institution.[72]

The "Global War on Terror" and the Law of War

On September 11, 2001, the Islamic terrorist group Al Qaeda hijacked four commercial jet airplanes, flying two of them into the World Trade Center in New York City and a third into the Pentagon in Washington, DC, killing as many as 2,800 people. (The fourth plane crashed in Pennsylvania.) The response of the US government was twofold—to install new security measures at home and to wage a "global war on terror" abroad. After invading Afghanistan and Iraq and overthrowing their respective governments, the USA instituted a world-wide program to detain and interrogate suspected Al Qaeda terrorists. Military commissions were resurrected to prosecute accused terrorists, and so-called "enhanced interrogation"—a euphemism for torture—was applied in American detention centers to extract information from prisoners.

Terrorism, of course, was not born anew on September 11, 2001. Federal Bureau of Investigation crime statistics reveal that, between 1968 and 1999, more than 14,000 international terrorist acts were carried out, claiming the lives of more than 10,000 victims.[73] Terrorism has been recognized as a breach of international humanitarian law since 1949, and the attacks of 9/11 would appear to qualify at least as crimes against humanity as defined by the Statutes of the ICTY, the ICTR, and the ICC. Violation of international law is not one-sided in this conflict, however, for in their use of torture against alleged terrorists, the organizers of the US interrogation program committed war crimes. Thus, both the initial provocation (the 9/11 attacks) and the US response (the torture of detainees) were violations of international customary law. Neither bodes well for future compliance with the Law of War in the twenty-first century.

Article 33 of the Fourth Geneva Convention of 1949 explicitly prohibits acts of terrorism against civilians, a prohibition applying to armies in enemy as well as in occupied territory. According to the ICRC's Commentary on Article 33, its purpose was to deter belligerents from employing "intimidatory measures to terrorise the population" as a means of preventing future attacks.[74] The ban covered acts by soldiers and civilians fighting on their behalf as well as civilians engaged in hostilities against an occupier. Additional Protocol II of 1977 extended the prohibition of terrorism against civilians or persons *hors de combat* to internal armed conflicts (Article 4(2)(d)). Other condemnations of terrorist acts against protected civilians may be found in Articles 51(2) (Protocol I) and 13(2) (Protocol II) (the articles are common to each of the Protocols).

The issue of charging terrorist acts as war crimes arose for the first time in a modern trial in the case of Stanislav Galić, a Bosnian Serb general and commander during the siege of Sarajevo (September 1992 to August 1994). At his trial before the ICTY in the early 2000s, he was charged with terrorism and with attacks on civilians for his involvement in sniping and shelling Bosnian residents. These acts, according to the Tribunal's verdict, violated Article 51 of Additional Protocol I, and could therefore be charged against the defendant as a war crime under Article 3 of the ICTY's Statute. To prove the crime of terror as a war crime, the Tribunal held that it must be proven the attack was "carried out with the primary purpose of spreading terror among the civilian population." Persuaded that this motive undergirded the siege of Sarajevo, and that Galić had exercised sufficient command and control of his troops, a majority of the judges found him guilty of terrorism as a violation of the Law of War, noting at the same time that his actions also met the definition of crimes against humanity under Article 5 of the ICTY Statute.[75] Hence, there is precedent for the view that attacks on civilians with the intent of spreading terror are both war crimes and crimes against humanity.[76]

The interrogation program that took shape in the wake of the 9/11 attacks and the American invasions of Afghanistan and Iraq was honeycombed with Law of War violations. The American interrogation program began with President George W. Bush's announcement of a national emergency on September 14, 2001, based on the September 11 attacks. Three days later, he issued a directive enabling the CIA to conduct covert operations without the need to seek specific authorization for them. Moreover, the directive expanded the CIA's extant program of "extraordinary rendition"—a policy that, in the view of American foreign policy scholar Chalmers Johnson, violated the UN Convention on Torture. If Johnson is correct, then the first torture-related war crime of the Bush administration was perpetrated less than six days after 9/11.[77]

The justification of a national emergency framed a second Bush order of November 13, 2001. Bush declared, "I have determined that an extraordinary emergency exists for national defense purposes, that this emergency constitutes an urgent and compelling government interest, and that issuance of this order is necessary to meet the emergency."[78] Bush asserted the necessity of detaining terrorist suspects and prosecuting them for war crimes in "military tribunals," which would not apply the rules of evidence observed in federal district courts; rather, any evidence deemed by the "presiding officer" to "have probative value to a reasonable person" would be admissible. Detainees would have neither the right to a jury trial nor to a unanimous verdict to convict. Appellate review was restricted to Bush or, if he so designated, the Secretary of Defense, Donald Rumsfeld. The order went on to vest these military tribunals with exclusive jurisdiction over detainees' trials. The detainees would have no legal recourse to US, foreign, or international courts.[79]

The Bush order of November 13, 2001 set the stage for the creation of special rules applicable to Al Qaeda members and their confederates. They would not enjoy US constitutional or international legal protections, nor could they be tried in a judicial venue other than military tribunals. Bush promulgated his order at a time when Taliban and Al Qaeda members were falling into the hands of US military forces in Afghanistan. Once captured, the detainees received treatment consistent with the Geneva Conventions—a fact that rankled with high-ranking officials in the Administration, who objected to extending Geneva's protections to Taliban and Al Qaeda fighters captured in Afghanistan. These events prepared the stage for a sequence of memoranda in early 2002 that were crucial to the evolution of American torture. The applicability of the Geneva Conventions was addressed in a memorandum of January 9, 2002, authored by two lawyers in the Office of Legal Counsel (a Justice Department office), Deputy Assistant Attorney General John Yoo and Special Counsel Robert J. Delahunty. The memo argued that, because "the Taliban was not a government and Afghanistan was not . . . a functioning State" during the US-Afghan war, Geneva did not apply to the detainees. Rumsfeld instructed General Richard Myers, Chairman of the Joint Chiefs of Staff, that Al Qaeda and Taliban detainees were not entitled to prisoner of war status under Geneva. He urged that US forces treat the detainees "humanely" and "in a manner consistent with the principles" of Geneva, but made such treatment dependent on the demands of "military necessity."[80]

Bush accepted the position of the Department of Justice that Geneva did not apply sometime on or around January 18, 2002. In the meantime, Secretary of State Colin Powell had registered a vigorous dissent from Rumsfeld's decision, advising that Bush reconsider his endorsement. On January 25, 2002, the President's counsel, Alberto Gonzales, submitted a memo to him defending the anti-Geneva views within the Administration. In this memo, Gonzales rehearsed Yoo's analysis holding that Afghanistan, as a "failed state," fell outside Geneva's protections. Stressing that the war on terror was "a new type of warfare" unforeseen by Geneva's authors, Gonzales affirmed that "a new approach in our actions toward captured terrorists" was necessary. In this new kind of war, "the ability to obtain information from captured terrorists" in order to prevent murderous attacks on Americans was essential. A "new paradigm" of international law had emerged after 9/11, one that "renders obsolete Geneva's strict limitations on questioning of enemy prisoners."[81] Gonzales's memo had found its mark. On February 7, 2002, Bush issued a memorandum to Administration officials reiterating the views of Gonzales and Yoo. "The war against terrorism ushers in a new paradigm," he wrote. "Our nation recognizes that this new paradigm ... requires new thinking in the law of war." The "new thinking" was the suspension of Geneva's Common Article 3 protections from application to Al Qaeda and Taliban detainees.[82]

Bush identified several reasons for denying these detainees "prisoner of war" status. Al Qaeda was "not a High Contracting Party to Geneva," as required by Common Article 3; furthermore, the Article applied only to "armed conflict not of an international character," a standard the war in Afghanistan failed to meet. Bush's third reason for refusing to treat the detainees as prisoners of war, however, struck a more ominous chord. He wrote that "the Taliban detainees are unlawful combatants and, therefore, do not qualify as prisoners of war under Article 4 of Geneva." The term "unlawful" or "enemy" combatants is not recognized in international law. The authors of the Geneva Conventions and the community of scholars who interpret them do not accept the designation of a prisoner as an unlawful combatant as a justification for avoiding Common Article 3. The term has an ephemeral history, having surfaced in only one prior case from the 1940s, *Ex Parte Quirin* (1942), in which the US Supreme Court approved the use of military commissions to try Nazi saboteurs captured within US territory as enemy combatants.[83] As used by the Administration, the term soon became inflationary. The journalist Jane Mayer writes of the term:

> ... the designation encompassed not just members of Al Qaeda and the Taliban but also anyone who associated with them, ... even if unwittingly. In 2004, a Bush Administration lawyer told a judge that, in theory, an enemy combatant could even be a "little old lady in Switzerland" whose charitable donations had been channelled, without her awareness, to Al Qaeda front groups.[84]

The simple identification of a suspect as an enemy combatant, on the Bush theory, removed that person from conventional legal protection. In federal lawsuits by detainees seeking access to US federal courts, the government argued for Bush's authority as Commander-in-Chief to deny ordinary legal rights to enemy combatants. The position staked in the government's briefs was that no branch of government could review the President's decisions in protecting the country from terrorist attack. In its brief in the *Hamdi* case (2004), the government characterized the enemy combatants label as a "quintessentially military judgment," one better entrusted to the armed forces than to Article III courts.[85]

In the months preceding August 2002, the Bush administration explored enhanced interrogation measures. In December 2001 William J. Haynes, General Counsel of the Department of Defense (DoD), sought information from another DoD office, the "Joint Personnel Recovery Agency" (JPRA), which for decades had trained American military personnel in resisting techniques of interrogation considered illegal under Geneva. The program overseen by JPRA was "Survival Evasion Resistance and Escape" (SERE). According to a JPRA instructor quoted in a Senate Armed Services Committee investigation, SERE was "based on illegal exploitation (under the rules listed in the 1949 Geneva Convention . . .) of prisoners over the last 50 years." Techniques included stripping students naked, contorting them into "stress positions," hooding them, depriving them of sleep, treating them like animals, and exposing them to loud music, flashing lights, and extreme heat or cold. Techniques also included slapping and waterboarding. Haynes's office enlisted the JPRA in assisting its development of a detainee interrogation program. Collaboration between JPRA and Haynes's office began in the spring of 2002.[86] In July 2002 JPRA furnished Haynes's office with a variety of materials from SERE training, including lists of techniques. The DoD Deputy General Counsel, Richard Shiffrin, testified before the Senate Armed Services Committee that Haynes's office wanted to "reverse engineer" the SERE techniques for interrogation of terrorist suspects. DoD's interests in gleaning intelligence from detainees ran parallel with similar efforts by the CIA, which sought approval from the National Security Council of its own interrogation tactics in the spring of 2002. The capture on March 28, 2002, of a "high-value detainee" in Pakistan, Abu Zubaydah, lent urgency to the CIA's request for official backing. ABC News reported at the time that the CIA informed top members of the Administration of Zubaydah's capture, among them Dick Cheney, National Security Advisor Condoleezza Rice, and Attorney General John Ashcroft. These persons endorsed the CIA's interrogation plan. The torture of Zubaydah began shortly thereafter and was conducted in an undisclosed location in Thailand. Mark Danner describes the opening stages of his interrogation:

> A naked man chained in a small, very cold, very white room is for several days strapped to a bed, then for several weeks shackled to a chair, bathed unceasingly in white light, bombarded constantly with loud sound, deprived of food; and whenever, despite cold, light, noise, hunger, the hours and days force his eyelids down, cold water is sprayed in his face to force them up.[87]

The CIA was not operating a renegade operation with Zubaydah's interrogation. CIA Director George Tenet briefed high-level Bush officials on the techniques used, which included slapping, pushing, deprivation of sleep, and "simulated drowning." The latter method, better known as "waterboarding," was applied in July 2002, after Bush officials authorized the CIA to employ "more aggressive techniques" on Zubaydah. ABC related that Tenet's briefings, designed to clothe the operation in legal cover, sometimes involved "choreographed" demonstrations of interrogation sessions.[88]

Bush officials were nonetheless apprehensive of the program's illegality. Alberto Gonzales, at that time the President's counsel, wanted a "golden shield" from the Justice Department, certifying that the interrogation techniques were legal and that CIA interrogators would be immune from prosecution. Foremost among their concerns was the Torture Convention of 1984 and its codification in 18 U.S.C. §2340 et seq. They turned to the Office of the Legal Counsel (OLC) at the Justice Department for their golden shield. Within the executive branch, a legal opinion from the OLC was authoritative. In prior administrations, when invited to prepare a legal opinion by the President, OLC had canvassed other departments within the government for feedback on the proposed action. On this occasion, OLC excluded the State Department from the process of review, a sign that the White House had a preconceived result in mind that it knew the State lawyers were reluctant to provide.[89] Instead, OLC consulted a reliable stalwart of executive authority, John Yoo, who had previously authored memoranda denying the applicability of the Geneva Conventions to Al Qaeda and Taliban detainees. On August 1, 2002, OLC issued two legal memoranda under the signature of Jay Bybee, the Assistant Attorney General. The first memo addressed "standards of conduct for interrogation under 18 U.S.C. §§2340–2340A." The second, substantially redacted memo responded to the CIA's request for review of interrogation tactics proposed for Al Qaeda members, which included waterboarding.[90]

After a short introduction, Yoo (the first memo's author) asserted that the federal anti-torture statute "requires that severe pain and suffering must be inflicted with specific intent" before a defendant's conduct rises to the level of torture. Further, Yoo held that the defendant "must expressly intend to achieve the forbidden act."[91] Without this "specific intent to inflict severe pain" as the "defendant's precise objective," the activity would not legally qualify as torture. Yoo could have stopped at this point, and simply concluded that the kind of interrogation contemplated by the White House would not be illegal under federal law so long as interrogators did not specifically intend to cause severe pain as their primary objective. For Yoo, however, the problem was that a jury might nonetheless find a specific intent to torture, insofar as juries "are permitted to infer from the factual circumstances that such intent is present."[92] In other words, the "golden shield" of immunity could be pierced. How could it be reinforced? Yoo argued that the federal statute did not apply to the proposed interrogation techniques. He buttressed his argument with a narrow construction of "torture," which he defined as physical pain of a severity "that would ordinarily be associated with a sufficiently serious physical condition or injury such as death, organ failure, or serious impairment of body functions."[93] Similarly, before the infliction of mental pain fulfilled the requirements for torture under the federal statute, it had to "result in significant psychological harm of significant duration, e.g., lasting for months or even years." Yoo's restrictive reading of the anti-torture statute sanctioned a wide range of extreme forms of coercive interrogation, among them waterboarding.

Of course, the danger remained that another branch of the government would see things differently. The federal judiciary might prosecute interrogators for violating §2340A. According to Yoo, however, applying the anti-torture statute would be unconstitutional if "it impermissibly encroached on the President's constitutional power to conduct a military campaign." He continued:

> As Commander-in-Chief, the President has the constitutional authority to order interrogations of enemy combatants to gain intelligence information concerning the military plans of the enemy. Any effort to apply Section 2340A in a manner that interferes with the President's direction of such core war matters as the detention and interrogation of enemy combatants thus would be unconstitutional.[94]

The Yoo/Bybee memos of August 1, 2002 exerted a direct influence on the evolution of American torture at Guantanamo Bay (Gitmo). As pressure from the White House to "get tough" with detainee questioning mounted in October 2002, Gitmo staff met with the CIA's Counter-Terrorist Center chief counsel, Jonathan Fredman, to discuss aggressive techniques adopted from the SERE program, among them sleep deprivation, death threats, and waterboarding. Participants in the meeting looked toward Fredman for legal advice on the applicability of anti-torture statutes. He replied in words fraught with Yoo's legal reasoning: "The language of the statutes is written vaguely. Severe physical pain described as anything causing permanent damage to major organs or body parts. Mental torture [is] described as anything leading to permanent, profound damage to the senses or personality." Fredman then said plainly: "It is basically subject to perception. If the detainee dies you're doing it wrong."[95]

The preceding account is only part of the story of American torture. Much more was to follow, including two authorizations of extreme interrogation techniques by Donald Rumsfeld (the first in early December 2002, the second in April 2003). The first authorization, providing the green light to twenty-hour interrogations, deprivation of light and auditory stimuli, removal of clothing, exploitation of phobias (such as dogs), and stress positions for up to four hours, led directly to preparation of a "Standard Operating Procedure" (SOP) at Gitmo in December 2002. The "premise" of the SOP, in its own words, was to approve the use of the SERE program tactics "to break real detainees during interrogation." The SOP was a how-to manual on slapping, stripping, and placing prisoners into stress positions, and mentioned other SERE techniques like "hooding," "manhandling," and "walling" (smashing against concrete walls).[96] Rumsfeld's authorization and the SOP following it triggered application of these techniques to Mohammed al-Khatani, whose interrogation began at Guantanamo on November 23, 2002 and continued until mid-January 2003. The Red Cross documented other cases of what it called "torture and/or cruel, inhuman or degrading treatment" on thirteen other detainees at secret CIA locations scattered across the world. For the Red Cross investigators, "the consistency of the detailed allegations provided separately by each of the fourteen adds particular weight to the information . . ."[97]

The methods solicited, devised, and approved by Bush officials, migrated to Afghanistan when Rumsfeld's December 2002 authorization was sent there from Gitmo sometime during that month. Rumsfeld's subsequent retraction had little effect on the interrogation program. Military interrogators in Afghanistan acting under the Rumsfeld memo adopted the Guantanamo techniques in January 2003, including forced nudity and "exploiting the Arab fear of dogs." The techniques then spread to Iraq after the US invasion of that country. According to a DoD Inspector General report, Special Forces in Iraq relied on an Afghanistan SOP from January 2003, which was in turn influenced by the "counterresistance" techniques approved in Rumsfeld's memorandum. The Afghanistan SOP "incorporated techniques designed for detainees who were identified as unlawful combatants. Subsequent battlefield interrogation SOPs included techniques such as yelling, loud music, and light control, environmental manipulation, sleep deprivation/adjustment, stress positions, twenty-hour interrogations, and controlled fear (muzzled dogs)." By the summer of 2003, Captain Carolyn Wood, the Interrogation Officer in Charge at Abu Ghraib, submitted the JPRA/ SERE techniques to her superiors as the proposed basis for all interrogation policy by US forces in Iraq. On September 14, 2003, following an August visit by the Guantanamo commander, Geoffrey Miller, the US Commander in Iraq, issued the command's first interrogation SOP. It authorized the familiar litany of stress positions, sleep deprivation, environmental manipulation, and the use of dogs.[98]

At US detention facilities in Afghanistan and Iraq, former detainees alleged systematic abuse that included hooding detainees, stripping them naked, attaching animal leashes to them, and forcing them into sexual positions. Photographs taken at the prison depicted US soldiers threatening Iraqi prisoners—and, in one case, apparently setting an attack dog on a detainee. An internal report prepared in February 2004 by Maj. Gen. Antonio Taguba documented assaults on detainees at Abu Ghraib by soldiers of the 372nd Military Police Company, among them sodomy with a broom stick, beating with a chair, and threatening prisoners with rape. In the report, Taguba noted that in excess of 60 percent of the civilian detainees were harmless and should have been discharged. Prisoners released from Bagram Air Base in Kabul meanwhile reported being kicked and degraded by female prison guards.[99] The perpetrators of the abuse claimed they were simply following the orders of military intelligence officers, CIA agents, and civilian contractors to "soften up" the detainees for interrogation. Their assertions were confirmed by Taguba's report, which found that military guards at Guantanamo Bay had been ordered to "set the conditions" for investigations by intelligence personnel. Taguba's report indicated that the Guantanamo model was later adopted at Bagram and Abu Ghraib, despite its violation of Army rules prohibiting guards from participating in interrogations.[100]

At the date of this writing, no one other than a handful of the lowest-ranking perpetrators has been held criminally accountable for torture, despite clear evidence that it was for a time the official policy of the American government. The examples of France in Algeria, the Vietnam War, and the American "Global War on Terror" show that the dark descent into wartime criminality is not confined to authoritarian regimes. Democracies, too—even those boasting historical associations with the Enlightenment and its doctrine of sacrosanct natural rights—are willing to discard the Law of War when their interpretations of military necessity so dictate.

Conclusion

From 1945 until the present, the Law of War has been codified in treaties and in the statutes governing ad hoc and permanent international tribunals. While the authors of the 1949 Geneva Conventions deliberately avoided the phrase "war crimes" in reference to the grave breaches listed within their provisions, they clearly intended that signatories would criminalize such acts and try offenders in their national courts. So, too, did Additional Protocol I, which not only reproduced the duty to criminalize grave breaches but explicitly referred to such violations as "war crimes." Important verdicts of the ICTY and ICTR—particularly the Tadić and Akayesu cases—have asserted the criminality under international law of "serious violations" as set forth in Common Article 3 and Additional Protocol II. Furthermore, affirmations by authoritative bodies like the ICRC and the US State Department have enlarged the scope of grave breaches warranting criminal prosecution. These statements sustain the trend in the Law of War since 1945 toward prohibiting a wider spectrum of actions during wartime as violations of international customary law.

If advocates of international prosecution find gratification in these developments, other events in recent history are far less encouraging. The growing incidence of terrorism threatens not only the well-being of global society but the international legal order on which it reposes. From Jacques Massu to Dick Cheney, pervasive social anxiety tilts the advantage in politics toward the critics of international law, and terrorist acts furnish spectacular, readily understandable support for their claims that doomsday will be at hand unless extreme measures are taken to defend national security. Not without irony, history has revealed that the immoderate responses of democratic societies to terrorist attacks in the name of an overriding military necessity pose a graver danger to the Law of War than terrorism itself.

CHAPTER 10
SINGERS OF SONGS OF EXPERIENCE: TRYING TO EXPLAIN WAR CRIMES IN WORLD HISTORY

In the film *Hannah and her Sisters*, Swedish actor Max von Sydow plays Frederick, a dyspeptic artist prone to outbursts of misanthropy worthy of Ambrose Bierce. Talking with his girlfriend Lee about a documentary film he watched about Auschwitz, Frederick declares:

> More gruesome film clips, and more puzzled intellectuals declaring their mystification over the systematic murder of millions. The reason they can never answer the question "How could it possibly happen?" is that it's the wrong question. Given what people are, the question is "Why doesn't it happen more often?"[1]

Frederick's grimly funny wisecrack applies with equal force to the occurrence of war crimes. Given the kinds of creatures we are and the atrocity-conducive environment of warfare, why wouldn't war crimes happen with dispiriting frequency? The answer to the question is the Law of War. As historian Adam Hirsch has written, restraint in combat is "inherently unstable due to the relentless pressure for greater violence."[2] Only a "precarious equilibrium of values" can prevent such restraint from "dissolving." Where an equilibrium of values has failed to materialize, as in the religious wars of early modern Europe, the Crusades, New World colonial wars, the German invasion of the USSR during World War II, or the USA's global war on terror, the centrifugal tendencies of warfare spin outward into uncontrolled violence.

World history is not interested in personal psychology as an explanation for historical events. A focus on the individual, or micro, level runs athwart the methodologies of world history, which engage with macro-level study of phenomena that span regions, cultures, and nations. Individual objects of study are relevant to the world historian only if they shed light on long-term transcultural and transregional interactions. Some world historians traverse cosmic time from the Big Bang to the present, while others analyze the histories of commodities like salt and silver or single persons, organizations, and ideas.[3] These modern-day definitions of the field are broadly congruent with the parameters drawn for "world civilization" by eminent historians like Fernand Braudel. For Braudel the concerns of criminologists with the causes of violent crime in a particular society at a particular time are remote from the world historian, whose spatial canvas is far larger and time-scale far longer than the social scientist's. The year-to-year and decade-to-decade vagaries of the crime rate are not her focus. Rather, the objects of her study are permanent (or semi-permanent) "structures" that in comparison with society undergo little or no significant change over the centuries. Braudel uses various terms to describe these structures: "collective psychology," "mental equipment" (quoting Lucien Febvre), "mentality," "a certain view of the world" with an origin in "the collective unconscious." He continues:

> These basic values, these psychological structures, are assuredly the features that civilizations can least easily communicate one to another. They are what isolate and differentiate them most sharply. And such habits of mind survive the passage of time. They change little, and change slowly, after a long incubation which itself is largely unconscious too.[4]

Such world historical methodologies would seem to preclude criminological inquiry into the causes of war crimes. The problem is straightforward: crimes are studied as social phenomena yet world history does not concern itself with the transient byproducts of society. Given this circumscribed definition, how might a world history of war crimes and their causes be undertaken? It would seem that an effort to understand war criminality from the perspective of world history must construe it as a behavior transcending single states, regions, and cultures. Structures inform and motivate this behavior that are diachronic, relatively stable, and global in their reach. Alternatively, a world historical approach might examine war crimes from the standpoint of comparative history, an approach that both documents their incidence in time while preserving the cultural and temporal uniqueness of their expression.

The latter approach of comparative history has consumed many of the chapters of this book. We have emphasized the singularity of the "Law of War" as it has appeared in the civilizations of antiquity, the Middle Ages, and modernity. In all epochs of the human story warfare, in common with every other aspect of culture, has reflected the cosmological beliefs of the people who wage it. At the same time, we have also studied the persistence of mental structures that breed extreme forms of violence unjustified by military necessity. The idea that a foe and his family may be exterminated as cultural outsiders is a prominent example. Our approach here, to borrow a metaphor from Braudel, is "blue-water cruising on the high seas of time, rather than prudent coastal navigation never losing sight of land."[5]

Braudel's nautical metaphor bears a certain resemblance to the differences between "mere conditions" and "proximate causes," two concepts that surface in both law and historical studies. A "mere condition," as described by the legal scholar Leo Katz, is a "necessary precondition" to an event in the absence of which the event would not have happened. In American law it has assumed the form of the "but for" test: but for the precondition, would the event we want to explain have taken place? Because there is a galaxy of factors essential to the occurrence of any event, Katz calls the but-for test the "naïve" theory of causation. He explains it in terms of the causes producing a four-alarm fire:

Suppose lightning strikes a building and sparks a fire, which consumes it. But for the presence of oxygen in the air, but for the dryness of the building, this would not have happened. Yet the cause of the fire isn't the oxygen, nor the dryness, but the lightning.[6]

The lightning is, in the language of the law, the proximate cause of the fire.

The distinction between conditions and causes is not confined to the law but appears in historical studies as well. It was the crux of the disagreement between two historians of the Second World War, A. J. P. Taylor and Hugh Trevor-Roper, who argued in the 1960s over the cause of the war's outbreak. According to Taylor, the true cause was the Treaty of Versailles ending the First World War and the interwar policies of the allied powers. Trevor-Roper hewed to a more conventional explanation, citing Hitler's decisions as the real cause of the war. In his discussion of their debate, Leo Katz notes that both historians agree that Versailles, allied policies, and Hitler's decisions were all "necessary links in the chain of events" leading to the war. Their disagreement turned on "whether only Hitler should be called the cause of the war and everything else a mere condition."[7]

Katz points out that historians tend to side with Trevor-Roper, that is, they "reject the naïve theory of causation." Of course, so, too, do common law courts, which distinguish between mere conditions and proximate causes, holding a defendant liable for an outcome only when he has directly caused it.[8] To recur to Braudel's nautical metaphor for a moment, historians like Trevor-Roper and common law judges are involved in "prudent coastal navigation" in which the nearest shore is always in view. This must be the case in both instances, otherwise we would be awash in a chaotic welter of real or potential causes. World historians, by contrast, are connoisseurs of chaos. Where historians studying specific historical events and courts tasked with imputing liability to actors for real-world results prize proximate causes, world historians sailing on the "high seas of time" are on the lookout for enduring structures that underlie the flux of centuries across territorial boundaries.

The discussion that follows here will focus on structures or conditions that more or less conform with Braudel's triangulation of world history as a discipline. In other words, these phenomena are collectively (but not individually) psychological, long-term, frequently unconscious, and spread out across regions, states, and cultures. Many, as I will suggest, are fundamental to human nature; others are the durable accretions of specific national and religious traditions unique to the cultures in which they are found.

One further point is worth mentioning before we delve into the deep strata on which war crimes in world history are layered. Excepting acts of violence attributable to battlefield frenzy, perpetrated without orders and indicative of a collapse of military discipline, war crimes do not fit into the working categories of criminology or criminal law. The reason is that both criminology and criminal law assume that the acts of perpetrators are deviant. Many war crimes, as we have seen throughout this book, do not match such a description. Indeed, far from deviating from social norms or military orders, perpetrators of war crimes often fulfill the orders of their superiors or act in accordance with the will or ethos of their group. Moreover, official involvement in war-related criminality is often a concomitant of war crimes; without a significant government role, the war crimes associated with the Holocaust, the Algerian and Vietnam wars, and the US invasion of Iraq are scarcely conceivable. Historically, criminology sought to explain why persons violated their community's norms while criminal law endeavored to define socially injurious actions and punish the offenders. War crimes, when committed in furtherance of social norms or government-backed orders, do not lend themselves to such analysis.

Years ago the German jurist Herbert Jäger, aware of the incompatibility of these and similar actions with traditional definitions of crime, invented a term for them, macrocriminality (*Makroverbrechen*). What distinguished macrocriminality from conventional wrongdoing was government involvement. Perpetrators of macrocriminality did not commit their crimes as individuals but in a manner "entirely conforming to the system and adapted to the situation within an organizational structure, machinery of power, or other collective context of action." Further, their crimes could only be committed within this very structure; no isolated person, group, or organization acting independently was capable of genocide or a war of aggression. Conventional criminal justice holds the individual offender responsible for her crimes, not the collective. Indictments are typically not returned "against peoples, states, machineries of power, governments, and political systems," although such collectives are always the perpetrators of "genocide, mass rapes as a systematic means of destroying an ethnic group, torture, and arbitrary executions." Because the quotidian criminal law is inapplicable to these offenses, Jäger argued for legal recognition of macrocriminality as a novel form of retribution, one that punished both the individual as a willing instrument of state crime and the government authority itself, whose aims the hands-on perpetrator strove to realize.[9]

The following synopses of theories advanced to explain extreme collective violence are geared toward macrocriminality in wartime and the antecedent conditions that enable it. In seeking deep tectonic structures underlying war-related atrocities, we will largely steer clear of proximate causation (such as war crimes committed on individual initiative without higher orders) or conventional criminology (i.e., sociological theories like social disorganization, learning theory, anomie, labeling theory, neoclassicism). It is not that such areas are unimportant but that they seem at best tangential to the concerns of a world history of war crimes. We begin with evolutionary-based theories before turning to the findings of cultural studies and social psychology.

David Livingstone Smith's dehumanization theory: bestializing the other

David Livingstone Smith, a professor of philosophy at the University of New England, has proposed the uncontroversial theory that dehumanization is a crucial facilitator of war crimes and genocide. What sets Smith's thesis apart as a unique contribution to understanding war crimes in world history is his insistence that attention be paid to humankind's evolutionary makeup. Six and a half million years ago a simian ancestor of human beings arose that was hostile toward hominoids living outside its group. This animal transmitted its violent, genetically-coded xenophobia to homo sapiens. As the human mind evolved, it developed a way of thinking that differentiated things into self-contained groups containing a unique quality, or "essence." Prehistoric humans, Smith writes, "concluded that what makes an animal an animal of a certain kind is its essence." He continues:

> Porcupines are porcupines because they have the porcupine essence. The members of every species have something inside of them that makes them members of that species.[10]

Upper Paleolithic cave art reveals that prehistoric humans portrayed themselves differently than animals, suggesting that they already ascribed a different essence to themselves as compared with the non-human realm. The notion of a unique human essence had two major effects: it counterbalanced the xenophobic urges inherited from homo sapiens' chimp-like ancestor and allowed for amicable intergroup relations, including trade and cultural exchange.[11]

In the midst of a thickening web of intercultural contact, tribes demarcated themselves from other groups by means of ethnic markers, or "distinctive forms of dress, behavior, and adornment." Over time these ethnic markers implanted in the minds of prehistoric peoples the view that other ethnic groups possessed a biological essence different from their own. The urge to "parse" the domain of organisms into natural kinds and draw conclusions from such categorizations fanned into roaring life the innate aggression toward outsiders that still flickered within the human mind. That mind now faced an internal schism: on the one hand, it saw a common human essence in cultural outsiders, accompanied by the belief that these persons should not be harmed; yet on the other it was instinctively hostile toward them precisely because they were outsiders. For Smith the solution to healing the schism and resolving the conflict was dehumanization.[12]

From early on primitive humans considered animals less deserving of humane treatment than people. The fossil record abounds with evidence of animal hunting, slaughter, and consumption. Not only were animals a food source but their body parts were used for clothing and ornamentation. Smith argues that, while cannibalism was extant, it was not widely practiced, nor was the conversion of human bodies into clothing, ornaments, and trophies common. From this Smith infers that early humans regarded animals as less valuable than people because they possessed an inferior essence. In order to harm members of their own species—members who possessed an essence that elevated them above the animal world and commanded respect—prehistoric people would have to strip them of this unique human quality. Flensed of their humanity, victims would be reduced to an animal-like status, fit to be hunted, brutalized, tortured, or killed.[13]

"By selectively dehumanizing other communities, humans found a way to get around their ambivalence. They could exclude ethnic groups from the charmed circle of a common humanity, slaughter them, and take their possessions, while at the same time enjoying the benefits of trade and affiliation with others."

D. L. Smith, Less than Human, *251*

Smith dates dehumanization to the Upper Paleolithic (50,000 to 10,000 years ago) or after. He argues that dehumanization gained traction among prehistoric people because it supplied a means by which the moral prohibition against killing human beings might be surmounted. Once essences were assigned to out-groups, interpreting their essences as subhuman and inferior buttressed the decision to harm them. Attribution of subhuman qualities to the enemy, in Smith's view, transformed him into an animal that could be attacked, plundered, and destroyed without remorse. The victim was portrayed in one of three feral categories: (1) as predators, (2) as parasites, or (3) as prey.

Out-group members portrayed as predators

Few people today face imminent risk of being killed by animal predators, but the environment in which our species evolved teemed with dangerous creatures fully capable of killing and eating them. Predaceous animals, as nature writer David Quammen notes, "were part of the psychological context in which our sense of identity as a species arose." He continues:

> Every once in a while, a monstrous carnivore emerged like doom from a forest or a river to kill someone and feed on the body . . . Among the earliest forms of human self-awareness was the awareness of being meat.[14]

Evil qualities were assigned to predatorial animals. They were not merely following instinctual drives implanted in them by their biology; they were malevolent beings associated with the devil and, during the European Middle Ages, the torments of hell. Medieval Europeans likened the "jaws of hell" to the maw of a behemoth carnivore. For all eternity the damned were devoured by dragons and bitten by serpents. Gigantic toads probed their chests with their boring beaks, seeking to rip out their hearts.[15] The ascription of diabolical traits to man-eating creatures had the carryover effect of demonizing out-group victims whenever they were reconceptualized as predators.

We have witnessed numerous examples in this book of how opposing armies are bestialized to enable their destruction. Assyrian kings and Egyptian Pharaohs equated the battle against the enemy with the hunt. The Egyptians identified predatory animals, foreigners, and rebels with chaos and disorder; the Pharaoh's defeat of each quite literally sustained the continuance of life on earth. The Zhou Dynasty in China also construed warfare in terms of a hunt, in which animals and war captives were sacrificed as demanded by the will of Heaven. Blood sacrifice was the object whenever the Maya conquered a hostile city-state, capturing its nobles after a military campaign interpreted as a royal hunt. Among the Spanish conquistadors the trope of native animality licensed both casual and malefic violence against indigenous populations. The Spaniards' techniques of mass annihilation included a method employed to kill dangerous wild animals—the use of hunting dogs to rip Native Americans to pieces. Apologists of Spanish imperialism like Juan Ginés de Sepúlveda spoke openly of their alleged subhumanity.

Colonial projects in Ireland and North America drew energy from similar discourses. Royal officials like Edmund Tremayne and Henry Sydney accused the Irish of being "unreasonable beasts" involved in murder, robbery, perjury, and irreligion. The charge of cannibalism was also laid to their account. In colonial New England military commanders described the Indians as "wicked imps" in league with the devil and as "roaring lions" scouring the land in search of prey. Civilian leaders like Solomon Stoddard advocated exterminating the Indians because they were wolves deserving of the treatment meted out to wolves. Cotton Mather agreed, holding that native peoples had joined the devil's plan to wipe out the Bay Colony and the Puritans. To repulse such existential threats, every act of self-defense was justified—including the murder of all Indian men, women, and children.

Out-group members portrayed as parasites

The image of the enemy as a parasite is akin to his portrayal as a predator; with either metaphor, the out-group becomes a sub-human, noxious force that has to be eliminated. The metaphor of the parasite, however, captures an effect on the onlooker different from that aroused by the metaphor of a predator. Where the predator construct evokes terror, the parasite construct evokes disgust. References to an opponent as a parasite are superabundant in the historical record. Yahweh demanded the destruction of Israel's enemies because of their "uncleanness." American bounty hunter H. L. Hall justified his murder of Indian children in 1859 with the aphorism that "nits would make a louse."[16] Hitler's *Mein Kampf*, written in the mid-1920s, is studded with identifications of the Jews with bacilli, the Black Death, vermin, bacteria, poison, vipers, adders, vampires, parasites, and devils. So intemperate and bitter are Hitler's words that the reader gradually realizes he is not speaking figuratively but literally: he is declaring that the Jews are not just *like* a deadly disease or a poisonous snake but are *in fact* the Black Death and vipers in human form. Both the socialists and the Jews were "poisoners" of the German people who had to be destroyed, much as vermin noxious to human beings must be exterminated.[17] In a 1943 speech in Poznan, given as the "Final Solution" was hitting its full stride, SS chief Heinrich Himmler returned to Hitler's language of Jewish parasitism. He defended the genocide of the Jews "because we have destroyed a bacillus, [and we did not want] to be infected by this bacillus and to die. I will never stand by and watch while even a small rotten spot develops or takes hold."[18]

Out-group members portrayed as prey

Human beings have only been cultivating crops for ten thousand years. For hundreds of thousands of years humans were hunters, and hunting seems to have quickened into a central component of our nature. The resemblance of hunting to warfare is so pronounced that their juxtaposition is found everywhere in the world's cultures. The logic of this resemblance means that warriors are tantamount to hunters and their opponents to prey. The reduction of the enemy to the level of a hunted animal hastens the process of dehumanization, setting in motion the chain of events ending in war crimes.

Imperial conquest of indigenous peoples was often the occasion for murdering them for sport. Las Casas reported, as we have seen, that Spanish soldiers placed bets on whether they could slice off the heads or sever the bodies of Indians with a single blow. In the late nineteenth-century European settlers in Australia and New Zealand formed shooting parties to hunt down and kill native peoples. In Australia young men sometimes spent their Sundays hunting aborigines for recreation. In other cultures hoarding body parts of a defeated enemy was not unusual. Taking scalps as trophies is an ancient custom practiced by the Scythians and by some North American Indian tribes.[19] Collecting human body parts, however, is not the monopoly of premodern peoples; as historian Paul Fussell learned while interviewing veterans for a book on the Second World War, American troops began collecting Japanese skulls during the Battle of Guadalcanal and continued until the end of the war, a habit that was by no means an exotic one.[20] (See Figure 34.)

For Smith dehumanization allows us to suspend our fraternal feelings towards other people as we unleash the cruel and aggressive drives instilled in us by our evolutionary past. It is the shadow side of human intelligence, an ambivalent gift that liberates our consciousness from pure instinct yet endows us with the ability to bypass our inhibitions about harming others. We weave tapestries of self-deceit by bestializing the Other, then inflicting on him the violence we typically reserve for the animal kingdom. The identity of the Other is protean: the peoples of the Seven Nations, barbarians, foreigners, heretics, infidels, indigenous peoples, Catholics, Protestants, Muslims, the Jews, Communists, capitalists, terrorists—the list would fill the New York phone book.[21] What each group

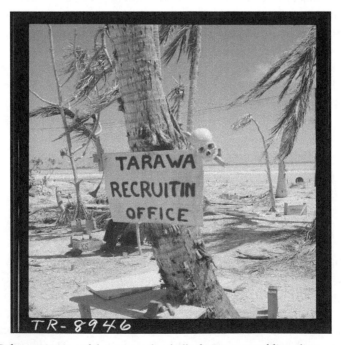

Figure 34 Dehumanization of the enemy: the skull of a Japanese soldier adorns a makeshift sign on the atoll of Tarawa, December 1943. © Wikimedia Commons (public domain).

shares is that, in the words of Paul Roscoe, it has "elicit[ed] killing responses appropriate toward nonhuman species."[22]

Jan Assmann's "Total Religion": fighting and dying for God

German Egyptologist Jan Assmann has argued cogently for a theory of religiously-inspired violence that is relevant to any exploration of war crimes in world history. Summed up *tout court* his thesis is that the origins of extreme religious violence in the Western world emerged from "total religion" during the last several centuries of the first millennium BCE. Assmann begins his analysis with the pre-exilic religions of antiquity, particularly the "cultic" religions of ancient Egypt and Israel. These archaic religions were centered entirely on their ritual practice, in which the priesthood played a dominant role. Because exactitude in ceremonial performance was essential, the expectation was that the priests, and not the population at large, would maintain their purity. Birth rather than personal adherence to religious laws determined membership in the religious community.[23]

The first watershed in the rise of total religion was the Pharaoh Akhenaton's revolutionary monotheism. Assmann describes it as "revolutionary" because it does not "evolve" from polytheism but "opposes [polytheism] in the sense of a revolution." Akhenaton's monotheism is new and stands in sharp relief against both polytheism and the "inclusive" monotheism of earlier religious forms. Conversion to the old religions of Egypt, Babylon, or Greece was unnecessary because the gods of each were convertible into the gods of the other; there was no need to choose "either Zeus or Amun." In revolutionary (or "exclusive") monotheism, however, each person stood before an "either/or" decision that would ultimately determine whether that person belonged to the religious community or not.[24] Failure to make the right choice would result in her demonization as spiritually impure.

While Assmann dates the first traces of revolutionary monotheism to Akhenaton in ca. 1350 BCE, the most decisive stage in its career does not take place until the end of the seventh century BCE with the collapse of the Assyrian Empire. Following Old Testament scholar Othmar Keel, Assmann contends that Jewish theologians "filled the vacuum" by ascribing to Yahweh the characteristics of royal absolutism under which they had suffered, in a bid to render Yahweh independent of all despots. Chief among these characteristics was the oath of loyalty whereby vassals bound themselves to obey the Assyrian king with complete fealty. The pledges of unconditional loyalty were political rather than religious. With the collapse of the Assyrian Empire, however, the Hebrews adopted the oaths as their own and, in assigning them to their god, transformed a political pledge into a religious duty of unswerving obedience. So thorough was this interpolation of an Assyrian political practice into Hebrew religion that the text of the loyalty oath was copied verbatim (although translated into Hebrew).[25]

In converting a political loyalty oath of despotic kings into a religious duty of obedience to Yahweh, Jewish theologians reformulated Yahweh as a draconian despot, one who now threatened nonconformist Jews with extreme violence for disobedience. According to Assmann, two scenes from the Torah exemplify Yahweh's absolutist demands on his people. The first appears in Exodus 32:6–28 and recounts Moses's orders

Figure 35 A sacred murder: Phinehas impaling Zimri and Cozbi. © History and Art Collection / Alamy Images.

to his Levite priests to kill 3,000 Israelites for their backsliding idolatry—an order that was fulfilled to the letter. The second is found in Numbers 25:1–13, in which a zealous priest, Phinehas, murders an Israelite man and his Midianite concubine by running a spear through them as they lay in coitus. These acts of extreme violence, both of them approved by Yahweh, reflect a seachange in the Hebrews' conception of God and their relationship as a people to him. Membership in the Jewish faith community was no longer defined by birth; henceforth it would be defined by strict observance of Jewish law, and those who deviated from it would be dealt with harshly, in a manner not unlike the punishment the Assyrian king imposed on his delinquent vassals.[26]

The "monotheism of loyalty" reflected in these two incidents pertained to intramural obedience to the Jewish law; it did not presuppose hostility toward the non-Jewish people of Canaan. Such hostility was instead found in what Othmar Keel has called the "anti-canaanism" of the Deuteronomic tradition, an attitude of murderous antipathy toward tribes like the Amorites and Perizzites already resident in Canaan at the time the Hebrews arrived. In Deuteronomy 7:1–6 Yahweh forbids the Hebrews from entering into alliances with these peoples, referred to collectively as the Seven Nations; instead, they were to be annihilated under the principle of the sacred ban (*herem*). The ban was truly genocide *avant la lettre*: no booty would be taken but everything living would be put to the sword, their city razed to the ground and rendered uninhabitable thereafter.[27] Why did such a fearsome treatment await the peoples of the Seven Nations? The Seven Nations posed a threat to the Israelites that other non-Jewish peoples did not—the danger that their religions would seduce the Hebrews, drawing them away from the covenant with Yahweh.[28]

Destruction of Cultural Objects

Figure 36 A giant Buddha image at Bamyan, Afghanistan. A UNESCO World Heritage Site, the statue was destroyed by the Taliban in 2001. © Wikimedia Commons (public domain).

Figure 37 Two women walk past the gaping cavity in which one of the Buddhas of Bamyan was housed. Built AD 507 and 554, they were until their destruction the largest statues of standing Buddha in the world. © Wikimedia Commons (public domain).

The theology of the covenant and the principles of Jewish law set forth in the priestly code developed after the conquest of Judah in 597 BCE. The Deuteronomic historians blamed Judah's fall on the Hebrews' breach of the covenant with Yahweh. From the pages of Deuteronomy emerges a distinctive narrative: so long as the Jewish people adhered to the law, Yahweh would shower blessings on them. If they did not, the result would be their ruin. This fateful template of Jewish history, excogitated in the centuries following the fall of the northern and southern kingdoms, would become an integral part of the language of violence targeting indigenous peoples over the next two millennia, used by the Spanish, New England Puritans, the Boers in South Africa, and Israeli settlers in the modern era.[29]

In the final two centuries BCE Deuteronomy's language of violence morphed into an outright criminalization of religious outsiders. In the Jewish apocryphal writings, mockery of heathen gods gives way to accusations of abhorrent heathen criminality and injustice, attributed in the Wisdom of Solomon to their worship of demonic idols. The indictment gleams with the gloss of venom; as Assmann notes, the writer has confused the physical image of non-Jewish gods with actual demons. The conflation of image and reality would give rise to an iconoclastic movement within Judaism, later to be transmitted to Judaism's tributaries, Christianity and Islam. Members of all these faiths will in later centuries identify the visual representations of foreign gods with devilish entities and from this identification draw the conclusion that, in destroying these images, they were simultaneously

Figure 38 The American destroyer, the USS *Cole*, being towed from the port city of Aden, Yemen, in late October 2000. On October 12, 2000, terrorists rammed the vessel with a 35-foot boat loaded with explosives, tearing a massive hole in the *Cole*'s hull. © Wikimedia Commons (public domain).

Figure 39 The devastating aftermath of a suicide car bombing in Baghdad. © Wikimedia Commons (public domain).

Figure 40 Results of a suicide truck bombing on the Canal Hotel in Baghdad, Iraq. © Wikimedia Commons (public domain).

destroying evil spirits. Iconoclasm has not faded into the brittle pages of ancient history but continues until the present day, carried out by the legatees of total religion, Islamic extremists. Iconoclasm surfaces in Christian history as well; as an Egyptologist, Assmann has personally witnessed the lingering traces of efforts by Christian zealots over the ages to vandalize Egyptian ruins. The deliberate destruction of cultural objects is now considered a war crime under international law.[30]

Criminalization of non-believers, identification of their gods with demons, and a flat rejection of the convertibility of gods so typical of pagan religions would lead Judaism toward an intolerant monotheism, one that branded Greek, Roman, Babylonian, and Egyptian pagans of Hellenistic antiquity as monstrous outsiders. Simmering just beneath the crust of this volatile monotheism was the churning lava of extreme violence, symbolized in Moses's execution of 3,000 Israelites for unbelief and Phinehas's divinely sanctioned murder of Zimri and Cozbi. In the final analysis, the violence inherent in the Deuteronomic narrative drew its potency from the model on which it was based—the Assyrian king's demands of unconditional obedience from his vassals. Jewish theologians appropriating this model extended to the realm of religion the claims of imperial absolutism. Total loyalty to the state becomes in the hands of the Deuteronomists total loyalty to the religion. A child of Judaism, Christianity will later retain much of its parent's condemnation of paganism while substituting for the schema of obedience and calamity a new narrative, i.e. the story of salvation and damnation. For the Hebrew covenant Christianity will substitute a dualism involving the end of the world and a final divine tribunal to judge humankind. Religion, which under paganism had been ancillary to politics, now subsumes politics and everything else; it has become "total religion."[31]

Assmann quotes Thomas Mann in *Joseph and His Brothers* that "God is differentiation." In Assmann's view, Mann's dictum applies to a unique feature of post-exilic monotheism—namely, its tendency to assign human beings to categories of "friend" and "foe" based on their religious affiliation. Politics of course had undertaken a similar sorting, yet the political foe could still be a treaty or trading partner. No such contact with the religious adversary was allowed. Total religion places all of society under the divine will; deviation from it is dealt with in accordance with Phinehas's response to intermarriage with unbelievers. The concepts of apostasy and heresy arise at this time to define non-observant Jews as internal threats.[32] Whether internal or external, the Other is an "enemy of God" who must be fought using divinely sanctioned violence.

Two religious phenomena important to the subsequent history of war crimes make their appearance during the Maccabean Revolt (167–160 BCE), a conflict fought on the Jewish side to repel the Hellenization of Judea. These phenomena are martyrdom and apocalypticism. Martyrdom, Assmann writes, is a corollary to killing for God, a theme central to 1 Maccabees. 2 Maccabees for the first time portrays martyrdom—"dying for God"—as the ultimate form of a life lived in accordance with Jewish law.[33] The topic arises as a reaction to demands by a pagan ruler that Jews perform acts contrary to their religious beliefs (like eating pork). The Jewish protagonists in 2 Maccabees reply, "We are ready to die rather than transgress the laws of our fathers."[34] In a subsequent book, 4

Maccabees, the Jewish heroes bear up under the persecution of King Antiochus Epiphanes, proclaiming the truth of their religion and the king's failure to defeat it.[35]

Martyrdom will go on to become a dominant motif in both Judaism and Christianity. Christian martyrs were distinguished by their passivity in the face of persecution. Under the Emperor Diocletian Christian martyrs, even those among them who had once been Roman soldiers, declined to defend themselves with violence. Rather, their admirers celebrated their actions as "struggles" (*athloi*) and the martyrs as "soldiers of the arena" and "athletes of God."[36] In Islam martyrs are specifically mentioned in the Quran, where they are denoted with the Arabic word *shuhada'*, or "witnesses" (the singular is *shahid*). One scholar of Medieval Islamic history, Michael Bonner, asserts that a fundamental difference separates a Christian from an Islamic martyr: the latter sheds the former's commitment to pacifism. "Instead of metaphorical soldiers of God," Bonner writes, "we have fighters who literally take up arms and use them." He continues:

> The Muslim texts of Tradition and Law repeatedly affirm that the martyrs (*shuhada'*) are those who die while fighting for the faith. Their sins are forgiven, though not their debts. They go immediately to Paradise, skipping the long wait for Resurrection and the "tortures of the grave" that others must undergo.[37]

Killing for God and dying for God are the two aspects of the religious fanatic. According to Assmann, they have served as oxygen to the blazing fires of religiously-inspired violence from the Maccabees to Bar Kokhba, Oliver Cromwell to Salafism.[38] Today, these two halves of total religion are conjoined in the person of the suicide bomber, a figure who both kills and dies for God.

The second religious phenomenon that arose during the Maccabean Revolt was apocalypticism, the belief that God will intervene to end human history and establish a new cosmic order.[39] Although its roots lay in Zoroastrianism,[40] in Judaic thought apocalypticism first appears in the Book of Daniel composed ca. 165 BCE, a premier text of apocalyptic Judaism. Assmann interprets the "Mene tekel" scene in Daniel 5 (in which a disembodied hand writes on a wall God's judgment against King Belshazzar) as the verdict of a divine world court portending the end of the world. Apocalypticism will seep into Christianity at its founding before spreading in later centuries to Islam. Along the frontier between Muslim and Byzantine armies, Islamic apocalypticism came into being during the Umayyad period (661–750 CE), encapsulated in prophetic writings that foretold a Byzantine invasion of the Syrian seacoast. This incursion, Islamic apocalypticists thought, would eventually lead to the fall of Constantinople to the Muslims and the end of the world.[41]

Assmann's concept of total religion implies that contemporary Islamic extremism is a repository of this persistent, transcultural, and transtemporal mental structure. If so, it may have achieved its supreme expression in the Islamic State of Iraq and Syria (ISIS), a splinter group of Al Qaeda that wants to found a caliphate in modern-day Iraq, Syria, and other Middle Eastern countries. As a militant offshoot of Sunni Islam called Salafism,[42] the leaders of the Islamic State strive to imitate the exemplary life of

Muhammed portrayed in the Qur'an and the hadith. The jihad it endorses targets both unbelieving outsiders and insufficiently pious insiders. Sh'ites are condemned as apostates because they are alleged to have forsaken the Prophet's example (the Islamic State considers their worship at the graves of imams and self-flagellation heretical). So, too, are Muslim leaders whose nations prefer human-made law to the divine law of Sharia. The Islamic State is therefore inherently genocidal. As journalist Graeme Wood has written, the capital sentence ISIS has pronounced against Shi'ites "means [that] roughly 200 million Shi'a are marked for death."[43]

The gruesome fantasy of wiping out 200 million people is sustained by a maniacal apocalyptic belief system. Whereas the leadership of Al-Qaeda—men like Osama bin Laden and his successor, Ayman al-Zawahiri—disdained Islamic apocalypticism, chalking it up to the fervor of the masses, the founders of the Islamic State are convinced the end times are imminent. A great leader, the Mahdi, would soon arrive to lead Muslim armies in victorious combat against the West. Once victory was achieved, the world would end. Graeme Wood sums up the Islamic State's eschatology as portrayed in its propaganda:

> [ISIS's apocalyptic doctrines] include the belief that there will be only 12 legitimate caliphs, and Baghdadi [first caliph of the Islamic State] is the eighth; that the armies of Rome will mass to meet the armies of Islam in northern Syria; and that Islam's final showdown with an anti-Messiah will occur in Jerusalem after a period of renewed Islamic conquest.[44]

ISIS leaders consider the Syrian city of Dabiq to be the future battlefield on which the forces of Islam will one day defeat the armies of Rome. Dabiq has become to Islamic State theology what Armageddon was to apocalyptic Christians. History ends in a sea of blood, a Medieval hellscape that, together with martyrdom, forms the irreducible nucleus of total religion. It is not for nothing that Assmann considers apocalypticism "the sharpest weapon in the strategy of a language of violence," the "common denominator of Western and Eastern, Christian and Islamic fundamentalism."[45]

Social psychology

Adorno's authoritarian personality theory

The appalling war crimes of the Second World War spurred postwar intellectuals, including social scientists and behavioral theorists, to search for the causes of such destructive behavior. Members of the Frankfurt School (a research group associated with the Institute for Social Research in Frankfurt a.M., Germany, whose approach to social theory was informed by Marxism), believed they found the answer in an "authoritarian personality" characteristic of highly prejudiced individuals. In their investigations, philosopher and social critic Theodor Adorno and his collaborators discovered that these people had undergone exceptionally harsh discipline in their childhood, meted out by

Adorno's F-Scale: The 9 Attributes of the Authoritarian Personality

1. Conventionalism

2. Authoritarian Submission

3. Authoritarian Aggression

4. Anti-Intraception (opposition to imaginative, subjective, or tender-minded people)

5. Superstition and sterotypy

6. Power and "toughness"

7. Destructiveness and Cynicism

8. Projectivity (projection outward of unconscious impulses)

9. Exaggerated concern with sex

Source: James Waller, Becoming Evil: How Ordinary People Commit Genocide and Mass Killing *(Oxford and New York: Oxford University Press, 2007), 82–83*

---

tyrannical fathers and rigid mothers. To elicit obedience the parents had reserved their affection, thereby producing insecurity in their children and a pronounced dependency on the parents. As adults the grown-up children retained these traits of insecurity and dependency, now expressed as an extreme submissiveness toward figures wielding power and authority. At the same time, Adorno et al. theorized, they harbored latent feelings of resentment toward their parents that had to be sublimated and redirected. The objects of their redirected hostility were minorities and persons they believed to be inferior to themselves in power. In this way, people with an authoritarian personality could reconcile the conflicting impulses boiling within themselves.[46] Adorno developed a list of traits constitutive of the authoritarian personality (reproduced in text box above).

Adorno's authoritarian personality model (referred to in the literature with the acronym "TAP") has been roundly criticized in the half-century since it was first formulated. Learning theorists have rejected it for its outmoded psychoanalytic framework. For learning theorists, the behavior of authoritarian people can be explained by studying the social norms they have absorbed from their families, schools, peers, and the larger society (including the media, churches, sports teams, etc.).[47] One study of sixteen Rorschach test administered at Nuremberg to top-ranking Nazi leaders found that they possessed only three of the nine traits of the F-Scale (anti-intraception, superstition/stereotypy, and projectivity).[48] Another study by sociologist and concentration camp survivor John Steiner surveyed two groups, former German army and SS members, using F-Scale criteria. Steiner found that the ex-SS men scored higher on the F-Scale than the soldiers. He theorized that violence-prone individuals possessed traits lying dormant in them until activated by external circumstances like Nazism. Once awakened, these "sleepers" responded to the call to actualize their latent inclinations toward extreme violence, flocking into Nazi organizations like the SS that best afforded an unfettered outlet for their aggressive urges.[49] Steiner's "sleeper" theory, like TAP generally, has been widely challenged. Psychologist Ervin Staub found Steiner's theory nugatory because most people, to one degree or another, were "sleepers" whose behavior was affected by their environment. In the final analysis, there was no need to resort to "authoritarian" sleepers because most of us are capable of wicked acts whether or not we have an authoritarian bent.[50] Historian George Browder, drawing on personnel files of SS men between 1932 and 1934, found no correlation between F-Scale attributes and the majority of the men he surveyed.[51]

If wartime atrocities are not due to the preexisting personalities of perpetrators, other causes lying outside personal psychology must be involved. As sociologist Zygmunt Bauman has put it, "cruelty correlates with certain patterns of social interaction much more closely than it does with personality features or other individual idiosyncrasies of the perpetrators. Cruelty is social in origin much more than it is characterological."[52] Bauman, like the political philosopher Hannah Arendt, does not focus on the characterological deficits of perpetrators but on the macro-processes of modernity: for Bauman, the reformist zeal of remaking the social world and the segmentation of action occasioned by the division of labor; for Arendt, the numbing of the conscience and moral insight that occurs in modern bureaucracies.[53] Both of these theoretical approaches have their adherents, and both have proven controversial. At best, however, neither would appear to stretch beyond mid-level officials receiving orders from above and relaying them for execution to levels below, and thus lack relevance as far as the direct, hands-on perpetrators are concerned. To explain how ordinary people can become extraordinary war criminals, other explanations are needed, such as those of social psychologists Stanley Milgram and Philip Zimbardo.

The Milgram experiment: ordinary people and malignant authority

Moved by the spectacle of Nazi atrocity, Yale psychologist Stanley Milgram undertook experiments on obedience in the early 1960s to test how far normal Americans would follow the orders of an authority figure to harm strangers. Milgram recruited psychologically ordinary people from the local community in New Haven, Connecticut and nearby communities, paying them $4.00 per day plus fifty cents for car fare to participate in an alleged experiment in how punishment affected learning. The ostensible purpose of the study was entirely bogus; the real aim was to explore the extent to which the test subject would administer painful electrical shocks to strangers when told to do so by a white-coated laboratory director.

The experiment consisted of a triad of participants: the "teacher," who was the naïve subject, the "learner," who was in on the true purpose of the study, and the director, who communicated orders to the teacher to transmit shocks of graduated intensity to the learner when he failed to report a correct answer to a series of questions. The electrodes attached to the learner's wrist and paste spread across the skin to avoid burns were fake; they were intended to create verisimilitude to persuade the teacher the experiment was

"I observed a mature and initially poised businessman enter the laboratory smiling and confident. Within 20 minutes he was reduced to a twitching, stuttering wreck, who was rapidly approaching a point of nervous collapse. He constantly pulled on his earlobe, and twisted his hands . . . And yet he continued to respond to every word of the experimenter, and obeyed to the end."

> Stanley Milgram, *"Behavioral Study of Obedience,"* Journal of Abnormal and Social Psychology *67 (1963), 377, quoted in Waller,* Becoming Evil, *110*

legitimate. The teacher and learner were situated in adjacent rooms close enough that the teacher could hear the groans of the learner. He/she was informed by the director that the shocks, while painful, were not life-threatening. The teacher confronted a bogus electrical panel equipped with thirty switches running from 15 to 450 volt shocks. The upper ranges were labeled as "Intense Shock," "Extreme Intensive Shock," "Danger: Severe Shock," and the most foreboding level, marked solely with a triple X. When the teacher pressed a switch s/he could hear buzzing and see flashing lights, a special effect designed to convince the teacher that a genuine shock was being sent to the learner.[54]

As the learner's mistakes piled up, the teacher administered shocks that mounted in their intensity with every wrong answer. When the 300 volt switch was pressed, the learner pounded on the walls. If the teacher expressed concern for the wellbeing of the learner, the director of the experiment (clearly representing authority) responded with one of four scripted answers: "Please continue"/"Please go on," "The experiment requires that you continue," "It is absolutely essential that you continue," and "You have no other choice, you *must* go on." Out of the forty subjects participating in the experiment, twenty-six, or 65 percent, complied with the director's commands to administer shocks up to the maximum level of 450 volts. As they ratcheted up the shock level, some of the teachers were robotic and impassive; others exhibited signs of emotional distress (sweating, trembling, stuttering, anxiously pacing the floor). Yet a significant majority of them obeyed the director's orders to the point, in their minds, of administering dangerous electrical shocks to strangers.[55]

Over the past half-century since Milgram ran his experiments, they have garnered broad national and international attention. As James Waller observes, the world's interest in the experiment was riveted by "the extreme willingness of adults to go to almost any lengths on the command of an authority."[56] The defense of obedience to authority has entered the world's courtrooms, used by defense counsel at the trial of William Calley (charged with participation in the My Lai massacre) and the 1989 murder trials of thirteen defendants in South Africa. Calley's invocation of the defense failed; nine of the South African murder defendants avoided capital punishment when the courts accepted "obedience to authority" as an extenuating factor.[57]

How relevant are Milgram's findings to macrocriminality? Waller summarizes the weaknesses of the Milgram experiment as applied to mass killings:

1. The teachers in the experiment were assured the "shocks" they administered were not harmful, whereas the destruction of human life is often the visible result—indeed, the purposed aim—of genocide and mass killing.

2. The teachers did not undergo a psychological process of devaluing the victims like the perpetrators of extreme violence frequently do.

3. The teachers often demonstrated mental distress and inward repugnance as they administered the fake shocks, in contrast with the calloused, and sometimes sadistic, affect of war criminals; and

4. The experiment was of far shorter duration than the extended time in which many war criminals carry out their atrocities, meaning that the teachers had little or no time to reflect on their actions.[58]

Important dissimilarities were also noted by Holocaust historian Christopher Browning in his celebrated study of rank-and-file perpetrators from a German reserve police battalion during the war. Like Waller, Browning thought the manifold differences between Milgram's experiment and the mass shootings carried out by the policemen complicated any straightforward application of Milgram's findings to the Holocaust. "None of Milgram's experimental variations exactly paralleled the historical situation at Józefów [a Polish town and site of a mass shooting of Jews]," Browning writes, "and the relevant differences constitute too many variables to draw firm conclusions in any scientific sense."[59]

Milgram himself was clearly aware of the implications of his study for Nazi crimes. At the same time, he recognized the limitations of his findings as applied to the Holocaust. The environment of the laboratory bore little resemblance to occupied Poland. Milgram's teachers were told the shocks would do no lasting harm to the learners; they neither acted under duress nor were they indoctrinated to devalue their victims. All of these features of the experiment differed sharply from the situation of Nazi killers, and indeed from the conditions under which most war criminals throughout history have perpetrated their crimes. The milieu of Nazi mass murder is the photographic negative of Milgram's laboratory: the killers, as objects of massive indoctrination by a totalitarian dictatorship, acted willfully to destroy the lives of their victims in the midst of a world war.[60]

These differences notwithstanding, Waller concedes that the "social and situational pressures" at work in the Milgram experiment, prodding ordinary people to obey the orders of an authority figure, *are* germane to extreme forms of wartime violence. He is less supportive of Milgram's theory of an "agentic state," in which the actor develops the view of him or herself as a tool of another person and therefore ceases to feel responsible. According to Waller, subsequent research has cast doubt on the agentic state thesis.[61] Waller's skepticism about efforts to explain extreme violence through internal personality dissociation also leads him to reject the "doubling" theory of psychiatrist Robert Jay Lifton, an idea that has gained numerous adherents since the publication of Lifton's book on Nazi medicine in 1986.[62]

Christopher Browning, like Waller, thinks that the fundamental insight of the Milgram experiment sheds light on the motivations of Nazi perpetrators. The variable of "direct proximity" to violence led to diminishing rates of obedience in the Milgram experiment and within Browning's reserve police battalion.[63] The shift from intimate killing in shooting operations to more detached, gas-induced mass murder in death camps encircled by barbwire reduced the men's sense of responsibility to the vanishing point. Moreover, Browning's policemen, like Milgram's teachers, disregarded their orders if left unsupervised; however, in neither case did they openly refuse compliance in the presence of authority. Browning's final verdict on the actions of the battalion is that the men were less moved to participate in atrocity by a submissiveness to authority than by a desire to "conform" to the group and measure up in the eyes of their comrades. As Browning writes, "Since the battalion had to shoot even if individuals did not, refusing to shoot constituted refusing one's share of an unpleasant obligation. It was in effect an asocial act vis-à-vis one's comrades."[64] Preservation of face through conformity to the expectations of the group was their true motive.

The Zimbardo prison experiment: good apples and rotten barrels

The actions of Milgram's teachers and the policemen of Reserve Police Battalion 101 highlight an all-important dynamic driving wartime atrocity: the power of the situation. Social-psychological research has shown that our social roles can become so deeply interiorized that they can reconstitute our psychological makeup. Perhaps the best known experiment on institutional cruelty and situational factors was conducted in August 1971 by psychologist Philip Zimbardo and his colleagues at Stanford University. Zimbardo paid twenty-one male undergraduates $15 a day to participate in a mock prison experiment set up at the university. Each was screened beforehand to ensure his psychological stability. The students were randomly assigned to play either guards or prisoners in the "prison," the "warden" of which was Zimbardo himself. Neither group was provided with guidelines for behavior prior to their arrival. Scheduled to last for two weeks, the experiment had to be terminated after only six days as the treatment of the prisoners rapidly descended into ever deeper levels of cruelty.[65]

From early on in the experiment, the participants fell quickly into the roles they were assigned. The meteoric suddenness of their adaptation may have been hastened by their clothing. The participants dressed in the garb appropriate to their status within the prison hierarchy: the prisoners in baggy gowns with their numbers etched on front and back, the guards in uniforms sporting reflective sunglasses and carrying billy clubs. (The guards were forbidden to use violence against the prisoners; the clubs were merely symbols of their authority.) Depression, outbursts of hysterical weeping, apathy, and resignation afflicted the prisoners in varying degree. Three were released after four days while a fourth had to be discharged after a psychosomatic reaction to the stressful conditions. Another prisoner, when told his request for premature release had been rejected ("denied parole"), meekly returned to his cell, seemingly unaware he could have left at any time of his own free will. Meanwhile, some of the guards began to exhibit sadistic and tyrannical attitudes toward the prisoners. Some one-third of them behaved in this manner. Without the benefit of instructions, they improvised methods to degrade

"Most dramatic and distressing to us was the observation of the ease with which sadistic behavior could be elicited in individuals who were not 'sadistic types.'"

Philip Zimbardo, quoted in Browning, Ordinary Man, *168*

and humiliate the prisoners. For these guards, their work was not an onerous burden that weighed heavily on their shoulders; rather, it was an activity they seemed to embrace and enjoy. A middle tier of guards acted "tough but fair" (sticking to the rules and not exerting themselves to torment the prisoners) while only two (20 percent) were deemed "good guards" who avoided punishing the prisoners or did favors for them.[66]

What are we to make of the Stanford prison experiment? For Waller, the experiment "demonstrated the evil that ordinary people can be readily induced into doing to other ordinary people within the context of socially approved roles, rules, and norms, a legitimizing ideology, and institutional support that transcends individual agency." Zimbardo's experiment revealed the depths of cruelty and sadism into which psychologically normal persons may sink, proving that brutality can be a consequence of a "social hierarchy committed to extraordinary evil." The depraved nature of the social context was the cause of the guards' cruelty, not their preexisting depravity. The warping effects of the situation were determinative.[67]

When the abuse of prisoners at the Abu Ghraib prison was exposed in 2004, the administration of President George W. Bush tried to pin the blame on the direct perpetrators—the low-ranking guards at the bottom of the military hierarchy. These soldiers were derided by Administration officials as "bad apples." In an interview with National Public Radio, Zimbardo challenged the metaphor of "bad apples" by contrasting it with an arresting counter-metaphor, that of a "bad barrel." As he told the NPR reporter, "We put good apples in a bad barrel. The barrel corrupts anything that it touches."[68] The bad barrel started at the very top with the policies of senior administration officials whom Zimbardo dubs "the architects." These included President Bush and Vice-President Dick Cheney, Secretary of Defense Donald Rumsfeld, and former CIA director George Tenet. Other rotten planks at the top of the barrel Zimbardo calls "the lawyers"—the President's team of legal advisors, Alberto Gonzales, John Yoo, Jay Bybee, William Taft, and John Ashcroft. Zimbardo refers to the military leaders setting the tone for the abuses as "the foremen:" Jeffrey Miller, Richard Sanchez, Janice Karpinski, and their staffs. At the bottom were "the technicians" tasked with implementing the administration's intelligence program. These were CIA agents, civilian contractors and soldiers in charge of interrogation, translators, medics, and military police.[69]

By its very design, the prison itself was a virtual incubator of excesses. The 400-foot tower rising from the heart of the prison made it an inviting target for insurgents. The staff were subjected to nightly mortar attacks and barrages of sniper bullets fired from adjacent buildings. At one point the prison was coming under siege on average 20 times per week, leaving parts of the edifice a charred ruin strewn with debris. The commander of Abu Ghraib, Army Reserve Brigadier General Janice Karpinski, seized every opportunity to absent herself from this hellish place, meaning that Abu Ghraib much of the time lacked a centralized command structure. As insurgents continued to be brought into the facility, the prisoner population soared. By November 2003 the population of Tier 1A, a section within Abu Ghraib set aside for detainee interrogation, had doubled, and by December it had tripled. Against the backdrop of constant attacks, few operating guidelines, and an exploding prison population indiscriminately mingled with children, the mentally ill, and detainees with contagious diseases, the contours of a humanitarian disaster slowly yet inexorably took shape. Already weakened by Karpinski's absences, the chain of command grew still more blurry when civilian contractors appeared in the prison, issuing orders to military policemen about the handling of prisoners to be interrogated. Military intelligence teams became the dominant force in Tier 1A. Consisting of CIA agents, linguists, and interrogators, the members of the intel teams wore plain-clothes with no indication of their identities. The interrogators violated a long-standing practice of restricting MPs to detention procedures by getting MP reservists involved in preparing detainees for questioning. The abuses that followed would shock the conscience of the world and inflict lasting damage to the honor and reputation of the United States.[70]

At the bottom of the rotten barrel were low-level, on-site military policemen. As a member of the defense team representing one of them, Ivan "Chip" Frederick, Zimbardo examined the defendant and found him psychologically normal. "This young man brought no pathology into that situation," Zimbardo writes. He continues:

> There is absolutely nothing in his record that I was able to uncover that would predict that Chip Frederick would engage in any form of abusive, sadistic behavior. On the contrary, there is much in his record to suggest that had he not been forced to work and live in such an abnormal situation, he might have been the military's All-American poster soldier on its recruitment ads.... The military could have used Staff Sergeant Ivan Frederick as a superpatriot who loved his country and was ready to serve it to the last drop of his blood. He could have been the best of apples in their good barrel.[71]

In May 2004 Frederick pleaded guilty to a miscellany of offenses in connection with his service at Abu Ghraib, including assault, maltreatment of detainees, and indecent acts. He was punished with an eight-year prison term, loss of rank and pay, and a dishonorable discharge. In the official narrative of the US government, Frederick was a deviant criminal. Zimbardo would have none of it. As in the mock prison at Stanford, the harsh conditions of Abu Ghraib facilitated the abuse. Attenuation of responsibility through a vacuum of senior leadership, coupled with a chaotic and blurry chain of command, eroded the ethical and professional norms that typically guide behavior. After the scandal came to light, a team of independent social psychologists conducted their own study of the prisoner abuses at Abu Ghraib, concluding that situational forces played a decisive role. These included (as summarized by Zimbardo) "conformity, socialized obedience to authority, dehumanization, emotional prejudices, situational stressors, and gradual escalation of abuses from minimal to extreme."[72]

It is comforting to think that, by sheer exertion of a good will, human beings can stand athwart the pressures of their social situation, imposing heroic moral outcomes on the play of events. The Stanford prison experiment and the Abu Ghraib prison scandal reveal such a view, however reassuring, as a fantasy. Many, perhaps even most, ordinary people will commit atrocity when the social context is conducive to it. A similar thesis has been advanced by Dave Grossman, who argues that the challenge of military leaders for centuries has been to resocialize ordinary men to discard their "innate human resistance to killing" their own species.[73] Evolutionarily and socially programmed as civilians to respect the lives of other people, soldiers are taught to embrace violence through specific techniques applied during their basic training, such as shooting at human silhouettes instead of bull's-eye targets. To deal with inevitable guilt over killing (as all ancient civilizations did through lustral rituals), modern armies "prepackage" defense mechanisms that allow killers to deny the harm they have done.[74] Grossman writes that this psychological training begins even before the soldier enters combat, and involves a "careful rehearsal and realistic mimicry of the act of killing," empowering the killer to deny he is taking a human life. Once habituated to killing the psychologically normal soldier may become addicted to it, diving headlong and with brio into the darker waters of wartime atrocity. Death and atrocity may come to hold a hypnotic allure for the soldier, as Grossman describes it:

> There are many benefits reaped by those who tap the dark power of atrocity. Those who engage in a policy of atrocity usually strike a bargain that exchanges their future for a brief gain in the present. Though brief, that gain is nonetheless real and powerful.[75]

Whether it is administering painful shocks to strangers, mistreating prisoners, killing enemy soldiers, or committing atrocities in wartime, the will to commit such acts cannot be said to be innate to the actors, at least not to most of them. Extreme violence can, and often does, arise from normal psychologies through perverse training/indoctrination and abnormal situational constraints.

Conclusion

In this chapter we have reviewed a handful of theories to explain how and why human beings have committed war crimes in world history, focusing on theories that stress long-term, persistent, and cross-cultural/cross-regional patterns of thought and behavior, patterns that are compatible with the methodologies of world historical analysis. The theories illumine an unconventional (but far from rare) type of criminal act called "macro-criminality," or non-deviant crimes committed on the orders of government authority. These theories were the evolutionary accounts of David Livingstone Smith to explain dehumanization of the Other, the cultural theory of "total religion" advanced by Jan Assmann to explain religiously-inspired war crimes, the dispositional theories of Theodor Adorno, John Steiner, and Robert Jay Lifton, which all stress unique features of perpetrators' psychologies, and the social-psychological analyses of Stanley Milgram and Philip Zimbardo, which emphasize the critical impact of situational factors on human beings' readiness to harm other people. Along the way, we have adverted to other theories seeking to grasp war crimes as historical and sociological phenomena: Zygmunt Bauman's and Hannah Arendt's implication of processes of modernity in war crimes, James Waller's belief that the social environment can actually rewire an individual's psychological makeup ("evil acts shape the self"), Christopher Browning's analysis of his reserve policemen's murder of Jews in terms of conformity to peer expectations, and Dave Grossman's thesis that soldiers must be trained to subdue their abhorrence of killing and that, in the midst of battle, psychologically normal soldiers may develop a taste for atrocity.

The thought of the social psychologists here (Milgram, Zimbardo, Waller, and non-psychologists who advance comparable views, such as Browning and Grossman) suggests a "blank slate" view of the human being.[76] In their insistence that personality aberrations are rarely the causes of extreme violence, these scholars place their emphasis squarely on situational and social factors. The student of war crimes, however, is advised to recall that human beings are not blank slates but the creatures of evolutionary development extending over vast stretches of time. The fact that the inculcation of racist ideology can intersect with latent receptors within each of us, activating our potentiality for hostility toward out-groups and leading to their dehumanization, is evidence that we are far from blank slates. The blank slate of course is a metaphor that has been with us for some time.[77] A better metaphor for human psychology may be the palimpsest—writing that has been imperfectly or incompletely erased to make room for a later writing, which is superimposed on the earlier text. Our psychologies consist of multiple layers of genetically-programmed behavioral tendencies that underlie our social personae. Sometimes, these partially effaced "writings" may become visible to us, as they did during the Abu Ghraib prison scandal. Without a preexisting openness to participating in carnage, the taste for atrocity would never express itself. In the absence of an ingrained distrust of the foreign and exotic, dehumanization and degradation of the Other would never be a concern.

We are the singers of songs of experience, not of innocence, and on the tablets of every human heart is written our deep evolutionary capacity for extraordinary good and extraordinary evil.

CONCLUSION: THE FUTURE OF
THE LAW OF WAR

In the literature on the Law of War, many scholars over the years have portrayed premodern warfare as lacking restraint. On this view, premodern warfare was a carnival of bloodlust, in which stronger armies ravaged the weaker and civilians alongside combatants frequently paid with their property, their freedom, and their lives. With the advent of the Enlightenment, as the story goes, the world's nations for the first time undertook efforts to restrain the violence of combat through law.[1] The history chronicled in this textbook, by contrast, has shown that warfare in the ancient world was seldom waged without some kind of inhibition, whether in the form of procedures required before the resort to armed conflict was legitimate or limitations imposed on the actions allowed during combat. Not until the nineteenth century were humanitarian considerations marshaled to temper the ferocity of battle. Even then, refinements in the technology of mass death, working in deadly synergy with the doctrine of military necessity, produced enormous numbers of casualties. Despite the promulgation of the Law of War in treaties and the judgments of international courts, warfare has never been more destructive as it has proven to be in the twentieth and now twenty-first centuries.

This somber development has given rise to criticisms challenging the efficacy of humanitarian principles as constraints on warfare. Although differing in their theoretical positions, the critics have in common a deep skepticism about the utility of international law as a humanizing force.[2] If the critics are right, then the modern Law of War is a sham that has not only failed to prevent the worst excesses of armed conflict but even accelerated them by attaching legal approval to hyperdestructive military practices. A more trenchant indictment of international humanitarian law is hard to imagine. However, are the critics right?

It may be impossible to gauge the full impact of the modern Law of War on military operations. As in any scientific experiment, we would have to compare the sample to be tested with a control group and chart the differences between them. For example, was humanitarian law feckless in restraining the violence of the First and Second World Wars? To know for sure, we would have to see the two events play themselves out twice: the first time under the influence of the Geneva and Hague Conventions, the second time detached from it. Obviously, such an experiment is impossible for human historians. On the other hand—less convincingly but much more practically—we can compare wars fought outside humanitarian law with others fought in accordance with it to determine whether the former produce more gratuitous suffering and bloodshed than the latter.

A consistent theme in the world history of war crimes is the ferocity of war waged against cultural outsiders. In such conflicts norms are often suspended, leading to wars of extermination. The Israelites waged annihilatory wars against the Seven Nations, who among the ancient Hebrews' foreign enemies were earmarked for destruction. The Greeks routinely suspended their Law of War when fighting against "barbarians" (non-Greeks) like the Persians. The Romans rarely tempered their warfare against the peoples of Italy during their conquest of the Italian peninsula, but whatever scant restraints they observed were discarded when Roman legions fought against non-Latin armies. The Muslims denatured their *jihad* when dealing with "Peoples of the Book of Scriptures" because of their cultural affinities with Islam; against the pagans, however, *jihad* was waged without remorse. Medieval Christians fought "mortal wars" against "enemies of the faith," in which quarter was deliberately withheld from opposing troops. Typically waged against Muslims and heretics, mortal wars were later mounted against the indigenous peoples of the New World, resulting in their decimation and sometimes the complete obliteration of native tribes from the face of the earth.

The same refrain rings through the modern era. Wherever the Law of War has been suspended, atrocities are the inevitable byproduct. This is especially visible in the guerrilla conflicts of the nineteenth century—the Spanish Peninsular Wars, the campaigns by and against the bushwhackers in Missouri, the repression of franc-tireurs in the Franco-Prussian War. By the First World War, a lawless conception of military necessity had hardened in the thinking of German policymakers, jurists, and military officers, which led them to forsake legal restraints when justified by the prospect of military victory. During the Second World War, Adolf Hitler's removal of Operation Barbarossa from the Law of War yielded a death rate of 58 percent of all Soviet soldiers in German captivity. First the French government and then the French military refused to apply Geneva to the rebellion in Algeria, breeding a full-fledged program of state terrorism and torture of captured insurgents. While the USA acknowledged the applicability of the Geneva Conventions to its war with North Vietnam, US security forces consciously suspended Geneva's rules as they administered the Phoenix program, knowing all the while that their actions were crimes under international law. Finally, the US torture program after 9/11 was abetted in no small degree by the declaration of the Bush Administration that Geneva did not apply in its struggle with Al Qaeda. Nonetheless, the awareness of government actors that their deeds were violations of peremptory norms under international law led them on a frantic quest for a "golden shield" against criminal prosecution.

In each of these examples from the world history of war crimes, perpetrators of extreme violence deliberately stripped their wars of normative restraint. The ensuing atrocities were not due to the Law of War but to its rejection. The fact that other conflicts fought in accordance with legal or normative prescription yielded fewer excesses demonstrates that the Law of War is a moderating influence on battlefield conduct. Intra-Greek wars tended to be less bloodthirsty than wars against non-Greeks; Roman campaigns against Latin peoples lacked the unalloyed ruthlessness of their wars with non-Latin peoples. Wars between Christian armies were inherently more humane than European wars with Muslims, heretics, and colonial peoples. Clashes during the Napoleonic wars between regular armies were on balance more restrained than the guerrilla wars in Spain; the same phenomenon recurred during the US Civil War, in which conventional battles were fought with a degree of reciprocal chivalry lacking from the guerrilla attacks and counter-insurgency in the border states. The behavior of the German army in both world wars was far more humane when fighting conventional battles than in situations German leaders had exempted from the Law of War. Similarly, wars waged by democracies after 1945 drifted into monstrous excess after suspension of the Law of War. Deviations from international legal restraints no more prove the inadequacy of the Law of War than the occurrence of crimes in civil society proves the inutility of domestic criminal law. On the contrary, a case could be made that law averted even worse outcomes in the troubled history of human conflict.

As we take leave of the world history of war crimes and the uneven efforts civilizations have undertaken to minimize them, one last point is worth mentioning. In the modern era, a distinction has often been drawn between international humanitarian law, which regulates war between states, and international human rights law, which regulates the treatment by states of their own citizens. The Law of War in world history rarely derived from humanitarian concerns but was anchored, as this book documents, in religious ceremonialism, social hierarchy, and ideas of reciprocity. Humanistic devotion to high ideals of mercy and charity is not required to be an adherent of the Law of War; a Kautilya or Machiavelli could be as much an advocate of restraint in warfare as a Gustave Moynier or Ashoka. Human rights law, by contrast, is of far more recent vintage, and stems from the humanitarian conviction that all human beings should be spared personal injury, degradation, or mistreatment at the hands of their government. The driving force of human rights law originates in a community concern to protect the basic rights of all people.[3]

In the decades following the Second World War, this distinction has grown vaporous. The criminalization of the Geneva Conventions' terms during internal conflicts—that is, in situations in which the benefits of international reciprocity are nonexistent—has forged a link between the Law of War and Human Rights law. Where the Law of War has traditionally focused on relations between belligerents and Human Rights on relations between governments and their citizens, the law governing internal conflicts abolishes this distinction. In the law of internal conflicts, war crimes and crimes against humanity converge.

Today, humanitarianism informs both the Law of War and Human Rights. It has not always been so, but the future of the Law of War now seems moored to the humanitarian concerns expressed in the Geneva and Hague Conventions. In these ideals lies our best hope of curbing humankind's dismaying talent for superfluous violence and ghastly self-destruction.

NOTES

Introduction

1. The scholarship on the Law of War is divided on whether warfare has been an activity bound by rules in world history. Two basic anthropological models have characterized scholars' conceptions of war: the view of war as a game (associated with Johann Huizinga) and the view of war as a hunt (associated with Walter Burkert). In this chapter, I follow the view that warfare emerged from human hunting practices. See Johann Huizinga, *Homo Ludens: A Study of the Play Element in Culture* (Boston, MA: Beacon Press, 1968); Walter Burkert, *Homo Necans: The Anthropology of Ancient Greek Sacrificial Ritual and Myth*, trans. Peter Bing (Berkeley: University of California Press, 1983); James Q. Whitman, *The Verdict of Battle: The Law of Victory and the Making of Modern War* (Cambridge, MA: Harvard University Press, 2012), 180–89.

2. Harold J. Berman, *Law and Revolution II: The Impact of the Protestant Reformations on the Western Legal Tradition* (Cambridge, MA: Belknap, 2006), 131–55, 188–90; John H. Langbein, *Prosecuting Crime in the Renaissance* (Cambridge, MA: Harvard University Press, 1974), 129–209; Henry S. Maine, *Ancient Law* (London: John Murray, 1861), 359–60; E. Adamson Hoebel, *The Law of Primitive Man* (Cambridge, MA: Harvard University Press, 1954), 259–60.

3. Lassa Oppenheim, *International Law, Vol. II: War and Neutrality* (New York: Longmans, 1906), 264–5. See also Daniel M. Segesser, "On the Road to Total Retribution? The International Debate on the Punishment of War Crimes," in *A World at Total War: Global Conflict and the Politics of Destruction, 1937–1945*, ed. R. Chickering, S. Förster, and B. Greiner (Cambridge: Cambridge University Press, 2005), 357.

4. John Fabian Witt, *Lincoln's Code: The Laws of War in American History* (New York: Free Press, 2012), 343.

5. Johann Caspar Bluntschli, *Das Moderne Völkerrecht der civilizierten Staaten als Rechtsbruch Dargestellt* (Nördlingen: C. H. Beck, 1872), §643a; O.A. Hathaway, P.K. Strauch, B.A. Walton, and Z.A.Y. Weinberg, "What is a War Crime?," *Yale Journal of International Law* 44, No. 1 (2019): 61.

6. Lassa Oppenheim, *International Law: A Treatise* (New York: Longmans, Green, & Co., 1906), 263–70.

7. Hathaway et al., "What is a War Crime?," 62.

8. Memorandum for the Judge Advocate General, Subject: Definition of the term "war crimes," Robert M. W. Kempner Papers, Box 142, Folder F3, Inclosure [sic] 1, Illustrative List of "War Crimes."

9. Hans Kelsen, one of the twentieth century's preeminent legal scholars , observed in 1944 that "[m]ost of the writers on international law maintain that war crimes constitute only penal offenses against national law, and that they have only 'municipal' [i.e. intra-state] character, since international law does not provide punishment of the offenders." Quoted in Hathaway et al., "What is a War Crime?," 60.

Notes

10. The criterion of seriousness is a staple of actions deemed to be extreme violations of the Law of War in world history. Hathaway et al. have posited a definition of war crimes heavily reliant on this criterion: "To be an international war crime," they write, "an act must meet two substantive criteria: it must be (1) a breach of [international humanitarian law] (2) that is serious. In other words, to be a war crime, an act must violate IHL, but not all violations of IHL are subject to criminal penalty—only those that are 'serious.'" Hathaway et al., "What is a War Crime?," 55. As we will see in chapter 9, the Geneva Conventions of 1949 avoided using the phrase "war crimes" altogether, preferring to refer to wartime atrocities as especially serious violations of IHL called "grave breaches." Not until Additional Protocol I of 1977 were "grave breaches" explicitly equated with war crimes.

11. Laurence Rosen, *Law as Culture* (Princeton, NJ: Princeton University Press, 2006), 3–9.

12. C. G. Jung, *Synchronicity: An Acausal Connecting Principle*, trans. R. F. C. Hull (Princeton, NJ: Princeton University Press, 1973).

13. William H. McNeill, "The Changing Shape of World History," *History and Theory* 34/2 (May 1995): 21.

14. i.e., sparing the life of a surrendered enemy.

15. i.e., the Geneva and Hague Conventions.

1 The Roots of the Law of War in World History

1. Quoted in Michael Fellman, *Citizen Sherman: A Life of William Tecumseh Sherman* (New York: Random House, 1995), 306.

2. Jean Guilaine and Jean Zammit, *Origins of War: Violence in Prehistory*, trans. Melanie Hersey (Malden, MA: Blackwell Publishing, 2005), 67–70.

3. Jean Guilaine and Jean Zammit, *Origins of War*, 86–9.

4. David Livingstone Smith, *The Most Dangerous Animal: Human Nature and the Origins of War* (New York: St. Martin's Press, 2007), 51.

5. John Keegan, *History of Warfare* (New York: Vintage, 1993), 122.

6. Keegan, *History of Warfare*, 118–25. Another early Neolithic farming community, Çatal Hüyük in modern-day Turkey (ca. 6700–5650 BCE), was even larger than Jericho, and like its Jordanian precursor it was constructed to withstand military attack.

7. For the classical exposition of "disenchantment" in modernity, see Max Weber, *The Sociology of Religion*, trans. Ephraim Fischoff (Boston: Beacon Press, 1993).

8. Mircea Eliade, *The Sacred and the Profane: The Nature of Religion* (New York: Harcourt, Brace & World, 1959), 93–94.

9. Gertrude Rachel Levy, *The Gate of the Horn: A study of the religious conceptions of the stone age, and their influence upon European thought* (London: Faber and Faber, 1948), 8.

10. David Lewis Williams, *The Mind in the Cave: Consciousness and the Origins of Art* (London: Thames and Hudson, 2004).

11. Henri Frankfort, *The Birth of Civilization in the Near East* (New York: Doubleday Anchor Books, 1956), 27.

12. Eliade, *The Sacred*, 12. Eliade's approach to sacrality may be helpfully distinguished from the German theologian Rudolf Otto, who conceived of the sacred as a frightening irruption into ordinary life that is experienced as both "terrifying" and "awe-inspiring" (*mysterium tremendum*

et fascinans). For Otto the divine is not encountered in the commonplaces of day-to-day existence; rather, it is radically discontinuous with everyday life and presents itself to the percipient as "completely other" (*ganz andere*). See Rudolf Otto, *Das Heilige: Über das Irrationale in der Idee des Göttlichen und Sein Verhältnis zum Rationalen* (Stuttgart/Gotha: Verlag Friedrich Andreas Perthes A.-G., 1923).

13. i.e. an ancient stepped pyramid in Mesopotamia and the area surrounding it.

14. Eliade, *The Sacred*, 35 ff. The idea of the cosmic pillar makes immediately intelligible the exclamation of the Kwakiutl initiate in his passage to manhood: "I am at the Center of the World!"

15. Eliade, *The Sacred*, 45.

16. Eliade, *The Sacred*, 46.

17. Eliade, *The Sacred*, 48. We can detect a flavor of the archaic identification of the enemy with darkness and chaos in Winston Churchill's "Finest Hour" speech, delivered to the House of Commons on June 18, 1940: "Hitler knows that he will have to break us in this island or lose the war. If we can stand up to him, all Europe may be freed and the life of the world may move forward into broad, sunlit uplands. But if we fail, then the whole world, including the United States, including all that we have known and cared for, will sink into the abyss of a new dark age made more sinister, and perhaps more protracted, by the lights of perverted science. Let us therefore brace ourselves to our duties, and so bear ourselves, that if the British Empire and its Commonwealth last for a thousand years, men will still say, 'This was their finest hour'." https://winstonchurchill.org/resources/speeches/1940-the-finest-hour/their-finest-hour/ (accessed March 12, 2019).

18. Eliade, *The Sacred*, 91.

19. Eliade, *The Sacred*, 103–04.

20. Hoebel, *Primitive Man*, 288–333; Stanley Diamond, "The Rule of Law Versus the Order of Custom," in Bonsignore et al, eds., *Before the Law: An Introduction to Legal Process* (Boston/New York: Houghton Mifflin, 2006), 233–8. I am following here the classical anthropological conception, which regards prehistoric society as passing through stages of development from bands, tribes, chiefdoms, to the early state. Keegan observes that contemporary anthropologists prefer a different, simpler scheme, which divides pre-state prehistoric societies into "egalitarian" and "hierarchical" stages. Keegan, *Warfare*, 103.

21. I will follow Henri Frankfort in using the term "Mesopotamians" to denote the Sumerians, Akkadians, Babylonians, and Assyrians.

22. Lewis Mumford, *The Myth of the Machine: Technics and Human Development* (New York: Harcourt, Brace, & World, 1967), 169.

23. Robert Bellah, *Religion in Human Evolution: From the Paleolithic to the Axial Age* (Cambridge, MA: Harvard University Press, 2011), 212.

24. Bellah, *Religion in Human Evolution*, 241.

25. Bellah, *Religion in Human Evolution*, 234.

26. Henri Frankfort, *Kingship and the Gods: A Study of Ancient Near Eastern Religion as the Integration of Society and Nature* (Chicago: University of Chicago Press, 1948), 6 and *passim*.

27. Leonard Woolley, *Ur "of the Chaldees,"* ed. P. R. S. Moorey (Ithaca: Cornell U. Press, 1982), 91.

28. Paul Wheatley, *The Pivot of the Four Quarters: A Preliminary Enquiry into the Origins and Character of the Ancient Chinese City* (Chicago: Aldine, 1971). See also Howard Spodek, *The World's History*, Volume I, *To 1500* (Upper Saddle River, NJ: Prentice Hall, 2000), 92–93; Bellah, *Religion in Human Evolution*, 252.

29. Bellah, *Religion in Human Evolution*, 234; Michael A. Hoffmann, *Egypt before the Pharaohs: The Prehistoric Foundations of Egyptian Civilization* (New York: Knopf, 1979), 336.

30. Originating as a club used to crush the skull of a wounded animal, the mace becomes a tool for dominating the king's opponents, be they unarmed farmers or enemy soldiers.

31. Guilaine and Zammit, *Origins of War*, 4. Bellah observes that the Pharaoh's role as the defender of cosmic order entailed a "smiting of the enemies," i.e., the destruction of foreign armies as a means of warding off the chaos they represent. Bellah, *Religion in Human Evolution*, 232–33.

32. Guilaine and Zammit, *Origins of War*, 2–3.

33. Quoted in Smith, *The Most Dangerous Animal*, 49.

34. Quoted in Guilaine and Zammit, *Origins of War*, 50.

35. Quoted in Bellah, *Religion in Human Evolution*, 222.

36. Assmann unfolds his interpretation of the changing nature of the Pharaoh's divinity in several works: see, e.g., Jan Assmann, *The Search for God in Ancient Egypt* (Ithaca: Cornell University Press, 2001); Assmann, *The Mind of Egypt: History and Meaning in the Time of the Pharaohs*, trans. Andrew Jenkins (Cambridge, MA: Harvard University Press, 2003).

37. Bellah, *Religion in Human Evolution*, 239.

38. Frankfort, *Birth of Civilization*, 54.

39. Jan Assman points out that the Egyptians lacked a word for "cosmos." Instead, they employed the hendiadys "heaven and earth." Here, in the interest of parallelism with our discussion of other cultures, we will use "cosmos" as a synonym for "heaven and earth." See Jan Assmann, *Tod und Jenseits im alten Ägypten* (Munich: C. H. Beck, 2010), 35.

40. Mircea Eliade, *A History of Religious Ideas: From the Stone Age to the Eleusinian Mysteries*, vol. 1 (Chicago: The University of Chicago Press, 1978), 91.

41. Frankfort, *Birth of Civilization*, 120.

42. Jan Assmann, *Ma'at: Gerichtigkeit und Unsterblichkeit im Alten Ägypten* (Munich: Verlag C.H. Beck, 2006), 35.

43. Ibid. The term "theopolitical order" is from Eric Voegelin, *Order and History*, vol. I: Israel and Revelation (Columbia and London: University of Missouri Press, 2001), 380.

44. Erik Hornung, "The Pharaoh," in *The Egyptians*, ed. Sergio Donadoni (Chicago: The University of Chicago Press, 1997), 284, 304; Eliade, *A History of Religious Ideas*, 91. Historian Rory Cox dates the association of the Pharaoh with the sungod Amun-Re even earlier (from the Middle Kingdom, 2055-1650 BCE). Rory Cox, "Expanding the History of the Just War: The Ethics of Ancient Egypt," *International Studies Quarterly* 61 (2017): 372.

45. Eliade, *A History of Religious Ideas*, 91; Colin Renfrew, *Prehistory: The Making of the Human Mind* (London: The Folio Society, 2013), 174. Likewise the Egyptian verb "khay" ("to shine") can mean either the sunrise or the Pharaoh's appearance at public ceremonies. Eliade, *A History of Religious Ideas*, 91.

46. Assmann, *Ma'at*, 9–10.

47. Assmann, *Ma'at*, 34.

48. Eliade, *A History of Religious Ideas*, 92. Re's battle against chaos is constant and his victory temporary, for it must be repeated every day as the sun temporarily vanquishes the darkness of night.

49. Erik Hornung, "The Pharaoh," 306.

50. Erik Hornung, "The Pharaoh," 306.

51. Erik Hornung, "The Pharaoh." The Egyptians may have prohibited night warfare because the glorious deeds of the Pharaoh would be obscured by darkness. Cox, "Just War," 374.

52. Cox, "Just War," 374.

53. Cox, "Just War," 376.

54. Quoted in Cox, "Just War," 376.

55. Cox, "Just War," 376.

56. Cox, "Just War," 378.

57. Quoted in Amnon Altman, "Tracing the Earliest Recorded Concepts of International Law. (3) The Ancient Near East in the Old Babylonian Period (2000–1595 BCE)," *Journal of the History of International Law* 10, no.1 (2008): 7.

58. Altman, "Tracing," 7.

59. Altman, "Tracing," 9–10.

60. I. J. Gelb, "Prisoners of War in Early Mesopotamia," *Journal of Near Eastern Studies* 32/1-2 (Jan.-Apr., 1973): 73–74. Gelb is by no means convinced that Rîmuš's account is historically accurate insofar as other Sumerian sources of the same period do not confirm the capture of war captives in such large numbers. This aside, Rîmuš's account likely reflects a widespread practice in Mesopotamia of killing enemy captives.

61. Gelb, "Prisoners of War," 82–83.

62. J. N. Postgate, *Early Mesopotamia: Society and Economy at the Dawn of History* (London & New York: Routledge, 1992), 255. See also Gelb, "Prisoners of War," 87.

63. Mark Edward Lewis, *Sanctioned Violence in Early China* (Albany: SUNY Press, 1990), 22–25.

64. Lewis, *Sanctioned Violence in Early China*, 38. See also Herrlee G. Creel, *The Origins of Statecraft in China* (Chicago: University of Chicago Press, 1970), 285–86.

65. Keegan, *Warfare*, 173.

66. Keegan, *Warfare*, 173.

67. Lewis, *Violence, passim*; Bellah, *Religion in Human Evolution*, 401.

68. Lewis, *Violence*, 18–19.

69. Lewis, *Violence*, 22–24.

70. Quoted in Lewis, *Violence*, 22–24.

71. Gary D. Solis, *The Law of Armed Conflict: International Humanitarian Law in War* (Cambridge and New York: Cambridge University Press, 2010), 4–5; M. Cherif Bassiouni, *Crimes against Humanity in International Criminal Law* (The Hague: Kluwer, 1999), 49.

72. Lewis, *Violence*, 127.

73. Bellah, *Religion in Human Evolution*, 405 ff.

74. The translations of ren and li are from Arthur Waley, *The Analects of Confucius* (London: Allen and Unwin, 1938).

75. Heiner Roetz, *Confucian Ethics of the Axial Age* (Albany: SUNY Press, 1993), 26–27.

76. Quoted in Bellah, *Religion in Human Evolution*, 413; Spodek, *World's History*, vol. 1, 204–5.

77. Lewis, *Violence*, 127–29.

78. Quoted in Bellah, *Religion in Human Evolution*, 414.

79. Quoted in Bellah, *Religion in Human Evolution*, 418.

80. Jean Guilaine and Jean Zammit, *Origins of War*, 422.

Notes

81. Guilaine and Zammit, *Origins of War*, 423 ff.

82. Quoted in Burton Watson, *Mo Tzu: Basic Writings* (New York: Columbia University Press, 1963), 40.

83. "Mozi." *Encyclopaedia Britannica Online*. Encyclopaedia Britannica Inc., 2013. Web. 24 May. 2013. http://www.britannica.com/EBchecked/topic/386700/Mozi

84. "Mozi."

85. *Mencius*, trans. D. C. Lau (Harmondsworth, UK, and New York: Penguin Books, 1970), 124.

86. *Mencius*, 68.

87. See *Mencius*, 86–87.

88. Lewis, *Violence*, 138 ff.

89. Bruce G. Trigger, *Understanding Early Civilizations: A Comparative Study* (New York: Cambridge University Press, 2003), 416.

90. Lewis, *Violence*, 222–232. The individual soldier was dissuaded from single acts of valor performed beyond the regulatory scope of the commander's guidance. The Greek reliance on such individual initiative, particularly from the front-line soldiers of the hoplite phalanx, had no counterpart in Han China.

91. i.e., the subcontinent of South Asia—modern-day India, Pakistan, Afghanistan, Bangladesh, Nepal, and Bhutan.

92. Bellah, *Religion in Human Evolution*, 488; Spodek, *World's History*, 232.

93. Bellah, *Religion in Human Evolution*, *Origins of War*, 493–94.

94. V. R. Ramachandra Dikshitar, *War in Ancient India* (New Delhi: Cosmos, 1999), 41. Significantly, the *Rigveda* did not distinguish between the forms of "just war" (*dharmayuddha*) and "unjust war" (*kutayuddha*), as do later Indian texts like the Book of Manu.

95. See, e.g., Clifford Geertz, "Local Knowledge: Fact and Law in Comparative Perspective," in *Local Knowledge: Further Essays in Interpretive Anthropology* (New York: Basic Books, 1983), 197; Bellah, *Religion in Human Evolution*, 519 ff.; H. S. Bhatia, *International Law and Practice in Ancient India* (New Delhi: Deep & Deep, 1977), 27, 123; W. S. Armour, "Customs of Warfare in Ancient India," *Transactions of the Grotius Society* 8 (1922): 78.

96. Wilhelm Halbfass, "*Dharma* in the Self-Understanding of Traditional Hinduism," in *India and Europe: An Essay in Understanding* (Albany, NY: SUNY Press, 1988), 310–33. See also Bellah, *Religion in Human Evolution*, 519 ff.

97. Halbfass, "*Dharma*," 317–18; Bellah, *Religion in Human Evolution*, 520.

98. Halbfass, "*Dharma*," 320–21; Bellah, *Religion in Human Evolution*, 520.

99. Geertz, "Local Knowledge," 196.

100. Geertz, "Local Knowledge," 198.

101. Dikshitar, *War in Ancient India*, 41 ff.

102. Thus, Bhatia insists, while the epics unconditionally condemn adharmic warfare, the apostle of Indian *Realpolitik*, Kautilya, released the warrior from the constraints of *dharmayuddha* if his opponent failed to respect them. Bhatia, *International Law*, 98–99. Dikshitar asserts that ancient Indian warriors were trained in both types of warfare, "and were expected to be well versed in all of them. The idea was to pay one in his own coin." *War in Ancient India*, 60–61.

103. L. R. Penna, "Humanitarian Law in Ancient India," *23 Mil. L. & L. War Rev* (1984): 235, 237.

104. Penna, "Humanitarian Law in Ancient India," 235, 237.

105. Penna, "Humanitarian Law in Ancient India," 236–37.

106. Dikshitar, *War in Ancient India*, quoting the Mahābhārata, 68.

107. Armour, "Customs of Warfare in Ancient India," 74.

108. M. K. Sinha, "Hinduism and International Humanitarian Law," *International Review of the Red Cross* 87 (858) (June 2005): 292; L. R. Penna, "Humanitarian Law in Ancient India."

109. Dikshitar, *War in Ancient India*, 68; Armour, "Customs of Warfare," 75.

110. Armour, "Customs of Warfare," 76–77.

111. The *Agni Purana*, written between 750 and 1000 CE, states that war captives were not to be enslaved but should be released once the war had ended. See, e.g., M. K. Sinha, "Hinduism," 292. This rule, if indeed followed, describes a practice that likely evolved centuries after the epics were composed. The evidence supports a practice among the ancient Indians of enslaving prisoners of war for at least a certain term.

112. Dikshitar, *War in Ancient India*, 72.

113. Quoted in Armour, "Customs of Warfare," 76.

114. H. S. Bhatia, *International Law*, 100–01.

115. Bellah, *Religion in Human Evolution*, 521.

116. Armour, "Customs of Warfare," 78. For a conflicting view, see Bhatia, *International Law*, 26, 93.

117. Bhatia, *International Law*, 31.

118. Bhatia, *International Law*, 98–99.

119. Bhatia, *International Law*, 173–74.

120. Kautilya moreover held that his tough-minded approach to inter-state relations would preserve a balance of power that would ultimately conduce to peace. See the discussion in Bhatia, *International Law*, 124.

121. Bellah, in *Religion in Human Evolution*, 546.

122. Will and Ariel Durant, *Our Oriental Heritage* (New York: Simon & Schuster, 1935), 446–47.

123. Bhatia, *International Law*, 134.

124. Bhatia, *International Law*, 129–30.

125. Sinha, "Hinduism and International Humanitarian Law," 291–92; Lakshmikanth Penna, "Traditional Asian Approaches: An Indian View," *Australian Yearbook of International Law*, vol. 9 (1985): 180 ff.

126. Lanni, "Laws of War," 486.

127. The "Seven Nations" comprised the Canaanites, the Jebusites, the Amorites, the Perizzites, the Hivites, the Hittites, and the Girgashites (Deuteronomy 7:1).

128. Deuteronomy 7:1–3 (*New English Bible*).

129. Deuteronomy 20: 10–14 (*New English Bible*).

130. Deuteronomy 20: 15–18 (*New English Bible*).

131. Numbers 31 (*New English Bible*).

132. This wholesale destruction of an enemy people was called the "solemn ban." The New English Bible describes it as "meaning that the city and all that is in it is to be offered as a holocaust to God . . .; no booty is allowed to be taken . . . and any deviation would be a sacrilege to be severely punished." *New English Bible*, 228n17. On the solemn ban (*herem*), see C. Brekelmans, *De Herem in Het Oude Testment* (Nijmegen: Centrale Drukkerij, 1959); P.D. Stern, *The Biblical Herem: A Window on Israel's Religious Experience* (Providence, RI: Brown Judaic Studies, 1991).

133. 1 Samuel 15:24–33.

134. Judges 1:6–7. In this case, the Israelites may have been punishing the Canaanite king in accordance with the law of talio: Adoni-bezek was notorious for removing the thumbs and toes of rival kings so as to render them unfit as warriors.

135. 1 Samuel 18:27–29.

136. See, e.g., M. G. Brett, "Genocide in Deuteronomy: Postcolonial Variations on Mimetic Desire," in *Deuteronomy and the Deuteronomic Literature: Festschrift C. H. W. Brekelmans*, ed. M. Vervenne and J. Lust (Leuven: Leuven University Press, 1997), 3–38; Y. Suzuki, "A New Aspect of ḥrm in Deuteronomy in View of an Assimilation Policy of King Josiah," *AJBL* 21 (1995): 3–27.

137. Jan Assmann, *Totale Religion: Ursprünge und Formen puritanischer Verschärfung* (Vienna: Picus Verlag, 2016), 51. Assmann notes the existence of archaeological evidence for the ban outside Hebrew culture. On the stele of King Mescha of Moab (mid-ninth century BCE) we read: "I attacked the city [of Atarot] and conquered it. And I killed all of the people of the city as victims for Kemosch and for Moab. [...] And I struck out by night and at dawn fought against [Nebo] until midday. And I took it and killed everyone: 7,000 men and slaves and women and prostitutes, because I had dedicated them to Kemosch."

138. Susan Niditch, *War in the Hebrew Bible: A Study in the Ethics of Violence* (New York: Oxford University Press, 1995), *passim*.

139. Assmann, *Totale Religion*, 122–25.

140. C. L. Crouch, *War and Ethics in the Ancient Near East: Military Violence in Light of Cosmology and History* (Berlin: Walter de Gruyter, 2009); Charles Trimm, "Recent Research on Warfare in the Old Testament," *Currents in Biblical Research* 10, no. 2 (2012): 187–88. On this topic, see also the citations in Trimm, 186.

141. T. A. Walker, *A History of the Law of Nations, Vol. I: From the Earliest Times to the Peace of Westphalia, 1648* (Cambridge: Cambridge University Press, 1899), 35 ff.

142. Walker, *Law of Nations*, 35. The fate of Saul and his sons is told in 1 Samuel 31:8–10.

143. Walker, *Law of Nations*, 35–36; 2 Kings 8:12.

144. Walker, *Law of Nations*, 36; 2 Kings 6: 21–23.

145. Bellah, *Religion in Human Evolution*, 306.

146. Deuteronomy 17:14–15, quoted in Bellah, *Religion in Human Evolution*, 312.

147. Bellah, *Religion in Human Evolution*, 312.

148. Bellah, *Religion in Human Evolution*, 316.

149. Eric Weil, "What is a Breakthrough in History?" *Daedalus* 104, no. 2 (Spring 1975): 21–36, cited in Bellah, *Religion in Human Evolution*, 281–82.

150. Deuteronomy 20:19–20. Walker writes that "we see the beginning of a definite Law of War" in this passage. *Law of Nations*, 36.

151. Adriaan Lanni, "The Laws of War in Ancient Greece," *Law and History Review* 26, no. 3 (Fall 2008): 472.

152. Rosalind Thomas, "Written in Stone? Liberty, Equality, Orality and the Codification of Law," in *Greek Law in Its Political Setting: Justifications, Not Justice*, ed. L. Foxhall and A. D. E. Lewis (Oxford: Clarendon Press, 1996), 31.

153. Lanni, "The Laws of War," 472.

154. Cicero, *Laws*, VI. 762 E.

155. Yvon Garlan, *War in the Ancient World: A Social History* (New York: W. W. Norton, 1975), 58; Lanni, "The Laws of War," 477. See also Lanni's primary source citations in notes 30–36, e.g., Pausanias, Xenophon, Polybius, Homer, Plutarch, and Thucydides.

156. Lanni, "The Laws of War," 478.

157. Plutarch, *Agis* 21, cited in Lanni, "The Laws of War," 487.

158. Thucydides, *The Peloponnesian War* (London: The Folio Society, 2006), 468–69. The citation is in Lanni, "The Laws of War," 487n91.

159. *The History of Herodotus*, transl. George Rawlinson (Chicago/London/Toronto: Encyclopedia Britannica, 1952), 205.

160. Lanni, "The Laws of War," 489.

161. Lanni defines the functions of each office: heralds were "professional messengers used to communicate with foreign states"; ambassadors were citizens "appointed to represent their polis and negotiate with a foreign state." Lanni, "The Laws of War," 478.

162. Lanni, "The Laws of War," 478; Garlan, *War*, 58. Lanni identifies the primary sources for this information about the sacred status of heralds: Homer in the *Iliad* (1/334), Pausanias (1.36.3), and Herodotus (7.133-6).

163. Lanni, "The Laws of War," 478; Garlan, *War*, 61.

164. Lanni, "The Laws of War," 478–79. See her references to the primary sources in footnotes 48 and 49 (Euripides, *Suppliant Women* 19, 311, 526, and Thucydides 4.97–101). The issue of the proper treatment of the enemy dead is at the heart of Sophocles's *Antigone*, where Antigone insists on her right to bury her dead brother, Polyneices, because burial fulfilled both the requirements of her family and the gods.

165. Plato, *Republic* 332a, cited in Lanni, "The Laws of War," 479n51.

166. Xenophon, *Cyropaedia* 7.5.73, and Aristotle, *Politics*, bk. 1, chap. 6, lines 6–7, 1255a6-8, both quoted in Lanni, "The Laws of War," 580nn54 and 55.

167. See, e.g., the catalogue of atrocities in W. Kendrick Pritchett, *The Greek State at War* (Berkeley: University of California Press, 1991), 218–19, 226–34, 247–71.

168. Herodotus 6.80; Thucydides 1.106, both cited in Lanni, "The Laws of War," 480nn57 and 58.

169. Lanni, "The Laws of War," 480.

170. Garlan, *War*, 71–72.

171. Lanni, "The Laws of War," 481; Garlan, *War*, 68–69.

172. Ober's theory is that these rules served the interests of the hoplite social class. The prohibition of non-hoplite arms like arrows ensured that the hoplite soldiers would receive exclusive honor for military victory. The rule limiting pursuit of retreating opponents was required to keep the hoplites massed together; dispersal of the soldiers would cause the hoplites to forfeit their military advantage. Another "common custom of the Hellenes" was the restriction of war to the summer months, a rule that enabled the hoplite soldiers, who were predominately farmers, to fight and return in time for the harvest. See Josiah Ober, "Classical Greek Times," in *The Laws of War: Constraints on Warfare in the Western World*, ed. M. Howard, G. J. Andreopoulos, and M. R. Shulman (New Haven, CT: Yale University Press, 1994), 13.

173. Hanson sets forth this traditional account in several scholarly works. See, e.g., Victor Davis Hanson, "The Ideology of Hoplite Battle, Ancient and Modern," in *Hoplites: The Classical Greek Battle Experience*, ed. Victor Davis Hanson (New York: Routledge, 1991), 3–14; Hanson, *The Western Way of War* (New York: Random House, 2005), 14–18, 36, 223; Hanson, *A War Like No Other: How the Athenians and Spartans Fought the Peloponnesian War* (New York: Random House, 2005), 299–300.

174. According to Ober, an adherent of the traditional account, the Peloponnesian War was decisive in this change because the Athenians relied on their naval power rather than a hoplite army for their military campaigns. Further, wars were now fought for longer periods of time and often by highly trained mercenaries carrying light arms, who disregarded the hoplite aversion to hot pursuit of a retreating foe. Ober, "Classical Greek Times," in 19, 23.

175. Lanni, "The Laws of War," 487, quoting Aristotle, *Politics* 1255a6–8.

176. Lanni, "The Laws of War," 486.

177. Thucydides, *The History of the Peloponnesian War* (London: Folio, 2006), 273–4 (4.97–98), quoted in Lanni, "The Laws of War," 473.

178. Thucydides, *History*, 182 (3.56), cited in Lanni, *Laws of War*, 473.

179. Polybius 5.9–10, cited in Lanni, *Laws of War*, 474.

180. Demosthenes XXIII, 82, quoted in Garlan, *War*, 38.

181. Garlan, *War*, 39.

182. Lanni, *Laws of War*, 475.

183. Herodotus, *History*, 237–38 (7.133–136), also cited in Lanni, "Laws of War," 475. Herodotus was unsure whether "the laying waste of [the Athenians'] city and territory" was indeed related to the murder of the Persian envoys or to some other cause. In this same account, Xerxes, king of the Persians, refused to deal with the Greeks as they had with his envoys; he would not stoop to such a depth of moral villainy in breaking "the laws which all men hold in common."

184. Pausanias 1.36.3, cited in Lanni, "Laws of War," 475n23.

185. See, e.g., Aeschylus, *The Oresteia: Agamemnon, The Libation Bearers, The Eumenides* (New York: Penguin Classics, 1984). The Greek lawgiver Solon (sixth century BCE) agreed with the Biblical view that the "sins of the fathers" would be transferred to their descendants. Lanni, "Laws of War," 475n24.

186. Coleman Phillipson, *The International Law and Custom of Ancient Greece and Rome* (London: Macmillan, 1911), 40.

187. *The Politics of Aristotle*, ed. and trans. Ernest Barker (Oxford/London/New York: Oxford University Press, 1958), 16 (I.vi.6).

188. Garlan, *War*, 71–72.

189. Ober, "Classical Greek Times," 13.

190. Ober, "Classical Greek Times," 18.

191. Thucydides, *Peloponnesian War*, 168–79 (3.36–50).

192. Lanni, "Laws of War," 482.

193. Excerpted in Joel Feinberg and Jules Coleman, eds., *Philosophy of Law* (Belmont, CA: Thomson-Wadsworth, 2004), 32.

194. Walker, *History*, 43.

2 The Law of War in Pre-Columbian America

1. Linda Schele and David Freidel, *A Forest of Kings: The Untold Story of the Ancient Maya* (New York: William Morrow and Co., 1990), 65.

2. On dualism in Western theology, see John Cobb, *God and the World* (Philadelphia: The Westminster Press, 1969), 69 ff.

3. Schele and Freidel, *Forest*, 65. One of the first proponents of the king as shaman thesis was Peter Furst in his 1976 article "Fertility, Vision Quest and Auto-Sacrifice: Some Thoughts on Ritual Blood-lettering Among the Maya," in *The Art, Iconography, and Dynastic History of Palenque, Part II: Proceedings of the Segunda Mesa Redonda de Palenque*, ed. Merle Green Robertson (Pebble Beach, CA: Robert Louis Stevenson School, 1976), 211–24.

4. Schele and Freidel, *Forest*, 67–70.

5. Schele and Freidel, *Forest*, 74–76. The myth of the Twins is recounted in the sacred Mayan scripture the Popol Vuh.

6. Schele and Freidel, *Forest*, 124–26; Mark A. Burkholder and Lyman L. Johnson, *Colonial Latin America* (New York: Oxford UP, 2001), 8.

7. On the distinction between territorial empires and city-states, see Trigger, *Understanding Early Civilizations*

8. Schele and Freidel, *Forest*, 146–49, 443n45.

9. Schele and Freidel, *Forest*, 147. The headwaters of the Tlaloc-Venus complex may have been Teotihuacán, from whom the Maya acquired the Tlaloc-Venus costume. See the discussion in Schele and Freidel, *Forest*, 159ff.

10. Schele and Freidel, *Forest*, 153.

11. Schele and Freidel, *Forest*, 452n66 and 464n76.

12. Burkholder and Johnson, *Colonial Latin America*, 13–14.

13. Benjamin Keen, *Latin American Civilization: History and Society, 1492 to the Present* (Boulder, CO: Westview, 2000), 6.

14. Curt Muser, *Facts and Artifacts of Ancient Middle America* (New York: E. P. Dutton, 1978), 76.

15. Nigel Davies, *The Aztecs* (London: Folio Society, 2000), 103–04, 184.

16. See, e.g., Burkholder/Johnson, *Colonial Latin America*, 18.

17. Davies, *The Aztecs*, 180.

18. Davies, *The Aztecs*, 114–15.

19. Davies, *The Aztecs*, 184–85.

20. See, e.g., Richard E. Blanton, "A Consideration of Causality in the Growth of Empire," in F. F. Burden et al, ed., *Aztec Imperial Strategies* (Washington, D.C.: Dumbarton Oaks, 1996), 219–25. While insisting that Aztec warfare was "profoundly conditioned by" the capture of prisoners for sacrifice, Davies concedes that other causes may have been involved. *The Aztecs*, 203.

21. Quoted in Keen, *Latin American Civilization*, 4.

22. Davies writes that, among other evidences of human sacrifice at Teotihuacán, the cult of the Flayed God was celebrated there. *The Aztecs*, 183. Burkholder and Johnson believe that the ferocity of the Aztecs may have been more proximately due to Toltec influences in the fusion of the Chichimec nobility with the Toltec aristocracy after 1246 CE. *Colonial Latin America*, 13.

23. Davies, *The Aztecs*, 183–84.

24. Ashley Kendell, "The Crow Creek Massacre: The Role of Sex in Native American Scalping Practices," in *Archaeological Perspectives on Warfare on the Great Plains*, Andrew J. Clark and Douglas B. Bamforth, eds., (Boulder, CO: University Press of Colorado, 2018), 321.

25. Robert H. Lowie, *Primitive Society* (New York: Boni and Liveright, 1920), 356.

Notes

26. R. H. Lowie, *An Introduction to Cultural Anthropology* (New York: Rinehart & Co., 1940), 221–22.

27. Clark Wissler, *Indians of the United States: Four Centuries of Their History and Culture* (New York: Doubleday and Company, 1941), 159.

28. Bernard Mishkin, *Rank and Warfare in Plains Indian Culture* (Seattle: University of Washington Press, 1940), 61–62.

29. W. W. Newcomb, "A Re-examination of the Causes of Plains Warfare," *American Anthropologist* 52/3 (July/Sept. 1950), 323.

30. Douglas B. Bamforth, "What Do We Know about Warfare on the Great Plains?", in *Archaeological Perspectives on Warfare on the Great Plains*, A. J. Clark and D. B. Bamforth, eds. (Boulder: University Press of Colorado, 2018), 21. The increase in intensity and scale of conflict is, for Bamforth, "the strongest pattern" in Plains warfare, apparent as early as 500 CE in the south and west.

31. See, for example, Jeffrey Blick's contention that such high casualty, systematic aggression was rare before contact with Europeans. J. P. Blick, "Genocidal Warfare in Tribal Societies as a Result of European-induced Culture Conflict," *Man* 23 (1988): 674–70. See also B. Ferguson, "Tribal Warfare," *Scientific American* 266 (1992): 108–16; idem and N. Whitehead, *War in the Tribal Zone* (Santa Fe: School of American Research Press, 1992), 113. Blick goes so far as to reaffirm the "war as game" construct of Crow warfare advocated by Lowie half a century before.

32. Frank Secoy, *Changing Military Patterns on the Great Plains* (New York: Augustin, 1952). Secoy's thesis is based on the testimony of a Cree Indian named Saukamapee who lived most of his life among the Blackfoot Indians in the third and fourth decades of the eighteenth century.

33. Douglas Bamforth, "Indigenous People, Indigenous Violence: PreContact Warfare on the North American Great Plains," *Man* 29 (March 1994): 110. On the role of dehumanization in producing atrocities during wartime, see infra, Chapter 10, p. 294 ff.

34. Kendell, "Crow Creek Massacre," 330.

35. Kendell, "Crow Creek Massacre," 330 ff.

36. Bamforth, "Indigenous People, Indigenous Violence," 100 ff. Bamforth notes that the mass murder at the Larson site falls within Blick's category of "genocidal" warfare.

37. This is the position of ethnohistorian Linea Sundstrom, who argues that Crow Creek was "more anomalous than representative of Plains Indian lifeways in the precontact era." Linea Sundstrom, "Coup Counts and Corn Caches: Contact-Era Plains Indian Accounts of Warfare," in *Archaeological Perspectives on Warfare on the Great Plains*, Andrew J. Clark and Douglas B. Bamforth, ed. (Boulder: UP of Colorado, 2018), 120–21.

38. Daniel K. Richter, "War and Culture: The Iroquois Experience," *The William and Mary Quarterly* 40/4 (Oct. 1983): 533–34; Wayne E. Lee, "Peace Chiefs and Blood Revenge: Patterns of Restraint in Native American Warfare 1500–1800, *The Journal of Military History*, Vol. 71, No. 3 (July 2007), 730–31.

39. Richter, "War and Culture," 534; Thomas S. Abler, "Iroquois Cannibalism: Fact not Fiction," *Ethnohistory* XXVII (1980): 309–16. Richter subscribes to a view of prisoner maltreatment not unlike the consensus theories of Émile Durkheim: for Richter public participation in the ritual abuse and killing of a war captive "promoted group cohesion and demonstrated to the Iroquois their superiority over their enemies."

40. Quoted in Richter, "War and Culture," 544.

41. Quoted in F.W. Hodge, G.P. Hammond, and A. Rey, eds., *Fray Alonso de Benavides' Revised Memorial of 1634* (Albuquerque: University of New Mexico Press, 1945), 43.

42. Elsie Clews Parsons, *Taos Pueblo* (Menash, WI: George Banta, 1936), 21. Jonathan Haas and Winifred Creamer write that scalp societies and dances were documented by anthropologists at other pueblo villages: Zia, Santa Clara, San Juan, San Ildefonso, Nambe, Hope, and several others. J. Has and W. Creamer, "Warfare among the Pueblos: Myth, History, and Ethnography," *Ethnohistory* 44/2 (Spring 1997): 246.

43. Adolf Bandelier, *Final Report of Investigations among the Indians of the Southwestern United States*, Part 1 (Boston: Papers of the Archaeological Institute of America, American Series, No. 3, 1890), 153.

44. The Zuni origin myth is retold in Matilda Cox Stevenson, *The Zuni Indians: Their Mythology, Esoteric Fraternities, and Ceremonies. Twenty-third Annual Report of the Bureau of American Ethnology* (Washington, D.C.: Government Printing Office, 1904), 34–35.

45. Stevenson, *The Zuni*, 55–56.

46. Leslie A. White, *The Pueblo of Santa Ana, New Mexico. Memoirs of the American Anthropological Association*, No. 43 (Menasha, WI: American Anthropological Association, 1942), 304.

47. Michael Lomatuway'ma et al., *Hopi Ruin Legends*, ed. and trans. Ekkehart Malotki (Lincoln, NE: University of Nebraska Press, 1993).

3 The Law of War in Rome, the Islamic World, and the European Middle Ages

1. Yvon Garlan, *War in the Ancient World: A Social History* (New York: W. W. Norton, 1975), 45–46.

2. Coleman Phillipson, *The International Law and Custom of Ancient Greece and Rome*, Vol. I (London: Macmillan, 1911), 336; John Rich, "Roman Rituals of War," in *The Oxford Handbook of Warfare in the Classical World*, ed. Brian Campbell and Lawrence A. Tritle (Oxford and New York: Oxford University Press, 2013), 560; Thomas Alfred Walker, *A History of the Law of Nations*, Vol. I (Cambridge: Cambridge University Press, 1899), 47; Alan Watson, *International Law in Archaic Rome* (Baltimore and London: The Johns Hopkins University Press, 1993), 53.

3. Rich, "Roman Rituals of War," 563–64.

4. Watson, *Archaic Rome*, 62–63.

5. Watson, *Archaic Rome*, 54.

6. Watson, *Archaic Rome*, 60. Our last reference to the fetials is found in Ammianus Marcellinus, 19.2.6.

7. The demand of the Romans that their wars be legally justified and divinely approved is widely discussed in the literature. See, e.g., Rich, "Roman Rituals of War," 564; Frederick H. Russell, *The Just War in the Middle Ages* (Cambridge: Cambridge University Press, 1975), 7–8; Robert C. Stacey, "The Age of Chivalry," in Michael Howard, George J. Andreopoulos, and Mark R. Shulman, eds., *The Laws of War: Constraints on Warfare in the Western World* (New Haven and London: Yale University Press, 1994), 27; Clifford Ando, "Aliens, Ambassadors, and the Integrity of the Empire," *Law and History Review* 26, no. 3 (Fall 2008): 496.

8. Quoted in Walker, *Law of Nations*, 48.

9. John Keegan, *A History of Warfare* (New York: Vintage, 1993), 265.

10. Walker, *Law of Nations*, 48.

11. Quoted in Keegan, *History of Warfare*, 265.

12. Keegan, *History of Warfare*, 265.

13. Walker, *Law of Nations*, 60–61.

14. Henry S. Maine, *Village Communities in the East and West* (London: John Murray, 1871), 193–94, cited in Phillipson, *International Law and Custom*, 71.

15. Frederick Carl von Savigny, *System des heutigen römischen Rechts*, Volume I (Heidelberg, 1840–51), 22; Theodor Mommsen, *Römisches Staatsrecht*, Volume III (Leipzig, 1887–8), 603–6. Both works are cited in Phillipson, *International Law and Custom*, 72 and 74, respectively.

16. Clifford Ando, "Aliens, Ambassadors, and the Integrity of the Empire," 497–98.

17. Phillipson, *International Law and Custom*, 331.

18. *Rhetoric*, I.13, quoted in Phillipson, *International Law and Custom*, 53.

19. Sophocles, *Antigone* II. 456–7, quoted in Phillipson, *International Law and Custom*, 53.

20. Quoted in Phillipson, *International Law and Custom*, 54.

21. Marcus Tullius Cicero, *Laws*, Book I, in *The Great Legal Philosophers: Selected Readings in Jurisprudence*, ed. Clarence Morris (Philadelphia: University of Pennsylvania Press, 1959), 46.

22. Cicero, *Laws*, Book I. 46.

23. Cicero, *On Duties*, Book III.28.

24. Cicero, *Laws*, 50–51.

25. Cicero, *Laws*, 50–51.

26. "Peregrine" is from the Latin *peregrinus*, or "foreign."

27. The "civil law," or *jus civile*, consisted of the Roman Law of the 12 Tables plus all subsequent legislation that enlarged it and authoritative judicial rulings that interpreted it. W. C. Morey, *Outlines of Roman Law, Comprising its Historical Growth and General Principles* (New York and London: G. P. Putnam's Sons, 1884), 69.

28. W. C. Morey, *Outlines*, 63; Barry Nicholson, *An Introduction to Roman Law* (Oxford: Oxford University Press, 1969), 4. On the relationship between the *jus gentium*, natural law, and the peregrine praetor, see Stephen C. Neff, *Justice Among Nations: A History of International Law* (Cambridge: Harvard University Press, 2014), 44–49. Neff contrasts Roman "global law" with that of the Chinese: for Neff, the Chinese construed global law as the decrees of a "single hegemon, the Chinese emperor," whereas the Romans identified it with the "idea of an impersonal and universal rule of law." (p. 48) The consequences were momentous. The differences in interpretation meant that international law would originate in Europe and not China.

29. Morey, *Outlines*, 66–7; C. E. Brand, *Roman Military Law* (Austin: University of Texas Press, 1968), 13–14.

30. Morey, *Outlines*, 70.

31. Morey, *Outlines*, 71.

32. William Harris, *War and Imperialism in Republican Rome* (Oxford: Oxford University Press, 1979), 48, quoted in Keegan, *History of Warfare*, 265–66.

33. Walker, *A History of the Law of Nations*, 61.

34. Thucydides, I.5, quoted in Garlan, *War in the Ancient World*, 32.

35. Garlan, *War in the Ancient World*, 33.

36. Garlan, *War in the Ancient World*, 36–37; Frederick H. Russell, *The Just War in the Middle Ages* (Cambridge: Cambridge University Press, 1975), 5.

37. Our principal sources for early Islamic views of the Law of War are the Qur'ān, the eighth- century biography of Ibn Ish. āq, and H. adīth, a record of sayings associated with Muhammad. The discussion of Islamic treatment of war captives is based on Lena Salaymeh, "Early Islamic Legal-Historical Precedents: Prisoners of War," *Law and History Review* 26/3 (Fall 2008): 521–44.

38. Muh. ammad Ibn Ish. āq, *The Life of Muh. ammad: A Translation of Ish. āq's rasūl Allāh*, trans. Alfred Guillaume (Karachi: Oxford University Press, 2004), 309, cited in Salaymeh, "Early Islamic Legal-Historical Precedents," 525.

39. Salaymeh, "Early Islamic Legal-Historical Precedents," 525.

40. Salaymeh, "Early Islamic Legal-Historical Precedents," 526.

41. Salaymeh, "Early Islamic Legal-Historical Precedents," 527.

42. Qur'ān 9:5, *The Holy Qur'ān*, 497, quoted in Salaymeh, "Early Islamic Legal-Historical Precedents," 529.

43. Muh. ammad ibn al-h. asan al-Shaybānī, *The Islamic Law of Nations: Shaybānī's Siyar*, trans. Majid Khadduri (Baltimore: Johns Hopkins Press, 1966), 100, cited in Salaymeh, "Early Islamic Legal-Historical Precedents," 530.

44. Quoted in Salaymeh, "Early Islamic Legal-Historical Precedents," 530–31.

45. Salaymeh, "Early Islamic Legal-Historical Precedents," 532.

46. Salaymeh, "Early Islamic Legal-Historical Precedents," 531.

47. On the failure of just war ideology to reduce the violence of war, see G. I. A. D. Draper, "The Interaction of Christianity and Chivalry in the Historical Development of the Laws of War," *The International Review of the Red Cross* (January 1965): 5 ff.

48. Noor Mohammad, "The Doctrine of Jihad: An Introduction," *Journal of Law & Religion* 3/2 (1985): 389; M. Khadduri, *War and Peace in the Law of Islam* (Baltimore: The Johns Hopkins University Press, 1955), 56–57.

49. Keegan, *A History of Warfare*, 193; Mohammad, "Jihad," 389–90.

50. Aristotle coined the phrase "just war" to designate armed conflict between the Greeks and non-Greeks (barbarians). According to Aristotle, war was only legitimate when it was waged in self-defense, to acquire an empire beneficial to the subjects of a territory, or to enslave inferior people undeserving of freedom (again, the barbarians). Russell, *The Just War in the Middle Ages*, 3–4.

51. Russell, *The Just War in the Middle Ages*, 11.

52. Period of relative peace established by Augustus (27 BCE–14 CE) and continuing through the reign of Marcus Aurelius (161–180 CE), affecting the Mediterranean, North Africa, and Persia.

53. Russell, *The Just War in the Middle Ages*, 12.

54. See, e.g., the Theodosian Code, 438 CE, http://www.fordham.edu/halsall/source/ theodcodeXVI. html (accessed October 13, 2014).

55. Russell, *The Just War in the Middle Ages*, 13.

56. Russell, *The Just War in the Middle Ages*, 20.

57. Russell, *The Just War in the Middle Ages*, 18–19; Richard S. Hartigan, "Saint Augustine on War and Killing," *Journal of the History of Ideas* 27 (1966): 195–204.

58. Russell, *The Just War in the Middle Ages*, 20–21. The story of Joshua's encounter with the Amorites is found in Numbers 21: 21–25.

Notes

59. Russell, *The Just War in the Middle Ages*, 22–3. See also Russell's citations to Augustine's texts in footnotes 19, 20, and 22 on p. 22 (*Against Faust, Confessions*, and *The City of God*).

60. Christopher Tyerman, *The Crusades: A Very Short Introduction* (Oxford: Oxford University Press, 2004), 75.

61. Tyerman, *The Crusades*, 73–74.

62. Keegan, *A History of Warfare*, 295.

63. Tyerman, *The Crusades*, 82.

64. Isidore, *Etymologiae*, XVIII, i, quoted in Maurice Keen, *The Laws of War in the Late Middle Ages* (London: Routledge, 1965), 66.

65. Keen, *The Laws of War*, 66.

66. See citations to each of these canonists' works describing just war theory in Keen, *The Law of War*, 66 notes 7–10.

67. Quoted in James A. Brundage, "The Hierarchy of Violence in Twelfth- and Thirteenth- Century Canonists," *The International History Review* XVII/4 (1995): 678.

68. Brundage, "The Hierarchy of Violence," 676–78.

69. Historian Robert Stacey mentions that, while it seldom happened, Roman War was sometimes fought between Christian armies. He cites the example of the French army at Crécy and Poitiers at the onset of the Hundred Years War, which was given orders to give no quarter. Likewise, French forces under Joan of Arc fought a Roman War at Orléans against the English. Robert C. Stacey, "The Age of Chivalry," *The Laws of War*, 33.

70. Augustine, *Epistolae*, CLXXXIX, 6, quoted in James A. Brundage, "The Hierarchy of Violence," 66.

71. Augustine, *Contra Faustum*, XII, 75, quoted in Brundage, "The Hierarchy of Violence," 69.

72. Bartolus, *Tractatus de Reprisaliis*, III, 2, and Nicholas of Tudeschi, *Lectura Super V Libros Decretalium, 2 Decretal.*, Tit. 24, cap. 39, both quoted in Brundage, "The Hierarchy of Violence."

73. Keen, *The Laws of War*, 105–106; Robert C. Stacey, "The Age of Chivalry," in *The Laws of War*, 33.

74. Keen, *The Laws of War*, 106; Stacey, "The Age of Chivalry," 34.

75. Keen, *The Laws of War*, 108–109; Stacey, "The Age of Chivalry," 38–39.

76. Keen, *The Laws of War*, 110.

77. James A. Brundage, *The Crusades, Holy War, and Canon Law* (Lawrence, KS: Variorum, 1991), 76.

78. Brundage, *The Crusades, Holy War, and Canon Law*, 78–79.

79. Brundage, *The Crusades, Holy War, and Canon Law*, 79.

80. Brundage, *The Crusades, Holy War, and Canon Law*, 81.

81. Brundage, *The Crusades, Holy War, and Canon Law*, 83–84.

82. Brundage, *The Crusades, Holy War, and Canon Law*, 84.

83. Brundage, *The Crusades, Holy War, and Canon Law*, 84.

84. Stacey, "Age of Chivalry," 30.

85. The French knights had surrendered to the Duke of Lancaster, John of Gaunt. John accepted their plea and accorded them full protection as his prisoners. *Oeuvres de Froissart*, ed. Kervyn de Lettenhove (Brussels 1869), cited in Keen, *The Law of War*, 1.

86. Froissart relates that Edward the Black Prince and his knights, in their efforts to punish the Bishop of Limoges for an alleged betrayal, struck down every man, woman, and child they encountered during the sack of Limoges, whether or not the hapless victims were involved in

the betrayal of Edward, and even though the victims begged for mercy on their knees. Jean de Froissart, *Oeuvres de Froissart*, vol. 8 (Brussels 1869), 38.

87. Stacey, "Age of Chivalry," 30.

88. Keen, *The Laws of War*, 23.

89. Keen, *The Laws of War*, 26–27. Like their counterpart in England, the French Courts of the Constable and the Marshals of France date back to the early fourteenth century.

90. Keen, *The Laws of War*, 27.

91. Keen, *The Laws of War*, 21–22.

92. Keen, *The Laws of War*, 22.

93. Stacey, "Age of Chivalry," 31–32.

94. Stacey, "Age of Chivalry," 37.

95. Keen, *The Laws of War*, 25–26.

96. Pedro Lopez d'Ayala, *Cronicas de Los Reyes de Castilla*, Vol. I (Madrid, 1779–80), 458–61, as retold in Keen, *The Laws of War*, 50–52.

97. Keen, *The Laws of War*, 51–52.

98. Keen, *The Laws of War*, 119.

99. *Chronique du bon Duc Louis de Bourbon*, ed. A-M. Chazaud, 143, quoted in Keen, *The Laws of War*, 120.

100. Keen, *The Laws of War*, 121–22.

101. Keen, *The Laws of War*, 123.

102. The language of Talbot's indictment is reproduced in Keen, *The Laws of War*, 124: Stafford had surrendered La Ferté Bernard "sans assault et sans engins . . . et de raison et par le droit darmes il a tout confisque et s'est rendu indigne." ("without assault and engines and on the basis of the law of arms everything is confiscated and he is made dishonorable").

103. Keen, *The Laws of War*, 87.

104. Keen, *The Laws of War*, 48–50.

105. Keen, *The Laws of War*, 50.

106. Burckhardt's story of Paolo Vitelli is retold in Theodore Draper, "The Interaction of Christianity and Chivalry in the Historical Development of the Laws of War," *The International Review of the Red Cross* (January 1965): 18.

107. Steven Runciman, *A History of the Crusades, Volume I: The First Crusade and the Foundation of the Kingdom of Jerusalem* (London: The Folio Society, 1994), 237.

108. For a more critical account of Muslim military actions during the Crusades, see David M. Crowe, *War Crimes, Genocide, and Justice: A Global History* (New York: Palgrave Macmillan, 2014), 19–20.

109. Runciman, *Crusades, Volume II: The Kingdom of Jerusalem and the Frankish East 1100–1187*, 379–80.

110. Runciman, *Crusades, Volume III: The Kingdom of Acre and the Later Crusades*, 46.

111. Draper, "Interaction," 12–13.

112. Runciman, *Crusades*, Volume III, 104.

113. Draper, "Interaction," 21.

114. Draper, "Interaction," 21.

4 Making Law in the Slaughterhouse of the World: Early Modernity and the Law of War

1. Theodor Meron, "Medieval and Renaissance Ordinances of War: Codifying Discipline and Humanity," in *War Crimes Law Comes of Age: Essays* (Oxford: Oxford University Press, 1998), 1. Meron states that the first multilateral agreement bearing on the Law of War was the first Geneva Convention of 1864. The first multilateral treaty having as its object the limitation of naval warfare was the Paris Declaration on Maritime War of 1856: http://www. icrc. org/applic/ihl/ihl.nsf/ Article.xsp?action=openDocument&documentId=473FCB0F41 DCC63BC12563CD0051492D (accessed December 28, 2013).

2. Meron, "Medieval and Renaissance Ordinances," 2.

3. Meron, "Medieval and Renaissance Ordinances," 2.

4. Meron, "Medieval and Renaissance Ordinances," 5–6. The quotation is from Charles VII's Ordinance, 5n31.

5. This text from the Ordinance of Charles VII is quoted in Meron,"Medieval and Renaissance Ordinances," 7.

6. Meron, "Medieval and Renaissance Ordinances," 8.

7. Meron, "Medieval and Renaissance Ordinances," 9.

8. Quoted in Meron, "Medieval and Renaissance Ordinances," 10. A complete copy of the Scottish Articles and Ordinances of War is available online: http://www.old.scotwars.com/ narra_ articles_of_warre.htm (accessed April 7, 2015).

9. Aristotle, *Politics* 1255a6–8.

10. Geoffrey Parker, "Early Modern Europe," in *The Laws of War: Constraints on Warfare in the Western World*, ed. Michael Howard, George J. Andreopoulos, and Mark R. Shulman (New Haven: Yale University Press, 1994), 45.

11. Frederic E. Wakeman, *The Great Enterprise: The Manchu Reconstruction of Imperial Order in Seventeenth-Century China*, 2 volumes (Berkeley: University of California Press, 1985), I: 558–65, 655–61, and 2:817–18, cited in Parker, "Early Modern Europe," 235n20.

12. Parker, "Early Modern Europe," 48.

13. Theodor Meron, *Henry's Wars and Shakespeare's Laws: Perspectives on the Law of War in the Later Middle Ages* (Oxford: Clarendon Press, 1993), 102.

14. These included crown-works, ravelins, and hornworks. See Geoffrey Parker, *Cambridge Illustrated History of Warfare* (New York: Cambridge University Press, 1995, revised and updated, 2008), 113.

15. *Henry V*, 3.2.7–18, quoted in Parker, "Early Modern Europe," 48.

16. Quoted in Parker, "Early Modern Europe," 49.

17. Jörg Friedrich, *Das Gesetz des Krieges,* 22–23.

18. The source for Friedrich's account is Friedrich Schiller, *Geschichte des Dreißigjährigen Kriegs*, Vol. II. Parker, on the other hand, attributes allegations of excesses during the sack of Magdeburg to "Protestant polemicists." Parker, "Early Modern Europe," 50.

19. Friedrich's estimate of the number killed at Magdeburg is based on Schiller, *Geschichte des Dreißigjährigen Kriegs*. Both *Encyclopedia Britannica* and Wikipedia offer death toll estimates between 20,000 and 30,000. Conventional textbooks on Western European history cite a figure of 20,000 killed in battle or in massacres after Magdeburg's fall. See, e.g., Anthony Esler, *The Western World: A Narrative History—Prehistory to the Present* (Upper Saddle River,

NJ: Prentice Hall, 1997), 300. Parker's estimate, by contrast, is far more modest ("thousands" were killed).

20. i.e., the rights by which persons and property captured during wartime are returned to their former status once the war is over.

21. Parker, "Early Modern Europe," 44.

22. The Gentili quotation is from Parker, "Early Modern Europe." The original citation is: Gentili, *De jure Belli*, 3.7 (Eng. Ed., 2:320).

23. François de La Noue, *Discours politiques et militaries*, ed. Frank E. Sutcliffe (Geneva: Droz, 1967), 391–401, 638–42 (originally published 1587), cited in Parker, "Early Modern Europe," 47.

24. Theodor Meron, *Bloody Constraint: War and Chivalry in Shakespeare* (Oxford/New York: Oxford University Press, 1998), 7.

25. Encyclopedia Britannica Online, "Massacre of St. Bartholomew's Day," http://www.britannica.com/EBchecked/topic/516821/Massacre-of-Saint-Bartholomews-Day (accessed October 7, 2014).

26. Parker, "Early Modern Europe," 43.

27. Alberico Gentili, *De Jure Belli Libri Tres*, ed. John C. Rolfe (Carnegie, 1933), 212, quoted in Meron, *Bloody Constraint*, 7.

28. Geoffrey Parker, "Dynastic War," in *The Cambridge Illustrated History of Warfare*, 161.

29. The quotation is from the French philosopher Joseph de Maistre as translated by Isaiah Berlin, *Freedom and its Betrayal: Six Enemies of Human Liberty* (Princeton and Oxford: Princeton University Press, 2002), 138.

30. Parker, "Early Modern Europe," 41.

31. The quotation is from the archive of the archbishopric of Mechelen (Belgium), reproduced in Parker, "Early Modern Europe," 48.

32. E. Symmons, *A Military Sermon, Wherein by the Word of God, the Nature and Disposition of a Rebel is Discovered* (Oxford, 1644), 35, quoted in Parker, "Early Modern Europe."

33. Parker, "Early Modern Europe," 52. See also Parker's citations in endnote 50.

34. Parker, "Early Modern Europe," 52.

35. Parker, "Early Modern Europe," 52–53.

36. Marquis Sfondrato to Don Miguel de Salamanca, June 4, 1640, quoted in Parker, "Early Modern Europe," 53.

37. Parker denotes with this phrase Swiss and south German military contractors who trained and maintained troops hired out under contract to European states. "Dynastic War," in *The Cambridge Illustrated History of Warfare*, 146–50.

38. Parker, "Early Modern Europe," 54.

39. Otto Ulbricht, "The Experience of Violence During the Thirty Years War: A Look at the Civilian Victims," in *Power, Violence and Mass Death in Pre-Modern and Modern Times*, ed. Joseph Canning, Hartmut Lehmann, and Jay Winter (Hampshire, UK/Burlington, VT: Ashgate, 2004), 102.

40. Ulbricht, "The Experience of Violence During the Thirty Years War," 106.

41. See the discussion in Ulbricht, "The Experience of Violence During the Thirty Years War," 106–107.

42. Ulbricht, "The Experience of Violence During the Thirty Years War," 124.

43. Ulbricht, "The Experience of Violence During the Thirty Years War," 112–13.

44. Parker, "Early Modern Europe," 54.

45. Parker, "Early Modern Europe," 55.

46. Parker, "Early Modern Europe," 55.

47. The "Dunkirkers" gained their name as privateers serving in the Dunkirk fleet, an element of Spain's Flemish fleet. During the Dutch War of Independence (1568–1648), the Dutch Republic's fleet was bent on the Dunkirkers' total destruction.

48. Francisco di Vitoria, *Relectiones Theologicae* (Lyons, 1587), 36–40; Thomas A. Walker, *A History of the Law of Nations, vol. I: From the Earliest Times to the Peace of Westphalia* (Cambridge: Cambridge University Press, 1899), 226–8.

49. Vitoria, *Relectiones*, 48, 49; Walker, *Law of Nations*, 228–29; Theodor Meron, *Henry's Wars and Shakespeare's Laws*, 82.

50. Vitoria, *Relectiones*, 52; Walker, *Law of Nations*, 229.

51. Francisco di Vitoria, "The Second Relectio on the Indians, or on the Law of War made by the Spaniards on the Barbarians," in *De Indis et de Jure Belli Relectiones*, J. P. Bate, trans. (Carnegie ed., 1917), 182 (45), quoted in Meron, *Henry's Wars*, 83.

52. di Vitoria, "The Second Relectio on the Indians," 183–84 (49), quoted in Meron, *Henry's Wars*, 83.

53. di Vitoria, "The Second Relectio on the Indians," 183–84 (49), quoted in Meron, *Henry's Wars*, 46.

54. di Vitoria, "The Second Relectio on the Indians," 184 (52), quoted in Meron, *Henry's Wars*, 43.

55. di Vitoria, "The Second Relectio on the Indians," 184–85 (52), quoted in Meron, *Henry's Wars*, 47.

56. Quoted in Wilhelm G. Grewe, *The Epochs of International Law*, trans. Michael Byers (Berlin/New York: Walter de Gruyter, 2000), 147.

57. Grewe, *Epochs*, 147.

58. di Vitoria, *Relectio prior de potestate Ecclesiae*, vol. 2, 75, cited in Grewe, *Epochs*, 148.

59. Grewe, *Epochs*, 208.

60. Balthasar Ayala, *De iure et Officiis Bellicis et disciplina militari*, libri III (Douai, 1582), 1.2, quoted in Parker, "Early Modern Europe," 43.

61. Ayala, *De iure et Officiis Bellicis*, libri III, 1.2, quoted in Grewe, *Epochs*, 208.

62. Meron, *Bloody Constraint*, 30–31.

63. Meron, *Bloody Constraint*, 31. According to Abraham Lincoln, obviously referring to the Civil War, "[I]n great contests each party claims to act in accordance with the will of God. Both *may* be, and one *must* be wrong."

64. Ayala, *De iure et Officiis Bellicis*, libri I, 4; Walker, *Law of Nations*, 248–49.

65. Quoted in Meron, *Henry's Wars*, 94.

66. Meron, *Henry's Wars*, 177–78.

67. On Ayala's assessment of ambassadorial immunity, see Meron, *Henry's Wars*, 178.

68. Grewe, *Epochs*, 184–5; Parker, "Early Modern Europe," 44. Ayala wrote: "Disobedience in the part of subjects and rebellion against the prince is treated as a heinous offense and put on a par with heresy." Ayala, *De iure*, 1.2.23 (16–17), quoted in Parker, 44.

69. Parker, "Early Modern Europe," 44; Walker, *Law of Nations*, 248.

70. Grewe, *Epochs*, 184–85.

71. W. S. M. Knight, "Ayala and His Work," *Journal of Comparative Legislation and International Law 4*, no. 4 (1921): 220.

72. Quoted in Knight, "Ayala and His Work," 221.

73. Grewe, *Epochs*, 208–209.

74. Theodor Meron, *War Crimes Law Comes of Age: Essays* (New York/Oxford: Oxford University Press, 1998), 125.

75. Francisco Suárez, *Selections from Three Works*, trans. G. L. Williams, A. Brown, & J. Waldron (Oxford: Oxford University Press, 1944), 816, quoted in Meron, *Bloody Constraint*, 26.

76. Suárez, *Selections from Three Works*, 816, quoted in Meron, *Bloody Constraint*, 37.

77. Suárez, *Selections from Three Works*, 850–51, quoted in Meron, *Henry's Wars*, 39.

78. Suárez, *Selections from Three Works*, 843, quoted in Meron, *Henry's Wars*, 94.

79. Suárez, *Selections from Three Works*, 845, quoted in Meron, *Henry's Wars*, 110. For both di Vitoria and Suárez, execution of "notorious" or "guilty" persons would conduce to security and peace by "terrifying" the survivors.

80. Meron, *Henry's Wars*, 43–44.

81. Suárez, *Selections from Three Works*, 813, quoted in Meron, *Henry's Wars*, 101.

82. Grewe, *Epochs*, 26. The distinction between *jus gentium* "between the nations" and "among the nations" goes back to di Vitoria's translation of the Roman jurist Gaius's definition of the *jus gentium*. Gaius wrote: "That which constitutes natural reason amongst all men, is called the law of nations." Some scholars have claimed di Vitoria mistranslated Gaius's words "amongst all men" as "between all the nations," thereby falsely suggesting the existence of an international law between states called the *jus gentium*. As Grewe observes, there can be no question that Suárez understood the distinction, one that has persisted since the later phases of the Roman Republic.

83. In Cicero's dialogue "Laws," for example, Atticus proclaims his conviction "that all men are bound together by a certain natural feeling of kindliness and good-will, and also by a partnership in Justice." Cicero, "Laws," in *The Great Legal Philosophers*, 46.

84. Hedley Bull, "The Emergence of a Universal International Society," in *The Expansion of International Society*, ed. Hedley Bull and Adam Watson (Oxford: Clarendon Press, 1984), 119.

85. Grewe, *Epochs*, 148.

86. Grewe, *Epochs*, 148.

87. John P. Doyle, *Collected Studies on Francisco Suárez, S.J. (1548–1617)* (Leuven, Belgium: Leuven University Press, 2010), 284–85.

88. Bull, "A Universal International Society," 120.

89. See, for example, Locke's statement in Chapter V of the *Second Treatise*, quoted in Ben Kiernan, *Blood and Soil: A World History of Genocide from Sparta to Darfur* (New Haven: Yale University Press, 2007), 243.

90. The phrase "Rules of natural Justice" equating natural law with land cultivation stems from an article in the *New York Weekly Post Boy* from 1746, and reflects the depth to which Locke's theories had permeated the attitudes of educated colonials toward westward expansion in North America. See Kiernan, *Blood and Soil*, 243–44.

91. Bull, "A Universal International Society," 120.

92. Walker, *A History of the Law of Nations*, vol. 1, 251–52.

93. Grewe, *Epochs*, 187.

94. Grewe, *Epochs*, 211; Meron, *Bloody Constraint*, 31.

95. Grewe, *Epochs*, 211; Alberico Gentili, *Three Books on the Law of War*, trans. John C. Rolfe (Oxford: Clarendon Press, 1933), 32, cited in Meron, *Bloody Constraint*, 31.

96. Grewe, *Epochs*, 212; Introduction to Gentili, *Three Books on the Law of War*, trans. and ed. Coleman Phillipson (Oxford: Clarendon Press, 1933), ii. 39a.

97. Meron, *Henry's Wars*, 50.

98. Grewe, *Epochs*, 212.

99. Grewe, *Epochs*, 212–13; Walker, *Law of Nations*, 260.

100. Walker, *A History of the Law of Nations*, 263.

101. Grewe, *Epochs*, 213; Walker, *A History of the Law of Nations*, 263. Gentili supported his hard stance on hostage execution with the argument that it would ensure the adherence of the enemy to his promises and minimize the incidence of treachery.

102. Gentili, *De jure Belli Libri Tres*, 211, 218, 223, quoted in Meron, *Henry's Wars*, 110–11, and 103, note 144; Meron, *War Crimes Law Comes of Age: Essays* (Oxford: Oxford University Press, 1998), 46. See also Grewe, *Epochs*, 213.

103. Gentili, *De jure Belli Libri Tres*, 216, quoted in Meron, *War Crimes Law*, 57.

104. Gentili, *De jure Belli Libri Tres*, 211–12, quoted in Meron, *War Crimes Law*, 58. While the massacre was regarded with horror at the time, Henry's contemporaries did not consider it a violation of the medieval Law of War. Even the French did not reproach Henry because they interpreted the slaughter as motivated by dire necessity, and admitted that they would have acted like the English in the same situation. For Gentili, on the other hand, no emergency could justify killing war captives.

105. Although rare, women sometimes fought as soldiers, most commonly to defend their cities when laid under siege. Sometimes, however, they served as military leaders, as did Joan of Arc, and in Germany the widows of officers killed in battle sometimes assumed the command of their late husbands' troops. According to medieval chivalry, women were presumed to be defenseless and hence shielded from armed assault—a presumption rebuttable when a woman took up arms. Meron, *Henry's Wars*, 95.

106. Grewe, *Epochs*, 214–15; Meron, *Henry's Wars*, 95–96; Walker, *Law of Nations*, 263–64. In drawing his class of protected persons, Gentili appeals to imperial Roman law (especially the Roman jurisconsult Arrian) and Roman canon law. In nearly all cases, these persons were immune to attack unless they acquired the attributes of combatants, such as carrying weapons.

107. di Vitoria's position appears to allow rape, albeit reluctantly, "as a spur to the courage of the troops." di Vitoria, "The Second Relectio on the Indians," 184–85, para. 52, quoted in Meron, *Henry's Wars*, 112.

108. Gentili, *De jure Belli Libri Tres*, II. 257, quoted in Meron, *Henry's Wars*, 112.

109. All quotations are from Gentili, *De jure Belli Libri Tres*, II. 99–101, quoted in Meron, *Henry's Wars*, 68. Gentili's prescient commentary on state responsibility anticipates Article 18 of the UN International Law Commission's draft articles on state responsibility. See Meron, *Henry's Wars*, 68n11.

110. Gentili, *De jure Belli Libri Tres*, II. 241–42, 243, quoted in Meron, *Henry's Wars*, 82. Gentili insisted that hostages were not prisoners of war; the latter was a category of protected persons. Walker, *Law of Nations*, 262–63.

111. The Italian jurist and Roman canon lawyer, John of Legnano, delineated the scope of reprisals allowed under the medieval Law of War. See Legnano, *Tractatus de bello, de represaliis et de duello*, ed. Thomas E. Holland (Washington, D.C., 1917), chapters 124–65, pp. 308–30, cited in Meron, *Henry's Wars*, 160. John's treatise was originally finished in 1360 but was only published in 1477.

112. Gentili, *De jure Belli Libri Tres*, II.232, quoted in Meron, *Henry's Wars*, 82. Geneva Convention III, Art. 13, forbids reprisals against prisoners.

113. Grotius, *The Rights of War and Peace*, III, chapter xi, pt. xvi(1), quoted in Meron, *Henry's Wars*, 161. Grotius wrote: "Nature does not sanction retaliation except against those who have done wrong. It is not sufficient that by a sort of fiction the enemy may be conceived as forming a single body."

114. Gentili, *De jure Belli Libri Tres*, I.Ch. 25, quoted in Grewe, *Epochs*, 307.

115. Quoted in Grewe, *Epochs*, 305. In this locution, pirates were "enemies," but not in the sense of a legitimate belligerent to whom duties are owed under the Law of War. Rather, pirates were illegal "enemies" of everyone.

116. Grewe, *Epochs*, 305. The German jurist and natural law scholar Samuel von Pufendorf cast his lot with Gentili on the piracy issue, reasoning that, because their atrocious crimes bespoke atheism, pirates could not invoke the Bible as a proof of their intention to adhere to an agreement; because their oath was defective, any treaty with them was null and void. Samuel von Pufendorf, *De iure naturae et gentium libri octo* (1672), Part 4, Ch. 2, 8, reproduced in *Classics of International Law*, vol. 17, ed. J. B. Scott (Carnegie Endowment, 1931).

117. The quotation is from Prolegomena 3 of the 1925 English translation of Grotius's treatise by F. W. Kelsey, quoted in Charles Edwards, "The Law of War in the Thought of Hugo Grotius," *Emory University Journal of Public Law* 19 (1970): 371–72.

118. Lassa Oppenheim, *International Law: A Treatise, vol. I—Peace*, ed. Hersh Lauterpacht (6th ed., London: Longmans, Green & Co., 1947), 87–88; *Encyclopedia Britannica Online*, s. v. Hugo Grotius, http://www.britannica.com/EBchecked/topic/246809/Hugo-Grotius/256632/ Life-in-exile-De-Jure-Belli-ac-Pacis (accessed February 25, 2014).

119. Grotius, *The Rights of War and Peace*, 705, quoted in Edwards, "The Law of War in the Thought of Hugo Grotius," 373.

120. See, e.g., Cicero, *Laws*, Book 1, 46.

121. Grotius, *The Rights of War and Peace*, Prolegomena 25, 26, quoted in Edwards, "The Law of War in the Thought of Hugo Grotius," 373–75.

122. See, for example, Cicero, *On the Commonwealth*, trans. G. Sabine (Columbus, OH: Ohio State University Press, 1929), 217; H. Paolucci, *The Political Writings of St. Augustine* (Chicago: Gateway, 1962), 163.

123. Grotius, *The Rights of War and Peace*, 171.

124. Grotius, *The Rights of War and Peace*, 565; Grewe, *Epochs*, 216.

125. Edwards, "The Law of War in the Thought of Hugo Grotius," 377.

126. Grotius, *The Rights of War and Peace*, Book III, Ch. XI, parts V and VI, quoted in Meron, *Henry's Wars*, 72–73.

127. Francisco Suárez, *De Legibus ac Deo Legislatore*, in *Selections from Three Works*, ed. J. B. Scott (Oxford: Clarendon Press, 1944), 353–54.

128. Grewe, *Epochs*, 195 (discussing Grotius's Prolegomena).

129. For critical views of Grotius's ambivalence, see Walker, *A History of the Law of Nations*, 335; Edwards, "The Law of War in the Thought of Hugo Grotius," 380.

130. Edwards, "The Law of War in the Thought of Hugo Grotius," 381.

131. "Therefore in the midst of divergent opinions we must lean towards peace." Grotius, *The Rights of War and Peace*, 560, quoted in Edwards, "The Law of War in the Thought of Hugo Grotius," 382.

132. Edwards, "The Law of War in the Thought of Hugo Grotius," 385; Grewe, *Epochs*, 194; Grotius, *The Rights of War and Peace*, I, chapter 2, VII. Rhadamanthus was a judge and punisher of the unjust in Tartarus (the Greek underworld).

133. Grotius, *The Rights of War and Peace*, 197–8, quoted in Edwards, "The Law of War in the Thought of Hugo Grotius," 387. Other skeptics include Van Vollenhoven, *The Three Stages in the Evolution of the Law of Nations* (The Hague: Martinus Nijhoff, 1919), 16 ff.; P. Remec, *The Position of the Individual in International Law According to Grotius and Vattel* (The Hague: Martinus Nijhoff, 1960), 117–18.

134. Edwards, "The Law of War in the Thought of Hugo Grotius," 387.

135. Grotius, *The Rights of War and Peace*, bk. III, ch. lii, pt. vi (1)–(3), quoted in Meron, *Henry's Wars*, 51.

136. Grewe, *Epochs*, 193.

137. Grotius, *The Rights of War and Peace*, ch. xi, pt. xiv(1), quoted in Meron, *Henry's Wars*, 79n13.

138. Grotius, *The Rights of War and Peace*, bk. III, ch. xx, pt. liii, quoted in Meron, *Henry's Wars*, 82.

139. Similarly, di Vitoria conceded the legitimacy of hostage execution when agreements for which they were sureties were breached. He insisted, however, that killing hostages was allowed only if they were combatants and not civilians (i.e., "they have borne arms"). di Vitoria, *Second Relectio on the Indians or on the Law of War made by the Spaniards on the Barbarians*, 181–82 (43), quoted in Meron, *Henry's Wars*, 82.

140. Grotius, *The Rights of War and Peace*, bk. iii, ch. 4, cited in Walker, *A History of the Law of Nations*, 314–15. Grotius observes that the reverse was sometimes the case, and that the law of nature permitted some military tactics forbidden by the law of nations, such as the use of poison to kill the enemy.

141. Quoted in Edwards, "The Law of War in the Thought of Hugo Grotius," 389.

142. Grotius, *The Rights of War and Peace*, bk. iii, ch. 11.

143. Grotius, *The Rights of War and Peace*, ch. 12.

144. Hersch Lauterpacht, "The Grotian Tradition in International Law," *Brit. Y.B. Int'l L.*, 23(1946): 46.

145. "If, in fact, the right of resistance should remain without restraint, there will no longer be a state, but only a non-social horde, such as that of the Cyclopes." Quoted in Edwards, "The Law of War in the Thought of Hugo Grotius," 390. Elsewhere, however, Grotius approves of forcible resistance to "atrocious cruelty" of such a magnitude that it jeopardized the survival of civil society. See, e.g., Grotius, *The Rights of War and Peace*, 156–7, cited in Edwards, "The Law of War," 393.

146. Grotius, *The Rights of War and Peace*, 504–505, quoted in Edwards, "The Law of War," 395.

147. Meron, *War Crimes Law Comes of Age*, 124.

148. See for example the principle of complementarity in Article 17 of the Rome Statute, which serves as the charter of the International Criminal Court.

5 Colonialism and the Law of War: Ireland and the Americas

1. Elbridge Colby, "How to Fight Savage Tribes," *The American Journal of International Law* 21/2 (April 1927), 283. In fact, Vitoria's position on the permissible treatment of non-Christians was far more nuanced. He wrote: "Even if the barbarians refuse to accept Christ as their lord, this does not justify making war on them or doing them any hurt." Quoted in Elizabeth A. Fenn, "Biological Warfare in Eighteenth-Century North America: Beyond Jeffery Amherst," *The Journal of American History* 86/4 (March 2000), 1574n45.

2. Quoted in Colby, "How to Fight Savage Tribes," 280.

3. U.S. Court of Claims in *Marks v. U. S.*, 28 Ct. Cl. 147 (1896).

4. Quoted in Colby, "How to Fight Savage Tribes," 280.

5. It is not the argument here that domination and plunder were the sole motives for Spanish actions toward native peoples in the New World. Recent scholarship on Iberian colonization has emphasized the diversity of aims and agendas underlying it, which were often non-violent and non-exploitative. The spectacular early conquests of Mexico and Peru could not be replicated in subsequent incursions into other parts of South America, where the Spanish had little choice but to cooperate with the decentralized indigenous societies they encountered. Because the methods and motives used effectively to overthrow complex and hierarchical kingships did not yield similar results elsewhere, the examples of Mexico and Peru should not be regarded as "paradigmatic" of Spanish colonial policy in the New World. See Wayne E. Lee, "Projecting Power in the Early Modern World: the Spanish Model?", in *Empires and Indigenes: Intercultural Alliance, Imperial Expansion, and Warfare in the Early Modern World*, ed. Wayne E. Lee (New York: NYU Press, 2011), 3, 6; Matthew Restall, *Seven Myths of the Spanish Conquest* (New York: Oxford University Press, 2003), 144-45; Michel R. Oudijk and Matthew Restall, "Mesoamerican Conquistadors in the Sixteenth Century," in *Indian Conquistadors: Indigenous Allies in the Conquest of Mesoamerica*, ed. Laura Matthew and Michel R. Oudijk (Norman: University of Oklahoma Press, 2008), 28–64. Despite these caveats, modern research tends to agree with the basic portrayal of the conquistadors as invidious in their motives and monstrous in their violence. Wayne Lee comments (summarizing the perspective of Matthew Restall): "[The early conquistadors] were men imbued with a crusading ideology, an energizing greed for hidden mineral wealth, and a profound, ends-of-the-earth, succeed-or-die desperation. Moreover, their consciences were fortified by an intricate and sustained religious-legalistic framework.... [W]hen resisted, they wielded violence swiftly, unhesitatingly, and with extraordinary cruelty." Lee, *Empires*, 5.

6. See the discussion in Kiernan, *Blood and Soil*, passim (but especially 78 ff.). The alleged inability of a victim group to farm was one of four enabling conditions of genocide in world history, according to Kiernan. The others were cults of antiquity, racism, and territorial expansionism.

7. Bartolome de las Casas, *History of the Indies*, Book 2, tr. Andrée Collard (New York, 1971), 99, quoted in Kiernan, *Blood and Soil*, 80.

8. Quoted in Kiernan, *Blood and Soil*, 81.

9. Quoted in David Livingstone Smith, *Less than Human: Why we Demean, Enslave, and Exterminate Others* (New York: St. Martin's Press, 2011), 76–77.

10. Quoted in Kiernan, *Blood and Soil*, 82.

11. Kiernan, *Blood and Soil*, 82. Some of the conquistadors, like Vasco Núñez de Balboa, resemble less a poisoner than a Nazi death camp commandant. Balboa urged the extermination of the Indians because they were an "evil breed" who should be "burnt to the last, young and old, so that no memory remains of such evil people." Quoted in Kiernan, *Blood and Soil*, 81. In one

Notes

Indian village subdued by Balboa and his men, forty Indian nobles were found dressed as women. Balboa accused them of sodomy and had all of them torn to pieces by dogs.

12. In 1493 the papacy issued decrees (bulls) conferring on Christian monarchs dominion over indigenous peoples. Christian rulers thereafter bore responsibility to convert them to Christianity. Burkholder and Johnson, *Colonial Latin America*, 37.

13. Quoted in Burkholder and Johnson, *Colonial Latin America*, 37.

14. Quoted in Kiernan, *Blood and Soil*, 89.

15. Kiernan, *Blood and Soil*, 90.

16. Kiernan, *Blood and Soil*, 90–91. Steel was a critical component of the Spaniards' success in destroying the Aztec empire: it was not only the staple of Spanish swords, daggers, lances, and crossbows but also of their ballistics. Cortes used cannon to—quite literally—wipe the buildings of Tenochtitlan off the face of the earth. Steel also reinforced the conquistadors' body armor, against which native weapons were often ineffectual. Add to this other advantages like the cultural differences in European vs. native approaches to warfare (the Spanish aiming to kill, the Indians to capture), conflicts among the tributaries of the empire that forestalled a united front of Mexican kingdoms and supplied the Spanish with fresh troops, Spanish access to horses, and the crippling effect of disease on Indian lives (smallpox broke out among the Aztec defenders during the last battle of Tenochtitlan), and Cortes's ability to overthrow the Aztec empire with relatively few men becomes easier to comprehend. On this topic, see Patricia Seed, "The Conquest of the Americas," in *The Cambridge Illustrated History of Warfare*, 132–45; Wayne Lee, "Projecting Power," 4–5.

17. Kiernan, *Blood and Soil*, 93–95; Burkholder/Johnson, *Colonial Latin America*, 59–60.

18. Kiernan, *Blood and Soil*, 95. Other scholars of the Spanish Conquest have not hesitated to brand it a holocaust: see, e.g., Gilbert M. Joseph and Timothy J. Henderson, ed., *The Mexico Reader* (Durham, NC: Duke University Press Books, 2003), 122; Mark Cocker, *Rivers of Blood, Rivers of Gold: Europe's Conquest of Indigenous Peoples* (New York: Grove Atlantic, 1998), 111; David Stannard, *American Holocaust: The Conquest of the New World* (New York: Oxford UP, 1993), 267.

19. J. G. Varner and J. J. Varner, *Dogs of the Conquest* (Norman, OK: University of Oklahoma Press, 1983), cited in Smith, *Less than Human*, 76.

20. Quoted in Smith, *Less than Human*, 76–77.

21. George M. Frederickson, *Racism: A Short History* (Princeton, NJ: Princeton University Press, 2002), 32–33. The French historian of anti-Semitism, Léon Poliakov, argued along similar lines, holding that in Spain "sectarian hatred" segued into "racial hatred." Léon Poliakov, *The History of Anti-Semitism*, vol. 2, *From Mohammed to the Marranos*, trans. Natalie Gerardi (Philadelphia: The University of Pennsylvania Press, 2003), 116 ff.

22. Smith, *Less than Human*, 78.

23. Quoted in Kiernan, *Blood and Soil*, 98. Remarkably, the Council of the Indies moderating the debate agreed with Las Casas; the Council's verdict, however, was never released to the public. The Church had already made its position clear, declaring in 1537 that New World peoples were full human beings with souls and that enslaving them was forbidden. Smith, *Less than Human*, 80.

24. Smith, *Less Than Human*, 79–80.

25. David Beers Quinn, *Raleigh and the British Empire* (London: Hodder & Stoughton, 1947); idem, *The Elizabethans and the Irish* (Ithaca: Cornell University Press, 1966); idem, "Ireland and Sixteenth-century European Expansion," *Historical Studies* I (1958), 20–32; Nicholas P. Canny,

"The Ideology of English Colonization: From Ireland to America," *The William and Mary Quarterly* 30/4 (October 1973), 575–98; Susan Juster, *Sacred Violence in Early America* (Philadelphia: University of Pennsylvania Press, 2017).

26. Sir John Davies, *A Discoverie of the True Causes why Ireland Was neuer entirely Subdued, nor brought vnder Obedience of the Crowne of England, Vntill the Beginning of His Maiefties happie Raigne* (London: A. Millar, 1612), 6. Davies was skeptical that the Normans and their successors had achieved a true "conquest" of Ireland due to inadequate military commitment, lack of political control, and the failure to subject all of Ireland to the English common law. He therefore referred to the "perfection" of conquest as occurring only in the sixteenth and seventeenth centuries, achieved for the first time by Elizabeth and James I.

27. The exception was the colonization of St. Leger in southwest Munster. Even in this instance, as Canny observes, the English charged that the lords of Munster were rebels whose land could be summarily seized. Canny, "The Ideology of English Colonization," 579.

28. David Edwards, "Beyond Reform: Martial Law and the Tudor Reconquest of Ireland," *History Ireland* 5/2 (Summer 1997), 16–17.

29. Canny, "The Ideology of English Colonization," 579–80.

30. Quoted in Kiernan, *Blood and Soil*, 198.

31. "Clandeboye" was a Gaelic Irish kingdom.

32. Kiernan, *Blood and Soil*, 198–200; Canny, "The Ideology of English Colonization," 580–81. Edwards reminds us that each of these massacres in the 1570s was conducted under the permissive terms of commissions of martial law, "passed under the royal seal in Dublin." Edwards, "Beyond Reform," 19.

33. Canny, "The Ideology of English Colonization," 581. As previously noted, David Edwards interprets the violence as part of the "state terrorism" initiated by the imposition of martial law in Ireland.

34. Kiernan, *Blood and Soil*, 201.

35. Edwards, "Beyond Reform," 19.

36. Quoted in Kiernan, *Blood and Soil*, 204.

37. Quoted in Kiernan, *Blood and Soil*, 205.

38. Quoted in Kiernan, *Blood and Soil*, 207. A "churl" was a Medieval English word for a peasant.

39. David Edwards, "'Some Days Two Heads, Some Days Four,'" *History Ireland* 17/1 (Jan.-Feb. 2009), 19–21.

40. Edwards, "'Some Days,'" 21.

41. Quoted in Kiernan, *Blood and Soil*, 210–11.

42. Canny, "The Ideology of English Colonization," 584–85.

43. Quoted in Kiernan, *Blood and Soil*, 197.

44. Frederick Jackson Turner, "The Significance of the Frontier in American History," in *The Frontier in American History* (New York: Henry Holt, 1921), 1–38.

45. On the impact of the frontier on the "American Way of War," see Erik Ringmar, "Francis Lieber, Terrorism, and the American Way of War," *Perspectives on Terrorism* 3(4) (December 2009), 52–60. For Ringmar the westering frontier moved into the Great Plains, stretched to the West Coast, then sprang overseas into the Philippines and Indochina. Everywhere the frontier went it constituted the native inhabitants along its edge as Godless barbarians who could be fought without restraint: the Cheyenne, the Apaches, the Comanches, the Sioux, Filipino guerrillas, and the Vietcong. Today,

we might add Afghanistan and Iraq to the list of overseas American frontiers, and so-called "enemy combatants" to the list of barbarians standing beyond the protections of international law.

46. Kiernan, *Blood and Soil*, 215.

47. Quoted in Alden T. Vaughan, "'Expulsion of the Salvages': English Policy and the Virginia Massacre of 1622," *William and Mary Quarterly* 35 (January 1978), 77. See also Kiernan, *Blood and Soil*, 222. Historian James Axtell discerns in the colonists' rejoinder to the Virginia Company "perhaps the first secular expression of genocidal intent." James Axtell, *The European and the Indian: Essays in the Ethno-history of Colonial North America* (New York: Oxford, 1981), 313.

48. Canny, "Ideology," 578. Canny writes that "men from the West Country were prominent in all English expansionist ventures of the seventeenth century." Their role in English colonialism has been an object of intense scholarly attention; see citations to the secondary literature in Canny, "Ideology," 578fn7.

49. Quoted in Ronald Dale Karr, "Why Should You Be So Furious?": The Violence of the Pequot War," *The Journal of American History* 85/3 (December 1983), 890.

50. One such exception was Miles Standish's horrific knife murder of Massachusett warriors in their own home in 1622.

51. Karr, "Violence," 895–96.

52. Karr, "Violence," 900. All of the preceding quotations are from Karr's article.

53. Karr, "Violence," 902; Kiernan, *Blood and Soil*, 228–29. The Puritans' actual declaration of war came in April 1637. Although the traditional Indian *jus ad bellum* was a stylized ritual involving a formal declaration followed by pro-war orations, the Pequots immediately responded to Endecott's provocation by attacking Fort Saybrook. The raid was intended as their declaration of war on the Bay Colony.

54. John Mason's lieutenant in the Pequot village massacre, John Underhill, described the Pequots' style of warfare as "more for pastime, then to conquer and subdue enemies." Quoted in Kiernan, *Blood and Soil*, 230.

55. Karr, "Violence," 891.

56. Francis Jennings, *Invasion of America: Indians, Colonialism, and the Cant of Conquest* (Chapel Hill: University of North Carolina Press, 1975), 211–13. On the *jus ad bellum* and *jus in bello* of the Pequots on the eve of the Pequot War, see Adam J. Hirsch, "The Collision of Military Cultures in Seventeenth-Century New England," *The Journal of American History* 74/4 (March 1988), 1190 ff.; Karr, "Violence," 903.

57. The context of the Puritan anabasis included Endecott's mission to kill and enslave the Block Island Indians. Moreover, in a letter to Winthrop Thomas Hooker urged him "to hasten execution, and not to do this work of the Lords revenge slackly." Jennings proposes the thesis that Mason's plan to exterminate the Pequot population as a whole was opposed by his lieutenants until the army chaplain endorsed the genocide, quieting their fears. Jennings, *Invasion*, 220. See also Alden Vaughan, *New England Frontier: Puritans and Indians, 1620–1675* (Norman, OK: University of Oklahoma Press, 1995), 143; Karr, "Violence," 904.

58. The attack on the Pequot village is widely retailed in the literature. Here, my sources are Kiernan, *Blood and Soil*, 229 ff.; Hirsch, "Collision," 1197 ff.; Karr, "Violence," 876 ff.

59. Quoted in Hirsch, "Collision," 1198. See also Kiernan, *Blood and Soil*, 232–33.

60. Kiernan, *Blood and Soil*, 234.

61. Hirsch, "Collision," 1187 ff. On the European military custom of fighting pitched battles, see James Q. Whitman, *The Verdict of Battle: The Law of Victory and the Making of Modern War*

(Cambridge, MA: Harvard University Press, 2012). Whitman, like Karr, rejects the thesis that premodern European warfare was restrained and chivalrous.

62. Hirsch, "Collision," 1204.

63. Karr, "Violence," 883.

64. Karr, "Violence," 908.

65. Quoted in Hirsch, "Collision," 1206.

66. Quoted in Smith, *Less than Human*, 82. This open demonization of the Indians had not always been the case but seems to have coincided with the passions aroused by the Pequot war.

67. On the mourning wars, see supra, Chapter 2, page 68 ff.

68. John Fabian Whitt, *Lincoln's Code: The Laws of War in American History* (New York: Free Press, 2012), 89–91.

69. Solomon Stoddard to Joseph Dudley, October 22, 1703, quoted in Hirsch, "Collision," 1208. One historian of seventeenth-century English colonialism, Susan Juster, has argued that hostile attitudes toward heterodoxy, sharpened in the conflict between Protestantism and Catholicism during the reconquest of Ireland, shaped ideas of "holy genocide" in North America. Susan Juster, *Sacred Violence in Early America* (Philadelphia: University of Pennsylvania Press, 2016).

70. Quoted in Patrick Brantlinger, *Dark Vanishings: Discourse on the Extinction of Primitive Races, 1800–1930* (Ithaca and London: Cornell University Press, 2003), 49.

71. The term "extinction discourse," which, in stripping indigenous peoples of their humanity marked them for extermination, is developed in Brantlinger, *Dark Vanishings*, 1 ff.

72. Emer de Vattel, *The Law of Nations*, ed. Bela Kapossy and Richard Whatmore (Indianapolis: Liberty Fund, 2008), 487. Although de Vattel's reference here is to "the Turks and other Tartars," the category of "savage" also included American Indians. See the discussion in Elizabeth A. Fenn, "Biological Warfare in Eighteenth-Century North America: Beyond Jeffery Amherst," *The Journal of American History* 86/4 (March 2000), 1574.

73. Quoted in Witt, *Lincoln's Code*, 93. In light of this rationale, we may more readily understand how Enlightenment tolerance of religious differences among Euro-Americans might be endorsed in colonial rhetoric while an "anti-Indian sublime" simultaneously instigated violence against native peoples during the 7 Years War. Peter Silver, *Our Savage Neighbors: How Indian War Transformed Early America* (New York: W. W. Norton & Co., 2008).

74. Karr, "Violence," 885. On the issue of equality of arms and its tendency to moderate conflict, see also Wayne E. Lee, "Peace Chiefs and Blood Revenge: Patterns of Restraint in Native American Warfare, 1500-1800," *The Journal of Military History* 71/3 (July 2007), 741.

75. Kelly L. Watson, *Insatiable Appetites: Imperial Encounters with Cannibals in the North Atlantic World* (New York: NYU Press, 2017).

76. Quoted in Hirsch, "Collision," 1210.

77. Jill Lepore, *The Name of War: King Philip's War and the Origins of American Identity* (New York: Vintage Books, 1999), 88–89.

78. Kiernan, *Blood and Soil*, 237.

79. Whitt, *Lincoln's Code*, 91; Patrick M. Malone, *The Skulking Way of War: Technology and Tactics Among the New England Indians* (Lanham, MD: Rowan and Littlefield, 2001); Hirsch, "Collision," 1210; Karr, "Violence," 909.

80. Lepore, *Name of War*, 175 ff.; Kiernan, *Blood and Soil*, 239 ff.

6 The Law of War in the Eighteenth and Nineteenth Centuries: Europe and the United States of America

1. R. R. Palmer and Joel Colton, *A History of the Modern World* (New York: Alfred A. Knopf, 1965), 10.

2. Palmer and Colton, *A History of the Modern World*, 117; Anthony Esler, *The Western World: A Narrative History, Prehistory to the Present* (Upper Saddle River, NJ: Prentice Hall, 1997), 323; J. H. M. Salmon, "Sovereignty, Theory of," in *Europe, 1450 to 1789: Encyclopedia of the Early Modern World*, vol. 5 (New York: Charles Scribner's Sons, 2003), 447.

3. Palmer and Colton, *A History*, 130. See also S. Baker, ed., *Halleck's International Law—Rules Regulating the Intercourse of States in Peace and War*, vol. 1 (London: Longmans, Green, 1928), 13–14; Oppenheim, *International Law*, vol. I, 682; J. G. Starke, *An Introduction to International Law* (London: Butterworths, 1963), 5–6. For a critique of this "Westphalian legal orthodoxy," see Stéphane Beaulac, "The Westphalian Legal Orthodoxy—Myth or Reality?" *Journal of the History of International Law* 2 (2000): 148–77 (arguing that the Treaties of Osnabrück and Münster did not create a system of independent states *de jure*).

4. Beaulac, 148–77.

5. Beaulac, 158.

6. Beaulac, 158.

7. Beaulac, 159–60; John A. Lynn, "States in Conflict," in G. Parker, ed., *The Cambridge Illustrated History of Warfare* (New York/Cambridge: Cambridge University Press, 1995), 164.

8. See, e.g., Guglielmo Ferrero, *Peace and War* (New York: Macmillan, 1933), 63–64, quoted in Gunther Rothenberg, "The Age of Napoleon," in Howard et al., *The Laws of War*, 86.

9. Carl von Clausewitz, *On War*, ed. and trans. Peter Paret and Michael Howard (Princeton: Princeton University Press, 1976), 75, 609–10, quoted in Rothenberg, "The Age of Napoleon," 86–87.

10. Roger Chickering, "Total War: the Use and Abuse of a Concept," in M. F. Boemeke, R. Chickering, and S. Förster, eds., *Anticipating Total War: The German and American Experiences, 1871–1914* (Cambridge: Cambridge University Press, 1999), 14.

11. John A. Lynn, "Nations in Arms 1763–1815," in *The Cambridge Illustrated History of Warfare*, 193. For Jörg Friedrich, the *levée en masse*, as an expression of the people's army, inaugurated modern warfare. J. Friedrich, *Das Gesetz des Krieges*, 48–49.

12. Chickering, "Total War," 15.

13. For a starkly differing view, see Whitman, *The Verdict of Battle* (arguing that the eighteenth-century pitched battle as a means of determining monarchical property and dynastic claims tended to moderate the violence of warfare).

14. Whitman, *The Verdict of Battle*, 22–23.

15. Rothenberg, "The Age of Napoleon," 87. See also J. Friedrich, *Das Gesetz des Krieges*, 41.

16. Geoffrey Best, *Humanity in Warfare* (New York: Columbia University Press, 1980), 60–1; Rothenberg, "The Age of Napoleon," 88.

17. Quoted in Rothenberg, "The Age of Napoleon," 88.

18. Rothenberg, "The Age of Napoleon," 88.

19. Quoted in David M. Crowe, *War Crimes, Genocide, and Justice: A Global History* (New York: Palgrave Macmillan, 2014), 42; Friedrich, *Das Gesetz des Krieges*, 53.

20. Friedrich, *Das Gesetz des Krieges*, 55; Rothenberg, "The Age of Napoleon," 88.

21. Malcolm Barber, *The Trial of the Templars* (London: The Folio Society, 2003), 23.

22. Mark Gregory Pegg, *A Most Holy War: The Albigensian Crusade and the Battle for Christendom* (Oxford/New York: Oxford University Press, 2008), 76–77, 100, 186.

23. Pegg, *A Most Holy War*, 78.

24. Chickering, "Total War," 20. See also Martin van Creveld, *The Transformation of War* (New York: Free Press, 1991), 37; Robert B. Asprey, *War in the Shadows: the Guerilla in History*, 2 volumes (Garden City, N.Y.: Doubleday, 1975).

25. Rothenberg, "The Age of Napoleon," 89, 91.

26. Rothenberg, "The Age of Napoleon," 91.

27. Rothenberg, "The Age of Napoleon," 90.

28. See Friedrich, *Das Gesetz des Krieges*, 58 ff.

29. Lynn, "Nations in Arms," 203–204.

30. Rothenberg, "The Age of Napoleon," 93.

31. Rothenberg, "The Age of Napoleon," 97.

32. Chickering, "Total War," 26. For Chickering, such "erasure" is "the salient theme in the military history of the past two centuries." On this topic, see also Michael Howard, *War in European History* (Oxford: Oxford University Press, 2009), 93; Geoffrey Best, *War and Society in Revolutionary Europe 1770–1870* (Montreal: McGill-Queen's University Press, 1998), 224.

33. i.e., the practice of bombing civilians in order to break their "morale." According to the Allied Combined Chiefs of Staff in 1943, bombing civilian centers would result in "the undermining of the German people to a point where their capacity for armed resistance is fatally weakened." Quoted in Charles Webster and Noble Frankland, *The Strategic Air Offensive against Germany, 1939–45* (East Sussex, UK: Naval & Military Press, 2006), 273.

34. Martin Bell, *In Harm's Way: Reflections of a War-Zone Thug* (London: Hamish Hamilton, 1995), 214–15, quoted in D. L. Smith, *The Most Dangerous Animal*, 2; von Clausewitz, *On War*, 76–77, 88–89, quoted in Chickering, "Total War," 24.

35. Lynn, "Nations in Arms 1763–1815," *The Cambridge Illustrated History of Warfare*, 205–13; Lynn Hunt, *Inventing Human Rights: A History* (New York/London: W. W. Norton & Co., 2007), 181–82; Michael Howard, *War in European History*, 93.

36. Russell F. Weigley, *Age of Battles: The Quest for Decisive Warfare from Breitenfeld to Waterloo* (Bloomington, IN: Indiana University Press, 2004), xvii, cited in Chickering, "Total War," 24.

37. Reinhold Niebuhr, *Moral Man and Immoral Society: A Study in Ethics and Politics* (New York: Charles Scribner's Sons, 1948), 44.

38. A process called "rifling."

39. Williamson A. Murray, "The Industrialization of War," in *The Cambridge Illustrated History of Warfare*, 218.

40. Keegan, *A History of Warfare*, 311–12.

41. Keegan, *A History of Warfare*, 312.

42. None of the governments involved in the conflict believed that tear gas was banned under the Hague Convention, which only prohibited "the use of projectiles the sole object of which is the diffusion of asphyxiating or deleterious gases."

43. Adam Roberts, "Land Warfare," in Howard et al., *The Laws of War*, 123–4; Martin Gilbert, *The First World War: A Complete History* (New York: Henry Holt, 1994), 143–44, 197–98, and *passim*; Adam Roberts and Richard Guelff, *Documents on the Laws of War* (Oxford/New York: Oxford University Press, 2004), 59–60.

44. James J. Sheehan, "The Problem of Sovereignty in European History," *The American Historical Review* 111(1) (February 2006): 7.

45. Sheehan, "The Problem of Sovereignty in European History," 8; Max Weber, *Economy and Society: An Outline of Interpretive Sociology* (Berkeley: University of California Press, 1978), 904 ff.

46. i.e., official authorization (via "letters of marque") of private ships to wage war at sea. The main activity of privateers was seizure of enemy merchant ships, a practice considered lawful until the nineteenth century.

47. Customary international law consists of principles that states adhere to out of a sense of legal duty, and that are consequently binding on other states whether or not they are parties to a treaty setting forth the customary principle. See, e.g., Theodor Meron, "Customary Law," in Roy Gutman and David Rieff, eds., *Crimes of War: What the Public Should Know* (New York/London: W. W. Norton & Co., 1999), 113.

48. Roberts and Guelff, *Documents*, 47; Lassa Oppenheim, *International Law: A Treatise*, vol. II, ed. H. Lauterpacht (London/New York: Longmans, Green & Co., 1944), 180.

49. The author of the account (published in 1862) was Jean-Henri Dunant, whose book *A Memory of Solferino* is considered the main impetus to the founding of the International Committee of the Red Cross in 1864.

50. Paul G. Lauren, *The Evolution of International Human Rights: Visions Seen* (Philadelphia: University of Pennsylvania Press, 2011), 69. Today, the ICRC provides aid to all persons in wartime and ensures that all sides in a conflict comply with international humanitarian law.

51. Convention for the Amelioration of the Condition of the Wounded in Armies in the Field, Geneva, 22 August 1864, http://www.icrc.org/ihl/INTRO/120?OpenDocument (accessed March 29, 2014).

52. Oppenheim, *International Law*, 281–82.

53. "Declaration Renouncing the Use, in Time of War, of Explosive Projectiles Under 400 Grammes Weight" (St. Petersburg Declaration), reproduced in Roberts and Guelff, *Documents,* 54–55.

54. Crowe, *War Crimes*, 84.

55. Project of an International Declaration concerning the Laws and Customs of War. Brussels, 27 August 1874, available at http://www.icrc.org/ihl/INTRO/135 (accessed April 1, 2014).

56. Quoted in Daniel Marc Segesser, "The International Debate on the Punishment of War Crimes," in *A World at War*, 356.

57. Segesser, "The International Debate on the Punishment of War Crimes," 355–56.

58. Preface, The Laws of War on Land. Oxford, 9 September 1880, available at http://www.icrc. org/applic/ihl/ihl.nsf/Article.xsp?action=openDocument&documentId=B06FB334DC14CB D1C12563CD00515767 (accessed April 1, 2014).

59. The Laws of War on Land, section III, Art. 84.

60. Crowe, *War Crimes*, 85.

61. Crowe, *War Crimes*, 85; Segesser, "International Debate," 357; Isabel Hull, "'Military Necessity' and the laws of war in Imperial Germany," in S. Kalyvas, I. Shapiro, and T. Masoud, eds., *Order, Conflict, and Violence* (Cambridge: Cambridge University Press, 2008), 357.

62. Hull, "'Military Necessity,'" 367. For a contrasting view that challenges Hull's thesis, see Alan Kramer, *Dynamic of Destruction: Culture and Mass Killing in the First World War* (Oxford/New York: Oxford University Press, 2007), *passim* (but particularly Chapter 4, 114–58).

63. Quoted in Hull, "'Military Necessity,'" 358.

64. Julius von Hartmann, "Militärische Nothwendigkeit und Humanität: ein kritischer Versuch," *Deutsche Rundschau* 13 (1877–8): 111–28 and 450–71; 14; 71–91, cited in Hull, "'Military Necessity,'" 359–61.

65. Hartmann, "Militärische Nothwendigkeit," 471, quoted in Hull, "Military Necessity," 360.

66. C. Lueder, "Krieg und Kriegsrecht im Allgemeinen," in F. v. Holtzendorff, ed., *Handbuch des Völkerrechts*, vol. 4 (Hamburg: A. G. Richter, 1889), 254, quoted in Hull, "'Military Necessity,'" 361. Other legal scholars subscribing to this interpretation included Christian Meurer, Emanuel Uhlmann, Franz von Listzt, and Karl Strupp. For citations to the works of these and other adherents of the German theory of military necessity, see Oppenheim, *International Law*, vol. I, 184n1.

67. Hull, "'Military Necessity,'" 362.

68. Oppenheim, *International Law*, vol. II, 449. The original provisions of the Russian draft (sections 69–71) stipulated that reprisals were permissible only if (1) enemy forces had committed "absolutely certain violations" of the Law of War; (2) they were narrowly tailored to the violations; and (3) they were ordered by the commanding officer.

69. Hull, "'Military Necessity,'" 363.

70. Hull, "'Military Necessity,'" 363.

71. Hull, "'Military Necessity,'" 373. Hull has expanded on her thesis in *A Scrap of Paper: Breaking and Making International Law during the Great War* (Ithaca/London: Cornell University Press, 2014), which builds on her earlier article as well as her previous monograph on German military culture in Southwest Africa, *Absolute Destruction: Military Culture and the Practice of War in Imperial Germany* (Ithaca and London: Cornell University Press, 2005). Both *Absolute Destruction* and *A Scrap of Paper* were critically acclaimed, yet her thesis of a German lawlessness based on an all-consuming doctrine of military necessity has invited its share of criticism. These include Samuel Moyn, "Book Review of *A Scrap of Paper* by Isabel V. Hull," *Wall Street Journal*, June 5, 2014, https://www.wsj.com/articles/book-review-a-scrap-of-paper-by-isabel-v-hull-1402010920 (accessed January 26, 2020); John W. Coogan, Review of Isabel V. Hull, *A Scrap of Paper*, H-Diplo, December 12, 2014, https://networks.h-net.org/node/28443/discussions/55267/h-diplo-essay-121-review-essay-scrap-paper-breaking-and-makingaccessed January 26, 2020); and Benjamin Ziemann, Review of Isabel V. Hull, *A Scrap of Paper*, H-Net Reviews in the Humanities & Social Sciences, May 2015, https://www.h-net.org/reviews/showpdf.php?id=44367 (accessed January 26, 2020). In a recent study of twentieth-century German crimes of state, historian Annette Weinke defends Hull's thesis against its critics: see Annette Weinke, *Law, History, and Justice: Debating German State Crimes in the Long 20th century* (New York/Oxford: Berghahn, 2019).

72. Crowe, *War Crimes*, 87.

73. Crowe, *War Crimes*, 88.

74. Quoted in Crowe, *War Crimes*, 88.

75. Preamble, Convention (II) with Respect to the Laws and Customs of War on Land and its annex: Regulations concerning the Laws and Customs of War on Land. The Hague, 29 July 1899, http://www.icrc.org/applic/ihl/ihl.nsf/Article.xsp?action=openDocument&documentId= 9FE084CDAC63D10FC12563CD00515C4D (accessed April 13, 2014).

76. Crowe, *War Crimes*, 89; Adam Roberts, "Land Warfare: From Hague to Nuremberg," in Howard, Andreopoulos, and Shulman ed., *The Laws of War*, 122.

77. Crowe, *War Crimes*, 89–90.

78. Roberts, "Land Warfare," 121.

79. Crowe, *War Crimes*, 90.

80. Crowe, *War Crimes*, 91; Roberts, "Land Warfare," 122; Roberts and Guelff, *Documents*, 67.

81. Roberts and Guelff, *Documents*, 68.

82. Roberts and Guelff, *Documents*, 69–82.

83. Crowe, *War Crimes*, 92.

84. Roberts and Guelff, *Documents*, 68.

85. Elihu Root, *Addresses on International Subjects* (Cambridge, MA: Harvard University Press, 1916), 103, quoted in Crowe, *War Crimes*, 81.

86. Halleck to Lieber, 6 August 1862, in Richard Shelly Hartigan, ed., *Lieber's Code and the Law of War* (New York: The Legal Classics Library, 1983), 78.

87. F. Lieber, "Guerrilla Parties Considered with Reference to the Laws and Usages of War," in Hartigan, *Lieber's Code*, 33.

88. Lieber, "Guerrilla Parties Considered with Reference to the Laws and Usages of War," in Hartigan, *Lieber's Code*, 34.

89. Lieber, "Guerrilla Parties Considered with Reference to the Laws and Usages of War," in Hartigan, *Lieber's Code*, 37.

90. Lieber, "Guerrilla Parties Considered with Reference to the Laws and Usages of War," in Hartigan, *Lieber's Code*, 43.

91. Lieber, "Guerrilla Parties Considered with Reference to the Laws and Usages of War," in Hartigan, *Lieber's Code*, 35.

92. Lieber, "Guerrilla Parties Considered with Reference to the Laws and Usages of War," in Hartigan, *Lieber's Code*, 35.

93. Lieber commented: "General Halleck seems to consider partisan troops and guerrilla troops as the same and seems to consider 'self-constitution' a characteristic of the partisan ..." Quoted in "Introduction," in Hartigan, *Lieber's Code and the Law of War*, 10.

94. Richard S. Hartigan, "Introduction," *Lieber's Code*, 10.

95. Lieber to Sumner, August 19, 1861, quoted in Hartigan, *Lieber's Code*, 2.

96. Lieber to Halleck, November 13, 1862, quoted in Hartigan, *Lieber's Code*, 13; Dietrich Schindler and Jirí Toman, eds., *The Laws of Armed Conflict: A Collection of Conventions, Resolutions and Other Documents* (Geneva, 1981), 10.

97. The committee consisted of four members, including General Ethan Allen Hitchcock, who served as chair. Lieber was the only non-military member of the board.

98. Richard S. Hartigan, "Introduction," in Hartigan, *Lieber's Code*, 14–15.

99. Article 5, "General Orders, No. 100," in Hartigan, *Lieber's Code*, 46.

100. Article 14, "General Orders, No. 100," in Hartigan, *Lieber's Code*, 48. Similarly, Abraham Lincoln justified his suspension of the writ of habeas corpus in 1861 with reference to national survival, reproving his critics: "Are all the laws but one to go unexecuted, and the government itself go to pieces, lest that one be violated?" Quoted in Jonathan Lurie, *Arming Military Justice*, vol. 1, *The Origins of the US Court of Military Appeals 1775–1950* (Princeton, NJ: Princeton University Press, 1992), 14.

101. Article 17, "General Orders, No. 100," in Hartigan, *Lieber's Code*, 49.

102. Article 22, "General Orders, No. 100," in Hartigan, *Lieber's Code*, 49. The "exigencies of war" notwithstanding, Lieber subsequently affirms that in modern European wars civilian immunity from military attack was "the rule" and denial of that immunity "the exceptions." See also Article 25.

103. Article 60, "General Orders, No. 100," in Hartigan, *Lieber's Code*, 57.

104. Article 28, "General Orders, No. 100," in Hartigan, *Lieber's Code*, 50.

105. Article 70, "General Orders, No. 100," in Hartigan, *Lieber's Code*, 58.

106. Article 80, "General Orders, No. 100," in Hartigan, *Lieber's Code*, 59.

107. Article 16, "General Orders, No. 100," in Hartigan, *Lieber's Code*, 48; Article 29, "General Orders, No. 100," in *Lieber's Code*, 50. The importance Lieber attached to restoring peace helps explain his well-known aphorism that it is more humane to fight wars with extreme (but not unnecessary) violence, so that the participants will be motivated to end the war. In his ringing phrase, "sharp wars are brief."

108. Article 31, "General Orders, No. 100," in Hartigan, *Lieber's Code*, 51.

109. Article 34, "General Orders, No. 100," in Hartigan, *Lieber's Code*, 51–52.

110. Article 38, "General Orders, No. 100," in Hartigan, *Lieber's Code*, 52.

111. Article 33, "General Orders, No. 100," in Hartigan, *Lieber's Code*, 51. Lieber begins Article 33 with the words, "It is no longer considered lawful . . .," suggesting that the practice of using the subjects of a conquered enemy as forced laborers was permitted in earlier eras.

112. Articles 51–52, in Hartigan, *Lieber's Code*, 55.

113. Article 65, in Hartigan, *Lieber's Code*, 57.

114. Articles 81–82, in Hartigan, *Lieber's Code*, 60.

115. The portions of Lieber's Code dealing with "irregulars" are consistent with the essay on guerrillas he had prepared earlier for Halleck. On April 22, 1863, Halleck communicated these principles to Union Army headquarters in Missouri, instructing district commanders and military judges that insurgents were not entitled to the Law of War. The key criterion setting "partisan soldiers" apart from "brigands or guerrillas" was the "organization and equipment of soldiers"; without them, the soldier enjoyed no protected status when captured. Instead, he was to be put on trial for brigandage before a military commission and, if convicted, put to death "according to the usage of nations." General Orders, No. 30, in Hartigan, *Lieber's Code*, 92–96.

116. Lieber to Halleck, May 20, 1863, in *Lieber's Code*, 108; Crowe, *War Crimes*, 82.

117. Introduction, *Lieber's Code*, 22; Theodor Meron, *War Crimes Law Comes of Age*, 139. For an analysis of the Lieber Code's impact on the Brussels Declaration, see Crowe, *War Crimes*, 84–85.

118. Quoted in Meron, *War Crimes Law Comes of Age*, 139–40.

119. Roberts and Guelff, *Documents*, 68.

120. Meron, *War Crimes Law Comes of Age*, 133–35.

121. Beth van Schaack and Ronald C. Slye, *International Criminal Law and its Enforcement* (New York: Foundation Press, 2010), 265.

122. The British and French incorporated the Hague Convention principles into their own military manuals, furnishing both excerpts of the Convention for their troops and glosses on them. Isabel Hull, *Absolute Destruction: Military Culture and the Practices of War in Imperial Germany* (Ithaca/London: Cornell University Press, 2005), 128.

123. Article 3, 1907 Hague Convention IV, in Roberts and Guelff, *Documents*, 70.

124. Theodor Meron, *The Humanization of International Law* (Leiden/Boston: Martinus Nijhoff, 2006), 116; Steven R. Ratner and Jason S. Abrams, *Accountability for Human Rights Atrocities in International Law: Beyond the Nuremberg Legacy* (New York/Oxford: Oxford University Press, 2001), 5.

125. Segesser, "International Debate," 356. Law professor Ziv Bohrer takes issue with this argument, countering that six pre-Second World War cases reaching back to the High Middle Ages show a "recurring 'outlawry format'" in the prosecution of international crimes. The six cases he cites are the trials of Conradin (1298), William Wallace (1305), Peter von Hagenbach (1474), the proposal to put Napoleon to death for waging war in violation of international treaties (1815), implementation of the Lieber Code (1861-65), and proposals to put the Kaiser and other accused war criminals on trial after the First World War. Bohrer's conclusion is that "[international criminal law] stretches for nearly a millennium." Ziv Bohrer, "International Criminal Law's Millennium of Forgotten History," *Law & History Review* 34 (2016): 393–485, available at SSRN: https://ssrn.com/abstract=3219242 (accessed February 1, 2020).

126. Peter Maguire, *Law and War: An American Story* (New York: Columbia University Press, 2001), 55–56.

127. Maguire, *Law and War*, 61–62.

128. Maguire, *Law and War*, 63–64.

129. See, e.g., the comments of Secretary of War Elihu Root, quoted in Maguire, *Law and War*, 65.

130. G. R. Elton, "Human Rights and the Liberties of Englishmen," *University of Illinois Law Review* No. 2 (1990): 332, 346.

7 The First World War and the Failure of the Law of War

1. The telegram of congratulations was sent to Paul Kruger, the president of the Transvaal, for repelling without German help a raiding party sent to the Transvaal by Cecil Rhodes.

2. Holger Herwig, *Hammer or Anvil? Modern Germany 1648–Present* (Lexington, MA/ Toronto: Heath, 1994), 178–79; Palmer and Colton, *A History of the Modern World*, 665.

3. Fritz Dickmann, "Die Kriegsschuldfrage auf der Friedenskonferenz von Paris 1919," *Historische Zeitschrift* 197(1) (August 1963): 13.

4. Dickmann, "Die Kriegsschuldfrage," 13.

5. Dickmann, "Die Kriegsschuldfrage," 15. Isabel Hull refers to this German blindness as a kind of cultural "autism." *Absolute Destruction*, 237. Like Dickmann, she regards Germany's "autism" as cutting it adrift from other European countries, particularly in its attitude toward military necessity and its reckless brinkmanship in international affairs.

6. See, e.g., the controversial thesis of Fritz Fischer, *Griff nach der Weltmacht: Die Kriegszielpolitik des kaiserlichen Deutschland 1914/18* (Düsseldorf: Droste Verlag, 1961), and *World Power or Decline: The Controversy over Germany's Aims in the First World War*, trans. Lancelot L. Farrar, Robert Kimber, and Rita Kimber (New York: W. W. Norton, 1965). For criticisms of the Fischer thesis, see Gerhard Ritter, *Der erste Weltkrieg: Studien zum deutschen Geschichtsbild* (Bonn: Schriftenreihe der Bundeszentrale für Politische Bildung, 1964); Egmont Zechlin, "Deutschland zwischen Kabinettskrieg und Wirtschaftskrieg," *Historische Zeitschrift*, 199/2 (October 1964): 347–458; Herwig, *Hammer or Anvil?*, 196.

7. Alan Kramer, *Dynamic of Destruction*, 6–8. German investigations into claims of brutality against Belgian civilians and the wanton destruction of buildings during the invasion found that Belgian civilians had staged armed attacks on German troops, thereby provoking reprisals. Unsurprisingly, the Belgians held their own investigations and arrived at a very different conclusion: German reprisals were premeditated and used to terrorize the Belgian population. Decades after the war, Franz Petri and Peter Schöller sought to resolve the issue so far as the evidence allowed. They found no merit in the Belgian thesis of a deliberate policy of terror; only after the outbreak of wild street-

shooting did the occupation troops resort to reprisals as a form of deterrence. On the other hand, they found little evidence of popular uprisings by Belgian civilians that would have justified reprisal. They categorically rejected the findings of the so-called "White Book" investigations of 1915 because the witness statements were falsified. Franz Petri and Peter Schöller, "Zur Bereinigung des Franktireurproblems vom August 1914," *Vierteljahrshefte für Zeitgeschichte* 9(3) (July 1961): 234–48.

8. Kramer, *Dynamic of Destruction*, 8.

9. Kramer, *Dynamic of Destruction*, 9–10.

10. Kramer, *Dynamic of Destruction*, 11.

11. Kramer, *Dynamic of Destruction*, 15.

12. Kramer, *Dynamic of Destruction*, 16.

13. James F. Willis, *Prologue to Nuremberg: The Politics and Diplomacy of Punishing War Criminals of the First World War* (Westport, CT/London: Greenwood Press, 1982), 27–28.

14. Quoted in Willis, *Prologue*, 31.

15. Willis, *Prologue*, 30; Paul Betts, "Germany, International Justice and the Twentieth Century," *History and Meaning* 17 (1/2) (July 19, 2005): 49.

16. Willis, *Prologue*, 33–34.

17. Willis, *Prologue*, 34–35.

18. Willis, *Prologue*, 54–55.

19. Willis, *Prologue*, 58; Dickmann, "Die Kriegsschuldfrage," 21–22.

20. Willis, *Prologue*, 63–64.

21. Willis, *Prologue*, 68; Dickmann, "Die Kriegsschuldfrage," 25.

22. Willis, *Prologue*, 68.

23. Dickmann, "Die Kriegsschuldfrage," 26.

24. Dickmann, "Die Kriegsschuldfrage," 26.

25. Dickmann, "Die Kriegsschuldfrage," 17, 19–20; Daniel Marc Segesser, "The Punishment of War Crimes Committed against Prisoners of War, Deportees and Refugees during and after the First World War," in Matthew Stibbe, ed., *Captivity, Forced Labour and Forced Migration in Europe during the First World War* (London/New York: Routledge, 2009), 138.

26. Dickmann, "Die Kriegsschuldfrage," 25–27.

27. Willis, *Prologue*, 41.

28. Willis, *Prologue*, 73–74.

29. Willis, *Prologue*, 73–75; Dickmann, "Die Kriegsschuldfrage," 36.

30. Willis, *Prologue*, 75–76. See also Dickmann, "Die Kriegsschuldfrage," 37.

31. Willis, *Prologue*, 77–78; Dickmann, "Die Krieggschuldfrage," 37–38.

32. Willis, *Prologue*, 81–82; Dickmann, "Die Krieggschuldfrage," 39–40.

33. Willis, *Prologue*, 83–84; J. W. Brügel, "Das Schicksal der Strafbestimmungen des Versailler Vertrags," *Vierteljahrshefte für Zeitgeschichte* 6(3) (July 1958): 263–64.

34. Willis, *Prologue*, 84–85.

35. Dickmann, "Die Kriegsschuldfrage," 5.

36. On this topic see Dickmann, "Die Kriegsschuldfrage," 7–8; Gerd Hankel, *Die Leipziger Prozesse: Deutsche Kriegsverbrechen und ihre strafrechtliche Verfolgung nach dem Ersten Weltkrieg* (Hamburg: Hamburger Edition, 2003), 31–32.

37. Brügel, "Das Schicksal," 267–69.

38. Willis, *Prologue*, 83, 86.

39. Betts, "Germany," 53.

40. The United Nations War Crimes Commission, *History of the United Nations War Crimes Commission and the Development of the Laws of War* (Buffalo: William S. Hein & Co., 2006), 46.

41. Willis, *Prologue*, 116, 128–29; Betts, "Germany," 53; Friedrich Karl Kaul, "Die Verfolgung deutscher Kriegsverbrecher nach dem ersten Weltkrieg," *Zeitschrift für Geschichtswissenschaft* 14 (1966): 23, 27–29; The United Nations War Crimes Commission, *History*, 46.

42. Willis, *Prologue*, 130–31; Kaul, "Die Verfolgung," 31.

43. Willis, *Prologue*, 133; Kaul, "Die Verfolgung," 31.

44. Willis, *Prologue*, 133–34; The United Nations War Crimes Commission, *History*, 48.

45. Willis, *Prologue*, 138; The United Nations War Crimes Commission, *History*, 49.

46. Quoted in Willis, *Prologue*, 137.

47. Willis, *Prologue*, 139–40; The United Nations War Crimes Commission, *History*, 49.

48. Willis, *Prologue*, 134–35; The United Nations War Crimes Commission, *History*, 51.

49. Willis, *Prologue*, 135–36; The United Nations War Crimes Commission, *History*, 50–51.

50. Willis, *Prologue*, 135–66. The Leipzig Imperial Court acquitted still other persons on the French list, including Lieutenant Adolf Laule and a Dr. Michelson (both acquitted in July 1922).

51. Willis, *Prologue*, 139–45.

52. Betts, "Germany," 53; The United Nations War Crimes Commission, *History*, 51.

53. Willis, *Prologue*, 146.

54. Gary Bass, *Stay the Hand of Vengeance: The Politics of War Crimes Tribunals* (Princeton/ Oxford: Princeton University Press, 2000), 116.

55. Bass, *Stay the Hand*, 124–25; Willis, *Prologue*, 154; Crowe, *War Crimes*, 112.

56. Bass, *Stay the Hand*, 126; Willis, *Prologue*, 154–56; Crowe, *War Crimes*, 112.

57. Bass, *Stay the Hand*, 126; Willis, *Prologue*, 154–56; Crowe, *War Crimes*, 112.

58. Talaat Pasha was shot down in Berlin in March 1921. Prince Said Halim Pasha met the same fate in Rome in December 1921, as did Dr. Behaeddin Shakir and Djemal Azmi (Berlin, April 1922) and Djemal Pasha (Tiflis, July 1922). It is suspected that Enver Pasha was dispatched by an Armenian during a skirmish in Central Asia in August 1922. Willis, *Prologue*, 163.

59. Quoted in UN War Crimes Commission, *History*, 287. See also Willis, *Prologue*, 138.

60. Eck and his co-defendants were charged with murdering the survivors of the *Peleus*, a Greek merchant ship. The British prosecutor argued his case with reference to the *Llandovery Castle* trial, quoting verbatim from the text of the Leipzig Imperial Court's verdict. All of the defendants were convicted and given punishments ranging from death to multi-year prison terms. See United Nations War Crimes Commission, *Law Reports of Trials of War Criminals*, vol. I (London: His Majesty's Stationery Office, 1947), 1–21.

8 The Second World War and the Triumph of the Law of War

1. Gerhard Weinberg, *A World at Arms: A Global History of World War II* (Cambridge: Cambridge University Press, 1994), 20.

2. Weinberg, *A World at Arms*, 21; Michael J. Lyons, *World War II: A Short History* (Upper Saddle River, NJ: Prentice Hall, 1994), 53.

3. Weinberg, *A World at Arms*, 21, 58.

4. Weinberg, *A World at Arms*, 21; Henry Friedlander, *The Origins of Nazi Genocide: From Euthanasia to the Final Solution* (Chapel Hill: The University of North Carolina Press, 1995), *passim*.

5. David M. Crowe, *The Holocaust: Roots, History, and Aftermath* (Philadelphia: Westview Press, 2008), 160; Alexander B. Rossino, *Hitler Strikes Poland: Blitzkrieg, Ideology, and Atrocity* (Lawrence, KS: University Press of Kansas, 2003), 22.

6. Michael S. Bryant, "Punishing the Excess: Sadism, Bureaucratized Atrocity, and the U.S. Army Concentration Camp Trials, 1945–1947," in Henry Friedlander and Nathan Stoltzfuss, eds., *Nazi Crimes and the Law* (Cambridge: Cambridge University Press, 2008), 67; Johannes Tuchel, "Planung und Realität des Systems der Konzentrationslager 1934–1938," in U. Herbert, K. Orth, and C. Dieckmann, eds., *Die nationalsozialistischen Konzentrationslager*, vol. 1 (Frankfurt a.M.: Fischer, 1998), 43, 48–49.

7. Eric Lichtblau, "The Holocaust Just Got More Shocking," *The New York Times Sunday Review*, March 1, 2013, http://www.nytimes.com/2013/03/03/sunday-review/the-holocaust-just-got-more-shocking.html?pagewanted=all&_r=0 (accessed June 13, 2014).

8. *U.S. v. Erhard Milch et al.*, in *Trials of War Criminals before the Nuernberg Military Tribunals*, Vol. II (Nuernberg: U. S. Government Printing Office, October 1946–April 1949), 353–888.

9. Michael S. Bryant, "Die US-amerikanischen Militärprozesse gegen SS-Personal Ärzte und Kapos des KZ Dachau 1945–1948," in Ludwig Eiber and Robert Sigel, eds., *Dachauer Prozesse: NS-Verbrechen vor amerikanischen Militärgerichten in Dachau 1945–1948* (Göttingen: Wallstein, 2007), 114–16.

10. Weinberg, *A World at Arms*, 209 ff.; Lyons, *World War II*, 131–32; Michael Bryant and Wolfgang Form, "Victim Nationality in US and British Military Trials: Hadamar, Dachau, Belsen," in *Justice, Politics and Memory in Europe after the Second World War*, vol. 2, ed. S. Bardgett, D. Cesarani, J. Reinisch, and J-D Steinert (London/Portland, OR: Valentine Mitchell, 2011), 20.

11. Crowe, *The Holocaust*, 197.

12. Hamburger Institut für Sozialforschung, ed., *Verbrechen der Wehrmacht: Dimensionen des Vernichtungskrieges* 1941–1944 (Hamburg: Hamburger Edition, 2002), 69.

13. Reproduced in Hamburger Institut für Sozialforschung, *Verbrechen der Wehrmacht*, 46–48.

14. Felix Römer, *Der Kommissarbefehl: Wehrmacht und NS-Verbrechen an der Ostfront 1941/42* (Paderborn: Ferdinand Schöningh, 2008), 13–15.

15. Christian Streit, *Keine Kameraden: Die Wehrmacht und die sowjetischen Kriegsgefangenen 1941–1945* (Stuttgart, 1991), 83–99, 100–105.

16. This figure likely understates the actual number of executions. See, e.g., Römer, *Kommissarbefehl*, 353.

17. Detlef Siebert, "Die Durchführung des Kommissarbefehls in den Frontverbänden des Heeres: Eine Quantifizierende Auswertung der Forschung," unpublished manuscript (2000), 13. According to Römer, the German Army in the East not only did not obstruct the order but broadly shared the ideological premises underlying it. *Kommissarbefehl*, 200–1. On the ideological affinities between the *Ostheer* troops and the Nazi leadership, see Omer Bartov, *The Eastern Front, 1941–45: German Troops and the Barbarisation of Warfare* (New York: Palgrave, 2001), 68–105; Christopher R. Browning and Jürgen Matthäus, *The Origins of the Final Solution: The Evolution of Nazi Jewish Policy, September 1939–March 1942* (Lincoln, NE/Yad Vashem, Jerusalem: University of Nebraska Press, 2004), 223.

18. Römer, *Kommissarbefehl*, 359.

19. Reproduced in Hamburger Institut für Sozialforschung, ed., *Verbrechen der Wehrmacht*, 58–60. A translation of the commissar order into English may be found in J. Noakes and G. Pridham, eds., *Nazism: A History in Documents and Eyewitness Accounts, 1919–1945*, vol. II (New York: Schocken Books, 1988), 1088–89.

20. Reproduced in Hamburger Institut für Sozialforschung, ed., *Verbrechen der Wehrmacht*, 54. For a translation of the "Guidelines for the Conduct of Troops in Russia" see Noakes and Pridham, *Nazism* II, 1090.

21. Bartov, *Eastern Front*, 107. According to Holocaust historian Christopher Browning, 6,000 Soviet prisoners of war died per day in German custody until the fall of 1941; by the spring of 1942, some 2 million were dead. *Origins*, 244.

22. Römer, *Kommissarbefehl*, 226, 235.

23. Bartov, *Eastern Front*, 110.

24. We can gain an inkling of the uniqueness of German policies in the east when we compare them with forbidden to harm French prisoners of war. In order to avoid gratuitous suffering, the rules of engagement prescribed conduct in accordance with the Law of War, as well as adequate food and transportation. In stark contrast with Barbarossa, the Law of War applied to the French campaign. Bartov, *Eastern Front*, 110.

25. Bartov, *Eastern Front*, 112–13.

26. Römer, *Kommissarbefehl*, 238–51.

27. Browning and Matthäus, *Origins*, 253–60; Crowe, *The Holocaust*, 199, 202.

28. Browning and Matthäus, *Origins*, 260.

29. Quoted in Browning and Matthäus, *Origins*, 260–61.

30. Browning and Matthäus, *Origins*, 261, 276.

31. Browning and Matthäus, *Origins*, 312–13.

32. Crowe, *The Holocaust*, 241 ff.; Michael S. Bryant, *Eyewitness to Genocide: the Operation Reinhard Trials, 1955–66* (Knoxville, TN: University of Tennessee Press, 2014), 2–8.

33. Robert Jan van Pelt and Deborah Dwork, *Auschwitz 1270 to the Present* (New York: W. W. Norton & Co., 1996), 130, 166–68.

34. van Pelt and Dwork, *Auschwitz*, 176–80.

35. van Pelt and Dwork, *Auschwitz*, Chapter 7, *passim* (197–235).

36. Quoted in van Pelt and Dwork, *Auschwitz*, 298.

37. van Pelt and Dwork, *Auschwitz*, 301–2; Browning and Matthäus, *Origins*, 421.

38. van Pelt and Dwork, *Auschwitz*, 254.

39. van Pelt and Dwork, *Auschwitz*, 302–303; Browning and Matthäus, *Origins*, 421.

40. van Pelt and Dwork, *Auschwitz*, 304–306.

41. van Pelt and Dwork, *Auschwitz*, 321–22.

42. van Pelt and Dwork, *Auschwitz*, 327–43.

43. US Department of State, *Foreign Relations of the United States: Diplomatic Papers 1941*, Vol. 1 (Washington, D.C.: Government Printing Office, 1960), 445ff.

44. See, for example, the letter from Dutch Ambassador Loudon, Luxembourg Minister Le Gallais, and Yugoslav Minister Fotitch to Cordell Hull, 30 July, 1942, in US Department of State, *Foreign Relations of the United States: Diplomatic Papers 1942*, Vol. 1 (Washington, D.C.: Government Printing Office, 1960), 46–47.

45. National Archives, Kew (London), FO 370/2899. See also Wolfgang Form, "Planung und Durchführung west-alliierter Kriegsverbrecherprozesse nach dem Zweiten Weltkrieg," in *Festschrift für Theo Schiller: Perspektiven der politischen Soziologie* (Wiesbaden, 2008), 233–53, 236.

46. Memorandum for Mr. Stettinius from J. W. Pehle, 28 August, 1944, National Archives Records Administration-College Park, RG 107, Entry 74A, Box 5, German War Crimes.

47. See, e.g., Gary J. Bass, *Stay the Hand of Vengeance*, 193.

48. "Memorandum of British Views on Policy to Be Adopted With Respect to War Criminals," US Department of State, *Foreign Relations of the United States: Diplomatic Papers, 1942,* Volume I (Washington, D.C.: Government Printing Office, 1960), 53–54.

49. "Task of the Commission: Investigation of Evidence and Compilation of Lists of Persons Wanted for Trial as War Criminals," US Department of State, *Foreign Relations of the United States: Diplomatic Papers, 1944,* Volume I, 1346. This was also the position of Sheldon Glueck, *War Criminals: Their Prosecution and Punishment* (New York: Alfred A. Knopf, 1944), 34.

50. "Memorandum of British Views on Policy to be Adopted With Respect to War Criminals," US Department of State, *Foreign Relations of the United States: Diplomatic Papers, 1942,* Volume I (Washington, D.C.: Government Printing Office, 1960), 53–54.

51. "The Polish Ministry for Foreign Affairs to the American Embassy near the Polish Government in Exile," US Department of State, *Foreign Relations of the United States: Diplomatic Papers, 1943,* Volume I (Washington, D.C.: Government Printing Office, 1963), 410.

52. Michael R. Marrus (ed.), *The Nuremberg War Crimes Trial 1945–46* (Boston/New York: Bedford Books, 1997), 23.

53. Winston S. Churchill, *The Second World War*, vol. 5, *Closing the Ring* (New York: Bantam Books, 1962), 319–20.

54. Martin Gilbert, *Winston S. Churchill, 1941–1945: Road to Victory* (London: William Heinemann, 1986), 1201–02.

55. Henry Morgenthau Jr., "Memorandum for President Roosevelt," in Marrus, *Nuremberg War Crimes Trial,* 24–55.

56. Henry L. Stimson, "Memorandum Opposing the Morgenthau Plan," in Marrus, *Nuremberg War Crimes Trial,* 26–27.

57. Michael S. Bryant, *Confronting the "Good Death:" Nazi Euthanasia on Trial, 1945–53* (Boulder, CO: University Press of Colorado, 2005), 67.

58. Bryant, *Confronting the "Good Death,"* 68; H. L. Stimson, E. R. Stettinius, Jr., and F. Biddle, "Memorandum for the President," in Marrus (ed.), *Nuremberg War Crimes Trial,* 30–32.

59. "Memorandum of Conversation of E. R. Stettinius Jr. and S. Rosenman with V. Molotov and A. Eden in San Francisco," in Marrus (ed.), *Nuremberg War Crimes Trial,* 35–37.

60. Russell M. Cooper, *American Consultation in World Affairs for the Preservation of Peace* (New York: Macmillan, 1934), 7–18.

61. "Document 24: Memorandum on Aggressive War by Colonel William Chanler," in Bradley F. Smith, ed., *The American Road to Nuremberg: The Documentary Record* (Stanford, CA: Hoover Institution Press, 1982), 69–74.

62. Charter of the International Military Tribunal, in *Trial of the Major War Criminals before the International Military Tribunal,* vol. I (Nuremberg, Germany: International Military Tribunal, 1947), 11; Protocol Rectifying Discrepancy in Text of Charter, 17.

63. Charter of the International Military Tribunal, in *Trial of the Major War Criminals,* vol. I, 12.

64. Robert H. Jackson, "Report to the President," in Marrus, ed., *The Nuremberg War Crimes Trial*, 40–42.

65. Article 24 (g), Charter of the International Military Tribunal, in *Trial of the Major War Criminals*, vol. I, 16.

66. Article 24 (j), in *Trial of the Major War Criminals*, vol. I, 16.

67. Telford Taylor, *The Anatomy of the Nuremberg Trials: A Personal Memoir* (New York: Alfred A. Knopf, 1992), 409, 567, 593.

68. See, e.g., Taylor, *The Anatomy of the Nuremberg Trials*; Ann Tusa and John Tusa, *The Nuremberg Trial* (New York: Skyhorse, 2010); Eugene Davidson, *The Trial of the Germans: An Account of the Twenty-two Defendants before the International Military Tribunal at Nuremberg* (Columbia, MO: University of Missouri Press, 1997); Whitney Harris, *Tyranny on Trial: The Evidence at Nuremberg* (New York: Barnes & Noble, 1995); Bradley F. Smith, *Reaching Judgment at Nuremberg: The Untold Story of How the Nazi War Criminals were Judged* (New York: Basic Books, 1977).

69. Judgment, *Trial of the Major War Criminals*, vol. I, 253–54; Theodor Meron, *The Humanization of International Law* (Leiden/Boston: Martinus Nijhoff, 2006), 9–10; The United Nations War Crimes Commission, *History*, 221.

70. S. Ratner and J. Abrams, *Accountability*, 81; Geoffrey Best, *War & Law Since 1945* (Oxford/ New York: Clarendon Press, 2002), 8; Meron, *Humanization*, 117; Oppenheim, *International Law*, vol. II, 282 ff.

71. Reproduced in Noakes and Pridham, eds., *Nazism*, vol. 2, 685.

72. Judgment, *Trial of the Major War Criminals*, vol. I, 186; Marrus, *Nuremberg War Crimes Trial*, 127–28.

73. Judgment, *Trial of the Major War Criminals*, vol. I, 225–26.

74. *Trial of the Major War Criminals*, vol. I, 226, 253.

75. *Trial of the Major War Criminals*, vol. I, 154.

76. *Trial of the Major War Criminals*, vol. I, 255 ff.

77. With the exception of Göring, who cheated the hangman by committing suicide in his jail cell.

78. Telford Taylor, "Nuremberg Trials: War Crimes and International Law," *International Conciliation* 450 (1949): 271.

79. Taylor, "Nuremberg Trials," 255–56.

80. William F. Fratcher, "American Organization for Prosecution of German War Criminals," *Missouri Law Review* 13(1) (January 1948): 66–67.

81. Taylor, "Nuremberg Trials," 272–73.

82. Taylor, "Nuremberg Trials," 273.

83. Bryant, *Confronting*, 75.

84. Preliminary Report to the Secretary of the Army by the Chief of Counsel for War Crimes, May 12, 1948, 2–3, quoted in Taylor, "Nuremberg Trials," 278.

85. For a penetrating account of the British role in providing the Americans with many of their medical defendants, see Paul Julian Weindling, *Nazi Medicine and the Nuremberg Trials: From Medical War Crimes to Informed Consent* (New York: Palgrave, 2004).

86. The exchange was not a one-way street: the US reciprocated by transferring Field Marshal Kesselring to the British for trial for war crimes committed in Italy.

87. Taylor, "Nuremberg Trials," 279.

88. Taylor, "Nuremberg Trials," 275.

89. Quoted in Taylor, "Nuremberg Trials," 289.

90. The British military courts adopted the same standard of *mens rea* ("guilty mind") in their Royal Warrant cases. In his instructions to the court in the *Burgholz* trial (No. 2), the British Judge Advocate stated that the "requirements of . . . *Mens Rea* are fulfilled if you find the accused either knew that they were doing wrong or ought to have known . . ." Cassese, *International Criminal Law*, 166n10.

91. "The fact that the defendant acted pursuant to order of his Government or of a superior shall not free him from responsibility."

92. Taylor, "Nuremberg Trials," 291.

93. Taylor, "Nuremberg Trials," 306. Flick was convicted of economic plunder under the second count, and he and another co-defendant (Steinbrinck) were also convicted under the fourth count (accessory to crimes against humanity committed by the SS) for their financial contributions to the SS, as well as fraternizing with the SS through an association called the "Circle of Friends."

94. Taylor, "Nuremberg Trials," 311–12.

95. Taylor, "Nuremberg Trials," 313–16; Cassese, *International Criminal Law*, 139.

96. Taylor, "Nuremberg Trials," 321–22; Beate Ihme-Tuchel, "Fall 7: Der Prozeß gegen die 'Südwest-Generale' (gegen Wilhelm List und andere)," in G. Ueberschär, ed., *Der Nationalsozialismus vor Gericht*, 145.

97. Opening Statement of François de Menthon, *Trial of the Major War Criminals*, vol. 5, 399.

98. Article 50, 1907 Hague Convention IV: Regulations, in Roberts and Guelff, *Documents*, 81.

99. Regrettably, neither the IMT nor the NMT considered that many of the reprisal shootings in the Balkans were inflicted on Serbia's Jewish and Sinti/Roma populations, which were almost entirely obliterated—a distinction that might have altered the judges' analyses.

100. Article 28, General Orders, No. 100 (the Lieber Code), in Richard S. Hartigan, ed., *Lieber's Code and the Law of War*, 50.

101. Telford Taylor, *Nuremberg and Vietnam: An American Tragedy* (New York: Bantam, 1971), 55–56.

102. Lassa Oppenheim, *International Law*, vol. II, 460.

103. Taylor, "Nuremberg Trials," 323. The judgment can be found in *Trials of War Criminals before the Nürnberg Military Tribunals*, vol. XI, "The Hostage Case" (Washington, D.C.: Government Printing Office, 1950). The portion of the verdict that discusses reprisals appears at pages 528 ff.

104. Taylor, "Nuremberg Trials," 324–25. Von Weichs was dismissed from the case due to illness; Franz Böhme committed suicide in his jail cell prior to arraignment.

105. Taylor, "Nuremberg Trials," 325.

106. Taylor, "Nuremberg Trials," 326–28.

107. The language of Military Tribunal V is reproduced in Alan Ryan, *Yamashita's Ghost: War Crimes, MacArthur's Justice, and Command Accountability* (Lawrence, KS: University Press of Kansas, 2012), 307–308.

108. See, e.g., Ryan, *Yamashita's Ghost*; Richard L. Yael, *The Yamashita Precedent: War Crimes and Command Responsibility* (Wilmington, DE: Scholarly Resources Inc., 1982), 124–27.

109. Cassese, *International Criminal Law*, 173, 205.

110. Cassese, *International Criminal Law*, 208–209.

111. Reproduced in Taylor, "Nuremberg Trials," 343.

112. Taylor, "Nuremberg Trials," 343.

113. Gary Bass, *Stay the Hand*, 29–31, 151 ff.

114. Jody Prescott and Joanne Eldrige, "Military Commissions, Past and Future," *Military Review* (March–April 2003): 43–45; A. W. Green, "The Military Commission," *Am. Journal of International Law* 42/4 (October 1948): 832–48.

115. See, e.g., the trial by military commission of eleven German civilians at Darmstadt on July 25, 1945, accused of killing three US prisoners of war (*U. S. v. Joseph Hartgen, Friedrich Wust, Margarete Witzler, et al.*).

116. UN War Crimes Commission, *Law Reports of Trials of War Criminals*, Vol. VI – "Trial of Martin Gottfried Weiss and 39 'Others'" (London: His Majesty's Stationery Office, 1949), 14.

117. Dachau embraced some eighty-five subsidiary camps ("subcamps"), such as Kaufering located twenty-five miles southwest of Munich.

118. "Trial of Martin Gottfried Weiss and 39 'Others'", 7.

119. "Trial of Martin Gottfried Weiss and 39 'Others'", 8.

120. *U. S. v. Hans Altfuldisch et al.*, Case no. 000-50-5, held at Dachau before a Military Government Court, March 29 to May 13, 1946.

121. "Trial of Martin Gottfried Weiss and 39 'Others'", 15.

122. "Trial of Martin Gottfried Weiss and 39 'Others'", 16–17.

123. Michael S. Bryant, "Dachau Trials–Die rechtlichen und historisichen Grundlagen der US-amerikanischen Kriegsverbrecherprozesse, 1942–1947," in H. Radtke et al., eds., *Historische Dimensionen von Kriegsverbrecherprozessen nach den Zweiten Weltkrieg* (Baden Baden: Nomos, 2007), 119.

124. See, e.g., Neil Boister and Robert Cryer, eds., *Documents on the Tokyo International Military Tribunal: Charter, Indictment and Judgements* (Oxford: Oxford University Press, 2008), xxxiii.

125. Crowe, *War Crimes*, 124.

126. Jonathan Fenby, *Chiang Kai-shek: China's Generalissimo and the Nation HE Lost* (Boston, MA: Da Capo Press, 2004, 214), cited in Crowe, *War Crimes*, 126.

127. Iris Chang, *Rape of Nanjing: The Forgotten Holocaust of World War II* (New York: Basic Books, 1997), 4.

128. Crowe, *War Crimes*, 129. Crowe cites the estimates of R. J. Rummel that, of the 19 million Chinese who perished in the Sino-Japanese War, as many as 1 million were prisoners of war.

129. Crowe, *War Crimes*, 131.

130. Crowe, *War Crimes*, 132.

131. Crowe, *War Crimes*, 133; John W. Dower, *War without Mercy: Race & Power in the Pacific* (New York: Pantheon Books, 1986), 234. In his book Dower shows that racism led to war crimes on both sides.

132. Crowe, *War Crimes*, 133; Tien-wei Wu, "A Preliminary Review of Japanese Biological Warfare Unit 731 in the United States," *Free Republic*, September 23, 2001, 4–5.

133. Crowe, *War Crimes*, 136; Yuma Totani, *The Tokyo War Crimes Trial: The Pursuit of Justice in the Wake of World War II* (Cambridge, MA: Harvard University Press, 2008), 60, 248.

134. For the recent scholarship on these trials, see Barak Kushner, *Men to Devils, Devils to Men: Japanese War Crimes and Chinese Justice* (Cambridge, MA: Harvard University Press, 2015), especially chapters 4 and 7.

135. Louis Fisher, *American Military Tribunals & Presidential Power: American Revolution to the War on Terrorism* (Lawrence, KS: University Press of Kansas, 2005), 144; Crowe, *War Crimes*, 223.

136. Ryan, *Yamashita's Ghost*, 47–49; Yael, *The Yamashita Precedent*, 30 ff.; Crowe, *War Crimes*, 198.

137. William Manchester, *American Caesar: Douglas MacArthur, 1880–1964* (Boston: Little, Brown, 1978), 412.

138. Yael, *The Yamashita Precedent*, 138.

139. Quoted in UN War Crimes Commission, *Law Reports of Trials of War Criminals*, vol. IV (London: His Majesty's Stationery Office, 1948), 3.

140. Crowe, *War Crimes*, 198; Ryan, *Yamashita's Ghost*, 63.

141. Cited in Crowe, *War Crimes*, 198–99.

142. These included reception of affidavits into evidence without a foundation, abbreviation of defense cross-examinations, and prohibition of criticisms in open court about faulty interpretations by the court interpreters. Yael, *The Yamashita Precedent*, 138.

143. Yael, *The Yamashita Precedent*, 139.

144. Robert H. Jackson was absent from the high court at this time, embroiled in prosecuting the major war criminals in Nuremberg.

145. The dissenting views of Rutledge and Murphy are summarized in UN War Crimes Commission, *Law Reports of Trials of War Criminals*, vol. IV, 49–75. The case citation is *In Re Yamashita*, 327 U.S. 1 (1946).

146. See, e.g., the trials of Soemu Toyoda and Takashi Saki cited in Cassese, *International Criminal Law*, 205n7.

147. Articles 86 and 87, Protocol Additional to the Geneva Conventions of 12 August 1949, and relating to the Protection of Victims of International Armed Conflicts (Protocol I), 8 June 1977, http://www.icrc.org/ihl/INTRO/470 (accessed July 23, 2014).

148. Cassese, *International Criminal Law*, 205.

149. Department of the Army, *The Law of Land Warfare* (Washington: Government Printing Office, 1956), 178–79, https://ia801506.us.archive.org/18/items/Fm27-101956/Fm27-101956.pdf (accessed July 23, 2014).

150. Colonel Howard's jury instructions are partially reproduced in both Yael, *The Yamashita Precedent*, 130, and Cassese, *International Criminal Law*, 166.

151. "Constructive" knowledge is knowledge the law presumes an individual possesses based on the information available to him/her. It is essentially an objective rather than subjective standard of *mens rea*.

152. The quoted language is excerpted from Cassese, *International Criminal Law*, 210. My summary of the case is based on the ICTY's "Case Information Sheet," Čelebići Camp (IT-96-21), *Mucić et al.*, http://www.icty.org/x/cases/mucic/cis/en/cis_mucic_al_en.pdf (accessed July 23, 2014).

153. Such as General Masaharu Homma, 14th Army commander at the Battle of Corregidor (1942). Like Yamashita, Homma was prosecuted by US military commission on a theory of command responsibility supporting forty-eight counts of war crimes. He was convicted in February 1946 and executed on April 3 of that year.

154. Article 5, IMTFE Charter, http://www.jus.uio.no/english/services/library/treaties/04/4-06/military-tribunal-far-east.xml (accessed April 12, 2015); Crowe, *War Crimes*, 205–6. The indictment would later add murder in counts 37–52 on the rationale that, as a transnationally recognized criminal offense, it would avoid criticisms of *ex post facto* and victors' justice.

155. Opening Statement of the Prosecution, quoted in Crowe, *War Crimes*, 207.

156. See, e.g., Richard H. Minear, *Victor's Justice: the Tokyo War Crimes Trial* (Ann Arbor, MI: University of Michigan Press, 1971) (concluding that the foundation of the trial in international law was dubious, the procedure deficient, and the history misconceived); Crowe, *War Crimes* (concluding that the Tokyo IMTFE is a negative example of how not to conduct an international war crimes trial). For a summary of Anglo-Japanese scholarship critical of the IMTFE, see Totani, *The Tokyo War Crimes Trial*, 246 ff.

157. "The Tokyo War Crimes Trials (1946–48)," http://www.pbs.org/wgbh/amex/macarthur/peopleevents/pandeAMEX101.html (accessed July 27, 2014); Crowe, *War Crimes*, 237–40. For a critique of Pal's dissent, see Saburō Ienago, "Futabi Pāru hanketsu ni tsuite: Mainia kyōju ni kotaeru" (On Pal's Judgment for the Second Time: My Response to Professor Minear), in *Rekishi to sekinin* (Tokyo: Chūō daigaku shuppanbu, 1979), 114–26.

9 Into the Twenty-First Century: War Crimes and their Treatment Since the Second World War

1. Roberts and Guelff, *Documents*, 299.

2. Article 13, 1949 Geneva Convention III, in Roberts and Guelff, *Documents*, 250.

3. Article 17, 1949 Geneva Convention III, in Roberts and Guelff, *Documents*, 251.

4. i.e., Article 8 of Geneva Conventions I, II, and III, and Article 9, Geneva Convention IV.

5. Article 10, Geneva Conventions I, II, and III, and Article 11, Convention IV, in Roberts and Guelff, *Documents*, *passim*.

6. Article 143, Geneva Convention IV, in Roberts and Guelff, *Documents*, 351.

7. G. I. A. D. Draper, "Wars of National Liberation and War Criminality," in Michael Howard, ed., *Restraints on War: Studies in the Limitation of Armed Conflict* (Oxford: Oxford University Press, 1979), 162; Thomas Buergenthal, Dinah Shelton, and David Stewart, *International Human Rights* (St. Paul, MN: West Publishing, 2009), 381.

8. Article 3, 1949 Geneva Convention IV, in Roberts and Guelff, *Documents*, 302.

9. The reluctance persists despite the assurance in Common Article 3 that applying its provisions will not affect the "legal status" of the belligerents.

10. Implicit in the democratic/nationalist movements of the eighteenth and nineteenth centuries, the principle of the self-determination of peoples was championed in Woodrow Wilson's 14 Points (1918), the Atlantic Charter (1941), and the UN Charter (1945).

11. George J. Andreopoulos, "The Age of National Liberation Movements," in M. Howard, G. Andreopoulos, and M. Shulman, eds., *The Laws of War*, 200–201.

12. G. I. A. D. Draper, *The Red Cross Conventions* (London: Stevens & Sons, 1958), 15n47.

13. Andreopoulos, "Age of National Liberation Movements," 207.

14. Intensification of US military involvement in Vietnam was marked by President Lyndon Johnson's commitment of 100,000 American troops in July 1965, followed by a second assignment of 100,000 troops in 1966. Stanley Karnow, *Vietnam: A History* (Harmondsworth/Middlesex: Penguin, 1984), 327.

15. Douglas Valentine, *The Phoenix Program* (Lincoln, NE: Author's Guild, 1990), 59–60.

16. Ruth Blakely, *State Terrorism and Neoliberalism: the North in the South* (Florence, KY: Taylor & Francis, 2009), 50.

17. Valentine, *Phoenix Program*, 312.

18. Quoted in Valentine, *Phoenix Program*, 382.

19. Valentine, *Phoenix Program*, 386.

20. Karnow, *Vietnam*, 602.

21. Karnow, *Vietnam*, 602.

22. Meron, *The Humanization of International Law*, 117.

23. Ratner and Abrams, *Accountability*, 85.

24. Geneva Convention I, Art. 49, II, Art. 50, III, Art. 129, and IV, Art. 146, http://www.icrc.org/applic/ihl/ihl.nsf/vwTreaties1949.xsp (accessed August 26, 2014).

25. For illustrative cases, see Ratner and Abrams, *Accountability*, 86n29 (citing the Čelebići and Blaskic judgments of the ICTY as augmenting the "grave breaches" language of the Conventions).

26. Jean S. Pictet, ed., *Commentary, IV Geneva Convention Relative to the Protection of Civilian Persons in Time of War* (Geneva: International Committee for the Red Cross, 1958), 593–94. The ICRC commentary is available online: http://www.loc.gov/rr/frd/Military_Law/ pdf/ GC_1949-IV.pdf (accessed August 26, 2014).

27. Meron, *The Humanization of International Law*, 117n96; Meron, "Rape as a Crime Under International Humanitarian Law," in *War Crimes Law Comes of Age: Essays* (Oxford/New York: Oxford University Press, 1998), 207–8; Catherine N. Niarchos, "Women, War, and Rape: Challenges Facing the International Tribunal for the Former Yugoslavia," *Human Rights Quarterly* 17/4 (November 1995): 682. Meron mentions some of the ICTY case law in which rape was charged as a grave breach of the Geneva Conventions: see the citations in *Humanization*, 117n96.

28. G. I. A. D. Draper, "Wars of National Liberation and War Criminality," in M. Howard, ed., *Restraints on War*, 141.

29. Roberts and Guelff, *Documents*, 419.

30. The Two Protocols were opened for signature by States Parties in Berne on December 12, 1977.

31. Part I, Article 1(4), Protocol Additional to the Geneva Conventions of 12 August 1949 (Protocol I), in Roberts and Guelff, *Documents*, 423.

32. See Roberts and Guelff, *Documents*, Article 3(a), Protocol I.

33. Roberts and Guelff, *Documents*, Article 3(a), Protocol I; 421.

34. See Article 85(3)(a)–(f), 1977 Geneva Protocol I, in Roberts and Guelff, *Documents*, 470–71.

35. Buergenthal et al., *Interntational Human Rights,* 390.

36. Ratner and Abrams, *Accountability*, 98–99.

37. Keith Suter, *An International Law of Guerrilla Warfare: The Global Politics of Law-making* (F. Pinter, Open Library), 170, 177.

38. Ratner and Abrams, *Accountability*, 100; Cassese, *International Criminal Law*, 54. See also the decision of the ICTY Appeals Chamber in the Tadić appeal, http://www.iilj.org/courses/documents/Prosecutorv.Tadic.pdf, as well as the Statute of the ICTY, Article 3, http://www. icty. org/x/file/Legal percent20Library/Statute/statute_sept09_en.pdf (both accessed August 31, 2014).

39. Ratner and Abrams, *Accountability*, 102; The Prosecutor v. Jean-Paul Akayesu, Case No. ICTR-96-4-T, http://www.unictr.org/sites/unictr.org/files/case-documents/ictr-96-4/trial-judgements/en/980902.pdf (accessed April 12, 2015); Art. 4, ICTR Statute, http://www.icls.de/dokumente/ictr_statute.pdf (accessed August 31, 2014).

40. Tadić Interlocutory Appeal, paragraph 70, http://www.icty.org/x/cases/tadic/acdec/en/51002. htm (accessed September 1, 2014).

41. Ratner and Abrams, *Accountability*, 88.

42. Statute of the ICTY, Article 3, http://www.icty.org/x/file/Legal percent20Library/Statute/ statute_sept09_en.pdf (accessed August 31, 2014).

43. Ratner and Abrams, *Accountability*, 93.

44. On the criteria for an "internal conflict" under Common Art. 3, see Ratner and Abrams, *Accountability*, 96.

45. Declaration (IV, 2) Concerning Asphyxiating Gases, 1899, http://lawofwar.org/Asphyxiating_ Gases_Declaration.htm (accessed January 5, 2015).

46. Roberts and Guelff, *Documents*, 155–57; Paul Kennedy and G. J. Andreopoulos, "The Laws of War: Some Concluding Reflections," in Howard et al., *The Laws of War*, 279n1.

47. Burrus Carnahan, "Weapons," in Gutman and Rieff, eds., *Crimes of War*, 379–80; David A. Rosenberg, "Nuclear War Planning," in Andreopoulos et al, eds., *The Laws of War*, 164–65.

48. Rome Statute of the International Criminal Court, http://legal.un.org/icc/statute/romefra.htm (accessed February 7, 2015); Cassese, *International Criminal Law*, 60.

49. Judgments of the Supreme Court of Canada, *R. v. Finta*, http://scc-csc.lexum.com/scc-csc/ scc-csc/en/item/1124/index.do (accessed September 4, 2014).

50. English version of the judgment of the Quebec Court of Appeal in *Munyaneza v. R.*, http:// www.scribd.com/doc/222658804/Court-of-appeal-judgment-for-Desire-Munyaneza (accessed September 4, 2014).

51. The text of the statute may be found at http://www.law.cornell.edu/uscode/text/18/2441 (accessed September 4, 2014).

52. Cited in Crowe, *War Crimes*, 342; Ethnic Cleansing and Atrocities in Bosnia, https://www. cia. gov/news-information/speeches-testimony/1995/ddi_testimony_8995.html (accessed April 20, 2015); Roger Cohen, "CIA Report on Bosnia Blames Serbs for 90 percent of the War Crimes," *The New York Times*, March 9, 1995, http://www.nytimes.com/1995/03/09/ world/cia-report-on-bosnia-blames-serbs-for-90-of-the-war-crimes.html (accessed April 20, 2015).

53. Buergenthal et al., *International Human Rights*, 400-1; About the ICTY, http://www.icty.org/ sections/AbouttheICTY (accessed September 4, 2014).

54. About the ICTY, http://www.icty.org/sections/AbouttheICTY (accessed September 4, 2014).

55. Buergenthal et al., *International Human Rights*, 402. See also the discussion in Cassese, *International Criminal Law*, 77–79, 119.

56. Beyond former Serbian and Yugoslavian President Slobodan Milošević, who died in his jail cell in 2006, the ICTY has indicted several prominent Bosnian Serb politicians and military leaders, including Radovan Karadžić (ex-president of the Bosnian Serb Republic), General Radislav Krstić (commander of the Bosnian Serb Drina Corps convicted of genocide in 2001), and General Ratko Mladić (commander of the Main Staff of the Bosnian Serb Army). For summaries of past ICTY cases and updates on pending ones, see http://www.icty.org/ (accessed September 6, 2014).

57. UN Security Council Resolution 955, http://daccess-dds-ny.un.org/doc/UNDOC/GEN/ N95/140/97/PDF/N9514097.pdf?OpenElement (accessed April 12, 2015). The ICTR is also authorized to conduct trials of defendants charged with genocide and war crimes perpetrated on the territory of neighboring countries. The charges stem from the mass murder of 500,000 to 800,000 Tutsis and 50,000 Hutus during a three-month period in mid-1994. Crowe, *War Crimes*, 349.

58. The ICTR shares its Appeals Chamber with the ICTY.

59. Articles 2, 3, and 4, Statute of the International Criminal Tribunal for Rwanda (November 8, 1994), http://www.icls.de/dokumente/ictr_statute.pdf (accessed September 11, 2014); Buergenthal et al., *International Human Rights*, 404.

60. *Prosecutor v. Akayesu*, Trial Chamber Judgment (September 2, 1998), ICTR-96-4-T, http://www.unictr.org/sites/unictr.org/files/case-documents/ictr-96-4/trial-judgements/en/980902.pdf (accessed April 12, 2015).

61. An unofficial paramilitary group that enjoyed the backing of the extremist Hutu government during the Rwandan genocide. At full strength it consisted of 30,000 members.

62. Crowe, *War Crimes*, 354–55. For summaries of these and other cases, as well as trials still pending, see http://www.unictr.org/en/cases (accessed January 6, 2015).

63. Proceedings of the Committee of Jurists, 1920, 748, quoted in Manley O. Hudson, "The Proposed International Criminal Court," *The American Journal of International Law* 32(3) (July 1938): 550.

64. Antoine Sottile, "The Problem of the Creation of a Permanent International Criminal Court," *Revue de droit international* 29 (October–December 1951): 272–73.

65. Manley O. Hudson, "The Proposed International Criminal Court," *The American Journal of International Law* 32(3) (July 1938): 550–51.

66. League of Nations Official Journal (1934), 1760.

67. Hudson, "The Proposed International Criminal Court," 552–53.

68. On these and other atrocities, see Ben Kiernan, *Blood and Soil: A World History of Genocide and Extermination from Sparta to Darfur* (New Haven, CT: Yale University Press, 2007).

69. Michael S. Bryant, "International Criminal Court," in G. Kurt Piehler, ed., *Encyclopedia of Military Science*, vol. 2 (Los Angeles: SAGE, 2013), 682–83. Information about the ICC, including a copy of the Rome Statute and the Court's Rules of Procedure, may be found on the ICC's website: http://www.icc-cpi.int/EN_Menus/icc/Pages/default.aspx (accessed April 20, 2015).

70. Structure of the Court, http://www.icc-cpi.int/EN_Menus/ICC/Structure percent20of percent20the percent20Court/Pages/structure percent20of percent20the percent20court.aspx (accessed January 24, 2015); Buergenthal et al., *International Human Rights*, 407.

71. Buergenthal et al., *International Human Rights*, 683.

72. Bryant, "International Criminal Court," 683.

73. Federal Bureau of Investigation, *Terrorism in the United States: 1999* (Washington, D.C.: US Government Printing Office, 2000), 15. Also available at http://www.fbi.gov/stats-services/publications/terror_99.pdf (accessed September 16, 2014).

74. Quoted in Cassese, *International Criminal Law*, 126.

75. Summary of Judgement, *The Prosecutor v. Stanislav Galić*, page 5, http://www.icty.org/x/cases/galic/tjug/en/031205_Gali_summary_en.pdf (accessed September 18, 2014). The defendant was convicted and sentenced to twenty years in prison.

76. International law requires that before acts of terrorism can be deemed crimes against humanity, they must satisfy two conditions: (1) they must be part of a broad-based and systematic attack on civilians, and (2) the perpetrators must know that their criminal acts are part of a systematic pattern of conduct. Cassese, for one, holds that the 9/11 attacks meet these requirements and would be chargeable as crimes against humanity under international law. For his discussion, see Cassese, *International Criminal Law*, 128.

77. Chalmers Johnson, *Nemesis: The Last Days of the American Republic* (New York: Metropolitan, 2006), 36.

78. Military Order of November 13, 2001, Detention, Treatment, and Trial of Certain Non-Citizens in the War against Terrorism, http://fas.org/irp/offdocs/eo/mo-111301.htm (accessed October 10, 2014).

79. Military Order of November 13, 2001, Detention, Treatment, and Trial of Certain Non-Citizens in the War against Terrorism.

80. On the events of December and January 2001–02, see Philippe Sands, *Torture Team: Rumsfeld's Memo and the Betrayal of American Values* (New York: Palgrave-MacMillan, 2008), 31–36; Memorandum for the Joint Chiefs of Staff, January 19, 2002, http://www.defense.gov/news/Jun2004/d20040622doc1.pdf (accessed October 10, 2014).

81. Memorandum for the President, January 25, 2002, http://www2.gwu.edu/~nsarchiv/NSAEB B/NSAEBB127/02.01.25.pdf (accessed October 10, 2014).

82. Memorandum for the Vice President et al., February 7, 2002, http://www2.gwu.edu/~nsarchiv/torturingdemocracy/documents/ (accessed January 6, 2015).

83. 317 U.S. 1 (1942).

84. Jane Mayer, "The Hard Cases," *The New Yorker*, February 23, 2009, 38.

85. Quoted in Kim Scheppele, "Law in a Time of Emergency: States of Exception and the Temptations of 9/11," *U. Pa. J. Const. L.* 6 (2003–04): 1001, 1053n208. The government's brief is available at: http://news.findlaw.com/hdocs/docs/hamdi/hamdirums120303gopp.pdf (accessed October 10, 2014).

86. Scheppele, "Law in a Time of Emergency," xiii–xiv.

87. Mark Danner, "US Torture: Voices from the Black Sites," *The New York Review of Books*, April 9, 2009, at 69, 73.

88. J. Greenburg, H. Rosenberg, and A. De Vogue, "Sources: Top Bush Advisors Approve 'Enhanced Interrogation,'" *ABC News*, April 9, 2008; Danner, "US Torture," 73.

89. Sands, *Torture Team*, 73.

90. The second memo of August 1, 2002, approved a list of hitherto classified techniques proposed by the CIA, including waterboarding.

91. Memorandum for Alberto Gonzales, Counsel to the President, August 1, 2002, 1, 3–7, http://www.justice.gov/sites/default/files/olc/legacy/2010/08/05/memo-gonzales-aug2002.pdf (accessed October 10, 2014).

92. Memorandum for Alberto Gonzales.

93. Memorandum for Alberto Gonzales. See also Sands, *Torture Team*, 72–75; David Cole, "What Bush Wants to Hear," *The New York Review of Books*, November 17, 2005, 10–11; Senate Armed Services Committee Inquiry, xv; Danner, "US Torture," 73.

94. Memorandum for Alberto Gonzales.

95. Senate Armed Services Committee Inquiry, xvii.

96. Senate Armed Services Committee Inquiry, xx. See also *ICRC Report on the Treatment of Fourteen "High Value Detainees" in CIA Custody*, 11 http://assets.nybooks.com/media/doc/2010/04/22/icrc-report.pdf (accessed October 10, 2014).

97. *ICRC Report*, 5.

98. *ICRC Report*, 5.

99. "The Military Archipelago," *The New York Times*, May 7, 2004, http://www.nytimes.com/2004/05/07/opinion/the-new-iraq-crisis-the-military-archipelago.html

(accessed October 10, 2014); Brian Whitaker, "US troops 'abusing Afghans,'" *Guardian Weekly*, March 11–17, 2004; Tania Branigan and Rosie Cowan, "Freed detainees accuse Britain and the US," *Guardian Weekly*, March 18–24, 2004; "Iraqi prison scandal expands," *The Toledo Blade*, May 22, 2004, 1; Seymour Hersch, "Torture at Abu Ghraib," *The New Yorker*, May 10, 2004, 46.

100. Seymour Hersch, "Torture at Abu Ghraib," 45.

10 Singers of Songs of Experience: Trying to Explain War Crimes in World HIstory

1. Internet Movie Database (IMDb), https://www.imdb.com/title/tt0091167/characters/nm0001884 (accessed December 25, 2019).

2. Adam J. Hirsch, "The Collision of Military Cultures in Seventeenth-Century New England," *The Journal of American History* 74, no. 4 (March 1988): 1209.

3. "What is World History?," https://www.thewha.org/about/what-is-world-history/ (accessed December 15, 2019). See also Heather Sharp, "After the Ideological Battles: Student Views on Sources Representing the Gallipoli Conflict," in *International Perspectives on Teaching Rival Histories: Pedagogical Responses to Contested Narratives and the History Wars*, ed. Henri Äström Elmersjo, Anna Clark, & Monika Vinterek (New York: Palgrave MacMillan, 2017), 235.

4. Fernand Braudel, *A History of Civilizations*, trans. Richard Mayne (New York: Penguin Books, 1995), 22.

5. Braudel, *A History*, 35.

6. Leo Katz, *Bad Acts and Guilty Minds: Conundrums of the Criminal Law* (Chicago: University of Chicago Press, 1987), 237.

7. Katz, *Bad Acts*, 238.

8. Katz, *Bad Acts*, 240.

9. Herbert Jäger, "Makroverbrechen als Gegenstand des Völkerstrafrechts: Kriminalpolitisch-kriminologische Aspekte," in *Strafgerichte gegen Menschheitsverbrechen*, ed. Gerd Hankel and Gerhard Stuby (Hamburg: Hamburger Edition, 1995), 327 ff.

10. Smith, *Less than Human*, 246.

11. Smith, *Less than Human*, 248–49.

12. Smith, *Less than Human*, 241, 250.

13. Smith, *Less than Human*, 251.

14. David Quammen, *Monster of God: The Man-eating Predator in the Jungles of History and the Mind* (New York: W. W. Norton & Company, 2003), 3.

15. Smith, *Less Than Human*, 256 (quoting Eileen Gardiner).

16. Quoted in Ben Kiernan, *Blood and Soil: A World History of Genocide and Extermination from Sparta to Darfur* (New Haven: Yale University Press, 2007), 353.

17. Christian Hartmann, Thomas Vordermayer, Othmar Plöckinger, and Roman Töppel, ed., *Hitler, Mein Kampf: Eine kritische Edition* (Munich/Berlin: Institut für Zeitgeschichte, 2016), passim (but especially 1:471 ff. and 1:791 ff.).

18. Quoted in Smith, *Less than Human*, 253–54.

19. See supra, p. 70 ff.

20. Smith, *Less than Human*, 259–61.

21. Smith notes that dehumanization, while "very widespread," may or may not be universal. "Although it has a form that cuts across cultures, its content in any given case is culturally determined." Smith, *Less than Human*, 265.

22. Paul Roscoe, "Intelligence, Coalitional Killing, and the Antecedents of War," *American Anthropologist* 109, no. 3 (2007): 490.

23. Jan Assmann, *Totale Religion: Ursprünge und Formen puritanischer Verschärfung* (Vienna: Picus Verlag, 2016), 18.

24. Assmann, *Totale Religion*, 169–70. On the interchangeability of polytheistic gods, see Franz Cumont, *Oriental Religions in Roman Paganism* (New York: Dover, 1956), 60.

25. Old Testament expert Eckart Otto has proven that parts of the Book of Deuteronomy are translations of a loyalty oath imposed on his subjects by Esarhaddon, king of Assyria from 680 to 669 BCE. Eckart Otto, *Das Deuteronomium: politische Theologie und Rechtsform in Juda und Assyrien* (Berlin/New York: de Gruyter, 1999). Assmann himself asserts that the Shema Israel— "Hear, O Israel: The Lord our God is one Lord" (Deuteronomy 6:4)—was derived from an Assyrian loyalty oath. Assmann, *Totale Religion*, 44.

26. Assmann, *Totale Religion*, 34 ff.

27. For a description of the ban, see Numbers 21:1 and Deuteronomy 20:15–18.

28. On the fear of infestation and seduction by the Seven Nations, see Exodus 23:31 ff.

29. Assmann, *Totale Religion*, 55. The remarkable persistence of Deuteronomic history as a catalyst of war crimes led one scholar, Ferdinand Deist, to speak of "the dangers of Deuteronomy." F. E. Deist, "The Dangers of Deuteronomy: A Page from the Reception History of the Book," in *Studies in Deuteronomy in Honour of C. J. Labuschagne*, ed. F. G. Martinez (Leiden: Brill, 1994), 13–29.

30. Assmann, *Totale Religion*, 66. In 2016 the International Criminal Court convicted Ahmad Al Faqi Al Mahdi, an Islamist militiaman in North Africa, of attacking religious buildings and monuments in Mali. It was the first case tried at the ICC that dealt with cultural destruction as a war crime. Information on the trial may be found at https://www.icc-cpi.int/mali/al-mahdi (accessed January 5, 2020).

31. Assmann, *Totale Religion*, 110, 122.

32. Assmann, *Totale Religion*, 151.

33. Assmann, *Totale Religion*, 153.

34. 2 Maccabees 7:2.

35. Michael Bonner, *Jihad in Islamic History: Doctrines and Practice* (Princeton and Oxford: Princeton University Press, 2006), 73.

36. Bonner, *Jihad*, 74.

37. Bonner, *Jihad*, 75.

38. Assmann, *Totale Religion*, 131.

39. Encyclopedia Britannica defines apocalypticism as comprising "eschatological (end-time) views and movements that focus on cryptic revelations about a sudden, dramatic, and cataclysmic intervention of God in history; the judgment of all men; the salvation of the faithful elect; and the eventual rule of the elect with God in a renewed heaven and earth." *Encyclopedia Britannica*, s.v. "apocalypticism," https://www.britannica.com/topic/apocalypticism (accessed January 7, 2020).

40. As Assmann argues in a different context, the roots of apocalypticism actually predate Zoroastrianism; they may be found in Egyptian religion, which entertained the idea of a last judgment at the end of time when the righteous would be rewarded with immortality and the wicked annihilated. See Jan Assmann, *Tod und Jenseits im alten Ägypten* (Munich: C. H. Beck Verlag, 2010), 100 ff.

41. Bonner, *Jihad*, 131–32. For additional secondary literature on Islamic apocalypticism, see the sources listed in Bonner, *Jihad*, 132n31.

42. An expert on terrorism, Jarrett Brachman, defines a Salafist as "a Muslim who rejects traditional religious authority in favor of a narrow body of teaching, including the Quran, and the literal model established by the life of the Prophet Muhammad and his followers in the *Hadith*. Most Salafists reject many dimensions of modernity and generally disavow those rulers who do not strictly implement Islamic law, or *Sharia*." Jarrett Brachman, *Global Jihadism: Theory and Practice* (London and New York: Routledge, 2009), 25.

43. Graeme Wood, "What ISIS Really Wants," *The Atlantic*, March 2015, available on-line, https://www.theatlantic.com/magazine/archive/2015/03/what-isis-really-wants/384980/. On the apocalyptic beliefs and rhetoric of ISIS, see William McCants, *The Isis Apocalypse: The History, Strategy, and Doomsday Vision of the Islamic State* (New York: Picador/St. Martin's Press, 2015). For a skeptical perspective on the genuineness of ISIS's apocalypticism, the reader is referred to Bernard Haykel, "The Seventh Annual Ernest May Memorial Lecture: The History and Ideology of the Islamic State," in *Blind Spot: America's Response to Radicalism in the Middle East*, ed. Nicholas Burns and Jonathon Price (Washington, D.C.: The Aspen Institute, 2015), 25–26.

44. Graeme Wood, "What ISIS Really Wants."

45. Assmann, *Totale Religion*, 156.

46. The German language has a term that perfectly captures Adorno's authoritarian personality—*Fahrradfahrer*, or "bicyclist." The bicyclist bows his head while kicking below. The metaphor conveys the behavior of someone who bows before superior authority while mistreating his supposed inferiors.

47. See, e.g., Bob Altemeyer, *Right-Wing Authoritarianism* (Winnipeg: University of Manitoba Press, 1981); Gerda Lederer, "Authoritarianism in German Adolescents: Trends and Cross-Cultural Comparisons," in *Strength and Weakness: The Authoritarian Personality Today*, ed. W. F. Stone et al. (New York: Springer Verlag, 1993), 182–98.

48. The unpublished study by Mark Resnick is cited in Waller, *Becoming Evil*, 87.

49. John M. Steiner, "The SS Yesterday and Today: A Sociopsychological View," in *Survivors, Victims, and Perpetrators: Essays on the Nazi Holocaust*, ed. J.E. Dimsdale (Washington, D.C.: Hemisphere, 1980), 359–403.

50. Ervin Staub, *The Roots of Evil: The Origins of Genocide and Other Group Violence* (New York: Cambridge University Press, 1989), 134.

51. George C. Browder, *Hitler's Enforcers: The Gestapo and the SS Security Service in the Nazi Revolution* (New York: Oxford University Press, 1996), 168.

52. Zygmunt Bauman, *Modernity and the Holocaust* (Ithaca: Cornell University Press, 1989), 166. For this reason, one of the mainstream theories of microcriminality, Anti-social Personality Order, is inapplicable to most war crimes outside a narrow band committed by psychopaths. As Waller avers, psychopaths are ill-suited to the strict discipline, hierarchy, and self-control of military life.

53. Bauman, *Modernity*; Hannah Arendt, *Eichmann in Jerusalem: A Report on the Banality of Evil* (New York: Viking Press, 1963). A more recent attempt to explore how modern administrative

structures are drawn into macrocriminality has been undertaken by Guy B. Adams and Danny L. Balfour, *Unmasking Administrative Evil* (New York/London: M. E. Sharpe, 2004). Yale law professor James Q. Whitman makes an argument analogous to Bauman's, contending that "wars enter their most dangerous territory not when they lose touch with chivalry but when they aim to remake the world." James Q. Whitman, *The Verdict of Battle*, 251.

54. Waller, *Becoming Evil*, 108.

55. Waller, *Becoming Evil*, 109. The study, compressed here for brevity, was even more detailed than I have presented. Milgram ran twenty variations of his experiment. In one variation he decreased the distance between learner and teacher; in another, the teacher had to force the hand of the learner onto the shock plate. In these situations Milgram found that rates of obedience declined. Nevertheless, in most of the variations Milgram ran compliance was strikingly high. Waller summarizes the overall results: "All told, it was difficult for Milgram to devise an experimental variation in which at least some subjects would not exhibit full obedience to the experimenter." Waller, *Becoming Evil*, 110.

56. Waller, *Becoming Evil*, 111. I can corroborate this observation anecdotally based on my teaching of the Milgram experiment in university classrooms, both within the USA and abroad. It continues to enthrall young people to the present day.

57. The cases are discussed in Waller, *Becoming Evil*, 111.

58. Waller, *Becoming Evil*, 111–12.

59. Christopher R. Browning, *Ordinary Men: Reserve Police Battalion 101 and the Final Solution in Poland* (New York: HarperPerennial, 1992), 174.

60. Browning, *Ordinary Men*, 174–75.

61. Waller cites as counterevidence a 1976 study by two German psychologists, who found no connection between their subjects' obedience and their allocation of responsibility. Waller, *Becoming Evil*, 115.

62. Robert Jay Lifton, *The Nazi Doctors: Medical Killing and the Psychology of Genocide* (New York: Basic Books, 1986). Lifton sought to account for the abominable crimes of Nazi medical professionals as products of psychological "doubling," whereby the perpetrator forms a second self which, in Jekyll and Hyde fashion, enables him to commit evil acts. As Waller glosses it, "it is the transfer of conscience to the second self that frees the primary self from responsibility." Waller, *Becoming Evil*, 120. What Lifton overlooks is the human tendency toward self-deception and self-justification—traits documented in juvenile delinquents by criminologists Gresham Sykes and David Matza. The creation of the second self is more likely a post hoc strategy devised by the perpetrator to avoid attribution of responsibility to himself. Sykes and Matza refer to such machinations as "neutralization techniques." Gresham M. Sykes and David Matza, "Techniques of Neutralization: A Theory of Delinquency," *American Sociological Review* 22, no. 6 (1957): 664–70. In a 2001 study, sociologist Alex Alvarez applied Sykes and Matza's theory of neutralization to perpetrators of genocide. Alex Alvarez, *Government, Citizens, and Genocide: A Comparative and Interdisciplinary Approach* (Bloomington, Indiana: University of Indiana Press, 2001): 114–29. If doubling is in fact a neutralization technique, then no second self comes into being as Lifton contends; instead, we are only faced with a subterfuge concocted after the fact to dodge accountability.

63. The role of proximity in extreme wartime violence is prominent in the scholarship; see, e.g., the influential studies by Dave Grossman, *On Killing: The Psychological Cost of Learning to Kill in War and Society* (New York/Boston/London: Back Bay Books, 2009), especially Section III, and Jonathan Glover, *Humanity: A Moral History of the 20th Century* (New Haven: Yale University Press, 1999), Chapter 10.

64. Browning, *Ordinary Men*, 184–85. Interestingly, Browning discounts the role of ideological indoctrination as a major contributing factor to the battalion's actions.

65. Details of the Zimbardo experiment appear in Waller, *Becoming Evil*, 236 ff.

66. Waller, *Becoming Evil*, 236–37; Browning, *Ordinary Men*, 168.

67. Waller, *Becoming Evil*, 237.

68. Philip Zimbardo, *The Lucifer Effect: Understanding How Good People Turn Evil* (New York: Random House, 2007), 331; Waller, *Becoming Evil*, 238. Lieutenant General Paul T. Milolashek, the Army inspector general, in his investigation of 94 cases of prisoner abuse in Iraq and Afghanistan, blamed all of them on the "unauthorized actions taken by a few individuals." Department of the Army, The Inspector General, *Detainee Operations Inspection*, available on-line, https://www.washingtonpost.com/wp-srv/world/iraq/abughraib/detaineereport.pdf (accessed January 16, 2020). On July 22, 2004, just one day after Milolashek's report was released, army leaders told a Senate subcommittee that abuses of detainees had been committed by a few "bad apples," insisting that neither their training nor military policy played a contributory role. Gerry J. Gilmore, "Bad Troops, Poor Leaders Responsible for Detainee Abuses," *DoD News*, July 22, 2004, https://archive.defense.gov/news/newsarticle.aspx?id=25668 (accessed January 16, 2020).

69. Zimbardo, *Lucifer*, 403.

70. In Tier 1A interrogators tried to pry information from an Iraqi general by soaking his teen-aged son, covering him with mud, and driving him naked from the prison. Two of the interrogators were accused of sexually assaulting a teenaged girl. So-called "ghost detainees"—prisoners believed to be high-level officials who were never officially registered as detainees—were beaten and tortured, and at least one of them was murdered by Navy SEALs. Zimbardo, *Lucifer*, 349–50. The report of prisoner abuse at Abu Ghraib by Major General Antonio Taguba, dated October 19, 2004, contains a detailed list of other war crimes committed on detainees, all in Tiers 1A and B: *Taguba Report: AR 15-6 Investigation of the 800th Military Police Brigade – Certified Copy*, October 19, 2004, available on-line, https://www.thetorturedatabase.org/document/ar-15-6-investigation-800th-military-police-investigating-officer-mg-antonio-taguba-taguba- (accessed January 16, 2020).

71. Zimbardo, *Lucifer*, 344.

72. S. T. Fiske, L. T. Harris, and A. J. Cuddy, "Why Ordinary People Torture Enemy Prisoners," *Science* 306 (2004): 1482–83, quoted in Zimbardo, *Lucifer*, 354.

73. Grossman, *On Killing*, xxxi.

74. Grossman, *On Killing*, 257–58. Grossman's approach seems to me to be akin to differential association theory, a cornerstone of learning theory. See Edwin H. Sutherland and Donald R. Cressey, "A Theory of Differential Association," in *Criminological Theory: Past to Present*, ed. Francis T. Cullen and Robert Agnew (Los Angeles: Roxbury, 2006), 122–24.

75. Grossman, *On Killing*, 209.

76. My point here is not that all these thinkers would identify as subscribers to the blank slate but that, in stressing the situational rather than dispositional factors involved in wartime atrocity, their theories entail it. Waller, in particular, is acutely aware of the mortgage of evolutionary psychology on human behavior. See Waller, *Becoming Evil*, 148 ff.

77. For an engaging *tour d'horizon* of the blank slate and a critical assessment of it, see Steven Pinker, *The Blank Slate: The Modern Denial of Human Nature* (New York: Viking Penguin, 2002).

Conclusion: The Future of the Law of War

1. Michael Bergner and Richard I. Miller, *The Law of War* (Lexington, MA: Lexington Books, 1975); Jean Pictet, *Development and Principles of International Humanitarian Law* (Springer,

Notes

1985), 6; Hilaire McCoubrey, *International Humanitarian Law: the Regulation of Armed Conflicts* (London: Dartmouth Publishing Co., 1990), 1–21; Geza Herczegh, *Development of International Humanitarian Law* (Budapest: Akademiai Kiado, 1984), 56–83; Robert Emmet Moffit, *Modern War and the Laws of War* (Tucson: Institute of Government Research, 1973).

2. See, e.g., Chris Jochnick and Roger Normand, "The Legitimation of Violence: A Critical History of the Laws of War," 35 *Harv. Int'l L.J.* 49 (1994); James Whitman, *The Verdict of Battle: The Law of Victory and the Making of Modern War* (Cambridge, MA: Harvard University Press, 2012).

3. Cassese, *International Criminal Law*, 65.

BIBLIOGRAPHY

Archives

Robert M. W. Kempner Papers, US Holocaust Memorial Museum.
National Archives, Kew (London).
National Archives/College Park, MD.

Published primary source materials

Ayala, Balthasar. *De iure et officiis bellicis et disciplina militari.* Three volumes. Douai, 1582.
Bluntschli, Johann Caspar. *Das Moderne Völkerrecht der civilizierten Staaten als Rechtsbruch Dargestellt.* Nördlingen: C. H. Beck, 1872.
Boister, Neil, and Robert Cryer, eds. *Documents on the Tokyo International Military Tribunal: Charter, Indictment and Judgements.* Oxford: Oxford University Press, 2008.
Department of the Army, The Inspector General, *Detainee Operations Inspection,* available on-line, https://www.washingtonpost.com/wp-srv/world/iraq/abughraib/detaineereport.pdf (accessed January 16, 2020).
de Vattel, Emer. *The Law of Nations,* edited by Bela Kapossy and Richard Whatmore. Indianapolis: Liberty Fund, 2008.
di Vitoria, Francisco. *Relectiones Theologicae.* Lyons, 1587.
———. "The Second Relectio on the Indians, or on the Law of War made by the Spaniards on the Barbarians." In *De Indis et de Jure Belli Relectiones,* translated by J. P. Bate. Carnegie edn., 1917.
———. *Relectio prior de potestate Ecclesiae.* Vol. 2. 1532.
Gentili, Alberico. *Three Books on the Law of War.* Translated by John C. Rolfe. Oxford: Clarendon, 1933.
Grotius, Hugo. *The Rights of War and Peace.* Edited and with an Introduction by Richard Tuck. 3 volumes. Indianapolis, IN: Liberty, 2005.
Hamburger Institut für Sozialforschung, ed. *Verbrechen der Wehrmacht: Dimensionen des Vernichtungskrieges 1941-1944.* Hamburg: Hamburger Edition, 2002.
Hartigan, Richard Shelly, ed. *Lieber's Code and the Law of War.* New York: The Legal Classics Library, 1983.
The Holy Qur'ān: English Translation of the Meanings and Commentary. Translated by 'Abdullah Yūsuf 'Ali. Al-Madīnah Al-Munawarah: King Fahd Holy Qur'ān Printing Complex, 1989–90.
Legnano, John of (Giovanni da Legnano). *Tractatus de bello, de represaliis et de duello.* Edited by E. Holland. Washington, D.C.: Oxford, 1917.
Locke, John. *Second Treatise of Government.* Seaside, OR: Watchmaker, 2011.
Marrus, Michael, ed. *The Nuremberg War Crimes Trial 1945–46.* Boston/New York: Bedford, 1997.
Mencius. Translated by D. C. Lau. Harmondsworth, UK, and New York: Penguin, 1970.
The New English Bible with Apochrypha. New York: Oxford University Press, 1972.
Noakes, Jeremy, and G. Pridham, eds. *Nazism: A History in Documents and Eyewitness Accounts, 1919-1945.* Vol. II. New York: Schocken Books, 1988.

Bibliography

Roberts, Adam, and Richard Guelff, eds. *Documents on the Laws of War*. Oxford/New York: Oxford University Press, 2004.

Root, Elihu. *Addresses on International Subjects*. Cambridge, MA: Harvard University Press, 1916.

Schindler, Dietrich, and Jirí Toman, ed. *The Laws of Armed Conflict: A Collection of Conventions, Resolutions and Other Documents*. Geneva, 1981.

Shakespeare, William. *Henry V*. New York: Washington Square Press, 2004.

Smith, Bradley F., ed. *The American Road to Nuremberg: The Documentary Record*. Stanford, CA: Hoover Institution Press, 1982.

Suárez, Francisco. *Selections from Three Works*. Translated by G. L. Williams, A. Brown, & J. Waldron. Oxford: Oxford University Press, 1998.

Symmons, E. *A Military Sermon, Wherein by the Word of God, the Nature and Disposition of a Rebel is Discovered*. Oxford, 1644.

Trial of the Major War Criminals before the International Military Tribunal. 42 volumes. Nuremberg, Germany: International Military Tribunal, 1947.

Trials of War Criminals Before the Nuernberg Military Tribunals Under Control Council Law No. 10. 15 volumes. Buffalo, NY: W. S. Hein (reprint edition), 1997.

United States. Department of State. *Foreign Relations of the United States: Diplomatic Papers 1941*. Vol. 1. Washington, D.C.: Government Printing Office, 1960.

———. *Foreign Relations of the United States: Diplomatic Papers 1942*. Vol. 1. Washington, D.C.: Government Printing Office, 1960.

———. *Foreign Relations of the United States: Diplomatic Papers 1943*. Vol. 1. Washington, D.C.: Government Printing Office, 1960.

———. *Foreign Relations of the United States: Diplomatic Papers 1944*. Vol. 1. Washington, D.C.: Government Printing Office, 1960.

von Clausewitz, Carl. *On War*, edited and translated by Peter Paret and Michael Howard. Princeton, NJ: Princeton University Press, 1976.

von Pufendorf, Samuel. *De jure naturae et gentium libri octo*. In *Classics of International Law*, edited by J. B. Scott. Volume 17. Washington, D.C.: Carnegie Endowment, 1931.

Classical sources cited

Aeschylus, *The Oresteia*. Ammianus Marcellinus, *Res Gestae*.

Aristotle, *Rhetoric; Politics; The Nicomachean Ethics*.

Cicero, *Laws*, Book I; *On Duties*, Book III; *On the Commonwealth*.

Demosthenes, *Speeches; Letters*.

Euripides, *Suppliant Women*.

Herodotus, *The History*.

Homer, *Iliad*.

Pausanias, *Description of Greece*.

Plato, *Republic*.

Plutarch, *Agis*.

Polybius, *The Histories*.

Sophocles, *Antigone*.

Thucydides, *The Peloponnesian War*.

Xenophon, *Cyropaedia*.

Medieval sources cited

Augustine, *Against Faust*; *Confessions*; *The City of God*; *Epistolae*.
Bartolus, *Tractatus de Reprisaliis*.
Isidore, *Etymologiae*.
Nicholas of Tudeschi, Lectura Super V Libros Decretalium.

Biblical sources cited:

Deuteronomy
Exodus
Numbers
The Book of Daniel
Wisdom of Solomon
1 Maccabees
2 Maccabees

Internet primary sources

Brief for the Respondents in Opposition, *Hamdi v. Rumsfeld*, http://news.findlaw.com/hdocs/
docs/hamdi/hamdirums120303gopp.pdf (accessed January 6, 2015).
Case Information Sheet, Čelebići Camp (IT-96-21), *Mucić et al.*, http://www.icty.org/x/cases/
mucic/cis/en/cis_mucic_al_en.pdf (accessed July 23, 2014).
Commentary, IV Geneva Convention Relative to the Protection of Civilian Persons in Time of War,
http://www.loc.gov/rr/frd/Military_Law/pdf/GC_1949-IV.pdf (accessed August 26, 2014).
Convention for the Amelioration of the Condition of the Wounded in Armies in the Field,
Geneva, 22 August 1864, http://www.icrc.org/ihl/INTRO/120?OpenDocument (accessed
March 29, 2014).
Convention (I) for the Amelioration of the Condition of the Wounded and Sick in Armed Forces in
the Field, Geneva, 12 August 1949, http://www.icrc.org/applic/ihl/ihl.nsf/Article.xsp?action=ope
nDocument&documentId=BAA341028EBFF1E8C12563CD00519E66 (accessed July 11, 2014).
Davies, John. *A Discoverie of the True Causes why Ireland Was neuer entirely Subdued, nor brought
vnder Obedience of the Crowne of England, Vntill the Beginning of His Maiefties happie Raigne*.
London: A. Millar, 1612, https://play.google.com/books/reader?id=GokvAAAAYAAJ&hl=en
&pg=GBS.PP5 (accessed May 12, 2020).
Department of the Army, *The Law of Land Warfare*. Washington: Government Printing Office,
1956, https://ia801506.us.archive.org/18/items/Fm27-101956/Fm27-101956.pdf (accessed
July 23, 2014).
18 U.S. Code § 2441 – War crimes, http://www.law.cornell.edu/uscode/text/18/2441 (accessed
September 4, 2014).
Ethnic Cleansing and Atrocities in Bosnia, https://www.cia.gov/news-information/speeches-
testimony/1995/ddi_testimony_8995.html (accessed January 6, 2015).
Geneva Convention I, Art. 49, II, Art. 50, III, Art. 129, and IV, Art. 146, http://www.icrc.org/
applic/ihl/ihl.nsf/vwTreaties1949.xsp (accessed August 26, 2014).
ICRC Report on the Treatment of Fourteen 'High Value Detainees' in CIA Custody, http://assets.
nybooks.com/media/doc/2010/04/22/icrc-report.pdf (accessed October 10, 2014).
IMTFE Charter http://www.jus.uio.no/english/services/library/treaties/04/4-06/military-
tribunal-far-east.xml (accessed April 12, 2015).

Bibliography

International Criminal Court, http://www.icc-cpi.int/EN_Menus/icc/Pages/default.aspx
  Memorandum for Alberto Gonzales, Counsel to the President, August 1, 2002, http://www.
  justice.gov/sites/default/files/olc/legacy/2010/08/05/memo-gonzales-aug2002.pdf
  Memorandum for the Joint Chiefs of Staff, January 19, 2002, http://www.defense.gov/news/
  Jun2004/d20040622doc1.pdf (accessed October 10, 2014).
Memorandum for the President, January 25, 2002, http://www2.gwu.edu/~nsarchiv/NSAEBB/
  NSAEBB127/02.01.25.pdf (accessed October 10, 2014).
Memorandum for the Vice President et al., February 7, 2002, http://www2.gwu.edu/~nsarchiv/
  torturingdemocracy/documents/ (accessed January 6, 2015).
Military Order of November 13, 2001, Detention, Treatment, and Trial of Certain Non-Citizens
  in the War against Terrorism, http://fas.org/irp/offdocs/eo/mo-111301.htm (accessed October
  10, 2014).
Paris Declaration on Maritime War of 1856, http://www.icrc.org/applic/ihl/ihl.nsf/Article.xsp?act
  ion=openDocument&documentId=473FCB0F41DCC63BC12563CD0051492D (accessed
  December 28, 2013).
Preamble, Convention (II) with Respect to the Laws and Customs of War on Land and its annex:
  Regulations concerning the Laws and Customs of War on Land. The Hague, 29 July 1899,
  http://www.icrc.org/applic/ihl/ihl.nsf/Article.xsp?action=openDocument&documentId=9FE
  084CDAC63D10FC12563CD00515C4D (accessed April 13, 2014).
Preface, The Laws of War on Land. Oxford, 9 September 1880, http://www.icrc.org/applic/ihl/ihl.
  nsf/Article.xsp?action=openDocument&documentId=B06FB334DC14CBD1C12563
  CD00515767 (accessed April 1, 2014).
Project of an International Declaration concerning the Laws and Customs of War. Brussels, 27
  August 1874, http://www.icrc.org/ihl/INTRO/135 (accessed April 1, 2014).
Protocol Additional to the Geneva Conventions of 12 August 1949, and relating to the Protection
  of Victims of International Armed Conflicts (Protocol I), 8 June 1977, http://www.icrc.org/
  ihl/INTRO/470 (accessed July 23, 2014).
Scottish Articles and Ordinances of War, http://www.old.scotwars.com/narra_articles_of_warre.
  htm (accessed April 7, 2015).
Senate Armed Services Committee Inquiry into the Treatment of Detainees in U.S. Custody,
  December 11, 2008, http://www.gwu.edu/~nsarchiv/torturingdemocracy/
  documents/20081211.pdf (accessed October 10, 2014).
Statute of the ICTR, http://www.icls.de/dokumente/ictr_statute.pdf (accessed September 11, 2014).
Statute of the ICTY, http://www.icty.org/x/file/Legal percent20Library/Statute/statute_sept09_
  en.pdf (accessed August 31, 2014).
Taguba Report: AR 15-6 Investigation of the 800th Military Police Brigade – Certified Copy,
  October 19, 2004, https://www.thetorturedatabase.org/document/ar-15-6-investigation-
  800th-military-police-investigating-officer-mg-antonio-taguba-taguba- (accessed January 16,
  2020).
UN Security Council Resolution 955, http://daccess-dds-ny.un.org/doc/UNDOC/GEN/
  N95/140/97/PDF/N9514097.pdf?OpenElement (accessed April 12, 2015).
United Nations, International Criminal Tribunal for Rwanda, http://www.unictr.org/en/cases
  (accessed January 6, 2015).
Winston Churchill, Finest Hour Speech, https://winstonchurchill.org/resources/speeches/1940-
  the-finest-hour/their-finest-hour/ (accessed March 12, 2019).

Periodicals

New York Weekly Post Boy (1746).

Herald Tribune International (1992).
The New York Times Sunday Review (2013).
Free Republic (2001).
The New York Times (1995; 2004).
The New York Review of Books (2002; 2009).
The New Yorker (2004; 2009). *ABC News (online)* (2008). *Guardian Weekly* (2004).
The Toledo Blade (2004).

Court cases

The Prosecutor v. Ahmad Al Faqi Al Mahdi, ICC-01/12-01/15, https://www.icc-cpi.int/mali/
    al-mahdi (accessed January 31, 2020).
Decision on the Defence Motion for Interlocutory Appeal on Jurisdiction (Tadić Case),
    International Criminal Tribunal for Yugoslavia Appellate Chamber, http://www.iilj.org/
    courses/documents/Prosecutorv.Tadic.pdf (accessed August 31, 2014).
Ex parte Quirin, 317 U.S. 1 (1942).
In re Yamashita, 327 U.S. 1 (1946).
Marks v. U. S., 28 Ct. Cl. 147 (1896).
Mucić et al., Čelebići Camp (IT-96-21), http://www.icty.org/x/cases/mucic/cis/en/cis_mucic_al_
    en.pdf (accessed July 23, 2014).
Munyaneza v. Regina, http://www.scribd.com/doc/222658804/Court-of-appeal-judgment-for-
    Desire-Munyaneza (accessed September 4, 2014).
The Prosecutor v. Jean-Paul Akayesu, Case No. ICTR-96-4-T, http://www.unictr.org/sites/unictr.
    org/files/case-documents/ictr-96-4/trial-judgements/en/980902.pdf (accessed April 12, 2015).
The Prosecutor v. Stanislav Galić, http://www.icty.org/x/cases/galic/acjug/en/gal-acjud061130.pdf
    (accessed April 12, 2015).
Regina v. Finta, http://scc-csc.lexum.com/scc-csc/scc-csc/en/item/1124/index.do (accessed
    September 4, 2014).
Trial of Henry Wirz, http://www.loc.gov/rr/frd/Military_Law/pdf/Wirz-trial.pdf (accessed
    October 8, 2014).

Secondary sources

Abler, Thomas S. "Iroqois Cannibalism: Fact not Fiction." *Ethnohistory* XXVII (1980): 309–16.
About the ICTY, http://www.icty.org/sections/AbouttheICTY (accessed September 4, 2014).
Adams, Guy B., and Danny L. Balfour. *Unmasking Administrative Evil*. New York/London: M. E.
    Sharpe, 2004.
al-Ḥasan al-Shaybānī, Muḥ ammad ibn. *The Islamic Law of Nations: Shaybānī's Siyar*. Translated
    by Majid Khadduri. Baltimore: Johns Hopkins Press, 1966.
Altemeyer, Bob. *Right-Wing Authoritarianism*. Winnipeg: University of Manitoba Press, 1981.
Altman, Amnon. "Tracing the Earliest Recorded Concepts of International Law. The Ancient
    Near East in the Old Babylonian Period (2000–1595 BCE)." *Journal of the History of
    International Law* 10, no. 1 (2008): 1–33.
Alvarez, Alex. *Government, Citizens, and Genocide: A Comparative and Interdisciplinary
    Approach*. Bloomington, Indiana: University of Indiana Press, 2001.
Ando, Clifford. "Aliens, Ambassadors, and the Integrity of the Empire." *Law and History Review*
    26, no. 3 (Fall 2008): 491–519.

Bibliography

Andreopoulos, G. J. "The Age of National Liberation Movements." In *The Laws of War: Constraints on Warfare in the Western World*, edited by M. Howard, G. J. Andreopoulos, and M. R. Shulman, 191–213. New Haven, CT: Yale University Press, 1994.

Arendt, Hannah. *Eichmann in Jerusalem: A Report on the Banality of Evil*. New York: Viking Press, 1963.

Armour, W. S. "Customs of Warfare in Ancient India." *Transactions of the Grotius Society* 8 (1922): 71–88.

Asprey, Robert B. *War in the Shadows: the Guerilla in History*. 2 volumes. Garden City, NY: Doubleday, 1975.

Assmann, Jan. *Ma'at: Gerichtigkeit und Unsterblichkeit im Alten Ägypten*. Munich: Verlag C. H. Beck, 2006.

———. *The Mind of Egypt: History and Meaning in the Time of the Pharaohs*. Translated by Andrew Jenkins. Cambridge, MA: Harvard University Press, 2003.

———. *The Search for God in Ancient Egypt*. Ithaca, NY: Cornell University Press, 2001.

———. *Tod und Jenseits im alten Ägypten*. Munich: C. H. Beck, 2010.

———. *Totale Religion: Ursprünge und Formen puritanischer Verschärfung*. Vienna: Picus Verlag, 2016.

Austin, John. "A Positivist Conception of Law." In *Philosophy of Law*, edited by J. Feinberg and J. Coleman, 24–35. Belmont, CA: Thomson-Wadsworth, 2004.

Axtell, James. *The European and the Indian: Essays in the Ethno-history of Colonial North America*. New York: Oxford, 1981.

Baker, S., ed. *Halleck's International Law—Rules Regulating the Intercourse of States in Peace and War*. Vol. I. London: Longmans, Green, 1928.

Bamforth, Douglas B. "Indigenous People, Indigenous Violence: Pre-Contact Warfare on the North American Great Plains." *Man* 29 (1994): 95–115.

———. "What Do We Know about Warfare on the Great Plains?" In *Archaeological Perspectives on Warfare on the Great Plains*, edited by A. J. Clark and D. B. Bamforth, 3–34. Boulder: University Press of Colorado, 2018.

Bandelier, Adolf. *Final Report of Investigations among the Indians of the Southwestern United States, Part 1*. Boston, MA: Papers of the Archaeological Institute of America, American Series, No. 3, 1890.

Barber, Malcolm. *The Trial of the Templars*. London: The Folio Society, 2003.

Bartov, Omer. *The Eastern Front, 1941–45: German Troops and the Barbarisation of Warfare*. New York: Palgrave, 2001.

Bass, Gary. *Stay the Hand of Vengeance: The Politics of War Crimes Tribunals*. Princeton/Oxford: Princeton University Press, 2000.

Bassiouni, M. Cherif. *Crimes against Humanity in International Criminal Law*. The Hague: Kluwer, 1999.

Bauman, Zygmunt. Modernity and the Holocaust. Ithaca: Cornell University Press, 1989.

Beaulac, Stéphane. "The Westphalian Legal Orthodoxy—Myth or Reality?" *Journal of the History of International Law* 2 (2000): 148–77.

Beers, David Quinn. "Ireland and Sixteenth-century Expansion." *Historical Studies* I (1958): 20–32.

———. *Raleigh and the British Empire*. London: Hodder & Stoughton, 1947.

———. *The Elizabethans and the Irish*. Ithaca: Cornell University Press, 1966.

Bell, Martin. *In Harm's Way: Reflections of a War-Zone Thug*. London: Hamish Hamilton, 1995.

Bellah, Robert. *Religion in Human Evolution: From the Paleolithic to the Axial Age*. Cambridge, MA: Harvard University Press, 2011.

Bergner, Michael, and Richard I. Miller. *The Law of War*. Lexington, MA: Lexington, 1975.

Berman, Harold J. *Law and Revolution II: The Impact of the Protestant Reformations on the Western Legal Tradition*. Cambridge, MA: Belknap, 2006.

Best, Geoffrey. *Humanity in Warfare*. New York: Columbia University Press, 1980.

———. *War & Law Since 1945*. Oxford/New York: Clarendon Press, 2002.

———. *War and Society in Revolutionary Europe 1770–1870*. Montreal: McGill-Queen's University Press, 1998.

Betts, Paul. "Germany, International Justice and the Twentieth Century." *History and Meaning* 17/1, no. 2 (19 July, 2005): 45–86.

Bhatia, H. S. *International Law and Practice in Ancient India*. New Delhi: Deep & Deep, 1977.

Blakely, Ruth. *State Terrorism and Neoliberalism: the North in the South*. Florence, KY: Taylor & Francis, 2009.

Blanton, Richard E. "A Consideration of Causality in the Growth of Empire." In *Aztec Imperial Strategies*, edited by F. F. Burden et al., 219–25. Washington, D. C.: Dumbarton Oaks, 1996.

Blick, J. P. "Genocidal Warfare in Tribal Societies as a Result of European-induced Culture Conflict." *Man* 23 (1988): 654–70.

Bluntschli, Johann Caspar. *Das Moderne Völkerrecht der civilizierten Staaten als Rechtsbruch Dargestellt*. Nördlingen: C. H. Beck, 1872.

Bohrer, Ziv. "International Criminal Law's Millennium of Forgotten History." *Law & History Review* 34 (2016): 393–485, https://ssrn.com/abstract=3219242 (accessed February 1, 2020).

Bonner, Michael. *Jihad in Islamic History: Doctrines and Practice*. Princeton and Oxford: Princeton University Press, 2006.

Brachmann, Jarrett. *Global Jihadism: Theory and Practice*. London and New York: Routledge, 2009.

Brand, C. E. *Roman Military Law*. Austin: University of Texas Press, 1968.

Branigan, Tania, and Rosie Cowan. "Freed detainees accuse Britain and the US." *Guardian Weekly*, March 18–24, 2004.

Brantlinger, Patrick. *Dark Vanishings: Discourse on the Extinction of Primitive Races, 1800–1930*. Ithaca and London: Cornell University Press, 2003.

Braudel, Fernand. *A History of Civilizations*. Translated by Richard Mayne. New York: Penguin Books, 1995.

Brett, M. G. "Genocide in Deuteronomy: Postcolonial Variations on Mimetic Desire." In *Deuteronomy and the Deuteronomic Literature: Festschrift C. H. W. Brekelmans*, edited by M. Vervenne and J. Lust, 3–38. Leuven: Leuven University Press, 1997.

Browder, George C. *Hitler's Enforcers: the Gestapo and the SS Security Service in the Nazi Revolution*. New York: Oxford University Press, 1996.

Browning, Christopher R. *Ordinary Men: Reserve Police Battalion 101 and the Final Solution in Poland*. New York: HarperPerennial, 1992.

———, and Jürgen Matthäus. *The Origins of the Final Solution: The Evolution of Nazi Jewish Policy, September 1939–March 1942*. Lincoln, NE/Yad Vashem, Jerusalem: University of Nebraska Press, 2004.

Brügel, J. W. "Das Schicksal der Strafbestimmungen des Versailler Vertrags." *Vierteljahrshefte für Zeitgeschichte* 6, no. 3 (July 1958): 263–70.

Brundage, James A. *The Crusades, Holy War, and Canon Law*. Lawrence, KS: Variorum, 1991.

———. "The Hierarchy of Violence in Twelfth- and Thirteenth-Century Canonists." *The International History Review* XVII, no. 4 (1995): 670–81.

Bryant, Michael S. *Confronting the "Good Death:" Nazi Euthanasia on Trial, 1945–53*. Boulder, CO: University Press of Colorado, 2005.

———. "Dachau Trials—Die rechtlichen und historischen Grundlagen der US-amerikanischen Kriegsverbrecherprozesse, 1942–1947." In *Historische Dimensionen von Kriegsverbrecherprozessen nach den Zweiten Weltkrieg*, edited by H. Radtke, D. Rössner, et al., 111–22. Baden Baden: Nomos, 2007.

Bibliography

——. *Eyewitness to Genocide: The Operation Reinhard Trials, 1955–66*. Knoxville, TN: University of Tennessee Press, 2014.

——. "International Criminal Court." In *Encyclopedia of Military Science*, edited by G. Kurt Piehler, 682–683. Volume 1. Los Angeles: SAGE, 2013.

——. "Punishing the Excess: Sadism, Bureaucratized Atrocity, and the U.S. Army Concentration Camp Trials, 1945–1947." In *Nazi Crimes and the Law*, edited by Henry Friedlander and Nathan Stoltzfuss, 63–85. Cambridge: Cambridge University Press, 2008.

——. "Die US-amerikanischen Militärprozesse gegen SS-Personal Ärzte und Kapos des KZ Dachau 1945–1948." In *Dachauer Prozesse: NS-Verbrechen vor amerikanischen Militärgerichten in Dachau 1945–1948*, edited by Ludwig Eiber and Robert Sigel, 109–25. Göttingen: Wallstein, 2007.

——, and Wolfgang Form. "Victim Nationality in US and British Military Trials: Hadamar, Dachau, Belsen." In *Justice, Politics, and Memory in Europe after the Second World War*, edited by S. Bardgett, D. Cesarani, J. Reinisch, and J-D. Steinert, 19–42. Volume 2. London/Portland, OR: Valentine/Mitchell, 2011.

Buergenthal, T., D. Shelton, and D. Stewart. *International Human Rights*. St. Paul, MN: West, 2009.

Bull, Hedley. "The Emergence of a Universal International Society." In *The Expansion of International Society*, edited by H. Bull and A. Watson, 117–26. Oxford: Clarendon, 1984.

Burkert, Walter. *Homo Necans: The Anthropology of Ancient Greek Sacrificial Ritual and Myth*. Translated by Peter Bing. Berkeley: University of California Press, 1983.

Burkholder, Mark A., and Lyman L. Johnson. *Colonial Latin America*. New York: Oxford University Press, 2001.

Canny, Nicholas P. "The Ideology of English Colonization: From Ireland to America." *The William and Mary Quarterly* 30, no. 4 (1973): 575–98.

Cassese, Antonio. *International Criminal Law*. New York/Oxford: Oxford University Press, 2003.

Chang, Iris. *Rape of Nanjing: The Forgotten Holocaust of World War II*. New York: Basic Books, 1997.

Chickering, Roger. "Total War: the Use and Abuse of a Concept." In *Anticipating Total War: The German and American Experiences, 1871–1914*, edited by M. F. Boemeke, R. Chickering, and Stig Förster, 13–28. Cambridge: Cambridge University Press, 1999.

Churchill, Winston. *The Second World War*. Vol. 5, *Closing the Ring*. New York: Bantam Books, 1962.

Cobb, John. *God and the World*. Philadelphia: The Westminster Press, 1969.

Cocker, Mark. *Rivers of Blood, Rivers of Gold: Europe's Conquest of Indigenous Peoples*. New York: Grove Atlantic, 1998.

Colby, Elbridge. "How to Fight Savage Tribes." *The American Journal of International Law* 21, no. 2 (1927): 279–88.

Cole, David. "What Bush Wants to Hear." *The New York Review of Books*, November 17, 2005.

Coogan, John W. "Review of Isabel V. Hull, *A Scrap of Paper*." H-Diplo, December 12, 2014, https://networks.h-net.org/node/28443/discussions/55267/h-diplo-essay-121-review-essay-scrap-paper-breaking-and-making (accessed January 26, 2020).

Cooper, Russell M. *American Consultation in World Affairs for the Preservation of Peace*. New York: Macmillan, 1934.

Cox, Rory. "Expanding the History of the Just War: The Ethics of Ancient Egypt." *International Studies Quarterly* 61 (2017): 371–84.

Crouch, C. L. *War and Ethics in the Ancient Near East: Military Violence in Light of Cosmology and History*. Berlin: Walter de Gruyter, 2009.

Creel, Herrlee G. *The Origins of Statecraft in China*. Chicago: University of Chicago Press, 1970.

Crowe, David. *The Holocaust: Roots, History, and Aftermath*. Philadelphia: Westview Press, 2008.

———. *War Crimes, Genocide, and Justice: A Global History*. New York: Palgrave-Macmillan, 2014.

Cumont, Franz. *Oriental Religions in Roman Paganism*. New York: Dover, 1956.

Danner, Mark. "US Torture: Voices from the Black Sites," *The New York Review of Books*, April 9, 2009.

Davidson, Eugene. *The Trial of the Germans: An Account of the Twenty-two Defendants before the International Military Tribunal at Nuremberg*. Columbia, MO: University of Missouri Press, 1997.

Davies, Nigel. *The Aztecs*. London: The Folio Society, 2000.

d'Ayala, Pedro Lopez. *Cronicas de Los Reyes de Castilla*. Vol. I. Madrid, 1779–80.

Deist, F. E. "The Dangers of Deuteronomy: A Page from the Reception History of the Book." In *Studies in Deuteronomy in Honour of C. J. Labuschagne*, edited by F. G. Martinez, 13–29. Leiden: Brill, 1994.

Diamond, Stanley. "The Rule of Law versus the Order of Custom." In *Before the Law: An Introduction to Legal Process*, edited by J. Bonsignore, E. Katsh, P. d'Errico, R. Pipkin, and S. Arons. Boston/New York: Houghton Mifflin, 2006.

Dickmann, Fritz. "Die Kriegsschuldfrage auf der Friedenskonferenz von Paris 1919. *Historische Zeitschrift* 197, no. 1 (August 1963): 1–101.

Dikshitar, V. R. Ramachandra. *War in Ancient India*. New Delhi: Cosmos, 1999.

Dower, John W. *War without Mercy: Race & Power in the Pacific*. New York: Pantheon Books, 1986.

Doyle, John P. *Collected Studies on Francisco Suárez, S.J. (1548–1617)*. Leuven, Belgium: Leuven University Press, 2010.

Draper, G. I. A. D. "The Interaction of Christianity and Chivalry in the Historical Development of the Laws of War." *The International Review of the Red Cross* (January 1965): 3–23.

———. *The Red Cross Conventions*. London: Stevens & Stevens, 1958.

———. "Wars of National Liberation and War Criminality." In *Restraints on War: Studies in the Limitation of Armed Conflict*, edited by Michael Howard, 135–62. Oxford: Oxford University Press, 1979.

Durant, Will and Ariel. *Our Oriental Heritage*. New York: Simon & Shuster, 1935.

Edwards, Charles. "The Law of War in the Thought of Hugo Grotius." *Emory University Journal of Public Law* 19 (1970): 371–97.

Edwards, David. "Beyond Reform: Martial Law and the Tudor Reconquest of Ireland," *History Ireland* 5/2 (Summer 1997): 16–21.

———. "'Some Days Two Heads, Some Days Four,'" *History Ireland* 17/1 (Jan.-Feb. 2009): 18–21.

Eliade, Mircea. *The Sacred and the Profane: The Nature of Religion*. New York: Harcourt, Brace, & World, 1959.

———. *A History of Religious Ideas*. Vol. 1, *From the Stone Age to the Eleusinian Mysteries*. Chicago: The University of Chicago Press, 1978.

Elton, G. R. "Human Rights and the Liberties of Englishmen." *University of Illinois Law Review* 2 (1990): 329–46.

Esler, Anthony. *The Western World: A Narrative History—Prehistory to the Present*. Upper Saddle River, NJ: Prentice Hall, 1997.

Federal Bureau of Investigation. *Terrorism in the United States: 1999*. Washington, D.C.: US Government Printing Office, 2000.

Fenby, Jonathan. *Chiang Kai-shek: China's Generalissimo and the Nation HE Lost*. Boston, MA: Da Capo Press, 2004.

Fenn, Elizabeth A. "Biological Warfare in Eighteenth-Century North America: Beyond Jeffery Amherst." *Journal of American History* 86, no. 4 (2000): 1552–80.

Ferguson, B. "Tribal Warfare." *Scientific American* 266 (1992): 108–116.

Bibliography

———, and N. Whitehead. *War in the Tribal Zone.* Santa Fe: School of American Research Press, 1992.

Ferrero, Giglielmo. *Peace and War.* New York: Macmillan, 1933.

Fischer, Fritz. *Griff nach der Weltmacht: Die Kriegszielpolitik des kaiserlichen Deutschland 1914/18.* Düsseldorf: Droste Verlag, 1961.

———. *World Power or Decline: The Controversy over Germany's Aims in the First World War.* Translated by L. L. Farrar, R. Kimber, and Rita Kimber. New York: W. W. Norton, 1965; London: Weidenfeld & Nicolson, 1975.

Fisher, Louis. *American Military Tribunals & Presidential Power: American Revolution to the War on Terrorism.* Lawrence, KS: University Press of Kansas, 2005.

Fiske, S. T., L. T. Harris, and A. J. Cuddy. "Why Ordinary People Torture Enemy Prisoners." *Science* 306, No. 5701 (2004): 1482–83.

Form, Wolfgang. "Planung und Durchführung west-alliierter Kriegsverbrecherprozesse nach dem Zweiten Weltkrieg." In *Perspektiven der politischen Soziologie im Wandel von Gesellschaft und Staatlichkeit: Festschrift für Theo Schiller,* edited by T. Schiller, T. Winter, and V. Mittendorf. Wiesbaden: VS Verlag für Sozialwissenschaften/GWV Fachverlage, 2008.

Frankfort, Henri. *Kingship and the Gods: A Study of Ancient Near Eastern Religion as the Integration of Society and Nature.* Chicago: University of Chicago Press, 1948.

———. *The Birth of Civilization in the Near East.* New York: Doubleday Anchor Books, 1956.

Fratcher, William F. "American Organization for Prosecution of German War Criminals." *Missouri Law Review* 13, no. 1 (January 1948): 45–75.

Frederickson, George M. *Racism: A Short History.* Princeton, NJ: Princeton University Press, 2002.

Friedlander, Henry. *The Origins of Nazi Genocide: From Euthanasia to the Final Solution.* Chapel Hill, NC: The University of North Carolina Press, 1995.

Friedrich, Jörg. *Das Gesetz des Krieges: das deutsche Heer in Rußland 1941–1945—Der Prozeß gegen das Oberkommando der Wehrmacht.* Munich: Piper, 1993.

Froissart, Jean. *Oeuvres.* Edited by Kervyn de Lettenhove. Brussels, 1869.

Furst, Peter. "Fertility, Vision Quest and Auto-Sacrifice: Some Thoughts on Ritual Blood-letting Among the Maya." In *The Art, Iconography, and Dynastic History of Palenque, Part II: Proceedings of the Segunda Mesa Redonda de Palenque,* edited by Merle Green Robertson, 211–24. Pebble Beach, CA: Robert Louis Stevenson School, 1976.

Garlan, Yvon. *War in the Ancient World: A Social History.* New York: W. W. Norton, 1975.

Geertz, Clifford. "Local Knowledge: Fact and Law in Comparative Perspective." In *Local Knowledge: Further Essays in Interpretive Anthropology,* 167–234. New York: Basic Books, 1983.

Gelb, I. J. "Prisoners of War in Early Mesopotamia." *Journal of Near Eastern Studies* 32, no. 1–2 (1973): 70–98.

Gentili, Alberico. *De Jure Belli Libri Tres,* edited by John C. Rolfe. Washington: Carnegie Endowment for International Peace, 1933.

Gilbert, Martin. *The First World War: A Complete History.* New York: Henry Holt, 1994.

———. *Winston S. Churchill, 1941–1945: Road to Victory.* London: William Heinemann, 1986.

Gilmore, Gerry J. "Bad Troops, Poor Leaders Responsible for Detainee Abuses." *DoD News,* July 22, 2004, https://archive.defense.gov/news/newsarticle.aspx?id=25668 (accessed January 16, 2020).

Glover, Jonathan. *Humanity: A Moral History of the 20th Century.* New Haven, CT: Yale University Press, 1999.

Glueck, Sheldon. *War Criminals: Their Prosecution and Punishment.* New York: Alfred A. Knopf, 1944.

Gombrich, Richard. *How Buddhism Began: The Conditioned Genesis of the Early Teachings.* London: Athlone, 1996.

Graham, A. C. *Disputers of the Tao: Philosophical Argument in Ancient China.* La Salle, IL: Open Court, 1989.

Greenburg, J., H. Rosenberg, and A. De Vogue. "Sources: Top Bush Advisors Approve 'Enhanced Interrogation,'" ABC News, April 9, 2008.

Grewe, Wilhelm G. *The Epochs of International Law.* Translated by Michael Byers. Berlin/New York: Walter de Gruyter, 2000.

Grossman, Dave. *On Killing: The Psychological Cost of Learning to Kill in War and Society.* New York/Boston/London: Back Bay Books, 2009.

Guilaine, Jean, and Jean Zammit. *Origins of War: Violence in Prehistory.* Translated by Melanie Hersey. Malden, MA: Blackwell, 2005.

Halbfass, Wilhelm. "Dharma in the Self-Understanding of Traditional Hinduism." In *India and Europe: An Essay in Understanding,* 310–33. Albany, NY: SUNY Press, 1988.

Hankel, Gerd. *Die Leipziger Prozesse: Deutsche Kriegsverbrechen und ihre strafrechtliche Verfolgung nach dem Ersten Weltkrieg.* Hamburg: Hamburger Edition, 2003.

Hanson, Victor D. "The Ideology of Hoplite Battle, Ancient and Modern." In *Hoplites: The Classical Greek Battle Experience,* edited by Victor D. Hanson, 3–14. New York: Routledge, 1991.

——. *A War Like No Other: How the Athenians and Spartans Fought the Peloponnesian War.* New York: Random House, 2005.

——. *The Western Way of War.* New York: Random House, 2005.

Harris, Whitney. *Tyranny on Trial: The Evidence at Nuremberg.* New York: Barnes & Noble, 1995.

Harris, William. *War and Imperialism in Republican Rome.* Oxford: Oxford University Press, 1979.

Hartigan, Richard S. "Saint Augustine on War and Killing." *Journal of the History of Ideas* 27 (1966): 195–204.

Hartmann, Christian, Thomas Vordermayer, Othmar Plöckinger, and Roman Töppel, ed. *Hitler, Mein Kampf: Eine kritische Edition.* Munich/Berlin: Institut für Zeitgeschichte, 2016.

Has, J., and W. Creamer. "Warfare among the Pueblos: Myth, History, and Ethnography." *Ethnohistory* 44, no. 2 (1997): 235–61.

Hathaway, O. A., P. K. Strauch, B. A. Walton, and Z. A. Y. Weinberg. "What is a War Crime?." *Yale Journal of International Law* 44, no. 1 (2019): 53–113.

Haykel, Bernard. "The Seventh Annual Ernest May Memorial Lecture: The History and Ideology of the Islamic State." In *Blind Spot: America's Response to Radicalism in the Middle East,* edited by Nicholas Burns and Jonathon Price, 21–28. Washington, D.C.: The Aspen Institute, 2015.

Herczegh, Geza. *Development of International Humanitarian Law.* Budapest: Akademiai Kiado, 1984.

Hersch, Seymour. "Torture at Abu Ghraib." *The New Yorker,* May 10, 2004.

Herwig, Holger. *Hammer or Anvil? Modern Germany 1648–Present.* Lexington, MA/Toronto: Heath, 1994.

Hirsch, Adam J. "The Collision of Military Cultures in Seventeenth-Century New England." *Journal of American History* 74, no. 4 (1988): 1187–1212.

Hodge, F. W., G. P. Hammond, and A. Rey, ed. *Fray Alonso de Benavides' Revised Memorial of 1634.* Albuquerque: University of New Mexico Press, 1945.

Hoebel, E. Adamson. *The Law of Primitive Man.* Cambridge, MA: Harvard University Press, 1954.

Hoffmann, *Egypt before the Pharaohs: The Prehistoric Foundations of Egyptian Civilization.* New York: Knopf, 1979.

Höffner, Joseph. *Christentum und Menschenwürde. Das Anliegen der spanischen Kolonialethik im Goldenen Zeitalter.* Trier, 1947.

Bibliography

Hornung, Erik. "The Pharoah." In *The Egyptians*, edited by Sergio Donadoni, 283–314. Chicago: University of Chicago Press, 1997.

Howard, Michael. *War in European History*. Oxford: Oxford University Press, 2009.

Huizinga, Johann. *Homo Ludens: A Study of the Play Element in Culture*. Boston: Beacon, 1968.

Hudson, Manley O. "The Proposed International Criminal Court." *American Journal of International Law* 32, no. 3 (July 1938): 549–54.

Hull, Isabel. *Absolute Destruction: Military Culture and the Practices of War in Imperial Germany*. Ithaca/London: Cornell University Press, 2005.

———. *A Scrap of Paper: Breaking and Making International Law during the Great War*. Ithaca/London: Cornell University Press, 2014.

———. "'Military Necessity' and the laws of war in Imperial Germany." In *Order, Conflict, and Violence*, edited by S. Kalyvas, I. Shapiro, and T. Masoud, 352–77. Cambridge: Cambridge University Press, 2008.

Hunt, Lynn. *Inventing Human Rights: A History*. New York/London: W. W. Norton, 2007.

Ihme-Tuchel, Beate. "Fall 7: Der Prozeß gegen die 'Südwest-Generale' (gegen Wilhelm List und andere)." In *Der Nationalsozialismus vor Gericht: Die allierten Prozesse gegen Kriegsverbrecher und Soldaten 1943-1952*, edited by Gerd Ueberschär, 144–54. Frankfurt a.M.: Fischer, 1999.

Isḥāq, Muḥammad ibn. *The Life of Muhammad: A Translation of Ishāq's rasūl Allāh*. Translated by Alfred Guillaume. Karachi: Oxford University Press, 2004.

Jäger, Herbert. "Makroverbrechen als Gegenstand des Völkerstrafrechts: Kriminalpolitisch-kriminologische Aspekte." In *Strafgerichte gegen Menschheitsverbrechen*, edited by Gerd Hankel and Gerhard Stuby, 325–54. Hamburg: Hamburger Edition, 1995.

Jennings, Francis. *Invasion of America: Indians, Colonialism, and the Cant of Conquest*. Chapel Hill: University of North Carolina Press, 1975.

Jochnick, Chris, and Roger Normand. "The Legitimation of Violence: A Critical History of the Laws of War." *Harvard International Law Review* 35 (1994): 49–95.

Johnson, Chalmers. *Nemesis: The Last Days of the American Republic*. New York: Metropolitan, 2006.

Joseph, Gilbert M., and Timothy J. Henderson, ed. *The Mexico Reader*. Durham, NC: Duke University Press, 2003.

Jung, C. G. *Synchronicity: An Acausal Connecting Principle*. Translated by R. F. C. Hull. Princeton, NJ: Princeton University Press, 1973.

Juster, Susan. *Sacred Violence in Early America*. Philadelphia: University of Pennsylvania Press, 2016.

Kahn, Paul. *The Cultural Study of Law: Reconstructing Legal Scholarship*. Chicago: University of Chicago Press, 1999.

Karnow, Stanley. *Vietnam: A History*. Harmondsworth, Middlesex: Penguin, 1984.

Karr, Ronald Dale. "'Why Should You be So Furious?': The Violence of the Pequot War." *Journal of American History* 85, no. 3 (1983): 876–909.

Katz, Leo. *Bad Acts and Guilty Minds: Conundrums of the Criminal Law*. Chicago: University of Chicago Press, 1987.

Kaul, Friedrich Karl. "Die Verfolgung deutscher Kriegsverbrecher nach dem ersten Weltkrieg." *Zeitschrift für Geschichtswissenschaft* 14 (1966): 19–32.

Keegan, John. *A History of Warfare*. New York: Vintage, 1993.

Keen, Benjamin. *Latin American Civilization: History and Society, 1492 to the Present*. Boulder, CO: Westview, 2000.

Keen, Maurice. *The Laws of War in the Late Middle Ages*. London: Routledge, 1965.

Kendell, Ashley. "The Crow Creek Massacre: The Role of Sex in Native American Scalping Practices." In *Archaeological Perspectives on Warfare on the Great Plains*, edited by Andrew J. Clark and Douglas B. Bamforth, 318–35. Boulder, CO: University Press of Colorado, 2018.

Kiernan, Ben. *Blood and Soil: A World History of Genocide from Sparta to Darfur*. New Haven: Yale University Press, 2007.

Khadduri, M. *War and Peace in the Law of Islam*. Baltimore: The Johns Hopkins University Press, 1955.

Knight, W. S. M. "Ayala and His Work." *Journal of Comparative Legislation and International Law* 4, no. 4 (1921): 220–27.

Koskenniemi, Marti. *The Gentle Civilizer of Nations: The Rise and Fall of International Law 1870–1960*. Cambridge: Cambridge University Press, 2001.

Kramer, Alan. *Dynamic of Destruction: Culture and Mass Killing in the First World War*. Oxford/New York: Oxford University Press, 2007.

Kushner, Barak. *Men to Devils, Devils to Men: Japanese War Crimes and Chinese Justice*. Cambridge, MA: Harvard University Press, 2015.

Langbein, John H. *Prosecuting Crime in the Renaissance*. Cambridge, MA: Harvard University Press, 1974.

Lanni, Adriaan. "The Laws of War in Ancient Greece." *Law and History Review* 26, no. 3 (Fall 2008): 469–89.

La Noue, François de. *Discours politiques et militaries*, edited by Frank E. Sutcliffe. Geneva: Droz, 1967.

Las Casas, Bartolome. *History of the Indies*, Book 2. Translated by Andrée Collard. New York: Harper & Row, 1971.

Lauren, Paul G. *The Evolution of International Human Rights: Visions Seen*. Philadelphia: University of Pennsylvania Press, 2011.

Lauterpacht, Hersch. "The Grotian Tradition in International Law." *British Yearbook of International Law* 23 (1946): 1–53.

Lederer, Gerda. "Authoritarianism in German Adolescents: Trends and Cross-Cultural Comparisons." In *Strength and Weakness: The Authoritarian Personality Today*, edited by W. F. Stone et al., 182–98. New York: Springer Verlag, 1993.

Lee, Wayne E. "Peace Chiefs and Blood Revenge: Patterns of Restraint in Native American Warfare, 1500–1800." *Journal of Military History* 71/3 (July 2007): 701–41.

———. "Projecting Power in the Early Modern World: the Spanish Model?" In *Empires and Indigenes: Intercultural Alliance, Imperial Expansion, and Warfare in the Early Modern World*, edited by Wayne E. Lee, 1–16. New York: NYU Press, 2011.

Lepore, Jill. *The Name of War: King Philip's War and the Origins of American Identity*. New York: Vintage Books, 1999.

Lewis, Mark Edward. *Sanctioned Violence in Early China*. Albany, NY: SUNY Press, 1990.

Lifton, Robert Jay. *The Nazi Doctors: Medical Killing and the Psychology of Genocide*. New York: Basic Books, 1986.

Lomatuway'ma, Michael, et al. *Hopi Ruin Legends*. Translated by Ekkehart Malotki. Lincoln, NE: University of Nebraska Press, 1993.

Lowie, Robert. *An Introduction to Cultural Anthropology*. New York: Rinehart & Co., 1940.

———. *Primitive Society*. New York: Boni and Liveright, 1920.

Lurie, Jonathan. *Arming Military Justice*. Vol. 1, *The Origins of the US Court of Military Appeals, 1775–1950*. Princeton, NJ: Princeton University Press, 1992.

Lynn, John A. "Nations in Arms 1763–1815." In *The Cambridge Illustrated History of Warfare*, edited by Geoffrey Parker, 186–213. New York/Cambridge: Cambridge University Press, 1995.

———. "States in Conflict." In *The Cambridge Illustrated History of Warfare*, edited by Geoffrey Parker, 164–85. New York/Cambridge: University of Cambridge Press, 1995.

Lyons, Michael J. *World War II: A Short History*. Upper Saddle River, NJ: Prentice Hall, 1994.

Maguire, Peter. *Law and War: An American Story*. New York: Columbia University Press, 2001.

Bibliography

Maine, Henry S. *Ancient Law. Its Connection with the Early History of Society and its Relation to Modern Ideas*. New York: Dorset, 1986 (reprint of 1861 first edition).

———. *Village Communities in the East and West*. London: John Murray, 1871.

Malone, Patrick M. *The Skulking Way of War: Technology and Tactics Among the New England Indians*. Lanham, MD: Rowan and Littlefield, 2001.

Manchester, William. *American Caesar: Douglas MacArthur, 1880–1964*. Boston: Little, Brown, 1978.

Mayer, Jane. "The Hard Cases." *The New Yorker* (February 23, 2009): 38–45.

McCants, William. *The Isis Apocalypse: The History, Strategy, and Doomsday Vision of the Islamic State*. New York: Picador/St. Martin's Press, 2015.

McCoubrey, Hilaire. *International Humanitarian Law: the Regulation of Armed Conflicts* London: Dartmouth Publishing Co., 1990.

McGehee, Ralph. "CIA and Operation Phoenix in Vietnam," http://www.serendipity.li/cia/operation_phoenix.htm (accessed August 25, 2014).

McNeill, William. "The Changing Shape of World History." *History and Theory* 34, no. 2 (May 1995): 8–26.

Meron, Theodor. *Bloody Constraint: War and Chivalry in Shakespeare*. Oxford/New York: Oxford University Press, 1998.

———. *Henry's Wars and Shakespeare's Laws: Perspectives on the Law of War in the Later Middle Ages*. Oxford: Clarendon Press, 1993.

———. *The Humanization of International Law*. Leiden/Boston: Martinus Nijhoff, 2006.

———. "Medieval and Renaissance Ordinances of War: Codifying Discipline and Humanity." In *War Crimes Law Comes of Age: Essays*. Oxford: Oxford University Press, 1998.

———. "Rape as a Crime Under International Humanitarian Law." In *War Crimes Law Comes of Age: Essays*. Oxford/New York: Oxford University Press, 1998.

Minear, Richard H. *Victor's Justice: The Tokyo War Crimes Trial*. Ann Arbor, MI: University of Michigan Press, 1971.

Mishkin, Bernard. *Rank and Warfare in Plains Indians Culture*. Seattle: University of Washington Press, 1940.

Moffit, Robert E. *Modern War and the Laws of War*. Tucson: Institute of Government Research, 1973.

Mommsen, Theodor. *Römisches Staatsrecht*. Vol. III. Leipzig, 1887–88.

Morey, W. C. *Outlines of Roman Law, Comprising its Historical Growth and General Principles*. New York and London: G. P. Putnam's Sons, 1884.

Moyn, Samuel. "Book Review of *A Scrap of Paper* by Isabel V. Hull." *Wall Street Journal*, June 5, 2014, https://www.wsj.com/articles/book-review-a-scrap-of-paper-by-isabel-v-hull-1402010920 (accessed January 26, 2020).

Mumford, Lewis. *The Myth of the Machine: Technics and Human Development*. New York: Harcourt, Brace, & World, 1967.

Muser, Curt. *Facts and Artifacts of Ancient Middle America*. New York: E. P. Dutton, 1978.

Murray, Williamson A. "The Industrialization of War." In *The Cambridge Illustrated History of Warfare*, edited by Geoffrey Parker, 216–41. New York: Cambridge University Press, 1995, revised and updated, 2008.

Neff, Stephen C. *Justice Among Nations: A History of International Law*. Cambridge, MA: Harvard University Press, 2014.

———. *War and the Law of Nations: A General History*. Cambridge: Cambridge University Press, 2005.

Newcomb, W. W. "A Re-examination of the Causes of Plains Warfare." *American Anthropologist* 52, no. 3 (1950): 317–30.

Niarchos, Catherine N. "Women, War, and Rape: Challenges Facing the International Tribunal for the Former Yugoslavia." *Human Rights Quarterly* 17, no. 4 (November 1995): 650–90.

Nicholson, Barry. *An Introduction to Roman Law*. Oxford: Oxford University Press, 1969.

Niditch, Susan. *War in the Hebrew Bible: A Study in the Ethics of Violence*. New York: Oxford University Press, 1995.

Noor, Mohammad. "The Doctrine of Jihad: An Introduction." *Journal of Law & Religion* 3, no. 2 (1985): 381–97.

Ober, Josiah. "Classical Greek Times." In *The Laws of War: Constraints on Warfare in the Western World*, edited by M. Howard, G. J. Andreopoulos, and M. R. Shulman, 12–26. New Haven, CT: Yale University Press, 1994.

Oppenheim, Lassa. *International Law*. Vol. II: *War and Neutrality*. New York: Longmans, 1906.

——. *International Law: A Treatise*, edited by Hersh Lauterpacht. Vol. I, *Peace*. London: Longmans, 1947.

Otto, Eckart. *Das Deuteronomium: politische Theologie und Rechtsform in Juda und Assyrien*. Berlin/New York: de Gruyter, 1999.

Otto, Rudolf. *Das Heilige: Über das Irrationale in der Idee des Göttlichen und Sein Verhältnis zum Rationalen*. Stuttgart/Gotha: Verlag Friedrich Andreas Perthes A.-G., 1923.

Oudijk, Michel R. and Matthew Restall. "Mesoamerican Conquistadors in the Sixteenth Century." In *Indian Conquistadors: Indigenous Allies in the Conquest of Mesoamerica*, edited by Laura Matthew and Michel R. Oudijk, 28–64. Norman: University of Oklahoma Press, 2008.

Palmer, R. R. and Joel Colton. *A History of the Modern World*. New York: Alfred A. Knopf, 1965.

Paolucci, H. *The Political Writings of St. Augustine*. Chicago: Gateway, 1962.

Parker, Geoffrey. "Dynastic War." In *The Cambridge Illustrated History of Warfare*, edited by Geoffrey Parker, 146–63. New York: Cambridge University Press, 1995, revised and updated 2008.

——. "Early Modern Europe." In *The Laws of War: Constraints on Warfare in the Western World*, edited by M. Howard, G. J. Andreopoulos, and M. R. Shulman, 40–58. New Haven, CT: Yale University Press, 1994.

Parsons, Elsie Clews. *Taos Pueblo*. Menash, WI: George Banta, 1936.

Pegg, Mark Gregory. *A Most Holy War: The Albigensian Crusade and the Battle for Christendom*. Oxford/New York: Oxford University Press, 2008.

Penna, L. R. "Humanitarian Law in Ancient India." *Military Law and Law of War Review* 23 (1984): 235–39.

——. "Traditional Asian Approaches: An Indian View." *Australian Yearbook of International Law* 9 (1985): 168–206.

Petri, Franz, and Peter Schöller. "Zur Bereinigung des Franktireurproblems vom August 1914." *Vierteljahrhefte für Zeitgeschichte* 9, no. 3 (July 1961): 234–48.

Phillipson, Coleman. *The International Law and Custom of Ancient Greece and Rome*. Vol. I. London: Macmillan, 1911.

Pictet, Jean S., ed. *Commentary, IV Geneva Convention Relative to the Protection of Civilian Persons in Time of War*. Geneva: International Committee for the Red Cross, 1958.

——. *Development and Principles of International Humanitarian Law*. New York: Springer, 1985.

Pinker, Steven. *The Blank Slate: The Modern Denial of Human Nature*. New York: Viking Penguin, 2002.

Postgate, J. N. *Early Mesopotamia: Society and Economy at the Dawn of History*. London & New York: Routledge, 1992.

Poliakov, Léon. *The History of Anti-Semitism*. Vol. 2, *From Mohammed to the Marranos*. Translated by Natalie Geradi. Philadelphia: The University of Pennsylvania Press, 2003.

Pritchett, W. Kendrick. *The Greek State at War*. Berkeley: University of California Press, 1991.

Quammen, David. *The Monster of God: The Man-eating Predator in the Jungles of History and the Mind*. New York: W. W. Norton, 2003.

Bibliography

Ratner, S. R., and J. S. Abrams. *Accountability for Human Rights Atrocities in International Law: Beyond the Nuremberg Legacy*. New York/Oxford: Oxford University Press, 2001.

Remec, P. *The Position of the Individual in International Law According to Grotius and Vattel*. The Hague: Martinus Nijhoff, 1960.

Renfrew, Colin. *Prehistory: The Making of the Human Mind*. London: The Folio Society, 2013.

Restall, Matthew. *Seven Myths of the Spanish Conquest*. New York: Oxford University Press, 2003.

Rich, John. "Roman Rituals of War." In *The Oxford Handbook of Warfare in the Classical World*, edited by Brian Campbell and Lawrence A. Tritle, 542–68. Oxford and New York: Oxford University Press, 2013.

Richter, Daniel K. "War and Culture: The Iroquois Experience." *The William and Mary Quarterly* 40, no. 4 (1983): 528–59.

Ringmar, Erik. "Francis Lieber, Terrorism, and the American Way of War." *Perspectives on Terrorism* 3, no. 4 (2009): 52–60.

Ritter, Gerhard. *Der erste Weltkrieg: Studien zum deutschen Geschichtsbild*. Bonn: Schriftenreihe der Bundeszentrale für Politische Bildung, 1964.

Roberts, Adam. "Land Warfare: From Hague to Nuremberg." In *The Laws of War: Constraints on Warfare in the Western World*, edited by M. Howard, G. J. Andreopoulos, and M. R. Shulman, 116–39. New Haven, CT: Yale University Press, 1994.

Roetz, Heiner. *Confucian Ethics of the Axial Age*. Albany, NY: SUNY Press, 1993.

Römer, Felix. *Der Kommissarbefehl: Wehrmacht und NS-Verbrechen an der Ostfront 1941/42*. Paderborn: Ferdinand Schöningh, 2008.

Roscoe, Paul. "Intelligence, Coalitional Killing, and the Antecedents of War." *American Anthropologist* 109, no. 3 (2007): 485–95.

Rosen, Laurence. *Law as Culture: An Invitation*. Princeton, NJ: Princeton University Press, 2006.

Rossino, Alexander B. *Hitler Strikes Poland: Blitzkrieg, Ideology, and Atrocity*. Lawrence, KS: University Press of Kansas, 2003.

Rothenberg, Gunther. "The Age of Napoleon." In *The Laws of War: Constraints on Warfare in the Western World*, edited by M. Howard, G. J. Andreopoulos, and M. R. Shulman, 86–97. New Haven, CT: Yale University Press, 1994.

Runciman, Steven. *A History of the Crusades*. Three volumes. London: The Folio Society, 1994.

Russell, Frederick H. *The Just War in the Middle Ages*. Cambridge: Cambridge University Press, 1975.

Ryan, Alan. *Yamashita's Ghost: War Crimes, MacArthur's Justice, and Command Accountability*. Lawrence, KS: University Press of Kansas, 2012.

Salaymeh, Lena. "Early Islamic Legal-Historical Precedents: Prisoners of War." *Law and History Review* 26, no. 3 (Fall 2008): 521–44.

Salmon, J. H. M. "Sovereignty, Theory of." In *Europe, 1450–1789: Encyclopedia of the Early Modern World*. Volume 5, 447–50. New York: Charles Scribner's Sons, 2003.

Sands, Philippe. *Torture Team: Rumsfeld's Memo and the Betrayal of American Values*. New York: Palgrave-Macmillan, 2008.

Schele, Linda, and David Freidel. *A Forest of Kings: The Untold Story of the Ancient Maya*. New York: William Morrow and Co., 1990.

Scheppele, Kim. "Law in a Time of Emergency: States of Exception and the Temptations of 9/11." *University of Pennsylvania Journal of Constitutional Law* 6 (2003–4): 1001–82.

Schiller, Friedrich. *Geschichte des Dreißigjährigen Kriegs*. Vol. II. Leipzig, 1793.

Secoy, Frank. Changing Military Patterns on the Great Plains. New York: Augustin, 1952.

Seed, Patricia. "The Conquest of the Americas," 132–45. In *The Cambridge Illustrated History of Warfare*, edited by Geoffrey Parker. New York/Cambridge: Cambridge University Press, 1995.

Segesser, Daniel M. "On the Road to Total Retribution? The International Debate on the Punishment of War Crimes, 1872–1945." In *A World at Total War: Global Conflict and the Politics of Destruction, 1937–1945*, edited by R. Chickering, S. Förster, and B. Greiner, 355–74. Cambridge, MA: Cambridge University Press, 2005.

———. "The Punishment of War Crimes Committed against Prisoners of War, Deportees and Refugees during and after the First World War." In *Captivity, Forced Labour and Forced Migration in Europe during the First World War*, edited by Matthew Stibbe, 134–56. London/ New York: Routledge, 2009.

Sheehan, James J. "The Problem of Sovereignty in European History." *The American Historical Review* 111, no. 1 (February 2006): 1–15.

Sharp, Heather. "After the Ideological Battles: Student Views on Sources Representing the Gallipoli Conflict." In *International Perspectives on Teaching Rival Histories: Pedagogical Responses to Contested Narratives and the History Wars*, edited by Henri Äström Elmersjo, Anna Clark, & Monika Vinterek. New York: Palgrave Macmillan, 2017.

Siebert, Detlef. "Die Durchführung des Kommissarbefehls in den Frontverbänden des Heeres: Eine Quantifizierende Auswertung der Forschung." Unpublished manuscript, 2000.

Silver, Peter. *Our Savage Neighbors: How Indian War Transformed Early America*. New York: W. W. Norton & Co., 2008.

Sinha, M. K. "Hinduism and International Humanitarian Law." *International Review of the Red Cross* 87, No. 858 (June 2005): 285–94.

Smith, David Livingstone. *Less than Human: Why we Demean, Enslave, and Exterminate Others*. New York: St. Martin's Press, 2011.

———. *The Most Dangerous Animal: Human Nature and the Origins of War*. New York: St. Martin's Press, 2007.

Solis, Gary D. *The Law of Armed Conflict: International Humanitarian Law in War*. Cambridge and New York: Cambridge University Press, 2010.

Sottile, Antoine. "The Problem of the Creation of a Permanent International Criminal Court." *Revue de droit international* 29 (October-December 1951): 267–359.

Smith, Bradley F. *Reaching Judgment at Nuremberg: The Untold Story of How the Nazi War Criminals were Judged*. New York: Basic Books, 1977.

Spodek, Howard. *The World's History*. Volume I, *To 1500*. Upper Saddle River, NJ: Prentice Hall, 2000.

Stacey, Robert C. "The Age of Chivalry." In *The Laws of War: Constraints on Warfare in the Western World*, edited by M. Howard, G. J. Andreopoulos, and M. R. Shulman, 27–39. New Haven, CT: Yale University Press, 1994.

Stannard, David. *American Holocaust: The Conquest of the New World*. New York: Oxford University Press, 1993.

Starke, J. G. *An Introduction to International Law*. London: Butterworths, 1963.

Staub, Ervin. *The Roots of Evil: The Origins of Genocide and Other Group Violence*. New York: Cambridge University Press, 1989.

Steiner, John M. "The SS Yesterday and Today: A Sociopsychological View." In *Survivors, Victims, and Perpetrators: Essays on the Nazi Holocaust*, edited by J. E. Dimsdale, 405–56. Washington, D. C.: Hemisphere, 1980.

Stevenson, Matilda Cox. *The Zuni Indians: Their Mythology, Esoteric Fraternities, and Ceremonies*. *Twenty-third Annual Report of the Bureau of American Ethnology*. Washington, D.C.: Government Printing Office, 1904.

Streit, Christian. *Keine Kameraden: Die Wehrmacht und die sowjetischen Kriegsgefangenen 1941–1945*. Stuttgart: J. H. W. Dietz, 1991.

Sundstrom, Linea. "Coup Counts and Corn Caches: Contact-Era Plains Indian Accounts of Warfare." In *Archaeological Perspectives on Warfare on the Great Plains*, edited by Andrew J. Clark and D. B. Bamforth, 120–41. Boulder: University Press of Colorado, 2018.

Bibliography

Suter, Keith. *An International Law of Guerrilla Warfare: The Global Politics of Law-making.* London: F. Pinter, 1984.

Sutherland, Edwin H., and Donald R. Cressey. "A Theory of Differential Association." In *Criminological Theory: Past to Present*, edited by Francis T. Cullen and Robert Agnew, 122–24. Los Angeles: Roxbury, 2006.

Suzuki, Y. "A New Aspect of ḥrm in Deuteronomy in View of an Assimilation Policy of King Josiah." *Journal of Biblical Literature* 21 (1995): 3–27.

Sykes, Gresham M., and David Matza. "Techniques of Neutralization: A Theory of Delinquency." *American Sociological Review* 22, no. 6 (1957): 664–70.

Taylor, Telford. *The Anatomy of the Nuremberg Trials: A Personal Memoir.* New York: Alfred A. Knopf, 1992.

———. *Nuremberg and Vietnam: An American Tragedy.* New York: Bantam, 1971.

———. "Nuremberg Trials: War Crimes and International Law." *International Conciliation* 450 (1949): 243–371.

Thomas, Rosalind. "Written in Stone? Liberty, Equality, Orality and the Codification of Law." In *Greek Law in its Political Setting: Justifications, Not Justice*, edited by L. Foxhall and A. D. E. Lewis, 9–32. Oxford: Clarendon Press, 1996.

Trigger, Bruce G. *Understanding Early Civilizations: A Comparative Study.* New York: Cambridge University Press, 2003.

Trimm, Charles. "Recent Research on Warfare in the Old Testament." *Currents in Biblical Research* 10, no. 2 (2012): 171–216.

Tuchel, Johannes. "Planung und Realität des Systems der Konzentrationslager 1934–1938." In *Die nationalsozialistischen Konzentrationslager*, edited by U. Herbert, K. Orth, and C. Dieckmann, 43–59. Volume 1. Frankfurt a.M.: Fischer, 1998.

Turney, Frederick Jackson. "The Significance of the Frontier in American History." In *The Frontier in American History.* New York: Henry Holt, 1921.

Tusa, Ann, and John Tusa. *The Nuremberg Trial.* New York: Skyhorse, 2010.

Tyerman, Christopher. *The Crusades: A Very Short Introduction.* Oxford: Oxford University Press, 2004.

Ulbricht, Otto. "The Experience of Violence During the Thirty Years War: A Look at the Civilian Victims." In *Power, Violence and Mass Death in Pre-Modern and Modern Times*, edited by J. Canning, H. Lehmann, and J. Winter, 97–127. Hampshire, UK/Burlington, VT: Ashgate, 2004.

United Nations, International Criminal Tribunal for the Former Yugoslavia, http://www.icty.org/ (accessed January 6, 2015).

United Nations War Crimes Commission. *History of the United Nations War Crimes Commission and the Development of the Laws of War.* Buffalo, NY: William S Heinemann, 2006.

———. *Law Reports of Trials of War Criminals.* 15 volumes. London: His Majesty's Stationery Office, 1947.

Valentine, Douglas. *The Phoenix Program.* Lincoln, NE: Author's Guild, 1990.

van Creveld, Martin. *The Transformation of War.* New York: Free Press, 1991.

van Pelt, Robert Jan, and Deborah Dwork. *Auschwitz 1279 to the Present.* New York: W. W. Norton & Co., 1996.

van Schaack, Beth, and Ronald C. Slye. *International Criminal Law and its Enforcement.* New York: Foundation Press, 2010.

Varner, J. G., and J. J. Varner. *Dogs of the Conquest.* Norman, OK: University of Oklahoma Press, 1983.

Vaughan, Alden T. "'Expulsion of the Salvages': English Policy and the Virginia Massacre of 1622." *William and Mary Quarterly* 35 (1978): 57–84.

———. *New England Frontier: Puritans and Indians, 1620–1675.* Norman, OK: University of Oklahoma Press, 1995.

Voegelin, Eric. *Order and History*. Vol. 1, *Israel and Revelation*. Columbia and London: University of Missouri Press, 2001.

Vollenhoven, Van. *The Three Stages in the Evolution of the Law of Nations*. The Hague: Martinus Nijhoff, 1919.

von Savigny, Frederick Carl. *System des heutigen römischen Rechts*. Vol. I. Heidelberg, 1840–1851.

Waley, Arthur. *The Analects of Confucius*. London: Allen and Unwin, 1938.

Wakeman, Frederic E. *The Great Enterprise: The Manchu Reconstruction of Imperial Order in Seventeenth Century China*. Vol. I. Berkeley: University of California Press, 1985.

Walker, T. A. *A History of the Law of Nations*. Vol. I, *From the Earliest Times to the Peace of Westphalia*. Cambridge: Cambridge University Press, 1899.

Waller, James. *Becoming Evil: How Ordinary People Commit Genocide and Mass Killing*. Oxford and New York: Oxford University Press, 2007.

Watson, Alan. *International Law in Archaic Rome*. Baltimore and London: The Johns Hopkins University Press, 1993.

Watson, Burton. *Mo Tzu: Basic Writings*. New York: Columbia University Press, 1963.

Watson, Kelly L. *Insatiable Appetites: Imperial Encounters with Cannibals in the North Atlantic World*. New York: NYU Press, 2017.

Weber, Max. *Economy and Society: An Outline of Interpretive Sociology*. Berkeley: University of California Press, 1978.

———. *The Sociology of Religion*. Translated by Ephraim Fischoff. Boston: Beacon Press, 1993.

Weigley, Russell F. *Age of Battles: The Quest for Decisive Warfare from Breitenfeld to Waterloo*. Bloomington, IN: Indiana University Press, 2004.

Weil, Eric. "What is a Breakthrough in History?" *Daedalus* 104, no. 2 (Spring 1975): 21–36.

Weinberg, Gerhard. *A World at Arms: A Global History of World War II*. Cambridge: Cambridge University Press, 1994.

Weindling, P. J. *Nazi Medicine and the Nuremberg Trials: From Medical War Crimes to Informed Consent*. New York: Palgrave, 2004.

Weinke, Annette. *Law, History, and Justice: Debating German State Crimes in the Long 20th century*. New York/Oxford: Berghahn, 2019.

Wheatley, Paul. *The Pivot of the Four Quarters: A Preliminary Enquiry into the Origins and Character of the Ancient Chinese City*. Chicago: Aldine, 1971.

Whitaker, Brian. "US troops 'abusing Afghans.'" *Guardian Weekly*, March 11–17, 2004.

White, Leslie A. *The Pueblo of Santa Ana, New Mexico. Memoirs of the American Anthropological Association, No. 43*. Menasha, WI: American Anthropological Association, 1942.

Whitman, James Q. *The Verdict of Battle: The Law of Victory and the Making of Modern War*. Cambridge, MA: Harvard University Press, 2012.

Williams, David Lewis. *The Mind in the Cave: Consciousness and the Origins of Art*. London: Thames and Hudson, 2004.

Willis, James F. *Prologue to Nuremberg: The Politics and Diplomacy of Punishing War Criminals of the First World War*. West Port, CT/London: Greenwood Press, 1982.

Wissler, Clark. *Indians of the United States: Four Centuries of Their History and Culture*. New York: Doubleday and Company, 1941.

Witt, John Fabian. *Lincoln's Code: The Laws of War in American History*. New York: Free Press, 2012.

Wood, Graeme. "What ISIS Really Wants." *The Atlantic*, March 2015. https://www.theatlantic.com/magazine/archive/2015/03/what-isis-really-wants/384980/ (accessed January 31, 2020).

Wooley, Leonard. *Ur "of the Chaldees,"* edited by P. R. S. Moorey. Ithaca, NY: Cornell University Press, 1982.

World History Association. "What is World History?" https://www.thewha.org/about/what-is-world-history/ (accessed December 15, 2019).

Bibliography

Yael, Richard L. *The Yamashita Precedent: War Crimes and Command Responsibility*. Wilmington, DE: Scholarly Resources, 1982.

Yoo, John. *The Powers of War and Peace: The Constitution and Foreign Affairs after 9/11*. Chicago: University of Chicago Press, 2006.

———. *War by Other Means: An Insider's Account of the War on Terror*. New York: Atlantic Monthly Press, 2007.

Zechlin, Egon. "Deutschland zwischen Kabinettskrieg und Wirtschaftskriege." *Historische Zeitschrift*, 199, no. 2 (October 1964): 347–458.

Ziemann, Benjamin. "Review of Isabel V. Hull, *A Scrap of Paper*." H-Net Reviews in the Humanities & Social Sciences, May 2015, https://www.h-net.org/reviews/showpdf.php?id=44367 (accessed January 26, 2020).

Zimbardo, Philip. *The Lucifer Effect: Understanding How Good People Turn Evil*. New York: Random House, 2007.

INDEX

Abu Ghraib, 289, 312–14, 315, 375 n.70
Adorno, Theodor, 11, 306–7, 315, 373 n.46
  see also authoritarian personality theory;
    Frankfurt School
ahimsā, 40
Agincourt, Battle of, 109, 133
Aguinaldo, Emilio, 195
Ai, people of, 88, 146
Akayesu, Jean-Paul, 274, 279–80, 290
Akhenaton, 24, 27, 299
Alba, Duke of, 111, 116, 120
Albigensians, 90, 113, 174–5
  see also heresy, punishment of
Alexander II, Tsar, 180
Alexander III, Pope, 94
Algerian War, 266–7, 294
Algonquin Indians, 16
Al-Nawawī, 85
Al-Qayrawānī, 85
al-Shaybānī, Muhammad ibn al-Hasan, 85
al-Zawahiri, Ayman, 306
Altman, Amnon, 29
Alva, Duke of, 166
Amada, Temple of, 27
Alvarado, Pedro, 63, 148–50
Amenophis II, 24, 25, 27
Amenophis III, 24
American National Military Tribunal (NMT) at
    Nuremberg, 242–50
  notable features of the NMT trials, 245–50,
    363 n.99
Amorites, 44, 88–9, 300, 327 n.127, 325 n.58
Amun-re (Egyptian solar deity), 23–4, 26,
    324 n.44
Anacaona, 144
Anderson, Bill, 189
Ando, Clifford, 78
Andreopoulos, George, 267
androlepsy, 124
apocalypticism, 304–6, 373 n.39, 373 n.40,
    373 n.43
Apophis (Egyptian mythological serpent), 24
Arawak Indians, 145
Arendt, Hannah, 11, 308, 315
Arikara Indians, the, 66–8
Aristotle, 49, 51, 53, 78, 80, 86, 102, 129, 151,
    335 n.50

Armenians
  assassination of Turkish perpetrators by, 217
  massacre of, 10, 204, 207, 216–17, 231, 358 n.58
armistice of Mudros, 216
Armstrong, William, 178
Artem illam, 94–5
Artha-shastras, 94–5
  see also Kautilya
Ashoka, 42–3, 102, 319
Asquith, Herbert Henry, 202
Assmann, Jan, 11, 23–4, 45, 299–306, 315, 324 n.36,
    324 n.39, 328 n.137, 372 n.25, 373 n.40
  see also total religion
Assyria, 18, 22, 30, 45–7, 55, 57, 132, 296, 299–300,
    304, 323 n.21, 372 n.25
Augustine, 8–9, 87–94, 96, 121, 130, 136, 146, 168,
    192
Aurelius, Marcus, 79, 335 n.52
Aurgelmir (slain Norse god), 17
Auschwitz-Birkenau, 222, 228–30, 291
Austerlitz, Battle of, 175
Austin, John, 54
authoritarian personality theory, 306–8, 373 n.46
  see also Adorno, Theodor; Frankfurt School
Awatovi, destruction of, 73
Ayala, Balthasar, 9, 82, 113, 123–6, 130–1, 137, 141,
    174, 340 n.68
Azmi, Djemal, 358 n.58
Aztecs, the, 8, 59–64, 74, 148, 168, 331 n.20,
    331 n.22
  and the cult of Huitzilopochtli, 8, 59–62, 63, 74
  and Feast of the Flayed God, 62–3, 331 n.22
  "Flower Wars" of, 61–2
  Teotihuacán and, 57, 63, 331 n.9, 331 n.22
  Valley of Puebla-Tlaxcala and, 61
  see also Alvarado, Pedro; Davies, Nigel; human
    sacrifice; Keen, Benjamin, Moctezuma II;
    Mexica, the; Tenochtitlan; Texcoco;
    Tlacopan; Vaillant, George C

Babylonians, 19–20, 22, 29, 46, 47, 55, 304, 323 n.21
Badr, Battle of, 84
Baldwin, William, 156
Bandelier, Adolf, 71
Bataan Death March, 255
Bauman, Zygmunt, 11, 308, 315
Bell, Martin, 176

Index

Index

Index

Index

Index